A Dictionary of Chemistry. Containing the Theory and Practice of That Science; ... Translated From the French. With Plates, Notes, and Additions, by the Translator. of 2

A Table of CHEMICAL CHARACTERS

△ Fire	Regulus of Antimony	c⊖^, Caustic vol. Alkali	A Powder
Air	Arsenic	Potash	E. Ashes
▽ Water	Regulus of Arsenic	Acids	B. A Bath
Earth	K Cobalt	Vinegar	BM, MB, Water-bath
f Fixable Air	N. Nickel	Vitriolic Acid	AB Sand bath
m Mephitic Air	SM Metallic Substances	Nitrous Acid	VB Vapor-bath
Clay	C Calx	Marine Acid	X. An Hour
Gypsum	Orpiment	Æ Aquafortis	A Day
c▽, Calcareous Earth	Cinnabar	R Æ Aqua Regia	A Night
CV, Quicklime	LC Lapis Calaminaris	Vol Sulphurous Acid	1 Month
Vitrifiable, or Siliceous Earths	⊗ Tutty	Phosphoric Acid	aaa, Amalgam
Fluors, or Fusible Earths	Vitriol	V Wine	To Distill
X Talk	⊖, ⊖, Sea-Salt	Spirit of Wine	To Sublime
M▽ Magnesia	8, Sal Gem	Rectified S.V.	To Precipitate
A▽, Earth of Alum	Nitre	Æ Ether	A Retort
∴ Sand	Borax	Lime Water	XX. An Alembic
☉ Gold	SS Sedative Salt	Urine	A Crucible
☽, Silver	Sal Ammoniac	Oil	SSS. Stratum Super-Stratum
♀ Copper	Allum	E. Essential Oil	CC Cornu Cervi Hartshorn
♃ Tin	Tartar	Fixed Oils	A Bottle
♄ Lead	Alkali	Sulphur	gr. A Grain
☿ Mercury	Fixed Alkali	Hepar of Sulphur	℈. A Scruple
♂ Iron	Volatile Alkali	Phosphorus	ʒ. A Dram
Ze Zinc	m⊖▽ Mild fixed Alkali	Phlogiston	℥. An Ounce
B. W. Bismuth	c⊖▽ Caustic fixed-Alkali	Soap	lb. A Pound
♁ Antimony	m⊖^ Mild vol. Alkali	[illegible]	dwt. A Penny weight
		[illegible]	
		Caput Mortuum	

Heywood Sculpt

A

DICTIONARY

A D Stone   OF

CHEMISTRY.

CONTAINING THE

THEORY and PRACTICE of that SCIENCE;

ITS APPLICATION TO

NATURAL PHILOSOPHY, | MEDICINE, AND
NATURAL HISTORY, | ANIMAL ECONOMY

WITH

Full Explanations of the QUALITIES and MODES of Acting of CHEMICAL REMEDIES.

AND

The Fundamental Principles of the ARTS, TRADES, and MANUFACTURES, dependent on CHEMISTRY.

TRANSLATED from the FRENCH.

WITH

PLATES, NOTES, and ADDITIONS, by the TRANSLATOR.

LONDON.

Printed for T. CADELL, and P ELMSLY, in the Strand, J ROBSON, in Bond-Street; and S BLADON, in Pater-noster-Row.
M,DCC,LXXI.

A

DICTIONARY

OF

CHEMISTRY.

VOL. I.

A—NE

A

DICTIONARY

OF

CHEMISTRY.

VOL. II.

NI—ZI.

A
PREFACE
BY THE
TRANSLATOR.

THE name of the Author of the French Dictionary of which this Work is a Translation, is not prefixed to it; nevertheless, it has been universally attributed to Mr. MACQUER, Professor of Medicine and Chemistry in the University of Paris, and Member of the Royal Academy of Sciences, who has very justly acquired amongst chemists a distinguished reputation. Whoever compares the stile and doctrines of this writer, in the works to which his name is prefixed, with those of the present Dictionary, will not hesitate to give his assent to the general opinion concerning the author.

The Work itself is not unworthy of Mr. MACQUER. It contains a very extensive knowledge of chemical history, facts, and opinions, and exact descriptions of the operations and instruments of chemistry. The facts and operations are well and fully explained, so far as the present state of chemical knowledge permits. The author has farther rendered his work of very extensive utility, as well as curiosity, by the applications which he has made of Chemistry to

Natural Hiſtory, Medicine, Pharmacy, Metallurgy, and all the numerous arts and trades, the operations of which depend on chemical principles In this comprehenſive plan is included whatever relates to Chemiſtry, and I believe we may juſtly affirm that this Dictionary contains more chemical knowledge than any one book extant.

Some perſons may perhaps diſapprove of treating Chemiſtry in an alphabetical order. The Author himſelf ſays in an Advertiſement prefixed to his Work, "that notwithſtanding the opinion of ſome learned perſons who adviſed "him to compile a Chemical Dictionary, he had been "doubtful of the propriety of that diſpoſition, but that, "upon farther reflection, it appeared to him leſs excep-"tionable, and even to be attended with ſome peculiar "advantages."

We muſt acknowledge that the form of Dictionary is a very imperfect one for teaching a ſcience, or "knowledge "of the relations of certain things to each other." But the Chemiſtry which is now known is ſcarcely entitled to the name of ſcience, ſo defined. It is at preſent little more than a collection of facts, the cauſes of which, and their relations to each other are ſo imperfectly underſtood, that it is not yet capable either of the ſynthetic or analytic modes of explanation. Among the advantages attending an alphabetical diſpoſition, the Author mentions that many articles have been inſerted in the Dictionary, which could not have been introduced in any other method. Hence we may certainly infer, that the connexion of theſe with the other parts of Chemiſtry was not perceptible, and conſequently that Chemiſtry is incapable of a more ſyſtematical arrangement. In this ſtate of knowledge, no kind of book ſeems to be more deſirable than a Dictionary with references to connected articles, in which the ſeveral parts of Chemiſtry are

are treated ſeparately, and ſo diſpoſed, that any article concerning which information may be wanted; may be eaſily found, and in which every thing relating to Chemiſtry may be inſerted.

When our knowledge ſhall be greatly extended, a more perfect arrangement may be admitted And now, ſince Chemiſtry is delivered from the obſcure jargon of alchemiſts, and from the narrow limits of one profeſſion, namely, the medical, from which it has received much of its advancement, ſince it is now juſtly conſidered as one of the moſt important branches of natural philoſophy, ſince it has become a more general object of ſtudy, and has lately been ſucceſsfully cultivated at home, but eſpecially abroad, by perſons who employ the advantages attending rank, opulence, leiſure, and philoſophical minds, to the acquiſition of knowledge, and improvement of uſeful arts, we may hope, that the number of chemical facts may be daily encreaſed; that thoſe diſcovered may be farther aſcertained and illuſtrated, and that ſome perſon of eminently perſpicuous genius may unfold the laws and cauſes of chemical combination and analyſis, collect and methodize the ſcattered facts, and form the ſeveral parts of Chemiſtry into one regular, connected ſcience.

We have already mentioned the merits of the original Dictionary of which this Work is a Tranſlation. But in a ſubject perhaps too extenſive for the labors of one man, many articles have been omitted, which ought to have been placed in a work that has ſo ample a title as the preſent; and a few errors have been committed, moſt of which have proceeded from the Author not having been acquainted with ſome very late diſcoveries, eſpecially thoſe important ones concerning *fixable air*, made by Dr. Black, Profeſſor of Chemiſtry

Chemistry in the University of Edinburgh, by Dr MacBRIDE, and by the Honorable Mr CAVENDISH

The Translator, induced by consideration of the utility of the plan, and of the merits of the execution of the original Dictionary, and by the hopes of rendering the work more compleat and less exceptionable than it is in the French language, by supplying some of the defects, and correcting the errors above-mentioned, publishes the present Translation with Notes and Additions.

With these intentions he has added considerably to some of the articles in this Dictionary, and has inserted many new articles. He considered that a Dictionary of Chemistry ought to contain histories of the chemical properties of all substances so far as they have been discovered: therefore to the general properties of animals, vegetables, and minerals, and of a few of the more important species of these, which are treated in the original Dictionary, he has added histories of the chemical analysis of many plants and of some animals, supposing that these analyses might lead to a knowledge of medicinal or other qualities, and to proper modes of employing these substances; and also histories of the chemical properties of all the several species of minerals, so far as they are known to him by the works of POTT, WALLERIUS, CRONSTEDT, VOGEL, LINNÆUS, BOMARE, HENCKEL, LEHMAN, and other authors, or by his own experience. The insertion especially of the chemical histories of minerals seemed to be necessary to the understanding of that branch of Natural History which treats of these substances, because the most intelligent Mineralogists agree, that by examination chiefly of chemical properties, and not of external forms, as LINNÆUS and others have unsuccessfully attempted, minerals ought to be distinguished into classes, orders, genera, and species.

He

He has particularly attended to the application of Chemistry to useful arts, and he thinks that some circumstances have enabled him to speak with knowledge on several of these subjects. Much more might have been added if he had not feared the too great encrease of the book, and that assertions unsupported by a name might have little authority *.

A knowledge of the forms of chemical instruments being essentially necessary, and not being capable of being well communicated merely by descriptions, we have supplied the defect of the original Dictionary in that respect, by adding Plates to this Translation.

Thus we have endeavoured to render this Dictionary more extensively useful, and less exceptionable than it is in the original language. If we have attained our purpose, we hope it will be considered as a work, from which Students of Chemistry may be taught the several parts of this useful and extensive branch of philosophy; Naturalists may learn the properties of those substances which they are so curious to discover and to distinguish; Students of Medicine and of Pharmacy may acquire a knowledge of the analysis and of the composition of remedies, and of the chemical properties of animal matters, from which they may draw inferences relating to animal economy, to medicinal qualities,

* The Translator purposes, if his attempts should be well received, to publish occasionally Supplements, in which the farther improvements which may be made in Chemistry shall be related, articles omitted shall be inserted, and errors which the Author or Translator may have committed, shall be corrected. Advantages may even be derived from the concealment of his name. An anonymous Author is not induced by love of consideration to invent new theories, for the establishment of which, facts, and experiments are too often misrepresented; nor is he, from a talic pride, prevented from renouncing his errors. Any assistance which may be offered (by sending to the Publisher) to supply defective or omitted articles, and to correct faults, shall be gratefully acknowledged.

This Note is omitted in the [illegible] Edition published and in octavo 177[illegible] - In 1779 some Additions to the Dictionary were published in octavo, and a second Edition with considerable Alterations of the Lecture on Gases, the [illegible] Edition of which is added to the octavo Edition of the Dictionary —

and to the proper modes of application of ſubſtances to the cure of diſeaſes, from which Metallurgiſts, Eſſayers, Refiners of Metals, Gilders, Dyers, Manufacturers of Wines, Spirits, Salt, Soap, Pot-aſh, Materials for Painting and Enamelling, Glaſs, Pottery, Porcelain, Perſons employed in the Arts called *Economical*, and in numberleſs others dependent on Chemiſtry, may learn the principles upon which their ſeveral operations depend, and be thereby enabled to improve and extend them; and laſtly, from which, as from a Repoſitory of Chemical Knowledge, Philoſophical Chemiſts may collect the facts and opinions already publiſhed, and thence may be aſſiſted to conduct their experiments, and to form their reaſonings for the farther advancement of Chemiſtry.

ADVER-

ADVERTISEMENT.

MANY good Treatiſes have been publiſhed on Chemiſtry, ſince that ſcience has been cultivated as a fundamental and eſſential part of Natural Philoſophy But none of theſe publications have the form of a Dictionary. Such a work, however, has been thought ſo deſirable by ſome men of learning and taſte for Chemical ſtudies, that they have adviſed me to undertake it. I confeſs that at firſt I did not much approve of their propoſal, as I thought that the connexion and mutual dependance of the parts of Chemiſtry, rendered this ſcience incapable of being treated with propriety in an alphabetical order But on further conſideration, and as I advanced in the execution of the work, I perceived that the form of a Dictionary was leſs imperfect, and even much more advantageous, than it ſeems to ſome men of learning

The alphabetical arrangement does indeed ſeem to interrupt and diſconcert the regularity of plan and ſyſtem, with which a ſcience ought to be treated But this fault may be remedied (as indeed it is in this work, and in other good Dictionaries of Sciences already publiſhed) by references to correſponding articles, and the connexion may, by this means, be reſtored. Beſides, this apparent want of order allows the readers to form ſuch plans to themſelves as they may judge proper, and they may poſſibly make a better choice than the author would have done.

Another advantage attends the treating of a ſcience in an alphabetical order. Names of a great number of things occur under their reſpective initial letters, which would be omitted, in any other method and thus the ſcience is rendered in many reſpects more compleat and extenſive.

I have only to add, that the readers of this work will eaſily perceive, that it is not a mere vocabulary, or dictionary of definitions, but rather a number of diſſertations, generally full and extenſive, on all the important objects of Chemiſtry, written with a deſign to accompliſh all thoſe intentions propoſed in the title-page.

A

PRELIMINARY DISCOURSE

CONCERNING THE

ORIGIN AND PROGRESS

OF

CHEMISTRY.

AS the Hiſtory of any Science ought to relate the labours, the diſcoveries, and the errors of the cultivators of that Science, and to ſhew the obſtacles which they have been obliged to ſurmount, and the miſtaken paths into which they have ſometimes been miſled, it cannot therefore fail of being very uſeful to perſons engaged in the ſame purſuits. This conſideration has induced us to give the following abridged Hiſtory of Chemiſtry. But that we may not repeat what ſome excellent authors have already copiouſly and accurately delivered, we ſhall here treat no further concerning the particular Hiſtory of Chemiſts, than as it tends to illuſtrate the general Hiſtory of Chemiſtry. Our intention is, to ſhew the ſeveral ſtates in which this Science has appeared, the revolutions it has undergone, and the circumſtances which have favoured or retarded its progreſs, in a word, we mean to diſplay a ſummary picture or repreſentation of Chemiſtry in different periods, from its origin to the preſent time.

Moſt authors who have written Hiſtories of Chemiſtry, have deduced its origin from the higheſt antiquity. They extend their reſearches into the firſt ages of the world, and pretend to diſcover ante-diluvian chemiſts But, like all the hiſtorians who have attempted to penetrate through the obſcurity of theſe remote ages, they have found nothing but fable, prodigy, and uncertainty

We do not now live in thoſe ages of credulity, when it could be with gravity maintained, and ſupported by the authority of apocryphal books, that angels and demons, ſmitten with love of women, diſcloſed to them the ſublimeſt parts of Sciences, and the profoundeſt ſecrets of Chemiſtry;

that the book containing theſe ſecrets was called *Kema*, from which Chemiſtry derived its name, beſides a thouſand other reveries of the ſame kind with the preceding, which are not worthy to be mentioned (*a*) All that can be truly and reaſonably ſaid on this ſubject, is, that the invention of ſeveral arts which depend on Chemiſtry, and are moſt neceſſary to men, is of the moſt remote antiquity The Sacred Scriptures mention that *Tubal-cain*, who lived before the Flood, made inſtruments of copper, and of iron This Tubal cain is believed to be the ſame perſon whom the heathen mythology afterwards admitted amongſt the gods by the name of *Vulcan*

Theſe hiſtorical traces have made *Tubal cain* be generally conſidered as the firſt chemiſt a title, which ought to be granted to him with reſpect to that kind of Chemiſtry only which he practiſed, not as a ſcience, but as an art, or a trade

No doubts will remain on this point, if we reflect on the nature and progreſs of the human mind For, what we call Science is the ſtudy and knowledge of the relations which ſubſiſt betwixt certain facts, which neceſſarily muſt be ſuppoſed to have been previouſly diſcovered But the diſcovery of theſe facts muſt have been effected merely by the deſire of gratifying the ſenſes For the moſt active and penetrating mind could have done little, in compariſon with the internal perception of a craving want, which muſt be obeyed If it had not been for the pleaſing and painful impreſſions excited in us by ſurrounding objects, we ſhould have remained ignorant of their moſt common properties Chance at firſt diſcovered ſome of theſe properties, and ſelf-love, from which ariſes an inſtinct more clear ſighted than reaſon itſelf, applied them to uſe The firſt men therefore being neceſſitous, muſt for that reaſon have been the firſt artiſts They ſeized on the beginnings of the arts by a natural effort, very different from that improved reaſoning, which alone can give birth to Science, and which requires the ſpace of ſeveral ſucceeding ages for its formation and perfection We may then conclude that the patriarch *Tubal cain* did no better deſerve the name of *Chemiſt*, than our founders and blackſmiths This concluſion is conformable with the text of Scripture, where he is called only, *malleator* and *faber*, which is to ſay, that he was no more than a mere artiſt, as all thoſe primeval men were, who acquired more knowledge than their contemporaries

(*a*) The author of *A Courſe of Chemiſtry*, who follows the principles of *Newton* and of *Stahl*, and is the firſt of our writers who have conſidered this Science in a manner truly philoſophical, has ridiculed with as much wit as juſtice theſe abſurdities, in an hiſtorical diſcourſe prefixed to his work, where the elegance of the ſtile is ſuitable to the importance which this learned author has given to his ſubject. [*Note of the Author*]

The

The idea which we here give of the original inventors of arts ought not to diminish the glory due to them. For, as the human understanding was then in its infancy, and as the Sciences did not yet exist, these inventors did all which they could possibly do. Although they were simple and rude workmen, yet they ought to be regarded as the greatest geniuses of their age. For the strength and extent of the understanding of men are less the work of nature than of the time and of the country where chance has placed them. If *Stahl* had lived before the Deluge, all the effort of that genius which unfolded the mysteries of nature by means of the most sublime Chemistry, would probably have been reduced to invent the method of forging an ax; and also the great *Newton*, who could measure the universe, and calculate infinites, might perhaps have exhausted the whole force of his mind in reckoning so far as the number ten, if he had been born among those American nations whose best arithmeticians cannot exceed three. Let me therefore repeat it, the first person who forged iron, or cast brass, altho' less expert than our meanest artists, was notwithstanding a great man, and no less deserving our elogiums than the most skilful and profound Chemist.

It has happened to Chemistry, as to the other arts. Before the invention of letters, an apprentice could only practise what he had learnt from his master by oral tradition, and he in the same manner transmitted his knowledge to his successor, like our present workmen, who write nothing, although the art of writing has been so long known. This most excellent art of writing was, like most others, discovered by the ancient Egyptians; and to this happy era may be truly referred the increase of human knowledge, and the birth of Science. Then, a real distinction appeared betwixt philosophers and artists. The latter proceeded in an uniform course, and confined themselves to practice, whereas the former carefully collected all the knowledge which could extend or adorn the human mind, made it the object of their researches, encreased it by meditation and reasoning, reduced it by writing into order, communicated it to each other, and, in a word, laid the foundation of philosophy. These illustrious men were the priests and the kings of a people who had wisdom enough to respect, and were therefore worthy to be governed by, such masters.

Amongst these royal philosophers, *Siphoas* is considered by Chemists as the founder of their Science. He lived, as it is believed, more than 1900 years before the Christian era. The Greeks, who received the Sciences from the Egyptians, knew him by the name of *Hermes*, or *Mercurius Trismegistus*. So numerous is the list recorded by Clemens Alexandrinus of this ancient philosopher's works, (none of which remain) that, in his time, considerable progress must have been made in the sciences. Yet among all that list not one treatise is professedly written on Chemistry, although we find some on every other Science, ex-

 cepting

cepting that one, which has received from him the name of *Hermetic Philosophy* In the library at Leyden some Arabian manuscripts said to have been written by Hermes are more directly on the subject of Chemistry Such, for instance, is that manuscript concerning poisons and antidotes, and another concerning precious stones But these compositions are justly considered as spurious, and less ancient (*b*). Probably, therefore, all the Chemistry known in the time of *Hermes* consisted of detached pieces of knowledge, the relations of which were undiscovered, and which therefore could not form a Science, although, at that time, Astronomy, Ethics, and some other Sciences had made considerable progress, as is evinced by the enumeration of the books of *Hermes*. We shall be less surprized at this observation, when we consider that some of the most important phenomena of Chemistry are very little obvious to our senses Hidden as they are by nature under a veil, like the springs of some precious machine, they are discoverable by those only who know to search for them, and by eyes exercised in that search If some of these singular and remarkable phenomena have been ever discovered by accident, they could only appear to these early philosophers as detached facts, the application and uses of which could not be perceived, because many other facts, essentially related to those discovered, were unknown.

These first Chemists, therefore, had no other resource than to collect the phenomena which came within their knowledge These they might reproduce at pleasure, either for use, or to excite the astonishment of the ignorant.

Such, without doubt, was the Chemistry of the first inventors of the Sciences, and such was the Chemistry which was taught to *Moses*, " instructed," as the Scriptures say, " in the wisdom of the Egyptians ," and which was afterwards taught to *Democritus*, who went to Egypt on purpose to learn the Sciences at their place of origin Both of these have

(*b*) Two illustrious Egyptians of the name of *Hermes* are recorded by ancient authors. The elder, who is supposed to be the same as *Mizraim*, the grandson of Noah, the *Hermes* of the Greeks, and the *Mercury* of the Romans, is considered as the founder of the Sciences And the younger *Hermes*, surnamed *Trismegistus*, who lived a housand years afterwards, restored the Sciences, after they had fallen into oblivion in consequence of a great inundation of the Nile. Of his numerous works none remains, excepting perhaps the Smaragdine Table No less than thirty-six thousand books are said to have been written under the name of Hermes But all these are not to be attributed to him. For, according to Jamblicus, a custom prevailed of inscribing all books of Science with the name of Hermes Some of these are preserved in great libraries, and a book, entitled, *The Works of Hermes*, was published at Venice, in Greek and Latin, 1531, and at Cologne, 1620, with notes by Annibal Rosellius Some authors deny the existence of Hermes, and maintain that his history is allegorical *See Deslandé's Histoire Critique de la Philosophie*, Tom. I. Livre I ch. 6.

been

been numbered among Chemists the former, because he dissolved the golden calf, and rendered it potable by the Israelites the latter, from the testimony of many ancient authors, and particularly of Pliny the Naturalist, who ascribes to Democritus a knowledge also of the magic arts (*c*)

Although we have advanced but little in the History of Chemistry, we cannot proceed without mentioning a singular madness which possessed Chemists It was a kind of epidemic malady, the symptoms of which shewed to what excess of folly the human mind could proceed, when influenced by a strong prepossession It excited chemists to surprising efforts, by which admirable discoveries were made, but it nevertheless impeded the advancement of Chemistry. Finally, the time when this malady began to be cured, which was not sooner than the last century, is the true era of the revival of this Science, and of its progress to perfection

It is evident, that I mean the passion for making gold From the time that this metal has become, by general convention, the representative of the value of all commodities, it has kindled a fresh fire in the furnaces of Chemists It appeared natural enough, that men skilled in the properties of metals, and accustomed to see them take a thousand various forms, should endeavor to produce the most beautiful and the most precious of all these metals. The wonders which they every day saw arise from their art, made them conceive hopes of adding this new prodigy to those which they had already effected They were at that time far from being capable of judging concerning the possibility of their undertaking, since even now that question is undecided. To blame their first trials, would be therefore unjust. But unfortunately this new object of their researches, was but too capable of producing a state of mind very different from the philosophical. it so engrossed their attention, that they lost sight of other objects: they imagined that to be the ultimate end and perfection of Chemistry, which in reality was only the solution of one chemical problem. their Science, far from being more extensive, was concentrated round a single point, to accomplish which they directed their labors. The desire of gain became their motive of action they were close and mysterious in a word, they had the character of tradesmen, and if they had succeeded, they would have been mere makers of gold, instead of being intelligent and skilful Chemists. But, unfortunately for them,

(*c*) Of all the Greeks who travelled into Egypt to acquire knowledge, *Democritus* only was admitted into their mysteries None of his writings are preserved. The Egyptian priests are said to have taught him many chemical operations, amongst which were the arts of softening ivory, of vitrifying flints, and of imitating precious stones. *Of Borrich. Senec. Epist.* 30

the

the trade at which they labored exiſted only in their imaginations. This circumſtance, however, by which they were deprived of a conſtant gain, diſtinguiſhed them from other artiſts, and rendered their ſituation ſomewhat ſimilar to men of ſcience. They therefore availed themſelves of this ſimilarity, and arrogated the titles of Philoſophers and of Chemiſts, in preference to all others, as is expreſſed by the Arabic particle *al*, which they added to the name of their ſcience, whence the words Alchemy and Alchemiſt, ſignifying *The* Chemiſtry, and *The* Chemiſt.

Theſe men were therefore an intermediate ſpecies betwixt philoſophers and artiſts. They had the name of the former, the character of the latter, and were indeed neither the one nor the other. In order to ſupport their reputation, they wrote books, like the philoſophers, on their pretended ſcience: but as character is never to be effaced, they wrote theſe books ſo obſcurely and unintelligibly, that they gave no more inſtruction concerning their art than if they had not written. Several of them ſeem ſenſible of the reproach to which they are juſtly ſubject in this reſpect, and endeavor to excite attention by declaring at the beginning of their books, that they mean to ſpeak clearly and plainly, which, however, they take care not to do. It is ſomething ſingular to ſee them, after having formally promiſed to reveal the moſt hidden ſecrets, expreſs themſelves more obſcurely than any of their predeceſſors.

We may eaſily judge what conſideration theſe people were held in, who did nothing and taught nothing: hence their hiſtory is as obſcure and confuſed as their writings. We do not even know the true names of moſt of them, the time when they lived, or whether the books attributed to them be genuine or ſpurious. In a word, every thing concerning them is involved in myſtery.

We ſhall not then enter into any detail about *Syneſius, Zoſimus, Adfar, Mortenus, Calid, Arnoldus de Villa Nova, Raymond Lully, Alanus Lillius, Johannes Meunius*, and numberleſs writers or pretended philoſophers, the enumeration of whoſe names would be tedious: but we ſhall haſten over this middle age of Chemiſtry, which is the moſt obſcure and the moſt humiliating part of its hiſtory. Thoſe who are deſirous of knowing what is related concerning the Chemiſtry of theſe times, true or falſe, may conſult the works of Borrichius, and the *Hiſtory of the Hermetic Philoſophy* by the Abbé Langlet de Freſnoy.

We ſhall content ourſelves with obſerving, that in this crowd of alchemical and unintelligible writers, there are a few who have expreſſed themſelves leſs obſcurely on certain experiments, and have given ſome intelligence. Such perhaps are *Geber*, the Arabian, *Roger Bacon*, an Engliſh Monk, who appears to have known gun-powder, and who was accuſed of magic, *Raymond Lully*, *Baſil Valentine*, and *Iſaacus Hollandus*, in whoſe writings ſomething may be decyphered concerning acid ſpirits, antimony, and perhaps other ſubſtances

Theſe valuable hints, which he ſmothered under a heap of riddles, are ſufficient to make us regret, that theſe laborious ſearchers into the philoſopher's ſtone have neglected to inform us of other pieces of knowledge, becauſe they were not immediately related to their object of enquiry The moſt eſſential ſervice which they could have rendered to Chemiſtry was, to relate their unſucceſsful experiments as clearly, as they have obſcurely related thoſe which they pretend to have been ſucceſsful

Such was the ſtate of Chemiſtry, or rather of Alchemy, till the ſixteenth century At that period, a famous Alchemiſt, called *Paracelſus*, a man of quick parts, extravagant, and impetuous, added a new ſpecies of folly to the follies of his predeceſſors Being the ſon of a phyſician, and himſelf a phyſician, he imagined, that by Alchemy an *univerſal medicine* might be diſcovered While he was boaſting, that he poſſeſſed the ſecret of prolonging his life to the age of Methuſalem, he died at the age of only forty eight years Before him indeed *Raymond Lully*, and other Alchemiſts, had dreamed of an univerſal medicine, but this famous chimera owed its credit chiefly to the eagerneſs and confidence of Paracelſus

This notion, abſurd as it was, gained many partiſans, and gave double force to the madneſs of Alchemiſts, ſo apt are men to believe what they wiſh to be true! Our philoſophers, without laying aſide their former inquiries into the tranſmutation of metals, and the making of gold, vied with each other in eagerneſs to diſcover the univerſal remedy, and perſuaded themſelves, that theſe ſeveral miracles might be effected by one chemical proceſs Many of them boaſted that their attempts had ſucceeded, and ſtiled themſelves *Adepts* Their books were now filled with receipts for making potable gold, elixirs of life, panaceas, or univerſal remedies, but were written in their uſual, that is to ſay, unintelligible language.

So many accumulated extravagancies had rendered Chemiſtry a pretended ſcience, or, as M Fontenelle ingeniouſly ſays, " a little truth was " ſo diluted in a large quantity of falſhood, that it became inviſible and " inſeparable To the few known properties of ſubſtances their imagi- " nations added others more dazzling Metals were ſuppoſed to ſympathiſe with planets, and with the principal parts of the human body. " an alkaheſt, or menſtruum, which had never been ſeen, was ſuppoſed " to be capable of diſſolving all ſubſtances the greateſt abſurdities were " reverenced, becauſe they were enveloped in myſterious darkneſs, in " which they were entrenched againſt the attacks of reaſon "

The notion of an univerſal remedy, although the moſt fooliſh that had entered the heads of Alchemiſts, was however the cauſe of the eſtabliſhment of rational Chemiſtry on the ruins of Alchemy

The

The fiery and enterprising *Paracelsus* had ventured to strike out a new road in the art of healing. He declaimed incessantly against the ancient pharmacy, in which were few or no Chemical remedies, and in a fit of madness he publickly burnt the writings of the ancient Greek and Arabian physicians, vaunting, at the same time, that, by his Chemical preparations, he could bestow immortality. His success, although inferior to his promises, was however prodigious. He made many surprising cures, and he applied, with great advantage, mercurial preparations against the venereal disease, which appeared about that time, and baffled the remedies of the ordinary pharmacy.

The real merit of Paracelsus excited many envious enemies, and the enthusiasm and foolish vanity with which he blazoned his skill, excited the admiration of others still more foolish.

Those physicians who had good sense enough to avoid these extremes, took the middle and wisest part. They were persuaded, that much dependance was not to be given to the sayings of a man who was foolish enough to despise the knowledge of all others, and to continually boast of his own discoveries, and therefore would not, like the mad partisans of Paracelsus, give implicit faith to his extravagant assertions. But, on the other side, they were convinced by his successful cures, that Chemistry could furnish excellent remedies, unknown before that time; and, like good citizens, they endeavoured to discover those remedies by an industry worthy of praise, since their motive was the good of mankind. They were, to speak properly, the inventors of a new Chemical art, the object of which was the preparation of medicines. They wrote what they knew concerning their art, because they were not mere artists, and they wrote clearly, because they were not Alchemists.

There were then two classes of Chemists, very different from each other.

While the *Rosicrusian fraternity*, *Cosmopolitanus*, *Espagnet*, *Beausoleil*, *Philalethes*, and many others, lost their time, their trouble, and their money, in prosecuting the foolish notions of *Paracelsus*, many valuable works were published by *Crollius*, *Quercetanus*, *Beguinus*, *Hartmannus*, *Vigani*, *Schroder*, *Zwelfer*, *Tachenius*, *Le Fevre*, *Glaser*, *Lemeri*, *Le Mort*, *Ludovicus*, and many others, who applied themselves to discover and describe new Chemical remedies.

The principal Faculties of Medicine, perceiving how important it was that remedies should always be prepared in one uniform manner, endeavored to fix and establish the processes: hence the many *Pharmacopeias* and *Dispensatories*, in which many excellent Chemical operations are described.

The greatest part of those *Chemical arts* which are exercised without literary

literary ſtudy, had, in the days of Paracelſus, arrived to a remarkable perfection, by a progreſs, ſlow indeed, but long, and uninterrupted from almoſt the beginning of the world. *Ores* of *metals* were then advantageouſly eſſayed and ſmelted. The methods were well known of allaying, diſſolving, and refining *metals* for the purpoſes of goldſmiths and of coinage. The compoſition of *glaſſes*, of *factitious cryſtals*, of *enamels*, and of various kinds of *earthen ware*, was underſtood. The preparation of *colors*, and their application to the purpoſes of dyeing, were known. *Fermentations*, by which *wine*, *beer*, and *vinegar*, were produced, and *diſtillations*, by which the ſpirituous, volatile and aromatic parts of plants were procured for the compoſition of *eſſences* and *perfumes*, were underſtood and practiſed: but all theſe arts were exerciſed by people who knew nothing but what related to their own buſineſs, and as they had never been deſcribed, ſo they were not all underſtood by any one perſon. All the parts of Chemiſtry did then exiſt, but the Science of Chemiſtry did not yet exiſt.

Happily the taſte for knowledge, which then began to ſucceed the jargon and ignorance of the preceding ages, awakened men of a philoſophic mind, and made them ſenſible how important it was to acquire and publiſh ſuch a number of uſeful facts. They ſurmounted all kinds of obſtacles, in order to diſcover and unravel the operations of workmen, who, though not Chemiſts, exerciſed the moſt eſſential parts of Chemiſtry.

The celebrated *Agricola* is one of the firſt and beſt authors of this kind. Born in a village of Miſnia, a country abounding in mines and metallurgic works, he has deſcribed them exactly and copiouſly. He was a phyſician, and was cotemporary to Paracelſus, but of a character very different. His writings are as clear and inſtructive as thoſe of Paracelſus are obſcure and uſeleſs. *Lazard*, *Erker*, *Schinder*, *Schlutter (d)*, *Henkel (e)*, and ſome others, have alſo written on metallurgy, and have deſcribed the art of eſſaying metals. *Antony Neri*, Doctor *Merret*, and the famous *Kunkel (f)*, who has enriched Chemiſtry with many fine experiments, have deſcribed very fully the arts of making glaſs, enamels, imitations of precious ſtones, and ſeveral other things.

The valuable Chemiſts whom we have mentioned, and even many who ſucceeded them, and whom we diſtinguiſh from the Alchemiſts, were not however entirely free from the illuſions of Alchemy. So true it is, that

(*d*) The works of *Schlutter* have been tranſlated into French by *Hellot*, and enriched by the obſervations of the Tranſlator, to whom Chemiſtry has many obligations.

(*e*) A part of *Henkel*'s works have been tranſlated into French by the *Baron d'Olbach*, one of the moſt zealous and illuſtrious benefactors of French Chemiſtry.

(*f*) The works of *Neri*, *Merret*, and *Kunkel*, are tranſlated into French by *Baron d'Olbach*.

that an obstinate and inveterate malady never disappears at once, without leaving traces behind. Thus, since the time of Paracelsus and Agricola, we have had many authors, in some respects rational Chemists, and in others Alchemists: *Kessler, Cassius, Rolfinkius, Orschal, Sir Kenelm Digby, Libavius, Van Helmont, Starkey, Borrichius*, are of this number. But they have sufficiently made compensation for this fault, by the number of interesting experiments which they have related.

As in the latter times of the authors above-mentioned, the Alchemical phrenzy began to draw near its crisis, it was attacked by many powerful antagonists, to whom rational Chemistry has many obligations, since by their writings, they contributed to rescue that science from an evil which at once disgraced it, and retarded its progress. Amongst these authors, are most distinguished the celebrated *Kircher*, a Jesuit, and the learned physician *Conringius*, who wrote with much success and reputation.

We are at length arrived at one of the most brilliant eras of Chemistry; I mean the time when its several parts began to be collected, examined, and compared by men of genius sufficiently extensive and profound to comprehend them all, to discover their principles, to perceive their relations, to unite them into one body of rational doctrine, and to lay the true foundation of Chemistry, considered as a Science.

Before the middle of the last age, this edifice was not begun to be erected, but the materials only had been collected. *Jam Barner*, physician to the king of Poland, was one of the first who arranged into order the principal Chemical experiments, and added rational explanations. His work is entitled *Philosophical Chemistry*. All the phenomena of this Science are there referred to the system of acids and alkalis which *Tachenius* had established, but which he had abused by extending too far: a fault very pardonable, when we consider how difficult it was for him to avoid it, who had discovered truths so general and so fertile in consequences as are the properties of these substances.

Bohnius, a Professor at Leipsic, published also a valuable Treatise of Rational Chemistry; but the reputation of these Philosophical Chemists has been almost eclipsed by the famous *Becher*, principal Physician to the Electors of Mentz and of Bavaria. This man, whose genius equalled his knowledge, appears to have seen, with a single glance, the immense multitude of chemical phenomena. By reflecting on these important objects, he invented the best and most satisfactory theory which has been ever published. This theory has had the honor of being adopted and commented upon by the greatest and most sublime of all the Philosophical Chemists.

By these titles the illustrious *Stahl*, principal Physician to the late King of Prussia, deserves to be distinguished. Born, as *Becher* was, with a strong

strong passion for Chemistry, which shewed itself in his early youth, he inherited a genius still superior to that of *Becher*. His imagination was as lively, as brilliant, and as active as that of his predecessor, and he had, besides, the inestimable advantage of being regulated by that philosophic and temperate wisdom, which effectually preserves from enthusiasm and illusion. The theory of *Becher*, which he has adopted almost entirely, has become, in his writings, of all theories the most enlightening, and the most conformable with the phenomena of Chemistry. Very different from those systems which are produced by imagination, without truth, and which experience destroys, the theory of *Stahl* is the surest guide that we can take for our conduct in Chemical researches, and the numerous experiments which are every day made, far from invalidating it, become new proofs for its confirmation.

Next to *Stahl* we place the immortal *Boerhaave*, though he excelled in a different way. This powerful genius, the honor of his country, of his profession, and of his age, threw light upon every subject which he treated. To the view which he took of Chemistry we owe the finest and most methodical analysis of the vegetable kingdom, his admirable Treatises on Air, on Water, on Earth, and particularly that on Fire, which is an astonishing master-piece, so complete, that the human understanding can scarcely make any addition to it.

Altho' the theories of the great men we have mentioned may contribute infinitely to the advancement of Chemistry, by explaining the causes and relations of the phenomena of that Science, we must however confess that they may produce a very contrary effect, if we deliver ourselves up to them with too much confidence, and extend their application beyond their true limits. Theories can only be useful so far as they arise from experiments already made, or lead us to new ones, for reasoning may be considered as the eye of a philosopher, but experience is his feeling, and this latter sense ought constantly to rectify the too frequent errors of the former. If experiments, undirected by theory, are only a blind feeling, theory without experiments is a deceitful and uncertain vision. Accordingly, the most important discoveries that have been made in Chemistry have been owing to the joint assistance of both.

A very convincing proof of this truth appears in the works of the illustrious literary societies, whose origin may be considered as the origin of experimental philosophy, and the true era of the expulsion of the barbarous jargon of the schools, of the illusions of judicial Astrology, of the extravagancies of Alchemy, which were only chimerical speculations, destitute of proof, or confused heaps of inconclusive facts.

The learned and profound Memoirs of those celebrated Societies will be ever the model of those who intend to advance the progress of Science, since

ſince there we always ſee experiments giving ſtability to theory, and theory giving light to experiment.

We have now the advantage of ſeeing the beſt days of Chemiſtry. The taſte of our age for philoſophical matters; the protection of Princes, the zeal of a multitude of illuſtrious and intelligent perſons attached by inclination to the ſtudy of this Science; the profound ſkill and ardor of modern Chemiſts, whom we do not attempt to praiſe, becauſe they are above our eulogiums, ſeem altogether to promiſe the greateſt and moſt brilliant ſucceſs. We have ſeen Chemiſtry drawing its origin from neceſſity, and receiving a ſlow and obſcure encreaſe from avarice. To true philoſophy it was reſerved to bring it to perfection.

A DICTIONARY

A
DICTIONARY
OF
CHEMISTRY.

I. ABSORBENT (*a*)
II ACETOUS (*b*)
III ACESCENT

This word may be employed to denote a matter, which either is turning sour, that is to say, acid, or which is slightly acid. *See* ACID (*c*)

IV ACID. Acids are of all saline substances the most simple, and consequently ought to be considered as *secondary principles* Their name is derived from their taste, which is acid or sour One of the marks by which they are easily known, is their property of changing into red the blue colors of an infusion of flowers of violets, or of the tincture of heliotropium (*d*)

If acids were separated from all moisture or water, and from all other substances not necessary to their saline essence, they would appear under a concrete

(*a*) ABSORBENT Those *earths* are called *absorbent*, which are capable of being combined with acids These are calcareous earths, ashes of burnt vegetable and animal substances, magnesia, and earth of alum. This class of earths might be more properly denominated *alkaline earths* *See* EARTH, MAGNESIA, ALUM

(*b*) ACETOUS *Acetous acid* is the same as vinegar *Acetous fermentation* is that fermentation by which vinegar is produced. *Acetous ether* is an ether made by means of vinegar. *See* VINEGAR, and ETHER.

(*c*) The word *acescent* can only be properly applied to denote the first of these meanings The second may be expressed by either of the words, *acidulous* or *subacid*

(*d*) This property of changing the blue, and of heightening the red colors of vegetables, is not common to all acids, for the volatile sulphureous acid destroys these colors · nor is it peculiar to acids, for alum, a neutral salt, produces the same effect.

or solid form. But generally they are liquid, because their affinity to water is so great, that when they contain no more than what is necessary to constitute them salts, they are strongly disposed to seize more water, whenever they can touch it, and as the atmosphere is always loaded with watery vapors, the contact of the air is solely sufficient to render acids fluid, by their rapid union with its moisture

Acids have a general tendency to unite with almost all substances, particularly with those which are either simple, or not much compounded, as phlogiston, alkaline salts, fixed and volatile, earths, (especially those called *absorbent*), metallic substances, water, and oil

Many substances are by chemists called *acids*, because they possess those general properties which we have mentioned But these substances differ from each other by properties peculiar to each

As acids from their tendency to unite, and to remain united with almost all other bodies, are never found single and pure, but must be obtained and separated by artificial operations from the bodies with which they happen to be combined, they have been distinguished by authors into classes, according to the substances whence they are extracted These classes are *mineral acids*, *vegetable acids*, and *animal acids* In Mr Geoffroy's Table of Affinities, those of acids are marked in the following order fixed alkali, volatile alkali, earths, metallic substances (*e*)

Very concentrated acids taken internally in a dose somewhat large, for instance, an ounce, or even much less, when the acid is susceptible of great concentration, are corrosive and genuine poisons Their best antidotes are alkaline substances, either saline or earthy, oils, alkaline soaps, large quantities of mild drink, as water, milk, mucilages These must be given copiously and speedily

Small doses of acids diluted with much water, so as to be agreeably acidulous, and blunted by some mild substance, as sugar, are excellent cooling and aperitive medicines, fit to quench excessive thirst, and lessen the acrimony of the bile They are chiefly useful in alkalescent dispositions, and in putrid, inflammatory fevers Their whole action seems to be exerted on the primæ viæ, for they are rendered unactive by the powers of digestion, by means of which they are combined with the earthy and oily parts of aliments and digestive juices. They would be certain poisons if they passed into the blood vessels with their acid qualities, at least with their acidity undiminished They would coagulate the blood, and would greatly irritate the nervous and sensible parts Malpighi killed a dog by injecting into the veins such a quantity of nitrous acid, as would not have hurt, if it had been swallowed Acids employed externally shew similar qualities, but more sensibly than when impaired by the digestive powers They are useful against alkalescent putridity (*f*)

(*e*) The *affinities or powers of union of acids* are, 1. Fixed alkali, 2 Calcareous earth, 3 Volatile alkali, and magnesia, the powers of union of these two being nearly equal, 4 Iron, zinc, copper, and perhaps some other metals, 5 Earth of alum, 6 The remaining metals.

(*f*) 1. The *common properties of acids* are, 1 They may be united with water This is not merely a dilution of acids, for by uniting them with a certain quantity of water, heat or cold is produced, and the mixed fluid acquires a specific gravity, different from the inter-

V. ACIDS (ANIMAL) This name is given to acids obtained from certain animal matters, as butter, fat, blood, ants, and moſt flies.

Theſe acids have been too little examined to enable us to judge whether they be eſſentially different from thoſe obtained from vegetables. But we are certain that they differ in the ſame circumſtances as the vegetable acids do from mineral acids; and probably, this difference proceeds from the ſame cauſe.

intermediate gravity of its component parts. From this union, therefore, a new compound is formed. 2. They may be combined with ſpirit of wine. *See* ÆTHER. 3. They may be combined with abſorbent earths. 4. They may be combined with alkaline ſalts. 5. They may be combined with metallic ſubſtances. Although every acid does not directly diſſolve every metallic ſubſtance, yet probably by concentration or dilution of the acid, diviſion of the metals by mechanical and chemical methods, by application of ſufficient heat, and other means, every metal may be acted upon by every acid. 6. They may be combined with phlogiſton, and with oils. 7. When they combine with theſe ſubſtances, they diſengage from them all or part of the fixable air which they contain. 8. They ſoften and diſſolve the ſolid parts of animals. 9. They coagulate moſt of the liquid parts of animals. 10. They change to red the blue, and heighten the red colors of vegetables, excepting volatile, ſulphureous acid, which deſtroys theſe colors. Probably this change of color proceeds from the action of acids upon the oily parts of vegetables; for oils are rendered red by ſufficiently concentrated acids. 11. They reſiſt fermentations. 12. They are not capable of being frozen by ſo ſmall a degree of cold as water is. 13. They produce cold when poured upon ice.

2. *As acids ſo powerfully attract water,* that they are never found pure and dry, but always in a fluid ſtate, when uncombined with earths, alkalies, or metals, we cannot eaſily aſcertain the quantity of acid contained in acid liquors. Homberg has attempted to eſtimate the quantity of acid contained in the acid ſpirits of vinegar, nitre, ſea-ſalt, and of vitriol, by combining theſe liquors with ſalt of tartar, ſo as to form neutral ſalts; imagining that the weight gained by that alkali from its union with acids, or the difference betwixt the weight of the ſalt of tartar and the neutral ſalt produced, was equal to the weight of real acid contained in the quantity of acid liquor employed. But as he did not conſider, that the air expelled from ſalt of tartar, during its combination with acids, makes a very conſiderable part of the weight of that alkali, the inferences from his experiments are not juſt; and the real quantity of acid contained in an acid liquor, is ſo much more than the quantity inferred by him, as the whole weight of the fixable air diſengaged from the ſalt of tartar. The quantity of fixable air contained in ſalt of tartar varies much according to the method of its preparation, and other circumſtances; but if we ſuppoſe that the fixable air in the ſalt of tartar, uſed by Homberg, was in as great a proportion as in the pearl-aſhes of Mr Cavendiſh, [Phil Tranſ. 1766] that is $\frac{284}{1000}$ of the whole weight of the alkali, by adding $\frac{284}{1000}$ of the alkali uſed in each experiment, we ſhall nearly find the true quantity of ſolid acid in each neutral ſalt. *The firſt column ſhews the quantity of each* of the acids employed to ſaturate an ounce of ſalt of tartar, and the ſecond column ſhews the quantities of the neutral ſalts produced.

1	2
Diſtilled vinegar, 14 oz	oz 1 dr 3 gr 36
Spirit of ſalt, oz 2. dr 5.	oz 1. dr 3 gr 14
Spirit of nitre, oz 1. dr 2 gr. 36	oz. 1 dr 3 gr 10
Acid of vitriol, dr 5.	oz. 1 dr 3 gr. 5

Homberg ſuppoſes, that in each of the neutral ſalts, the quantities of which are mentioned in the ſecond column, the quantity of contained alkaline ſalt is equal to an ounce, and the quantity of contained acid is equal to the remaining weight; whereas by

which constitutes the difference betwixt the vegetable and mineral acids; namely, the combination of oily particles with the former (g)

The *phosphoric acid*, obtained from urine, appears, for the same reason, to belong to this class of animal acids But it has properties so different from those

by our proposed method of correction, supposing still that the quantity of fixable air in his salt of tartar was $\frac{284}{1000}$ of the whole weight, we shall find that of the oz 1 dr 3 gr 5 of vitriolated tartar in the last mentioned instance of the table, dr 5 gr 44 were fixed alkali deprived of its air, and dr 5 gr 21 were acid Hence we may perceive that the quantities of alkali and of acid in the several neutral salts, the weights of which are expressed in the second column of the table, are very nearly equal *See* AIR (FIXABLE)

3. The *known acids* are, 1 Vitriolic acid 2 Nitrous acid 3 Marine acid 4 Acetous acid 5 Vinous acid, or tartar 6 Essential acid of vegetables 7 Acid obtained by distillation of vegetables 8 Acid of bitumens 9 Acid of borax 10 Acid obtained by distillation of oils, resins, and fats 11 Phosphoric acid 12 Acid of ants and other insects 13 Acids of healthy and of diseased stomachs of animals. 14. Acid of perspirable matter of diseased animals Perhaps the number of acids is much larger, or perhaps some of these are only modifications of other primary acids, or lastly, as Stahl supposes, they are all modifications of the one only primary acid, namely, that of vitriol *See the theory of acids under the article* SALT

(g) The acid of ants may be perceived by smell, on turning up an ant-hill in spring or summer When these insects are irritated, they discharge a fluid which has an acid taste and smell Water, or spirit of wine, in which they are agitated, becomes acidulous. Part of this acid is so volatile as to rise by distillation with spirit of wine, in which ants had been immersed, but the greatest part of it is so fixed, as to remain united with the residuous phlegm All the acid may be extracted by water, and rendered capable of rising by distillation with that fluid in a water-bath From 24 ounces of fresh ants were obtained by distillation, without addition, eleven ounces and two drams of acid spirit, some urinous salt and spirit, some empyreumatic oil, and a residuum, consisting of earth and fixed salt This acid is found to have the general properties of acids. With fixed alkalies it forms neutral crystals, oblong, and deliquescent These crystals being distilled by a violent fire, yielded a liquor scarcely acid, and another liquor urinous or ammoniacal From the residuum dissolved in water, by filtration and evaporation, were obtained large crystals which did not deliquiate, and had the general properties of fixed alkalies In this experiment the acid seemed to disappear But by pouring oil of vitriol on these alkaline crystals, white vapors were disengaged, although no acid spirit could be obtained by distillation From these white vapors, and from the facility with which this salt crystalizes, Mr. Margraaf, from whom these and the following experiments on the acid of ants are extracted, suspects the existence of a latent acid The acid of ants formed with volatile alkali an ammoniacal fluid, which, like the combination of the same alkali with vinegar, could not be reduced to a concrete or solid state With quicklime, chalk, and coral, it formed dry crystals.

This acid did not precipitate silver, lead, or mercury, from nitrous acid, hence it has no analogy to marine acid Nor did it precipitate quicklime from marine acid, and hence it has no analogy to vitriolic acid

As a menstruum, this acid acted weakly upon copper, and strongly upon iron and upon zinc, but it did not act, or very little, upon silver, lead, tin, regulus of antimony and bismuth Its combination with iron crystallized, in which respect it differs from vinegar It dissolved the calxes of copper, silver, zinc, and lead, but not the calxes of tin, regulus of antimony, bismuth, or of mercury, which last calx it converted to fluid quicksilver Upon the whole (says Margraaf), we may perceive a resemblance in many respects, though not in all, betwixt this acid and the acetous *See the Memoirs of the*

of all other acids, that it deserves to be considered as a distinct acid *See* PHOSPHORUS

VI ACIDS (CONCRETE) These are saline, solid substances which have the general properties of acids Such are, *crystals of tartar*, *essential salts of vegetables*, particularly of those which are acid, the *volatile acid salt of amber*, and of some other *bitumens*, and *flowers of Benjamin*

VII ACID *of* VINEGAR. *See* VINEGAR

VIII ACIDS (FLUOR), Are those which are generally, or always in a fluid state, such are the volatile vitriolic, nitrous, marine acids, and those obtained by distillation from vegetable and animal substances

IX ACID (MARINE) This is so called, because it is generally obtained from sea-salt, though it may be also procured from *Sal-gem*, or *fossile salt*, and from the salt of saline fountains and pits, since all these salts are different from sea-salt, only as to their origin

The marine acid, as well as the nitrous and vitriolic, is never found alone and pure, but it is always combined with an alkali, so as to form a neutral salt, which is dissolved copiously in the sea, to which it gives a salt taste

This neutral salt is also found crystallized in large transparent masses within the earth, and is then called *Sal gem*, or *fossile salt*

It is also dissolved in the waters of some *wells* or *fountains*, which may be owing to these waters communicating by subterraneous passages with the sea, or to their passing through mines of *Sal-gem*

The marine acid has all the general properties of saline acid substances

It differs from the vitriolic acid in the following circumstances it is more light and volatile, it has smell and color, it emits vapors, it has less affinity with fixed alkalies and absorbent earths, and, like the nitrous acid, it forms with absorbent earths no salts but such as are deliquescent

It differs from the nitrous acid by its color, which is more yellow and less red, by the whiteness of its vapors, which are visible only in open air, by its smell, which resembles saffron, by a weaker affinity with absorbent earths and fixed alkalies *(h)*

The marine acid cannot be so much concentrated as the vitriolic and nitrous acids, because it is more volatile

This acid cannot be so easily combined with phlogiston as the vitriolic and nitrous, and we are not certain that some medium is not requisite for such a combination

Although the properties of the marine acid are as well known as those of nitrous and vitriolic, yet chemists are far from understanding the nature of this saline substance equally well Becker, according to his theory of acids, attributes the distinguishing properties of the marine acid to that principle which

the Berlin Academy, vol 4 1749, or the *Opuscules Chemiques de Mr Margraaf*

Insects armed with stings, as bees, wasps, and hornets, when irritated, discharge an acid liquor

(h) Marine acid differs from the nitrous in another instance, besides those mentioned in the text It readily dissolves metallic calxes, which are little affected by nitrous acid. Hence it extracts from most colored earths and stones the metallic calxes, by which the color of these substances is produced

he calls *mercurial earth*. But he supports his opinion by no other proofs, than by some appearances excited by the union of this acid with metallic substances, in which also he supposes this mercurial earth to be a component part. But as the existence of this mercurial earth in marine acid, or in metallic substances, is not demonstrated, nor even sufficiently indicated; and as Becker has explained himself very obscurely and confusedly on this subject, what he has said does not merit a deliberate discussion. Stahl, therefore, who was too judicious to be satisfied with appearances and probabilities, abandoned, in some measure, this part of Becker's theory, and only expresses a wish that the existence of the mercurial earth could be as well ascertained as the existence of phlogiston.

This great chemist, however, appears to be convinced of the primary identity of all saline substances; that is to say, he believed that they all were the vitriolic acid disguised by some mixture. He assures us, even, that he has been able to transmute acids into each other; that is, to change the vitriolic acid into the nitrous and marine; and to reduce these back again into the vitriolic. But he has not published his experiments on this subject, perhaps because he had not sufficiently ascertained the processes, or that he chose to reserve to himself such important discoveries. The possibility, therefore, of these transmutations of acids is not yet determined. *(i)*

The properties of the marine acid, above-mentioned, indicate nothing more than that it participates of the nature of both the vitriolic and nitrous acids.

Its combination with phlogiston, which, of all its properties, might assist us more in our investigation, has not been sufficiently explained.

The unsuccessful attempts made by M. Margraaf, a celebrated chemist of the academy of Berlin, to combine the marine acid pure and crude, as he calls it, with phlogiston, with a view to compose phosphorus, are so many fresh causes of uncertainty, and additional motives to endeavor the illustration of this important object. *See* PHOSPHORUS.

Marine acid combined to the point of saturation with marine alkali, called also mineral or fossil alkali, forms a neutral salt, crystalizing in cubes, of an agreeable, salt taste. *See* COMMON SALT under the article SALT.

With volatile alkali it forms a neutral, crystalized, and very pungent salt. This salt is semi volatile, and may be sublimed with a certain degree of heat. It is called *Sal ammoniac*. *See* AMMONIAC.

Metallic substances are in general more difficultly dissolved by the marine than by the vitriolic and nitrous acids, because the first has less affinity than the other two with phlogiston, which is the medium of union betwixt metals and acids.

Marine acid, when fluid, however much concentrated, and assisted by any heat, cannot dissolve gold, silver, platina, or mercury, in their natural or metallic state. It combines however very well and intimately with silver and mercury by two methods. One of these is called the dry method or cementation, because the acid then, in some measure, is dry, and exposed to the greatest heat it is capable of receiving. *See* PARTING (CONCENTRATED) and SUBLIMATE

(i) Concerning the identity of acids, see the article SALT. Concerning the transmutation of marine acid into the acid of nitre, *see* also ACID (NITROUS).

(COR-

(CORROSIVE). The second method is called the *humid way*, and consists in separating these metals from their solutions in nitrous acid. See LUNA CORNEA, and PRECIPITATE (WHITE).

This acid, when pure and unmixed, cannot by any known method dissolve gold or platina. But when it is mixed with the nitrous acid, it forms a menstruum called *aqua regia*, which readily dissolves these metals. See AQUA REGIA. From combinations of aqua regia with gold or platina, metallic salts are formed susceptible of crystalization. See GOLD, and PLATINA. (*k*)

Pure marine acid dissolves sufficiently well tin, lead, copper, iron, zinc, and bismuth; and less easily regulus of antimony: and it forms with these metals different salts, the properties of which see under the articles TIN, LEAD, &c. (*l*)

The general phenomena, most remarkable in the combination of marine acid with metallic matters, are;

1. It dissolves these substances with less heat and effervescence, and with fewer vapors, than nitrous acid does. This observation is true, even with respect to those metals which it dissolves most readily, as copper and iron.

2. It forms with all the metals which it dissolves, excepting iron and copper, salts capable of crystalization. The cause of this property is, that generally it takes from metals much less of their phlogiston than the nitrous acid does.

3. The metals with which it contracts the strongest union, as silver, lead, mercury, and the regulus of antimony, are actually those with which it unites most difficultly. We must here observe, that marine acid separates silver, lead, and mercury, from the nitrous acid in which they had been previously dissolved; and when it is once united with these metals, they adhere more strongly to it, than they did to the nitrous acid. This has given occasion to Becker and other chemists to advance, that in marine acid, and in the last mentioned metals, there is more of that principle which they call *mercurial earth*, than in any other acids or metals. And to this abundance of mercurial earth, they attribute the stronger connection of marine acid, and the mentioned metals, which are distinguished from all others by the appellations *white*, *lunar*, and *mercurial*.

4. Marine acid has the property of volatilising, or carrying off with it in sublimation or distillation, entirely or partly, the metals with which it is united, those particularly with which it forms the strongest union, as mercury, regulus of antimony, silver, and lead. See SUBLIMATE (CORROSIVE), LUNA CORNEA, BUTTER of ANTIMONY, and PLUMBUM CORNEUM.

5. Marine acid, though in some respects less strong than the vitriolic or nitrous, forms with metallic substances, and particularly with the last mentioned metals, with which it adheres most firmly, *metallic salts*, much more corrosive than those formed by the other two acids. See CAUSTICITY.

(*k*) By two methods gold and platina may be rendered soluble in marine acid: 1. by previous solution in aqua regia, and precipitation from that menstruum by means of an alkali; or, 2. by a previous calcination with tin or bismuth.

(*l*) Marine acid, when boiling, dissolves arsenic. Regulus of cobalt, and the semimetal called nickel, are also soluble in marine acid: the solution of the former is reddish yellow, which is changed to green by application of heat; and the solution of the latter is of a deep green color.

The

The greatest part of these phenomena, peculiar to marine acid, evidently proceeds from the difficulty with which it unites with phlogiston, and to the smallness of the quantity of that principle which it takes from metallic substances

However, these phenomena, thus collected, may, by being compared together, furnish matter for curious speculations concerning the famous mercurial earth of Becker, which, according to him, is the third principle of metallic substances Besides, in most solutions of metals by marine acid, a singular smell, resembling the smell of garlic, or of arsenic, is exhaled but, according to Becker, arsenic contains abundantly the mercurial principle

The difficulty with which marine acid combines with the inflammable principle, is the reason why this acid acts so little upon oils and oily substances It seems to have no power over these substances when it is fluid and united with a certain quantity of water What it would produce, if it were artfully applied to these oleaginous matters in its highest degree of concentration, with the help or considerable heat, is not known Very interesting researches remain yet to be made upon this subject

It appears that the inflammable principle, when intimately united with water, as in ardent spirits, is in the favorable state for combination with marine acid, although many more difficulties are found in making this combination with the marine acid, than with the vitriolic or nitrous

Marine acid, mixed with spirit of wine in all proportions, and even frequently distilled with it, is much less intimately combined than the other two acids, and proportionably loses less of its acidity than they do *See* SPIRIT of SALT (DULCIFIED)

Lately, however, marine acid has been applied to spirit of wine in such a manner, that from their union results a liquor which has the distinguishing properties of ether, and is a true *marine ether* M *Baumé*, an able artist, and excellent observer, was the first who published that he had succeeded in making this combination His method was by applying the vapors of highly concentrated marine acid to the vapors of spirit of wine, by means of a convenient apparatus of vessels. The detail of this fine experiment may be seen in his *Dissertation on Ether*

Since his time, an illustrious and learned lover of chemistry * has found a method of making marine ether with infinitely more facility, and more abundantly, by distilling along with spirit of wine the *smoaking spirit of Libavius*, which is nothing more than highly concentrated marine acid, charged with a considerable quantity of tin, which it had carried up with it in distillation *See* SPIRIT (SMOAKING) of LIBAVIUS

M Pott, in his dissertation de *acido salis vinoso*, and other chemists, mention the mixture of some metallic salts, containing concentrated marine acid, such as butter of antimony, with spirit of wine The phenomena which accompanied these mixtures, shewed that these substances re acted considerably on each other, and consequently were intimately combined

* The Marquis de Courtanvaux

These

These phenomena, and particularly the easy production of marine ether, by the smoaking spirit of Libavius, prove that the marine acid which has been combined with metallic substances, is in the fittest state for its intimate combination with spirit of wine, and for the formation of an ether. Does it acquire this property, by depositing along with the metals a portion of some of its principles, for instance, of its mercurial earth, or by carrying off some of the principles of the metals? To me the latter seems certainly the method, and that the metallic principle which it carries off is the phlogiston of the metals. The best means of deciding this interesting question, is to combine the acid with several metallic substances, particularly with those which contain much phlogiston and easily part with it, as zinc, regulus of antimony, tin, and iron, and then to separate the acid from these substances, not only to try whether ether can be made by the acid thus prepared, but also to ascertain by the other means which chemistry affords, whether the acid be really by this method combined with a portion of the phlogiston of the metals. Mr Pott, as well as Stahl, affirms a fact which confirms these notions, and which well deserves to be ascertained, which is, that the properties of the nitrous acid may be given to the marine by combining the latter with iron. But it is very certain, that the principal difference betwixt these two acids, proceeds from the quantity of phlogiston which enters as a principle into the composition of the nitrous. *See* ETHER (MARINE).

The affinities of marine acid, according to Mr Geoffroy's table, are in the following order: tin, regulus of antimony, copper, silver, mercury. According to Mr Gellert, its affinities are placed thus: phlogiston, zinc, iron, copper, tin, lead, bismuth, regulus of antimony, mercury, arsenic. This table shews also that it does not dissolve gold, and partly dissolves silver by the dry method. (*m*)

(*m*) The affinity of tin is greater than that of copper to marine acid, according to Mr Geoffroy's table, and less, according to Mr Gellert's table. I have observed that tin readily precipitates copper from this acid, and also from aqua regia. Mr Gellert is therefore mistaken. The affinities of this, and also of other acids to metals, vary in different circumstances. Thus, for instance, although marine acid unites generally with copper or with iron, preferably to mercury, or regulus of antimony, yet if either of these latter metallic substances be added to a mixture of sea-salt and vitriol, green or blue, and considerable heat applied, the marine acid of the sea salt, disengaged from its basis by the acid of the vitriol, will not unite with the iron or copper of the vitriol, but with the mercury or regulus of antimony, and along with them will be raised by the force of the fire, forming mercury sublimate, or butter of antimony.

Mr Hellot found, that by repeatedly drying and distilling the mother water of sea-salt, more and more marine acid could be obtained without addition.

Marine acid renders calcareous earths and metals soluble in spirit of wine, but not volatile alkali, as nitrous acid does, nor fixed alkali, as acetous acid does.

Marine acid, together with burning phlogiston, gives a reddish yellow flame. The marine acid of mercury corrosive sublimate, combined with copper, forms a fusible mass, which kindles like sulphur, and burns with a blue flame. The phosphorus of Homberg, which is a combination of the marine acid of sal ammoniac with calcareous earth, to which a portion of the inflammable principle of the sal ammoniac adheres, is luminous

X ACIDS (MINERAL) Mineral acids are those which are obtained from minerals, or substances dug from the earth, such as *sulphur*, *bitumens*, *alum*, *selenites*, *vitriols*, *clays*, all which contain *vitriolic acid*, the *nitrous earths*, from which nitrous acid is obtained, and *Sal-gem*, sea-salt, or *common salt*, which furnish marine acid

There are then three mineral acids, the vitriolic, nitrous, and marine These acids are generally more simple, less volatile, more susceptible of concentration, and stronger than the acids obtained from animals or vegetables Hence their power of decomposing all the neutral salts whose acids are of the latter kind, of disengaging these acids, and of substituting themselves in their place by uniting with the substance, which together with the animal or vegetable acid had formed the neutral salt *See* ACID, ACID (VITRIOLIC), ACID (NITROUS), ACID (MARINE)

XI ACID (NITROUS) Nitrous acid has all the general properties of saline acid substances, mentioned under the article Vitriolic Acid *See* ACID (VITRIOLIC) But it differs from vitriolic acid in the following circumstances

1 It is lighter than the vitriolic The weight of the most concentrated nitrous acid, which can be obtained by ordinary means, is to the weight of water as 19 to 12 See a memoir of Mr Rouelle concerning the inflammation of oils, in the Memoirs of the Academy for the year 1747

2 It is of a yellowish-red flame color

3 It is less fixed than vitriolic acid, and cannot therefore be ever obtained in a concrete form, when unmixed

4 It perpetually exhales in vapors of the same color as itself

5. Its smell and taste are peculiar and distinguishing

6 When highly concentrated, it strongly attracts the moisture of the air, but less strongly than vitriolic acid highly concentrated

7 When concentrated nitrous acid is mixed with water, a considerable heat and ebullition are produced from the activity with which these two substances combine While they are mixing, a singular and curious phenomenon appears, which is, that the liquor assumes a blue or deep green color, while the vapors continue still of their original yellowish red. M Beaumé has made this observation

This blue color, as the same chemist has remarked, disappears in a few days, if the nitrous acid has been diluted with much water

Concentrated nitrous acid is very corrosive It tinges the skin with a yellow color, which does not disappear till the epidermis comes off It is successfully employed to corrode and gradually destroy warts, and uninflamed, indolent tumors

nous when struck in the dark. From these facts, together with the preparation of marine ether, we may perceive that marine acid is capable of uniting with phlogiston, and that a marine sulphur might probably be formed, if the volatility of marine acid did not prevent the application of heat sufficient for the forming of that combination

Homberg found, that marine acid corrodes glass more than any other acid For the process of obtaining marine acid, see SPIRIT of SALT.

If the opinion of Becker, Stahl, Junker, and all the scholars of Stahl be true, that there is only one primitive acid, whence the rest are formed, and that this most simple acid, the principle of all others, is the vitriolic, then it follows that nitrous acid is nothing else than vitriolic acid, changed by the union of some other principle Further, these chemists think that nitrous acid is formed from the vitriolic combined, by means of the putrid fermentation, with a certain quantity of phlogiston To prove their opinion, they give the following reasons

1 That the nitrous acid is obtained from nothing else than materials impregnated with putrid juices of animal and vegetable substances, which are known to abound with phlogiston whereas vitriolic acid exists, not only in most minerals, and in the very earths and stones, which are fittest to form a matrix for the generation of nitrous acid, but also in the atmosphere, as appears from the experiment of exposing to the air linnen soaked in a lixivium of alkaline salt, which in a certain time is found to be changed into vitriolated tartar

2 There is a great analogy betwixt those properties of the nitrous and volatile vitriolic acids, by which each of these acids differs from vitriolic acid, and volatile vitriolic acid is evidently vitriolic acid changed by union with phlogiston

This volatile vitriolic acid differs from vitriolic acid by its volatility, by its smell, by its weaker adhesion to alkaline salts, by the greater solubility and different form of the crystals resulting from its union with alkaline salts

But these properties are the same which distinguish nitrous acid from the vitriolic Besides, the volatile vitriolic and nitrous acids resemble each other, and differ from vitriolic acid in the following respects 1 They produce a much greater alteration on the colors of vegetables than the vitriolic does and 2 The salts formed by their combination with fixed alkali resemble each other, and are equally different from vitriolated tartar

Several new interesting experiments might be made to determine more particularly the analogy betwixt the volatile vitriolic and nitrous acids The salt resulting from the combination of volatile vitriolic acid and absorbent earths might be examined, in order to discover whether it be deliquescent, like the salt from the combination of the same earth with nitrous acid, and in what other circumstances these two salts resemble each other, and differ from the vitriolic salt with earthy base, or selenites This inquiry would be still more interesting, as the nitrous salts with earthy bases have also been little examined *See* SALTS (NITROUS) *with* EARTHY BASES

Nitrous acid is one of the most powerful menstruums in chemistry not that it is the strongest acid, for in strength it is inferior to vitriolic acid, and even in certain circumstances to marine acid but on account of the facility, of the quickness, and of the activity with which it dissolves most substances

The bodies upon which it acts most forcibly are, phlogiston, alkalies fixed and volatile, metallic substances and earths, particularly of the calcareous and absorbent kinds

Nothing can equal the impetuosity with which nitrous acid joins itself to phlogiston It is so great, that probably nitrous acid has a stronger affinity with phlogiston than the vitriolic has and it is probable too, that

 this

this proceeds from the phlogiston being one of the principles of nitrous acid

The phenomena exhibited by nitrous acid with all matters containing phlogiston, are different according to the state of these matters, and of the acid itself

When the phlogiston of the substances applied to nitrous acid is in small quantity, and inveloped in much uninflammable matter, and when the nitrous acid is diluted in much water, from which it cannot disengage itself in the act of combination, then it dissolves these substances always with more facility, quickness, and activity than the other acids, all circumstances being supposed alike, but it dissolves them without decomposing itself, and forms along with them new combinations But when the substances to which the nitrous acid is applied, contain much phlogiston, as sulphur, oils, charcoal, and many metallic matters, and when the nitrous acid is dephlegmated as much as is possible, or when it can, in the very act of combination, become dry, and receive at the same instant the heat of ignition, whether this heat be applied to it, or it be generated by the violence of the re-action, then does the nitrous acid, in this state of heat and dryness, combine itself intimately with the phlogiston, and form with it a kind of sulphur or nitrous phosphorus, which is instantaneously inflamed and decomposed in such a manner, that not only the phlogiston, but also the nitrous acid itself, is entirely burnt and destroyed And this combustion is effected differently from all others, without the necessity of access of air Hence the inflammations, the detonations, the explosions, which always happen when all these circumstances concur *See* DETONATION *of* NITRE *with sulphur, &c* GUNPOWDER, FULMINATING POWDER, FULMINATING GOLD, INFLAMMATION *of* OILS

Nitrous acid forms with fixed vegetable alkali a neutral crystalizable salt, called *nitre*, or *salt-petre* *See* NITRE

With marine or fossil alkali it forms a crystalizable salt, called *cubic*, or *quadrangular nitre*, from the figure of the crystals *See* NITRE (CUBIC)

With volatile alkali it forms a neutral salt, capable of crystalizing, called *ammoniacal nitre*, or *nitrous sal ammoniac* This salt has the property of detonating without addition of phlogiston, because phlogiston is contained in the volatile alkali *See* AMMONIAC (NITROUS) *(n)*

Nitrous acid dissolves with much facility and readiness all calcareous and absorbent earths, and forms with them neutral salts not capable of crystalization, undoubtedly because of the small adhesion of this acid with the earths These salts, when dried and exposed to the air, deliquiate or melt into a liquor They are called *nitre with earthy base*, or *nitrous selenites*

The action of nitre upon other earths is not yet well known *See* NITRE *with* EARTHY BASIS

Nitrous acid attacks and dissolves in general all metallic substances, gold and platina excepted, which it also dissolves when it is united with marine acid, which is likewise incapable of dissolving these metals without the assistance of nitrous acid

(*n*) This ammoniacal salt, formed by the acid of nitre, is soluble in spirit of wine, in which respect it differs from vitriolic and marine ammoniacal salts

The

The phenomena presented by nitrous acid in metallic solutions are very numerous The particulars must be seen under the articles of each metal We shall only here make some general observations upon this subject

1 Nitrous acid, in dissolving metallic substances, emits a great quantity of red vapors, and, *cæteris paribus*, produces more heat than when it dissolves alkaline salts or earths, which can only be attributed to the phlogiston of metallic substances

2 There are metallic substances with which nitrous acid forms salts capable of crystallization and detonation Such are particularly silver, lead, mercury, and bismuth With most other metals, as with copper, tin, iron, and regulus of antimony, it forms deliquescent metallic salts, which partly are decomposed spontaneously by the separation of the metallic part This difference proceeds from the greater or less quantity of phlogiston, which the nitrous acid takes from the metals in solution Those metals from which it takes little phlogiston, form with it more intimate combinations, because they retain a good deal of that principle which is the medium of union betwixt their earth and the acid On the contrary, the solution of the metals from which this acid takes much phlogiston, is attended with much more ebullition and violence and when the acid is strong, when the quantities of the acid and metal are large, and the metal reduced to filings or grains, then the heat, the boiling, and the vapors are carried to their highest point, almost to inflammation It is even probable that a real inflammation might be produced, if the experiment were pushed far enough

A remarkable phenomenon which has not been attended to, is, that the metals from which nitrous acid takes least phlogiston, are those which form with it the most corrosive salts, so that mercurial nitre and the nitre of lead are true poisons This remark may help to explain the corrosive quality, or causticity, which the combinations of the mineral acids with metallic substances generally have *See* CAUSTICITY

Nitrous acid is easily combined with all oils, and with all oily and inflammable matters It acts upon these matters more slowly and weakly, in proportion as it is more diluted with water It thickens them, and forms with them resinous or saponaceous compounds, according to their nature and the proportion of the acid When the acid is very concentrated, it burns and inflames them *See* INFLAMMATION *of* OILS

It easily unites, even when much diluted with water, with spirit of wine. It combines intimately with that substance, and thereby loses much of its acidity It is then called *spirit of nitre dulcified*, which *see*

With proper proportions and management, it changes part of the spirit of wine into a liquor which has the principal properties of vitriolic ether *See* ETHER (NITROUS)

The affinities of nitrous acid are, according to Mr Geoffroy's table, iron, copper, lead, mercury, silver and according to Mr Gellert, phlogiston, zinc, iron, regulus of cobalt, copper, bismuth, lead, mercury, regulus of antimony, silver, arsenic, and tin The tin is there said to be only partly soluble, undoubtedly because of the abundant precipitation of the earth of the

tin,

tin, which the nitrous acid deprives of its phlogiston, and in some sort calcines rather than dissolves. *See* TIN. (*o*)

XII. ACID (PHOSPHORIC). *See* PHOSPHORUS.

XIII. ACID (VOLATILE SULPHUREOUS, or VOLATILE VITRIOLIC). This is nothing else than vitriolic acid diluted with water, and weakly united to the inflammable principle. The properties of this acid are then the same *essentially* as those of vitriolic acid. *See* ACID (VITRIOLIC). But the phlogiston which is united with the volatile acid makes it differ considerably from the pure vitriolic acid.

It differs from vitriolic acid, 1. By its smell, which is so active and penetrating, that it can instantaneously suffocate and kill animals. This smell is the same as that of lighted sulphur. As vitriolic acid, when pure and free from phlogiston, has no smell, it appears that the smell of volatile vitriolic acid is caused by its phlogiston; and this is one of the best proofs of the opinion of Stahl and other chemists, who think that phlogiston is the principle of all odors. This opinion will appear even demonstrated, when we consider that no odoriferous substance can be found, in which it is not easy to shew the presence of phlogiston. *See* PHLOGISTON.

2. The volatile acid differs from the vitriolic by its volatility. The latter is the most fixed of the mineral acids, and is for that reason the most susceptible of concentration: but the volatility of the former is so great, that it cannot be much concentrated. This property proves that phlogiston is a principle essentially volatile.

3. The volatile acid is infinitely weaker than vitriolic acid; not only because it cannot be so much concentrated, but also because by its combination with phlogiston it is rendered less simple, and consequently less capable of affinity with other bodies. Therefore, the neutral salts formed by it with alkalies, are easily decomposed by vitriolic acid, and also by all other acids, even the weakest amongst the vegetable.

4. The neutral salt which results from the union of volatile vitriolic acid and fixed alkali, differs much from vitriolated tartar with respect to the figure of its crystals, which are long and needle-like, arranging themselves together in form of tufts or shrubs. Its taste also is different from that of vitriolated tartar, and it is more soluble in water: all these properties shew in a

(*o*) Nitrous acid forms with copper, a green, with iron, a reddish, with lead, a yellow, and with silver, bismuth, mercury, and zinc, colorless solutions. Tin it dissolves imperfectly, and it corrodes regulus of antimony to a white powder. With regulus of cobalt it forms a red, and with nickel a green solution. It dissolves arsenic, and, according to Henckel and Neumann, forms with it a gum-like substance. Dr. Brandt found that by particular management it can dissolve gold. *See* GOLD. It has little effect on metallic calxes. Nitrous acid combined with chalk forms the phosphorus of Baldwin. *See* PHOSPHORIC STONES. Cohobated and distilled with quicklime, it emitted an inflammable vapor. *See Mr. Pott's Dissertation on the Solution of Quicklime by Nitrous Acid.* With ice this acid produces cold remarkably. Concerning the origin of nitrous acid, *see* NITRE *and* SALT; and for the process of obtaining it, *see* SPIRIT *of* NITRE.

neutral

neutral salt the weak union of its acid and base This salt is called the *sulphureous salt of* STAHL. *See* SALT (SULPHUREOUS)

5 The action of volatile vitriolic acid is much more evident than of vitriolic acid upon the colors of vegetables, as appears by pouring an equal quantity of each of the two acids into the tincture of violets, or of heliotrope, of cochenille, Brasil wood, &c In all these instances, the tinctures into which volatile vitriolic acid has been poured, will have lost much more of the intensity of their colors than the other tinctures, that is to say, their colors will be more changed, enlivened, and heightened This effect is produced to such a degree by this acid, that it destroys most colors, and makes them disappear entirely in time This property renders it very useful in several arts, by giving to certain matters, for instance to wools and silks, a degree of whiteness to which they could not be otherwise brought For this purpose, these matters are exposed in a close place to the fumes of burning sulphur, from which, as we shall afterwards see, much of this acid exhales *See* SULPHUR

Although volatile vitriolic acid differs essentially from nitrous acid, since the former is nothing else than vitriolic acid disguised by the addition of phlogiston, which is but weakly united to it, nevertheless, it is necessary to remark, that all the properties now recited of the volatile acid, make it resemble nitrous acid as much as they distinguish it from vitriolic acid From this remark may be drawn one of the strongest presumptions in favor of Stahl's opinion concerning the nature of nitrous acid. This great chemist thinks, that vitriolic acid, which he therefore calls the *universal acid*, is the principle of all other acids, and the most simple of all He thinks that nitrous acid is particularly nothing else than vitriolic acid combined by means of putrefaction with a certain quantity of phlogiston, but in a manner very different, and infinitely more intimately than the phlogiston is combined in volatile vitriolic acid For this latter combination is so weak, that it is decomposed by contact of air, so that the most strong and penetrating volatile vitriolic acid, by exposure in open vessels, loses in a little time all its smell and volatility, and becomes entirely similar to a pure and weak vitriolic acid The same phenomenon takes place when the volatile acid is combined with an alkali Hence the sulphureous salt of Stahl, exposed for a while to free air, loses all the properties which distinguish it from vitriolated tartar, and becomes no wise different from it

The true reason of the weakness of adhesion of the phlogiston in volatile vitriolic acid, is the presence of the aqueous principle, above the quantity of water essential to vitriolic acid This principle always resists a strong and intimate union of phlogiston with any body

This is so true, that if vitriolic acid deprived of all water except what is essential to it, be applied to any matter containing phlogiston, volatile vitriolic acid is not then produced, but true sulphur, in which the phlogiston adheres more strongly *See* SULPHUR On the contrary, when a vitriolic acid, overcharged with superfluous water, is combined with a matter containing phlogiston, volatile vitriolic acid is constantly produced, and never sulphur, except that in the very act of combination the vitriolic acid be deprived of all its superabundant water.

The

The great facility which vitriolic acid has to combine with phlogiſton, even when ſuperfluous water is mixed with it, furniſhes many methods of producing abundantly this volatile vitriolic acid

Stahl propoſes two The firſt is, by burning ſulphur as ſlowly and gently as poſſible The acid which exhales in this operation is very volatile, very phlogiſticated, and very ſuffocating, for two reaſons 1 Becauſe of the little activity with which the ſulphur burns, the inflammable principle is not entirely conſumed, but a portion of it remains united to the acid and, 2 *Becauſe when the vitriolic acid, which in ſulphur is in its higheſt degree* of concentration, and even in a ſtate of perfect dryneſs, diſengages itſelf by degrees, during the ſlow burning of the ſulphur, it finds in the air a portion of water which it greedily ſeizes, and which renders it fit to be changed with the remaining phlogiſton into volatile vitriolic acid When ſulphur is burnt haſtily and ſtrongly, little or no volatile vitriolic acid is produced, principally becauſe then almoſt all the inflammable principle of the ſulphur is deſtroyed by this perfect inflammation

This firſt method of obtaining the volatile vitriolic acid is the beſt and eaſieſt, when it is not intended to collect it, but to apply it to ſome body as ſoon as it is produced, as, for example, to kill inſects or noxious animals, to whiten wools and ſilks, to ſulphurate wines, or to produce the ſulphureous ſalt of Stahl *See* SALT (SULPHUREOUS *See* alſo SULPHUR) But this method is improper for collecting the volatile acid, becauſe ſulphur cannot burn in cloſe veſſels

The ſecond method propoſed by Stahl for obtaining the volatile vitriolic acid, is by diſtilling green or martial vitriol in a cracked retort, to which a receiver is properly luted By this method a conſiderable quantity is produced and collected, becauſe, 1 The phlegm of the martial vitriol ſupplies the neceſſary water to the vitriolic acid, and, 2 Enough of the phlogiſton of the burning coals paſſes through the crack of the veſſel, to form volatile vitriolic acid. This method, though very good in itſelf, is ſubject to a very great inconveniency in practice, which is, that when cracked retorts are expoſed to the fire with the greateſt caution, they are very apt to break ſtill more, and entirely to fall in pieces, by which the operation is ſpoiled

This inconveniency may be avoided by diſtilling in a good retort, not cracked, a mixture of vitriolic acid, or ſubſtance containing it, and any matter capable of furniſhing at once water and phlogiſton Thus ſpirit of wine, oils, fat, reſins, &c mixed and diſtilled with vitriolic acid, can always furniſh a good quantity of ſtrong volatile vitriolic acid *See* OIL and ETHER (VITRIOLIC)

This acid ought to be kept in cryſtal glaſs bottles, cloſed exactly with glaſs ſtoppers, and to be as little as poſſible expoſed to air, becauſe vapors always exhale from it when ſo expoſed, by which its ſtrength is impaired from the diſſipation of part of its phlogiſton

This great facility which the phlogiſton has to ſeparate itſelf from volatile vitriolic acid, is the cauſe of the exceeding difficulty, and even impoſſibility of determining preciſely the quantity of phlogiſton neceſſary to convert any given quantity of vitriolic acid into volatile vitriolic acid In general, we know that very little is required; a ſingle drop of oil being capable of converting, by diſtillation, a large quantity of vitriolic acid into very ſtrong volatile acid

It

It is no less difficult to determine certainly and precisely the properties of this acid as a menstruum of different substances, as, for example, earths and metals This difficulty also proceeds from the facility with which it parts with its phlogiston, and consequently changes its nature, which it does more or less in the act of combination with the substances it dissolves It is an acid perpetually changing, and which we cannot be certain of having the same at different times

These difficulties ought not to prevent trials of such combinations, hitherto little known. Because in an important and essential enquiry, which may throw new light upon the theory of acids and phlogiston, even approximations become important and essential

XIV ACID (TARTAREOUS) *See* TARTAR, and CREAM *of* TARTAR

XV ACIDS (VEGETABLE) All acids obtained from vegetable matters are so called Such are the juices of four fruits, wine turned four, or vinegar, crystals of tartar, all the essential, acid, concrete salts, procured by crystallisation from the expressed juices of plants, and lastly, all the acids obtained from vegetable substances in analysing them by distillation

These acids differ from mineral acids in being less simple, less fixed, less susceptible of concentration and weaker, qualities, which proceed from their union to a certain quantity of oil, with which they are so intimately combined, that they cannot be separated from it but by very nice and studied operations Hence all the neutral salts formed by these acids may be decomposed, either by the mere action of the fire, or by any mineral acid whatever

The particulars of what is here advanced in general on their properties and principles, may be seen under the articles of the principal vegetable acids

XVI. ACID (VITRIOLIC) was so named, because, formerly, it was chiefly obtained from martial vitriol It is, according to the very probable opinion of Becker and of Stahl, the simplest of all acids, and consequently the simplest of all saline substances When it is as pure as can be obtained, it is entirely free from smell and color, that is to say, in these respects, it resembles water

It possesses most eminently all the properties characterising saline, and particularly acid substances.

It tastes exceedingly four, and it sets the teeth on edge

It changes to red the color of syrup of violets, of tincture of heliotropium, &c

It is very susceptible of concentration, that is, much of the water unnecessary to its saline essence may be raised by distillation *See* CONCENTRATION

The specific gravity of this acid, when much concentrated, is very great. It is more than double the specific gravity of water, sometimes is 17 to 8, and perhaps might be further concentrated M Hellot, in pushing strongly the distillation of martial vitriol, obtained towards the end of the operation a vitriolic acid so concentrated, that it was solid and crystalline Some chemists have given to vitriolic acid so concentrated as to become concrete, the name of GLACIAL, or ICY OIL *of* VITRIOL

Vitriolic acid highly concentrated is less fluid than water. It pours ropey like oil, and feels to the fingers greasy. These two last properties have occationed the ancient chemists to call it *Oil of Vitriol* This name is very improper, since it is not inflammable, nor has any peculiar properties of oils *See* OILS. Its oily consistence is owing to the great approximation of its parts, and its apparent unctuosity proceeds from the same cause, joined to this, that as it is a very powerful dissolvent, it attacks and dissolves effectually a portion of the unctuous substance of the skin which it touches

The very strong and concentrated vitriolic acid is not only much heavier, but also much more fixed than water Hence it is capable of receiving, when exposed to fire, a degree of heat greatly superior to that of boiling water, and which almost amounts to a red heat

This acid when well concentrated, (which we suppose here all along) unites itself to water with an astonishing activity and impetuosity If two or three ounces of it be mixed with as much pure and cold water, the re-action of these two substances on each other is so strong, that instantly a boiling arises, attended with many vapors, and a noise similar to that of a red-hot iron plunged into water The heat resulting from the re-action of these two cold liquors is so great, that in an instant it equals, and even much surpasses the heat of boiling water Some chemists have attributed this heat to a disengagement of the igneous particles contained in vitriolic acid This is not true, except they only mean the igneous particles contained in this acid, as in all other substances, and which are set in motion by all collisions, but not any superabundant igneous particles peculiar to this acid, since no experiment demonstrates their existence

The concentrated vitriolic acid, exposed to the atmosphere, attracts moisture so much, that its bulk is considerably encreased, and it becomes mixed with twice its weight of water (*p*)

It may be combined with the inflammable principle or phlogiston, and thereby form two compounds, differing from each other in the quantity of phlogiston, and in the closeness of the union

The first, which is the result of a combination of weak vitriolic acid with a small quantity of phlogiston, is called volatile, sulphureous, or vitriolic acid *See* ACID (SULPHUREOUS), and the second, which arises from an intimate union of vitriolic acid, freed from all water above what is necessary to its essence as a saline substance, with about a seventh part of its weight of pure phlogiston, is called *Sulphur* *See* SULPHUR

Earths are more or less soluble by vitriolic acid, according to their natures, and form with it different salts, or earthy saline compounds of different properties, according to the kinds of earths employed Particular management is requisite to combine vitrifiable earths with vitriolic acid, and the salts resulting

(*p*) Dr Gould relates, that three drams of concentrated vitriolic acid acquired by imbibing moisture from the air, in 57 days, an increase of six drams and a half, and that in general this acid acquires increase of weight in a compound ratio of the largeness of the surface exposed, and of the humidity of the atmosphere. Neuman found that an ounce of this acid, by exposure to air during a year, had imbibed more moisture than six times its original weight For the method of obtaining this acid, *see* SPIRIT *of* SULPHUR, CLYSSUS *of* SULPHUR, and CONCENTRATION *of* VITRIOLIC ACID from their combination have not yet been sufficiently examined. *See* VITRIFIABLE EARTHS and LIQUOR of FLINTS

Calcareous earths may be dissolved without any previous preparation by vitriolic acid This solution is made with moderate effervescence, and from this combination results an earthy saline compound, susceptible of crystallization, whose principles are so intimately combined, that the saline properties of the vitriolic acid are almost entirely masked by those of the earth which is the prevailing principle (*see* AFFINITY, , so that this neutral vitriolic salt with earthy basis has no sensible taste, and is scarcely soluble in water according to Mr Baumé's experiment, one grain only of it could be dissolved in an ounce of water This want of saline properties, which appears common to all vitriolic salts with bases of calcareous earth, has occasioned them to be distinguished by the name of *Selenites*, from other combinations whose saline properties are more obvious *See* SELENITES.

Alum is a vitriolic salt with earthy basis, but it differs considerably from Selenites This difference proceeds from the nature of its earthy basis, which is not calcareous, but argillaceous *See* ALUM

Vitriolic acid may be combined and saturated with vegetable fixed alkali and from this combination is formed a neutral salt, capable of being crystallized, bitter, hard, and not easily soluble in water Several names have been given to this salt from the several substances whence its alkaline basis was extracted, at a time when these alkalies were supposed to differ from each other These names are, *Sal de duobus*, *vitriolated tartar*, *arcanum duplicatum* *See these words*, and ALKALI (VEGETABLE)

With the alkaline basis of sea salt, called marine or fossil alkali, the vitriolic acid forms a neutral, crystalizable salt, called *Glauber's salt*, which differs from vitriolated tartar in the figure of its crystals, its greater solubility in water, the quantity of water contained in its crystals, and its property of drying in the air, or losing much of its water, by which the crystals lose their transparency, their solidity, and are reduced into a white meal, called *effloresce* *See* ALKALI (MARINE), and SALT *of* GLAUBER.

Volatile alkali combined to the point of saturation with a vitriolic acid, forms a neutral ammoniacal salt, and crystalizable, called *Salt (Vitriolic Ammoniac)*, *which see*, and ALKALI (VOLATILE)

Vitriolic acid being more simple and more powerful than the nitrous and marine acids, separates them from the alkalies to which they are united, and substitutes itself in their place. *See* NITRE and SALT (COMMON)

In general, this acid acts upon all metallic substances, and dissolves them with phenomena peculiar to each It forms with them neutral salts with metallic bases capable of crystalizing, to all which salts M Macquer thinks proper in his course of chemistry to give the general name of *vitriol*, and to specify the different vitriols by the name of the metallic matters which enter into their composition Thus, for example, he proposes to call the combination of vitriolic acid with silver, *vitriol of silver*, or *lunar vitriol*, and the combination of the same acid with mercury, *vitriol of mercury*, &c in the same manner as the neutral metallic salts formed by the union of vitriolic acid with iron and with copper, are called *vitriol of copper*, and *vitriol of iron*, or *martial vitriol* *See* VITRIOL

 Thus,

This acid, in consequence of its great affinity with the inflammable principle, attacks the phlogiston of metals when it dissolves them, and separates part of it from those which are capable of being deprived of it; consequently it calcines them more or less according to their nature, and to the manner of making the solution, and adheres to them proportionably less, as it has taken from them a greater quantity of their phlogiston. We may conclude from these phenomena, that vitriolic acid dissolves metals chiefly by means of their phlogiston; or that this principle is a medium of union between this acid and metallic earths.

The most general phenomena accompanying the solutions of metallic matters in vitriolic acid by the humid method, are, 1. The effervescence and heat, which are commonly moderate. 2. The vapors; many of which are the volatile vitriolic acid, as in the solution of mercury; or they are inflammable vapors, as in the solution of iron. 3. The formation of concrete sulphur, as in the solution of tin. See *the particular details of all these solutions of metallic matters by vitriolic acid, under the article of each metallic substance, and at the word* VITRIOL. (*q*)

It appears from what has been said on the combinations of vitriolic acid with all the substances with which it can form a neutral salt, that all these neutral vitriolic salts are susceptible of crystallization. This property is peculiar to vitriolic acid, and probably proceeds from the intimacy of union contracted betwixt this acid and the substances which it dissolves.

Concentrated vitriolic acid acts with considerable force on all oils and concrete oily matters. It boils and grows warm when added to them. It partly

(*q*) Diluted vitriolic acid dissolves iron and zinc speedily, and copper very slowly. Boiling concentrated vitriolic acid dissolves copper, and partly dissolves and partly corrodes silver, tin, mercury, and lead. Vitriolic acid does not directly dissolve gold, but precipitates it from aqua regia, which precipitate is soluble in vitriolic acid. It lessens the volatility of mercury and of arsenic; and the fusibility of lead, zinc, bismuth, and regulus of antimony. It dissolves the calxes of most metals. It also dissolves the semimetal, regulus of cobalt, but not nickel.

Although vitriolic acid has a strong power to combine with iron, yet its adhesion to it when dissolved seems to be very weak. Thus Mr Margraaf found, that by boiling a solution of green vitriol in a copper vessel, or with filings of copper, part of the iron was deposited, and in its place part of the copper was dissolved. This experiment is so much more remarkable, as a diluted vitriolic acid has no sensible effect upon copper in a short time. The acid therefore by its previous solution of iron seems to have been so changed, as to be rendered capable of dissolving copper. This experiment does not contradict the general rule by which the power of union of vitriolic acid is affirmed to be greater to iron than to copper, but may be explained from the slight adhesion of the inflammable principle to the earth of iron; by which property salts formed by this metal with vitriolic or nitrous acids are continually decomposing; the phlogiston, which is the medium of union betwixt acids and earths, escaping into the air or combining with the acid, and the calx of iron separating from the acid, in form of a red sediment. This decomposition of martial vitriol, and martial nitre, and also of some other metallic salts subject to the same change, is accelerated by application of heat, air, moisture, and, as Mr Margraaf's experiment seems to indicate, by the application of another metal, as copper. Mr Margraaf has not given his sentiments concerning the cause of the alteration produced upon the acid in his experiment, by which it is rendered capable of dissolving copper. Is it by absorption of the phlogiston of the iron, that it becomes volatile vitriolic acid, and thereby acquires new properties as a menstruum?

decomposed

decomposes them, blackens, and in some sort burns them From these mixtures many fumes exhale, which have a mixt smell of burnt oil, and very suffocating volatile vitriolic acid See the detail and explanation of these phenomena at the word OIL

Vitriolic acid, when very weak, does not appear to have any action upon oils, because its superfluous water, with which it strongly adheres, hinders it from combining with these substances, to which the water cannot be united However, the union of such a weak vitriolic acid with oil, does not seem impossible *See* OIL.

Concentrated vitriolic acid shews, when mixed with spirit of wine, many very interesting phenomena, and which vary according to the proportions of these two acids, and the management employed

Without distillation, it entirely combines in substance with spirit of wine, without occasioning any decomposition, that is to say, it does not combine with any of the principles of the spirit of wine preferably to the rest It loses its acidity by this union, and is rendered greatly milder Hence it is called *Dulcified Vitriolic Acid* It has also been called WATER of RABEL, which *see*

When spirit of wine and vitriolic acid are distilled together, the latter decomposes the former, takes possession of its aqueous principle, reduces a part of it into a middle substance betwixt ardent spirits and oil, to which the name *Ether* has been given, and lastly, the acid reduces the spirit of wine into a true oil, which has been improperly called *Sweet Oil of Vitriol* *See* the words SPIRIT (ARDENT), ETHER, ETHER (VITRIOLIC), and SWEET OIL *of* VITRIOL

Vitriolic acid is no where in nature found pure, that is, unmixed with any other matter This proceeds from its capacity to dissolve, and to combine with a great variety of different substances

Thus vitriolic acid is found naturally combined, 1 With an inflammable substance, then it is in form of sulphur or bitumen, or, 2 With earthy substances in form of selenites, aluminous and argillaceous matters, or, 3 With metallic substances, in form of natural vitriols, or, 4 With alkaline salts, in form of neutral vitriolic salts with alkaline bases But it is almost only with the fossile or marine alkali that the vitriolic acid is ever found naturally combined, because this alkali is most generally diffused, and is indeed almost the only natural alkali Vitriolic acid is therefore found in form of Glauber's salt Natural Glauber's salt is chiefly found in those waters which contain common salt *See* SALT (COMMON) and WATERS *of* SALT FOUNTAINS

Vitriolic acid, combined with vegetable fixed alkali, forming vitriolated tartar, or with volatile alkali, forming vitriolic ammoniac salt, otherwise called the secret ammoniac salt of Glauber, can be found but very rarely, and by particular decompositions and combinations, as, for example, by burnings

From what has been said concerning the states in which vitriolic acid is naturally and habitually found, we may perceive that it cannot be obtained alone and pure without particular artful operations, that is, by decomposing those bodies which contain most of it, and from which it may be easiest procured These bodies are *Sulphur* and *Vitriols*. *See these words for the extraction of Vitriolic Acid*

Upon

Upon considering the several substances with which vitriolic acid is found naturally combined, an interesting question arises concerning the original and primitive state of this acid For as sulphur is spread in very large quantities within the earth, and that by its burning or decomposition, its acid separated from its phlogiston becomes capable of combination with earthy and metallic substances, as happens actually in the fabrication of vitriols and of alum, we may consider whether all vitriolic acid has been originally in the state of sulphur, and if one part of this sulphur being consumed or decomposed by natural causes, as happens in volcanos, its acid has formed all the vitriols and vitriolic salts with earthy bases, which are found formed in the earth, or whether, as we know by the experiment of the artificial composition of sulphur, that vitriolic acid quits every other substance in order to combine with phlogiston, all this acid was originally combined with earthy and metallic substances, and these vitriolic salts, meeting matters abounding in phlogiston, have been decomposed to form all the sulphur found in the earth This question cannot certainly be decided but by the profoundest researches into the natural history of these several bodies

The affinities of vitriolic acid according to Mr Geoffroy's table are, phlogiston, fixed alkali, volatile alkali, earths, iron, copper, and silver and according to Mr Gellert's table, phlogiston, fixed alkali, volatile alkali, earths, zinc, iron, copper, silver, tin, lead, mercury, bismuth, regulus of antimony, and arsenic

XVII ACIDS (VOLATILE). Those acids are so called which are more volatile than most other acids, which volatility proceeds either from an union of some phlogiston, or of some attenuated oil Such are the volatile vitriolic acid, the acid spirits of some acrid vegetables, as the roots of squills, according to Mr Cartheuser, the acids which rise when butter or fat are distilled, and others similar

XVIII ADEPT is the name assumed by those alchemists who pretended to have discovered the philosopher's stone *See* STONE (PHILOSOPHER'S).

XIX. ADOPTER *See* RECEIVER

XX AFFINITY. By affinity (*r*) is understood that tendency which the constituent or integrant parts of bodies have to unite, and that power by which they adhere when united

The definition of affinity shews that it is not a word void of meaning The power with which the parts of bodies tend to unite with each other, and their adhesion when united, are very sensible and palpable effects, since this power cannot be destroyed but by another power as real and more considerable It is

(*r*) By the terms *affinity* and *elective attraction*, we ought to understand the power by which the constituent parts of bodies unite, and not to suppose that this power is exerted by any similarity and homogeneity of parts, or by any mechanical traction, as these terms seem to imply The cause of this power, or the manner in which this union of constituent parts, is produced, is unknown to us To these terms, therefore, another less exceptionable, namely, *the power of combination*, may be substituted In our author's definition of affinity is comprehended not only the power of union of the constituent parts of bodies, which is the proper object of chemistry, but also the power of union of the integrant parts of bodies, which he calls the affinity of aggregation, and which is treated of by writers on natural philosophy and mechanics under the terms,

attraction,

besides demonstrated by numberless experiments, as, for example, by the adhesion of two bodies applied to each other, whose surfaces are finely polished, by the tendency which two drops of water, or of oil, mercury, or of any other fluid, have to run together and unite into one mass, by the convex or spherical figure which drops of fluids assume, when their form is not given them by containing vessels or other body, and when they are supported by bodies with which they are not disposed to unite all which effects happen even in a vacuum, and demonstrate the affinity which the integrant parts of bodies solid, or fluid, have to each other

The affinity of the constituent parts or principles is demonstrated by the detail of all the phenomena in chemistry

We do not here enquire into the cause of this great effect, which is so general, that it may itself be considered as the cause of all combinations, and may serve to explain them It may perhaps be a property as essential to matter as its extent and impenetrability, of which we can say no more, than that such properties do exist On this subject the works of Newton, Freind, Keil, and the Abbé Marcuzzi, may be consulted These authors have endeavored to illustrate these obscure subjects by calculation We shall be satisfied with observing the most remarkable laws, according to which the principles of bodies unite and combine, in consequence of this property

M Macquer distinguishes several sorts of affinities Not that he believes there are distinct species of affinities, for it is very certain, that it is but one and the same property of matter, differently modified according to different circumstances, but only that he may better distinguish and remark the phenomena occasioned by this property, in the detail of the combinations and separations which it effects in the most general and most important operations of chemistry

By *simple affinity* he means the disposition to unite and adhere, which is observed between the integrant and homogeneous parts of the same body, or between the heterogeneous parts of two different bodies The simple affinity is therefore distinguished into two kinds

The first kind of simple affinity produces the *union of aggregation*, that is to say, that the body resulting from this union is of the same nature, but of larger size M Macquer calls it the *affinity of aggregation*, as, for example, when several loose particles of the same metal or of the same earth are united together by fusion, so as to form but one mass *See* AGGREGATION

The second kind of simple affinity, producing the union and adherence of heterogeneous parts, different in their natures, from which results a new compound body, whose properties are different from those of the two principles

attraction, gravitation, and cohesion. Whether these two unions are produced from the same cause differently modified, as our author affirms, I know not, but their effects are so different, that they deserve to be considered separately the union of integrant parts being only an apposition of these parts, which are capable of being disjoined by mechanical means, and without any change produced upon their properties, and the union of constituent parts, or combination, being attended with considerable changes of properties, and being incapable of disjunction by mechanical means *See the article* COMPOSITION *of* BODIES, and the following *Note*

from which it was formed, is called *affinity of composition*, because a new body is actually composed. If, for example, the primitive integrant parts of vitriolic acid be united with those of iron, a new body results from this union, which is neither vitriolic acid nor iron, but a compound of the two, called *martial vitriol*.

The following remarks may be made on simple affinities.

1. That the affinity of aggregation resists the affinity of composition. For it is evident that the force which makes the homogeneous and integrant parts of a body adhere together, hinders them from separating, in order to join the parts of another body.

2. Hence it follows, that if the adhesion of aggregation between the integrant parts of a body be weakened or destroyed, the affinity of composition is thereby facilitated, that is, the affinity which they have to join the parts of another body.

3. That as the hardness of a body supposed simple and homogeneous depends only on the adhesion of aggregation betwixt its integrant parts, if this adhesion be destroyed by separating their parts from each other, as by reducing them into fine powder, or still more by diffusing them in a liquid, with which they have no adhesion, or less than they had to each other, they may then be combined with the parts of another body, more or less easily, in proportion as they have been more or less separated by this mechanical division.

4. As different bodies are more or less susceptible of this mechanical division, whether artificial or natural, by which their integrant parts are more or less separated from each other, hence arises a great difference betwixt these bodies in their greater or less facility of combining with other bodies.

5. This facility of combining with another body does not, however, determine solely the degree of affinity betwixt these two bodies. For experience shews that principles or constituent parts of certain compounds, which unite together very readily and easily, have however but a weak adhesion, which is destroyed by the smallest effort of analysis, or chemical decomposition, while other principles which can be united only with great difficulty, and by studied means, contract together an union much stronger, and much less apt to be dissolved. Mercury, for instance, unites much more easily with nitrous acid than with the marine, but yet it adheres much more strongly to the latter than to the former.

Hence we ought to conclude, that we cannot positively determine that one body has no affinity with another body, because no means are known of uniting them. On the contrary, it appears certain that all natural bodies have a certain degree of affinity, and facility of uniting with each other, and a certain degree of adhesion when they are united, and consequently, that there are no combinations really and absolutely impossible, but that this degree of affinity varies according to the different states in which these bodies are found.

However, as the want of union betwixt two bodies prevents their affinity from shewing itself, we may consider bodies which we cannot combine as having no affinity together, until chemistry be so far advanced as to make combinations which now seem impossible. Thus, for instance, oil is said to have no affinity with water, nor lead with iron, nor iron with mercury, because, in fact, these bodies cannot be directly united together in chemical operations. Thus any affinity which they may have together is to us of no consequence.

On

On the contrary, as the affinities of bodies which may be united together, produce in chemical operations effects proportionable to their facility of union, and to their force of adhesion when united, we may consider the affinity of bodies in general, as being in a compound ratio of these two properties.

The last remark we can make on the simple affinity of composition, furnishes a very useful and very general fundamental law, by which we may discover, even without decomposition, the principles of which bodies are composed. The remark is, that all compound bodies have properties partaking of the properties of the principles of which these bodies are composed. Thus, for example, the union of two principles, of which one is fixed, and the other is volatile, forms a compound, whose degree of fixity or volatility is intermediate betwixt those of the two principles.

The same may be said of all the other properties, such as gravity, opacity, transparency, ductility, hardness, fluidity, &c. and even of the affinities. So that, supposing we knew perfectly the properties of the principles of a compound, we might by examining the properties of this compound, discover its principles, even although its analysis were impossible.

We must however allow that this rule, although very general, is subject to a considerable number of restrictions and modifications, which depend on a number of particular circumstances. For example, it happens sometimes that the operation by which two principles are united changes or even annuls some of the properties of these principles: it happens too that sometimes their union developes new properties, which cannot be immediately perceived in either of the principles. But such changes are never so compleat as to lead one into gross mistakes concerning the principles; therefore they do not prevent the rule from being sufficiently general, to be an excellent guide in many chemical enquiries. (s)

Where more than two bodies act upon one another, the *affinity* may be called *complicated*; and from the definition given, it appears that all these complicated affinities must be of the kind called *Affinity of Composition*.

(s) The rule mentioned in the text is so far from being general, that perhaps the reverse of it may be considered as a general rule; and a change of properties, and a production of new properties, may be considered as criterions, by which compound bodies, chemically combined, may be distinguished from bodies formed merely by mixture or apposition of integrant parts; in which latter compound bodies, the properties are intermediate betwixt the properties of the several component parts, and no new properties are produced. Thus, three parts of copper combined by fusion with one part of tin, forms a body more hard, more brittle, and more sonorous, than either of the constituent metals. Its hardness, therefore, its brittleness, and its sonorousness may be considered as new properties. Its color is much whiter than the intermediate color, and its specific gravity is greater than the intermediate specific gravity. Further, the properties of bodies are in many instances destroyed or annulled by chemical combination. Thus the acrimony and deliquescency of acids and of alkalies are almost entirely annulled by combining these two kinds of substances together. Every body chemically combined may furnish facts which refute the general proposition mentioned in the text. Bodies formed by mixing, not by chemically combining several substances together, as, for instance, a liquor formed by mixing wine and water, partake of the qualities of each ingredient, proportionably to the quantity of it employed. *See* COMPOSITION *of* BODIES, *and* AGGREGATION.

First, we ought to consider that complicated affinity in which only three principles act. Experience indicates the following observations.

If a principle be added to two other principles united together, phenomena of composition or of decomposition happen, which differ according to the affinities of these three bodies to each other.

1. Sometimes the third supervening principle is united to the other two, and forms together with them a compound consisting of three principles. For example, if to a mass composed of gold and silver, some copper be added, this third metal is united to the other two, and forms with them a compound consisting of three principles, namely, gold, silver, and copper. Thus it happens, when the third supervening principle has with the two others an affinity equal, or almost equal to the affinity which these two principles have to each other.

2. The same thing also happens sometimes, although the third supervening principle has no affinity with one of the two principles originally united. But then it is necessary that this supervening principle should have, with the other of the two principles, an affinity equal to the affinity subsisting between those two principles originally united. And in this case, that principle which serves to connect and unite the two which could not otherwise be united, is called an *intermedium*. This affinity may also be called the *affinity of intermediums*. For example, if water be added to the compound called *liver of sulphur*, which consists of two principles, sulphur and fixed alkali, it unites with the water, dissolves in it without being decomposed, and forms a new compound consisting of three principles, namely, sulphur, fixed alkali, and water. The water and sulphur could not by themselves form any union; but as fixed alkali has a great affinity with both sulphur and water, it serves upon this occasion as an intermedium to unite these two substances together. It is necessary to remark, that in this affinity of intermediums, the affinity of the principle which serves as an intermedium is weakened, because it is divided betwixt two bodies; and that the union contracted with them is less strong than if it were united to one of them only.

3. Sometimes a third principle, when added to a compound consisting of two principles, does not unite but with one of these two principles, and obliges the other to separate itself entirely from the principle with which it was originally united. In this case a total decomposition happens of the first compound, and a new combination of the remaining principle with the supervening principle, from which a new compound results. This happens when the supervening principle has little or no affinity with one of the principles of the compound, and when it has with the other, an affinity much stronger than that which subsists betwixt the two first principles. For example, when an alkali is added to a solution of a metallic matter in an acid, as it has more affinity with the acid than with the metal, it seizes the acid, and obliges it to quit the metal, which therefore precipitates, because the metal has much less affinity than the alkaline salt has to the acid.

4. It happens sometimes that a principle, which, in consequence of the affinity we have been discoursing of, has been separated from another principle, may again resume its place with the principle, as it was originally, and dispossess the supervening principle. This affinity, which is called *reciprocal*, on account of

of its reciprocal effects, takes place when the two principles which are alternately separated from the third principle by each other, have with this third principle, an almost equal affinity, and that their separation is procured by particular circumstances relative to some of their properties.

All that has been said concerning the affinities of three principles may be applied to affinities of four principles, due regard being had to the changes produced by the introduction of a fourth principle. It is evident, for example, that in place of one decomposition and one new composition, which can result from the different degrees of affinity of three principles, the affinities of four principles forming two new compounds, may, by a mutual change, produce two decompositions and two new combinations. This always happens when the sum of the affinities, which each of the principles of the two compounds has with the principles of the other, surpasses the sum of the affinities subsisting betwixt the principles forming the two first compounds. This sort of affinity, where there is a double exchange of principles, may be called *double affinity*. Examples of these affinities are often met in chemical operations and mixtures; and without a knowledge of them, it would be impossible to explain many singular phenomena of decomposition. For example, it happens often that two principles, neither of which could singly effect the disunion of the principles of a compound, because their affinities are each of them inferior to the affinity betwixt the principles of that compound, become nevertheless capable of procuring this decomposition when they act in concurrence. For this purpose, it is sufficient, as we have already said, that the sum of affinities which the two decomposing principles have with the principles of the body to be decomposed, should surpass the sum of the affinity betwixt the principles of the decomposing body, and the affinity betwixt the principles of the body to be decomposed. See examples of this play of affinities at the words BLUE (PRUSSIAN), and SALT (NEUTRAL ARSENICAL).

We shall pursue no farther these remarks upon affinities; because the affinities of bodies compounded of many principles are much less strong and less sensible in chemical operations; or because this science is not yet sufficiently advanced to have observed and distinguished them all. What we have said is sufficient to form just ideas on the theory of all the important phenomena which are exhibited by the fundamental experiments, and to conduct to many new discoveries.

XXI. AGARIC (*t*)

XXII. AGATE (*u*)

(*t*) AGARIC is a fungus growing on the trunk of the common larch tree, from which turpentine is obtained. Three-fourths of it is a resinous substance, and the remainder is a slimy mucilaginous earthy matter, so tenacious as scarcely by any method to be dissolved by water.

(*u*) AGATE is a flint variegated with different colors blended together, and sometimes with colored lines and dendritical figures, as the *mocha stone*, which is a variety of agate, or with red spots, as the *sardea* or *St Stephen's gem*, which also are varieties of this stone. For the chemical properties of agates, *see* EARTHS (VITRIFIABLE). By fire the *color* of a white agate, called *chalcedony*, was rendered whiter, and the color of a black agate was not changed. Colors may be given to agates, or their natural colors may be changed. Mr du Fay, in the Memoirs of the Academy of Sciences, 1728, relates, that to chalcedony a saturated solution of silver in strong spirit of

XXIII AGGREGATION In order to have a clear idea of what chemists mean by the words *aggregation*, *aggregate*, *aggregated bodies*, we must attend to the difference betwixt what natural philosophers call *constituent parts* and *integrant parts* of bodies The constituent parts are, properly speaking, the principles of bodies These are substances differing in nature from each other, which, by their union and mutual combination, really *constitute* mixed bodies, which partake of the properties of their constituent parts. For example, the constituent parts of common salt are an acid and an alkali, which ought to be considered as the principles of this salt at least as its proximate principles. *See* PRINCIPLES As this acid and alkali are what really constitute common salt, and are the parts, to the union of which it owes its existence and properties, it is evident that the constituent parts cannot be disunited from each other, without destroying and decomposing it so that after such a disunion, the salt will no longer exist, but only the acid and the alkali of the salt, which are very different from the salt, and from each other

On the contrary, the *integrant parts* of bodies do not absolutely differ from each other, nor do they differ, as to the nature and principles, from the body into whose mass they enter By the integrant parts of a body are to be understood the smallest molecules or particles into which this body can be reduced without decomposition We may conceive that a neutral salt, for instance, common salt, may be divided into molecules still smaller and smaller, without any separation of the acid and alkali which constitute the salt, so that these molecules, however small, shall always be common salt, and possessed of all its essential properties If we should now suppose that these molecules are arrived at their utmost degree of smallness, so that each of them shall be composed of one atom of acid and of another atom of alkali, and that they cannot be further divided without a separation of the acid and alkali, then these last molecules are those which Mr Macquer in his Chemical Lectures calls *primitive integrant molecules*

In the same manner that we conceive that a body may be divided into its primitive integrant molecules, without any change of its nature, or other alteration than a diminution of its bulk, so we may also easily perceive, that if these pri-

nitre gave a reddish brown color, to oriental agate a blacker stain, and changed the yellow spots of an agate to purple The stone after the application of the metallic solution ought to be placed in the sun, and the color may be rendered more intense by repeating the application of the solution The liquor spreads so much on the stone, that neat designs cannot be made on it Dr Lewis proposes to remedy this inconvenience by covering the stone over with etching wax, and the lines intended to be stained cut through this ground, in the manner of etching copper plates The colors given to these stones may be destroyed by fire or by aqua fortis, and the colors thus destroyed by aqua fortis are recoverable by exposure to the sun. Agates and other stones may be stained black by applying to them a solution of copper in aqua fortis, and afterwards exposing them to a red heat in a crucible See *Lewis's Commerce of Arts* Mocha stones may be imitated by moistening the smooth surface of an agate with a solution of copper, and on the middle of this surface setting an iron nail upright on its head The iron absorbs the acid from the copper, and the copper forms ramifications If the nail be then removed, and the corroded iron carefully washed off by dipping the stone in water, the vegetations may be rendered by a red heat, of a black color These vegetations are not fixed in the stone, which ought therefore to be covered with a plate of crystal glass.

mitive integrant molecules, which are all homogeneous and of the ſame nature, and which are ſuppoſed ſeparated from each other, ſhould be brought to unite and combine together, no new body, that is, a body of different nature, will reſult from this union, but only a more conſiderable maſs of the ſame body that is to ſay, for inſtance, that if the primitive integrant molecules were common ſalt, their reunion would ſtill form common ſalt, only in a maſs ſo much larger, as there is a greater number of theſe molecules united together But it is the union of theſe homogeneous parts, of theſe primitive integrant molecules, which modern chemiſts have called *aggregation*, and they have called *aggregates* bodies conſidered as reſulting from their primitive integrant parts, in oppoſition to the names *mixts* and *compounds*, which they have given to bodies conſidered as reſulting from the union of their conſtituent parts, which are ſubſtances heterogeneous, and of different natures

The name of integrant parts, which has been given to thoſe whoſe union forms aggregates, agrees well with them, becauſe, in fact, this union is a kind of addition or integration (if ſuch a word may be uſed) of a certain number of parts of the ſame kind, whence reſults a ſum, or a whole

It is very eſſential to obſerve on the ſubject of aggregation, that we ſhould have a very falſe idea of it, and entirely oppoſite to chemical phenomena, if we underſtood by this word nothing but a ſimple juxtapoſition of the integrant parts of bodies for beſides that, there muſt be a real adheſion and intimate union of theſe ſame parts with each other, ſo that they cannot be ſeparated but by ſome force ſuperior to that by which they are united A heap of ſand, for example, if we conſider the grains of ſand as its integrant parts, cannot be regarded as an aggregrate, becauſe theſe grains are only *juxtapoſited*, and have no real adheſion together, ſo that the reſiſtance which they oppoſe to their ſeparation can only proceed from their gravity, and is not the effect of adheſion, or tendency to each other

In the ſecond place, it is neceſſary to obſerve on the ſubject of aggregation, that the force of adheſion of the integrant parts of different bodies varies much, according to the nature of theſe bodies, ſome of them adhering very ſtrongly, and others very weakly, and that thoſe which adhere weakly are generally the eaſieſt to be diſſolved, conſidering that the ſolution of a body, or its combination with another body of a different nature, cannot be effected but ſo far as the integrant parts of theſe bodies are ſeparated, or their aggregation broken, which is partly done by the operations of art, but chiefly by the action of menſtruums

All theſe conſiderations on the aggregation of bodies, although very ſimple in themſelves, are of the greateſt importance in the theory and practice of chemical operations. Becker and Stahl were the firſt who explained theſe ideas, which have been ſince illuſtrated and extended by the beſt modern chemiſts *See the words*, AFFINITY, COMPOSITION, SOLUTION, DECOMPOSITION, DIVISION *of* BODIES

XXIV A I R Air is a fluid inviſible, inodorous, inſipid, imperceptible to all our ſenſes but the touch, and is conſidered as a ſimple elementary body, and primary principle, becauſe it cannot be altered or decompoſed by any known methods

The

The air is always in form of a fluid, though perhaps that fluidity is not essential to it But it is certain that no cold has ever yet been produced, natural or artificial, strong enough to deprive it of its fluidity

We cannot flatter ourselves that we can have air, any more than the other elements, in perfect purity On the contrary, it is always found mixed with more or less of foreign substances, proceeding from a perpetual exhalation of volatile matters, and particularly of water, with which it has even a certain degree of adhesion (*x*)

The primary integrant parts of air, although certainly very small, yet are not so small as those of water, and even those of other liquids less simple, such as spirit of wine and oils at least, these liquids pass easily enough through the pores of several substances, such as paper, the skin, &c through which the air does not pass, or passes with difficulty

The experiments of Mr Boyle, and more particularly those of Dr Hales, related in his Vegetable Statics, prove that most vegetable and animal matters contain a prodigious quantity of air , and scarcely credible, if the effects it produced were not so considerable and sensible Chemical experiments also give us many occasions not only of observing these phenomena, but also of ascertaining the quantity of air disengaged, or absorbed in several operations (*y*)

It appears that air, as well as other primary principles, is found in bodies in two different states that is to say, that in certain bodies, and in certain circumstances, it is merely dispersed and interposed betwixt the integrant parts of those bodies, but without adhering to these parts, or at least adhering but very weakly This air, which may be separated by means purely mechanical , such as the operations of the air-pump, compression, or shaking , and which besides possesses all its other properties , ought not to be considered as one of the elements of those bodies in which it exists But that portion of air which cannot be separated from many bodies but by analysing them, and by employing such means of decomposition as chemistry furnishes , which, besides while it remains in those bodies, is deprived of one of its essential properties, its elasticity, which it does not recover till it is disengaged , this air, I say, ought truly to be considered as one of the elements or constituent parts of these bodies

(*x*) Air not only *adheres* to water, as the text says, but chemically combines with it, and probably with many other volatile matters The dissolving power of air, as of other menstruums, is encreased by heat , and hence upon an access of cold, the air deposits part of its water which it kept dissolved while its heat was greater The water deposited becomes then visible, forming fogs, or condensing upon any cold body, as upon glass windows This dissolving power of air is also effected by other circumstances besides heat for we find that in equal heats air sometimes imbibes water faster than at other times Dr Gould found that vitriolic acid saturated with water by long exposure to air, did sometimes lose and sometimes gain weight, according as the air was disposed to deposit or dissolve moisture By what circumstances this dissolving power of the air is effected, and how these various states of the atmosphere affect the health of vegetables and animals, are subjects worthy of enquiry

(*y*) Whether the permanently elastic vapors produced in distillations and other operations be really atmospherical air altered by its union with the bodies from which it is disengaged, has not been hitherto shewn It has been called fixed or fixable air *See* AIR (FIXABLE)

The properties of pure air, and which occaſion many effects in chemiſtry, are

1. Its *expanſive power*, that is to ſay, that it is capable of great rarefaction, and of occupying a ſpace thirteen times larger than its original ſize, when it is expoſed to the greateſt poſſible heat. This great expanſibility of air, added to the prodigious quantity of it which is diſengaged in many chemical analyſes and mixtures, occaſions frequently violent exploſions, againſt which an intelligent artiſt ought always to be on his guard. *(w)*

2. Its *compreſſibility*, that is to ſay, that the effect contrary to that we have been mentioning, is produced upon it by means of cold and of preſſure.

3. Its *elaſticity*, which is nothing elſe than the force with which it endeavours to reſume its natural condition, when it is violently rarefied, compreſſed, or condenſed, and the effort which it makes for that purpoſe upon bodies which oppoſe its re-eſtabliſhment.

4. Its *weight*, which determines it to fall impetuouſly into all the ſpaces into which it can have acceſs, and which are unoccupied by air, or more ponderous bodies. The experiments which demonſtrate all theſe properties of the air are ſo numerous and deciſive, that nothing is better known and illuſtrated in natural philoſophy. On this ſubject may be conſulted the works of Paſcal, Boyle, Mariotte, Abbé Nollet, and, in a word, of all the experimental philoſophers. It is only neceſſary to obſerve here, that the ſpecific gravity of air is to that of water, nearly as 1 to 850.

5. The faculty which the air has of conſiderably *facilitating the evaporation* of volatile matters ſublimed by the fire. It is a well-eſtabliſhed fact in chemiſtry, that the acceſs of air greatly accelerates all evaporations and diſtillations. We ſee, for example, that by directing the blaſt of bellows upon the ſurface of any volatile body evaporating by means of fire, as water, antimony, mercury, &c. that the ſmoke or vapors of theſe bodies are very ſenſibly increaſed. It is alſo certain that any diſtillation of a liquor, as of water, is much haſtened, by directing upon its ſurface in the inner part of the alembic, the wind of a ventilator, as an Engliſh author has propoſed. *See* DISTILLATION and EVAPORATION. *(z)*

(w) Air is expanded ⅓ of its bulk by the heat of boiling water. *See the Hiſtory of the Academy of Sciences* 1699. Hales found that the air in a retort, when the bottom of the veſſel was juſt beginning to be red-hot, was expanded to twice its former ſpace, and in a white or almoſt melting heat it occupied thrice its former ſpace or more; and Mr Robins, a very accurate experimental philoſopher, found that air was expanded by the heat of iron juſt beginning to be white to four times its ſize. As greater expanſions cannot be well eſtimated, I preſume there is an error in that part of the text to which this note refers, where the air is ſaid to be capable of expanſion to thirteen times its ordinary bulk.

(z) Air accelerates evaporation by its diſſolving power, which is indeed the principal or only cauſe of evaporation, if by that word we mean the eſcape of any fluid with leſs heat than is neceſſary to convert it into vapor in a vacuum. By the ſame power air may alſo accelerate diſtillations, in which the heat is ſufficient to raiſe the fluid into vapor in a vacuum; but if the air be cold, it will probably more impede the diſtillation by cooling the ſurface of the fluid, and condenſing part of the vapor, than accelerate the eſcape of vapor by its diſſolving power.

6 Lastly, the most singular property of air, and at the same time one of the most interesting in chemistry, is, that no combustible substance can burn without its access, and that the more strongly it is impelled against burning bodies, the more rapid is the combustion Hence it follows, that as the most part of chemical operations cannot be performed without the assistance of fire, a constant current of air more or less strong, and in a certain direction, is necessary to produce the heat requisite in these operations These currents of air are procured by bellows applied either to a forge, or to a melting furnace, or they are procured merely by the construction of the furnaces, which is done in such a manner, that by means of a space left in the upper part of the furnace, in which the heat keeps up a perpetual vacuum, the external air is determined and forced to enter by the ash-hole, to fill the vacuum above, and consequently forms a current which constantly passes through the fire, and which is so much more strong and rapid as the vacuum of the furnace above is greater That is a fundamental principle from which general rules may be deduced, applicable to the construction of all possible furnaces. *See* BELLOWS, FORGE, and FURNACE

Boerhaave, in his Treatise on Fire, and M Genke, Doctor of Physic, and Member of the Royal Academy of Berlin, who has also given a very large Dissertation on Fire, in a very good work, printed in 1741, entitled *Fundamenta Chymiae Rationalis*, are of opinion, that the access of air is necessary to the combustion of substances, because, by its weight and spring, it keeps the flame constantly applied to the combustible body, and encreases their contact

But this theory does not sufficiently explain why combustible bodies may be kept red-hot in close vessels, without any consumption, because then it cannot be doubted but that the matter of fire is, by the movement excited during ignition, continually applied and even impelled upon the combustible body, without its burning or consuming It has then all the appearance of a body burning and penetrated by fire, but it is by an extraneous fire that it is so penetrated, its own inflammable matter is not consumed, and rests unalterable in midst of a most intense fire

However this be, it is very certain that the access of air is indispensibly necessary to maintain the combustion of bodies But it is at the same time very difficult to find the true cause of this fact The phenomena of combustion seem to prove, that the air materially concurs to the production of flame, and makes a part of it for a given quantity of air can maintain only during a limited and determinate time, the combustion of a certain quantity of inflammable matter If, for example, a lighted wax candle be placed under an inverted glass bell, which is joined exactly to its support, the flame of the wax candle subsists during a certain time, so much longer as the bell is larger, but constantly diminishing till at length it is extinguished, because the quantity of air contained in the bell being a determinate quantity, and not capable of being renewed, cannot serve but for a certain quantity of combustion Another phenomenon worthy of observation in this experiment is, that after the extinction of the wax candle, a real vacuum is formed under the bell, which is then as strongly pressed upon its support, as if a vacuum had been made by an air pump, which proves demonstrably that the air which it included

included, materially concurred to the production of flame, since, if it were not so, the air being greatly rarified by the heat within the bell, would, on the contrary, make an effort to raise itself, and would escape violently as soon as it could (a)

If we reflect but a little on these phenomena, many questions occur very interesting, but at the same time very difficult of solution In fact, does the air, which disappears in this experiment, form a new compound with the inflammable principle of the burnt body by a new combination? If it be so, what is this compound? and what becomes of it? or is the air itself a necessary pabulum or food of flame? is it decomposed by the act of combustion? If so, the air, is not a simple body what then is the nature of its principles? and what becomes of them?

XXV AIR (FIXABLE) (b)

XXVI ALABASTER The name Alabaster is given to stones externally resembling marble, of a hardness nearly equal, but inferior, and

(a) A partial vacuum only is formed by this experiment Dr Mayow found that $\frac{1}{30}$th part of the elasticity of the air in a close vessel was destroyed by the burning of a candle till it was extinguished, and Dr Hales found this diminution of elasticity of air, by the same means, to be $\frac{1}{20}$th part Dr Hales also found that $\frac{1}{10}$th part of the elasticity of air contained in a close vessel was destroyed by burning sulphur All the air contained in close vessels in these experiments was not, however, rendered fixable by the burning of the candle till it ceased to flame, for Mr Cavendish found that $\frac{1}{9}$th part of fixable air was sufficient to render a quantity of common air unfit for the maintenance of the flame of a candle. See Phil Transf 1766

(b) AIR (FIXABLE) By this term we mean those permanently elastic vapors which are disengaged from almost all bodies when decomposed by distillation, from vegetable and animal substances by fermentations, and from many matters during their combination with other substances

This subject is one of the most interesting in chemistry. Little more was known concerning it, than that permanently elastic fluids were producible from the substances, and by the methods mentioned in the above definition, till lately that the phenomena attending the combination of these fluids with, and their expulsion from those substances, together with some other properties, have been investigated by experiments The author of this Dictionary seems to have been unacquainted even with those discoveries which were published before this work Of these the most important have been deduced by Dr Black, from experiments so conducted and related, that his treatise may be considered as an excellent specimen of the best method of investigating and demonstrating chemical truths *See Essays Physical and Literary, published at Edinburgh*

The discoveries already made enable us to explain many chemical phenomena We shall have frequent occasions to supply the defects of the text in this particular, and to correct some errors that prevailed in the theory of chemistry till lately The subject is still new, and much may be expected from further experiments

Some fixable air is *inflammable*, and some is *not inflammable* We shall treat first of the latter kind, to which the name *fixed*, or *fixable air*, has been more peculiarly applied

An uninflammable permanently elastic fluid may be produced by various methods, and from various substances As the identity or diversity of the kinds of the several fluids thus variously obtained has not been yet ascertained, we shall mention what we know of each separately, distinguishing them only by the methods of their production

1. A permanently elastic fluid may be obtained *from alkaline substances by combining these with acids*, or *by calcination* Alkaline substances seem to have a power of combination with this fluid, and with it form compounds, some of the properties of which are different from the properties of these substances when uncombined. This power of combination

ſuſceptible of a ſimilar, but leſs lively and ſparkling poliſh Some alabaſters are white, and others are veined and colored, like marbles When theſe ſtones are well poliſhed, their ſemitranſparency, which is more ſenſible than that of marble, gives them the appearance of agates

is nevertheleſs weaker than that which alkaline ſubſtances have to acids, nor is it ſtrong enough to reſiſt the action of fire Hence this fluid or fixable air may be diſengaged from thoſe ſubſtances by acids, or by fire, when the alkaline ſubſtance is ſufficiently fixed to receive a violent heat When alkaline ſubſtances have been by any means deprived of this fixable fluid, and are expoſed to an atmoſphere in which particles of it float, they readily abſorb it, unleſs they have been previouſly combined with ſome other ſubſtance, as an acid, with which they preferably unite, and again reſume their former ſtate Hence all native alkaline ſubſtances are combined with this fluid Thus, calcareous earth combined with this air forms the ſeveral maſſes of lime-ſtone, marble, chalk, and other ſtones and earths of this claſs When any of theſe ſubſtances are deprived, by calcination or otherwiſe, of the fluid or air with which they are combined, they then become pure uncombined calcareous earth, or *quicklime* Alſo fixed alkaline ſalts, obtained by incineration of vegetables, are found to contain much fixable fluid, unleſs they have been perfectly calcined, and volatile alkali, obtained by diſtillation of animal or of ſome vegetable ſubſtances, is ſaturated with this fluid The principal differences which have been obſerved betwixt theſe ſubſtances combined, or not combined with fixable air, are, 1 By combination with fixable air they are rendered ſuſceptible of cryſtallization, which they are not when uncombined Hence the uniform texture of marbles, calcareous ſpars, cryſtals of vegetable or of mineral alkali, is deſtroyed by extrication of this air 2 By combination of alkaline ſubſtances with fixable air, their power of combination with all other matters which are incapable of expelling from them this air, is diminiſhed Hence, by this combination, the ſolubility of calcareous earth in water is deſtroyed hence fixed alkali is leſs diſpoſed to deliquiate, or imbibe moiſture from the atmoſphere hence volatile alkali, which when combined is ſo ſtrongly diſpoſed to unite with water that it cannot be obtained in a ſolid or concrete ſtate, is rendered ſolid and cryſtalliſable hence the power of alkaline ſalts to diſſolve oil is greatly diminiſhed, ſo that ſoap-boilers find it neceſſary, in the preparation of ſoap, to deprive their ſalts, by quicklime, of all the fixable air with which they happen to be united hence the cauſticity of calcareous earths is deſtroyed, and of alkaline ſalts is diminiſhed, and hence, theſe ſubſtances when combined with fixable air are diſtinguiſhed by the epithet *mild*, and when uncombined by the epithet *cauſtic* 3 Alkaline ſubſtances combined with fixable air effervelce with acids, which they do not, when rendered perfectly cauſtic, this effervelcence being cauſed by the fixable air, which is diſengaged by acids from theſe ſubſtances

This fixable air may be extricated from ſome alkaline ſubſtances by others, with which it has a ſtronger power of combination, and with which it does then actually combine Thus mild volatile alkali may be deprived of its air, or rendered cauſtic by applying to it uncombined magneſia, fixed alkali, or calcareous earth, while theſe ſubſtances unite with that air, and are thereby rendered mild Magneſia may be deprived of its air by cauſtic fixed alkali and calcareous earth and laſtly, mild fixed alkali may be rendered cauſtic by quicklime or cauſtic calcareous earth, which is thereby rendered mild Thus by adding a mild fixed alkali to lime-water, which is a ſolution of cauſtic calcareous earth in water, the calcareous earth will take the fixable air from the alkali, will become mild, conſequently unſoluble in water, and hence will be precipitated.

Fixable air has a weaker power of combination than acids have with alkaline ſubſtances hence theſe ſubſtances may be deprived of their fixable air by acids, and accordingly, when calcareous earth is precipitated from marine acid by a cauſtic alkali, it is found to be in a cauſtic ſtate, or quicklime

The quantity of fixable air contained in marble was found by Mr Cavendiſh, (Phil Trans. 1766) to be $\frac{407}{1000}$ of the whole, in

volatile

Naturaliſts diſagree in their opinions about the kinds of ſtones which ought to be called *alabaſters* For ſome authors give this name to certain ſtones which are abſolutely calcareous, while others give it to ſtones of a gypſeous nature Of the latter claſs of naturaliſts is Mr Pott, who admits no calcareous alabaſter, and

volatile ſal ammoniac, $\frac{523}{1000}$, and in cryſtals of ſalt of tartar $\frac{423}{1000}$

The ſpecific gravity of this fixable air was found by Mr Cavendiſh's experiments to be to that of water as 1 to 511, or to the ſpecific gravity of atmoſpherical air, when this is 800 times lighter than water, as 1 $\frac{5}{100}$ to 1

This fixable air is noxious to animals, and extinguiſhes flame These properties probably do not proceed from its interception of common air, but from ſome peculiar quality, for Mr Cotes found by experiments, that fixable air was more injurious to animals than a vacuum, and from Mr Cavendiſh's experiments we find that $\frac{1}{9}$ of fixable air, mixed with atmoſpherical air, occaſioned the extinction of the flame of a candle

2 A permanently elaſtic fluid or fixable air is produced *by diſſolving metallic ſubſtances in acids* From iron, zinc, and tin, diſſolved in the vitriolic or marine acids, an inflammable air is produced, of which we ſhall treat afterwards From all other metallic ſubſtances, and from theſe above mentioned diſſolved in other acids, uninflammable airs are produced An air alſo adheres to metallic ſubſtances precipitated by mild alkalies or earths, which they receive from theſe precipitating matters, and which gives them greater than their original weight To adhering air Dr. Black attributes the fulminating property of the precipitate called *fulminating gold*

3 An elaſtic fluid or fixable air is produced *by combining concentrated acids with oily, and reſinous ſubſtances, with ſpirit of wine and with water* Theſe ſubſtances are alſo capable of abſorbing the fixable air of alkaline matters. Thus oil of olives was found to abſorb an equal bulk of it, ſpirit of wine 2 $\frac{1}{4}$ times its bulk, with the heat of 46° of Fahrenheit's thermometer Water alſo abſorbed this air more copiouſly in cold than in hot weather With a boiling heat, and even by expoſure to common air during a few days, it parted with the air it had abſorbed

4 A fixable air is obtainable *from animal, vegetable, and ſome mineral ſubſtances by diſtillation* By this method Dr Hales procured from a cubic inch of deer's horn thirty-three grains of air, from Indian wheat $\frac{1}{4}$ of its weight, from well-water $\frac{1}{6}$, from Pyrmont water $\frac{2}{3}$, from nitre $\frac{1}{8}$, from tartar $\frac{1}{3}$, and from ſalt of tartar $\frac{1}{6}$ of the reſpective weights of theſe ſubſtances

5 A fixable air is extricated from water merely *by taking off the preſſure of the atmoſphere* An air may alſo be extricated by the ſame method from lime-water, which muſt be different from the air of alkaline ſubſtances, elſe it would precipitate the calcareous earth from the water, as Dr. Black has remarked

6 Fixable airs are produced by the *vinous, acetous, putrefactive, and probably by all other fermentations* Dr Hales found that 42 cubic inches, of ale, which had been fermenting thirty-four hours, did continue to emit air from the 2d of March to the 9th of June following, ſometimes more and ſometimes leſs according to the heat of the weather, and that upon a ſudden change of weather from hot to cold, it reſorbed air The whole quantity of air emitted was 639 cubic inches Theſe airs are alſo deleterious to animals, and extinguiſh flame.

7 *Atmoſpherical air is rendered unfit for reſpiration, or combuſtion, by having been inſpired by animals or vegetables,* and is therefore probably reduced to the ſame, or to a ſimilar ſtate with ſome of the above mentioned fixable airs

8 *Atmoſpherical air is rendered unfit for reſpiration or further combuſtion, by having aſſiſted the combuſtion of ignited inflammable bodies* A conſiderable part alſo of its elaſticity is deſtroyed by this combuſtion for by burning a candle in a cloſe veſſel till it ceaſed to burn from want of freſh air, the air contained in the veſſel loſt, according to Dr Hales, $\frac{1}{18}$th, and according to Dr Mayow, $\frac{1}{30}$th part of its elaſticity Theſe effects are not produced upon air merely by heat, for we find from Mr Hawkſbee's experiments, that air was not altered by paſſing through a heated glaſs tube, but was rendered noxious to animals by paſſing through heated tubes

firmly maintains his opinion in his Lithogeognosia against Linnæus, Konig, Bruckman, and several other authors, who class alabaster along with marbles and calcareous stones

It cannot be doubted that the stone which Mr Pott called alabaster, and which he chemically examined, is actually gypseous His experiments evidently

of brass and iron, glass being an incombustible substance, and metals, at least those called imperfect, being capable of calcination, which is a combustion, or dissipation of their inflammable principle Whence does this alteration of atmospherical air proceed? Is it that part of the atmospherical air is converted into fixable air, by combining with the phlogiston or some part of the burning substances?

9 A permanently elastic fluid or fixable air is produced *by deflagration of nitrous acid with any inflammable substance* In this operation the acid disappears, and an elastic vapor is produced May we not thence infer, that the acid is converted by combination with some other substance, probably with the inflammable matter, or by decomposition of its own substance, into elastic vapor? The author of this Dictionary in the article DETONATION OF NITRE adopts the opinion of Stahl, that the explosion of nitre with inflammable matter is produced by rarefaction of water contained in nitre or its acid This rarefaction does contribute to the effect produced, but is not the sole or principal cause for the vapor of water is condensible by cold into a liquor similar to the water from which it was formed, whereas the vapor of which we now treat is permanently elastic Stahl did indeed maintain that the water was by this operation changed into air, but we have not sufficient reasons to believe the possibility of such a conversion in any instance, and in this instance we know that the water of the nitre is, after the explosion, condensed, and forms what is called a *clyssus* *See* CLYSSUS OF NITRE, and DETONATION OF NITRE

This elastic fluid was found by Mr Robins to occupy, when compressed by the atmosphere and reduced to the same heat, a space equal to 250 times the space occupied by the gun-powder before explosion And as the elasticity of air appeared from his experiments to be encreased four times by the heat of iron just beginning to be white, if this fluid be equally affected by heat as air is, its elasticity in the instant of explosion is about 1000 times greater than the pressure of the atmosphere, a force sufficient to produce the effects of gun-powder

These are the known kinds of permanently elastic fluids extricated from substances, in which they existed so combined, that their elasticity was either destroyed or counteracted by a superior force The properties of these fluids have not been sufficiently investigated, to enable us to determine whether all or several of them be of the same or different kinds Do not, however, the elastic fluids produced by combustion, and extricated from alkaline substances, seem to be of the same kind, since a caustic alkali may be rendered mild by exposure to the former fluid? Are not these two elastic fluids probably of the same kind with that obtained from some metals, or, at least, have they not some principle common to them all, since metals deprived of their fixable air, or of the principle which renders atmospherical air fixable, by calcination, or by solution in acids, may be reduced to their proper metallic state by applying combustible substances, and since several instances are given, by authors, of the reduction of metallic calxes by chalk, and other mild calcareous earths? Have not the fluids separable from all aline and metallic substances some analogy with acids? Like acids, they readily unite with, and effect the crystallization of those substances As a weaker acid is extricated from those substances by a stronger, so is this air by all known acids Are not the elastic fluids produced by the deflagration of nitre, and by the combustion or alkalization of tartar, and of other vegetable acid salts, formed from the acids of these substances combined with the inflammable principle? Whether these or many other conjectures, which might be made, be just or not, we may easily perceive that a judicious prosecution of this subject may tend to explain many important facts in chemistry

Concerning

demonſtrate it. But, on the other ſide, it does not appear leſs certain, that the name *alabaſter* has been very anciently given to ſtones undoubtedly calcareous The greateſt part of the antique vaſes and buſts, although univerſally called alabaſter, are of this kind They are readily and entirely ſoluble in ſpirit of nitre with great efferveſcence, and are convertible by fire into quicklime

The truth is, that ſculptors and artiſts, who work upon marble and alabaſter, ſeem to have given indiſcriminately the name *alabaſter* to ſtones which have only an external reſemblance to each other; that is to ſay, to ſtones which, to the other external qualities of marble, join alſo a more cryſtalline and more tranſparent appearance Thus theſe artiſts have confounded under one name ſtones of very different kinds, and hence, among thoſe called alabaſters, ſome are truly calcareous, and others entirely gypſeous Therefore if ſtones are to be named from their external appearances, we ought, in order to avoid a confuſion of two ſubſtances entirely different, to admit two kinds of alabaſters, one kind calcareous, of which the greateſt part of vaſes and buſts are made which are called alabaſter, and the other kind gypſeous, which is alſo uſed in ſculpture, and is that which Mr Pott examined, and to which he aſſigns excluſively the name alabaſter

Theſe difficulties being explained, chemiſts and naturaliſts are at liberty to take which ſide they pleaſe They will always be underſtood when they diſtinguiſh in this manner the ſubſtances concerning which they write.

This being eſtabliſhed, the kind of ſtone which may be called calcareous alabaſter, has eſſentially all the properties of calcareous ſtones, for which reaſon, it is neceſſary to conſult, upon this ſubject, the articles EARTHS (CALCAREOUS) and QUICKLIME We ſhall only obſerve here, that it appears demonſtrated, as M. d'Aubenton has advanced, that the differences obſervable betwixt calcareous alabaſter and marble, proceed only from the different manners in which theſe

Concerning the *antiſeptic* qualities of fixable airs, *ſee* PUTREFACTION

Inflammable permanently elaſtic fluids may be obtained by diſſolving zinc, iron, or tin in marine or dilute vitriolic acids 350 ounce-meaſures of air were obtained from an ounce of zinc diſſolved in vitriolic acid, and alſo from the ſame quantity of zinc diſſolved in marine acid 412 ounce-meaſures of air were obtained from an ounce of iron diſſolved in vitriolic acid, and 202 ounce meaſures of air from an ounce of tin diſſolved in marine acid

This inflammable air was not abſorbed by water, or by fixed or volatile alkalies

Like other inflammable ſubſtances, it is only combuſtible by acceſs of atmoſpherical air, of which it requires an equal quantity for that purpoſe

It was found by experiment to be eleven times lighter than atmoſpherical air, when the weight of this was to that of water as one to 800 Hence the quantity of air obtained from zinc, as above mentioned, was nearly $\frac{1}{24}$th part of the ſemi-metal

An inflammable permanently elaſtic air is alſo producible from putrefying vegetable and animal ſubſtances One grain of this air was obtained from 7640 grains of putrefying gravy broth, which contained about 163 grains of ſolid matter The loſs of weight ſuſtained by this broth was much greater The remaining part muſt have been according to Mr Cavendiſh (from whoſe paper on factitious air, Phil Tranſ 1766, all the above mentioned facts on inflammable air are copied) uninflammable fixable air, and ſome matter which communicated color and ſmell to ſoap-leys

An inflammable permanently elaſtic fluid is frequently obſerved in mines, and is dangerous to miners Theſe fluids are called *Damps* See *the article* DAMPS

two

two ſubſtances are formed, marble being of ancient formation, and the product of a depoſition of calcareous particles accumulated upon each other in banks and large maſſes while calcareous alabaſter is formed alſo of calcareous particles, but in the way of filtration, and of *ſtalactites*, of which large enough maſſes are found to make vaſes, buſts, and even ſtatues This difference in the formation of theſe two matters is ſufficient to explain the cauſe of the greater tranſparency of calcareous alabaſter In fact, if a piece of calcareous ſtalactites be cut and poliſhed, no difference can be perceived betwixt it and works made of calcareous alabaſter

As to the ſtone called *gypſeous alabaſter*, it has all the properties of gypſeous ſtones, and therefore it is neceſſary to conſult upon this ſubject the articles Gypsum and Plaster

XXVII ALCHEMY This term has been employed by the pretended adepts, and by ſearchers after the philoſopher's ſtone, to diſtinguiſh that kind of chemiſtry the knowledge of which they flattered themſelves was reſerved for them alone The adepts conſider chemiſtry as a vulgar ſcience, which ſcarcely contains the firſt elements of the myſterious ſcience of alchemy. But hitherto they have produced nothing which, in the judgment of ſenſible men, can give the leaſt grounds to ſuch a pretenſion True chemiſts conſider alchemy as an imaginary ſcience, and thoſe who are devoted to it as perſons who, from want of better inſtruction, quit a reality for the ſake of a ſhadow

XXVIII ALEMBIC An alembic or *ſtill* is a veſſel employed in diſtillations. There are ſeveral kinds differing from each other, either as to their form, or the matter of which they are compoſed

The moſt frequent uſe of alembics is for diſtillations of very volatile principles drawn from ſeveral ſubſtances, particularly from vegetables When the principles intended to be procured by diſtillation have no conſiderable action upon metals, and when they are ſuſceptible of riſing with a degree of heat which does not exceed, or but little, the heat of boiling water, copper alembics well tinned in their internal ſurface are employed

The moſt convenient of theſe alembics, and which may be employed for many kinds of diſtillation, are compoſed of the following pieces The firſt is a kind of pot deſigned to contain either the matters intended for diſtillation, or water, in which is immerſed another ſmaller veſſel of the ſame form, and made to contain the matters intended for diſtillation by the water-bath Theſe pieces of the alembic are called in general *cucurbits*, becauſe formerly they were of an oblong form, upright, contracting themſelves in their upper part, and diminiſhing into a kind of neck, which made them reſemble a cucurbit, or gourd, or a *bladder*, by which latter name alſo they have been diſtinguiſhed

The cucurbits of copper alembics uſed now have no reſemblance to this form on the contrary, they are broad, not very deep, and wide This new form of cucurbits is much more advantageous, as by it the diſtillations are much accelerated, with equal heat The reaſon of this is, that the quickneſs of diſtillation is always proportionable to the quickneſs of evaporation, and that as evaporation is always made at the ſurface of bodies, the more ſurface theſe bodies preſent, the more quick and eaſy will be the evaporation But the broad and wide form of modern cucurbits is infinitely more proper for the expoſing of much

much surface of the bodies contained, and particularly of liquid bodies, than the form of the ancient cucurbits, which were high and strait

The first of these two pieces is of copper, that it may resist the action of the fire the second is generally of tin, and ought to be so shaped, that it can enter exactly into the former piece, and that they should fit so well as to render any luting unnecessary

There ought to be a small pipe or neck at the upper part of the first piece, which may be exactly closed, and through which water or other fluid may be introduced at pleasure,

The third piece of the alembic is called the *capital*, because it is a kind of head This piece has the form of a hollow cone It is furnished with a gutter or channel, which is placed along its inner and lower circumference

This capital has also in its lower part a kind of neck, which ought to enter so exactly into either of the two former pieces, as no luting shall be necessary Lastly, it ought to have a pipe, called the *beak*, which opens inwardly into the gutter

This beak ought to be from fifteen to eighteen inches externally, and so inclined, that it shall make with the neck of the alembic an angle of about sixty degrees

The fourth piece of a copper alembic is called the *refrigeratory* It is a kind of bucket, surrounding the capital, to which it is exactly soldered in its lower part In this, near its bottom, is inserted a cock The use of the refrigeratory is to contain cold water to facilitate the condensation of vapors circulating in the capital Its cock serves to empty the water when it is become too hot, that it may be supplied with cold

As in copper alembics the refrigeratory and capital are joined, they may be considered as making only one piece However, it is necessary to distinguish them, first, because their uses are very different, and, secondly, because the refrigeratory is not essential to the alembic Several chemists, good operators, are doubtful concerning its utility, particularly since the custom was introduced of applying worms to alembics

The *worm* is a long, tin, spiral pipe, included in a copper bucket, so that its upper and lower extremities shall come out of the bucket by two holes, round which they are well soldered The upper extremity of the worm receives the beak of the alembic, and its lower extremity enters into a receiver fitted to it The bucket containing the worm is filled with cold water, which cools and condenses the vapors passing through it The principal advantage which this refrigeratory has over that surrounding the capital, is, that it is not subject to retard or even to stop the distillation, as this latter one is for this inconvenience has been observed to happen, whenever the capital of the alembic has been exposed to a certain degree of cold There is in M Beaume's Elements of Pharmacy a very exact description, and a good engraving of a copper alembic with its worm

The alembics described are of great use for the distillation of the *spiritus rector* of vegetables, of their *distilled waters*, of their *essential oils*, of pure *ardent spirits*, of spirits charged with the odoriferous principles of plants, and also for many other distillations of this kind But as it is frequently necessary to distill in alembics acid and saline liquors capable of attacking metals, glass alembics are employed

employed for such distillations and these are generally composed of only two pieces, namely, a cucurbit, and a capital, which is fitted above and joined by luting There are glass cucurbits, high and strait, which may be useful for the distillation of certain very volatile substances Others are made shallow and broad, and these have the same advantages from their form as the metal ones have

To avoid the luting of the capital with the cucurbit, these glass alembics have been made of one entire piece The capital of these alembics, which are of crystal glass, ought to have an opening at its top, which may be exactly closed with a crystal stopper ground with emery This opening is intended for the introduction of matters to be distilled, and for the extraction of the residuums after distillation These alembics of one piece, although sometimes convenient, are seldom employed on account of their dearness, and of the difficulty of introducing, and of extracting solid matters

There are also made cucurbits of stone-ware, and of glazed earthen ware, which are useful in many cases *See* at the word DISTILLATION several observations relative to the form and matter of alembic *See Plate* I

XXIX ALKAHEST This is a name given by ancient chemists to a pretended universal menstruum Such a menstruum either does not exist, or else there is not any body in nature which may not become an alkahest For although certain substances have not hitherto been combined with others, the daily discoveries in chemistry of combinations formerly believed impossible, seem to prove, that by certain management, and certain circumstances, any substance may be combined with all others, or, in other words, that all bodies may be dissolved by any single substance (c)

XXX. ALKALESCENT. This word is employed to denote a matter slightly alkaline, or which begins to turn to the alkaline and putrid fermentation

XXXI ALKALI (FIXED) Fixed alkali is a substance composed of acid, of earth, and of a little phlogiston, and whose principles have to each other a weaker adhesion, than the principles of any acid have to each other There are several kinds of saline alkaline substances These are vegetable alkali, mineral or fossil alkali, and volatile alkali They are all called by the general name *Alkali*, because the following properties are common to them all

1 Alkalies may easily be obtained dry and concrete, and freed from all water unnecessary to their saline essence (d) When they are in this state,

2 They produce heat by adding water to them

3 They attract the moisture of the air, and deliquiate into a liquor (e)

4 They change the color of syrup of violets into green, whether they be dry or fluid

(c) Kunckel very well shews the absurdity of searching for an universal solvent by asking, "If it dissolves all substances, in what vessel can it be contained?"

(d) Volatile alkali retains water so strongly that it cannot be obtained dry, unless by combining it with fixable air, and then it becomes crystallizable. The fixed alkalies may be rendered dry by application of heat, but are only chrystallizable by help of fixable air *See* AIR (FIXABLE)

(e) Mineral alkali does not deliquiate by exposure to air, but on the contrary, when chrystallized, it becomes dry, and loses the water which is necessary to its chrystalline state.

5. They

5 They have an acrid, burning taſte, ſo much ſtronger as they are purer and dryer. This taſte has ſomething *urinous* and hence they are called by ſome chemiſts *urinous ſalts* They are alſo called *lixivial ſalts*, becauſe the method of obtaining fixed alkalies conſiſts in lixiviating the aſhes of certain vegetable ſubſtances

6 They partly exhale with water, particularly when boiled in open air

7 When they are dryed and re-diſſolved, ſome earth is always ſeparated from them

8 They may be fuſed by a moderate heat

9 When fuſed, they diſſolve all earths

10 When added to earths and particularly to thoſe called vitrifiable earths, and expoſed to a ſufficient degree of heat, they and the earths become glaſs *See* VITRIFICATION.

11 When added in a large proportion to the earths, with which they are fuſed or vitrified, they communicate to theſe earths all their own properties *See* LIQUOR OF FLINTS.

12 They effervеſce and unite with acids to the point of ſaturation more perfectly and more intimately than pure abſorbent earths, and from this union reſult different neutral ſalts

13 They decompoſe all ſalts with baſes of earths, metals, or volatile alkali They ſeparate theſe baſes, and unite with the acids of the ſalts, with which they form new neutral ſalts This is an example of ſtronger affinity, from whence reſult a new decompoſition and a new combination

Alkaline ſalts being ſubſtances pretty ſimple, as well as acids, are powerful ſolvents They are capable of combining not only with all acids and with all earths, as we have ſaid, but alſo with ſulphur and with oily matters With ſulphur they form a ſulphureous ſoap, ſoluble in water, called *liver of ſulphur*, which *ſee*

With oils, fat, reſins, &c they form compounds, which have been called *ſoaps* In each of theſe combinations, the alkali is a medium by which the inflammable ſubſtance, naturally unſoluble, and even immiſcible in water, becomes miſcible and ſoluble in that liquid *See* SOAP

Theſe ſaline ſubſtances can act alſo upon ſpirit of wine, when they are deprived of all the water unneceſſary to their eſſence as ſalts. Alkalies, in that ſtate, applied to ſpirit of wine, firſt deprive it of its ſuperfluous water, afterwards, when in a proper proportion, they act upon its own ſubſtance, by combining with it, and cauſing ſeveral alterations, and even a decompoſition of its parts *See* SPIRIT *of* WINE (TARTARISED), and TINCTURE *of* SALT *of* TARTAR

Laſtly, alkalies act upon metallic ſubſtances with more or leſs facility, according to their natures, and the different means employed, which ſhall be mentioned under the ſeveral articles of the alkalies and metals

N B. All that has been ſaid above concerning alkalies, may be applied to all the ſeveral kinds of alkalies, even to thoſe called *volatile*, excepting thoſe properties which depend upon fixity Hence this article is applicable to alkalies in general But it is neceſſary to obſerve, that a very juſt idea cannot be formed of theſe generalities, without entering into the details of what concerns the ſeveral kinds *See* for the *affinities* of fixed alkali, and for its *medicinal virtues*, the word ALKALI (FIXED MINERAL)

XXXII ALKALI (FIXED VEGETABLE). This name is given to all fixed alkalies obtained by burning any vegetable ſubſtances, and which have not the properties of the alkali, which is the baſis of common ſalt, which has been called the alkali of common ſalt, the *marine alkali, mineral or foſſil alkali*

The common method of obtaining fixed alkalies from vegetable ſubſtances, conſiſts in burning theſe ſubſtances freely and in open air, till they be reduced to aſhes *See* COMBUSTION *of* PLANTS After which theſe aſhes are lixiviated with very pure water, till the water comes from them inſipid. This lixivium is evaporated to dryneſs, and what remains is the fixed alkaline ſalt of the plant, which may be deprived of its ſuperfluous water and ſuperfluous phlogiſton by calcination with a long and gentle fire

Fixed alkalies obtained from any vegetable matters when well prepared and carefully purified by means hereafter to be deſcribed, are all exactly alike, and have the ſame properties, ſo that they are only one and the ſame kind of ſaline ſubſtance But as it is very difficult to procure this ſalt in its utmoſt degree of purity, and as, in this reſpect, there is a difference betwixt thoſe obtained from different vegetable matters, ſome of them being naturally purer or more eaſily ſuſceptible of purification than others, and further, as ſufficient attention has not been given to the means of perfectly purifying theſe alkalies, two inconveniences have happened The firſt is, that ſeveral chemiſts have imagined that there was an eſſential difference betwixt alkalies obtained from different plants and the ſecond is, that other chemiſts have attributed to alkalies in general, ſeveral properties not belonging to them as alkalies, but to certain foreign ſubſtances adhering to them We here conſider the vegetable alkali perfectly purified and after we have enumerated its principal properties, we will treat of its origin, of its formation, and of the means of purifying it

Fixed vegetable alkali has all the properties related under the article ALKALI (FIXED)

It is ſolid or concrete, like an earthy ſubſtance, of a fine white color, without tranſparency, or cryſtalline and regular ſhape, becauſe, in fact, it is not ſuſceptible of cryſtallization *(f)*, of no ſmell while it is dry, but of a ſlight lixivial ſmell when moiſtened with water It has a violent, ſharp, burning, cauſtic and urinous taſte, that is to ſay, that when put in the mouth, it diſcovers a taſte of putrefied urine, which is cauſed by the diſengagement of volatile alkali from animal ſubſtances

Here it is proper to obſerve, that when it is required to taſte fixed alkali, it is convenient to diſſolve and dilute it in much water, which only leſſens its ſtrength without altering its character otherwiſe, the tongue might be bliſtered, becauſe calcined alkali is powerfully cauſtic, and quickly corrodes and deſtroys all animal matters *(g)*

Fixed alkali, expoſed to air, attracts moiſture, with which it reſolves, or deliquiates into a white tranſparent colorleſs liquor like pure water Fixed alkali

(f) Fixed vegetable alkali does not ſo readily cryſtallize as mineral alkali does It is nevertheleſs cryſtallizable by expoſing it to fixable air, with which it combines and forms cryſtals *See* AIR (FIXABLE)

(g) The cauſe of this is, that by calcination fixed alkali is deprived of a part of its fixable air, and is thereby rendered more ſoluble, and conſequently more cauſtic *See* AIR (FIXABLE)

attracts

attracts thrice its quantity of moisture, according to Gellert *Chemie Metallurgique, Tom 1 p 26*

The same thing happens if it be purposely dissolved in water But in this latter case, at the first instant of the mixture, a pretty strong heat is excited, by the activity of the union of alkali and water This heat, however, is much less than what arises from the mixture of concentrated vitriolic acid and water

Every time that fixed alkali is dissolved in water, a portion of indissoluble matter remains If the solution be filtered, it passes very clear but after some time, it begins to be turbid, and small flocks are formed in it of a matter which falls to the bottom of the vessel, and cannot afterwards be redissolved This matter is of the same nature as the first substance which we observed remains undissolved, and is nothing else than a portion of the earth of the alkali, which is separated every time that the salt is calcined and dissolved The part which at first passes through the filter, and which afterwards renders the liquor turbid, is that part which was the most attenuated, and most adhering to the alkaline salt This earth thus separated, is no longer in a saline state, and consequently becomes indissoluble in water like pure earths

Alkali dissolved in the smallest possible quantity of water, forms a liquor less fluid, more thick, and unctuous than pure water, and which passes with more difficulty through the filter, from the quantity of saline matter with which the water is charged When it is touched and rubbed betwixt the fingers, it appears to have a fat and oily nature, which proceeds from the greasy particles of the skin dissolved by it. These properties have occasioned it to be called, but improperly, an *oil*, by ancient chemists *See* Oil *of* Tartar It ought to be called the *Liquor of alkaline salt*

Dry fixed alkali, exposed to a moderate fire, that is, a little more than cherry red, sustains its action pretty well, altho' it fuses, and diminishes in quantity But by a very violent fire, the greatest part of it is dissipated in vapors, or even all of it, if the heat be sufficiently long and intense It is easy to be convinced of this by observing the pots in which glass is melted in glass-houses Above these pots a perpetual smoke may be seen, which can proceed only from the fixed alkali which enters into the composition of glass, the other matters which enter into that composition being infinitely more fixed than it

Fixed alkali is a very powerful solvent In the dry way, and by help of proper heat, it dissolves all calcareous, vitrifiable, argillaceous, gypseous, and metallic earths, and in certain proportions, and nearly in equal parts, it changes most of these into different kinds of hard, solid, and transparent glasses *See* Glass, Vitrification, Crystal-Glass.

When a third or fourth part only of earth is added to it, they more readily fuse, and unite together and as the alkali is the prevailing principle in the new compound which results from this union, so its properties also prevail Hence it renders the earths so dissolved, soluble in water, and in acids, susceptible of attracting the moisture of the air, &c. *See* Liquor *of* Flints

The alkali appears to have no action by the humid way upon substances purely earthy, but it has upon quicklime, to which it gives, and from which it receives, very singular alterations When it is liquid, and treated with this sub-

 stance,

ſtance, it becomes infinitely more cauſtic and more fuſible than it was before *See* LIXIVIUM *of* SOAP-BOILERS, CAUTERY *(b)*

Fixed vegetable alkali unites with the vitriolic acid violently and with great efferveſcence The union of theſe two ſaline ſubſtances is very ſtrong and very intimate, and from thence reſults a perfect neutral ſalt, which is *vitriolated tartar*, *See* TARTAR (VITRIOLATED)

With nitrous acid it forms *nitre*, a neutral cryſtallizable ſalt, the properties of which ſee under the word NITRE

With marine acid, fixed vegetable alkali forms a particular kind of common ſalt, reſembling in many reſpects the natural common ſalt, but differing from it in others, and chiefly in its taſte, which is much leſs agreeable than that of common ſalt The differences betwixt theſe two ſalts are cauſed by the difference of their alkaline baſes, natural common ſalt having for its baſis a particular kind of fixed alkaline ſalt, which differs conſiderably from the fixed vegetable alkali The kind of common ſalt formed with this latter alkali and marine acid is called *regenerated common ſalt*, or SALT (FEBRIFUGAL) *of* SYLVIUS *See* that article

Fixed vegetable alkali unites alſo very well with vegetable acids, and with them forms different neutral ſalts, according to the nature of theſe acids With the acid of vinegar, it makes a neutral deliqueſcent ſalt, of a very pungent taſte, called, *regenerated tartar*, or *Terra foliata tartari*, ſee theſe words With the concrete vegetable acid, or cream of tartar, it forms a neutral cryſtallizable ſalt called *tartariſed tartar*, or *Salt (vegetable)*, which ſee

Laſtly, fixed vegetable alkali unites alſo and forms true neutral ſalts with any ſubſtances, which, though not pure acids, do however act as acids with relation to alkalies Such is the ſedative ſalt, with which this alkali forms a particular kind of *Borax* *See* BORAX and SALT (SEDATIVE) Such alſo is arſenic, with which it unites to the point of ſaturation, and forms a very ſingular, neutral, cryſtallizable ſalt, the properties of which were firſt obſerved by M Macquer, who gave it the name of *neutral arſenical ſalt* *See* SALT (NEUTRAL ARSENICAL)

Fixed vegetable alkali diſſolves ſulphur in all its ſubſtance; that is, it unites with both the acid and the phlogiſton of which this mineral matter is compoſed It only diminiſhes the adheſion of theſe two conſtituent parts of ſulphur This union of alkali with ſulphur may be made in the humid way and in the dry way, but much better in the latter Hence reſults a particular ſaponaceous body, called *liver of ſulphur*, which is a powerful ſolvent of all metallic ſubſtance *See* LIVER *of* SULPHUR

Metallic ſubſtances are capable of being attacked and diſſolved by pure alkali Some of them, ſuch as iron, and particularly copper, need only to be digeſted in the liquor of alkaline ſalt, to be perfectly diſſolved Moſt of the others require to be previouſly diſſolved by acids but by means of this ſolution in acids they become very ſoluble in alkali For this purpoſe it is neceſſary to pour ſome drops of metallic ſolution into a very ſtrong liquor of alkaline ſalt at firſt a precipitate is formed, which diſappears when the liquor is agitated, thus the

(b) The cauſticity which alkaline ſalts acquire by being treated with quicklime, is occaſioned by this ſubſtance depriving them of fixable air, to which it has a ſtronger power of combination than they have. *See* AIR (FIXABLE).

acid

acid metallic solution is to be continued to be poured in at different times into the alkaline liquor, till this latter cannot any longer dissolve the precipitate

All metals are not by this method dissolved with equal facility, and in equal quantities by fixed alkali The lunar metals, namely, silver, mercury, and lead, are dissolved by it with more difficulty and in less quantity than the solar metals, such as gold, platina, tin, copper, and especially iron This last metal gives to the alkali while it is dissolving a beautiful saffron color, approaching to red This solution of iron by alkali was first published by Stahl, and by him called *martial alkaline tincture* See TINCTURE (MARTIAL ALKALINE) *of* STAHL

It is proper to observe upon the subject of the solubility of metals in fixed alkali, 1 That in order to its success, it is very necessary that the previous solution of metal in an acid should be very acid, and very far from the point of saturation In whatever manner the operation is done, it always fails in making the martial alkaline tincture of Stahl, if a very saturated solution of iron in nitrous acid be employed M Macquer and Mr Beaumé have ascertained the necessity of this management, which is not observed by Stahl or any other chemist

2 Most of these metallic solutions in alkali preserve their limpidity only during a certain time after which they become turbid, and a deposition is then formed, of the same color as the solution This deposition is nothing else than a portion of the dissolved metal which separates from the solvent, as happens to several solutions of metals in acids

3 A very illustrious chemist recommends for the solution of metals in fixed alkali, particularly of gold, silver, mercury, zinc, and bismuth, an alkali phlogisticated and fit to make Prussian blue But this is the precise way to fail in the operation This able chemist has been led into error by some of those circumstances, which are but too frequent in chemistry, and against which it is impossible for the most intelligent persons to be always guarded Some details upon this subject may be seen under the articles BLUE (PRUSSIAN), *and* TINCTURE (MARTIAL ALKALINE) *of* STAHL

By fusion and by the dry way, fixed alkali dissolves and vitrifies all metallic calxes, or earths deprived of phlogiston, perhaps even it is capable of dissolving the metals uncalcined

Fixed vegetable alkali unites easily with oils and oily substances, and communicates to them its property of mixing well with water With them it forms saponaceous compounds, partaking of the properties of oil, and of those of alkaline salt, as has been said under the article of alkali in general *See* the word SOAP

As to the origin of fixed vegetable alkali, it is disputed whether it exists ready formed in vegetables previously to their combustion, by which it is obtained, but which in this supposition does only disengage substances which envelope and disguise it, or whether vegetables contain only the materials proper for its formation, which consequently takes place in the act of burning, and whether it be, properly speaking, produced by fire

There are reasons for and against these two opinions, and they are so strong on both sides, that there are grounds to believe that both of them are true, that is to say, that the fixed alkali obtained after burning a vegetable, did partly exist ready formed in that vegetable before it was burnt, and that the other part was produced by the very act of combustion

The proof of the former part of this proposition is, that from most plants neutral salts whose bases are fixed vegetable alkali, such as vitriolated tartar and nitre, may be actually obtained without burning And still more M Beaume, upon a particular examination of the plant called *corona solis*, found that this plant when well cultivated furnished not only a very considerable quantity of perfect nitre, very susceptible of crystallization and detonation, the base of which consequently was fixed vegetable alkali, but also a large quantity of this alkali, disengaged from any acid, well distinguished, and possessed of all its properties An alkali then does exist in vegetables previous to burning It remains to be examined whether this alkali existing in plants previous to burning, be truly one of their principles and constituent parts, or only a foreign and unnecessary substance What renders the latter opinion probable, is that the quantity of alkali in plants, whether disengaged or united to an acid in neutral salts, is very variable, and that it appears to depend solely on culture and on the nature of the soil so that it frequently happens, that the same plants which contain much alkali when these two circumstances favor its introduction, contain none at all in contrary circumstances

As to the second proposition concerning the origin of fixed vegetable alkali, which is, that a great part of this alkali is produced and combined by the act of combustion, it is established by several proofs seemingly incontestable The observation of the circumstances concurring to the production of alkali by burning, demonstrates that this alkali is in great measure formed by the vegetable acid, which, during the deflagration of vegetables, combines in a particular manner with a portion of their earth and inflammable principle

The following observations will render this truth evident

1 When vegetables capable of furnishing ashes containing much alkali, are decomposed by other means than combustion, scarcely any other saline matters are obtained from them but fluor acids, or what are properly called essential salts, which are nothing else than concrete acids rendered solid by a portion of oil and earth

2 When vegetables are deprived of a part of their acid by distillation, or by extraction of their essential salts, the quantity of fixed alkali obtained from their ashes is as much less, as the quantity of acid previously taken away was greater

3 The matter of extracts containing almost all the acid of the vegetables used for that extraction, and the essential salts of vegetables are, of all vegetable matters, those which furnish the greatest quantity of fixed alkali by burning in open air The concrete acids particularly are changed by this process almost entirely into fixed alkali A striking example of this is seen in the combustion of tartar, which is one of those concrete acids

4 Oils and oily concretions, which contain little acid and earth, leave after burning a scarcely sensible quantity of fixed alkali

5 Plants which contain a very volatile acid, and those from which no acid is obtained by distillation, such as mustard seed, leave also in their ashes but an almost insensible quantity of fixed alkali

6. All

6 All vegetables, even those which in their natural state furnish ashes containing much fixed alkali, when burnt, after their acid has been altered by a complete putrefaction, leave ashes entirely free from alkali

We cannot therefore but conclude, after having attended to these facts, that the greatest part of the fixed vegetable alkali is produced from the acids of vegetables

We ought also, after what has been said on the origin and production of fixed alkali, to perceive the reason, why vegetable matters, which have undergone decoctions or long macerations in much water, as floated wood, leave but little or no alkali in their ashes The water has dissolved and carried off either the alkali ready formed, or their acids and essential salts, which, as we have seen, are the principal materials of its composition

Fixed alkali prepared by the incineration of vegetable substances, and by lixiviating and evaporating to dryness, is very far from the degree of purity requisite in exact chemical experiments.

It is almost always altered, 1 By some remaining inflammable principle, which could not be entirely consumed during the burning, 2 By a portion of superabundant earth, 3 By the mixture of different saline matters as fixed as itself, which partly or entirely elude the action of the fire These saline matters are either some neutral salts, which are frequently found in plants, such as vitriolated tartar, Glauber's salt, common salt, and sometimes a little nitre or a portion of fixed mineral alkali 4 As iron is diffused in almost all bodies, and particularly in greater or less quantity in the ashes of vegetables, as Mr Geoffroy has proved, and further, as iron is very soluble by fixed alkali, this saline substance is subject to be altered by mixture with iron

Fixed alkali is discovered to be phlogisticated, or altered by a superabundance of inflammable matter, 1 By its color not being perfectly white, and by its lixivium or solution in water being more or less yellow, or red instead of being absolutely colorless, 2 By the smell of its lixivium, which is always so much stronger, as it is more phlogisticated, 3 By its degree of causticity, which is always so much less as it retains more superabundant inflammable matter, 4 Lastly, by its property of forming Prussian blue, by precipitating solutions of iron in acids, when it is much phlogisticated See upon this last article, BLUE (PRUSSIAN)

There are two methods of purifying fixed alkali thus altered, that is, of depriving it of all the superabundant inflammable matter it contains The first is by calcination, according to the general rules and with all the attentions necessary to be observed in calcining by fire. *See* CALCINATION

The second method of purifying fixed alkali from superabundant inflammable matter consists in applying to it a body on which it cannot act, and which has a stronger affinity than it with this inflammable matter M Beaumé first practised this second method This able observer, having perceived that when he evaporated in silver vessels red and phlogisticated alkaline lixiviums, these vessels were more and more tarnished, till at length the surface of the silver became quite black, and that the lixivium lost its color in proportion as the silver acquired it, carried this experiment as far as possible, and at length, by renewing the surface of the silver contiguous to the alkaline lixivium, he deprived this lixivium of all its color, and rendered it entirely white This lixivium being

then

then evaporated to dryness, furnished an alkali very white, very caustic, and free from all superabundant phlogiston Besides the practical method of dephlogisticating alkaline salt, which this experiment suggests, it also confirms a truth demonstrated by M Macquer in his theory of Prussian blue, namely, that metallic substances may be charged with a superabundant quantity of inflammable matter, and that they are capable of taking it from fixed alkali by the humid way *See* BLUE (PRUSSIAN)

The second substance which alters fixed alkali is a superabundant earth As this earthy substance is not soluble in water when alone, and as it has but a weak adhesion to the alkali, it may be easily separated by drying it once or twice by solutions and filtrations But this purification must not be carried too far, because the alkali itself is capable of decomposition by this method, in detaching itself at every drying or calcination from a part of its earthy principle.

As to the saline matters which by their mixture alter the purity of the fixed alkali, they can be separated by no chemical process but by crystallization This method is founded on the incapacity of the alkaline salt to crystalize, and on its property of decomposing and of converting into crystallizable salts, all uncrystallizable and deliquescent salts with which it may be mixed It is then necessary to evaporate to the convenient point, the alkaline liquor from which these foreign salts are to be separated, and to let it cool at several different times to favor the crystallization of those salts which are best crystallized in the cold, or to continue the evaporation for those salts which, like common salt, can only be crystallized by this method *See* CRYSTALLIZATION But it is manifest, that this method, however carefully performed, is incapable of procuring a perfect separation of all the extraneous salts from the alkali, since while this continues fluid, it always remains mixed with a small quantity of crystallizable salts, which are dissolved by part of the same water which keeps the alkali fluid, and that the separation by crystallization cannot take place but when all is evaporated to dryness It is then impossible to separate completely from the alkaline salt, the last small portions of extraneous salts with which it was mixed Notwithstanding this, the degree of purity to which the alkaline salt may be brought by this method is considerable, and sufficient for most of the operations of the arts, and even for many operations in chemistry

It is still more difficult to purify the alkali from iron No practical method is known for this purpose When therefore a very pure alkali is required, it is proper to choose such substances as furnish a salt the least impure For in this respect there is a great difference betwixt the substances from which it may be obtained, as will appear when we enumerate summarily the several alkalies most frequently used

Fixed alkali being of great use, and much employed in arts, as it is the basis of soap and leys, and much used in dying, making of glass and saltpetre, is procured from matters which furnish a great deal of it, and at a small expence

The most common alkali, and at the same time the least pure, is that of the ashes of common hearths These ashes are employed for lixiviums, in the manufacture of salt-petre and in glass houses where common bottle-glass is made

In

In the Northern countries, where wood is plentiful, it is burnt on purpoſe, as well as many plants, to procure from their aſhes a ſtrong but very impure alkali, called *Pot-aſh*. This alkali is always much phlogiſticated, and contains many of the ſaline matters above mentioned. Pot-aſh is employed for the purpoſes related. It is alſo uſed by dyers in ſome of their operations. Pot-aſh may be purified ſo far as to become a very good alkali by the methods mentioned. (*t*)

The dregs and leys of wine being dried and burnt, leave aſhes abounding in alkaline ſalt, called in French, *cendre gravelée*. This alkali is not only in great quantity in theſe aſhes, but likewiſe when the matters furniſhing it are properly and carefully burnt, it is the pureſt of all thoſe which are in commerce. It

(*t*) The great conſumption of pot-aſh renders it a matter of importance. We ſhall therefore deſcribe the methods of preparing it.

In ſome parts of Germany it is prepared from the ſame wood of which charcoal is made. A number of tubes, made of plate iron, or of copper or braſs, are ſo diſpoſed in the pile of wood intended to be burnt into charcoal, that the water, acid, and oil, which are obtained in ordinary diſtillations, ſhall, when ſeparated from the wood by fire, paſs through theſe tubes into buckets placed to receive theſe liquors. The oil is then to be ſeparated from the acid liquor, which is then to be boiled in copper or iron veſſels, and the reſiduum dried and calcined. By this calcination, the acid ſalt is alkalized. This method, and the preparation of ſalt of tartar by calcining tartar, ſhew that vegetable alkali is produced by converſion of an acid to an alkali. How is this converſion effected?

The moſt common method of making pot-aſh, is by burning large piles of wood, lixiviating the aſhes by boiling in copper veſſels, decanting the lixivium when clear, and boiling in other copper veſſels till the liquor be evaporated and a reddiſh ſolid ſalt obtained, called *black pot-aſh*, which by calcination in ovens with a heat not intenſe enough to fuſe it, is dephlogiſticated and rendered white. If any of it has been fuſed, it will have a greeniſh blue color.

Another method of preparing pot aſh, and which may be conveniently uſed in a large manufactory of it, is deſcribed by Kunckel. The aſhes of wood are put into a large tub, near the bottom of which is inſerted a cock, and to prevent the aſhes from filling up the cock, the bottom is covered with ſtraw and pieces of ſmall wood. Water is to be poured on the aſhes, and is the next day to be let off through the cock into another veſſel. The aſhes may be again elixated with more water till all the ſalt be diſſolved. The weaker leys are to be poured on freſh parcels of aſhes till they can receive no more ſalt. The ley is then to be evaporated in an iron pan, and the brown ſalt is to be dephlogiſticated by calcination in a furnace or oven with a heat not intenſe enough to fuſe it.—Some perſons ſoak ſtraw in the ley obtained by lixiviating wood-aſhes with water, and by drying and burning this ſtraw they obtain a ſalt without the trouble of boiling the ley. The alkaline ſalt called *pearl aſh* has a whitiſh pearl color, and is almoſt entirely ſoluble in water. The Ruſſia pot-aſh is dark-colored, hard, not eaſily deliqueſcible, and contains (as Dr Lewis ſays) more than half its weight of an earth unſoluble in water. Scheffer, in the Swediſh Memoirs for the Year 1759, ſays, that from 100lb of Ruſſian pot-aſh he obtained 92½ lb of alkaline ſalt, and 7½ lb of neutral ſalts. Dr Home found that Ruſſia pot-aſh contained a conſiderable quantity of quicklime. From experiments made by Brandt (*Memoires Suedoiſes* 1749), and from the preference given to it by ſoap-boilers, it appears to be more cauſtic, and more powerfully to diſſolve oils, than purer pot aſh rendered cauſtic by quicklime. Ruſſian pot-aſh is ſaid to be prepared by burning wood with a cloſe ſmothering heat, making a ley from the coarſer part of the aſhes, and moiſtening therewith the finer part into the conſiſtence of a paſte, ſtratifying this paſte with ſome of the more inflammable kinds of wood, and ſetting the pile on fire. The neutral ſalts found in pot-aſh are chiefly vitriolated tartar, ſea ſalt, with which latter ſalt pot-aſh is frequently adulterated to increaſe its weight.

it contains iron, it is in an insensible quantity, and it is naturally free from mixture of extraneous salts therefore dyers and other manufacturers whose operations require a pure alkali, prefer these to any other alkaline ashes.

Fixed Alkali *of* Tartar

TARTAR, which is nothing but the concrete acid or essential salt of wine, being properly burnt, is almost entirely changed into an alkaline salt, very strong, and the purest of all, and which therefore has been reasonably preferred by chemists to any other It is called the *Alkaline Salt of Tartar*, or simply *Salt of Tartar* Hence this name has become in some measure synonimous with that of alkali

Salt of tartar is made by wrapping up in wet brown paper the tartar intended to be burnt, and placing these parcels so wrapped up in a furnace, by beds or strata, together with strata of charcoal, alternately, and by setting fire to the whole, and continuing the fire till no more blackening smoak rises

As tartar is almost entirely changed into alkaline salt, it preserves after incineration a certain consistence, and retains the form it had before burning, which makes it easy to collect it properly But too great heat must be prevented in burning tartar, otherwise the alkali would melt and flow to the bottom of the furnace, where it would mix with the impurities of the charcoal To avoid this inconvenience a furnace entirely open may be employed, in which the charcoal may burn freely, but without any strong current of air to render the heat too intense. On the other side, as fire is generally more intense in great than in small operations, where proportionable quantities of combustible matters are used, when much tartar is to be burnt, it is proper to diminish the quantity of charcoal, to prevent too great heat, and the consequent fusion of the alkali

When tartar is sufficiently burnt, a lixivium must be made from it till the water poured on it receives no more taste It must then be filtered, evaporated, dried and calcined, according to the directions given to obtain the alkali of tartar in its greatest purity

Fixed Alkali *of* Nitre

THE basis of nitre being a fixed alkaline salt of the nature of the vegetable alkali, and the acid of this salt being capable of decomposition and total destruction by deflagration, we may obtain separately its alkali, called *alkalised or fixed nitre*, by burning or detonating it with combustible matters As this combustion is very rapid, and as it is alkalised almost instantaneously by detonation, it has been also called extemporaneous alkali.

Those vegetable substances only which contain an acid yield an alkaline salt by incineration From mustard and other vegetables which yield a volatile alkali and no acid by distillation, no fixed alkali can be obtained

The ashes of firs, pines, and all trees which contain much resin and essential oil, yield a small quantity only of fixed alkali by elixation The cause of this seems to be, that the acid of these trees is very volatile, and together with a volatile inflammable matter forms the essential oils and resins See Resins.

The

The matters most convenient and most frequently used for the deflagration of nitre are charcoal and tartar The alkali made by deflagration of nitre with charcoal is called NITRE *fixed by* CHARCOAL *See* this article for the method requisite

Nitre and tartar burnt together produce a very strong alkali, which is a mixture of the alkali of nitre and of the alkali of tartar, both which are entirely of the same nature They are confounded together by the name NITRE *fixed by* TARTAR *See* that article, and FLUX (WHITE)

These alkalies of nitre, when well prepared, are very pure, and fit for the nicest operations in chemistry

All these several kinds of alkali, when perfectly purified, have entirely the same properties, and ought to be regarded only as one and the same alkali, which ought to be called *Fixed Vegetable Alkali* The purification above mentioned of this alkali is attended with considerable difficulties in practice The chief of these difficulties is in the evaporation and drying of the alkaline lixiviums, and this relates to the vessels employed in these operations Vessels made with the imperfect metals are unfit, because they are liable to the action of the alkaline salt Silver vessels are the fittest of all for this purpose but it is not very certain that this metal is incapable of being acted upon by alkali

Glazed earthen vessels, such as common pottery-ware, cannot be employed, because they are not, and cannot be sufficiently baked The alkaline lixivium passes through them as easily as through a filter If vessels not metallic are to be used, they ought to be of glass or porcelaine, or made of pure clay, and baked in a violent fire, such as that kind of pottery called stone-ware These vessels perfectly resist the action of alkalies, but they are very liable to be cracked by heat

Well-prepared fixed alkali ought to be preserved, either dry or fluid, in crystal-glass bottles, with glass stoppers When the fluid alkali is used, it must be gently decanted from the sediment deposited at the bottom of the bottles

XXXIII ALKALI (MINERAL *or* FOSSIL), or ALKALI (MARINE) This is a saline, alkaline, fixed substance, serving as a basis to the acid of common salt, and forming with it the native neutral salt which is dissolved in large quantities in the sea, and known by the names *Common Salt* and *Sea-Salt* As this salt is a natural production, and belongs neither to the vegetable nor animal kingdoms, it has been ranged amongst minerals, and therefore called mineral alkali notwithstanding that a considerable quantity of this salt may be obtained from the ashes of several vegetables But its origin is always the same, and it is not to be considered a vegetable substance; for we shall see that mineral alkali obtained from vegetables, proceeds always from common salt contained in these vegetables After we have mentioned the properties of this alkali, we shall describe the method of procuring it in its greatest purity

Fixed mineral alkali has essentially and fundamentally all the properties of fixed vegetable alkali It has the same taste and the same fixity It dissolves all the same substances, and exhibits with them very similar phenomena It melts and vitrifies all earths, and is altered by quicklime in the same manner It combines with all acids to the point of saturation, and with them forms neutral salts It has the same action as fixed vegetable alkali on metallic substances, and forms soaps with oils and oily matters, therefore, in order to have a just idea of the alkaline properties of this saline substance, it is very necessary to read exactly and entirely what has been said under the articles ALKALI and ALKALI (FIXED VEGETABLE) But it also differs very considerably from fixed vegetable alkali by several properties peculiar to it, and it is upon these properties we are chiefly to insist in this article

Fixed mineral alkali, which we here suppose to be in its greatest purity, differs from fixed vegetable alkali

1 By its taste, which is a little less fiery and corrosive but this difference is very slight

2 When dried, it does not attract the moisture of the air sufficiently to form a liquid, as fixed vegetable alkali does

3 If it be dissolved in water, when it is dry and calcined, it does not heat the water nearly so much

4 When dissolved in water, and its solution evaporated and cooled, it coagulates into crystals, precisely as neutral salts do In this it differs considerably from fixed vegetable alkali, which is absolutely deliquescent, and not crystallizable *(k)*

The crystals of mineral alkali contain much water, and have but little adhesion to this water, for most of it is dissipated by exposure to open air By this dissipation of water the crystals lose their form and transparency, which were owing, as of all neutral salts, to the water contained *See* CRYSTALLIZATION

Crystals of mineral alkali thus deprived of their water, fall into a white powder therefore, to preserve them, they must be put into bottles as soon as they are drained

The differences related betwixt the vegetable and mineral alkalis show that this latter possesses saline properties in a less eminent degree, which probably proceeds from the abundancy of its earthy principle

5 Fixed mineral alkali dissolves by fusion, and vitrifies all earths like the vegetable alkali But it has been observed, that it vitrifies earths better, and renders the glass more solid and durable Probably this proceeds from the greater fixity of the mineral alkali, from its containing an earth less combined, and also from its want of the deliquescent quality

6 With vitriolic acid, mineral alkali forms a neutral crystallizable salt called *Glauber's salt*, which differs from vitriolated tartar in the following circumstances. 1 Its crystals are of a different figure and larger size 2 They contain more water 3 They are more soluble in water 4 Their adhesion to the water of their crystallization is less, insomuch that this salt by exposure to air loses its water, and consequently its form and transparency, and becomes a white powder, as the mineral alkali does also when exposed to air *See* SALT *of* GLAUBER As the same acid is in Glauber's salt and in vitriolated tartar, the differences above related must proceed from their alkaline bases therefore all the properties which distinguish Glauber's salt from vitriolated tartar are to be considered as the dif-

(*k*) We have observed in a note upon the former article, that fixed vegetable alkali is crystallizable by exposure to fixable air.

ferences

ferences betwixt the vegetable and mineral alkalis The same observation may be applied to all combinations of mineral alkali with the other acids, of which we are now going to speak

7 With nitrous acid, mineral alkali forms a particular kind of nitre, susceptible of detonation and of crystallization, but it differs from ordinary nitre, or that which has for its base fixed vegetable alkali, in the figure of its crystals, which, instead of being like long needles, are solids, each of which has six rhomboidal faces, that is to say, two angles of each face are acute, and the other two obtuse This figure, which is somewhat similar to that of a cube, has occasioned this salt to be called *cubic* or *quadrangular nitre* This figure is caused by the mineral alkali *See* NITRE (QUADRANGULAR)

8 With marine acid, mineral alkali forms common salt, the crystals of which are perfect cubes. This salt differs from the neutral salt formed by the combination of the same acid with vegetable alkali chiefly by its taste, which is infinitely more agreeable *See* SALT (COMMON).

9 Mineral alkali forms with the acid of vinegar a neutral salt entirely different from the *terra foliata tartari*, which is deliquescent and not crystallizable, while the former crystallizes well, and does not attract the moisture of the air This salt has no particular name *See* SALT (NEUTRAL) *Composed of the* ACID *of* VINEGAR *and of* MINERAL ALKALI

10 With the concrete tartareous acid, mineral alkali forms a neutral crystallizable salt, differing from that made with the same acid and vegetable alkali, or *vegetable salt*, by the figure of its crystals, which are also much larger and finer. *See* SALT (VEGETABLE)

11 Mineral alkali very well dissolves oils and oily matters, and with them forms saponaceous compounds, as the vegetable alkali does But soaps made with this latter alkali remain soft, and do not acquire such consistency and hardness as those made with mineral alkali. This difference is certainly caused by the property which mineral alkali has of crystallizing *See* SOAP *(l)*

It is probable, that if we were to examine attentively the combinations of marine alkali with sulphur and metallic substances, sensible differences might be discovered from similar combinations made with vegetable alkali The discovery of these differences could not fail to throw new light upon the nature of this alkali But I do not believe that sufficient experiments have been made on this subject *(m)*

Several celebrated chemists have, however, made considerable researches into the nature of marine alkali The person who has done most in this way is M Duhamel de Monceau, a member of the Academy of Sciences. He has published

(l) The difference mentioned in the text does certainly not proceed from the crystallizing quality of mineral alkali, for this salt cannot be formed into a hard soap till it has been deprived of its crystallizing quality by quicklime, which, by absorbing its fixable air, renders it caustic, and incapable of forming crystals *See* AIR (FIXABLE) The greater hardness of soaps made with mineral alkali than of those made with vegetable alkali, probably proceeds from that property of mineral alkali by which it has a weaker power of combination with water than vegetable alkali has

(m) A remarkable difference has been observed by Margraaf between the mineral and vegetable alkalies, namely, that platina may be precipitated from its solution in aqua regia by the latter, but not by the former.

in

in ſeveral memoirs, a detail of many experiments made to decompoſe common ſalt, that he might obtain the alkaline baſis ſingle and pure, for the purpoſe of examining its properties Common ſalt not being capable of decompoſition merely by the action of fire, and without the application of another ſubſtance, it was neceſſary to find ſome ſubſtance which could carry off the marine acid, without combining itſelf with the alkaline baſis As phlogiſton produces this effect very well on thoſe neutral ſalts which are compoſed of a fixed alkali and vitriolic or nitrous acids, it was natural to try the ſeparation of the marine acid by the ſame intermediate ſubſtance This M Duhamel did, but without ſucceſs, altho' in his experiment he employed every reſource of the moſt enlightened chemiſtry The ſame thing happened to Mr Margraaf, who tried without ſucceſs to combine marine acid with phlogiſton, in order to produce phoſphorus It appears, then, that art does not yet furniſh any method of decompoſing common ſalt by phlogiſton

It is nevertheleſs probable that this decompoſition is not impoſſible, and that it even takes place every day in the combuſtion of maritime plants of the *kali* kind, all of which contain ſea-ſalt, and when burnt, furniſh a conſiderable quantity of cryſtallizable alkali, which being combined with the vitriolic and nitrous acids forms Glauber's ſalt and cubic nitre, entirely ſimilar to thoſe formed from the decompoſition of common ſalt by theſe two acids It is very probable that this cryſtallizable alkali obtained from the aſhes of maritime plants, proceeds from a portion of ſea-ſalt contained naturally in theſe plants, a part of which is decompoſed by the burning, for it is certain that no trace of a diſengaged alkali can be obſerved in theſe plants previouſly to their incineration

However that be, it is certain that this cryſtallizable alkali obtained from the aſhes of maritime plants, is entirely of the ſame nature as the natural alkaline baſis of ſea-ſalt This is a truth which no chemiſt queſtions But diſputes have ariſen concerning the ſaline alkaline nature of this ſubſtance

The inquiries of M. Duhamel had proved to him, that it had the principal marks of a ſaline alkali, he concluded that it really was ſuch. On the contrary, the celebrated Mr Pott, who has alſo made many experiments on this matter, has always maintained that it was only a pure earth, without the properties of an alkaline ſalt This diverſity of ſentiments has occaſioned a literary diſcuſſion betwixt theſe two learned gentlemen, of that kind which always turns out to the advantage of ſcience, as it has occaſioned a great number of beautiful experiments, which greatly illuſtrate this matter

The ſtrongeſt proof brought by Mr Pott in ſupport of his opinion may be found in the eclairciſſements given to the ſequel of the French tranſlation of his Lithogeognoſia Mr Pott ſays, " that by a fixed or volatile alkali an inſipid and " perfectly inſoluble earth may be precipitated from the mother water of ſea-ſalt " This earth united to the vitriolic acid forms a Glauber's ſalt perfectly ſimilar to " that prepared from ſea-ſalt This Glauber's ſalt produces with charcoal a ſa- " line alkaline body, which is not precipitable by fixed vegetable alkali, which " alſo happens preciſely to Glauber's ſalt prepared with ſea-ſalt This alkaline " ſalt is not produced by the vitriolic acid, nor by the charcoal, but principally " from this ſaline earth, which for that reaſon may be called an *alkaline earth*, " nearly approaching a ſaline ſtate, and which is capable of taking from acids a

" proper

" proper portion of their most subtle parts, by combination with which it be-
" comes a genuine alkali "

As to what remains, it appears that, after the properties of fixed alkaline salts and of the basis of sea-salt have been established, it is easy to decide the question Nothing can be said more sensibly on this subject than the following quotation from the learned and judicious translator of Mr. Pott's Lithogeognosia " This " question is now reduced to a dispute about words, since Mr Duhamel agrees " with Mr Pott that the basis of sea-salt differs from the fixed alkali of nitre and " others similar, and that Mr Pott agrees with Mr Duhamel, that it differs " from common absorbent earths. But hitherto it seems that Mr Duhamel's " expression is more just and conformable to the definition of saline substances "

From all this we ought to conclude, that the basis of sea salt is neither a pure earth, nor an alkali similar to that obtained from vegetables, but a saline alkaline substance of a peculiar nature, and if conjectures may be allowed on the nature of this alkali, I should be inclined to believe, that it differs from the vegetable alkali, either because a larger quantity of earth enters into its composition, or because its earthy principle is united to it more intimately

Further, it appears that the basis of common salt is truly of a saline nature, from its successful and even advantageous application to all the same purposes in the arts as fixed vegetable alkali, as has been said above

The only practical method of procuring this alkali in great quantities is by the incineration of maritime plants These ashes contain much mineral alkali, when the plants happen to grow in a favorable soil and climate, and the mineral alkali is found to be more or less pure, according to the nature of the plants and of the soil These ashes are generally known in commerce by the name *Soda* This soda is employed in arts without purification, hence there is observed a great difference betwixt different sodas, some of which are much better than others (*n*)

As the chemical affinities and the medicinal virtues of the mineral and of the vegetable alkalis are the same, we proceed to mention what is most material on these subjects

The *affinities of fixed alkali*, according to Mr Geoffroy's table, are in the following order vitriolic acid, nitrous acid, marine acid, vinegar, sulphur

Mr Gellert's table is more extensive, and is as follows Phlogiston, vitriolic acid, nitrous acid, marine acid, vegetable acid, zinc, iron, copper, lead, tin, regulus of antimony, regulus of cobalt, arsenic and bismuth, Gold and silver are marked in this table as indissoluble by fixed alkali

As fixed alkalis are the greatest absorbents of acids, they are proper for all those maladies described by Boerhaave as proceeding from a spontaneous acid

(*n*) Mineral alkali is found lying upon the ground in the island of Teneriff, and in many other countries The Spanish ashes called *barigha*, or *soda*, are produced by burning kali, varech, or fucus maritimus, alga marina, and other maritime plants, previously dried, in pits dug in the ground. The fire employed is so violent as to fuse the ashes into one large and hard bluish mass From these plants Henckel obtained, by boiling in water, evaporating and crystallizing, a considerable quantity of marine salt. Stahl, Gellert, and other authors, prefer this salt to vegetable alkali, for the formation of glass, durable, and not attackable by acids But Kunckel observes, that the impurities mixed with common soda, or barigha, give a bluish color to glass, and render it liable to crack, when cooled. Stahl observes, that the same effect is produced by common pot-ash The mineral alkali, as has been observed in the text, makes a finer, harder soap than vegetable alkali It is also said to be more effectual in the reduction of metallic calxes

They

They are even preferable to absorbent earths, (although these latter are more frequently used) in cases where, notwithstanding signs of acidity, a putrescent disposition is apprehended, which is not at all impossible, because they are, like all saline matters, antiseptic, according to the observations of Dr Pringle But if the putridity was advanced to alkalescency, which is very rare, they would be very hurtful, because they would encrease this alkaline acrimony

It must not be supposed that fixed alkalis taken internally enter the blood-vessels with their alkaline qualities If that happened, they would be true poisons, as acids are, since they quickly kill animals into whose veins they are injected

The human constitution, which cannot suffer the presence of any sensible and disengaged acids or alkalis, at least to a certain degree, in our fluids, acts upon alkalis taken internally by combining them in digestion with the acids of aliments, or with their oily parts, forming soaps, in which conditions only they can arrive at the blood

Pure alkalis ought never to be prescribed but in small doses, as from half a grain to two grains, when they are incorporated with solid medicines and in small bulk, but they may be given from one to six grains, if they be diluted, on account of their causticity, in a pint of some watery vehicle These saline substances are dissolving, aperitive, and lithontriptic They are not much employed for these qualities, but are principally used to correct resinous purgatives, which they do very well, by giving to these medicines a saponaceous quality Externally applied, these alkalis are resolvent, discutient, and caustic *(o)*

XXXIV ALKALI (VOLATILE) Volatile alkali is a saline substance procured by decomposition, from all animal, and from some vegetable substances, and by putrefaction from all these matters *(p)*

This saline substance is called *alkali*, because in fact it has all the general properties of saline alkalis, as the sharp, caustic and burning taste, the property of

(o) Dr. Smith, in a treatise *de motu musculari*, mentions an extraordinary fact which he affirms to have ascertained by repeated experiments, namely, that of the many substances which he mentions, acid, alkaline, and corrosive, mineral alkali and compounds formed of it, were alone capable of stimulating or irritating the muscles of frogs, by immediate application to them, which were exposed for the sake of making these experiments

(p) The plants from which volatile alkali is obtainable by distillation are chiefly of the cruciform kind This salt is obtained by distilling all kinds of clays, (as Brandt says) many calcareous earths, chiefly that kind called Lapis suillus, and some mineral waters. Sal ammoniac, which contains volatile alkali, is sublimed in volcanos Sal ammoniac may be produced from soots of burning vegetable or animal substances, and even of mineral coal. Authors mention various methods by which volatile alkali may be produced As a knowledge of these may assist us to form a theory concerning this saline substance, we shall relate some of them Volatile alkali may be produced by heat, 1 From a mixture of quicklime with vitriol, or with alum, or with tartar *Pott* 2 From a mixture of any essential oil with vitriolic acid and fixed alkali *Id* 3 From nitre detonating with charcoal *Id* 4. From a combination of marine acid with quicklime *Id* 5 From magnesia alba by distillation *Dr Black* 6. From tartar *Id* 7 From deliquiated salt of tartar poured on white salt of vinegar *German Ephemerides, Pott, Ludovici, and Hoffman* 9 From sea-salt combined with putrefying substances *Pott* 10 From sea-salt distilled with charcoal *Id* 11 From sea salt distilled with quicklime *Id* 12 From salt of Sylvius distilled with fixed alkali. *Beck and Peterman* 13. From sea-salt distilled with clay *Brandt* 14 From rust of iron distilled. *Bourdelin.*

tinging

tinging violets with a green color, of combining with acids to the point of saturation, and forming with them different neutral salts, most of which are crystallizable, of separating all earthy and metallic matters from their union with acids, lastly, of dissolving by the humid way, almost all substances soluble by other alkalis

This alkali is called *volatile*, because in fact it is very much so Its volatility is owing to a portion of attenuated, very subtle, and very volatile oil, which enters into its composition as one of its principles, as is proved by its distinguishing properties

Volatile alkali differs according to the substances whence it is procured, and according to the manner of obtaining it These differences proceed from some principles superabundant and extraneous, particularly, several oils from which it is not at first exactly depurated But all volatile alkalis, however obtained, and from whatever substances, may be so purified by the method which shall be soon described, that no difference remains amongst them, and hence we ought to conclude of this substance, as well as we did of the various kinds of fixed alkali, that it is single, identical, and always similar to itself, when sufficiently purified

Pure volatile alkali differs from fixed alkali, first, by its greater volatility, which is so great that it may be entirely sublimed or dissipated by a heat much less than the heat of boiling water, by its smell, which is only an effect of its volatility the smell of this salt is strong, very penetrating, and so pungent, that it cannot be endured above an instant, without suffocation or fainting, its vapor excites a cough, and brings tears into the eyes. It is this salt which occasions the pungent smell observed in necessary-houses at changes of weather

This alkali differs also from the fixed by its less force, hence fixed alkalis are capable of decomposing all those salts whose bases are volatile alkali, of separating it from their salts, and of setting it at liberty

Volatile alkali unites perfectly with water, to which it has even a strong affinity, and with it retains fluidity it is then called volatile alkaline spirit When it contains no superabundant water, it is in a concrete form, and is crystallized, in which it differs from fixed vegetable alkali (q)

All acids unite and effervesce with volatile alkali to the point of saturation, forming neutral salts generally called *ammoniacal salts*

Ammoniacal salts have an infinitely stronger and more pungent taste than salts whose bases are fixed alkali, because volatile alkali unites with acids less intimately These neutral salts are semi-volatile, that is, they may be sublimed by a sufficiently strong heat, and this property they owe to the volatility of their alkaline basis

The ammoniacal salt which volatile alkali forms with vitriolic acid is crystallizable, and is called *vitriolic ammoniacal salt*, or *secret ammoniacal salt of Glauber*, from the name of the chemist who discovered it *See these words.*

The kind of nitre formed by volatile alkali and nitrous acid is also crystallizable, and has the peculiar property of detonating alone, when heated sufficiently, without addition of any matter containing phlogiston, as is necessary for

(q) Volatile alkali, by combination with fixable air, is crystallizable, uncombined, it cannot be obtained in a solid state.

the detonation of ordinary nitre This phenomenon proves the existence of the inflammable principle in volatile alkali This nitre, whose basis is volatile alkali, is called *ammoniacal nitre*, or *nitrous ammoniacal salt* *See these words*

With marine acid, volatile alkali forms also a neutral crystallizable salt, called *Sal Ammoniac*. This is the most used, and first known of the ammoniacal salts, and from which the name has been derived to the others *See* SAL AMMONIAC

Volatile alkali may be combined with sulphur, with which it forms a kind of volatile liver of sulphur, the preparation of which is given by Hoffman *See* LIVER *of* SULPHUR

Most metallic matters are attacked, and more or less dissolved by volatile alkali, but copper is of all metals the most easily and copiously dissolved by it To dissolve this metal nothing more is requisite than to digest its filings in liquid volatile alkali The solution acquires a beautiful blue color

This solution exhibits a curious and interesting phenomenon, which is, that if the bottle containing it be well corked, the blue color grows fainter, and at length entirely disappears, so that the liquor becomes colorless like water But if the same bottle be then uncorked, the upper part of the solution from its contact with the external air resumes its color, and this color is gradually communicated to the rest of the liquor Thus may this blue color be made to appear and disappear alternately, as often as is required, by corking and uncorking the bottle

Other metallic matters are not nearly so easily attacked by volatile alkali as copper is These solutions have even not been much examined

When metals are previously dissolved and divided by acids, they are then infinitely more susceptible of solution by volatile alkali For this purpose it is sufficient to pour into some strong alkaline spirit some drops of metallic solution At first a precipitate is formed, which soon disappears upon agitating the liquor, and is redissolved by the volatile alkali That this experiment should succeed, it is necessary that the metallic solution should have a considerable excess of acid, that is, that the acid should not be nearly saturated with the metal By this method, copper and mercury are dissolved in greater quantity than other metals

In whatever manner the copper be dissolved by this salt, it always communicates a blue color, very beautiful and deep This property renders the alkaline spirit a proof liquor to discover copper, and render it sensible when it could not, from the smallness of its quantity, be perceptible by other methods Thus a little volatile alkali may be poured into any mineral water, containing too small a quantity of copper to be otherwise perceptible The blue color which this water assumes discovers the presence of copper

Volatile alkali, added gradually to a metallic solution, seizes the acid of the solution, and precipitates the metal The most singular metallic precipitate made by volatile alkali is that of gold previously dissolved in aqua regia This precipitate is of a yellow color, and is one fourth part heavier than the gold employed (*r*) When heated to a certain degree, it detonates and fulminates with a most terrible explosion It is called *fulminating gold* *See* GOLD (FULMINATING)

(*r*) Dr Black, in his Essay upon Magnesia, attributes the encrease of weight which metallic precipitates gain, to adhering fixible air, which they receive from the precipitating alkalis To this adhering air he also attributes the fulminating property of the precipitate called *Fulminating Gold*

Mercury

Mercury dissolved in spirit of nitre and precipitated by volatile alkali, is of a slate color This color proceeds from the inflammable matter of the volatile alkali The other metallic precipitates made by volatile alkali have nothing singular none of them fulminates like the precipitate of gold, even that of platina does not, tho' this metal possesses so many of the properties of gold. (s)

Volatile alkali, as well as fixed, acts upon oils, and forms with them different saponaceous compounds, hence this salt may be employed to scour and clean from grease, and lixiviums made of quicklime and urine which contain much volatile alkali, are used in some arts This alkali is nevertheless less easily united with oils than fixed alkali is, and particular management is necessary to bring it to a saponaceous state. *See* SPIRIT (VOLATILE AROMATIC OILY), and EAU DE LUCE. These are the principal saponaceous compounds made with volatile alkali

Volatile alkali, when first separated from animal and vegetable matters, is, as we before observed, very impure It is particularly depraved by much empyreumatic oil, which is united with it into a state perfectly saponaceous, and which it renders soluble in water It may be separated from this superfluous oil by distilling it with a very gentle fire, either alone, or mixing with matters capable of absorbing and retaining the oil, as fixed alkalis and absorbent earths are But the most efficacious method of purifying it is, to reduce it to sal ammoniac, and then to decompose this salt, by any of the proper mediums for the disengagement of the volatile alkali By this method it is obtained in its greatest purity, because, in its combination with the acid, it perfectly separates itself from all extraneous matter *See* SAL AMMONIAC, *for the purification of volatile alkali, and for several of its essential properties* (t)

The affinities of volatile alkali, according to Mr Geoffroy's table, are, vitriolic acid, nitrous acid, and marine acid According to Mr Gellert's table they are, phlogiston, vitriolic, nitrous, and marine acids, vinegar, zinc, iron, copper, bismuth, mercury, silver, and gold

(s) From Mr Margraaf's Experiments, published in the Berlin Memoirs for the year 1745, we find that gold, silver, bismuth, zinc, and copper, dissolved in their proper acid solvents, may be first precipitated from these, and afterwards redissolved by volatile alkali, that these metals precipitated by fixed alkalis may be again dissolved by volatile alkali, and that mercury, lead, and tin, were not dissolved by volatile alkali applied in the same manner. Brandt says, that volatile alkali occasions a coagulation of a solution of iron in nitrous acid, which is soon redissolved, and that the same alkali precipitates iron from vitriolic acid He also says, that regulus of cobalt cannot be precipitated from nitrous acid, nor arsenic from aqua regia, by volatile alkali Volatile alkali has no effect upon any metal not previously dissolved by acids, excepting copper, iron, and lead, the first of which it dissolves perfectly, a very small quantity of the second, and the third is very slowly changed by it into a kind of mucilage See POTT *sur la Dissolution des Corps*

(t) To the properties above-mentioned of volatile alkali, we may add, 1 That pure or caustic volatile alkali, that is, uncombined with fixable air, or the spirit of sal ammoniac obtained by quicklime, is soluble in spirit of wine, and that mild volatile alkali is not soluble in that spirit, hence if a strong solution of mild volatile alkaline salt be added to spirit of wine, the water of the solution will combine with the spirit, and the salt will be precipitated, forming what is called *Offa Helmontii* 2 Mild volatile alkaline salt requires four times its quantity of water to dissolve it caustic volatile alkali, as we have already observed, is always combined with water 3 Volatile alkali deflagrates with nitre, which proves that it contains an inflammable matter

Volatile alkali is employed in medicine as a powerful stimulant and exciter, when applied so that the person shall inhale the vapors of it Thus it is applied in faintings, syncopes, apoplexies, and in all lethargic diseases, in which the nervous parts are benumbed and unbraced In these cases it is usually applied in bottles, either in a concrete form called *English Salt*, or in a fluid form, and reduced to a semi-saponaceous state by mixture with oil of amber, when it is called *Eau de Luce* *See* SALT (ENGLISH), and EAU DE LUCE

It may also be taken internally in these cases, particularly in apoplexies and lethargic diseases, but in small doses, as from two or three grains to six, and added to stimulant mixtures Taken in this manner, it sometimes is a powerful sudorific.

M Bernard de Jussieu has discovered that this saline substance is a specific against the bite of vipers, having cured as it were miraculously, by means of eau de luce, a student of medicine, to whom this accident happened, while he was botanizing

XXXV ALKALISATION This name is applied to operations by which alkaline properties are communicated to bodies, or to those by which alkali is extracted from bodies which contain it, or in which it may be formed. For example, *spirit of wine* is said to be *alkalised* when it has been digested upon alkali, a part of which it dissolves, and thence acquires alkaline properties On the other hand, when a neutral salt is decomposed in order to obtain its alkaline basis, this salt is said to be alkalised Thus nitre, deprived of its acid by detonation with inflammable matters, as charcoal, tartar, metals, so that nothing remains but its alkali, is called *Nitre alkalised by Charcoal*, or *by Tartar*, &c

Vegetable substances, when reduced to ashes, may also be said to be alkalised, because these ashes contain fixed alkali *See* the detail of particular alkalisations, under the articles of the different ALKALIS

XXXVI ALKOHOL This name has been given to any impalpable powder *See* PORPHYRISATION

It has also been given to highly rectified spirit of wine *See* SPIRIT *of* WINE

XXXVII ALLAY This word is employed in chemistry to signify the union of different metallic matters

As an infinity of different combinations may be made according to the nature, the number, and the proportions of the metallic matters capable of being allayed, we shall not here enter into the detail of the particular allays, all which are not yet nearly known Those which are used, as *Bronze*, *Tombac*, *Brass*, *White Copper*, &c may be found under their particular names, and what is known concerning other allays may be partly found under the names of the different metals, and semimetals, and partly in this article

Metallic substances cannot unite directly with earthy matters, not even with their own earths, when deprived of their inflammable principle, and consequently of their metallic properties But in general it may be said, that all metals may be allayed with each other, although more or less easily, and although some of them have not yet been made to unite

As metals are bodies naturally solid, the first condition for their union is, that they be fused They then unite, like all bodies which reciprocally dissolve each other, and from these combinations new compounds result, which have the mixt properties of the component substances. *See* COMPOSITION (CHEMICAL)

In

In these metallic allays, as in almost all other metallic combinations, phenomena appear which depart from the general rules of combinations. Thus it is observed, that some of the properties of metals forming an allay are altered, encreased, or diminished by their union. The ductility, for instance, of a metallic composition is generally less than the ductility of the component metals alone and pure. The density or specific gravity of metals and semimetals is also changed by allaying them with each other. Sometimes the specific gravity of the compound is intermediate betwixt the specific gravity of the component metals, sometimes it is less, and frequently greater: this depends upon the nature of the metals. The same observation may also be applied to the colors resulting from the allays of metals.

Metallic allays are either *natural* or *artificial*. The first are those made by nature, such as most minerals, containing several metals allayed with each other. Native gold is always more or less allayed with silver, and native silver with gold.

Artificial allays are those made expresly for different uses, or for the sake of examining their properties.

Although the allays of different metallic matters are of great importance to the theory and to the practice of chemistry, yet all the researches which the subject deserves, and is capable of, have not been made. Mr Gellert is one of those who have done most in this way. In his *Metallurgic Chemistry* there are a great number of experiments, which we shall relate here summarily. The experiments made for the allaying of semimetals with metals are his own, and were undertaken to determine the specific gravities of these allays. He relates the others before known, from chemical writings, and particularly from a Dissertation of Mr Kraaft exprefly on this subject. We shall refer the allays of mercury with other metals, called Amalgams, to the word AMALGAM.

Gold may be easily united with silver, and in all proportions. Mr Gellert says, that this allay is nearly of an intermediate gravity betwixt the gravities of the two metals, and but a very little augmented. This allay is of no use in the arts: on the contrary, as pure metals are always more ductile than allays, in the arts where ductility is requisite, as in wire-drawing, gold-beating, the purest metals are chosen. (u)

Silver may be easily allayed with copper, and in all proportions: copper also unites in the same manner with gold. Gellert observes that the allay of silver

(u) The component metals of which metallic allays are formed may be either chemically combined, that is, mutually dissolved by each other, or mechanically mixed, that is, diffused through each other by the action of fire, or they may be partly combined, and partly diffused, if the proportion of their quantities to each other be different from that which is necessary for their combination. For most, if not all, metals can be only combined with each other in certain proportions, as is very observable in those, the fusion of which requires very different degrees of heat. But those which may be kept fused in nearly the same degrees of heat may be mixed together in almost any proportion, and will be nearly uniformly diffused throughout the metallic mass when hastily cooled. As metallic allays have not been before considered in this manner, no experiments have been made to determine the proportions with which they can combine, nor can we easily establish rules by which this kind of combination can be ascertained. Those, however, which appear to me most probable, for distinguishing this combination, are, 1

Wher

and copper is of a greater than the intermediate gravity, but that the allay of gold and copper is of a gravity less than intermediate Copper renders gold and silver harder and more sonorous, without much diminution of their ductility It has even the remarkable property of rendering these two metals less susceptible of losing their ductility by the vapor of charcoal, which they are very liable to do, copper also heightens the color of gold These properties of copper relatively to gold and silver render its allay with these metals of great use to gold and silver-smiths; because it makes them firmer, and fitter for working and chasing, and also for making money, for the same reasons, and for the payment of the Prince's duties, and for compensation of the expences of coining The quantity of copper allayed with gold and silver for these different uses varies according to the different countries, but in each country it is fixed, and always the same

Iron allays well with silver, and still better with gold Gellert observes, that the gravity of an allay of gold and iron is less than the intermediate The affinity of these two metals is very great, for gold facilitates its fusion, which indi-

When an allay possesses properties which neither of its component metals had 2 When the properties, as the specific gravity, color, hardness, &c of the allay, are not in an intermediate degree betwixt the same properties of the component metals, according to the proportion of these metals to each other 3 When the component parts of an allay are not separable from each other by eliquation, that is, by applying a heat capable of fusing one of them only, nor by keeping the whole mass in fusion, with a heat not more intense than is necessary for that purpose, but insufficient to occasion an ebullition, and by cooling the melted mass very slowly When therefore, according to these rules, a metallic allay has no properties but those which its component metals had, when its density, color, hardness, elasticity, fusibility, and other properties, are precisely in an intermediate degree betwixt those of its component metals, and lastly, when its component metals may be separated from each other by eliquation, or by giving them such a fluidity and rest as that they may separate according to their respective densities, we may then, with probability, pronounce that this allay is composed of parts not chemically combined and when to an allay, which by these rules is composed of metals chemically combined, a quantity of one of the same kinds of metal of which the allay is composed, be added, and, upon examination, the new allay be found to possess no properties but such as are intermediate betwixt the first allay and the added metal, and to be separable by eliquation, or by their different densities, we may then consider this new allay as a mass consisting of metals partly combined, and partly diffused That the allay mentioned in that part of the text to which this note refers, namely, that of gold with silver, does not consist of parts chemically combined, or else that but a very small proportion of each of these metals can be combined with the other, appears probable from the following reasons 1 The density of the allay is very nearly intermediate between the densities of the component parts 2 The silver and gold are not uniformly and equally distributed through the whole mass This inequality is proved by an experiment of Mr Hellot He melted a mass of 20 pounds, containing 55 parts of silver and one part of gold, and poured it into three separate masses, each of which was found by essay to contain a different proportion of gold from the two others 3 Gold and silver kept in gentle fusion are separable from each other, merely by their different densities Mr Homberg kept equal parts of gold and silver in gentle fusion a quarter of an hour, and found, upon breaking the crucible, two masses, of which the upper was pure silver, and the lower the whole gold allayed with ⅕th part of silver He repeated the experiment with nearly the same event, and twice he obtained the two metals perfectly separated from each other *See a note to the article* AFFINITY

cates

cates a strong disposition to unite Gellert observes upon this occasion, that therefore gold is fitter than copper for soldering fine works of iron and steel (w) Iron unites difficultly with copper, and in small proportion It renders copper paler The portion of iron which does not unite with copper forms a separate regulus, which, however, strongly adheres to the surface of the regulus of copper The degrees of affinity of iron with other metals, according to Gellert's table, but reversing the order in which he has placed them, (that is to say, beginning by those with which it has the strongest affinity, which seems to be the most natural order) are, gold, silver, and copper.

Tin, according to the same author, unites with all metals, and renders them brittle, iron and lead it alters least in this respect (x) But gold and silver are so affected by tin, that its vapor alone is capable of destroying the ductility of a large quantity of these metals, as is well known to artificers

The allay of tin with gold and silver is then of no use, on the contrary, it is carefully avoided, but with copper tin forms an useful compound, known by the name of *Bronze* The specific gravity of allays of silver and of copper with tin is greater, and that of gold with tin is less than the intermediate The affinities of tin with other metals, according to Gellert's table, (only reversing his order, which we shall always do) are iron, copper, silver, gold

Lead unites with all metals, excepting iron, with which no method has been found to unite it Gellert observes, that this property of iron with regard to lead renders it fit to separate this latter metal from others, provided that the metal from which it is to be separated has not a greater disposition to unite with lead, than the iron has to unite with it This is certain, that lead may serve as an intermedium by which iron may be separated from other metals for instance, from silver For if a sufficient quantity of lead be melted with silver allayed with iron, it will easily seize upon the silver, and separate the iron from it, which will then swim upon the surface of the two melted metals

The allays of gold and of silver with lead have a greater specific gravity, and the allays of copper and of tin with lead have a less specific gravity, than the intermediate

The allay of lead with other metals is used for the essays of ores, for refining, and for liquation *See* LIQUATION

Lead and tin are allayed together to form a solder for pipes and other works of lead

The affinities of lead with other metals, according to Mr Gellert's table, are, silver, gold, tin, copper.

Zinc may be allayed with all metallic matters, excepting bismuth, with which it cannot unite, according to Mr Gellert This semimetal, when united with metallic substances, gives fusibility to those which are less fusible than itself The density of allays of gold, of silver, of copper, and of lead with zinc is greater, and that of allays of the same semimetal with tin, iron, and regulus of antimony, is less than intermediate

(w) A very small quantity of iron renders gold hard, brittle and pale So hard are some mixtures of iron and gold, that they are said to have been formed into razors Three or four parts of iron and one part of gold compose an allay nearly as white as silver

(x) Equal parts of tin and iron form a white but brittle mass.

The allays of zinc with most metallic matters are not used in the arts, but that with copper is very much This allay forms *Brass*, *Tombac*, *Prince's Metal*, *Pinchbeck*, &c

The affinities of zinc with other metallic matters are, according to Gellert's table, copper, iron, silver, gold, tin, lead *partly*, that is, it does not unite with lead in all proportions

Bismuth unites with all metals, and with most semimetals It has so great action upon other metallic substances, that it sensibly facilitates their fusion (y) Bismuth renders all the metals with which it is united brittle It does not unite with zinc, nor, according to Mr Gellert, with arsenic When melted along with zinc, it remains at the bottom of the crucible, as being the heavier of the two, and when they are cooled, they are found forming two distinct reguli adhering strongly to each other Gold, silver, lead, and regulus of antimony form with bismuth allays of greater, and iron forms an allay of less, than intermediate density, and copper forms with it an allay of intermediate density

The allays of bismuth are not in use, excepting some particular metallic compositions for mirrors

The affinities of bismuth with other metals are, according to Mr Gellert's table, in the following order iron, copper, tin, lead, silver, gold

" Cobalt" *, says Mr Gellert, " may be allayed with all metals and semi " metals, but it acts little upon lead and silver When equal parts of lead and " cobalt are melted together, these two substances are found only adhering to " each other, the lead being, in consequence of its greater specific gravity, at " the bottom of the crucible, and the cobalt above it, so that it seems pro- " bable that they are not at all combined But if the same cobalt be melted, " after it has been thus treated, with iron, which seems to be the most readily " united with it of all the metals, a small regulus of lead is found at the bottom " of the crucible, because iron and lead do not unite At first, we might be " apt to believe that silver and cobalt do not unite together In fact, if two " parts of cobalt, and one part of silver be melted together, the silver is found " at bottom and the cobalt above, only adhering to each other But the silver " is become more brittle, of a greyish color, and the cobalt is become whiter " than before If this silver be cupelled, the part of the cobalt united with it " will attach itself to the cupell in form of a circle, and the silver will be found

(y) Bismuth greatly encreases the fusibility of some metals, as appears from the following table of Dr Lewis, in which the degrees of heat are marked in numbers according to Fahrenheit's scale

600 Mercury boils
540 Lead melts
460 Bismuth melts
410 Tin melts
390 Tin 8 parts, bismuth 1 part, melt.
330 Tin 2 parts, bismuth 1 part, melt
Tin 3 parts, lead 2 parts, melt
280 Tin and bismuth, equal parts, melt.
212 Water boils

An allay composed of two parts of lead, three parts of tin, and five parts of bismuth, may be melted with considerably less heat than the most fusible of those mentioned in the above table

* Note By *Cobalt* Mr Gellert certainly means what we call Regulus of Cobalt, for Cobalt properly called is a mineral composed of other substances besides the regulus of cobalt, as sulphur, arsenic, bismuth, silver, and unmetallic earths *See* COBALT.

" to

" to have lost an eighth part of its weight, which will be found upon essaying " the cobalt, and examining how much silver it contains " *Metallurgic Chemistry*, *Tom* I

These experiments of Mr Gellert's prove, that regulus of cobalt cannot be united to lead and to silver in all proportions, but only in small quantity The same may be said of bismuth, with which, says Mr Gellert, cobalt is very easily united for Mr Beaume, who has made many experiments on the regulus of cobalt, has observed, that when this regulus is melted with bismuth, these two metals are found separate, the bismuth being at the bottom of the crucible and the cobalt above it

The allays of the regulus of cobalt are but little known, and not used in the arts

In Mr Gellert's table the affinities of regulus of cobalt with metallic matters are in the following order copper, iron, tin, zinc, regulus of antimony, bismuth and lead, silver, and arsenic, partly

Regulus of antimony may be allayed with almost all metallic substances Mr Gellert says, that the density of allays of this regulus with iron, tin, or zinc, is less than intermediate, and that the density of allays of this regulus with silver, copper, lead, and bismuth, is greater than intermediate He observes also, that the magnetic property of iron is much more diminished by an allay of this metal with regulus of antimony than with any other metallic substance

Allays of regulus of antimony are little used in the arts It is used for some compositions for speculums An allay of this semimetal with iron, tin, and copper, is made for the preparation of a medicine called *Lilly of Paracelsus*, or *Tincture of metals* *See* Lilly *of* Paracelsus

The affinities of the regulus of antimony with metallic substances are placed by Mr Gellert in the following order zinc, copper, tin, lead, silver, gold Bismuth is so placed in the table as to denote its incapacity of uniting with the regulus of antimony

Arsenic, or its regulus, unites with most metallic matters Mr Gellert says, that it whitens iron, but the allay resulting from thence is very brittle Copper is also rendered very white by mixture with arsenic This is the *white tombac* which resembles silver Mr Gellert affirms, that this allay, notwithstanding it contains arsenic, is sufficiently ductile and malleable, which is very remarkable But if it contain too much arsenic, it is brittle, and blackens in its surface Arsenic united with tin is partly reduced to a powder like ashes, in which much arsenic remains The rest of the tin is very brilliant, foliated, and externally resembling zinc, without being possessed of any of its properties Tin also becomes much harder and more sonorous by this union Lead united with arsenic smokes and swells more quickly with a moderate fire than it does alone a part of it is dissipated in form of a thick smoke, another part is changed into a glass of a reddish yellow color, and the remaining lead is brittle, and dark-colored Arsenic unites with silver, and renders it brittle It does the same to gold, and also deprives it of its color, rendering it pale It unites very difficultly with cobalt, with which it forms a black, shining matter. Lastly, Mr Gellert (from whom all this is extracted) says, that bismuth cannot be united with arsenic.

In this author's table of affinities, the metallic substances capable of uniting with arsenic are placed in the following order, which is the same as that for the regulus of antimony zinc, iron, copper, tin, lead, silver, gold, regulus of antimony

The allays of arsenic used in the arts are white tombacs, and some compositions for speculums

It is necessary to remark on the subject of arsenical allays, that this singular substance has the property of uniting with metals even when deprived of phlogiston, and in an unmetallic state This proceeds from its saline character, and from its property of taking phlogiston from the imperfect metals and from the semimetals, consequently there ought to be a difference betwixt the allays made with white crystalline arsenic, and those made with the regulus of arsenic *See* ARSENIC, and REGULUS *of* ARSENIC (z) It is proper to observe, that chemists who treat of metallic allays differ much from each other in the descriptions they give of the results of their experiments, as may be seen in the particular articles of each metallic matter, which ought to be consulted on this subject. But these varieties are not surprising, when we consider the difficulty of the matter, and the great obstacles which prevent perfect exactness in these experiments All who have operated much in chemistry will easily perceive, that, without reckoning the difference of proportions of the metals employed in the allays, which must greatly affect the results, others much more considerable would occur, depending on the purity of the metals, on the greater or less quantity of phlogiston with which many of them are capable of being united, on the very variable destructibility and volatility of many metallic matters, and lastly, on the just degrees of heat, which are of considerable consequence, and which it is almost impossible to determine precisely

From these observations we ought to conclude, that, in order to make a set of accurate experiments on metallic allays, and which may be depended upon, it is, in the first place, necessary that all the metallic matters to be employed be exceedingly pure, which is a matter of great difficulty in the second place, it is proper to make all the fusions in vessels perfectly close, to prevent the alteration, the burning, and the destruction of those metals which are liable to those events lastly, to determine carefully the precise degree of heat requisite for the best combination of metallic matters with each other But it does not appear that any person has hitherto done this great and important work, it is to be wished that it was undertaken How many fine experiments may then be made upon all these allays, to discover their properties!

What has been already done in this matter is, however, sufficient to establish some general truths Several have been explained in the beginning of this article Another evidently results from the experiments of M Kraaft and M. Gellert it is this, That as the union of all other bodies, so in that of metallic substances, some are more easily soluble, and in all proportions, others more or

(z) The author of the Dictionary has omitted, in the enumeration of allays, those of platina, and of the semimetal discovered by Mr Cronstedt, called *Nickel* For those of platina, *see* the article PLATINA *Nickel* may be allayed with all metallic substances excepting silver, mercury, and zinc By means of nickel the two semimetals bismuth and regulus of cobalt may be united It whitens copper and gold, and it renders the malleable metals hard and brittle

less

lefs difficultly, and only in certain proportions, and laftly, others appear incapable of uniting in any manner

On thefe two latter cafes it is very important to obferve, that this property which certain metallic matters have of diffolving others in certain proportions only, is very capable of impofing on the operator, and of perfuading him that one metal cannot be united with another, becaufe he fees after the fufion two diftinct reguli, while in fact there is a quantity though frequently a very fmall one, of one of the metals united with the other This is fimilar to what happens in the combination of fpirit of wine with oils, and of water with ether Chemifts believed long that ether was infoluble in water, becaufe when thefe two liquors were put in the fame veffel they conftantly feparated, the ether, being greatly the lighter of the two, rifing upwards, and floating on the furface of the water But the Count de Lauragais, having examined the matter more attentively, and in a truly chemical manner, demonftrated, in a memoir read at the Academy of Sciences, of which he is a member, that ether is really foluble in water, but only in a certain proportion *See* ETHER This being eftablifhed, perhaps we fhould find, if we were to examine all the mixtures of metallic fubftances, that thofe which have hitherto been confidered as incapable of union are, neverthelefs, very capable of it, but only in certain proportions, and if fome are found which cannot by ordinary fufion be united, we might ftill try to break their aggregation more compleatly, and to apply them to each other in this condition, as the Count de Lauragais has done with fulphur and fpirit of wine. *See* COMBINATION, COMPOSITION (CHEMICAL)

XXXVIII ALUDELS Chemifts give this name to certain pots or capitals which are open at both the upper and lower ends, and may be inferted and applied above each other, fo that the whole fhall form a pipe or tube more or lefs long according to the number of aludels compofing it The aludel which terminates this tube above ought to be clofed in its upper part, or to have but a very fmall opening The tube compofed of thefe aludels is nothing but a kind of capital or head, which may be enlarged or lengthened at pleafure, and adapted to a cucurbit This apparatus is intended to collect and retain dry and volatile matters, which may be reduced into flowers by fublimation It may be employed for the preparation of flowers of fulphur, of arfenic, of antimony, of benjamin, &c *See* SUBLIMATION *See alfo* PLATES

XXXIX ALUM Alum is a cryftallizable falt compofed of vitriolic acid united with an argillaceous earth This falt has an auftere, fweetifh, and ftrongly aftringent tafte This ftrong tafte proceeds from the ftrength of union betwixt the acid and its bafe being lefs than in other vitriolic falts with earthy bafes, fuch, for example, as felenites, which has no fenfible tafte Mr Beaumé has even obferved, that the acid of alum is not exactly faturated, for it is certain that it reddens turnfol and blue paper

This falt diffolves fufficiently well in cold, but in much larger quantity in boiling water (*a*) It is confequently fufceptible of cryftallization by the evaporation and cooling of the water in which it is diffolved The figure of the cryftals of this falt varies, like that of other falts, according to the circumftances concurring during the cryftallization When its folution, evaporated to the cryftal-

(*a*) Neuman fays, that alum requires ten times, and other authors fay requires fourteen times, its weight of water to diffolve it

lizing point, is made to cool slowly, the greatest part of its crystals are found to be triangular pyramids, whose four angles seem cut off Alum retains half its weight of water in crystallizing

This great quantity of water in the crystals of alum, together with its property of greater solubility in hot water, is the cause that when put in an earthen or iron vessel, on a good fire, it enters into a liquefaction, which gradually diminishes as the water evaporates When it is entirely evaporated, which is not soon, the alum which had swelled much during this operation, remains dry and friable, it is then called *Calcined Alum* After this evaporation, it may be again dissolved in water, and crystallized as before

Although the acid of alum appears, as its taste and solubility indicate, to be less intimately combined with its basis than the acid of selenites, yet but a very small quantity of it can be disengaged by the strongest fire Mr Geoffroy put some calcined alum into an earthen retort, and exposed it to a most violent fire continued during six days and six nights, and from five pounds of alum thus treated he obtained only three ounces of vitriolic acid, although it is certain that this salt contains a much greater proportion of acid, as we shall soon see The acid thus obtained by distillation from alum is called *Spirit of Alum*, and does not differ from pure vitriolic acid

Alum may be easily decomposed by several intermediate substances

First, as the acid of alum is certainly the vitriolic, all substances which have a greater affinity than earths to vitriolic acid, are capable of uniting with it, and of separating from it its earthy basis

Alum, therefore, treated properly with any matter containing phlogiston, may be decomposed, its acid uniting with it, and forming artificial sulphur *See* SULPHUR

It is by means of this artificial sulphur, which forms during the calcination of alum with any vegetable or animal matter, that the *pyrophorus of Homberg* is made, which has the property of burning merely by contact of air *See* PYROPHORUS

In the second place, all saline alkalis are capable of decomposing alum This decomposition may be made in the humid way If then any alkali be added to a solution of alum, the liquor immediately becomes turbid and white, and a sediment is formed, which is the earth of alum separated from its acid by the intervention of alkaline salt On the other side, the new salt formed by the union of the acid of alum with the alkali, may be crystallized by evaporating the liquor. If fixed vegetable alkali was employed for this precipitation, vitriolated tartar is formed if mineral alkali was employed, Glauber's salt is formed This decomposition of alum is a very convenient method of preparing these two salts Lastly, if volatile alkali be employed for this precipitation of the earth of alum, vitriolic ammoniacal salt will be formed

Calcareous earths, and even some metallic substances, are capable of decomposing alum The former are so, because their affinity is greater than that of the argillaceous earth of alum with the vitriolic acid, and the latter, for instance iron and zinc, are so, because of the slight adhesion of their phlogiston.

It appears that Mr Geoffroy was the first who discovered that iron could decompose alum, and this he did by boiling alum in an iron pot This experiment of Mr Geoffroy is found in the Memoirs of the Academy of Sciences

What

What has been said concerning these different decompositions of alum proves incontestably, that the acid of this salt is the pure vitriolic, and this truth has been known a considerable time, but till lately, the nature of the earthy basis of alum was not precisely and distinctly understood For a long time it was considered by chemists as a calcareous earth but accurate experiments have since shewn, that calcareous earths, united with vitriolic acid, formed selenites and not alum, which are entirely different, and that the earth of alum could not decompose sal ammoniac, nor be converted into quicklime, nor had any of the distinguishing properties of calcareous earth These experiments have been made by Pott, Margraaf, and Baron This last chemist, struck with the differences betwixt earth of alum and calcareous earth, and with the resemblance betwixt alum and most vitriolic salts with metallic bases, has given a Memoir to the Academy of Sciences, in which he conjectures that this earth of alum is of metallic nature

On the other side, there were experiments which prove, that the earth of alum was contained in clays Mr Geoffroy and Mr Hellot had said, that, by digesting clays with vitriolic acid, they had obtained salts of the nature of alum Hellot, having employed a clay as an intermediate substance in the distillation of the ether of Frobenius, perceived that the vitriolic acid of this mixture had deprived the clay of all its argillaceous properties, by taking from it an earth, which being again separated from this acid by an alkali, had all the properties of pure clay. *See Memoirs of the Academy for the year* 1739 Mr Pott, who quotes in his Lithogeognosia this experiment of Mr Hellot, having satisfied himself with regard to the properties of the alum obtained by digesting vitriolic acid upon clay, had concluded that the earth of alum is of an argillaceous nature *See Pott's Lithogeognosia* Mr Gellert in his Metallurgic Chemistry, and especially Mr Margraaf, in three dissertations upon alum, had mentioned the same experiments, and had drawn from them the same conclusions Lastly, Mr Macquer, in a Memoir read at the Academy in 1762, *concerning clays and their fusibility when joined to calcareous earth*, after having quoted the above citations, which are extracted from that memoir, places the affair beyond doubt, by adding his own experiments and observations to those already made I add," says this chemist, " to all these testimonies, that having made an accurate examination of the properties of the earth of alum, separated from every acid, I am " convinced, by all the proofs to which I have submitted it, that it has an entire " and perfect resemblance to the purest clay that is, to clay perfectly separated " from vitriolic acid and all sandy matter I have observed, that earth of alum, " properly prepared, has all the argillaceous properties attributed to it by the " above-mentioned chemists, and particularly a very binding quality I have " also observed, that this earth is very difficultly dried, and that it strongly re" tains the last portions of moisture. By drying, its bulk is considerably dimi" nished, which occasions it to be much cracked It receives a polish, like all " fat clays, when rubbed with a smooth body If it be exposed suddenly to fire " before it be perfectly dried, it decrepitates strongly, and bursts with great " noise, like clays When it has been gradually heated, and then exposed to " a violent fire, I have observed that it has acquired a flinty hardness, and that " by this baking and hardening in the fire it has contracted to one half in all its " dimensions

" Notwithstanding

" Notwithstanding this hardening, and great contraction of its size by fire, " it is remarkably refractory It resisted the greatest violence of fire that I " was able to expose it to without shewing the least tendency to melt Having " mixed it with fritts of crystal-glass, and different fluxes, such as fixed alkaline " salts, nitre, borax, glass of lead, I have found that these matters melted and " vitrified, without melting this earth, so that it has always communicated an " opacity to all the glasses resulting from these mixtures

" A very remarkable property of this earth, but which, like the foregoing " properties, is common to it with clays, particularly when very pure, is, that " though its color be very white, yet this whiteness cannot be preserved for " when it is moist it greedily absorbs all greasy, and consequently coloring par- " ticles from contiguous bodies When exposed to moderate fire, it begins to " blacken, then it becomes more or less white, according to the nature of its " coloring matter but to whiten it thus, it ought not to be entirely closed, but " to have a free communication with external air Lastly, if the fire be en- " creased sufficiently to harden well and bake this earth, then in whatever man- " ner, and with whatever attention it may have been prepared, it never fails to " resume so much more color as it is heated more intensely It takes all sorts " of tints, yellowish, greenish, bluish, grey, brown, and some I have seen be- " come quite black I have already observed, that the same thing happens to " natural clays, when well deprived of sand

" This property denotes a very great disposition in this earth of uniting with " the principle of inflammability, and of retaining it strongly when once united " This may give occasion to conjecture that the earths of metals, and those " which are disposed to metallisation, are essentially of argillaceous nature, and " this idea adds a new probability to the opinion of Mr Baron, who, in a me- " moir upon the earth of alum, conjectures that this earth is of metallic nature, " although not really reducible into metal, at least by any processes hitherto " ascertained, and sufficiently known

" However that be, it appears well ascertained by the chemical experiments " quoted above, and by mine, that earth of alum is a pure clay, free from all " mixture of vitrescible earth, and that all natural clays are mixtures of greater " or less quantities of this pure argillaceous earth, which is capable of com- " bining with vitriolic acid, and of forming with it alum, and of another sub- " stance of different nature, which in its natural state cannot combine with vi- " triolic acid, and which Mr Margraaf considers as a true sand, as indeed it " has all the marks of that kind of earth

" From all this it may be inferred, that in all natural clays there is only this " portion capable of forming alum with a vitriolic acid, which is a true argilla- " ceous earth, and that the other portion is of a nature entirely different" *See* CLAY

Alum is capable of decomposing nitre and common salt, in consequence of the vitriolic acid it contains The nitrous and marine acids may even be obtained more pure by means of alum than of any other substance

All the alum which is in commerce is extracted by different operations from several pyritous, earthy, or stony matters, containing the vitriolic acid and the earth proper for forming this salt

The

The pyrites or pyritous matters from which alum is extracted, ought to have effloresced in open air, or to have been calcined in the fire, to allow the vitriolic acid of the sulphur which they contain to disengage itself This acid meeting in the pyrites itself the argillaceous earth proper to form alum, does in fact there combine with it and form that salt, which is afterwards extracted by lixiviation, evaporation, and crystallization, as is practised for all salts Much of these pyrites or pyritous stones furnishing alum are found in Sweden, England, Germany, and France, and they are worked by the general processes we have mentioned But to have a clear idea of what passes in these operations, it is necessary to know pyrites, and its nature, for which reason see the word PYRITES

XL ROCK-ALUM The alum which is extracted from pyritous mineral matters is seldom very pure, on account of the vitriolic metallic substances always contained in pyrites I have examined many of these alums, and by the proofs made of them, I have found that they always contained a greater or less quantity of martial vitriol This alum is in commerce called rock-alum, because much of it is extracted from pyritous rocks or stones It appears that the names *Ice-alum* and *Rock-alum* are synonimous and confounded in commerce, because there is no difference in the price Frequently these alums, which are in great masses, like stones, (which may also have contributed to the name Rock-alum) have a reddish tinge These are the impurest, and contain most martial vitriol

A large quantity of pure alum is extracted from the neighbourhood of Puzzoli, near Naples, at a place called *Solfatara* See SULPHUR

The Abbé Nollet, who visited this place, and examined the works established there, says, in the Memoirs of the Academy, that the matter from which the alum is extracted, is an earth similar in its consistence and color to the marle found in the same plain I have examined this earth, and have found that it has the appearance, and nearly the consistence of white marle but it differs essentially from marle in not effervescing with nitrous acid

Caldrons of lead, two feet and a half in diameter, and as much in depth, are filled with this earth or stone to three quarters of their contents These caldrons are sunk so as to be almost on a level with the ground under a great shed, at about the distance of four hundred paces from the sulphur furnaces Water is thrown into each caldron, till it rises three or four inches above the earth The natural heat of the ground of this place is sufficient to heat the matter, as it makes Mr Reaumur's Thermometer rise thirty-seven degrees and a half above the freezing point and thus fuel is spared By means of this digestion, says the Abbé Nollet, the saline part is disengaged from the earth, and rises to the surface, whence large crystals are extracted

The alum in this state is mixed with much impurities It is carried to a building at the entry into the Solfatara, and it is dissolved with hot water in a great stone vessel shaped like a funnel The alum is there crystallized again by the heat only of the ground, and becomes purer

XLI PLUME-ALUM This name is given to two very different substances One is a matter truly saline, which tastes and dissolves in water like alum, and crystallizes in form of feathers This kind of alum, which is native, is found crystallized in grottos where aluminous mineral waters pass Mr. Tournefort observed it in his voyage into the Levant It is rare, and not

found

found in commerce. The other matter to which the name of plume alum has been very improperly given, is nothing elſe than a *friable amianthus* or *aſbeſtus* (*b*).

XLII. ROMAN ALUM. In the territory of Civita Vecchia, about fourteen leagues from Rome, is found a hard ſtone whence a great deal of very fine and pure alum is extracted. The place where this ſtone is found and manufactured, is called *Alumiera della Tolſa*. This ſtone, which is neither pyritous nor calcareous, is manufactured by calcining it, as limeſtone is, for twelve or fourteen hours, after having broken it in pieces. This ſtone thus calcined is laid in ſeveral heaps upon places ſurrounded by ditches filled with water. It is ſprinkled with this water three or four times each day, for forty days, or till the calcined ſtone enters into a kind of effervеſcence, and is covered with a reddiſh efflorеſcence. Then the ſtones are boiled with water in caldrons to diſſolve all the alum which is formed, and the water is then evaporated to the point of cryſtallization. This water is made to flow quite hot into oaken veſſels, where, by cooling, a great quantity of irregular cryſtals are formed of a pale reddiſh tinge. In this ſtate the Roman alum is ſold. It is not in large maſſes like rock-alum, but in lumps of the ſize of almonds, nuts, or eggs. This alum is alſo mixed with much reddiſh duſt. I have carefully examined the purity of Roman alum, and I have found it to exceed much the purity of rock-alum. It contains no metallic or vitriolic matters; and is therefore preferred for certain dyes, the beauty of which is hurt by the ſmalleſt quantity of martial vitriol. Its price alſo is greater than that of rock-alum. (*c*)

Alum is very uſeful in ſeveral arts, and chiefly in dying, to which it is eſſentially neceſſary, as it heightens the intenſity and luſtre of moſt colors. It is even abſolutely neceſſary to give ſolidity to all thoſe colors which reſide in gummy ſubſtances. Without alum, theſe dyes would be only confuſed ſtains, which might be waſhed out by water. *See* DYING.

Alum is an aſtringent drug of powerful efficacy; conſequently it is proper for diſeaſes where the principal indications are to fortify and conſtringe, as

(*b*) Alum is ſometimes found native with a lanuginous or plumoſe appearance, and it is then called *plume alum*. It is probably formed by the decompoſition of pyrites, or ſome compound containing ſulphur, and clay. By the diſſipation of the phlogiſton of the ſulphur, the vitriolic acid is diſengaged, and unites with the argillaceous earth, forming alum.

The name *plume-alum* is alſo frequently given to a ſtriated ſtone of the aſbeſtus kind, called alſo *falſe aſbeſtus*. *See* ASBESTUS.

Laſtly, this name is given by Baſil Valentine, and other alchemical authors, to a compound formed of arſenic united with vitriolic acid.

(*c*) A remarkable circumſtance attends the cryſtallization of alum, namely, that good cryſtals of this ſalt cannot be formed, unleſs an alkaline lixivium or urine be added to the lixivium of alum when ſet to cryſtallize. Chemiſts ſuppoſed that by adding theſe alkaline matters, ſome metallic or impure earthy ſubſtance which prevented the cryſtallization was precipitated; but Mr Margraaf found by experiments that he could not form good cryſtals by combining vitriolic acid with earth of alum, with calcined alum, or with clay, unleſs he added a lixivium of fixed or volatile alkali, or urine. He ſuppoſes that theſe alkaline lixiviums produce their effect either by engaging a ſuperabundant acid, or ſome greaſy matter which prevents the cryſtallization.

for

for immoderate menstrual and lochial discharges, losses of blood, fluor albus, diarrheas, hæmorrhages, vomitings of blood, and even some kinds of hemoptoes But it is necessary to observe on the subject of this remedy, and even of all other astringents, that they ought only to be prescribed by intelligent physicians, who can distinguish whether or not these diseases proceed from or are accompanied with inflammation, or too great plenitude for in these cases, astringents, so far from being useful, must be pernicious, and increase the cause of the evil Alum is improper in these maladies, but when it is evident that they proceed from a mere relaxation, or from a rupture of the vessels in these cases it has excellent effects

As alum is one of the strongest astringents, and as it is even somewhat caustic, several intelligent physicians, as Mr Cartheuser, and Mr Baron, in his Notes on Lemery's Chemistry, prohibit the internal use of it, notwithstanding which it is every day used successfully in the above mentioned cases However, it is prudent to administer alum at first in very small doses only, as two or three grains, except in very urgent cases, where it may be given to ten or twelve It may be given either alone, or joined with other astringent or blunting medicines, according to the particular indications

Alum being susceptible of decomposition by all alkaline and calcareous matters, it must not be mixed with these substances, when intended to act as an astringent Alum is often used externally, it constringes and fortifies considerably the parts to which it is applied consequently it is an efficacious repellent, and is useful in collyriums and in astringent gargarisms When calcined, its powder is sprinkled on soft and fungous flesh, which prevents the cicatrisation of ulcers It absorbs their moisture, dries and consumes them

XLIII A L U M I N O U S Whatever contains alum, or partakes of the nature of that salt is called aluminous

XLIV A L K A N E T (*d*)

XLV A L M O N D S (*e*)

XLVI A L O E S (*f*)

XLVII A L T H E A (*g*)

(*d*) Alkanet The cortical part of the root of this plant, which is a kind of Bugloss, contains a red colorific matter, capable of being extracted by oils, by wax, and by spirit of wine Wax thus colored, applied to warm marble, leaves a red stain

(*e*) Almonds, *sweet* and *bitter*, contain an expressible oil and farinaceous earth The bitter part of bitter almonds is not expressed with the oil, but may be dissolved by digestion in aqueous and in spirituous liquors, and with these may be distilled Waters distilled from bitter almonds, or from most other bitter vegetables, fruits, and flowers, which have a similar flavor to them, are poisonous to birds, to some animals, and have sometimes been so to men

(*f*) Aloes is an inspissated bitter juice extracted from the leaves of a plant of the same name It is partly gummy, and partly resinous, and the gum and resin are so well mixed together, that most of the juice is soluble either in aqueous or spirituous menstruums

(*g*) Althea, or *Marsh-mallow* Two ounces of the root of althea yielded, with water, ten drams and fifty grains of mucilaginous extract, and afterwards, with spirit, forty-one grains of resin The same quantity of that root treated first with spirit gave six drams of a resinous extract, a considerable part of the mucilage dissolving in that menstruum along with the resin The remainder boiled in water gave five drams and forty-eight grains of pure mucilage The indissoluble earthy part was one-fourth part of the root, and one half of the leaves of althea *Neuman*

XLVIII. AMALGAM. This word is applied to the allays of metallic matters with mercury.

Mercury being a metallic substance cannot contract any union with earthy matters, not even with the earths of metals when deprived of their phlogiston, and their metallic form. But it is capable of being allayed more or less easily with almost all metallic substances.

As mercury is habitually fluid, as it ought to be considered as a metal perpetually in fusion, and as it is sufficient for most combinations that one of the two bodies that are to be combined be fluid, it follows that without the help of heat, mercury may be amalgamated with many metallic substances. There are two methods generally used of making amalgamas. The first is merely by trituration, and without heat. The second is by fusing the metal which is to be amalgamated, and by adding to it, when fused, the intended quantity of mercury.

Metals, by their union with mercury, become friable and capable of being pulverized, when the mercury is only in small quantity. But when the mercury is added in larger quantities, the metals are by it reduced to kinds of paste, which has no ductility nor tenacity.

Of all metals, gold has the greatest affinity to mercury, and unites with it most easily. For this purpose nothing more is requisite than that the mercury should be slightly rubbed on a piece of gold, or that it remain some time in a golden vessel. The surface of the gold which has touched the mercury becomes white as silver, and if the gold is thin, its consistence is destroyed in that place, so that it very easily breaks. But the amalgamation of mercury with gold is considerably accelerated by dividing the gold into very small parts or very thin plates. All metals ought to be so divided, when they are to be amalgamated by trituration without fusion or heat. *(b)*

Silver may be amalgamated nearly in the same manner as gold. Mr Gellert has observed a singular and remarkable phenomenon in this amalgam, which is, that its specific gravity is not only greater than the intermediate specific gravity of the mercury and of the silver but that it is even greater than the specific gravity of mercury, although silver be greatly lighter. *See* SILVER *and* MERCURY.

Mr Gellert ascertained this fact, not only by observing that the amalgam of silver sinks to the bottom of a vessel containing mercury, but also by the exactest hydrostatical experiments. *See his Metallurgic Chemistry. Tom. I.*

The amalgams of gold and silver, and particularly the first, are much used for the separation of these two metals from their ores, or rather from the earthy

(b) As an amalgam of gold is much used for gilding metals, we shall mention that the plates or grains of that metal may be more easily and perfectly amalgamated by applying them red hot to the mercury, which ought also to be previously heated till it begins to smoke, and by stirring the mixture with an iron rod till the gold disappears, which will be very soon. When the quantity of mercury is so large that the mass is fluid when cold, the superfluous part of it may be separated by passing it through soft leather: this contains a very small portion of gold. The remaining amalgam has the consistence of butter, and contains about one part of mercury to two parts of gold, but is nearly as white as silver.

and

and stony matters with which they are mixed *See* ORES *of* GOLD, and of SILVER These amalgams are also used for some kinds of *gilding* and *silvering* See these two words The amalgam of silver is also employed for the *Arbor Dianæ* *See* ARBOR DIANÆ

The amalgamation of all metals with mercury is much facilitated by heat But the amalgamation of those metals which unite difficultly with mercury cannot be effected without heat For this purpose, the mercury ought to be heated till it begins to rise in vapors, and the metals of difficult fusion, which we suppose to have been previously divided into small parts, ought to be made red by fire, and quickly triturated with the hot mercury As to the metals which melt before they become red, such as tin and lead, it is sufficient to melt them, and to throw the mercury upon them, stirring a little the mixture and thus the amalgam is made in an instant

It would be very imprudent to melt metals which require a great heat for their fusion, as copper, for instance, and to add mercury to this melted metal, with an intention to make an amalgam, because not only the greatest part of the mercury would be dissipated in vapors before it could be united to the metal, but also because there would be great danger of explosion from the mercury, which being a rarefiable and volatile body, is capable, like all such bodies, of producing this effect, when they are suddenly exposed to too great heat

Mercury amalgamates difficultly with copper, more difficultly with regulus of antimony, not at all with iron (*r*), nor, as Mr Gellert says, with cobalt. But with all the other metals and semi-metals it may be easily amalgamated

The amalgam of mercury with tin is much used for covering one of the surfaces of mirrors, and thus rendering them capable of representing images more sensibly and perfectly *See* TINNING *of* LOOKING-GLASSES This amalgam is also used for the preparation of mercury-balls, intended to purify water *See* BALLS (MERCURY).

Bismuth when amalgamated with mercury has the singular property of so attenuating lead added to this amalgam, that a great part of this metal may be passed through leather along with the mercury Mr Cramer advises, in order to make this experiment succeed, to melt the lead first with the bismuth, and to this mixture to add the mercury He further says, that if this amalgam be digested several days, the bismuth will be separated, and will leave the attenuated lead united to the mercury

Regulus of antimony can, as was said above, very difficultly, be united with mercury Mr Gellert says, that to make this amalgam succeed, the regulus ought to be put into hot mercury, and the whole covered with water But that when the regulus of antimony has been prepared by means of iron, or an alkaline earth, this amalgam may be made much better, so that the regulus shall not separate, after standing some time, from the mercury, as it usually does

(*r*) Dr Lewis observes, that mercury adheres to, and coats the ends of iron pestles used for the trituration of amalgams, and that a plate of tough iron may be rendered brittle by keeping it immersed in mercury during some days This experiment did not succeed with me. Hence he infers, that mercury is not incapable of acting upon iron.

The affinities of metallic fubftances with mercury are placed, according to Mr Geoffroy, in the following order gold, filver, lead, copper, zinc, regulus of antimony

According to Mr Gellert's table, they are, gold, filver, bifmuth, zinc, tin, lead, copper, regulus of antimony

As the amalgams of mercury are true allays of metallic fubftances, all the general properties of allays are applicable to them *See* ALLAY

XLIX AMBER. *See* BITUMEN

L AMBERGRISE Is a fubftance of a grey color, which moft chemifts and naturalifts have claffed amongft bitumens, rather from its properties and the principles it yields by diftillation, than from any certain knowledge of its origin For it does not appear that any truly foffil ambergrife is known, and that any is found in commerce, but what is procured from the Indian feas upon which it floats in the neighbourhood of the Molucca iflands

Mr Cartheuler thinks that ambergife ought certainly to be confidered as a bitumen, and he is determined to this opinion from the analyfes made of it by feveral chemifts, and particularly by Neuman From which analyfes it appears, that the fame principles were obtained from ambergrife as from amber, that is to fay, phlegm, a volatile acid, partly fluid and partly folid, oil, and a little coaly matter

Befides, ambergrife is nearly as difficultly foluble as amber and other bitumens in different menftruums but it differs from amber in this, that it is much fofter, is not fmooth, nor is capable of taking a polifh Further, it is not tranfparent, and is capable of fufion The heat of the hands alone is fufficient to foften it like wax It alfo leaves much lefs coaly refiduum than amber, after diftillation All thefe properties denote that ambergrife is much more oily than amber

The agreeable fmell of ambergrife renders it ufeful in perfumes Mufk however is always joined with it, or fubftituted for it, not becaufe mufk is cheaper, for it alfo is very dear, but becaufe its fmell is greatly ftronger, and goes farther in the preparation of perfumes

Ambergrife is alfo ufeful in medicine It has the fame general virtues as all the odoriferous fubftances, from the fpiritus rector or highly attenuated and volatile oil, which is the principle of their fmell It enters into the compofition of many cordial, fudorific, and alexiterial waters It is alfo faid to be a venereal ftimulant But its chief virtue confifts in its antifpafmodic and fedative quanties fimilar to thofe of mufk and caftor, and in its power of relieving certain hyfterical, convulfive, and other nervous affections It may be taken inwardly from half a grain to ten or twelve grains or more For, as to dofes, there can be no fixed rules about remedies and difeafes of thefe kinds

LI. AMMONIAC (SALT) All neutral falts compofed of any acid faturated with volatile alkali, may be called ammoniac falts But the name *Sal-ammoniac* is more efpecially appropriated to the neutral falt refulting from the union of the acid of common falt with volatile alkali All the other ammoniacal falts are fpecified by particular epithets, as *vitriolic ammoniacal falt*, *nitrous ammoniacal falt*, and *vegetable ammoniacal falt* We fhall fpeak fucceffively of thefe feveral falts

All ammoniacal falts have the general propeities of neutral falts, compofed of acids and alkalis, But they differ from the neutral falts whofe bafes are fixed,

fixed alkalis, by their more pungent taste, which proceeds from the less adhesion of acids in general with volatile alkali than with fixed alkali, in the second place, by their less fixity, all the ammoniacal salts being semi volatile, that is, capable of subliming to a certain height, when exposed to a strong enough fire This property proceeds from the volatility of their alkaline bases Lastly, ammoniacal salts are susceptible of decomposition by many substances not capable of producing the same effect on neutral salts whose bases are fixed alkali, as we shall see by a more particular examination of the properties of these salts

The most generally known and used ammoniacal salt is that which contains the acid of common salt This salt, when very pure, is very white, semitransparent, capable of forming feather like crystals, or of subliming in close vessels into a compact striated mass

This salt is easily soluble in water It deliquiates into a liquor when exposed some time to a moist air It is one of the salts which produce the most cold during its solution in water This generation of cold is so much as to sink the thermometer eighteen or twenty degrees, and even more, according to the temperature of the atmosphere It appears that the hotter this temperature is, the greater cold is generated, which proceeds from the greater and quicker solubility of this salt in warm than in cold water Mr Gellert [*Metallurgic Chemistry, tom* 1] says, that if any gum or resin be boiled in water impregnated with sal ammoniac, these substances will be dissolved in it It is not surprizing that gums should be thus dissolved, considering that water is their proper menstruum But as pure water does not at all attack resins, their solution in Mr Gellert's experiment must proceed from the sal ammoniac

Sal ammoniac cannot be decomposed merely by the action of fire in close vessels, because it then entirely sublimes, as we have already observed To decompose it therefore, we must employ some intermediate substance capable of disengaging either its acid or its alkali

The acids having, from their several affinities, the same relations to volatile alkali as they have to fixed alkali, (*See* ALKALI VOLATILE) it follows that sal ammoniac ought to furnish the same phenomena of decomposition by the vitriolic and nitrous acids, as common salt does These two acids then are capable of decomposing sal ammoniac, by separating its acid, which passes alone in distillation, and by uniting themselves with the volatile alkali, with which the first forms a vitriolic ammoniacal salt, and the second a nitrous ammoniacal salt

It is proper to observe upon the decomposition of sal ammoniac by nitrous acid, 1 That the marine acid does not rise singly in distillation, but is always accompanied with a good deal of nitrous acid, which rises in consequence of its volatility, and, together with the marine acid disengaged from the sal ammoniac, forms an *aqua regia* 2 That in this operation great management, slowness, and precautions are necessary, particularly if smoking spirit of nitre be employed, because the vapors which pass are more expansible, and less condensible than the pure vapors of the nitrous or of the marine acids, which difference undoubtedly proceeds from the reaction of these two acids upon each other 3 That it is very necessary to attend carefully to the fire towards the end of the distillation, and when the matter remaining in the retort begins to be dry, because it is a nitrous ammoniacal salt, which has the property of detonating alone, and with

little

little heat Prudence therefore requires that the distillation be not pushed to perfect dryness There is scarcely any operation in chemistry so liable to an explosion as this is *See* AMMONIAC (NITROUS SAL)

Sal ammoniac is also capable of decomposition by many substances, which, by uniting with its acid, set at liberty its volatile alkali

These substances are calcareous earths, quicklime, fixed alkalis, and metallic matters The most essential phenomena which this salt exhibits, when treated by these different matters, are the following

If powdered sal ammoniac be mixed with twice its weight of any calcareous earth, of chalk for example, also powdered, and the mixture be distilled with a proper apparatus, (*See* DISTILLATION) a large quantity of volatile alkali will pass into the receiver, in a concrete form, very white and very beautiful, lining all the inside of the receiver, and when the operation is over, we shall find in the retort a mass containing all the acid of the sal ammoniac, engaged and retained in the calcareous earth if consequently this caput mortuum be lixiviated, in order to dissolve all its saline part, we shall find that this lixivium is impregnated with much marine salt with earthy basis See for the properties of this salt ACID (MARINE), and SALT (MARINE) *with* EARTHY BASIS

In this operation a true decomposition happens of the sal ammoniac by the intervention of the calcareous earth Mr Duhamel seems to have been the first who discovered and published this decomposition He has observed, that the volatile alkali of the sal ammoniac, when it disengages itself in this operation, carries off with it a part of the calcareous earth We shall soon see that it also carries off part of other substances employed to disengage it.

Mr Beaumé, who has since repeated this experiment with his usual accuracy, and in great quantities, has observed, that a quantity of volatile alkali may be obtained by this distillation equal in weight to the sal ammoniac employed, altho' it be certain, that there is nearly as much marine acid as volatile alkali contained in sal ammoniac (*k*)

This salt treated with quicklime is still more easily decomposed than with uncalcined calcareous earth To make this decomposition, and to obtain the volatile alkali, powdered sal ammoniac must be quickly mixed with twice its weight of quicklime, slaked by exposure to air, and the mixture must be quickly put into a great stone-ware retort, to which a receiver must be immediately

(*k*) Mr Duhamel and other authors have attributed this great encrease of weight gained by volatile alkali, during its separation from the marine acid in the decomposition of sal ammoniac, by intervention of chalk, or other mild calcareous earth, or mild fixed alkali, to part of the substance of the earth, or fixed alkali, being carried along with the volatile alkali The substance which volatile alkali does receive from these intermediate matters is not, as these authors have supposed, earthy, or alkaline, but is the fixable air which is separated from them, when they combine with the acid of the sal ammoniac In this operation, therefore, we have an instance of what our author calls *double affinity*, (*See* AFFINITY) the acid of the sal ammoniac combining with the earthy part of the chalk, or with the saline part of the mild alkali, and the volatile alkali of sal ammoniac combining at the same time with the fixable air of the chalk, or of the mild alkali That this addition of fixable air to the volatile alkali is sufficient to render its weight equal to that of the sal ammoniac employed, appears from Mr Cavendish's experiments, which shew, that more than half of the weight of mild volatile alkali is fixable air *See* AIR (FIXABLE), and ALKALI (VOLATILE.)

luted *See* DISTILLATION. The action of the quicklime upon the sal ammoniac is so quick, that a good deal of volatile alkali is disengaged as soon as the two matters are mixed together, which obliges the operator to take care not to expose himself to breathe the vapors The heat must also be attended to in this distillation, particularly at the beginning, because then it is performed almost without fire

It is very remarkable that volatile alkali obtained by intervention of quicklime, never is, nor can be, in a concrete form, by any method It is always liquid, and is called *volatile spirit of sal ammoniac* It is evident that it is by means of the water contained in a large quantity in the flaked lime, and in which the volatile alkali is dissolved, that it thus appears in a liquid state, but it is certain that this saline matter so strongly adheres to this water, that it cannot be separated without some intermediate substance, and that, on the other side, this same water is so necessary to its separation from the marine acid by the intervention of the lime, that Mr Duhamel could not obtain volatile alkali by trying to decompose sal ammoniac with quicklime in the state it is in when newly calcined, and still hot from the kiln, and consequently perfectly dry (*l*)

This volatile alkali, although it be diffused in much water, is still more active and more penetrating than that which is obtained by the intervention of other substances in a dry and concrete state Mr Beaumé has observed, that the volatile spirit of sal ammoniac made with quicklime, when poured into a solution of any salt with earthy basis, does not produce the same effects as the same alkali of sal ammoniac which has been disengaged by calcareous earths or fixed alkalis, and which may always be procured in a concrete state, as this latter volatile alkali easily decomposes these salts with earthy bases, and occasions a copious white precipitate to fall from their solutions, while the former does not appear to produce any effect, but only occasions a very light whitish cloud (*m*)

These differences prove that a singular alteration is produced upon volatile alkali by quicklime, and this alteration is probably caused by the quicklime depriving it of part of its inflammable principle by help of which it seems crystallizable, and consequently by a partial decomposition of it Another phenomenon, no less important, supports this opinion, which is, that if volatile spirit of sal ammoniac be frequently distilled from new quicklime each time, we may easily perceive that there is a considerable quantity of it entirely decomposed by each

(*l*) The volatile alkali obtained by this process is caustic or uncombined with fixable air, and is therefore, as we have observed under the article VOLATILE ALKALI, always in a liquid state This liquid volatile alkali may also be obtained by employing caustic fixed alkali instead of the quicklime From Mr Duhamel's experiment mentioned in the text, by which he found that volatile alkali could not be obtained in this process, unless water was combined with the quicklime, it appears probable, that this operation also is an instance of double affinity, and differing only from the former operation in this respect, that in this process the volatile alkali receives water, and in the former it receives fixable air, from the calcareous earth

(*m*) Caustic or uncombined volatile alkali does not precipitate calcareous earths from acids, because its power of combination with acids does not seem to be stronger than that of those earths But mild volatile alkali acts upon salts with bases of calcareous earth, by what our author calls double affinity, that is, its alkaline part combines with the acid of those salts, while its fixable air combines with the calcareous earth.

distillation,

diſtillation, and that, on the other ſide, if, as Mr Duhamel did, we lixiviate quicklime in a large quantity of water, till it makes no longer cream of lime, nor has the properties of quicklime, and if the lime thus decalcined, and reduced to the ſtate of mere calcareous earth, be employed for the decompoſition of ſal ammoniac, we ſhall then obtain a concrete volatile alkali as if a calcareous earth had been uſed, which had never been calcined. *See* QUICKLIME. *(n)*

When ſal ammoniac is decompoſed by the intervention of quicklime, in the retort is found a ſaline earthy matter, that is, a part of the quicklime above what was neceſſary for the decompoſition, and another part ſaturated with the acid of ſal ammoniac, and forming a ſort of ſea ſalt with earthy baſis, which ſeems to be ſimilar to that ſalt formed by uniting marine acid with an uncalcined calcareous earth, but which ought to differ from it in many reſpects, and particularly by a ſtronger adheſion of the acid to the quicklime. *(o)* This ſalt, when dry, is called improperly *fixed ſal ammoniac*, and when deliquiated into a liquor, it is called *oil of lime*, or *liquid ſhell*.

Fixed alkali, either vegetable or mineral, eaſily decompoſes ſal ammoniac, and ſeparates from it by diſtillation the volatile alkali in a concrete ſtate, if there be little or no water in theſe matters: but if theſe matters contain water, or if water be deſignedly added, the alkali, which is more volatile than the water, paſſes firſt, partly in a concrete ſtate, then the water which riſes diſſolves it wholly or partly, according to the quantity of water, and it is thus reduced to a liquid ſtate. Mr Duhamel obſerves, that in this diſtillation alſo the volatile alkali carries off with it a portion of the fixed alkali which is employed to diſengage it. *(p)*

The ſalt remaining in the retort after this diſtillation is common ſalt, entirely ſimilar to ordinary ſea ſalt, if the fixed alkali employed was the mineral alkali, and ſimilar to regenerated ſea-ſalt, or ſalt of Sylvius, if the vegetable fixed alkali was employed. *See* SALT (COMMON).

Moſt metallic ſubſtances alſo act upon ſal ammoniac, and are capable of decompoſing it.

Silver, copper, iron, tin, lead, and mercury, well mixed with this ſalt, and diſtilled together, diſengage its volatile alkali. The ſemimetals alſo produce the ſame effect. After the diſtillation is finiſhed, the metal is found combined with the acid of ſal ammoniac. Thus ſilver becomes *luna cornea*, and lead becomes *plumbum corneum*. In this manner Mr Margraaf prepared his *plumbum corneum* which he employed in his operation for phoſphorus. *See* PLUMBUM CORNEUM, and PHOSPHORUS.

A remarkable thing occurs in this decompoſition of ſal ammoniac by lead, for which Mr Margraaf requires a calx of lead, ſuch as minium, rather than lead itſelf

(n) Mr Duhamel evidently reduced his quicklime to mild calcareous earth, that is, combined it with fixable air, we need not, therefore, wonder that the volatile alkali which he obtained was alſo mild, or combined with that air.

(o) The ſalt formed by decompoſing ſal ammoniac with quicklime is preciſely the ſame as the ſalt formed by uniting marine acid with uncalcined calcareous earth: for the acid, uniting with uncalcined calcareous earth, deprives it of its fixable air, and reduces it to the ſame ſtate as the calcined earth, or quicklime is in.

(p) See the note (l).

itself, for the conveniency of the mixture, which is, that the volatile alkali which passes over in the distillation, altho' very strong and much dephlegmated, is always in a liquid or fluor state, which shews, that upon this occasion, as in many others, metallic calces produce the same effect as quicklime

As to mercury, it very certainly decomposes sal ammoniac, and separates its volatile alkali But if more sal ammoniac was added than the mercury can decompose, this undecomposed part of the salt remains united with the combination of marine acid with mercury, and cannot by crystallization or sublimation be separated from thence This fact has been ascertained by Mr Macquer, of which a detail is given in his Memoir upon the *Count de la Garaye's Tincture of Mercury*, printed in the collection of the Academy of Sciences in the year 1755

Junker says, that regulus of antimony treated with sal ammoniac disengages the volatile alkali, and is converted into butter of antimony

It is proper to observe on this occasion, of the decomposition of sal ammoniac by earthy and metallic substances, which unite with its acid and disengage its volatile alkali, that as the volatile alkali thus disengaged is capable of separating in its turn all these same substances united to an acid, and even to the marine acid, there seems to be something contradictory in the affinities of volatile alkali, and of earthy and metallic substances Mr Baron, in his Memoir upon Borax, and Mr Macquer, in his Elements of Practical Chemistry, explain these effects in a plausible manner, by the great difference of the fixity and volatility of these substances It appears nevertheless that the subject is still somewhat obscure, and requires a more particular examination

If, instead of mixing with sal ammoniac sufficient quantities of copper, iron, and even of most other metals, and with proper circumstances for the decomposition, these metals were employed in a smaller quantity, and that the heat was immediately raised sufficiently intense for sublimation, the sal ammoniac would then be obtained sublimed, or flowers of undecompoſed sal ammoniac would be raised, containing some part of the metals By this method chemical preparations or medicines are made, which are named from the metals employed Thus flowers of sal ammoniac impregnated with copper are called *ens veneris*, those impregnated with iron, are called *martial flowers of sal ammoniac*, or *martial flowers*, or *ens martis* See *these words*

There are also other properties of sal ammoniac which ought to be mentioned here

This is one of those salts which are soluble in spirit of wine Mr Macquer, in the above quoted memoir, has determined that thirty-two parts of well rectified spirit of wine are necessary for the solution of one part of sal ammoniac

Sal ammoniac acts considerably on mercury sublimate corrosive It dissolves this salt and unites with it, and occasions no decomposition to either of the salts From the union of these two salts, a mixed salt is produced which chemists have called *Salt Alembroth* See this word.

Sal ammoniac is employed advantageously in many arts. It is particularly useful in the tinning of copper and iron *See* TINNING It is also employed in the fusion of gold, because it has been observed to exalt and heighten the color of that metal

If sal ammoniac be treated with nitre in a crucible, and with a red heat, the nitre is observed to deflagrate to a certain point. This phenomenon proceeds from the inflammable matter which enters into the compoſition of the volatile alkali, which is the baſis of the ſal ammoniac. It is alſo this ſame inflammable principle which produces the good effects of ſal ammoniac in the tinning of metals.

Sal ammoniac is found ready formed in volcanos, or in their neighbourhood. It is called *native ſal ammoniac*, but it is in too ſmall quantity to furniſh the demands of artiſts. The ſal ammoniac ſold in commerce is made in great manufactories for this purpoſe.

The method of manufacturing ſal ammoniac was long unknown. Mr Le Maire and Mr Granger were the firſt who explained the proceſs, in very circumſtantial memoirs upon this ſubject communicated to the Academy of Sciences. An extract of theſe memoirs may be found in Mr Macquer's Elements of Practical Chemiſtry, for which reaſon, we will only briefly mention, that in Egypt, where moſt of the ſal ammoniac is made which is in commerce, ſoot is employed for this purpoſe, which is produced by burning the dung of cows and camels, which are the ordinary fuels of that country. This ſoot is put into large glaſs veſſels arranged near each other in oblong furnaces. The fire is raiſed gradually, that all the volatile principles of the ſoot may be driven off, then the fire is encreaſed towards the end, by which the ſal ammoniac is ſublimed, the materials of which were contained in the ſoot, the glaſs veſſels are then broken to get out the loaves of ſal ammoniac, which are formed upon the upper interior parts of the glaſs veſſels. Theſe loaves or cakes, as they are found at the ſhops of druggiſts, weigh from three to five or ſix pounds. They are more or leſs blackened by a quantity of fuliginous or ſooty matter, which riſes with the ſal ammoniac in the ſublimation. *See* SOOT.

Sal ammoniac may be purified from this extraneous matter by the means commonly employed for the purification of ſalts, that is, by diſſolving in water, filtrating, cryſtallizing, and by ſubliming a ſecond time, if this ſhould be thought neceſſary. Sal ammoniac is then obtained perfectly white and pure. Sal ammoniac may be made by combining marine acid to the point of ſaturation with volatile alkali, obtained from the diſtillation of animal or vegetable ſubſtances, and by filtrating, cryſtallizing, and ſubliming the ſaline matters thus combined. But this ſal ammoniac would coſt more than the price it is generally ſold for. Although the volatile alkali uſed for this proceſs, ſolid or liquid, be very impure and impregnated with much empyreumatic oil, from which it is difficult to purify it, yet the ſal ammoniac obtained from it by this method is very pure and good, becauſe the volatile alkali, when it combines with an acid, ſeparates itſelf from all the ſuperabundant oil with which it was at firſt combined: hence the volatile alkali obtained by decompoſing ſal ammoniac is better diſengaged from all ſuperabundant oily matter than what is obtained by any other method. But we muſt obſerve, that the volatile alkali obtained from ſal ammoniac always carries off with it ſome of the ſubſtance employed for the decompoſition. This circumſtance muſt produce different effects in chemical experiments, to which attention ought to be given. *(q)*

(q) To the above article we ſhall add, 1. Sal ammoniac requires four times its quantity of water to diſſolve in that liquid. 2. Its volatility is diminiſhed ſo much by repeated ſublimations, that it remains half fluid at the bottom of the ſubliming veſſel, and when ſal ammoniac was repeatedly ſublimed together with mercury corroſive ſublimate,

LII AMMONIACAL SALT (VITRIOLIC) This is a neutral salt composed of vitriolic acid saturated by volatile alkali

This salt may be made by several different methods

1 By combining vitriolic acid with disengaged volatile alkali

2 By decomposing sal ammoniac by vitriolic acid in Glauber's manner If this latter method be used, a marine acid is obtained by distillation, strong in proportion to the concentration of the vitriolic acid employed, and in the retort the vitriolic ammoniacal salt remains, which *Glauber* called his *secret sal ammoniac*

3 By decomposing all vitriolic salts with earthy or metallic bases, by means of volatile alkali *See* ALKALI (VOLATILE)

This salt has the properties of sal ammoniac, with the differences depending on their different acids. It is semi-volatile, it may be entirely sublimed, it cannot be decomposed in close vessels without some intermediate substance, it has a sharp taste, it easily dissolves in water, and is susceptible of crystallization This ammoniacal salt is not used in arts or in medicine Glauber attributes many wonderful properties to it, which it certainly does not, so eminently at least, possess

LIII AMMONIAC SALT (NITROUS) This salt is composed of nitrous acid saturated with volatile alkali It is found in earths, or plasters where nitrous acid is generated, when these earths have imbibed a sufficient quantity of putrid animal or vegetable substances to furnish volatile alkali to the generating nitrous acid.

Nitrous ammoniacal salt may be made, as the vitriolic, by three methods

1 By combining to the point of saturation nitrous acid with volatile alkali

2 By decomposing sal ammoniac by means of nitrous acid

3 By decomposing nitrous salts with earthy or metallic bases, by means of volatile alkali *See* ALKALI (VOLATILE)

Nitrous ammoniacal salt has a very pungent taste, is soluble in water, capable of forming beautiful needle-like crystals, like those of ordinary nitre

This salt has the singular property of detonating alone, when exposed to a certain degree of heat, and without the necessity of addition, as in ordinary nitre, of inflammable matter *It seems even to inflame with less heat than nitre mixed* with inflammable matter does

This property proceeds from the phlogiston or inflammable matter which enters as a principle into the composition of the volatile alkaline basis of this salt This property also furnishes a decisive proof of the existence of this inflammable matter in volatile alkali.

This inflammability of nitrous ammoniacal salt renders it incapable of sublimation, like the other ammoniacal salts, as an explosion would certainly happen

mate, and the residuum of each preceding operation mixed with the sublimed salt, the whole matter became quite fixed in the fire, and would no longer rise from the bottom of the glass *Neuman.* 3 The degree of heat necessary to volatilize sal ammoniac is a little below that of ignition, nearly the same with which lead is melted. 4 Pott says, that a small quantity of sal ammoniac may be produced by distilling sea-salt with charcoal or with lum, or by distilling marine acid with Armenian bole 5 The same author affirms, that the inflammability of sulphur is destroyed by subliming it with twice its quantity of sal ammoniac in the operation Chemists do not seem to have examined particularly the properties of this salt, neither is it used in arts or in medicine, If this curious salt were to be more particularly examined, the operator would need the greatest circumspection to avoid explosions

LIV AMMONIACAL SALT (VEGETABLE) This name is given to all neutral salts formed by combinations of volatile alkali with vegetable acids But these salts are hitherto little known, although they deserve to be examined That saline combination formed by volatile alkali and vinegar is called *Spirit of Mindererus*

LV. AMMONIACAL SALT (ANIMAL) As the fat of animals contains much acid, (*See* FAT) an ammoniacal salt might be formed by combining this acid with volatile alkali, which might be properly called animal ammoniacal salt. But this combination has not yet been made, or examined.

Lastly, the phosphoric salt, or native salt of urine, belongs to the class of ammoniacal salts, and as its acid appears to be peculiarly animal, it would also be in this sense a true animal ammoniacal salt *See* SALT (FUSIBLE) *of* URINE.

LVI AMMMONIAC (FIXED) *(r)*

LVII AMMONIAC (GUM). *(s)*

LVIII AMETHYST *(t)*

LIX AMIANTHUS) *(u)*

LX ANALYSIS Chemists understand by the word analysis, the decomposition of a body, or the separation of the principles and constituent parts of a compound substance

Chemistry furnishes several means for the decomposition of bodies These means are all founded on the differences of the properties belonging to the different principles of which the body to be analysed is composed Thus, for example if a body be composed of several principles, some of which have a great, and others a moderate degree of volatility, and, lastly, others are fixed, its most volatile parts may be first separated, by a graduated heat, in distilling vessels, and then the parts which are next in volatility will pass over in distillation, and lastly, those parts which are fixed, and capable of resisting the action of fire, will remain at the bottom of the vessel As this analysis cannot be made but by means of fire, it is called the *Analysis by fire*.

(r) FIXED AMMONIAC is a name given to the residuum formed by decomposing sal ammoniac with a calcareous earth It is a salt compoled of that earth and marine acid *See* SALT (MARINE) *with* BASIS *of* CALCAREOUS EARTH

(s) GUM AMMONIAC is a gum resin, from an ounce of which six drams may be dissolved by spirit of wine, or six drams two scruples and a half may be dissolved by water *Neuman*

(t) AMETHYST This is a violet-colored, frequently yellowish or reddish, pellucid gem, the seventh in degree of hardness from diamonds, fusible by fire, which also destroys its color. It is found amongst quartz, and is probably only a colored quartz crystal This stone may be imitated by adding to a fritt of crystal-glass eight parts of magnesia and one part of zaffre

(u) AMIANTHUS is the lightest and softest of all stones It consists of fibres parallel or interwove, so flexible, that cloth has been formed of them By a strong heat it is whitened, hardened so as to be capable of striking fire with steel, and rendered brittle It has generally been considered as unfusible by fire, but Mr D'Arcet, in a Memoir of the French Academy for the year 1766, affirms, that by a violent and long continued fire it is fusible, and that it forms a black glass. This stone is insoluble by acids,

It

It is proper to observe, that this method of analysing does not succeed equally well upon all bodies, and that it is very imperfect upon some bodies, which being composed of principles of very different degrees of volatility, might seem well adapted to it. This particularly happens when the principles of substances analysed by this method have a great adhesion with each other, because in this case a volatile principle drags along with it a portion of the fixed principle, which would never have been raised by the degree of heat employed without this adhesion, and as it were, participation of the volatility of the former to the latter. Frequently, therefore, the principles obtained by this method of analysis are in part still united with each other, and are far from the proper degree of purity. In this case it is necessary to have recourse to new distillations, rectifications, and purifications, to obtain them sufficiently pure and separated from each other. This inconvenience particularly attends the analyses by fire of most animal and vegetable substances, in which analyses very volatile acids and alkalis are often procured, still united with much superfluous heavy oil. The best method of avoiding this inconvenience, or at least of diminishing it as much as possible, is to manage very carefully the fire, for it is evident that a too strong fire would readily confound all the principles of the substance to be analysed.

A second no less important remark concerning the analysis by fire, is, that by this method the *proximate principles* of very compound bodies, such as most vegetables, cannot be obtained, because these proximate principles being themselves very compound, and of a delicate mixture, cannot, for the most part, support the action of fire without a total or partial decomposition, or, at least, without receiving such considerable alterations that they can no longer be known. This inconvenience chiefly attends those proximate principles which are not possessed of great volatility, as we may see from the example of mild and fat oils, of gummy, resinous, saponaceous, and extractive parts of vegetables. These principles cannot ever be procured by distillation such as they were in the plant.

These inconveniences have induced chemists, particularly the modern, to search for other methods of decomposing bodies and separating their principles.

They have found one method which wonderfully supplies in many cases the defects of the analysis by fire.

This second method of decomposing bodies is founded on the different degrees of solubility in most menstruums, which the different principles possess. Thus when a body is compounded of several substances, one of which, for instance, is soluble only by spirit of wine, a second is soluble only by water, and a third is soluble only by ether, these substances may be very easily separated from each other, by submitting successively the compound body to the action of these menstruums, each of which dissolves that particular substance to which it has an affinity, and from which it may be afterwards easily separated. This method of analysis is excellent to separate without any sensible alteration the greatest part of the proximate principles of vegetables, and to obtain them as they exist in the plants. If, for instance, a vegetable matter contain gum, resin, and an oil or oily concretion not soluble in spirit of wine, we may first deprive it by water of its mucilaginous and gummy parts, which may afterwards be obtained in their natural state merely by evaporation of the water, then, by applying to this vegetable matter spirit of wine, we may extract its resinous parts, and lastly, we may, by treating it with ether, separate its oily part, which could not be dissolved the water or the spirit of wine. It is afterwards easy to obtain the substances dissolved by the ether and spirit of wine, pure and free from their menstruums, either by evaporation, or by addition of much water, which separates the oily and resinous parts. See SPIRIT *of* WINE, and ETHER.

As this method of separating the principles of bodies is solely founded on the action of menstruums, this kind of analysis has been called ANALYSIS *by* MENSTRUUMS.

What has been said on this subject is sufficient to make its great utility appear. We may add, that in some cases this is the only analysis which can be applied, and by which a perfect and compleat separation can be effected. If, for example, the body to be analysed consists of two substances which equally resist the action of fire, as gold and silver, it is evident that these two substances cannot be separated from each other but by means of a menstruum which can only dissolve one of them. Thus, by exposing a mass composed of gold and silver to aqua regia, which dissolves the gold only, or to nitrous acid, which dissolves only the silver, the separation of these two metals may be effected. The operation called *Parting* ought then to be considered as the true analysis by menstruums. See PARTING.

We may say the same of all decompositions and precipitations which are made in numberless chemical operations by intermediate substances, either by the humid method, or by the dry, in different fusions. In all these cases, the intermediate substance employed effects the precipitation or separation of the body intended to be separated, by really dissolving another body to which the former was united. Thus the analysis by menstruums is at least of as extensive utility as the analysis by fire, since it takes place in almost all the operations of chemistry.

It is true, that in many cases the analysis by menstruums, as well as that by fire, is incomplete. This inconvenience happens when there is in the compound body to be analysed some intermediate substance, by means of which the menstruum is rendered capable of acting upon some of the principles, which it ought not to do, in order to have a complete and perfect separation. But these inconveniences may be prevented or repaired.

Frequently it is necessary, in order to make a perfect analysis of bodies, to unite these two methods by fire and by menstruums: the one may be made to assist the other, and from these combined means a decomposition results much more perfect, and more accurate, than could have been obtained by either of them separately. If, for instance, we intended to separate from spirit of wine superabundant quantities of oil and water which are generally united with it, we ought, instead of distilling it alone, to mix with it some fixed alkali, or very dry earthy matter, and then to proceed to the distillation: these alkaline or earthy substances acting upon the oil and water will retain and fix them, by which means the spirit of wine is allowed to rise much purer in distillation.

We shall say nothing more here upon analysis in general. This subject is so extensive, that to make particular applications of it, we should be obliged to consider all the objects in chemistry. Those who know the use of general principles will easily apply these to particular operations, and longer details would be fatiguing and useless to others. It is nevertheless proper to mention the general

neral articles which are related to this *See* DECOMPOSITION, DISTILLATION, SUBLIMATION, PRECIPITATION, EXTRACTION, SOLUTION.

LXI. ANGELICA (*w*)

LXII. ANIMAL (*x*)

LXIII. ANIME (*y*)

LXIV. ANISE (*z*)

LXV. ANNOTTO (*a*)

LXVI. ANTIMONY. Antimony is a mineral of a metallic, shining, leaden color, the masses of which have no determinate figure, but are composed of long, brittle, parallel needles. It is composed of a semimetallic substance called its *regulus*, united with sulphur, as most metallic substances are in their mineral state.

There are two kinds of antimony, namely, that which is called *native* or *mineral*, and is in the same state as when it is dug out of the earth; and *fused antimony*, so named, because it has been actually fused in order to separate it from adhering stones and earths. This operation, which ought rather to be called liquation than fusion, considering these words in their metallurgic sense, is made in great perfection upon the grounds whence antimony is dug. The process is very simple and easy. It consists in placing the mineral in earthen pots, pierced in their bottoms with small holes. These pots are placed in a furnace, where they receive the necessary heat for the fusion of the antimony. As it is very fusible, (for it melts before it is red) this degree of heat is much less than is necessary for the fusion of the earthy and stony matters mixed with it. The antimony thus melted runs through the holes at the bottom of the pots and is received in other pots placed below, and defended from the heat as much as is possible. The antimony is allowed to cool and fix in these receivers, from which it therefore takes its form of cakes, in which it is sold. The countries which furnish most antimony are Hungary and Auvergne, whence the names *Hungarian antimony*, and *Auvergne antimony*. Antimony is also found in other countries, and in different forms, upon which subject consult the article ORE *of* ANTIMONY.

(*w*) ANGELICA. The root of this plant contains an essential oil, and a resinous matter. *Neuman.*

(*x*) ANIMAL KINGDOM. *See* KINGDOM.

(*y*) ANIME, according to Neuman, is a resin totally soluble in spirit of wine. It is called improperly *gum anime*. Other authors mention two substances to which this name is given, one of which is brought from India, and is resinous: the other is brought from Brasil, and is similar in appearance and insolubility in spirit of wine or in water, to the substance called *gum copal*. All the anime which is to be found in shops of druggists is of this latter kind, and if it does not proceed from the same tree as gum copal, is scarcely distinguishable from it.

(*z*) ANISE. The outer thin skin of the seeds of this plant contains an essential oil and the kernel itself contains an inodorous, insipid, expressible oil. *Neuman.*

(*a*) ANNOTTO is a red mass extracted by infusion in water, and fermentation from the pellicles of the seeds of an American tree. To water this mass gives only a pale brownish-yellow color, and is very little soluble in that liquid. It readily dissolves in spirit of wine, and gives a bright orange color: hence it is useful as an ingredient in varnishes and lacquers. By alkaline salts it is rendered soluble in water, without any change produced upon its color. Wool and silk boiled in this solution acquire a deep, but not durable orange dye. Its color is not changed by alum or by acids, but is discharged by soaps, and is destroyed by exposure to air. It is said to be an antidote to the poisonous juice of manioc, or cassada.

As

As many remedies of great consequence are prepared from antimony, and as alchemists have supposed it essential to the *great work*, a very great number of chemical operations have been made upon this mineral, the results of which are distinguished by particular names We shall here give a summary account of these operations, and shall make references for the particular details and explanations

The metallic part of antimony is disengaged from its sulphur by several methods The first and simplest is torrefaction, commonly called *Calcination of Antimony* It consists in exposing crude antimony, grossly powdered, in a flat and shallow earthen vessel, to the action of a moderate fire, taking care to stir it constantly During this calcination, the sulphur, being less fixed than the metalline part, is gradually evaporated The calcination is continued till no more sulphureous vapors rise What remains after the calcination is the metallic part of the antimony separated from the mineral sulphur, and even deprived of part of its own inflammable principle This substance is much more fixed and less fusible than antimony, because in general metallic earths are so much more fixed and less fusible as they are deprived of more of their inflammable principle It is called *Calx of Antimony* It is of a grey ash color When taken internally it is violently emetic and purgative, which antimony is not, because its metallic earth is inveloped by sulphur, and thereby deprived of most of its properties

Calx of antimony, exposed to a great heat in a crucible, melts and appears when cold a hard, compact, brittle, shining mass This melted matter is sometimes transparent, and of a more or less deep hyacinthine color It is then called *Glass of Antimony*, because it has the appearance and properties of a vitrified substance

Sometimes calx of antimony, when fused and cooled, becomes an opake brown mass It is then called *Liver of Antimony*

These differences proceed from the greater or less quantity of inflammable principle which remains united with the metallic earth of the antimony They consequently depend on the length and accuracy of the calcination

When this calcination has been slight, and much inflammable matter remains united with the earth of antimony, then the calx produced is capable of melting with less heat, and the result is liver of antimony, which ought to be considered as an intermediate matter betwixt the vitrified and metallic states

If the calcination has been more compleat, the calx is of more difficult fusion, and the result from it is a vitrified substance

Lastly, if the calcination has been as perfect as is possible, the remaining calx is still more refractory, and is even incapable of fusion and vitrification

The calx, the liver, and the glass of antimony, are violently emetic The phenomena which they shew when treated with chemical agents, are so much more similar to those exhibited by the regulus of antimony, as they approach more to the reguline state, that is to say, as they are more perfectly deprived of mineral sulphur, and less deprived of their inflammable principle

These three preparations of antimony being treated in close vessels, and fused with matters capable of furnishing phlogiston, such as the black flux, are reduced not into antimony as they were originally, but into a semi metallic, hard, brittl brittle ſubſtance, of a dull white color, and compoſed of ſhining facets This ſubſtance is called *Regulus of Antimony* The cauſe of this change is, that by calcination this mineral is deprived of all the ſulphur which is found united with its ſemi-metallic or reguline ſubſtance, and that this ſulphur is not reſtored to it in the reduction above-mentioned If then it be intended to reſtore the properties of antimony to its calx, liver, glaſs, or regulus, it ought to be combined by fuſion not only with phlogiſton, but alſo with a proper quantity of mineral ſulphur

Antimony may be diſengaged from its ſulphur, and at the ſame time reduced either into regulus, liver, or white calx entirely deprived of its phlogiſton, by ſeveral other proceſſes, much ſhorter and more expeditious than calcination, which is always very long

If a mixture of four parts of crude antimony pulveriſed, three parts of tartar, and one part and a half of nitre, be projected at different times into a large red-hot crucible, and ſurrounded with burning coals, and when the detonation is finiſhed, the fire raiſed ſo as the matter ſhall be fuſed, then upon breaking the crucible when cool, a maſs is found conſiſting of two diſtinct ſubſtances, and which may be ſeparated from each other by the ſtroke of a hammer The lower ſubſtance is the reguline metallic part, and is called *Regulus of Antimony* The ſubſtance lying above this is called *Scoria of the Regulus of Antimony* This ſcoria is alkaline and acrid it attracts the moiſture of the air, and is compoſed, 1 Of the alkalis of the nitre and of the tartar alkaliſed by each other in the operation, 2 Of a portion of the ſulphur of the antimony, which during the operation united with the alkali and formed a liver of ſulphur, 3 A portion of reguline ſubſtance of antimony diſſolved by this liver of ſulphur, 4 Laſtly, ſome vitriolated tartar which was formed by a part of the acid of the ſulphur combining during the detonation with the fixed alkali

From the ſolution of the ſcoria of the regulus of antimony in water, a yellow reddiſh matter is depoſited in a certain time, which is nothing elſe than a part of the ſulphur and of the regulus of antimony which quit the alkali without ſeparating from each other, conſequently it is a kind of *Kermes* When the ſolution of this ſcoria is ſaturated with any acid, a pretty large quantity of reddiſh matter is precipitated, which is compoſed, like the former, of ſulphur and reguline parts This matter is called SULPHUR (GOLDEN) of ANTIMONY, *which ſee*

Theſe two precipitates, and particularly the latter, are very emetic, although in them the reguline part is, as in antimony, which has no emetic quality, united with a large portion of ſulphur The true reaſon of this difference is, that in crude antimony the ſulphur is much more intimately and ſtrongly united to the ſemi metallic part than it is in the golden ſulphur

Moſt metals, as iron, copper, tin, lead, and ſilver, have a greater affinity to ſulphur than the regulus of antimony has Hence this regulus may be precipitated in fuſion, and its ſulphur may be ſeparated by means of theſe metals. The regulus thus obtained is called the *Regulus of the Metals* The name of the particular metal employed to make this precipitation is added Thus it is called, the *Regulus of Tin*, the *Regulus of Copper*, the *Martial Regulus*, according

ing to the metal uſed in the operation Iron is moſt frequently employed to make this regulus, becauſe of all metals it has the greateſt affinity to ſulphur, and for that reaſon ſeparates moſt eaſily and perfectly the reguline part *See* REGULUS *of* ANTIMONY (MARTIAL).

If inſtead of detonating antimony with a ſufficient proportion of nitre to obtain the regulus, equal parts of theſe two ſubſtances are employed, then, after the detonation, no regulus will be found at the bottom of the crucible, but a brown, opake, brittle maſs, of no metallic appearance, in a word, ſimilar to that maſs which is obtained by melting the calx of antimony alone, when too little dephlogiſticated to be capable of vitrification This maſs is, properly ſpeaking, the ſubſtance called *Liver of Antimony*, from its color, which ſomewhat reſembles that of the liver of animals By this proceſs the liver is always made in ſmall chemical laboratories But it is ſaid that in Holland, where many chemical operations are objects of manufacture, the liver of antimony is made by melting the calx of this mineral alone, ſufficiently dephlogiſticated The liver of antimony prepared by either of theſe methods is a violent emetic and purgative Several diſpenſatories require it to be employed in the preparation of *emetic tartar* *See this word* It is alſo uſed to purge horſes

When in this operation of liver of antimony by nitre, the matter has been well fuſed, it is obſervable that the maſs found upon breaking the crucible is compoſed of two diſtinct ſubſtances. The liver of antimony, being the heavier of the two, is at the bottom, and above it lies a lighter and more ſaline matter, called the *ſcoria*, which may be ſeparated by a hammer. This ſcoria is nearly of the ſame nature as that of the ordinary regulus It is very acrid and alkaline, and contains vitriolated tartar, and liver of ſulphur, by which ſome liver of antimony is kept diſſolved A golden ſulphur of antimony may be alſo precipitated from this ſcoria by any acid

When in the operation of the liver of antimony, the fuſion has not been ſufficient, or the mixture has been cooled too ſuddenly, then the ſcoria remains mixed with the liver of antimony, which it in ſome meaſure keeps diſſolved

Laſtly, in detonating antimony with thrice its weight of nitre, after the operation, a maſs perfectly white and void of color is found This maſs is a mixture of calx of antimony with certain ſaline matters. Theſe are, 1 Nitre alkaliſed by the phlogiſton of the ſulphur, and of the regulus of antimony, 2 Vitriolated tartar, proceeding from a portion of the acid of the ſulphur, combined with the alkali of the nitre, 3 A portion of nitre undecompoſed

As to the calx of antimony obtained by this operation, it is perfectly white, becauſe entirely deprived by nitre not only of all the mineral ſulphur, but alſo of its own phlogiſton

This calx well waſhed, ſo as to be cleanſed from the ſalts, is called *Diaphoretic Mineral, Diaphoretic Antimony*, and *White Calx of Antimony* It is neither emetic nor purgative, for which reaſon a diaphoretic quality has been attributed to it

The white calx of antimony is not ſoluble in acids It is exceedingly fixed, and often refractory, being capable of ſuſtaining the greateſt violence of fire without vitrifying or melting All theſe properties, ſo different from thoſe of the

the regulus, the liver, and the glass of antimony, proceed from its being entirely divested of phlogiston by nitre

The quantity of nitre employed in this operation is more than sufficient to dephlogisticate entirely all the earth of the antimony, since in the scoria is found some nitre undecomposed, because there was not phlogiston enough in the antimony for that purpose

These phenomena of the calcination of antimony, which are conformable to those of all other metallic calcinations, prove in a satisfactory manner, that metallic matters owe their volatility, their fusibility, and their solubility in acids to their phlogiston

The mass remaining in the crucible after the detonation, in the operation of diaphoretic antimony, and which consequently contains the calx of antimony and the salts resulting from the operation, receives aperitive, and even purgative qualities from the salts contained in it. It is called *Unwashed Diaphoretic* It forms also the substance called the *Flux of Rotrou*

When the result from the detonation of diaphoretic antimony is washed, in order to cleanse it from the salts, the water dissolves not only the saline matters, but also the finest part of the calx of antimony adhering to these salts This matter separates and precipitates in form of a very white and fine powder, for which reason it has been called *Pearl-Matter* It has also been named the *Ceruss of Antimony*, and very improperly the *Fixed Sulphur of Antimony* For it is evident from the nature of the operation, that no sulphur can remain in it, nor even any inflammable matter. The pearl matter also gives no marks of sulphur contained, and has absolutely the same properties as diaphoretic antimony, and if it differs in any thing, it is in being more perfectly calcined

The white calx of antimony and the pearl-matter may be reduced into regulus by fusion in close vessels, with a reducing flux, as black flux, but only in part, and with considerable loss

In all these operations, where antimony is exposed to a fusing heat, a considerable quantity of volatile matter rises in smoke, and adheres in form of a meal or fine powder to any cold body it meets This is called *Flowers of Antimony*, which are nothing else than the semi-metallic part of the antimony, more or less deprived of the sulphur and phlogiston, but never entirely of the latter for which reason, they are violently emetic

In the chemical operations for procuring these flowers, only antimony itself or its regulus are employed For this purpose a convenient apparatus and vessels are used *See* FLOWERS *of* ANTIMONY, and FLOWERS *of* REGULUS *of* ANTIMONY

When crude antimony is boiled in a lixivium of fixed alkali, a liver of sulphur is formed from the combination of this alkali with the sulphur of the antimony, by which the metalline part of the antimony is dissolved But the alkali, by its being dissolved in water, having but a slight union with the sulphur, this antimoniated liver of sulphur cannot be kept suspended in the water, when the heat of that fluid is less, or much less than is sufficient to make it boil. Hence when the liquor cools, it becomes turbid, and a brick-colored sediment falls down, which has been called *Kermes Mineral.* This precipitate drags down along with it, according to a general rule of all precipitates a portion of the alkali by which it was kept diffolved But this portion of alkali is very fmall For this reafon alfo the kermes cannot be kept diffolved but in very hot water Hence it appears that kermes is nothing but an antimoniated liver of fulphur, containing the fmalleft poffible quantity of alkali, or a fuperabundant quantity of fulphur and regulus of antimony

Kermes may alfo be made by fufion, that is, by melting in a crucible dry alkaline falt and crude antimony, and then diffolving the combination in boiling water The fame phenomena appear, as in the preceding operation, and for the fame reafons

Kermes is a preparation of great utility and importance in medicine *See the details, the preparation of Kermes, and the theory of it more extenfively, as well as its medicinal virtues, at the article* KERMES MINERAL

Acids difficultly diffolve regulus of antimony To diffolve it by the vitriolic acid, the fame procefs muft be ufed as in the folution of mercury by this acid for the preparation of turbith mineral that is, to employ a very concentrated acid, and to diftill in clofe veffels The fame phenomena alfo occur in this operation as in that for turbith mineral a very fuffocating fulphureous acid rifes , and as Mr Geoffroy obferves, a true fulphur fublimes, and adheres to the neck of the retort a white faline tumefied mafs remains in the veffel When the veffels are unluted, a white fume iffues like the fmoking fpirit of Libavius Thefe phenomena of the production of volatile fulphureous acid, and of concrete fulphur, are evidently effects of the combination of the vitriolic acid with the phlogifton of the regulus of antimony

The nitrous acid does, properly fpeaking, only corrode and dephlogifticate the regulus of antimony, which it converts into a white calx It diffolves a little better this reguline part, when it is applied to the antimony itfelf This folution, as Mr Geoffroy obferves, acquires a blueifh greenifh color When only a fufficient quantity of acid is employed, it may be feen to infert itfelf betwixt the ftriæ of the antimony, and there form fmall cryftals.

Marine acid does not fenfibly act upon antimony nor its regulus It only detaches from the antimony, in lumps, fome light and fulphureous flocks

Aqua regia moft directly and completely diffolves regulus of antimony. For this operation, it is proper to employ an aqua regia compofed of four parts of fpirit of nitre, and one part of fpirit of falt This menftruum is digefted in a fand-bath with a gentle heat upon bits of regulus of antimony, which are added fucceffively, fo that one fhall not be added till the former are diffolved By means of this management, directed by Mr Geoffroy in the Memoirs of the Academy of Sciences, aqua regia can diffolve about a fixteenth part of its weight of regulus of antimony This folution has a beautiful golden color, which difappears by the evaporation of white fumes continually rifing from it

The aqua regia above defcribed is alfo very proper to diffolve the reguline part of crude antimony, and the folution even fucceeds better in this way This is applicable to all the folvents of the regulus of antimony

The combination of marine acid with regulus of antimony, which fucceeds ill by applying this acid directly to the femi metal, may be much better made

made by employing a marine acid previously combined with mercury in corrosive sublimate

When regulus of antimony or powdered crude antimony is mixed with corrosive sublimate, and this mixture distilled, the marine acid, having a stronger affinity with regulus of antimony than with mercury, quits the latter metallic substance to unite with the former, and from this a combination results which passes in distillation, and has a butyraceous appearance It is a very corrosive metallic salt, and is called the *Butter of Antimony*

When the regulus is employed to make the butter of antimony, the mercury is separated from the acid of the corrosive sublimate, and passes over in its metallic and fluid state towards the end of the operation, and when the fire is encreased

But if antimony has been employed to make this butter, a cinnabar may be sublimed, by increasing the fire after the butter of antimony has passed over in distillation This cinnabar results from the union of the sulphur of the antimony with the mercury, and is called *Cinnabar of Antimony* See BUTTER *and* CINNABAR *of* ANTIMONY

Butter of antimony is then the result of a combination of the metallic part of antimony with marine acid in its highest degree of concentration, and is therefore a powerful caustic It may be rendered liquid by a small quantity of water, but if diluted with much water, then the greatest part of the regulus separates from the menstruum, and precipitates in the state of a white powder, which has been called *Powder of Algaroth*, and *Mercury of Life* See *these words*

The powder of algaroth is a very violent emetic Mr Beaume has ascertained, by very accurate experiments, that when it is sufficiently washed it does not retain a particle of marine acid

The liquor in which the powder of algaroth is precipitated contains all the marine acid of the butter of antimony, with a portion of the reguline part, which may be separated from it by precipitation with an alkali This liquor has been named *Philosophical Spirit of Vitriol*; which name is improper, since it contains no vitriolic acid

Nitrous acid poured upon butter of antimony dissolves it easily, and even violently When this solution has been made gradually and cautiously, a transparent solution is obtained, impregnated with much regulus of antimony

As in this operation the added nitrous acid forms with the marine acid, already united with the regulus in the butter of antimony, an aqua regia, and as aqua regia is the best solvent of this semi metallic substance, a new solution takes place by the addition of this nitrous acid, entirely similar, as to its concomitant phenomena, to the solutions of metals by this acid, not previously dissolved by any other This new solution is even so impetuous, that when the quantity of matter is considerable, it is apt to be thrown violently out of the containing vessels

Butter of antimony is entirely changed by its union with nitrous acid This acid, as is usual, seizes upon the inflammable part of the regulus of antimony which the marine had left unchanged it diminishe the adhesion of the marine acid with the regulus Hence it happens that this new combination of regulus

of

of antimony with the acids of aqua regia, when dried and calcined, no longer possesses the volatility of the butter of antimony. Instead then of subliming or passing in distillation without decomposition, as the butter does, the new compound resists the action of fire, is decomposed, lets its acids escape, and remains in the state of a white powder.

If fresh nitrous acid be twice poured upon this white powder, and each time the matter evaporated and calcined, the regulus of antimony is then reduced to a white earthy substance, indissoluble in the nitrous acid, entirely fixed and unfusible, and possessed of no emetic or purgative qualities. This preparation has been called *Bezoar mineral*. See *this word*.

This operation is one of those which proves most sensibly the power of the nitrous acid to calcine metallic substances, by depriving them of their phlogiston. It also proves that it is chiefly by means of this phlogiston that the nitrous acid dissolves these substances, since it cannot dissolve bezoar mineral, diaphoretic antimony, nor any other similarly dephlogisticated metallic substances.

LXVII. ANNEAL. Annealing consists in making metals red-hot which have become hard and stiff by frequent percussion, or by a strong compression, in order to restore their former malleability and tractability. All metals have the singular property of becoming more or less hard, untractable, and unmalleable, after they have been struck some time with a hammer. It seems as if something happened to them similar to the effect produced by the tempering of steel. Metals thus affected become more elastic than before, but, at the same time, more brittle. They are more sensibly affected in this manner in proportion as they are naturally harder. Copper is so much affected, and even gold and silver, by hammering, that they soon cease to be malleable, and are apt to split and crack, instead of being extended, under the hammer. This labor therefore must be often interrupted, to soften and restore malleability to metals. This is effected by making them red-hot, which the workmen call *annealing*. Thus heat produces the same effect on metals in the state described, as it does upon tempered steel: for if the hardest tempered steel be made red-hot, and cooled slowly, it becomes as tractable and ductile as the softest iron.

There is also an annealing for works made of glass. It consists in placing them, while newly made and still hot, in an oven or furnace, where they very slowly cool. This annealing for bottles and other glass utensils is quite necessary to render them serviceable, for all glass which is cooled suddenly is liable to be broken, not only by the least change of heat and cold, but even by the slightest force.

LXVIII. APYROUS. This word is applied to denote that property of some bodies, by which they resist the most violent fire without any sensible alteration. Apyrous bodies ought to be distinguished from those which are *refractory*. Refractory substances are those which cannot by violent heat be fused, whatever other alteration they may sustain. But a body, properly speaking, apyrous, can neither be fused by heat, nor can undergo any other change. Hence it follows, that all apyrous substances are also refractory, but that every refractory substance is not apyrous. Very pure calcareous stones, for instance, are refractory, because they never melt without addition of other substance: but they are not apyrous, because by fire their weight is considerably diminished, the adhesion of their integrant parts is destroyed, and all their essential properties are changed

changed by their conversion into quicklime On the contrary, a very clear and pure diamond is apyrous, because the strongest fire is incapable not only of melting it, but also of producing upon it any other sensible alteration, so that a diamond which has been a long time exposed to the most intense heat, is found to be the same in all respects as it was before

Perhaps there is no body in nature essentially and rigorously apyrous This too is very probable, but it is sufficient that there be bodies apyrous relatively to the degree of fire which art can produce, to entitle them to that name

LXIX AQUA-FORTIS Aqua fortis is a name given by artists and manufacturers to nitrous acid, from its dissolving power As it is not the concentrated and smoking nitrous acid which is employed in the arts, it seems that the name aqua fortis may be retained by that acid which has not these qualities

Most artists who use nitrous acid, call the purer and stronger kind, which is also considerably dearer, by the name of *Spirit of Nitre* For the properties of this acid, *see* ACID (NITROUS), and for the distillation of it, *see* SPIRIT *of* NITRE

In the manufacture of soap, the caustic alkaline lixivium is called also the *strong water*, or *soap-lees*, or *lixivium of soap-boilers* *See* LIXIVIUM.

LXX AQUA-REGIA Aqua-regia is a mixture of the nitrous and marine acids. These two acids are mixed to obtain a menstruum capable of acting upon certain bodies which no pure acid can dissolve, or but imperfectly, particularly gold and platina cannot be dissolved in their aggregated state by any other acid than by aqua-regia. Tin and regulus of antimony are better and more easily dissolved by aqua regia than by any other acid

This menstruum may be made either by merely mixing the spirit of nitre with spirit of salt, or by dissolving in spirit of nitre a salt containing marine acid, and particularly sal ammoniac and common salt Lastly, it may be well made by distilling nitrous acid from either of these salts, because nitrous acid, being capable of disengaging marine acid from these salts, does actually disengage it, either by simply dissolving them in nitrous acid, or by distillation

The only difference betwixt the several sorts of aqua regia, prepared in these different manners, is, that the aqua-regia made by merely dissolving sal ammoniac or common salt in nitrous acid contains ammoniacal or cubic nitre, and that these neutral salts do not exist in the aqua-regia made by mixture of the two acids, or by distillation

The presence of these neutral salts in aqua-regia does not injure its dissolving powers Thus, as the aqua-regia which contains them is the easiest prepared, and least expensive, it is more generally used than the others But it is necessary to observe, that the ammoniacal nitre in the aqua-regia may occasion considerable differences in the nature of the precipitates made from solutions of metals in this menstruum, by separating from these precipitates any of those metallic substances which it is capable of dissolving, and also by a portion of it adhering to precipitates For instance, gold precipitated by a fixed alkali from an aqua regia made by mixing the pure nitrous and marine acids, does not fulminate, whereas it does fulminate when precipitated from an aqua-regia made by dissolving sal ammoniac in nitrous acid. *See* PRECIPITATES, and GOLD (FULMINATING)

The

The mixture of the nitrous and marine acids presents a very singular and remarkable phenomenon, which is, that the vapors of this mixture are more expansive and more difficult to be confined than the vapors of either of the acids before mixing This proves a re action of these acids upon each other This phenomenon is very little sensible when the acids employed contain much superabundant water, but is more manifest in proportion as these are more concentrated I have observed, that upon mixing moderately smoaking nitrous and marine acids, which had remained without occasioning any disturbance in their bottles, an aqua-regia has been formed infinitely more smoaking, and which has made the stopper fly out of the containing bottle, particularly in weather somewhat warm Mr Beaumé, when distilling a pretty strong nitrous acid upon sal ammoniac, observed, that the vapors which passed were so elastic, that notwithstanding every precaution that could be taken in such a case, it was impossible to continue the distillation

As to the proportions of nitrous and marine acids, or of sal ammoniac, which ought to be employed for the preparation of aqua-regia, there are no established rules. Common aqua-regia is made by dissolving four ounces of sal ammoniac in sixteen ounces of nitrous acid But these proportions ought to be varied according to the nature of the solutions intended

To dissolve, for example, the greatest possible quantity of platina, the best proportion is equal parts of the two acids.

To dissolve the greatest quantity of regulus of antimony, the aqua regia ought to be composed of four parts of nitrous acid to one of marine.

In general, the greater the proportion of marine acid, or of sal ammoniac, is in aqua regia, the less are the imperfect metals, and particularly tin calcined and precipitated by it. An aqua-regia, composed of two parts of spirit of nitre and one part of spirit of salt or of sal ammoniac, makes a clear solution of nearly an equal weight of tin, without forming any precipitate but for this purpose, the operation must be performed slowly, and heat must be avoided as much as possible *See* GOLD, PLATINA, TIN, and REGULUS *of* ANTIMONY *(b)*

LXXI AQUA-SECUNDA This is nothing else than aquafortis diluted with much pure water It is employed in several arts to clean the surface of metals and of certain stones, and for some other purposes

LXXII AQUA VITÆ. Aqua-vitæ is the spirituous part obtained by a first distillation from wine, or any other liquor which has undergone the vinous fermentation It is properly speaking, ardent spirit, or spirit of wine

To make the aqua vitæ that is sold in commerce, wine is put in large copper alembics or stills, to which worms are fitted, and the distillation is so conducted

(*b*) Aqua-regia does not dissolve silver but when the quantity of marine acid contained in the aqua-regia is very small, the acid of nitre does then dissolve silver, which is immediately afterwards attacked by the marine acid, with which it forms the metallic salt called *luna cornea*, and is precipitated Aqua-regia dissolves a larger quantity of lead than marine acid. All the other metals it perfectly dissolves According to Gellert's table, the substances which aqua-regia dissolves are placed in the following order, beginning with those to which it most powerfully unites Phlogiston, zinc, iron, regulus of cobalt, copper, tin, arsenic, bismuth, mercury, lead, regulus of antimony, gold In this table copper is erroneously placed before tin, as the latter metal readily precipitates the former

that

that the liquor flows out of the beak of the still in a constant stream, and is continued till this liquor begins to be no longer inflammable

It is evident that this distillation, being hastily and unartfully performed, can only furnish a very impure spirit of wine, mixed with several of the other principles of the wine employed Thus aqua-vitæ contains much superabundant water, and much oil of wine, substances entirely foreign to what is properly called spirit of wine

These heterogeneous matters contained in aqua vitæ prevent it from being employed in chemical operations. To purify it, and change it into spirit of wine, it must be again distilled and rectified *See* SPIRIT *of* WINE

LXXIII AQUILA ALBA (*c*)

LXXIV ARBOR DIANÆ The arbor Dianæ is the result of a chemical operation by which particles of silver, previously dissolved in nitrous acid, are capable of arranging themselves in the form of a shrub Chemists have called this *Arbor Dianæ*, from the silver which they also call Diana or the Moon The following process given by Lemeri for making the arbor Dianæ succeeds well

" Take an ounce of fine silver, dissolve it in a sufficient quantity of spirit of " nitre, very pure and moderately strong, mix this solution of silver in a mat- " trass with about twenty ounces of distilled water, add to this mixture two " ounces of mercury, and let the whole remain at rest During a space of about " forty days, a kind of silver tree will be formed upon the mercury, with " branches resembling vegetable ramifications "

As this process is very long, we shall here add another much shorter, taken from a memoir of Mr Homberg, and quoted by Mr Baron, in his edition of Lemeri's Chemistry

" Make an amalgam without heat, of four drams of filings of silver, or, still " better, of silver-leaf, and of two drams of mercury (*See* AMALGAM), dis- " solve this amalgam in four ounces, or a sufficient quantity, of spirit of nitre " pure and moderately strong, dilute this solution in about a pound and a half " of distilled water, shake the mixture, and preserve it in a bottle with a glass- " stopper when this preparation is to be used, an ounce of it is to be put into a " phial together with about the size of a pea of an amalgam of gold or of silver, " which ought to be soft as butter, and the whole is to remain at rest soon " afterwards, small filaments are to be seen issuing from the small amalgam, " which quickly encrease, branch out on both sides, and take the form of " shrubs "

This experiment, which is generally considered merely as curious and amusing, is founded on many of the essential properties of the substances employed As mercury has a stronger affinity than silver to nitrous acid, it obliges this metal to separate and precipitate But in this precipitation there are two essential particulars the first is the color of the silver precipitated, which on this occasion appears in its natural form and metallic brilliancy The cause of this is, that it was precipitated by a metallic substance, for it appears, that in general this happens whenever one metal is precipitated by another metal, whereas

(*c*) AQUILA ALBA is a name given to sweet mercury. *See* MERCURY (SWEET)

metals precipitated by any other substance are always in form of calxes, or earthy precipitates, without any metallic appearance. See PRECIPITATION.

The second remark to be made on the precipitation of silver in this experiment is, the singular arrangement taken by the particles of silver on the surface of the mercury one after another, according as they are separated from the nitrous acid. We cannot but perceive in this phenomenon a very sensible effect of the attraction or affinity of the integrant parts of the same substance, or of two similar substances to each other. In fact, it can only proceed from this affinity which the particles of silver first separated from the nitrous acid have with the mercury, that they rather attach themselves to the surface of that metallic substance, than to any part of the vessel or of the liquor; and it also proceeds from this tendency which the particles of silver have to each other, that those which are afterwards separated from the nitrous acid adhere to the particles already attached to the mercury, and to each other, rather than to any other body.

As to the necessary conditions for this experiment of the arbor Dianæ, it has been already recommended to employ very pure silver, nitrous acid, and water, because the greatest part of the extraneous matters with which these substances are generally mixed, are capable of precipitating the silver, which in the present experiment ought not to be separated but by mercury. See SILVER, and PARTING.

In the second place, it is absolutely necessary to dilute in much water the solution of silver; 1. To avoid the formation of crystals of silver, which might take place if this solution was too concentrated, these being a crystallization of silver in a saline state, very different from the arbor Dianæ which is required. See CRYSTALS of SILVER. 2. Because if the solution of silver was concentrated, the particles of silver would be precipitated too fast, and in too great quantity, by which they would be prevented from applying themselves regularly to each other, and would be thrown down confusedly.

In the third place, it is necessary that the nitrous acid should be saturated with silver before it is diluted with water, otherwise the unsaturated part of the acid must first dissolve its proper quantity of silver or mercury, before the precipitation can take place, which would lengthen the experiment so much more, as the quantity of water with which the solution was diluted was greater.

LXXV. ARCANUM CORALLINUM. This is nothing else than *red precipitate*, on which spirit of wine has been two or three times burnt, with an intention of rendering it milder. See PRECIPITATE (RED).

LXXVI. ARCANUM DUPLICATUM. This Latin name, which signifies *the double secret*, is one of the most generally known salts. It is the salt composed of vitriolic acid united with vegetable fixed alkali, and therefore does not differ from the *Sal de duobus*, and *vitriolated tartar*. See TARTAR (VITRIOLATED).

LXXVII. ARCHIL. *(d)*

(d) ARCHIL, ARCHILLA, ROCELLA, or ORSEILLE, is a white moss which grows in the Canary and Cape de Verd islands, and according to Linnæus, on the western coast of England. From this plant is prepared by grinding and moistening with volatile alkali, a beautiful purple dye, which is not durable, but is chiefly used to give a bloom as it is called,

LXXVIII ARGENTUM MUSIVUM (e)

LXXIX ARRACK (f)

LXXX ARSENIC Arsenic, or *white arsenic*, is, properly speaking, nothing but the flowers or calx of regulus of arsenic

This substance has singular properties, which render it the only one of its kind

It is at once a metallic earth and a saline substance It resembles all metallic calxes in its capacity of combining with phlogiston, and of being thereby changed into a true semimetal

But it very essentially differs from all metallic calxes and earths

1 In being constantly volatile, whereas all other calxes of metals, and even of the most volatile semimetals, are very fixed when deprived of phlogiston

2 Metallic calxes, so far from being soluble in water, are even for the most part indissoluble in the strongest acids White arsenic, on the contrary, is soluble, not only in all acids, but also in water itself, as saline matters are

According to Mr Brandt, (*Acta Eruditorum Upsal de Semimetallis*, 1733) arsenic may be dissolved in fourteen or fifteen times its weight of water, by help of a boiling heat, and transparent yellow crystals may be obtained by evaporating this solution

3 Metallic calxes, when perfectly calcined, (the calx of the regulus of antimony not excepted) are entirely free from smell, taste, or other action upon the human body On the contrary, arsenic always preserves a strong alliaceous smell, and when put on the tongue, it excites an impression of acrimony and heat, which produces an involuntary spitting, when taken internally, or even when applied externally, it produces the most terrible and violent effects of a corrosive poison

4 No kind of earth, nor even the metallic earths, can contract an union with metallic substances Arsenic easily unites with all metals and semimetals, with the same degrees of affinity that the regulus of antimony does, that is to say, in the order following, according to Mr Cramer Iron, copper, tin, lead, silver, gold

It is proper to observe, that arsenic renders all the metals with which it is united brittle It renders gold of a greyish color in its broken surface, silver of a deep grey, and copper white Tin becomes by mixture with arsenic much harder and more unfusible Lead becomes very hard and very brittle, and it changes iron into a blackish mass These observations are taken from Mr. Brandt's Memoir quoted above

called, to other colors By adding solution of tin to an infusion of archil in water, a durable scarlet dye is produced, as Mr Hellot says The color of archil may be extracted by water, by volatile spirits, or by spirit of wine It loses its color in glass tubes hermetically sealed, and resumes it upon exposure to air A solution of archil in water gives a permanent and deep stain of a purplish color to marble

(e) ARGENTUM MUSIVUM or MOSAICUM is a mass consisting of silver-like flakes, used for the coloring of plaster figures, and for other purposes, as a pigment It consists of an amalgam of equal parts of tin, bismuth, and mercury It is to be mixed with white of eggs, or spirit varnish, and then applied to the intended work, which is afterwards to be burnished

(f) ARRACK is a vinous spirit obtained by distillation in the East-Indies, from rice or sugar, as is said, fermented with the juice of cocoa nuts.

5 The more metallic calxes are deprived of phlogiston, the more unfusible they are rendered On the contrary arsenic is always very fusible Its volatility alone prevents its perfect fusion It volatilizes, vitrifies, and scorifies all solid bodies, excepting gold, silver, and platina

6 Earths and metallic calxes have no action upon nitre, which (as is observed under the article *Nitre)* can be decomposed only by phlogiston, by vitriolic acid, and by sedative salt Arsenic decomposes nitre with the greatest facility, not by combining with and destroying its acid, as phlogiston does, but by disengaging it, and uniting in its place with the alkali, as the vitriolic acid and sedative salt do

Stahl and Kunkel both knew this property which arsenic possesses of decomposing nitre, and of disengaging its acid

Stahl directs how to prepare by means of arsenic a very volatile nitrous acid, extremely concentrated, of a penetrating fetid smell, and blue color, although its vapors are red This color, according to Mr Beaumé's observation, is caused by the water which must necessarily be put in the receiver to condense the vapors of this very strong and difficultly condensible acid

Kunkel also directs to make an aqua-fortis similar to that of Stahl, but by a much clearer and simpler process, since he decomposes nitre by arsenic alone, whereas Stahl employs in his mixture a martial vitriol calcined till it becomes red, and does not use pure arsenic, but a combination of equal parts of arsenic with antimony and sulphur, a combination which the chemists have called *Pirimeson*, or *Lapis de tribus*

These two chemists contented themselves with examining the properties of the spirit of nitre, which they procured by means of arsenic, and nobody had examined the residuum in the retort after distillation

This matter, being worthy of attention, has been resumed by Mr Macquer, who has particularly examined the decomposition of nitre in close vessels by arsenic, and the new kind of salt remaining in the retort after the distillation of the nitrous acid

These researches, the detail of which has been given in two memoirs printed in the collection of the academy, discovered to him that arsenic, by combining with the basis of nitre, after having chased the acid from it, forms with this alkali a kind of salt perfectly neutral, which he has called *neutral arsenical Salt* *See* SALT (NEUTRAL ARSENICAL)

Another decomposition of nitre by arsenic was known by chemists, and consequently also another combination of arsenic with the basis of nitre, called by some chemists, *Arsenic fixed by Nitre*, or *Nitre fixed by Arsenic*, but this latter combination differs from the arsenical salt of Mr Macquer in this, that it is not a neutral salt, and that it preserves, on the contrary, all the properties of an alkali *See* NITRE FIXED *by* ARSENIC

Mr Macquer has also made another combination of arsenic with deliquiated fixed alkali Mention is made of it also under the article *Salt (Neutral Arsenical)* There the differences are shewn betwixt these two combinations, although formed of the same substances

White arsenic, although very volatile, is partly fixed by the adhesion which it contracts with different sorts of earths, and even so far as to sustain a vitrifying heat It facilitates the fusion of many refractory matters, hence it enters into the composition

composition of several glasses, to which it gives much whiteness and clearness, nearly in the same manner as borax and the sedative salt do but it also has the same inconvenience, namely, that glass, in which a considerable portion of arsenic enters, is very quickly corroded by the air

Dyers employ white arsenic in several of their operations, but the effects it produces are not yet well known, and require a particular examination Arsenic and its regulus, being capable of combining with all metals, is employed for several metallic compositions, such, for instance, as *white copper*, and *white tombac* See these words

Arsenic is employed successfully for making, together with copper and tin, metallic compounds of a beautiful white color, and of a very dense and close texture, and consequently capable of receiving a fine polish, of reflecting well the rays of light, and of being formed into metallic mirrors

From what has been said concerning the properties of arsenic, we may conjecture that this substance is a metallic earth of a particular nature, intimately combined with a saline and even acid principle, which has never been separated from it by any chemical trial, which accompanies it in its combination with phlogiston when it takes a metallic form, and which adheres to it when, by the burning of this phlogiston, it becomes again white arsenic

Thus Becker, without having been acquainted with all the properties of white arsenic, gives an idea of it very analogous to this conjecture He defines it in his *Subterranean Physics*, "a substance composed of the earth of sulphur which "is in common salt," (by which he seems to mean the acid of sea salt) "and "of a metal joined to it" In another place, he calls it "a coagulated aqua-fortis" And as he imagined he could trace every where his mercurial earth, or at least something mercurial, he calls mercury a fluid arsenic He considers mercury and metals precipitated by marine acid, for instance, *luna cornea*, as different kinds of artificial arsenic

Arsenic combines with sulphur, and forms with it a compound of a yellowish tinge, more or less red according to the quantity of sulphur with which it is united It is of a beautiful yellow color when the sulphur is only a tenth part of the mixture, and is then called *yellow arsenic* when the sulphur is a fifth part of the mixture, it is of a very beautiful red color, and it is then called *red arsenic* The mixture of sulphur renders it a little more fixed and more fusible Thus red arsenic may be melted, and by this means acquires transparency it then resembles a ruby, and has therefore been called *Ruby of sulphur*, or *arsenical ruby*

All these compounds of arsenic and sulphur are artificial They are prepared by mixing and subliming these two substances together in the proportions abovementioned, or, still better, in subliming together the sulphur and arsenic of minerals containing these two substances

Natural compounds are also found, which are combinations of sulphur and of arsenic, nearly of the same colors as the red and yellow artificial arsenics They come from the East, from Transylvania, and Turkey The yellow are called *orpiment*, *orpin*, and *yellow rizagal* the red are called *sandaracl*, *realgar*, or *red rizigal*

Agricola, Mathiole, Schroder, seem to have confounded the red and yellow artificial arsenics with the native, and after them most chemists and naturalists have alſo confounded them, a confuſion for which they have been reproached by Hoffman, chiefly becauſe he was convinced that native orpiment and realgars are not poiſonous, like the yellow and red artificial arſenics, from experiments which he had made on purpoſe.

On this ſubject we muſt remark, that, notwithſtanding Hoffman's experiments, which were made only once or twice upon dogs, it would be very imprudent to give the native orpiment or realgars internally particularly as all chemical trials ſhow that they contain an arſenical principle, and that Hoffman himſelf agrees, that when they have been expoſed to fire, they become very violent poiſons

Hoffman alſo remarks, that the ancient phyſicians did not ſcruple to give internally orpiment and realgar, and juſtifies them from the reproaches thrown upon them by moderns But we muſt obſerve, that the ancients were unacquainted with white, red, and yellow arſenics, which have been well known only within theſe two hundred years, and that if they had known the effects of theſe poiſons, and their reſemblance to the native orpiments and realgars, they would probably have been leſs bold Diſtruſt is as commendable as boldneſs is blameable in thoſe matters, the almoſt inſenſible differences of which may occaſion the moſt troubleſome accidents For this reaſon, we cannot approve of the ſingular ſecurity with which ſo great a phyſician, as Hoffman was, endeavors to inſpire a confidence for ſo ſuſpicious drugs as native orpiment and realgar

We do not however mean to ſay, that there is no eſſential difference betwixt native orpiment and yellow arſenic It is even agreed that the arſenic contained in the orpiment is better united with the ſulphur, and is beſides in a leſs proportion for one part of orpiment appears to be compoſed of a ſparry ſtone and mica, from which it receives a foliated and ſhining form

When arſenic is combined with ſulphur, a part of the ſulphur may be ſeparated from it merely by ſublimation, becauſe it is more volatile But ſome of the ſulphur always remains united with the arſenic, from which it cannot be ſeparated but by an intermediate ſubſtance

Fixed alkali and mercury are two intermediate ſubſtances proper for this operation

When fixed alkali is uſed, it muſt previouſly be deliquiated or reſolved into a liquid, and with this the ſulphurated arſenic is to be made into a paſte This paſte is to be ſublimed in a proper veſſel with a heat gradually raiſed The arſenic then ſublimes in white flowers When too much alkali is added, leſs arſenic is obtained becauſe ſome of the arſenic is retained by the part of the alkali which is unſaturated with ſulphur A liver of ſulphur is found at the bottom of the veſſel after the operation.

When mercury is employed for this ſeparation, it muſt be triturated and mixed with the ſulphurated arſenic, and the mixture ſublimed Firſt the arſenic riſes, then cinnabar All the metallic matters which have a ſtronger affinity than mercury to ſulphur may ſeem capable of being employed for this purpoſe, but there are two objections

1 They have alſo a conſiderable affinity with arſenic, and mercury has none

2. Arſenic

2 Arsenic has the remarkable property of taking from all metallic matters, excepting gold, silver, and mercury, a part of their phlogiston, so that it would be sublimed half regulified

In the operation by mercury, a part of the cinnabar frequently rises with the arsenic, which makes it necessary to sublime it a second time

Arsenic is soluble in all acids, and with them forms combinations which have not yet been sufficiently examined The vitriolic acid has the property of rendering it much more fixed than it naturally is an effect which it also produces upon mercury

If a mixture of arsenic and concentrated vitriolic acid be distilled together, a vitriolic acid is obtained, which, as Mr Macquer observes, has sometimes the exact smell of marine acid When this solution is distilled till no more acid rises, the retort is then almost red-hot, and no arsenic is sublimed, but it remains fused at the bottom of the retort, and when it is cold, it is found to be one heavy, compact mass, brittle and transparent as crystal glass This kind of arsenical glass exposed to the air soon loses its lustre from the moisture it attracts, which dissolves and partly deliquiates it This deliquium is extremely acid

Arsenic treated with phlogiston in a proper manner combines with it, and assumes all the properties of a very volatile semi-metal, of a white shining color more or less upon the grey This substance is called *Regulus of Arsenic* *See this word for the manner of making this regulus, and for its properties*

The arsenic sold in commerce is brought chiefly from the cobalt works in Saxony for making *Zaffer*, and *Smalt* Cobalt contains much arsenic, which must be separated from it by a long torrefaction, and which would be lost but for a particular contrivance for the collecting it

For this purpose, cobalt is roasted in a vaulted oven, to which is adjusted a long crooked chimney The arsenic in vapors passes along this chimney, and is there collected, the arsenic which attaches itself to the coldest and most distant part of the chimney is in form of a white or grey powder, called *Flowers*, or *Meal of Arsenic*, whereas that part of the arsenic which adheres to the hottest part of the chimney, and least remote from the furnace, sustains there a kind of fusion by which it is reduced into compact, heavy, white masses resembling white enamel These masses of white arsenic are almost always interrupted by yellow or greyish veins and strata These colors proceed from a little sulphur or phlogiston with which this part of the arsenic is still united.

As arsenic is seldom obtained in the great works entirely free from sulphureous or phlogistical particles, if it be required perfectly pure in operations of chemistry or of arts, it must be again sublimed after mixing it with some intermediate substance capable of absorbing its inflammable parts, such as fixed alkali or absorbent earth

Arsenic is a very violent corrosive poison it produces always the most painful symptoms and fatal effects, whether it be taken internally or applied externally It ought never to be employed medicinally, although some people, not very intelligent, give small doses of it in obstinate intermittent fevers, which it effectually cures, but is always attended with bad consequences to the patients, such as phthisis, and other no less troublesome diseases

Persons

Persons poisoned by arsenic suffer acute pains in their bowels, violent vomitings, cold sweats, syncopes, and convulsions, which are always followed by death, unless prevented by speedy remedies The best antidotes to this poison are large quantities of diluting and softening drinks, as mucilages, oil, milk Perhaps absorbent and alkaline matters would also produce good effects, from the property which arsenic has of combining with, and in some measure of being neutralized by, these substances

When the bodies of persons killed by arsenic are examined, their stomachs and intestines are found covered with red, black, livid, inflamed and gangrenous spots Frequently also arsenic is found there in substance, which may easily be distinguished by its alliaceous smell, when put on burning coals, or a red-hot iron

Mr Geoffry's table does not shew the affinities of arsenic In Mr Gellert's they are zinc, iron, copper, tin, lead, silver, gold, and regulus of antimony *(g)*

LXXXI ASA-FŒTIDA *(h)*

LXXXII ASBESTUS *(i)*

LXXXIII ASHES This name is generally applied to the substance remaining of bodies containing an inflammable matter, of which they have been deprived by burning, or calcination in open air Thus workmen, without understanding chemistry, and induced merely by analogy or resemblance, apply

(g) Neuman relates that arsenic precipitated almost all metallic solutions, but most of them very slowly Silver, iron, copper, tin, lead, mercury, bismuth, were precipitated from aqua fortis, and gold from aqua regia Solutions of mercury corrosive sublimate, of copper in aqua regia, of zinc in aqua-fortis, and of regulus of antimony suffered no precipitation Solutions in vitriolic acid of zinc and of iron were precipitated, of copper very little Sugar of lead, and solutions of sulphur with quicklime or fixed alkali were precipitated The same author further relates, that arsenic was not precipitated from its solution in vitriolic or nitrous acids by oil of tartar or by volatile alkali, but it was precipitated from marine acid by oil of tartar

Arsenic is used for many purposes, by dyers, as an ingredient in compositions for scarlets and other fine reds, by goldsmiths, for enamelling, by makers of glass, for promoting the fusion of fritt, and the clearness and transparency of glass, by potters, for a white glazing, by essayers, in form of glass, for promoting the scorification of ores which contain tin and antimony, for the preparation of compound metals, and for whitening copper and brass *Neuman* says, that a beautiful metal like the finest steel may be made by melting cast iron with arsenic, glass, and a little tin, and that a metal resembling silver may be made from iron, tin, arsenic, and perhaps a little copper Mr Brandt (*Act Upsal* 1733) proposes to make a varnish for ships, of arsenic with pitch, sulphur, or rosin, to preserve the timber from rotting, and from worms

(h) ASA-FOETIDA is a gum-resin, from four ounces of which rectified spirit is capable of extracting two ounces six drams and a half of resinous extract, and water, one ounce three scruples and a half of gummy extract Four ounces of asa-fœtida, distilled either with water or with spirit, yielded above a dram of essential oil, in which its peculiar smell resides *Neuman*

(i) ASBESTUS is a grey, greenish or blackish stone, possessed of the same chemical properties as amianthus, and is therefore referable to the same class of earths. *See* AMIANTHUS The chief differences betwixt those two stones are, that asbestus is heavier than amianthus, and its fibres are more hard and brittle

False asbestus is a name given to plume-alum *See* ALUM (PLUME)

the

the name of *ashes* to metallic earths thus calcined Pewterers, for example, give the name *Tin-ashes*, to the earth of this metal which in fusion has been deprived of its phlogiston and metallic properties If workmen had always applied names as properly as they have done this, they could not have been blamed *See* COMBUSTION

LXXXIV ASH-HOLE The ash hole is the lowest part of a furnace, and is intended to receive the ashes falling from the fire, and to give a passage to the air which is to be introduced into the furnace, to keep up the combustion *See* FURNACE

LXXXV ATHANOR Chemists have distinguished by this name a furnace so constructed that it can always maintain an equal heat, and which shall last a long time without addition of fresh fuel

The body of the athanor has nothing in it particular, and is constructed like ordinary furnaces But at one of its sides, or its middle, there is an upright hollow tower, which communicates with the fire-place by one or more sloping openings This tower ought to have a lid which exactly closes its upper opening

When the athanor is to be used, as much lighted coal is put in the fire-place as is judged necessary, and the tower is filled to the top with unlighted fuel The tower is then to be exactly closed with its lid. As fast as the coal in the fire-place is consumed, that in the tower falls down and supplies its place As the coal contained in the tower has no free communication with the external air, it cannot burn till it falls into the fire-place

The athanor being much celebrated and used by ancient chemists, it has been particularly described by many authors, and was formerly found in all laboratories At present this furnace is much less employed, and is even neglected The reason of this is, that all the ancient chemists were in search of the art of making gold, and being excited by this powerful desire, and confidence of success, they spared no trouble nor expence to accomplish their design They undertook without hesitation, operations which required great length of time and unremitted heat Whereas now, these alluring hopes having vanished, the cultivators of chemistry have no other view than to extend and perfect the theory of this essential part of natural philosophy This motive, although undoubtedly much nobler than the former, seems however to be less powerful over most men For now, all long and laborious operations whence chemistry might receive great advantages, are neglected, as being tiresome and disgustful There is, in fact, a considerable difference betwixt the hope of explaining a philosophical phenomenon, and that of obtaining an ingot of gold capable of producing many others Hence the instruments employed in long operations, and particularly the athanor, are now much neglected , and also because the fuel in the tower is apt to stick there or fall down at once in too great quantity. The *Lamp-furnace*, which is a true athanor, may be successfully employed in operations which do not require much heat *See* FURNACE (LAMP). (*k*)

LXXXVI AURUM MOSAICUM (*l*)

LXXXVII AZURE The word azure, which at present signifies in general a fine blue color, was formerly appropriated to *Lapis Lazuli*, called

(*k*) *See* PLATES.

azure-stone, and to the blue prepared from it But since a blue has been extracted from cobalt, custom has applied to it the name of azure, although it differs considerably from the former, and is incapable of being used for the same purposes, and particularly for painting in oil. The former at present is called *Lapis Lazuli*, or only *lapis*, and the blue prepared from it for painting in oil, is called *Ultramarine*

The name *azure* is generally applied to the blue glass made from the earth of cobalt and vitrifiable matters This glass, which is called *Smalt* when in masses, is called azure only when it is reduced to a fine powder Several kinds of azure are distinguished, according to its degrees of beauty, by the names of *Fine Azure*, *Powdered Azure*, and *Azure of Four Fires* In general, the greater the intensity of color and the fineness of powder, the more beautiful and dear it is Azure is employed to color starch, hence it has also been called *Starch-Blue* It is used for painting with colors and for a blue enamel *See* COBALT, SMALT, ZAFFRE *See also* LAPIS LAZULI.

(*l*) AURUM MOSAICUM, or MUSIVUM, is a mass consisting of beautiful gold colored flakes, prepared by amalgamating tin with half its quantity of mercury, mixing this amalgam when cold with half its quantity of sal ammoniac, and the same quantity of flowers of sulphur, and by exposing the whole mixture to fire in a matrass, by which means a sal ammoniac and cinnabar will be sublimed, and the residuum is the aurum mosaicum, or mosaic gold, weighing about $\frac{1}{12}$ more than the tin originally employed It is used as a pigment and for mixing with glass to imitate the spangles of lapis lazuli, for which latter purpose shining talk is also employed.

B.

LXXXVIII BALANCE (HYDROSTATICAL) The hydroſtatical balance is an inſtrument by which the ſpecific gravity of bodies is determined. For this purpoſe it is neceſſary to find how much any given weight of a body, whoſe ſpecific gravity is required, loſes of its abſolute gravity when plunged into a fluid. All liquid ſubſtances are proper to determine ſpecific gravities, becauſe theſe gravities are only relative but water has been generally employed for this purpoſe, becauſe it is the moſt common liquid, and moſt conſtantly of a nearly uniform weight

When a body is to be weighed in water, it is ſuſpended to one of the arms of a balance, to the other arm of which is fixed an ordinary ſcale, and in this ſcale weights are to be put ſufficient to maintain an equilibrium with the body ſuſpended in air The weight neceſſary for this purpoſe is to be obſerved and remembered. Then the ſame body ſtill ſuſpended at the arm of the balance, and counterpoiſed by the weights in the ſcale, is to be immerſed in water, by which the equilibrium is deſtroyed, and the balance inclines to the ſide of the weights. The weights are therefore to be diminiſhed till an equilibrium is reſtored with the body ſunk entirely in water The difference betwixt the weights of the ſame body weighed in air and in water, determines its ſpecific gravity.

It is proper to obſerve upon this ſubject, 1 That water can determine the ſpecific gravity of bodies only which are ſpecifically heavier than itſelf For it is certain, that if they were lighter than water they could not ſink in it by their own weight, which is neceſſary for the experiment. In this caſe it is neceſſary to employ ſome liquid lighter than water ſuch as ethereal oils, ſpirit of wine, or ether

2 It is proper to remark on the ſubject of the hydroſtatical balance, that it can be employed conveniently for ſolid bodies only, becauſe the fluids cannot be weighed in water but by means of ſome veſſel which muſt be immerſed along with them But this veſſel having its peculiar ſpecific gravity would render a troubleſome calculation neceſſary Another method is then generally uſed to determine the ſpecific gravity of liquids

3 If the ſolid body, whoſe ſpecific gravity is to be determined, be ſoluble in water, as, for inſtance, a lump of ſalt, water could not be employed for this experiment, becauſe a quantity of it would be diſſolved during the time of weighing, by which an error would be occaſioned ſo much greater as there was more

of

of the soluble body dissolved. In this case then it is necessary to use some other liquid which cannot dissolve the body, or else not to employ the hydrostatical balance, but the same method by which the specific gravity of liquids is discovered. *See* GRAVITY, GRAVITY (ABSOLUTE), GRAVITY (SPECIFIC).

LXXXIX. BALLS (MARTIAL). Martial Balls are a mixture of filings of iron and of cream of tartar formed into a solid consistence and form of a ball, which is used to impregnate water or other liquids with iron dissolved by the tartareous acid. To make these balls, one part of filings of iron and two parts of powdered cream of tartar are mixed well together, and put into an earthen or iron vessel with some water. This mixture is to be stirred from time to time, till it becomes almost dry, and then it is to receive more water, and to be stirred as before. This treatment is to be continued till it acquires, when nearly dry, somewhat of the consistence and tenacity of softened rosin. Then it is to be rolled up into the form of a ball, which is generally kept tyed up in a rag, and when intended to be used, it is to be infused in water, till it gives some color to that liquid.

The infusion of martial balls is tonic, vulnerary, discutient, and aperitive, and is employed both internally and externally. *See* IRON.

Iron being soluble in all acids, is attacked in this preparation by the tartareous acid, which reduces it to a kind of neutral salt not crystallizable. This salt would remain liquid, and would form a *soluble martial tartar*, called *Tartarised Tincture of Mars*. If proper proportions of filings of iron and cream of tartar be used, and treated long enough for an entire and complete combination, nothing would be obtained but a liquor or *magma*, which could not be preserved in a solid form, but would be continually moist. Therefore in the martial ball there is a good deal of the cream of tartar and filings of iron not combined together, by which its solidity is preserved.

Hence it follows that the infusion of the martial ball is entirely of the same nature as the tartarised tincture of Mars, and therefore these preparations may be substituted for each other. *See* TINCTURE *of* MARS (TARTARISED).

XC. BALLS (MERCURIAL). Mercurial balls are an amalgam of mercury and tin, sufficiently solid to be moulded, and to preserve a given form.

The method of making them is by adding mercury to melted tin, and pouring the fluid mass into a round and hollow mould.

These balls are employed to purify water, in which they are boiled, for which purpose travellers often carry some along with them.

XCI. BALLOON. This name is given to glass bottles, or receivers, which are generally round like hollow spheres, or like foot-balls, called in French, *Balons*, whence they are named.

In a laboratory there ought to be balloons of different sizes, capable of containing from a quart of water to fifteen or twenty pints. The large balloons are employed in distillations in great, being capable of containing much, and having necks wide enough to admit those of large retorts. For the contrary reasons, small balloons are employed when a little matter is to be distilled.

Large balloons are also necessary when the vapors disengaged during the distillation are very elastic and difficult to be condensed, because such vapors would not

not find in small vessels sufficient space to circulate and condense; hence they would either burst the vessel, or if a vent was given them to prevent that accident, they would be entirely dissipated and lost Notwithstanding the size of the balloons employed, so much air is disengaged during the distillation of certain hard bodies, vegetable and animal, such as wood, tartar, hartshorn, &c and the vapors of certain acids, such as the smoking spirits of nitre and of sea-salt, are so elastic and expansible, that a small hole in the side of the balloon is necessary to give vent to those vapors when necessary Afterwards this hole, which ought to be about half a line in diameter, is to be closed with a peg of wood, or some lute

It is to be wished, that in the glass-houses where chemical vessels are made, it was the custom always to make such holes in the balloons, which might easily be done by a pointed instrument, while the glass is still hot and soft Instead of this practice, chemists are themselves obliged to drill holes through the balloons with considerable difficulty and hazard of breaking This operation is performed in the following manner

The most convenient part for drilling this hole is nearer the neck than the bottom of the balloon, and for this purpose one of those bubbles which are always found in glass is chosen

This bubble is first of all cut or broke by the pointed angle of a flint, and afterwards the hole is to be completed by turning this pointed flint always in the same place. Mr Beaumé observes, that when an entry is once made by the flint, the hole may be better finished by a triangular drill with a strong hard tempered steel point, because the angular points of the flint are continually breaking, by which the operation is prolonged (m)

For certain operations balloons with two necks placed opposite to each other are used One of these ought to be large enough to receive the neck of the retort, and the other to enter the neck of a second balloon. These two joinings must be well luted together *See* LUTE

This apparatus is called *Enfiladed Balloons* Their use is to encrease the whole space of the receiver, because any number of these may be adjusted to each other, and as they communicate with each other, their capacity is so much larger as their number is greater But good artists seldom use so troublesome an apparatus The only one of these vessels which is generally used, is a small oblong balloon with two necks, which is to be luted to the retort and to the great balloon It serves to remove this receiver from the body of the furnace, and to hinder it from being exposed to too great heat This small balloon with two necks is called an *Adopter* As this adopter is larger in its middle than at either extremity, it serves also to receive solid bodies, and to prevent them from passing with the liquids into the great balloon It is chiefly in distillations of volatile concrete salts that the adopter serves for this last purpose. *See* DISTILLATION and RECEIVER

(m) Such pierced balloons, receivers and retorts are commonly made in English glass-houses But as chemists may have occasion to drill holes through glass vessels, we shall observe, that this operation may be best performed with a copper drill and emery, as a steel instrument occasions vibrations apt to break the glass.

XCI BALSAM. By balsams are meant oily, odoriferous, and aromatic matters, liquid, but somewhat thick, which flow spontaneously from certain trees, or from incisions made on purpose to obtain a larger quantity.

These balsams, which may more particularly be called *natural balsams*, to distinguish them from some compositions also called balsams, derive their liquidity and smell from a greater or less quantity of essential oil which they contain, and which may be extracted by distillation with the heat of boiling water. *See* OILS (ESSENTIAL)

Balsams may be even considered as true essential oils, which have lost some of their odoriferous principle, and of their finest and most volatile part When they are deprived of their remaining part of volatile oil, their residuums exactly resemble those which remain after the rectification of essential oils These residuums are true resins, from the analysis of which the same principles are obtained as from natural resins, and these last are nothing but balsams exhausted by time, or by the action of the air, and of the sun, of all their odoriferous and volatile parts

There are several kinds of natural balsams They do not essentially differ from each other, but only in the smell and degrees of consistence The same kind of balsam also frequently differs with respect to the degrees of these two qualities.

The principal natural balsams are the *balsam of Mecca*, or the *white balsam*, which is the most rare and dear of all, the *balsams of Tolu* and of *Peru in shells*, both which Mr Beaumé considers as the same kind of balsam, with this difference, that the first is liquid, and the second is almost dry, the *balsam of Copahu*, or of *Copaiba*, vulgarly *Capivi*, *liquid styrax*, or *storax*, and *turpentines* *See for an example of the analysis and properties of all these balsams the word* TURPENTINE

XCII. BALSAM *of* SULPHUR The balsam of sulphur is a solution of sulphur in oil

Sulphur, from the quantity of phlogiston it contains, is insoluble in water and aqueous liquors but it is capable of dissolving in oils, which also contain much phlogiston

All oils, either expressed or essential, can dissolve sulphur to make this solution, the oil ought to be poured on the sulphur in a matrass placed in a sand-bath, and sufficient heat applied to melt the sulphur, according to Mr Beaumé's observation, who kept these two substances a very long time together in a less heat, without perceiving any sign of solution

While the oil is dissolving the sulphur, it acquires a reddish or brown color, an acrid and disagreeable taste, and a strong fetid smell like that of the combination of oil with vitriolic acid

As water can dissolve only a determinate quantity of some salts, and as this quantity is greater when the water is warm than when cold, so also oils can dissolve only a determinate quantity of sulphur, and this quantity is greater when heat is applied hence it happens, that when an oil is saturated with sulphur, by a suitable heat, a part of the sulphur thus dissolved separates from the oil, when the solution cools, and coagulates at the bottom of the vessel in a crystallized form, in the same manner as some salts do, which having been dissolved in boiling water, crystallize on the application of cold

The

The portion of sulphur remaining dissolved in oil is in a singular state, the adhesion of its constituent parts, namely, the vitriolic acid and phlogiston, seems to be much diminished by the union they contract with the principles of the oil Its vitriolic acid unites with the watery part of this oil, and thus these two principles have no longer the necessary relation to each other for the formation of sulphur See SULPHUR

It is certain at least, that all these changes happen when the balsam of sulphur is distilled This is proved by the analysis which Homberg made of this combination for by distilling it with a very slow fire he obtained a volatile sulphureous acid, a vitriolic acid more or less strong and sulphureous, some oil, partly fluid and partly thick, and a charry residuum, but no sulphur This is a proof that the sulphur was decomposed in the experiment, as all the same products are obtained from a combination of vitriolic acid with oil, when the oil is in too great quantity relatively to the acid

The balsams of sulphur are named from the particular oils which enter into their composition Thus if a balsam of sulphur be made with the essential oil of turpentine, it is called *terebinthinated balsam of sulphur*, if it be made with the essential oil of aniseed, it is called the *balsam of sulphur with oil of aniseed* These are the two most used The balsam of sulphur made with oil of nuts is called *Rullond's balsam of sulphur* See SULPHUR

XCIII BASALTES (a)

XCIV BASIS, or BASE Any body which is dissolved by another body, which it receives and fixes, and with which it forms a compound, may be called the basis of that compound Thus, for example, the bases of neutral salts are the alkaline, earthy, and metallic matters which are saturated by the several acids, and form with them these neutral salts In this sense it is that these neutral salts are called *salts with earthy bases*, *salts with alkaline bases*, *salts with metallic bases*, also the appellations, *basis of alum*, *basis of nitre*, *basis of Glauber's salt*, *basis of vitriol*, &c. signify the *argillaceous earth*, which, with the vitriolic acid, forms alum, the *vegetable alkali*, which, with the nitrous acid, forms nitre, the *mineral alkali*, which, with the vitriolic acid, forms Glauber's salt, and the *metal*, which, with the vitriolic acid, forms a vitriol because these substances are supposed to be fixed, unactive, and only yielding to the action of the acids, which they fix, and to which they give a body and consistence

It is proper, for the conveniency of chemical language, to retain these expressions but these bases must not be considered as really unactive, for in every combination and solution the several bodies which unite are equally active, their action being reciprocal They dissolve each other, so that it is as proper to say, as Mr Gellert observes, that a metal or an earth dissolves an acid, as that an

(a) BASALTES is a heavy, hard stone, chiefly black or green, consisting of prismatic crystals, the number of the sides of which is uncertain It is called by English miners *cockle*, and by Germans *schorl*. Its specific gravity is to that of water, as 3000 or upwards to 1000 It is considered by Wallerius as a species of the *corneus*, or *horn rock* Cronstedt enumerates it among the earths which he called *Garnet earths* Basaltes frequently contains iron, and consists either of particles of an indeterminate figure, or of a sparry, striated, or fibrous texture Black basaltes is called *Lapis Lydius*, and is used as a touchstone to shew the colors of metals Basaltes has a flinty hardness, is unsoluble by acids, and is fusible by fire See GARNET.

acid dissolves a metal or an earth, although this latter mode of expression be more general. It is even probable that the dissolving power which the more weighty and fixed bodies have is really much stronger than that of bodies less weighty and fixed. This is certainly so if the tendency to unite be only an effect of the general attraction or gravitation of all particles of matter to each other. *See* COMBINATION and SOLUTION.

XCV. BATH. Chemists call several matters which they employ to transmit heat, *Baths*. The matters most frequently used for this purpose are water and sand.

When water is employed it is called *Balneum Mariæ*, or *water-bath*. The water bath is much used, and is convenient for many operations.

As water, when exposed to fire in any vessel from which it can evaporate, does only receive a determinate degree of heat, which always remains the same, when once it has arrived to the boiling heat, it follows, that by the water-bath a degree of heat always equal may with certainty be transmitted. Further, this degree of heat being incapable of burning, or of communicating an empyreumatic quality to matters susceptible of it, the water-bath has also the advantage of not exposing substances to this inconvenience. The water-bath may likewise be employed successfully for all degrees of heat inferior to that of boiling water. *See* ALEMBIC, *for the structure of the water bath.*

When vessels in which distillations and digestions are made, are placed in sand, then a *sand-bath* is formed. This intermediate substance is also very convenient to moderate the too great activity of the naked fire, and to transmit any degree of heat from the weakest to a red heat. As this bath is attended with less trouble, and requires less apparatus than the water-bath, it is much used in laboratories. For the sand-bath nothing is requisite but an earthen or iron vessel filled with fine sand. This vessel is fitted in to a furnace, and is capable of containing the cucurbits, retorts, matrasses, or other vessels containing the matter to be operated upon.

The only baths now generally used in chemistry are those mentioned, the water and sand-baths, because they are the most convenient, and are sufficient for all the operations which do not require a naked fire.

Ancient chemists, who had all a tincture, more or less, of alchemy, and who for that reason were much more careful and laborious in their operations, used many different baths, in order to apply precisely the required degree of heat. They used the vapor of water, ashes, dung, the substance remaining after the squeezing of grapes, and whatever they imagined most proper for their purposes: hence the names of *vapor-bath*, *ash-bath*, *dung-bath*, *bath of a horse's belly*, &c. But, as we have said, an intelligent and experienced artist may very well perform all the chemical operations, which do not require a naked fire, by means of the water and sand-baths. *See* DISTILLATION *and* DIGESTION.

The word *bath* is also used in another sense to signify the fusion of metallic matters in certain operations: thus, for example, in refining or cupelling, the metals are said to be *in bath*, when they are melted. When gold is purified by antimony, this semimetal melted is called by some chemists the *bath of gold*. Alchemists, who consider gold as the king of metals, call antimony, *the bath of the king only*, *balneum solius regis*, because, in fact, gold only can resist the action of antimony. *See* PURIFICATION *of* GOLD *by* ANTIMONY.

XCVI.

XCVI. BDELLIUM (*o*)

XCVII. BEE-GLUE (*p*)

XCVIII. BEER. Beer is a ſpirituous liquor made from any farinaceous grain, but generally from barley. It is, properly ſpeaking, the wine of barley. The meals of any of theſe grains being extracted by a ſufficient quantity of water, and remaining at reſt in a degree of heat requiſite for the ſpirituous fermentation, naturally undergo this fermentation, and are changed into a vinous liquor. But as all theſe matters render the water mucilaginous, fermentation proceeds ſlowly and imperfectly in theſe liquors. On the other ſide, if the quantity of farinaceous matter be ſo diminiſhed that its extract or decoction may have a convenient degree of fluidity, this liquor will be impregnated with ſo ſmall a quantity of fermentable matter, that the beer or wine of the grain will be too weak, and have too little taſte.

Theſe inconveniences are remedied by preliminary operations which the grain is made to undergo.

Theſe preparations conſiſt in ſteeping it in cold water that it may ſoak and ſwell to a certain degree, and in laying it in a heap with a ſuitable degree of heat, by means of which, and of the imbibed moiſture, a germination begins, which is to be ſtopped by a quick drying, as ſoon as the bud ſhews itſelf. To accelerate this drying, and render it more compleat, the grain is ſlightly roaſted, by making it paſs down an inclined canal ſufficiently heated.

This germination, and this ſlight roaſting, changes conſiderably the nature of the mucilaginous fermentable matter of the grain. The germination attenuates much, and in ſome meaſure totally deſtroys the viſcoſity of the mucilage, and it does this, when not carried too far, without depriving the grain of any of its diſpoſition to ferment. On the contrary, it changes the grain into a saccharine ſubſtance, as may be perceived by maſhing grains beginning to germinate. The ſlight roaſting contributes alſo to attenuate the mucilaginous fermentable matter of the grain. When the grain is thus prepared, it is fit to be ground, and to impregnate water with much of its ſubſtance without forming a glue, or viſcous maſs. The grain thus prepared is called *malt*. This malt is then to be ground, and all its ſubſtance, which is fermentable and ſoluble in water, is to be extricated by means of hot water. This extract or infuſion is ſufficiently evaporated by boiling in caldrons, and ſome plant of an agreeable bitterneſs, ſuch as hops, is at that time added, to heighten the taſte of the beer, and to render it capable of being longer preſerved. Laſtly, this liquor is put into caſks, and allowed to ferment; nature performs the reſt of the work, and is only to be aſſiſted by the other moſt favorable circumſtances for the ſpirituous fermentation. *See* FERMENTATION (SPIRITUOUS).

XCIX. BEN (*q*)

(*o*) BDELLIUM is a gum reſin, from an ounce of which may be extracted by water ſix drams and two ſcruples, or by ſpirit two drams. *Neuman.*

(*p*) BEE-GLUE is a ſoft, unctuous, glutinous matter employed by bees to cement the combs to the hives, and to cloſe up the cells. *Neuman.*

(*q*) BEN-NUTS yield, by expreſſion, much oil, which, from its property of not becoming rancid, at leaſt for years, is uſed as a menſtruum for the extraction of the odoriferous part of flowers of jaſmin, violets, roſes, hyacinths, lillies of the valley, tuberoſes, jonquils, clove-july flowers, and others, which, like theſe, yield little or no

 eſſential

C. BENJAMIN *Benjamin*, or *Benzoin*, is a resin of an agreeable aromatic smell, from which an essential salt, or volatile, concrete, crystallized acid, called *flowers of Benjamin*, is obtained by sublimation. *See* FLOWERS *of* BENJAMIN As to its other principles, it is similar to other resins *See* RESIN

CI BERYL (*r*)

CII BEZOAR MINERAL Bezoar mineral is the earth of the regulus of antimony deprived of all its phlogiston by the action of the nitrous acid and by calcination

The ordinary process to make this preparation consists in dissolving butter of antimony in a sufficient quantity of nitrous acid, or till the phenomena of solution cease If more nitrous acid be added than is necessary for the solution, no inconvenience follows, as we shall presently see

When the solution of butter of antimony is made, it is to be evaporated to dryness in a glass or stone-ware vessel more nitrous acid is then to be poured upon it, rather too much than too little, because an excess of this does no harm this solution is to be evaporated, as at first, and the same operation is to be repeated a third time, after which the matter being dryed, is to be calcined for half an hour, till, according to Lemery, a very slight acidity only remains

This operation, which was invented for the preparation of a remedy, furnishes phenomena very worthy of attention, and fit to illustrate the essential properties of the nitrous and marine acids The following remarks then are to be made on this subject Aqua-regia being the most active menstruum of regulus of antimony, and spirit of nitre, in which the butter of antimony is dissolved, forming an aqua-regia with the marine acid contained in this butter, a new solution is made of the reguline part, which after this is no longer united with the marine acid only, but with the nitrous and marine acids jointly, that is, with aqua-regia. When this solution is not hurried too much, it is clear and limpid, and this is the best method of having the greatest possible quantity of regulus of antimony perfectly dissolved by aqua-regia

As upon this occasion, the nitrous acid finds the integrant parts of the regulus of antimony separated from each other by the interposition of the parts of the marine acid, and consequently the aggregation of the regulus of antimony broken, this nitrous acid seizes upon all the parts of the regulus with so much more facility and almost instantaneously hence it happens that unless the nitrous acid be gradually added, and at long intervals, the solution is made so impetuously, that all the matter is apt to rise instantly over the containing vessel with effervescence, which happens in most solutions, and which proceeds from disengaged air The

essential oil by distillation, but impart their fragrance to expressed oils The method of impregnating oil of ben with the odor of flowers is this Some fine carded cotton is dipt in the oil, and put in the bottom of a proper vessel On this is spread a thick layer of fresh flowers, above which more cotton dipt in oil is placed, and thus alternately flowers and cotton are disposed, till the vessel (which may be made of tin, with a cover to be screwed on to it, or of porcelain) is full By digestion during 24 hours in a water-bath, the oil will receive the odor of the flowers

(*r*) BERYL, or AQUA-MARINA, is a polygonous pellucid gem, the tenth from a diamond in hardness, of a sea green color, and fusible by fire This gem may be imitated by adding, at several different times, to twenty pounds of crystal-glass, made without magnesia, and well purified from glass-gall, six ounces of calcined brass or copper, and a quarter of an ounce of prepared zaffre

quantity

quantity of air in this solution is very great. Dr Hales has ascertained that thirty-six cubic inches of air are disengaged from the solution of half a cubic inch of butter of antimony in as much nitrous acid; but this must vary according to the manner of making the solution. Is it even certain that it is air which is thus disengaged, and not some other substance reduced to elastic vapor?

However it be, the new combination of regulus of antimony with the acids of aqua-regia is very different from the butter of antimony. The presence of the nitrous acid produces an entire change. This metallic substance is no longer united with a single acid, incapable of depriving it of its phlogiston, and which, by its intimate union, communicates to the semimetal its volatility. The nitrous acid cannot unite with the regulus of antimony without depriving it of a large portion of its inflammable principle. The regulus thus half calcined can no longer have the same adhesion to the marine acid, therefore if this new combination be exposed to the action of fire, the marine acid, which now scarcely adheres to this altered metallic matter, far from raising it, as when it was combined with no other acid, does with great facility evaporate, and the nitrous acid, which adheres still less than the marine acid to this metallic earth, quits it still more easily, and continues to deprive it more and more of its inflammable principle.

The same effects ought to take place still more upon the new additions and evaporations of the nitrous acid, therefore, after all these operations, nothing remains but an earthy white matter, absolutely fixed, unfusible, and insoluble in acids, which has no longer any emetic or purgative qualities, nor any taste, if sufficiently calcined. It is, in short, a true calx of antimony, entirely similar to diaphoretic antimony, except that to this latter preparation a small portion of the earth of the alkaline basis of nitre adheres, which is not to be found in bezoar mineral; hence we ought to conclude, that nitrous acid produces the same effects upon the regulus of antimony by the humid, as it does by the dry way.

When bezoar mineral is prepared for the purposes of medicine, it is proper not to calcine it too much, otherwise it would probably have no virtue. When it is moderately calcined, as Lemery prescribes, it may have the sudorific virtue ascribed to it, from the small quantity of acid and perhaps of phlogiston adhering to it. It is this sudorific virtue, truly or falsely ascribed, which has occasioned the name of bezoar mineral, because the animal bezoar is considered also as a sudorific.

It is evident from what has been said concerning the nature of the bezoar mineral, and what passes during its preparation, that the marine acid contained in the butter of antimony is entirely lost, and not essential to the operation, since the nitrous acid alone is capable of depriving the regulus of antimony of all its phlogiston, and of reducing it to a white calx entirely similar to bezoar mineral. Instead then of employing butter of antimony, which requires a preliminary and expensive preparation, the nitrous acid may be directly poured upon the powdered regulus, and its action assisted by heat. This acid readily corrodes the semimetal, without dissolving it; because it deprives it of its phlogiston while it attacks it, and quickly reduces it to a white calx.

When this acid is carried off, and more acid poured on, and this repeated several times, till the matter is at last calcined, a white calx of antimony is obtained entirely similar to bezoar mineral.

CIII BILE (s)

CIV BISMUTH Bismuth, called also *tin-glass*, and by some naturalists *marcasita officinarum*, is a semimetal somewhat similar to the regulus of antimony It appears to be composed of cubes formed by the application of plates upon each other Its color is less white than that of the regulus of antimony, and has a reddish tinge, particularly when it has been exposed to the air

It is the heaviest of the semimetals, and loses in water about a ninth part of its weight

It is also very fusible, and melts a long time before it is red-hot

Bismuth is semi-volatile, like the other semimetals When exposed to the fire, flowers rise from it, it is calcined, and converted into a litharge and glass nearly as lead is It may even be employed, like that metal, to the purification of gold and silver by cupellation

It easily combines with sulphur, and is thereby reduced into a striated mineral like antimony

It amalgamates with mercury, and, according to Mr Wallerius, it has the singular property of so attenuating tin, silver, and especially lead, when any of these metals are added to this amalgam, that a part of them passes along with the mercury through chamois leather This sufficiently proves that this method of purifying mercury is insufficient (*Wallerius's Mineralogy*)

Mr Cramer, on the contrary, says that only lead, and not the other metals, can be so disposed by bismuth as to pass along with the mercury He adds, that the lead must be previously united by fusion with the bismuth, and that if the amalgam be digested during some days, the bismuth is separated, and the lead is left attenuated with the mercury

This semimetal is not equally soluble in the several acids

The vitriolic acid does not, properly speaking, dissolve bismuth If a part and a half of bismuth be mixed with one part of concentrated vitriolic acid, the whole distilled to dryness, and the residuum washed with water, the liquor drawn off is of a red yellow color, but from which nothing can be precipitated by alkalis hence it may be suspected that the vitriolic acid attacks only the inflammable part of bismuth, and does not dissolve its metallic earth

The nitrous acid dissolves bismuth very well

The marine acid attacks and dissolves bismuth a little, but slowly and difficultly Alkalis form a precipitate with marine acid in which bismuth has been digested a certain time

This semimetal does not very sensibly detonate with nitre It is, nevertheless, calcined by this salt, as all the imperfect metals and semimetals are

Two parts of nitrous acid dissolve with heat and effervescence one part of bismuth The solution is clear, limpid, and rose-colored It coagulates into small crystals as soon as it cools

(s) BILE *of* ANIMALS is an oily, viscid, saponaceous fluid, diffusible in water, and when thus diluted, more putrescent than other animal fluids Inspissated bile may, by heat, be first melted, and then decomposed, yielding by distillation an urinous spirit, a volatile salt, much empyreumatic oil, and a residuum containing a considerable quantity of fixed alkali Acids also decompose it, are thereby neutralized, and precipitate from it a resinous matter, not soluble in water, but partly soluble in spirit of wine

This

This solution ought to be made gradually, to avoid too great commotion and effervescence

Water alone being added to this solution, precipitates the bismuth The precipitate is of a very beautiful white, and is commonly called *magistery of bismuth*, and by some artists *Spanish white*, being the same which is used as a paint for the skin

To have this white very beautiful, an aqua-fortis must not be employed, which is adulterated by a mixture of vitriolic acid, for this latter acid gives it a greyish cast

If the nitrous acid has dissolved but little bismuth, much more water is necessary to effect a precipitation

This magistery ought to be well washed, to deprive it as much as possible of the adhering acid, and preserved in a well closed bottle, because this semimetal, when thus divided, has, like silver and lead, the property of easily combining with phlogiston in vapor, and of becoming black by that addition hence the skin of women painted with this white may be rendered quite black by the phlogistic vapors which rise from putrefying matters, necessary houses, sulphur, liver of sulphur, bruised garlic, &c

Alkalis also added to the solution of bismuth occasion a white precipitate of this semimetal, but not so beautiful as when water only is used, because the purest alkalis contain some phlogiston, which gives more or less color to the precipitate

Some authors recommend a solution of sea-salt in water for the making of this precipitate But Mr Pott, in his Dissertation on Bismuth, has shewn that the marine acid does not precipitate this semimetal, and separate it from the nitrous acid, as it does silver, lead, and mercury

Thus, although bismuth resembles lead in many of its properties, as the younger Mr Geoffroy has shewn in the Memoirs of the Academy, so that some chemists have called it the lead of the semimetals, it appears, that, besides want of ductility, it differs essentially from that metal in other respects

Lemeri says, that if the solution of bismuth be used to write with as an ink, that the writing does not appear, but that it becomes very black, when moistened with the deliquiated liquor of the scoria of regulus of antimony This solution is therefore a sympathetic ink The reason of this phenomenon is founded on what we have observed concerning the property which bismuth has, when much divided, of easily imbibing a superabundant quantity of phlogiston, and by that means of acquiring a black color

The scoria of regulus of antimony is almost entirely liver of sulphur The alkali of this liver precipitates the bismuth from the solution employed to write with,, and the sulphur or phlogiston, disengaged from the liver, blackens the bismuth, which therefore becomes visible

It is evident after this explanation, that it is needless to have recourse to the solution of scoria of regulus of antimony in this experiment, for it only acts as a liver of sulphur, and the portion of regulus of antimony contained in this scoria contributes nothing to the success the liver of sulphur alone may therefore be as well employed

Bismuth readily unites with all metallic matters, excepting, according to Mr Gellert, zinc and arsenic, and all the allays are rendered more fusible by bismuth

muth This chemist places the affinities of metallic matters with bismuth in the following order iron, copper, tin, lead, silver, and gold (*t*)

CV BISTRE (*u*)

CVI BITTERN (*w*)

CVII BITUMEN Bitumens are oily matters, of a strong smell, and of different consistences, which are found in many places within the earth

There is only one liquid bitumen known it is called *petroleum*, because it is an oil which actually flows from clefts in certain rocks, and it is gathered in wells dug in certain grounds and mountains *See* PETROLEUM

Solid bitumens are *Amber*, called also *Karabe*, or *yellow amber*, *Jet*, *Asphaltum*, or *bitumen of Judea*, and fossil or *pit coal*

All these bitumens, when distilled, furnish phlegm, an acid liquor frequently sulphureous, a thin oil like petroleum, a volatile acid and concrete salt, (of which amber gives the largest quantity) a black and thick oil, and lastly, a charry residuum, more or less earthy and copious, according to the nature of the particular bitumen analysed Fossil coal furnishes the largest quantity of this residuum From this analysis it appears, that bitumens are composed, like all other vegetable and animal concrete oily matters, of an oil and an acid They differ in general from resins by their greater solidity, by their smell, which is stronger, and not like the aromatic smell of resins, by their insolubility in spirit of wine, by the volatile sulphureous acid, and finally, by the concrete acid obtained in their analysis

The origin of bitumens is an interesting question, concerning which naturalists are not agreed, some imagining that they essentially belong to the mineral kingdom, and others that they proceed originally from vegetable substances We

(*t*) 1 Bismuth, like iron, is said to *occupy, when fused, a less space than when solid* 2 It is *fusible* with a heat of 460° of Fahrenheit's thermometer 3 It greatly *encreases the fusibility of some other metals* Thus, an allay consisting of equal parts of tin and bismuth is fusible with a heat of 280° of Fahrenheit's scale 4 Equal parts of *gold* and *bismuth* form a brittle regulus colored like bismuth Equal parts of *bismuth* and *silver* form a mass not so brittle as the former A small portion of bismuth encreases the brightness, hardness, and sonorousness of *tin* The color of *copper* is rendered less red, but not white, by bismuth Equal parts of *bismuth* and *lead* form a dark grey compound Bismuth may be united with *iron* by a strong heat It does not unite with *zinc* or with *regulus of cobalt*, or only in a small proportion 5 The *uses* of bismuth are, for making *pewter* with tin, for *soldering* some metals, for *printers types* (Homberg advises one part of bismuth and one of tin to be added to twelve parts of the common composition, which is one part of copper, one part of regulus of antimony, and five parts of lead), for *foils for mirrors*, the common mixture for this being one part of tin, one part of lead, two parts of bismuth, and ten parts of mercury, for *anatomical injections*, equal parts of lead, tin, and bismuth, to which some add a little mercury, forming a mixture sufficiently fusible, for *imitating silvering on wood*, for which purpose it is ground, applied with whites of eggs, and burnished, for *purifying gold and silver by cupellation*, for which it is preferable to lead, as it more effectually destroys imperfect metals, promotes the vitrification of earths and calxes, and combines with sulphur, forming a very fusible mass, and lastly, for *rendering some metals fitter for being cast into moulds*, as a small portion of it encreases their fusibility

(*u*) BISTRE is a brown pigment, consisting of the finer parts of wood-soot separated by water from the grosser

(*w*) BITTERN is the bitter saline liquor which remains after the crystallization of sea-salt in sea-water, or the water of salt springs *See* WATER (SEA)

must allow this latter opinion to be the most probable: for, first, no body the origin of which is certainly mineral, contains the smallest portion of oil. Even sulphur, which of all minerals approaches most to the nature of bitumens, and which all the ancient chemists have considered as such, does not contain, as Stahl has demonstrated, the smallest vestige of oil.

2dly, It is probable that the qualities by which bitumens differ from resins and other oily matters, vegetable and animal, are either the natural effects of time upon these oily matters converted into bitumens, or of an alteration produced upon them by mineral acids; or rather they are the effect of both these causes united.

Thirdly, by combining mineral acids with vegetable oils, compounds may be formed much resembling natural bitumens, and to which perhaps nothing but a sufficiently long digestion is wanting to render them true bitumens.

Fourthly, we cannot doubt that the vegetable and animal matters continually destroyed on the surface of the earth, the juices of which are capable of penetrating further, must introduce into the earth much oily matter, which, in time, may become bitumen.

Besides, natural history proves that many entire vegetables and animals have been buried in large quantities, and even at considerable depths, by the various accidents and revolutions which have happened upon the earth; for under ground immense beds of turf are daily found, and large banks of half-decomposed, bituminous, and petrified fossil wood, which can be nothing else but considerable portions of the surface of the earth, thus buried by accidents too ancient to be remembered. All these matters are sufficient to furnish the earth with a large quantity of truly oily substance, which probably can be formed only in the organised bodies of vegetables and animals.

Junker describes, after Neuman, the Prussian amber mines, which are the richest known. First, at the surface of the earth is found a stratum of sand. Immediately under this sand is a bed of clay filled with small flints of about an inch diameter each: under this clay lies a stratum of black earth or turf, filled with fossil wood, half-decomposed and bituminous: this stratum is extended upon a bank of minerals containing little metal, excepting iron, which are consequently pyrites: lastly, under this bed the amber is found scattered about in pieces, or sometimes accumulated in heaps.

If we add to all this, that in amber are frequently included insects and fragments of plants, we shall find a further probability that bitumens are of vegetable original.

It is true that amber, petroleum, and other bitumens are found in grounds where no fossil vegetable matters exist; but it is easy to conceive that these matters may have been destroyed, and their appearance changed by time, particularly as the different natures of soils contribute much to the preservation or destruction of vegetable and animal substances.

Those bitumens which are sufficiently compact to be cut and polished, such as amber and jet, are formed into toys and ornaments, as necklaces, heads for canes, buttons, and mourning ear-rings.

Bitumens

Bitumens are alſo uſed for the preparation of very ſolid and beautiful oil varniſhes. For this purpoſe amber is chiefly uſed. *See* AMBER *and* VARNISH. (*x*)

CVIII. BLACKNESS. (*y*)

(*x*) Notwithſtanding the reference made in the text to *amber* and *varniſh*, both theſe articles are omitted by the author: we ſhall therefore make ſome addition concerning *amber varniſhes*.

A *fine black varniſh* may eaſily be made by diſſolving amber previouſly melted in a crucible till it is rendered black, in boiling linſeed oil. But the ſolution of amber without decompoſition, by which its color is altered, in linſeed or other expreſſed oils, is more difficult, and has been unſucceſsfully attempted by Neuman and other chemiſts. Hoffman ſays, that he reduced amber and oil of olives to a gelatinous maſs by placing the glaſs-veſſel containing them in Papin's Digeſtor, one third part of which was full of water. The experiments of Dr Stockars are more deciſive. He ſays, that, by continuing a ſimmering heat during twelve hours, and by confining the vapors as much as ſtone-ware veſſels would bear, powdered amber was perfectly diſſolved in expreſſed oils, in turpentine, and in balſam of copaiba. He prevented the veſſels from burſting, by making ſmall notches in the corks with which he ſtopped them. The ſolutions of amber in oils of rape ſeed and of almonds had a fine yellow color; in oil of linſeed a golden color; in oil of poppy a yellowiſh red; in oil of olives a beautiful red; in oil of nuts a deeper red; in oil of bays a purpliſh red. Solutions of amber in turpentine and balſam of copaiba had a deep red color, and when cooled, formed hard brittle red maſſes. All theſe ſolutions were eaſily miſcible with ſpirit of turpentine. Thoſe made with oils of linſeed, bays, poppies, and nuts, with balſam of copaiba, and with turpentine, being diluted with four times their quantity of ſpirit of turpentine, formed hard, tenacious, gloſſy varniſhes, which dried ſufficiently quick. See *Dr Stockars's Specimen Inaugurale de Succino, Leyden*, 1760.

Amber may be rendered clear and pellucid by two methods: 1. By cementing lumps of it with ſand, during 40 hours, in an iron pot. 2. By digeſting them during 20 hours in boiling rape-ſeed oil.

A *tincture* may be extracted from amber by rectified ſpirit of wine, or by ſweet ſpirit of vitriol.

From 16 oz. of coarſe amber Neuman obtained *by diſtillation*, eleven ounces ſix drams of oil, four drams and a half of ſalt, (*ſee* SALT *of* AMBER) one ounce and a half of water, and nearly one ounce of caput mortuum.

(*y*) BLACKNESS. Dr Lewis, in his *Philoſophical Commerce of Arts*, has written copiouſly concerning the ſubſtances capable of communicating blackneſs. What we ſhall ſay on this ſubject ſhall be chiefly extracted from that work.

The *native black coloring materials* are, 1. *Black chalk*, or *black marking ſtone*; which ſeems to be a ſlaty bituminous ſubſtance, unſoluble by acids, and capable of being rendered friable and red by fire. It ſtains freely. When powdered, it does not loſe its blackneſs, and may then be formed with oil into a paſte, or with water into a ſlimy maſs; which properties render it uſeful to painters. 2. *Pitcoal* mixed with oil produces a browniſh black. 3. *Black ſand* found in Virginia, ſtrewed upon writing while yet wet, dries and gives luſtre to the ink. This ſubſtance might be uſed in oil painting to give a ſparkling black. What this ſubſtance is Dr Lewis has not mentioned. I have eſſayed a black ſparkling powder uſually ſold for ſtrewing upon writing, and found it to conſiſt of minute particles of the lead-ore called *galena*. 4. *Black-lead*, the color of which is rather a deep ſhining blue than a black, is ſmooth and unctuous, and hence is uſed, as ſoap and oil are, to prevent the friction of machines. It is unſoluble by acids, and unfuſible by fire. In cloſe veſſels it is unalterable by fire; but by a long calcination in an open fire it is moſtly volatiliſed, emitting, according to Lawſon, (*Diſſertatio de Nihilo*) inflammable blue flowers, and the reſiduum is a yellow calx, which being reduced by Mr. Queſt, (*ſee Swediſh Acts*, 1754) ſeemed to be a mixture of iron and tin. Black lead may be readily mixed with melted ſulphur, and of this compoſition pencils are formed much inferior

CIX. BLACK-JACK (z)

CX. BLOOD. Blood is well known to be a red liquor in most animals,

ferior to those made of slips of entire black lead fitted into pieces of cedar wood. 5. *Black vegetable juices.* The excellent black varnish of China and Japan is a native juice exsuding from incisions made in certain trees, one of which is said to be that, the fruit of which is brought to Europe, called *anacardium*. Anacardium contains a black juice which gives to linnen and cotton a reddish brown stain, which, by exposure to air, becomes black, and is incapable of being discharged by washing or boiling with soap or alkaline leys. The oriental varnish is said by others to be produced from the tree called *toxicodendron*. 6. *Cuttle-fish* contains, in a distinct vessel, a fluid as black as ink, and which is said to be fit for the same purposes.

The black coloring materials produced by fire are, 1. *Charcoal*, which, entire or powdered, is used as a pigment. For this purpose artists use the smaller branches of trees, chiefly of the softer woods, as willows and vines, freed from the bark and pith. The coal of horns and other animal substances is glossier and deeper colored than vegetable coals. That of ivory is superior to the rest. 2. *Soots* are softer than coals, and more easily miscible with oil or water. A part of wood soot is soluble in water. From an infusion in wood soot in water is prepared the brown pigment called *bistre*, used for painting in water-colors. The finest of the soot blacks is *lamp-black*, usually prepared by burning in an oven the dregs and pieces of pine-bark left in the process for making common rosin. Soots prepared by burning small pieces of wood or of mineral bitumens very slowly under a copper pan, were found by Dr Lewis to be not different from those prepared from oils and resins, and, like these, contained nothing soluble in common water, as the soot collected in common chimneys does. *See* SOOT.

The *black-coloring materials produced by mixture* are, 1. A solution of green vitriol in water, added to an infusion of galls or some vegetable astringent, is the basis of black inks, and black dyes for the uses of callico printers, tanners of leather, hatters, dyers, &c. The color given by this mixture adheres permanently to silk and wool, but may be discharged from linnen and cotton by washing. If the water employed for dissolving the vitriol, or infusing the galls, have been distilled, or if it be common spring water, or fresh rain water, the color produced will be bluish; and if the water has any putrid or alkaline quality, the color produced will have a purple or reddish tinge. The blackness given by galls is much improved by addition of logwood. All vegetable astringents do not produce blackness by mixture with solution of green vitriol. Thus the Peruvian bark is said to give a greenish color. *See* INK. 2. A *solution of silver* in nitrous acid gives black stains to solid white animal substances, to agates, and some other stones, afterwards exposed to the sun and air. Bones and hair at first receive no stain, but sooner or later, as they happen to be more or less exposed to the sun and air, they become of a reddish or purplish color, which gradually changes to a brown, and afterwards to a black. Mr Schultze (*Act. Natur. Curios. vol. I.*) says, that white chalk moistened with solution of silver, by exposure to the sun, acquires a purplish black color on its surface, which color may be interrupted by threads shading parts of the chalk. If the chalk, thus moistened with solution of silver, be dried in the shade or by fire, no color will be produced. No color was given by this method to white clay, talk, or plaster of Paris. The action of solar light also gives a dark color to the white precipitate of bismuth, and to sweet mercury. 3. A black stain is given to paper or other white substances by *solutions of lead in acid*, when these substances are afterwards exposed to phlogistic or sulphureous vapors. *See* INK (SYMPATHETIC). *Calxes of lead melted with sulphur* form a black or blackish mass useful for taking casts from medals, as it is less brittle than sulphur alone. Mr Le Blon found that a black color may be produced by mixing blue, red, and yellow pigments, and Mr Cartel directs that fifteen parts of blue should be mixed with five parts of red, and three of yellow, and that each of these colors should be very deep. Dr Lewis tried such mixtures, but produced only a brownish or greyish black.

(z) BLACK-JACK, or BLEND, is a mineral, called also *false galena*. *See* GALENA (FALSE).

circulating in their vessels during life, and the common source whence all the necessary and superfluous animal liquors are derived (a)

Blood newly drawn from a sound animal gives no sign of an acid or alkaline quality. It has a sweetish and somewhat saline taste. When left to itself, it coagulates, and quickly passes to a fermentation at first a little acid, and afterwards entirely putrid, in the same manner as all other perfectly animalised substances.

This liquor contains nothing volatile by the heat of boiling water, but a pure phlegm. Thus when blood is distilled in a water-bath, it is only dried, not entirely decomposed. By this drying it loses ⅞ of its weight. The residuum being distilled in a naked fire, yields volatile alkali, and animal oil, at first thin, and afterwards thick. In the retort a charry residuum remains, which can difficultly be reduced to ashes, from the lixiviation of which a little common salt may be obtained.

From this analysis, which is almost all that chemists have done to discover the nature of the blood, it appears that this liquor contains the same principles as all other perfectly animalised matters. But a more accurate examination might probably be made of it by separating at first from each other several different substances, of which the blood is only a collection or mixture, and then by analysing each of these substances, as has been done with milk.

In fact, the blood being opake, or not very transparent, appears to be, as milk is, nothing else than a mixture of several heterogeneous matters confounded together, without being dissolved by each other. It is known, that, when the blood is no longer circulated in the vessels of the animal, but left at rest in a vessel, it coagulates and separates spontaneously into a red mass, and a white liquor, or serum, in which the red mass floats; and that by washing, the red part of this mass may be carried off, and the remaining matter is white and gelatinous. There are then three distinct matters in the blood which seem to correspond with those contained in milk; that is, the serum of the blood corresponds with the whey of milk; the white gelatinous matter, with the cheesy part; and lastly, the red globules with the butyraceous substance.

It is so much more probable that the red part of the blood is oleaginous, as anatomists, who have examined the blood by microscopes, have observed that this red part is composed of globules swimming in a white liquor; and as all oily matters, when well mixed, but not dissolved in a watery fluid, have this globular appearance. (b)

This being established, if the blood were to be examined more exactly than it has hitherto been, it would probably be necessary to begin by separating from each other the three above-mentioned substances, each of which ought afterwards to be subjected to experiments and analyses, as has been done with milk. It is probable that this method of analysing blood would throw new light upon its

(a) The color of blood, like that of many other substances, is affected by exposure to air, by which it acquires a scarlet tinge. Arterial blood has this scarlet color, which it has acquired by passing through the lungs in respiration. The blood flowing through the veins has a deeper and less vivid red color. It acquires the scarlet color by exposure to air, and arterial blood loses its vivid red color by exclusion from air.

(b) The red particles of blood are said to have an annular form.

nature

nature and principles, which are yet very imperfectly understood, as well as those of other animal matters.

The purely gelatinous parts of the blood are probably not different from any other animal jelly; but it is to be presumed that some peculiar salt might be obtained from the serous parts, as have been from milk and from urine; and that the red globular part would be found to be oleaginous. The acid, or volatile alkaline principles which would be obtained from the red part of the blood would determine whether or not it is a truly animal oil, or fat. If it be true, as Mr Homberg and Mr Macquer affirm, that some acid may be obtained by analysing the blood, it would probably be found to belong to this red substance.

Lastly, it is evident that whatever knowledge could be acquired on this subject by well-conducted experiments, must extend and encrease an interesting branch of our knowledge, namely, that concerning animal economy. *(c)*

CXI. BLUE *(d)*

(c) Dr Fordyce, in his very excellent Elements of the Practice of Physic, says, that the white gelatinous matter of the blood, or *coagulable lymph*, continues fluid while circulating with any degree of heat betwixt 30 and 120° of Fahrenheit's thermometer; but that it is coagulated very soon after it is taken out of the body in any heat, in motion, or in rest; and that its coagulation may be prevented by saturating the blood with sea-salt, or perhaps with some other neutral salts. The coagulum is rendered soluble in boiling water, by putrefaction, by concentrated acids, caustic alkalis, calcareous earths, and by some metallic salts. He observes also, that the coagulable lymph is more fluid, and is not so easily coagulable when the arteries of the person from whom the blood is drawn act more strongly than they usually do; in which case, the red particles and this lymph can separate more exactly from each other according to their densities, the former falling to the bottom, and the greatest part of the latter forming upon the upper surface a very viscid tough mass called the *buff*. By putrefaction the coagulable lymph and serum are converted into a mucilaginous matter, not coagulable by any of the methods recited above, which mucilaginous matter may be converted by further putrefaction into saline substances and calcareous earth. The red part of the blood is readily soluble in water, but not in serum, nor in a saturated solution of neutral salts. By the first stage of putrefaction this red part of blood is broken down into smaller particles, its color is rendered darker, and afterwards it is converted to a mucilage soluble in serum.

(d) BLUE COLORING MATERIALS. No blue materials for dying consist of animal or mineral substances. Concerning the blue glass called *smalt*, prepared from the ore or regulus of cobalt; the preparation of iron called *Prussian blue*; and the preparation of lapis lazuli called *ultramarine* or *azure*, *see* SMALT, AZURE, *and* BLUE (PRUSSIAN). The *blue color of flowers* is so perishable as to be of little use in dying. It is extracted from many by infusion in water, but not in spirit. It is changed by acids to a red not more durable than the original blue; by marine acid to the most florid red; and it is changed by alkalis and by lime-water to a green, which afterwards becomes a yellow. The green by lime-water is the more permanent and beautiful, and has been formed into lakes for painting. The two principal vegetable substances used for dying of a blue color are *indigo* and *woad*. These are feculæ or sediments deposited by fermentation from infusions of the leaves of the plants *anil*, and *woad*, or *glastum*. Hellot thinks, that a similar blue dye might be obtained from most other vegetables, and that the green of vegetables is caused by a mixture of blue and yellow coloring particles, of which the blue is the most durable, and least affected by fermentations. The colors given by both indigo and woad are at first green, but are soon changed, by exposure to air, to blue. A blue tincture may be made from *nephritic wood*, which has not been applied to any use. The *essential oils of camomile, milfoil, pimpinella nigra*, are blue, and by keeping become green and yellow. *See* DYING.

 CXII

CXII BLUE (PRUSSIAN) Prussian blue is a precipitate of iron with a superabundant quantity of phlogiston, from which it receives a very beautiful color.

This blue, which is successfully used in painting, was discovered, like most other things, by accident, and about the beginning of this century

A chemist of Berlin having successively thrown upon the ground several liquors from his laboratory, was much surprised to see it suddenly stained with a most beautiful color He then recollected what liquors he had thus thrown upon each other, and having made a similar mixture in a vessel, he saw the same blue color appear As he perceived that this discovery might be profitable to him, he did not publish the process, but prepared this blue for the use of painters, who found that it might be substituted for ultramarine, a very dear color, and from that time made much use of it

An account of this blue, called *Prussian* or *Berlin blue*, from the place where it was made, was published in the Berlin Memoirs for 1710, but no description was given of the process for making it

Several chemists undoubtedly attempted to discover it accordingly it was discovered, and in the year 1724 Dr Woodward published it in the Philosophical Transactions The process succeeds very well, and is as follows

Alkalise together four ounces of nitre and as much tartar *See* ALKALI (EXTEMPORANEOUS) Mix this alkali well with four ounces of dried bullock's blood, and put the whole in a crucible covered with a lid in which there is a small hole calcine with a moderate fire till the blood be reduced to a perfect coal, that is, till it emits no more smoke or flame capable of blackening any white bodies that are exposed to it increase the fire towards the end, so that the whole matter contained in the crucible shall be moderately, but sensibly red

Throw into two pints of water the matter contained in the crucible, while yet red, and give it half an hour's boiling, decant this first water, and pour more water upon the black and charry coal till it becomes almost insipid mix together all these waters, and reduce them by boiling to about two pints

Also dissolve two ounces of martial vitriol, and eight ounces of alum in two pints of boiling water mix this solution when hot, with the preceding lixivium, also hot A great effervescence will then be made The liquors will be rendered turbid, and will become of a green color more or less blue, and a precipitate will be formed of the same color Filtrate, in order to separate this precipitate, upon which pour spirit of salt, and mix them well together, by which means the precipitate will become of a fine blue color It is necessary to add rather too much spirit of salt than too little, and till it no longer encreases the beauty of the precipitate The next day wash this blue till the water comes off from it insipid, and then gently dry it Such is the process by which Prussian blue is made Chemists, after having discovered it, endeavored to find the theory of it, and to explain the appearances in the several operations of the process There have been several opinions concerning the nature of Prussian blue

Mr John Brown of the Royal Society of London thinks, that this blue is the bituminous or phlogistic part of iron, disengaged by the lixivium of bullock's blood, and applied to the earth of alum. This opinion has been adopted by Dr Geoffroy in the Memoirs given by him on this subject, which are found in the collection of the Academy of Sciences for the year 1725

The Abbé Menon, a correspondent of the Academy of Sciences, in Memoirs printed amongst the collection of the *Sçavans Etrangers*, published by the academy, advances and endeavors to prove that Prussian blue is nothing but iron entirely freed from all saline matter by the phlogiston of the alkaline lixivium, and precipitated with its natural color, which, he pretends, is blue. He thinks that the use of the alum is to diminish the intensity of the color by the whiteness of its earth.

Lastly, Mr Macquer, having examined this matter in all its extent, has published a memoir amongst those of the Academy of Sciences for the year 1752, in which he concludes, after having related many experiments, that Prussian blue is nothing but iron impregnated with a superabundant quantity of phlogiston, which it receives from the phlogisticated alkaline precipitant. The experiments and discoveries made by this chemist are as follow.

Mr Macquer first observes that very pure alkaline salts separate iron, as they do all metallic substances, from acids; and that iron so precipitated has a color more or less yellow, and is soluble by acids.

If, on the contrary, this precipitation of iron be made by an alkali previously calcined with an inflammable matter, then a precipitate is formed, more or less green or blue, as the alkali was more or less phlogisticated.

If an acid be poured upon this green precipitate, experiments shew that this acid dissolves one part of it, and does not act upon the other. This proves that the green precipitate is not homogeneous, but a mixture of two precipitates, one of which is soluble, and the other is insoluble by an acid.

As the precipitate which resists the action of acids is very blue, when separated from that which the acid has dissolved, and as the green color of the mixed precipitate is a mixture of yellow and blue, the author concludes that the part dissolved by the acid is yellow, and consequently that this portion of green precipitate is entirely similar to the iron which pure alkalis separate from acids.

As to the blue precipitate, as it not only resists the action of acids but also of magnets, it might not be known to be iron, if a slight calcination did not at once deprive it of its blue color, and render it entirely similar to other iron.

These facts prove that Prussian blue is nothing but iron united with some matter which gives it a blue color, and the property of resisting the action of acids and of magnets.

Mr Macquer has further discovered that fire is not the only means by which the Prussian blue may be deprived of all the properties, by which it differs from ordinary iron.

A very pure alkali produces also the same effect. He has also discovered, that the alkali which has thus deprived the Prussian blue of all the properties which distinguish it from ordinary iron, becomes by that operation entirely similar to the phlogisticated alkali used for the preparation of Prussian blue.

These facts seem to demonstrate that Prussian blue is nothing else than iron, which becomes blue by impregnating it with with a matter which the alkali is capable of giving to it or of separating from it, according to circumstances; that is to say, that when the alkali is impregnated with this matter, and is applied to iron dissolved in an acid, it then combines with this acid, and precipitates the iron, to which it transfers at the same time the matter which changes the iron into Prussian blue. But if on the contrary Prussian blue be applied to pure alkali,

alkali, then this alkali entirely dissolves the coloring matter of the Prussian blue, and takes it from the iron, which is thus reduced to its ordinary condition

By a more particular examination of this alkali, impregnated with the coloring matter of Prussian blue, either by calcination with an inflammable matter, or by taking the color from Prussian blue itself, Mr Macquer found that its alkaline properties were so much more weakened, as it was impregnated with a larger portion of this coloring matter This induced him to presume, that by giving it a sufficient quantity of Prussian blue to discolor, it might be entirely saturated with this coloring matter and the event entirely answered his expectation

By applying much Prussian blue to an alkali, this latter was so saturated that it no longer discolored the blue when boiled together, and upon trial, was found to possess no longer any alkaline qualities

A solution of iron by any acid poured into this alkali, saturated with the coloring matter of the Prussian blue, forms immediately a precipitate, not green, composed of yellow and blue, the former of which must be separated by an acid from the latter to obtain this of a pure blue color, as in the ordinary process for the preparation of Prussian blue, but a single homogeneous precipitate, and a perfect Prussian blue This effect ought necessarily to happen, because the saturated alkali contains no part purely alkaline which can occasion a precipitate of soluble iron, as pure alkalis do

But an essential phenomenon, and not observed by any former chemist, is, that it is not merely by the action of the acid, which dissolves the iron, that the coloring matter is applied to the iron, and thus the Prussian blue formed, but that the affinity of this matter to iron contributes also to produce this effect The author has demonstrated this truth by the following decisive experiment

If any pure acid be poured upon an alkali perfectly saturated with the coloring matter of Prussian blue, this acid contracts no union with this alkali, nor is any-ways neutralized, and consequently is incapable of separating the coloring matter of Prussian blue It only procures this separation when it is united with iron, the affinity of which to the coloring matter, being joined to the affinity of the acid to the alkali, form a sum of affinities capable of occasioning the separation of which we treat

In this operation, therefore, there is a very distinct example of the effect of double or united affinities *See* AFFINITY This example is even so much more compleat, as it is amongst the most general that chemistry furnishes For according to Mr Macquer's observations, iron is not the only metallic substance the affinity of which being united with that of the acid, procures the separation of the coloring matter of the Prussian blue from the alkali, but any metallic substance dissolved in any acid separates the phlogistic matter from all alkalis, fixed or volatile This is ascertained by Mr Macquer's experiments, a detail of which may be seen in his memoir

Another no less important phenomenon, which none of the chemists who have endeavored to explain the theory of Prussian blue had observed, is, that earths have not the same affinity as metallic substances with the phlogistic matter of Prussian blue Hence if an alkali saturated with this coloring matter be poured into a solution of alum, no decomposition is effected, nor is any precipitate formed

formed The a[illegible] remains unchanged

After this experiment Mr Macquer reasonably concludes, that the alum added in the operation of Prussian blue does not directly contribute to the production of this blue The purpose to which it serves is as follows

This chemist proved by many experiments, that alkaline salt can never be entirely saturated with the colouring matter of Prussian blue by calcination This being established, it is certain that alkalis, calcined with inflammable substances to make the proper lixivium for Prussian blue, still remain alkaline Hence it happens that when they are mixed with a solution of green vitriol, they form by their purely alkaline part a yellow precipitate, so much more copious as this purely alkaline part is itself more copious But nothing is more capable of spoiling the color of the portion of iron precipitated in Prussian blue than a mixture of this yellow or olive-colored precipitate, therefore a large quantity of acid must be employed, that this yellow precipitate may be entirely dissolved if we mean to have a very fine blue

Part of these inconveniencies is avoided by mixing a solution of alum with a solution of green vitriol By this means, the purely alkaline part of the lixivium is mostly employed to precipitate a greater or less quantity of the earth of alum, and consequently the quantity of yellow ferruginous precipitate is much diminished But the earth of alum being of a fine shining white does not in the least alter the purity of the blue color, but enlivens it, and lessens its intensity, which is frequently no inconvenience, because the Prussian blue, when it is not of the finest color, is always too dark and black

It follows from what has been said, that when Prussian blue is to be made with a lixivium not saturated, it is a matter of indifference whether the green precipitate is to be again dissolved, or the alkaline part of the lixivium saturated with alum or with an acid, before the precipitate is formed The only difference which can proceed from these modes of management is, that in the former case all the part of the precipitate which is not Prussian blue is redissolved by an acid, whereas in the latter case, this mixed precipitation is prevented, and nothing is thrown down but true Prussian blue

It is proper to observe, concerning the theory of Prussian blue, that most alkalis obtained from the ashes of vegetables, being combined by their combustion with a portion of inflammable matter, are capable of furnishing a quantity of Prussian blue proportionable to the quantity retained by them of this inflammable matter, even without the necessity of mixing them with a solution of iron, because they always contain a little of this metal dissolved, some of which may be found in almost all vegetables, therefore it is sufficient for this purpose to saturate them with an acid These materials which form Prussian blue in alkaline salts occasion their impurity, and require much trouble to be perfectly separated

Some chemists had even perceived the production of this blue in the saturation of alkaline salts, before the discovery of the Prussian blue and Henkel particularly, who had observed it in the saturation of sal soda, or fossil alkali, recommended to chemists an enquiry concerning the nature of this blue Thus chemists had already acquired some sort of knowledge on this subject, and therefore the Prussian blue could not have long remained unknown, even if accident

dent had not presented it in so striking a manner to the chemist of Berlin, who was the first who prepared it in sufficient quantity for the uses of painters

CXIII B O L E Boles, or bolar earths, are clays which adhere to the tongue, when applied dry, and which are colored, yellow and red, by a ferrugineous earth *See* CLAY

CXIV B O L O G N I A N S T O N E *See* STONE

CXV. B O N E S (*e*)

CXVI B O R A X Borax is a saline matter, with all the properties of a neutral salt

It is soluble in water, and crystallizable nearly as alum is, with this difference only, that it requires a little more water for its solution, and retains somewhat less in its crystallization.

When exposed to fire, it at first undergoes the liquefaction occasioned by the water of its crystallization, and is then calcined, as alum is, but is not so much swelled and rarefied during the operation

If the fire be increased to a melting heat, the borax is pretty easily fused, and is converted into a vitreous matter, or saline glass and when it is mixed with earths of any kind, it acts as a flux, and converts them into more or less transparent glasses according to their natures *See* VITRIFICATION

Glass of borax is very friable, easily tarnishes in the air, and becomes mealy, nearly as the alkaline basis of sea-salt does It is entirely soluble in water, and when the solution of it is evaporated, borax is again formed in crystals, as it was before its fusion

Borax then suffers no decomposition by fire, even in open vessels, and certainly, therefore, not in close ones

But it may be decomposed by the vitriolic, nitrous, and marine acids, which unite with the saline alkaline matter which is its basis, and form with it exactly the same neutral salts as those which result from the union of these acids with the marine alkali, that is to say, the vitriolic acid forms Glauber's salt, the nitrous acid forms cubic nitre, and the marine acid forms sea-salt

When acids combine thus with the alkaline basis of borax, they separate from it a saline substance of a singular nature, and little understood, called *Sedative Salt* *See* SALT (SEDATIVE)

We are far from knowing as much concerning borax as is desirable We are even ignorant of its origin, which might supply the want of a perfect analysis, and give light to the nature of this saline substance

As borax is not found in Europe, it is brought from the East-Indies in a state which only requires a slight purification, which is given to it by the Dutch and

(*e*) BONES are totally soluble in concentrated acids of vitriol, nitre, and sea-salt, and may be softened by these or acetous acids diluted From two ounces of ox-bone Neuman obtained by distillation two drams of empyreumatic phlegm, one dram of volatile urinous spirit, two scruples of volatile alkali, two scruples of fetid oil, and one ounce, three drams, and two scruples of residuum Dr Lewis observes, that bones exposed to a heat gradually raised are rendered white, opake, and friable, and when exposed suddenly to a violent heat, are rendered hard, semi-transparent, and sonorous Bones and horns may be stained by the common dying infusions and decoctions of vegetable and animal substances, and by metallic solutions

Venetians

Venetians who are the chief merchants of it But it is not yet known whether this matter be a natural or an artificial substance, nor whence, nor how it is obtained

Our ignorance concerning borax is certainly owing to the interest, which they, who make a lucrative commerce of it, have to keep every thing concerning its origin secret

However that be, notwithstanding the resources which chemists posess of discovering what is hid from them by their experiments, it appears that they were long in a state of indifference concerning borax Satisfied with employing it in their operations, in which it is very useful as a flux, they long used it without attempting to subject it to proper proofs for the discovery of its nature.

In the writings of Becher and Stahl we scarcely find any thing concerning borax The examination by chemical means of this substance, which ought to excite the curiosity of chemists, has been begun only in these latter times, and it is to the praise of the French, that almost all the knowledge we have concerning it we owe to them alone

Homberg was amongst the first who undertook a set of experiments on borax, by which the sedative salt was discovered, which was a new substance, and entirely unknown before him Homberg obtained the sedative salt from borax, by distilling it with vitriol, and imagining that he discovered a sedative or quieting power in it, he called it the *Narcotic Salt of Vitriol*, or *Sedative Salt* This chemist did not well understand the theory of his experiment, but that is not surprising in matters so new

The younger Lemeri, who after Homberg made many experiments on borax, discovered that sedative salt may be obtained from it not only by the vitriolic acid, but also by the nitrous and marine acids This discovery was the more important, as it naturally led to further but he seems to have been prevented by other pursuits from continuing this subject as it ought to be

Homberg and Lemeri obtained sedative salt only by distillation or sublimation, which, particularly in this case, was a long and embarrassing operation M Geoffroy has improved upon their discoveries, by shewing the method of obtaining the same salt from borax by acids with evaporation and crystalliza ion only, in greater quantity and with less trouble We are also obliged to him for having first demonstrated that borax contains the basis of sea-salt This truth he has firmly established, by obtaining a true Glauber's salt by mixing vitriolic acid with a solution of borax

Lastly, Mr Baron, Member of the Academy of Sciences, and of the Faculty of Medicine at Paris, proved by many experiments that sedative salt of borax may be obtained by means of vegetable acids, which had not been done before him He has also proved, that sedative salt is not a combination of an alkaline matter with the acid employed to obtain it, but that it exists ready formed in borax, of which it is a principle or constituent part, that the acids employed to extract it do only disengage it from the alkali with which it is united, that this alkali is entirely similar to that of sea salt, that sedative salt may be re united with its alkali, and again form borax, which is a compleat proof that borax is nothing else than a compound of sedative salt, and marine alkali.

Nothing more then remains to have, on the nature of borax, all the knowledge we can desire, than to discover what this sedative salt is The experiment by which Mr Baron found that this salt is capable of decomposing nitre and marine salt, by separating the acids of these salts by help of fire, seems to shew that vitriolic acid is one of the principles of the sedative salt But to prove this decisively, the sedative salt itself must be decomposed This is the subject of Mr. Bourdelin's late admirable experiments Although this able chemist has not been able to accomplish his purpose by all the methods which the most profound chemistry can suggest, his experiments are nevertheless useful, as they may prevent others from employing their time and labor in making them, and also because they make us better acquainted with the properties of the sedative salt *See* SALT (SEDATIVE) *(f)*

CXVII BRAINS *(g)*

CXVIII BRANDY *(h)*

(f) *Borax*, when crude, as it is brought from the East-Indies, is called *Tincal* In this state, it consists of small, yellow, glutinous crystals It is said to be refined by lime water Refined borax consists of large, white, eight sided crystals, each of which is composed of small, soft, bitterish scales It is difficultly soluble in water, to which it gives a glutinous quality, and hence is used by dyers to give a gloss to silks It is also soluble in spirit of wine, to the flame of which it gives a green color By repeatedly moistening it, while it is considerably heated, it may be entirely sublimed Borax renders all earths and stones fusible by fire, and hence is used for the essaying of ores It also facilitates the fusion of metals, and is particularly useful when small particles of metal mixed with dirt and ashes are to be melted together, as it promotes the fusion of the metal, and the vitrification of the other matters, by which the particles of metal may disengage themselves, and collect into one mass It is further useful in the fusion of metals, as it defends their surfaces from the combined action of air and fire, by which imperfect metals are calcined Crucibles in which gold and silver are melted ought to be previously glazed on their inner surfaces with borax, that when the metals are poured out, no particles may adhere to the sides of the crucibles Gold is rendered pale by fusion with borax, which effect is prevented by adding a little nitre or sal-ammoniac, or is remedied by remelting the gold with either of these salts Dr Lewis observes, that borax also renders brass and Prince's-metal pale, and at the same time acquires a deep red color This color it probably receives from some part of the copper contained in these compound metals, as it acquires the same red color by fusion with copper Borax is not, as some suppose, a substance capable of reducing or reviving calcined metals, but is used with the intentions above described A principal use of borax is to facilitate the soldering of metals, which it does by accelerating the fusion of the surfaces of the metals to be joined, and by clearing them from any calx or other matter by which they might be prevented from being perfectly applied to each other Borax is also used for the preparation of some fine glasses, and imitations of precious stones, because the glasses prepared by fusing it with earths are very hard, compact, bright, and very transparent, but by long exposure to air they lose much of their lustre, become cloudy, and when the quantity employed has been large, even opake

(g) BRAINS From 16 oz of ox's brains, Neuman obtained by distillation six ounces, two drams, and two scruples of a colorless phlegm, four ounces and four scruples of a volatile, empyreumatic spirit, which being rectified, produced two scruples of a volatile, concrete salt, and one ounce of caput mortuum, from which, by elixation, were procured 25 grains of fixed salt

(h) BRANDY is an ardent spirit distilled from wine For its properties, *see* SPIRIT It may be imitated by adding to very pure malt spirits some dulcified spirit of nitre

CXIX

CXIX. BRASS (*t*) Brass, called also *Latten*, is a mixture of very pure copper, with a fourth part of very pure zinc, by which the color of the copper is rendered of a fine golden yellow. This is undoubtedly the most useful and necessary of all the mixtures of copper and other metals, chiefly on account of the copper's preserving so much of its ductility, when combined with that proportion of zinc.

(*t*) BRASS. As the manufacture of brass is important in commerce, a detail of the process by which it is made may be acceptable. The calamine is previously to be prepared by cleansing it from adhering earth, stone, or other matters; by roasting or calcining it; and by grinding it into a fine powder. The calcination, by which moisture and small portions of sulphur and other volatile matters are dissipated, may be performed either in a reverberatory furnace, in which the calamine is kept till it be thoroughly red hot, and that this heat may be more equally given to it all at the same time, it ought to be frequently stirred; or by setting fire to a conical pile, composed of horizontal layers of calamine, and of charcoal placed alternately one upon the other, and of a lower stratum consisting of large pieces of wood, in which lower stratum are four horizontal channels, through which the air maintaining the fire passes to the center, and thence arises through a chimney or perpendicular empty space, left for that purpose, along the axis of the conical pile. If the calcining heat be too intense or too long continued, part of the contained zinc may be dissipated; and if it be not sufficiently intense, or long enough continued, the volatile matters will not be entirely expelled, and the texture of the stone will not be sufficiently broken to prepare it for the subsequent grinding. The length of time and degree of heat requisite for the calcination of calamine, are different according to the qualities of that mineral. The calamine thus cleansed, calcined, and ground, is to be mixed with about a third or fourth part of powder of charcoal, or of pit-coal, as is done in some parts of England. The malleability of the brass is diminished by the use of pit coal, which is therefore employed only for the preparation of coarser kinds of brass. To this composition of calamine and coal some manufacturers add common salt, by which the process of making brass is said to be hastened. In Goslar, where the cadmia adhering to the inner sides of furnaces is employed, instead of native calamine a small quantity of alum is added, by which they pretend the color of the brass is heightened. With this composition, and with thin plates or grains of copper, the crucibles are to be nearly filled. The proportion of calamine to the copper varies according to the richness of the former, but is generally as three to two. The copper must be dispersed through the composition of calamine and coal, and the whole must be covered with more coal till the crucibles are full. The crucibles thus filled are to be placed in a furnace sunk in the ground, the form of which furnace is that of the frustum of a hollow cone. At the bottom of the furnace, or greater basis of the frustum, is a circular grate, or iron plate. This plate is covered with a coat of clay and horse-dung to defend it from the action of the fire, and pierced with holes, through which the air maintaining the fire passes. The crucibles stand upon the circular plate, forming a circular row with one in the middle. The fuel is placed betwixt the crucibles, and is thrown into the furnace at the upper part of it, or the lesser basis of the frustum. To this upper part or mouth of the furnace is fitted a cover made of bricks or clay, kept together by bars of iron, and pierced with holes. This cover serves as a register. When the heat is to be encreased, the cover is to be partly or entirely taken off, and a free draught is permitted to the external air, which passes along a vault under ground to the ash hole, through the holes in the circular grate or plate, betwixt the crucibles, and through the upper mouth along with the smoke and flame into an area where the workmen stand, which is covered with a large dome or chimney through which the smoke and air ascend. When the heat is to be diminished, the mouth of the furnace is to be closed with the lid, through the holes in which the air, smoke, and flame pass. The crucibles are to

Although zinc be only a semi-metal, and consequently not ductile, and although metallic mixtures be generally less ductile than the pure metals of which they are composed, zinc seems to be an exception to this rule in its combination with copper; for it has the property of uniting with that metal in a large proportion, as of a third, or a fourth, without sensibly diminishing the ductility of the copper. But as this property is quite peculiar to zinc, it is evident that it is necessary, in order to make good brass, that the copper and zinc be, each of them, in their greatest purity.

If such zinc as is procured in the smelting of ores be melted with copper, as in some mixtures commonly used, we might indeed obtain a very fine colored brass, but it would be brittle and unmalleable. It would only be a mixture of that kind called *tombacs*, because this zinc is never very pure. *See* ZINC.

This inconvenience is avoided in making brass, by a kind of cementation with the ore of zinc, which is lapis calaminaris. This process is performed in the following manner.

A cement, composed of one part and a half of good lapis calaminaris and powder of charcoal triturated together, and moistened with water, is put into an earthen pot or crucible. Then one part of very pure copper beat into

to be kept red-hot during eight or ten hours, and in some places much longer, even several days, according to the quality of the calamine, during which time the zinc rises in vapor from the calamine, unites with the copper, and renders that metal fusible by considerably less heat than it is alone. To render the metal very fluid, that it may flow into one uniform mass at the bottom, the fire is to be encreased a little before the crucibles are taken out for the pouring of the fluid metal into moulds. From sixty pounds of good calamine and forty pounds of copper, sixty pounds of brass may by this process be obtained, notwithstanding that a considerable quantity of zinc is burnt and dissipated during the operation, as we may learn from the blue flame round the mouths of the crucibles and furnaces, from the flowers of zinc which adhere to the inner sides of the furnace, and from the blue color communicated to the crucibles. The quantity of brass obtained has been considerably augmented since the introduction of the method now commonly practised of using granulated copper, by which a larger surface of this metal is exposed to the vapor of the zinc, and consequently less of that vapor escapes. For the granulation of the copper, a cylindrical wooden reservoir is made, four or five feet deep, in which a circular brass or copper bottom may be raised or lowered, by means of a chain. This reservoir is covered with a copper lid, in the middle of which is a hole half a foot in diameter, intended to receive an iron ladle pierced with holes, and coated with clay. The reservoir being filled with water, the melted copper is poured through the holes in the ladle into the water, where it is broken by its fall into smaller drops or grains, is rendered solid by the cold water, and is collected in the moveable bottom, which is afterwards to be raised by the annexed chain, that the granulated copper may be taken out.—The above is the process generally employed for making brass. But to make the finer and more malleable kinds of brass, besides the choice of pure calamine and pure copper, some manufacturers cement the brass a second time with calamine and charcoal, and sometimes add to it old brass, by which the new is said to be meliorated.

Brass is brittle when hot, but is so ductile when cold that it may be drawn into very fine wire. Its beautiful color, its hardness, its malleability, its fusibility, by which it may be easily cast into moulds, and its quality of being less subject to rust or verdigrise than copper, render it fit for the fabrication of many utensils.

plates,

plates, is placed over the cement, and the whole is covered with charcoal dust The crucible is then closed, and is heated only enough to make it gradually become red When the flame of the coals has acquired a cupreous color, an iron rod is introduced into the crucible, to try if the copper be melted under the cementing powder If that be the case, the action of the fire is moderated, and in a few minutes the crucible is taken out.

When it is cooled, the copper is found to have become yellow, and to have received an augmentation of a fourth, and sometimes of a third of its weight, and is nevertheless very malleable

This process is, as we see, a kind of cementation, in which the zinc is raised from its ore in vapors, and combines with the copper This method is advantageous, principally because the other metallic matters, and particularly the iron, from which lapis calaminaris is seldom free, do not rise in vapors, and consequently cannot combine with the copper

In order to effect this purpose more certainly, the cementing powder may be mixed up with clay into a paste, which being put in the bottom of the crucible, is to be covered with plates of copper and charcoal powder, proceeding as is directed above The copper, penetrated by the vapors of the zinc which pass through the paste, melts upon the surface of the paste, and does not mix with the other metals, which always alters the color and ductility of the brass These processes are from M Cramer

The advantages of converting copper into brass are, that its weight is augmented one fourth part, that its color is changed to one more agreeable, as it approaches the color of gold, that it is more fusible, and lastly, that it is less subject to rust, because zinc is less susceptible than copper of being altered by the action of air and of water

Although zinc be fixed to a certain degree in brass by the adhesion it contracts with the copper, yet when brass is melted and exposed to a violent fire during a certain time, the zinc dissipates in vapors, and even flames away, if the heat be strong enough, and if the heat lasts long enough, all the zinc will be evaporated and destroyed, so that what remains is copper

Copper, or copper converted into brass, or in any other form, but particularly when penetrated by any salts and reduced into verdigrise, produces always, when taken internally, the most troublesome consequences, and becomes a poison For this reason it is dangerous to use copper utensils and vessels for the purpose of cookery, and in many places they begin to be disused

For the same reason also, none of the preparations of this metal are ever employed medicinally by prudent physicians It appears, however, to enter into the composition of a remedy much used, the *Lilly of Paracelsus*, or *Tincture of Metals* but in fact, it is certain that the spirit of wine, employed for the preparation of this medicine, dissolves nothing of the calx of copper, or of the other calxes of metallic substances digested in it Mr Beaumé convinced himself of this fact by a most accurate examination of the *Lilly of Paracelsus*

The best remedies for persons poisoned by verdigrise are, mild, watery, mucilaginous, and oily drinks, given quickly and copiously, which ought to be immediately succeeded by evacuants to carry off the poison as fast as is possible.

The use of copper then in medicine is confined to external applications It is stimulant, tonic, and detersive Verdigrise enters into the ungentum Egyptiacum, into several plasters, the collyrium of Lanfranc, and the green balsam of Metz A blue water for the eyes is made with copper and sal ammoniac, which is called *Celestial water*.

CXX BREAD The grains of all vegetables are almost entirely composed of substances very proper for the nourishment of animals, and amongst grains those which contain a farinaceous matter are the most agreeable and most nutritive

Man, who appears to be designed by nature to eat of all substances which are capable of nourishing him, and still more of vegetables than animals, has, from time immemorial, and in all parts of the earth, used farinaceous grains as the principal basis of his food but as these grains cannot be without difficulty eaten by men in their natural state, this active and intelligent animal has gradually found means not only to extract the farinaceous part, that is, the only nutritive part of these grains, but also to prepare it so that it becomes a very agreeable and wholesome aliment, such as the bread we now generally eat

Nothing appears so easy at first sight as to grind corn, to make a paste with the flour and water, and to bake this paste in an oven They who are accustomed to enjoy the advantages of the finest human inventions, without reflecting on the labor it has cost to compleat them, think all these operations common and trivial However, it appears very certain, that for a long time men no otherwise prepared their corn than by boiling and forming compact, viscous cakes, not very agreeable to the taste, and of difficult digestion, before they were able to make bread of good taste and quality, as we have now It was necessary to invent and compleat ingenious machines for grinding corn, and separating the pure flour with little trouble and labor, and that inquiries, or rather some happy chance, which some observing person availed himself of, should discover that flour mixed with a certain quantity of water is susceptible of a fermentation, which almost entirely destroys its viscidity, heightens its taste, and renders it proper to make a light bread, very agreeable to the taste, and of easy digestion

This essential operation, on which the good quality of bread depends, is entirely of the province of chemistry It would add to the honour of the ancient cultivators of chemistry, to attribute to them so useful and important a discovery, but unhappily it is too probable that they had no share in it The ancient chemists were engaged in other pursuits than that of bread and other common objects They hoped to make gold; and what is bread in comparison with gold?

However that be, to the fortunate invention of raising the paste before baking we owe the perfection of the art of making bread This operation consists in keeping some paste or dough, till by a peculiar spirituous fermentation it swells, rarefies, and acquires a smell and taste quick, pungent, spirituous, somewhat sour, and rather disagreeable. This fermented dough is well worked with some fresh dough, which is by that mixture, and moderate heat, disposed to a similar, but less advanced fermentation than that above-mentioned By this fermentation the dough is attenuated and divided, air is introduced into it, which

which being incapable of disengaging itself from the tenacious and solid paste, forms in it small cavities, raises and swells it hence the small quantity of fermented paste which disposes the rest to ferment, is called *leaven*, from the French word *lever*, signifying to raise.

When the dough is thus raised, it is in a proper state to be put into the oven, where, while it is baked, it dilates itself still more by the rarefaction of the air, and of the spirituous substance it contains, and it forms a bread full of eyes or cavities, consequently light, and entirely different from the heavy, compact, viscous, and indigested masses made by baking unfermented dough,

The invention of beer, or wine of grains, furnishes a new matter useful in the making of bread This matter is the froth which forms upon the surface of these liquors during fermentation When it is mixed with dough, it raises it better and more quickly than ordinary leaven It is called *yeast* or *barm* By means of this the finest, lightest bread is made It often happens that bread made with leaven dough has a sourish and not agreeable taste, which may proceed from too great a quantity of leaven, or from leaven in which the fermentation has advanced too far This inconvenience does not happen to bread made with yeast, because the fermentation of this substance is not too far advanced, or because more attention is given to that finer bread

It may be asked, why, since dough is capable of fermenting spontaneously and singly, as we see from the leaven, a substance is added to dispose it to ferment The true reason is, that all the parts of a fermenting substance do not ferment at the same time, nor to the same degree, so that some parts of this substance have finished their fermentation while others have not yet begun The fermentable liquors which contain much sugar, as hydromel, and must of wines, give proofs of this truth, for, after these liquors have become very vinous, they have still very distinctly a saccharine taste but all saccharine matter is still susceptible of fermentation, and, in fact, if vinous hydromel, or must, or even new beer, be distilled, so that all their ardent spirit shall be separated, and the residuums diluted with water, we shall see a second fermentation take place, and a new quantity of ardent spirit formed.

The same thing precisely happens to dough, and still more sensibly, from its viscosity and want of fluidity, so that if it be left to ferment alone, and without the help of leaven, as the fermentation proceeds very slowly and successively, the parts which ferment first will have become sour and vapid before all the rest be sufficiently attenuated and changed, by which the bread will acquire a disagreeable taste

A mixture of a small quantity of leaven with dough effectually prevents this inconvenience, because the effect of this leaven, and of all fermenting substances, is to dispose to a similar fermentation all matters capable of it, with which it is mixed, or rather, by means of leaven, the fermentation of all the parts of such substances is effected more nearly at the same time

Bread well raised and baked differs from unfermented bread, not only in being less compact, lighter, and of a more agreeable taste, but also in being more easily miscible with water, with which it does not form a viscous mass, which circumstance is of great importance in digestion

CXXI BRONZE Bronze is a compound of copper and tin, to which sometimes other metallic substances, particularly zinc, are added.

Bronze

Bronze is brittle, hard, and sonorous It is employed for various uses, as for making bells, cannons, and statues, and the proportions of the component metals are varied to suit the several uses to which it is applied

The compound of copper and tin has a greater than the intermediate specific gravity Two ounces of a metal composed of four-fifths of pure copper, and one fifth of pure tin have seven grains and the tenth of a grain more of specific gravity, than the same quantities of these two metals not allayed have (k) This proves that in the union of copper and tin there is a penetration of parts, that is, that one metal enters into the pores of the other Perhaps even this effect is reciprocal

Many chemists, and particularly Glauber and Becker, have a long time ago remarked, that the specific gravities of metallic allays differed more or less from what they ought to be, if there were no penetration, and that sometimes the effect is contrary. But lately this matter has been treated with more precision Several good chemists, such as Eisporn, Hahn, Krafft, and Gellert, have given results of well conducted experiments on this subject *See Gellert's Metallurgic Chemistry See the words* ALLAY, GRAVITY (SPECIFIC)

Mr Tillet, member of the Royal Academy of Sciences, observes, in his Memoir concerning the ductility of metals, that when the mixture of copper with tin is made in the proportions above-mentioned, the color of the copper is entirely annulled and covered by that of the tin, although the quantity of copper be four times the quantity of tin This singular effect cannot be understood without admitting a total change in the size and disposition of the pores of the compound metal, which consequently is a new proof of the reciprocal penetration of the two metals

As tin is less sensible to the action of salts, of moisture, and of the air, than copper, it is also less liable to rust hence bronze is less apt to be covered with verdigrise than pure copper is This is one reason why this allay is used for cannons, statues, and works exposed to the air and weather

The greater fusibility of bronze than of copper is also an advantageous property, and much facilitates the casting of large works, as statues, bells, and cannon

Lastly, a phenomenon worthy of attention is, that tin, though greatly softer and less sonorous than copper, nevertheless renders this metal, by being allayed with it in a proper proportion, more hard and more sonorous hence this allay is used for bells.

The operation by which large works of bronze are cast is sufficiently simple For this purpose a brick furnace is used, nearly of the shape of an oven for baking bread The floor of this furnace is concave, and consists of a composition of sand and clay In this hollow floor the metals to be fused are put The furnace has three openings

The first is a lateral mouth, at which enters the flame of wood placed in a second furnace on one side of the first the second opening is a chimney placed on the side opposite to the mouth, by means of which the flame is drawn over

(k) The author means, I suppose, that a metallic mass, weighing two ounces, composed of four-fifths of copper and one fifth part of tin, weighs, in water, 7 1/10 grains more than the same quantities of these two metals would together weigh, in water, if not allayed

the metal The third opening is a hole which is opened and shut at pleasure, through which the inner part of the furnace may be occasionally inspected, that the state of the metal may be observed When the metal is in the state required, a fourth opening is then unclosed, communicating with the hollow floor, and through which the melted metal flows by channels into the moulds prepared to receive it

CXXII BRYONY (*l*)

CXXIII BURDOCK (*m*)

CXXIV BUTTER Butter is the fat, oily, and inflammable part of milk This kind of oil is naturally distributed through all the substances of the milk, in very small particles, which are interposed betwixt the caseous and serous parts, amongst which it keeps itself suspended by a slight adhesion, but without being dissolved It is in the same state in which oil is, in emulsions, hence the same whiteness of milk and emulsions, and hence by rest the oily parts separate from both these liquors to the surface, and form a cream. *See* EMULSION

When butter is in the state of cream, its proper oily parts are not yet sufficiently united together to form a homogeneous mass They are still half separated by the interposition of a pretty large quantity of caseous and serous particles The butter is compleatly formed by pressing out these heterogeneous parts by means of continued percussion It then becomes an uniform soft mass

Fresh butter, which has undergone no change, has scarcely any smell, its taste is mild and agreeable, it melts with a weak heat, and none of its principles are disengaged by the heat of boiling water These properties, together with that of not inflaming but with a heat greater than that of boiling water, capable of decomposing it, and reducing it to vapors, prove that the oily part of butter is of the nature of the mild, fat, and fixed oils obtained from many vegetable substances by expression *See* OILS (SWEET EXPRESSED)

The half fluid consistence of butter, as of most other concrete oily matters, is caused by a considerable quantity of acid, united with the oily part but this acid is so well combined, that it is not sensible while the butter is fresh, and has undergone no change, but when it grows old, and undergoes some kind of fermentation, then the acid is disengaged more and more, and this is the cause that butter, like oils of the same kind, becomes rancid by age

The acid of butter is more quickly and sensibly disengaged by fire If butter be exposed to a degree of fire strong enough to make it smoke, vapors are exhaled from it insupportably acrid, which draws tears from the eyes, and excite coughing, as may be daily observed in kitchens These vapors are nothing else than the disengaged acid The remaining part of the butter after this operation has a strong taste, very different from its former mildness, because the part of the acid which is not exhaled is become sensible and half-disengaged by

(*l*) BRYONY. From two ounces of this plant Neuman obtained by water ten drams of gummy extract, and from the same quantity he obtained by spirit two drams two scruples and a half of resinous extract

(*m*) BURDOCK ROOT From 16 drams of this root Neuman extracted by water 7 drams 52 grains, and from an equal quantity of it by spirit he extracted 5 drams and 10 grains.

the action of the fire. The same thing precisely happens when butter is distilled in a retort

To decompose butter by distillation, a much greater heat than that of boiling water must be applied to it acid vapors are then raised of considerable volatility and acrimony These vapors are accompanied with a small portion of oil, which being that part which is mostly deprived of its acid, does not congeal, then a second oil of a red color passes, which congeals when cold, and which becomes more and more thick as the distillation advances Lastly, a small quantity of charry matter remains in the retort, which in an open fire can be scarcely burnt entirely, and reduced to ashes

If the congealed oil in the receiver be again distilled, more acid and fluid oil are obtained Thus the whole of it may be reduced into acid and fluid oil by repeated distillations

The acid obtained is accompanied with phlegm, particularly at first, and with a portion of oil united with it, which it renders soluble in water, and to which it partly owes its volatility It is owing to this oil that the acid has the empyreumatic smell of burnt butter

There are many essential remarks to be made upon this analysis of butter by distillation, because it presents exactly the same phenomena as the analysis of all other concrete oily matters of the same kind, such as wax, suet, cacao, butter, sperma-ceti, and may be considered as a specimen of the decomposition of all these matters

First, it is necessary that these distillations should be made slowly, and with the precise degree of heat necessary for continuing a moderate distillation, because when the distilation is too much hurried, the acid has not time to separate itself, and the concrete oily matter passes almost entirely into the receiver without suffering any decomposition but whatever management be employed, a considerable part of this half-decomposed matter always passes, which must be subjected to future distillations in order to reduce it to fluid oil

Secondly, when the distillation is too much hurried, the acid passes in white sensible vapors from the quantity of oil united with it For the same reason, towards the end of the distillation, when the fire must be raised, the acid always passes in this form of white sensible vapors

Thirdly, at each distillation, made of butter, or of its congealed oil, there is always a portion of oil entirely decomposed, and thus the quantity continually diminishes, and sensibly

This quantity of entirely decomposed oil is proportionable to the quantities of phlegm, acid, charry residuum, or earthy phlogisticated matter, which are obtained at each distillation, and are the proximate principles of the oil This remark is applicable to the distillation of any oil *See* Oil

We ought also to observe in general upon this analysis of butter, that this matter, although derived from animal bodies, does not yield a particle of volatile alkali, neither does the fat of animals, which proves that these substances are not assimilated to other animal substances, all which, when decomposed, furnish volatile alkali, without excepting the oils obtained from these substances

Butter is constantly used in food, from its agreeable taste, but to be wholesome, it must be very fresh, and free from rancidity, and also not fried or burnt,

burnt, otherwise its acrid and even caustic acid being disengaged, disorders digestion, renders it difficult and painful, excites acrid, empyreumatic belchings, and lastly, introduces much acrimony into the blood. Some persons have so delicate stomachs, that they are even affected with these inconveniences by fresh butter and by milk. *See* MILK. This observation is also applicable to oil, to fat, to chocolate, and in general to all oleaginous matters.

CXXV. BUTTER *of* ANTIMONY. Butter of antimony, called by some chemists the *glacial oil of antimony*, is composed of marine acid united with the reguline part of antimony.

This is one of the combinations which cannot be made directly, that is, by the application of pure and liquid marine acid to the regulus of antimony; for in this manner the marine acid, however strong, dissolves none, or almost none, of the regulus: but when the acid is in its highest degree of concentration, reduced almost to dryness, as it is in several combinations, and when the body to which it is united has a less strong affinity to it than the regulus of antimony has, then it quits that body to unite with the regulus, and forms the butter of antimony.

Marine acid united with mercury has all the above-mentioned conditions, wherefore butter of antimony may be made by mixing together corrosive sublimate and regulus of antimony, both well powdered, and by applying a certain heat and distillation.

Lemeri, the most exact of the operators who have written, says, that the best proportion of corrosive sublimate and regulus of antimony is sixteen parts of the former to six parts of the latter. He observes, that this mixture frequently becomes very hot, some time after it has been made. This heat proceeds from the re-action of the two matters upon each other even without fire.

To proceed to the distillation of butter of antimony, this mixture must be put in a retort of convenient size, the neck of which ought to be large and short; this retort is to be placed in a furnace with a sand-bath; a receiver is to be luted, and the distillation is to be carried on at first by a gentle fire, which is to be encreased as more heat becomes necessary to continue the operation; a heavy liquor rises, which congeals in the receiver when it cools: this is the butter of antimony. The operation is stopped when it appears that it cannot be continued without a great encrease of heat, by which fluid mercury would be distilled instead of butter of antimony.

If then it be required to obtain this mercury, which is a very pure mercury, revived from corrosive sublimate, before the fire is encreased, it is proper to remove the receiver, and apply another containing some water.

It is evident, that as the marine acid only unites with the regulus of antimony by disengaging itself from the mercury of the corrosive sublimate, this latter metal ought to appear in its proper fluid form; but as it is less volatile than the butter of antimony, it does not rise till this has passed, and the fire be encreased.

Butter of antimony may also be made by using antimony itself instead of its regulus, because the acid of corrosive sublimate attacks as easily the regulus of antimony in the antimony itself, although it be there united with sulphur, as when it is pure: but it is evident, that in this case more antimony must be used, than the requisite quantity of regulus in the preceding operation. Lemeri

 observes,

obſerves, that twelve parts of antimony are neceſſary for ſixteen parts of corroſive ſublimate

When butter of antimony is made by this latter method, it more readily congeals, and is more ſolid than when made with the regulus

Mr Baron, in his notes on Lemeri's Chemiſtry, ſays, that this proceeds from the greater quantity of acid contained in the butter made with the regulus than in that made with antimony This matter would require a particular examination

However that may be, a part of this butter made with antimony always congeals in the neck of the retort, and is frequently accumulated there in ſufficient quantity to block up the paſſage, by which means the confined vapors may occaſion an exploſion This inconvenience is prevented by applying a hot-coal near the neck of the retort, by which the butter is melted, and made to flow into the receiver

It is evident, that when the butter of antimony is made with antimony, if the diſtillation be continued after the butter has paſſed, we ſhall not then obtain fluid mercury, but a combination of mercury with the ſulphur of the antimony, that is, a cinnabar will be ſublimed This is called the *cinnabar of antimony* *See* MERCURY, SULPHUR, *and* CINNABAR

This cinnabar makes its appearance towards the end of the operation by red vapors As ſoon as theſe are ſeen, the receiver ought to be changed

The butter of antimony made by either of theſe operations, eſpecially by the latter, is generally rendered more or leſs impure by ſome fluid mercury, or by ſome cinnabar, which are raiſed along with it but it is eaſily purified from theſe extraneous ſubſtances by a ſecond diſtillation with a gentle heat, when it paſſes very white and pure This ſecond diſtillation, as all other repeated diſtillations and ſublimations for the purifying of ſubſtances, is called *rectification*

Sweet ſublimate, *mercurial panacea*, and *white precipitate*, are alſo mercurial combinations with marine acid, and, like the corroſive ſublimate, are capable of being decompoſed by means of regulus of antimony, and of forming with it kinds of butter of antimony But Lemeri obſerves, that theſe butters are leſs cauſtic than that made with corroſive ſublimate, undoubtedly becauſe theſe mercurial compounds contain leſs marine acid

Laſtly, butter of antimony may be made with *luna cornea*, which is a combination of ſilver with very concentrated marine acid, which is nearly in the ſame ſtate as it is in corroſive ſublimate, (*ſee* LUNA CORNEA), becauſe the marine acid has leſs affinity with ſilver than with regulus of antimony This butter is called the *lunar butter of antimony*

Butter of antimony then contains a very concentrated marine acid, which is not ſo intimately engaged with the regulus of antimony as to loſe all its properties, hence we may account for the property which the butter of antimony has of attracting moiſture from air, and for its cauſticity, for it is ſtrongly corroſive, and is applied, like lapis infernalis, to ulcers and to carious bones *See* CAUSTICITY

This metallic ſalt has been called *butter*, from its conſiſtence, which is nearly the ſame as that of butter, and from the facility with which it meltswith a very gentle heat

Butter

Butter of antimony ought to be claſſed amongſt the ſalts which are at once cryſtallizable and deliqueſcent, for however confuſed the maſs ſeems after diſtillation, it is in fact a heap of very ſmall cryſtals.

By the operation of butter of antimony, and its properties, ſeveral eſſential properties of the marine acid and of regulus of antimony are diſcovered.

Firſt, although the marine acid has a great affinity with this ſemimetal, it cannot diſſolve it, but when highly concentrated. This phenomenon is analogous to thoſe preſented by the marine acid with mercury and with ſilver, to both which it has a great affinity, but which it cannot diſſolve unleſs it be very highly concentrated, or applied to them when their aggregation is broken, as we ſee by the operations of making *white precipitate*, *corroſive ſublimate*, *luna cornea*, and of the *concentrated parting*. See *all theſe words*.

Secondly, the property which the butter of antimony has of not being decompoſed by fire alone, as the metallic ſalts are which contain the vitriolic and nitrous acids, depends on the great adheſion which the marine acid contracts with the regulus of antimony, as it generally does with other metallic matters, and on its property of volatilizing them, or carrying them along with it in diſtillation, which we ſee happens in corroſive ſublimate, luna cornea, ſmoking ſpirit of Libavius, and many other chemical operations, in which the moſt fixed metals are carried off by marine acid.

Thirdly, the butter of antimony is by the affuſion of water changed in its nature, or rather is divided into two parts, one of which is perfectly diſſolved by the water, and another part is precipitated, being inſoluble by water. The diſſolved part contains its greateſt poſſible quantity of acid, and the precipitated part contains the leaſt poſſible quantity of acid. This latter part, when well waſhed, is called *mercurius vitæ*, or *powder of algaroth*. *See* POWDER *of* ALGAROTH.

Mr Beaumé pretends, that the powder of algaroth is improperly ſaid to contain the leaſt poſſible quantity of acid, ſince, by a ſufficient lavation, he has been able to deprive it of every veſtige of an acid.

Butter of antimony is ſoluble in nitrous acid, and this ſolution is made with great violence: afterwards, by evaporation of the acids, a white calx of antimony is formed, called *Bezoar mineral*. See *that word*.

CXXVI. BUTTER *of* ARSENIC. Butter of arſenic, called alſo *corroſive oil of arſenic*, is a combination of marine acid with arſenic. This combination is made by a proceſs ſimilar to that of the butter of antimony. According to Lemeri, equal parts of butter of arſenic and corroſive ſublimate ought to be pulveriſed, well mixed, and diſtilled together, by which a butyraceous liquor is obtained ſimilar to butter of antimony in its external appearance.

When the diſtillation cannot be continued without conſiderably encreaſing the fire, the receiver ought to be taken off, and another receiver, in which there is ſome water, adapted to the retort, then, upon raiſing the fire, fluid mercury may be obtained. *See* BUTTER *of* ANTIMONY.

This experiment ſhews that the affinity of marine acid to arſenic is greater than to mercury. In this operation the mercury is revived from the corroſive ſublimate.

It

It is evident that this butter of arsenic must be a most violent caustic. It ought not to be ever used, from its poisonous quality. *See* ARSENIC.

It does not appear that this combination of marine acid with arsenic has been carefully examined by any chemist.

CXXVII. BUTTER *of* CACAO. Butter of cacao is an oily, concrete, white matter, of a firmer consistence than butter, or even than suet. This substance is extracted from the kernel of a fruit called *cacao*, with which *chocolate* is made.

As the butter of cacao is a true congealed oil, it cannot be obtained without a heat sufficient to melt it. The best method is to bruise the cacao, and to boil it in water. Almost all the superabundant and uncombined oil, which this substance contains, is liquefied, and separated from the parenchyma and extractive part, and as it is lighter, it swims on the surface of the liquor in which it is left to congeal, that it may more easily be taken off. This butter is generally mixed with some broken solid bits of the cacao fruit, from which it may be purified by melting with a very gentle heat without water, in a pretty deep vessel, and by keeping it thus melted, long enough for an entire separation of the matters to take place according to the specific gravities. By this method, a very white and pure butter of cacao may be obtained.

This oily concrete substance has a very mild taste, it has no aromatic smell, it does not rise in distillation without a heat superior to that of boiling water, by distillation it is partly decomposed, lastly, it does not flame, till it is sufficiently heated to be reduced into vapors. As these are precisely the properties of mild and fat oils obtained from vegetable and animal matters by expression only, the butter of cacao must be undoubtedly ranged in this class, and as it is concrete, it is analogous to other concrete oily matters of the same nature, such as wax, fat, butter of milk, &c. also it presents the same phenomena when decomposed and attenuated by distillation. For the reason of this *see* BUTTER.

Butter of cacao has quite the same medicinal properties as all the mild expressed oils. It is emollient and blunting when not rancid, it enters into the composition of pomatums. *See* OILS (SWEET EXPRESSED).

CXXVIII. BUTTER *of* WAX. Butter of wax is nothing but half-decomposed wax, that is, wax deprived of a part of its acid by distillation. As this acid is the cause of the consistence of the oily part of wax, the reason is evident that the butter is softer than the wax itself. It has a strong smell, and, when left exposed to the air, it does not resume its consistence, in which it essentially differs from resinous matters. *See* WAX.

CXXIX. BUTTER *of* TIN. *Butter of tin* is a name given by some chemists to a combination of tin with the concentrated marine acid of corrosive sublimate.

Tin, as well as the regulus of antimony, has a stronger affinity to marine acid than mercury has. If then corrosive sublimate and tin, reduced to small parts, be mixed together, these two substances will act upon each other even without the application of heat, so that in time the mixture becomes moist, and attracts the humidity of the air. If these substances be distilled together immediately after their mixture, the corrosive sublimate is much more quickly decomposed

decomposed by the tin, the marine acid quits the mercury to unite with the tin, the greatest part of which it carries off along with it In this distillation a kind of *marine salt with basis of tin* passes over Part of this combination is in form of a liquor which smokes continually, even when cold. This is called the *smoking spirit of Libavius* Another part is raised in a concrete form, which more particularly deserves the appellation of *butter of tin*, although it seems that several chemists give this name indifferently to the liquor or concrete matter, or to both of them at the same time. *See* SPIRIT (SMOKING) *of* LIBAVIUS

CXXX BUTTON By the word *button* is meant the metal which is collected generally in a roundish mass at the bottom of a crucible after fusion, or which remains in the cupels after cupellation.

C.

CXXXI. CADMIA The name of *Cadmia*, or *Calamine*, is given to several different substances What is called the *Cadmia of the furnaces* is a matter which is sublimed when ores containing zinc, like those of Rammelsberg, are smelted This cadmia consists of the flowers of zinc sublimed during the fusion, and adhering to the inner surfaces of the walls of furnaces, where they suffer a semi-fusion, and therefore acquire some solidity So great a quantity of these are collected, that they form very thick incrustations, which must be frequently taken off The name of *Cadmia of furnaces*, has also been given to all the soots and metallic sublimates formed by smelting in the great, although there certainly are great differences in these matters *See* SMELTING *of* ORES

Several authors call *Native* or *Fossil Cadmia*, a sort of stone or mineral, containing zinc, iron, and sometimes other substances It is of a yellow or reddish colour, and is also called *Calamy*, *Calamine*, or lapis calaminaris. Both this mineral and the *Cadmia of Furnaces* are used for the preparation of brass. *See* BRASS

Lastly, some chemists have given the name of *Fossil Cadmia* to a mineral containing arsenic, frequently bismuth, silver, and particularly the semi-metal, the calx of which being melted with vitrifiable matters, forms a beautiful blue glass This mineral is better known by the name *Cobalt*, which only ought to be given to it, to avoid the confusion attending the application of the same name to different substances *See* COBALT.

CXXXII CALAMINE *See* CADMIA, and ORES *of* ZINC

CXXXIII CALAMUS AROMATICUS (*n*)

CXXXIV CALCINATION The calcination of a body is, properly speaking, the exposing of it to the action of fire, to produce some change upon it.

The principal effects of fire in chemical operations are to carry off the volatile principles, and to separate them from the fixed, or to occasion the combustion of inflammable matters Hence it follows that bodies are calcined either to

(*n*) CALAMUS AROMATICUS The root of this plant has an agreeable flavour, and peculiar taste, both which are caused by an essential oil, of which two scruples were obtained by distillation from 16 ounces of the dry root *Neuman*

deprive

deprive them of some volatile principle, or to destroy their inflammable principle, and sometimes for both of these purposes

We have examples of the first kind of calcination, in exposing calcareous earths and stones to the fire, to convert them into quicklime, which is effected by the entire evaporation of the watery principle contained in this kind of earth. *See* QUICKLIME

The calcination of *Gypsum*, of *Alum*, of *Borax*, and of several other *Salts*, by fire, which deprives them of the water necessary for their crystallization, the roasting of minerals, by which the fire carries off the sulphur, arsenic, and other volatile contents, ought to be referred to the first kind of calcination.

We have an example of the second kind of calcination, by exposing imperfect metals to fire; by which they lose their inflammable principle, their form, and metallic properties, and are changed into earthy matters called *Metallic Calxes*

It is necessary to observe, that this second calcination differs essentially from the first, as the changes produced by it upon imperfect metals are not effected by evaporation, but by decomposition and destruction of their phlogiston It is therefore a *combustion*, and not a *volatilisation* of their inflammable principle

Hence it follows, that the first kind of calcination may succeed without the contact of air and in close vessels, although it is more quick and complete in open vessels, from a property of air, by which it greatly accelerates the evaporation of volatile bodies *See* AIR But as the second kind of calcination is a true combustion, like that of all inflammable bodies, it requires all the conditions necessary for combustion, and particularly the free access of air *See* COMBUSTION *and* CALXES (METALLIC)

There are many bodies, in the calcination of which an evaporation of volatile parts happens, and also a destruction or deprivation of their inflammable principle, although without any sensible combustion of this latter. Such particularly are all combinations of imperfect metallic matters with vitriolic and nitrous acids when these bodies are exposed to fire, their acid evaporates, and at the same time carries off with it their inflammable principle We have examples of this kind of calcination in exposing to fire *Martial Vitriol* and *Bezoard Mineral*

As vitriolic acid, and still more nitrous acid, deprive the imperfect metals of more or less of their phlogiston even without fire, several of these metals, particularly iron, copper, tin, regulus of antimony, are reduced, after they have been dissolved in these acids, to a state similar to that of calcination with access of air, that is to say, they become earths, not possessed of metallic properties, which they cannot resume without the addition of phlogiston Hence most chemists consider acids as capable of calcining these metals, and they accordingly call earths of metals which have been dephlogisticated by acids, without fire, *Calxes*

Lastly, nitrous acid, when engaged in a fixed alkali, that is, nitre having the property of inflaming when applied to a combustible substance with a red heat, and of making the phlogiston of these bodies burn, becomes a very powerful agent for the calcination of many substances, and particularly of imperfect metals and charry matters. *See* NITRE. We have a very good example of this kind of calcination in the preparation of diaphoretic antimony

This calcination of metals by nitre is effected partly by a dephlogistication similar to that by nitrous acid in humid solutions, and partly by combustion which does not hinder it from succeeding without access of air, and in close vessels, from the peculiar property of nitre in this respect See NITRE

It is proper to observe, that certain preparations of gold and silver are improperly called calxes, because they are not truly calcined, no method being known by which they can be deprived of their phlogiston See GOLD, SILVER, *and* METALS (PERFECT)

What is improperly called *Calx of Gold*, is nothing but gold reduced into very fine particles, either by amalgamation with mercury, or by its separation from other solvents Most of these improper names, found in such numbers in chemistry, proceed from the ignorance of ancient chemists, and still more of alchemists, who all believed, for example, that they had processes for decomposing and calcining gold. Nothing is more equivocal than the pretended calcinations of perfect metals We cannot, however, affirm its impossibility Some facts even seem to make it probable, such as the destruction of gold in the focus of Thirsnhausen's great lens, an account of which is published by Homberg in the Memoirs of the Academy of Sciences, and the calcination of gold by long reverberation, in the manner of Isaacus Hollandus. But if the most simple and easy experiments of chemistry require frequent repetition to be sufficiently established, certainly these, which are exceedingly difficult and laborious, require great attention See COMBUSTION, *for some essential observations regarding the second kind of calcination*

CXXXV. CALXES *of* METALS Metalic calxes are earths of metals deprived of their phlogiston, and consequently of their metallic properties

All metallic substances, excepting gold, silver, platina and mercury, are susceptible of being deprived of their inflammable principle by several methods

The first method is by burning their phlogiston in open air, and by a calcination, or rather a combustion similar to that of all other combustible matters *See* CALCINATION *and* COMBUSTION

The second method is by applying to metals acids capable of depriving them of their phlogiston, such as vitriolic acid, and particularly nitrous acid This kind of calcination of metals is made in the humid way, and by solution *See* SOLUTION

The third method is by nitre, with which metallic matters may be detonated This third method, which is composed of the two former, is the most efficacious and expeditious *See* NITRE, *and* DETONATION *of* NITRE.

The earths of metals deprived of phlogiston by any of these methods have properties peculiar to each, concerning which the articles of the several metallic substances ought to be consulted, but they also have properties general and common to all These are the following

Not only calcined metals lose the characteristic properties of metals, but also the following changes are effected The more perfectly metallic matters are calcined, the more they lose of their fusibility, so that very fusible substances, such as tin and regulus of antimony, are rendered by a perfect calcination, (that is, till they become very white) bodies absolutely infusible, and which may be

classed

classed amongst those that are refractory Hence it is proved that phlogiston is the principle of fusibility of metals

In proportion as metallic substances lose their phlogiston, they become more fixed This property is less sensible in metals, from their fixity, than in semi-metals, all which are very volatile when in their metallic state, and the calxes or earths of which become exceedingly fixed, as we see very evidently from the example of diaphoretic antimony, which resists the most violent fi e without the least loss, and which recovers all its volatility, if it be restored to its reguline state by addition of phlogiston. This proves that phlogiston is a principle essentially volatile, and that it communicates its volatility to certain bodies with which it is combined

Metallic earths become less soluble in acids, and particularly in nitrous acid, by being deprived of phlogiston, as we may perceive from crocus martis when well calcined, from calxes of tin, of regulus of antimony, &c Hence we are led to conclude, that the solubility of metallic substances by acids, and particularly by nitrous acid, depends on the intervention of phlogiston for if calxes be reduced by adding phlogiston, the metals resulting from that reduction will then recover their solubility.

What we have said concerning the general changes produced by calcination of metallic matters, upon their fusibility, their fixity, and solubility, may also be applied to their opacity, their specific gravity, in a word, to all their metallic properties, which are always diminished so much more in metallic calxes, as they are more perfectly dephlogisticated This seems to indicate, that if an entire and perfect calcination of metallic sustances could be effected, they would then have no metallic property, and perhaps they would not specifically differ from each other, and only be one and the same kind of earth This is certain, that when the calcination of metals has been too long continued, their calxes become irreducible, or at least much more difficultly reducible, and this reduction is always made with loss, so that the quantity of metal originally calcined is never again obtained

Although metallic calxes are essentially different from calx of stone or quicklime, they have nevertheless some similar properties, particularly those which relate to fixed and volatile alkalis Thus, for example, fixed alkalis receive from metallic calxes the same causticity and properties as from quicklime, and volatile alkali may be separated from sal ammoniac by metallic calxes, and particularly by minium, as it may by quicklime, and it receives the same changes, that is, it becomes more penetrating, is always fluid, and cannot be reduced to a concrete state, when treated with a sufficient quantity of these matters *See* QUICKLIME.

CXXXVI CAMOMILE (o).

(o) CAMOMILE In the cup of the flowers of camomile resides a small quantity of blue essential oil The flowers contain also a saline substance which being extracted by decoction in wine, precipitated silver and mercury from nitrous acid, and these precipitates were different from luna cornea and corrosive sublimate *Neuman* Camomile flowers have been found by Dr Pringle's experiments to possess eminently an antiseptic quality.

CXXXVII CAMPHOR Camphor is a vegetable, concrete, very volatile substance, and inflammable, as essential oils are, of a strong smell, and easily soluble in spirit of wine.

From all these properties, camphor perfectly resembles resins; but on the other side, it essentially differs from them in this, that when exposed to fire in close vessels, it is entirely sublimed without suffering any decomposition, and without leaving any residuum of coal or other matter Although it has a strong taste, it has not the acrimony of essential oils the most caustic alkalis do not act upon it the vitriolic and nitrous acids dissolve it, but without effervescence, heat, inflammation, scorching, or other sensible change, even when these acids are concentrated

Nitrous acid dissolves camphor without commotion, and the solution is clear and limpid It is called *Oil of Camphor* When it is mixed with too much water, the mixture becomes turbid and milky, because the acid has a stronger affinity with water than with camphor The camphor then quits the acid, and appears in white flocks, which soon precipitate to the bottom of the containing vessel, their weight being encreased by some adhering acid But when this acid is taken off by the water, the flocks of camphor rise to the surface, and there float When they are compleatly washed and dried, they are found to be camphor entirely similar to what it was before this solution and precipitation This is a manifest proof that camphor receives no change from the nitrous acid, which, however, of all acids, acts the most powerfully upon oily matters *See* OILS (ESSENTIAL) *and* RESINS, *for the resemblances and differences betwixt camphor and these substances*

It follows from what has been said concerning the properties of camphor, that this singular substance, although it has many of the essential properties of oils and resins, is not, however, comparable to any of those which are known, and forms a class apart As, excepting its concrete state, camphor approaches more to the nature of ether, precisely by those very properties in which it differs from oils, it is to be presumed that this substance is analogous to ether, as Mr Macquer conjectures in his Elements of Chemistry *See* ETHER.

All the camphor which is sold comes from India and Japan It is procured from a kind of laurel called *Laurus Camphorifera*, great numbers of which grow in the island Borneo A long time this tree was believed to be the only vegetable containing camphor, but several modern chemists, and particularly Mr Cartheuser, have discovered, that many aromatic plants, as thyme, rosemary, sage, and almost all the labiated kind, contain a substance of the nature of camphor, which may be extracted, although in very small quantities

Camphor when first extracted from its tree is mixed with many impurities, and is then called *Rough Camphor* The Dutch, who chiefly make a trade of it, purify it by sublimation in glass matrasses

Camphor is used in medicine as sedative and antispasmodic It succeeds well in many convulsions, and other nervous affections. This quality is common to it, and to all other ethereal, oily, volatile substances, such as *Ether*, *Dippel's Animal oil*, *highly rectified Essential Oils*, *Musk*, *Castor*, *Opium*, and other similar substances Hoffman has observed and commended, more than any other physician, the sedative powers of camphor. This substance is also very successfully used

used as a powerful antiseptic, and when dissolved in spirit of wine, is employed against gangrenes

CXXXVIII. CANTHARIDES (p)

CXXXIX. CAP. The piece which terminates the top of a melting furnace is called the *Cap*. This piece has the form of an oblong dome. In one side there is a large oval door, intended for the introduction of a considerable quantity of coal at a time, because this kind of furnace consumes a great deal, and must be quickly supplied. The upper part of the cap is terminated by a tube or chimney, which may be lengthened at pleasure by the addition of other tubes adjusted to each other. *See* FURNACE (MELTING).

CXL. CAPITAL. The *Capital* or *Head* is the upper part of an alembic. *See* ALEMBIC.

CXLI. CAPUT MORTUUM. This is a Latin name given to fixed and exhausted residuums remaining in retorts after distillations.

As these residuums are very different, according to the substances distilled, and the degree of heat employed, they ought to be specified more particularly by adding a term denoting their qualities, as, for example, we might say, *Earthy Residuum*, *Clarry Residuum*, *Saline Residuum*, &c. This method is more accurate and distinct, and is chiefly used by modern chemists.

CXLII. CARDAMOM (q).

CXLIII. CARDUUS (r).

CXLIV. CARMINE (s).

CXLV. CARNELIAN (t).

CXLVI. CASE HARDENING (u).

(p) CANTHARIDES. These insects contain a very acrid resinous substance, six grams and two scruples of which were extracted by spirit of wine from four ounces of cantharides. The stimulating power of cantharides is caused by this substance, and not, as some imagine, by a volatile alkali, of which they yield less by analysis than some other animal substances, and none without the action of fire. *Neuman.*

(q) CARDAMOM. An ounce of the seeds of the lesser cardamom contain about a scruple of essential oil, by which their pungency and aromatic smell are caused, with fourteen grains of resinous extract, and forty-five grains of mucilage. *Neuman.*

(r) CARDUUS BENEDICTUS. From four ounces of the leaves of this plant may be obtained about 4½ drams of resinous extract by means of spirit of wine, or from the same quantity of leaves, about 6½ of mucilaginous extract by means of water. In the juice of this plant, after proper depuration and evaporation, saline crystals similar to tartar are formed. *Neuman.*

(s) CARMINE is a red pigment prepared by dissolving cochineal in an alkaline lixivium, and precipitating the solution by alum. It consists, therefore, of the coloring matter of cochineal adhering to the earth of alum.

(t) CARNELIAN, *Carneolus*, or *Sardus*, is a semi-transparent reddish agate. *See* AGATE.

(u) CASE-HARDENING of iron is a superficial conversion of that metal into steel by the ordinary method of conversion, namely, by cementation with vegetable or animal coals. This operation is generally practised upon small pieces of iron wrought into tools, and instruments, to which a superficial conversion is sufficient, and it may be performed conveniently by putting the pieces of iron to be case-hardened, together with the cement, in an iron box, which is to be closely shut and exposed to a red heat during some hours. By this cementation, a certain thickness from the surface of the iron will be converted into steel, and a proper hardness may be afterwards given by sudden extinction of the heated pieces of converted iron in a cold fluid. *See* STEEL.

CXLVII CASSIA (x)

CXLVIII CASTOR (y)

CXLIX CAUSTIC (COMMON). Common caustic is a fixed alkaline salt, sharpened by quick-lime, and deprived of all moisture by drying and fusion The alkali employed for this preparation is generally potash A lixivium is made with quick lime, like that of the soap-boilers, called soap-leys *See* LIXIVIUM *of* SOAP BOILERS This lixivium is to be evaporated to dryness in a copper or silver vessel Afterwards the dry matter is to be put into a crucible, and exposed to fire till it flow like melted wax Then it is to be poured into a balon, and quickly cut into pieces, while it is still hot and moist, and is to be speedily put into a glass bottle, well closed with a glass stopper

An alkali thus treated is much more caustic than ordinary fixed alkali It is also more fusible, and attracts the moisture of the air much more readily, for which reason it ought to be cut and put into bottles, while it is yet hot, otherwise it would become very soon moist

This alkali when applied to the skin during half or three quarters of an hour, corrodes it, and forms a painful eschar, like that produced by burning. It is employed to open issues, which formerly were much used, but were afterwards almost abolished They have since been brought again into frequent use, and justly, for they are serviceable by evacuating vicious fluids which resist other remedies But at present common caustic is not much used for the opening of issues, because it occasions a quick and long pain The common method at present is to make an incision with a knife, and to promote the suppuration by methods well known in surgery

The causticity of common caustic must not be believed to proceed from a perfect drying and concentration of the alkali This concentration does indeed augment its causticity, but we are no less certain, that independantly of that, alkalis treated with quick-lime are much more active and caustic, even when they are fluid, than any other alkalis This is evident from the effects of the lixivium, or ley of soap boilers, which almost instantaneously corrodes and destroys all animal matters This causticity then is caused by some particular change produced upon alkalis fixed or volatile by quick-lime, which change probably consists in depriving them of some unctuous matter, which invelops and blunts their saline principle. *See* ALKALI (FIXED), ALKALI (VOLATILE), AMMONIAC SALT, SPIRIT (VOLATILE) *of* SAL AMMONIAC, LIXIVIUM *of* SOAP-BOILERS

CL CAUSTIC (LUNAR) Lunar caustic, or *Lapis Infernalis*, is a caustic made by taking from lunar crystals all their water of crystallization by fusion.

To make the lunar caustic, crystals of silver are to be put into a Hessian crucible, which ought to be large in proportion to the quantity to be used, be-

(x) CASSIA. The fruit called *Cassia Fistularis* contains a sweet saline substance, soluble in water or in spirit of wine *Neuman*

(y) CASTOR Two drams and a scruple of extract may be obtained from an ounce of castor by spirit of wine, or by water By distillation with water, the peculiar smell of the castor is given to the water hence we may probably infer that it contains an essential oil By distillation with spirit of wine, none of this peculiar smell is given to the spirit *Neuman*

cause

caufe a confiderable fwelling and frothing happens in the beginning of this fufion The crucible is to be placed in a furnace which ought to draw little air, and furrounded by a very fmall quantity of lighted coals, becaufe thefe cryftals are very fufible, and too great heat would be prejudicial to the preparation of the lunar cauftic This matter is then to be very quickly liquified In the beginning particularly, the heat ought to be moderate, otherwife a part of the matter might flow over the crucible, and deflagrate like nitre upon the coals, by which the filver would be reduced While the ebullition gradually diminifhes, the fire is to be encreafed, and when the matter is brought to a perfect and tranquil fufion, it is to be caft into an iron mould previoufly heated and greafed in its inner furface The lunar cauftic is there to be left till it is fixed and cold, and then it is to be put into a bottle with a glafs ftopper The lunar cauftic ought to be formed into fmall cylindrical pieces, like pencils, of about a line in diameter, and the furgeon who ufes them puts them in a crayon or pencil cafe, to prevent his fingers being injured by touching them The mould for the lunar cauftic is fo made as to give them that form It confifts of five or fix hollow cylinders, placed vertically and parallel to each other, to which a gutter is adapted, by means of which the matter is poured into them This mould is compofed of two pieces which exactly fit each other, in each of which the fame number of hollow femi-cylinders correfpond to thofe of the other By this difpofition, when the lunar cauftic is caft and cooled, it is obtained in entire cylinders, by feparating the two pieces of the mould.

The lunar cauftic muft be poured as foon as it is in tranquil fufion, for that degree of heat is fufficient to carry off its acid, which may be obferved to diffipate in fumes, and confequently, if it was left in the fire long after it is thus fufed, it would lofe fome of its caufticity, which it entirely owes to this acid

The operation for lunar cauftic fhews two remarkable phenomena The firft is the black color affumed by the cryftals of filver thus fufed I believe this color proceeds from a part of the phlogifton of the nitrous acid, which attaches itfelf to the filver fuperficially, and which always gives a black color to this and other white metals, fuch as mercury, lead, and bifmuth, when it is thus united to them

The other remarkable phenomenon is a certain fymmetry of arrangement, or cryftallization, which lunar cauftic takes when it cools and becomes folid If a pencil of lunar cauftic be broken into pieces, its inner fubftance may be obferved to be compofed of needles or radii paffing from the circumference to the center, much like the infide of the round ferruginous and fulphureous pyrites. This phenomenon is common to all bodies of a certain degree of fimplicity of compofition, which pafs without agitation from a liquid to a folid ftate, and is a fpecies of cryftallization Perhaps the fame phenomenon occurs in many other neutral falts in which it has not yet been remarked. *See* CRYSTALLIZATION

Lunar cauftic ought to be made with tefted filver If filver allayed with copper be ufed, the cryftals of filver ought to be well drained upon brown paper, by which they will be freed from the folution of copper, and will become white This folution of copper in nitrous acid when dried is alfo cauftic, but lefs fo than lunar cauftic It alfo has the inconvenience of becoming moift in the air *See* SILVER, CAUSTICITY, *and* CRYSTALS *of* SILVER.

CLI.

CLI CAUSTICITY. By this word is denoted a quality belonging to several substances, by the acrimony of which the parts of living animals may be corroded, and destroyed Bodies which have this quality, when taken internally are true poisons The causticity of some of these, as of *arsenic*, is so deadly, that even their external use is proscribed by prudent physicians

Several others, as *nitrous acid*, *lapis infernalis*, or *lunar caustic*, *common caustic*, *butter of antimony*, are daily and successfully used to consume excrescences, to destroy fungous flesh, to open issues, &c They succeed very well when properly employed, and skilfully managed

The causticity of bodies depends entirely on the state of the saline, and chiefly of the acid matters which they contain When these acids happen to be at the same time much concentrated, and slightly attached to the matters with which they are combined, they are then capable of acting, and are corrosive and caustic Thus fixed and volatile alkalis, although they are themselves caustic, become much more so by being treated with quicklime, because this substance deprives them of much fat or inflammable matter, which binds and restrains the action of their saline principle (z) By this treatment then, the saline principle is more disengaged, and rendered more capable of action Also, all combinations of metallic matters with acids, form salts more or less corrosive, because these acids are deprived of all their superabundant water, and are besides but imperfectly saturated by the metallic matters

Nevertheless, some other circumstance is necessary to constitute the causticity of these saline metallic matters For the same quantity of marine acid, which when pure and diluted with a certain quantity of water should be incapable of producing any harm, shall however produce all the effects of a corrosive poison when it is united with mercury in *corrosive sublimate*, although this sublimate shall be dissolved in so much water, that its causticity cannot be attributed to the concentration of its acid.

This effect is attributed by some chemists to the great weight of the metallic parts with which the acid is united This opinion is very probable, since the causticity is nothing but its dissolving power, or its disposition to combine with other bodies, and this disposition is nothing else than attraction, which is one and the same thing as weight or gravitation

CLII CAWK (a)

CLIII CEMENT All those powders and pastes are called *cements*, with which any body is surrounded in pots or crucibles, and which are capable, by help of fire, of producing changes upon that body Hence the expressions *to cement*, and *cementation*

The principal cements are the *royal cement*, which is used to separate silver from gold in the operation called *Concentrated Parting*, [*See* PARTING

(z) The substance which quick-lime takes from alkaline salts, by which the dissolving power of these salts is encreased, is fixable air *See* AIR (FIXABLE)

(a) CAWK is a white, very dense, sparry substance, unsoluble in acids, and fusible by fire It is generally found in or near lead-mines. If an ounce or two ounces of cawk be thrown red-hot upon sixteen ounces of melted antimony, and the fusion continued about two minutes, a regulus weighing fifteen ounces will be obtained hard and white *See Phil Trans. Num* 110 This experiment Dr. Lewis has frequently repeated with success.

TRATED) the cement for converting iron into steel (*see* STEEL), the cement for converting certain glass into porcelain (*see* GLASS *and* PORCELAIN), the cement for converting copper into brass, *see* BRASS

Cements may be made of many various kinds, and for various purposes, by varying the materials of the compositions Cementation is generally a very powerful method of producing changes upon bodies, or of forming combinations which could not otherwise be easily effected, because in this operation the active matters of the cement are in a state of dryness, are reduced into vapors, and assisted by considerable heat.

CLIV CEMENT-COPPER (*b*)

CLV CENTAURY (*c*)

CLVI CERUSS, or WHITE LEAD Cerufs is a kind of rust of lead which has been corroded and half-dissolved by vapors of vinegar To make cerufs, leaden plates rolled spirally, so that the space of an inch shall be left betwixt each circumvolution, must be placed vertically in earthen pots of a proper size, containing some good vinegar These leaden rolls ought to be so supported in the pots, that they do not touch the vinegar, but that the vapor of this acid may circulate freely betwixt the circumvolutions these pots are to be covered, and placed in a bed of dung, or in a sand-bath, by which a gentle heat may be applied The acid of vinegar, which very well dissolves lead, being thus reduced into vapors, easily attaches itself to the surface of these plates, penetrates them, and is impregnated with this metal, which it reduces to a beautiful white powder called *Cerufs* when a sufficient quantity of it is collected on the surface of the plates, the rolls are taken out of the pots, and unfolded, the cerufs is then taken off, and they are again rolled up, that the operation may be repeated

This management is very ingenious, because the plates of lead thus disposed present the greatest surface to the vapors of vinegar, while they occupy the least possible space

As in this operation the acid of vinegar is overcharged with lead, this metal thus changed into cerufs, is not properly in a saline state, hence cerufs is not in crystals, nor is soluble in water but a saline quality would render it unfit for painting, for which it is chiefly employed

Cerufs ground and prepared for painting is called *white lead* It is the only white hitherto found fit for painting in oil. The discovery of another white for this purpose is desirable, not only from its faults as a paint, but also from its injuring the health of persons employed in its manufacture, by affecting them with a severe disease, which lead and all its preparations frequently occasion, called the *colic of minerals*, or the *colic of painters*

Cerufs, like the other preparations of lead, is drying, sedative, and lenient, as such it is employed, but only externally It is an ingredient in many oint-

(*b*) CEMENT, *or* ZIMENT COPPER, is copper precipitated from vitriolic waters by iron The name is derived, as is said, from a vitriolic water in Hungary called ziment

(*c*) CENTAURY. The leaves of the lesser centaury contain a bitter substance soluble by water, or by spirit of wine The green color of the plant resides in the resinous part, being extracted by spirit of wine, but not by water.

 ments,

ments, plaisters, and other pharmaceutical preparations designed for external maladies.

As lead is much divided in cerufs, and is already penetrated with a certain quantity of acid of vinegar, its saturation with this acid may be easily completed, by dissolving cerufs in distilled vinegar Thus the lead is entirely reduced to a saline state From this saturation a crystallizable neutral salt with metallic basis results, called *sugar* or *salt of lead* *See* SUGAR *of* LEAD

CLVII. CERUSS *of* ANTIMONY This name is given by some chemists to a pearl colored matter, or white earth, which separates from the water with which diaphoretic antimony has been washed It is the finest part of the white calx of antimony, which has been dissolved by the alkali of nitre formed in this operation The peculiar earth of the alkali, some of which always separates after every calcination and solution, probably makes a part also of the cerufs of antimony *See* DIAPHORETIC MINERAL

CLVIII. CHALK Chalk is a calcareous earth, found in form of friable stones, and therefore cannot be polished as marble and other hard calcareous stones may. Chalk is also found in powder This substance has all the properties which characterize calcareous earths *See* EARTHS (CALCAREOUS)

CLIX CHALK (BLACK (*d*)

CLX CHARACTERS Chemical characters are signs invented to represent the principal substances and operations in a concise manner These signs ought to be understood, because they are used by many authors, and in tables of affinities *See the* PLATES.

CLXI CHEESE. Cheese is the mucilaginous or gelatinous part of milk As the milk of all animals is a true emulsion, the cheese or caseous part of milk is an intermediate substance by which the oily or butyraceous part of this liquor is divided, and suspended in the serous part Thus cheese is in milk what mucilage is in emulsions or milky juices of vegetables, but although it has some properties common with mucilages, it differs in other respects, particularly in its want of ductility, or its viscidity, and in its property of coagulating by heat and by acids

Milk is composed of three very different substances, butter, cheese, and whey. These substances are only well mixed together, but not combined, since they are capable of a spontaneous separation or analysis but this separation is not entire and exact, except it be procured by methods peculiar to each of these substances *See* BUTTER, MILK, *and* WHEY

To have cheese as pure as is possible, fresh milk, after the cream is well taken off, must be curdled by runnet, or by cream of tartar, the whey then must be well drained from it, and it must be frequently washed with much pure water

If it be then exposed to distillation with a graduated heat, at first a phlegm arises which has a slight smell of milk or of cheese, without any marks of an acid or of an alkaline quality. This phlegm arises with the heat of boiling water,

(*d*) CHALK (BLACK), *humus nigra pictoria*, *atramentum fossile*. This is a light, earthy, flakey substance used for drawing black lines on paper, and for mixing with oil or water for the use of painters. It is calcinable by fire to a reddish white earth It is unsoluble by acids, and seems to be a bituminous slate Wallerius says, that in Sweden, near Huneberg, a black earth is found as diffusible in water as Indian ink.

and

and when the heat is encreased an oily and saline spirit arises. The saline part of this spirit is generally a volatile alkali Afterwards a small quantity of empyreumatic oil arises, which is at first fluid, and becomes more and more thick and fetid Concrete volatile alkali also arises in this distillation, and at length when the retort is very red-hot, and nothing more rises, a considerable quantity of coal remains This coal is of that kind which cannot be burnt without very great difficulty

From this analysis of cheese, which resembles the analysis of all animal matters, this substance appears to be the most animalised part of the milk, for butter and whey furnish other principles, and particularly much acid We must, however, observe, that cheese made of the milk of frugivorous animals may furnish acid, instead of volatile alkali This difference depends perhaps on the nature of the aliments used by the animals from which the milk is taken, and also of their temperaments, dispositions, and nature of their digestions, for, in general, the state of the acid, and its greater or less disposition to be transformed into volatile alkali, are very variable in the animal kingdom, particularly in those animals which live only on vegetables, and in their milk, which still more approaches a vegetable nature

This matter, although very interesting, has been much neglected by chemists We find, in the Elements of Practical Chemistry, an analysis of cheese produced from cows milk, and in that analysis no mention is made but of an acid, which shews the variations that may happen in this matter We wish it were examined as accurately as it deserves, but for this purpose many experiments which require much time and favorable circumstances ought to be made, which could not be done without having several cows of different ages, fed with different herbs and grains, at different periods from their having calved, and at different seasons of the year *See* MILK

CLXII CHEMISTRY Chemistry is a science, the object of which is to discover the properties of bodies by analysis and by combination

The advantages resulting from this science are too manifest and too numerous to require an enumeration in such a work as this.

CLXIII CHERT *(e)*

CLXIV CHRYSOLITE *(f)*

CLXV CINNABAR. Cinnabar is of two kinds, one is native, the other is artificial

(e) CHERT, *or* CHERTZ, *petrosilex semipellucidus, lapis corneus, hornstein of the Germans.* Chert is a semi-transparent stone of the siliceous kind *See* its chemical properties under the article EARTH (VITRIFIABLE). It is generally less hard and of a coarser texture, than common flints. Large quantities of chert are found in beds of limestone, as flints are found in beds of chalk, with this difference, that flints consist of loose nodules, and chert often forms large masses of the rock They are used as grinding stones for grinding calcined flints, and other hard substances, but have too smooth and close a texture for the grinding of corn

(f) CHRYSOLITE is a pellucid, yellowish-green stone or gem, the sixth in hardness from diamonds, yet susceptible of impression from a file By fire it suffers no other change than loss of color. It is probably a species or variety of topaz Its chemical properties *see* under the article EARTH (VITRIFIABLE) This gem may be imitated by adding twenty grains of crocus martis to two ounces of crystal-glass, and six ounces of minium.

Native cinnabar is a heavy and brittle mineral, of a very deep red color when it is in a lump, and consists of shining, needle-like, parallel striæ

This mineral is composed of mercury and sulphur, as will be proved when we shall relate its analysis It is, properly speaking, mercury mineralised by sulphur, or a true ore of mercury

Cinnabar cannot be attacked in the humid way by any chemical agent It is volatile, so that, when exposed to fire in close vessels, it is entirely sublimed, without suffering any decomposition The sublimation may be repeated any number of times without any change upon the substance

If cinnabar be exposed to the action of fire, with access of air, it is decomposed by the burning of its sulphur, and then the mercury disengages itself in vapors, but as these vapors are not easily to be collected, and as many of them would be lost by this method of decomposition with access of air, another method is employed of decomposing cinnabar in close vessels, by means of some substance to which sulphur has a greater affinity than to mercury Many substances are known to be possessed of the quality required for this purpose

Fixed alkalis, quicklime, calcareous earths, iron, copper, tin, lead, silver, bismuth, and regulus of antimony, have a greater affinity than mercury has to sulphur, and consequently are capable of decomposing cinnabar Of these substances iron is found to be the most convenient, and is therefore most used for the decomposition of small quantities of cinnabar When this decomposition is to be made, equal parts of filings of iron and cinnabar are to be well mixed together, and put into a retort, which is to be exposed in a furnace to a naked fire, or in a sand-bath so disposed that a sufficiently strong heat may be applied, a receiver containing water is to be adapted to the retort, and the distillation to be promoted The mercury disengaged from the sulphur by means of iron is raised into vapors, most of which are condensed in the receiver, at the bottom of which, under the water, they appear changed into fluid mercury, a small part of the mercury remains much divided, and floats on the surface of the water in form of a black powder, which must be carefully collected, and mixed with the mass of fluid mercury, with which it easily incorporates, this mercury, which is then to be strained through closely woven linen, is very pure It is called *mercury revivified from cinnabar*, and this reduction is called *revivification of mercury from cinnabar* In the retort is found a mass composed of the iron employed, and of the sulphur of the cinnabar, or if, instead of iron, some other substance was employed, it would be found after the operation united with the sulphur Thus if an alkali or calcareous earth has been employed, an earthy or alkaline liver of sulphur will be found *See* SULPHUR

By weighing the cinnabar employed in this process, and the mercury obtained by it, this mercury is found to be seven-eighths of the whole cinnabar Thus in cinnabar seven parts of mercury are united with one part of sulphur

From a knowledge of the constituent parts of cinnabar we may learn a method of composing an artificial cinnabar entirely similar to the natural For this purpose, mercury and sulphur must be fused and triturated together till they unite well, and form a black body called *Ethiops mineral* *See* ETHIOPS MINERAL This Ethiops mineral is then to be sublimed, but we must observe, that the operation is attended with some difficulties, so that a beautiful and perfect cinnabar, in which the mercury and sulphur are exactly proportioned, cannot be obtained

obtained by the first sublimation. The first sublimate is always overcharged with sulphur, which gives it a black color. The reason of this is, that more sulphur is necessarily employed to make the ethiops mineral than is sufficient to form cinnabar: but by each subsequent sublimation some of that superfluous sulphur is separated, till at length, by five or six sublimations, it becomes entirely similar to native cinnabar. (g)

CLXVI. CINNABAR *of* ANTIMONY. An artificial cinnabar may also be obtained from the decomposition of corrosive sublimate by antimony. This operation is performed by mixing together and distilling these two compound substances. The marine acid of corrosive sublimate, which has a stronger affinity to regulus of antimony than to mercury, quits this latter substance to combine with the former, with which it forms a new compound called *butter of antimony*, that passes by distillation into the receiver. *See* BUTTER *of* ANTIMONY.

Also the mercury of the corrosive sublimate, being disengaged from its marine acid, unites with the sulphur of the antimony likewise disengaged from its regulus, and these two substances, thus united, are sublimed in form of cinnabar after the butter of antimony has been distilled: but although in this process the mercury is not previously united with the sulphur into an ethiops, the same superfluity of sulphur is perceived in the cinnabar produced by this as by the former operation, because the quantity of antimony necessarily employed for the compleat decomposition of corrosive sublimate, contains more than the requisite quantity of sulphur for the formation of perfect cinnabar with the quantity of mercury contained in the corrosive sublimate. This inconvenience is to be remedied by the method directed in the former process, that is, by repeating the sublimation till the cinnabar becomes perfect, and entirely similar to the native. It is called *cinnabar of antimony*, because its sulphur has been furnished by antimony.

The chief use of cinnabar is for painting. Although this body be composed of sulphur, the color of which is a light citron, and of mercury which is white as silver, it is nevertheless of an exceeding strong red color. Lumps of it are of a deep brown red, without brilliancy. But when the too great intensity of its color is diminished by bruising it and dividing it into small parts, (which is a method generally used to lessen the intensity of all colors) the red of the cinnabar becomes more and more exalted, flame-colored, and exceedingly vivid and brilliant. In this state cinnabar is called *vermilion*.

Cinnabar is often employed as an internal medicine. Hoffman greatly recommends it as a sedative and antispasmodic, and Stahl makes it an ingredient in his *temperant powder*. Other very intelligent physicians, and particularly Mr Cartheuser, deny that cinnabar taken internally has any medicinal quality. Their opinion is grounded on the unsolubility of cinnabar by any menstruum. This question concerning the utility of cinnabar taken internally cannot be decided without new researches and experiments. But cinnabar is certainly used

(g) Hoffman says, that cinnabar may be produced without sublimation by shaking or digesting a little mercury with volatile tincture of sulphur, by which means the mercury imbibes the sulphur from the volatile spirit, and forms with it a deep red powder, the color of which is not inferior to that of ordinary cinnabar.

successfully

successfully to procure a mercurial fumigation, when that method of cure is proper in venereal diseases For this purpose cinnabar is burnt in an open fire on red-hot coals, by which the mercury is disengaged, and forms vapors, which being applied to the body of the diseased person, penetrate through the pores of the skin, and produce effects similar to those of mercury administered by friction

When fumigations of cinnabar are applied, the patient ought not to be exposed to breathe the vapors of the mercury and of the burning sulphur, which might injure him *See* MERCURY *and* SULPHUR *(h)*

CLXVII CINNAMON *(i)*

CLXVIII CIVET. *(k)*

CLXIX CLAY, *or* ARGILLACEOUS EARTH, is a particular kind of strong earth, considerable banks of which are found almost every where, at greater or less depths. The general properties and characteristics of pure clay are

1. This earth makes no sensible effervescence with acids, although it be capable of solution by acids, as we shall see

2 Clay being moistened with water, imbibes some of that liquid, swells, and mixes with it

3 When it is mixed with no more than the necessary quantity of water to reduce it to a moderately soft paste, it is so ductile as to be capable of being worked upon a potter's wheel, and of being formed in moulds. By these means vessels may be made of it which keep their form

4 Clay is dense, compact, and close When its surface is rubbed with a polished body, it also becomes polished

5 If it be exposed when moist to a gentle heat, it gradually dries and contracts, that is, its dimensions become less, hence it is very apt to crack *(l)* It retains moisture pretty strongly, and difficultly allows the last portions of it to escape

6. If clay be heated much, and quickly, before it be perfectly dried, it bursts with loud noise from the effort made by the water rarefied and changed into vapor, to escape from the parts of this tenacious earth which invelop it Thus this bursting and cracking do not happen, if the clay exposed to heat contain water enough to render it soft, because then the water finding much less resistance from the clay, only separates the argillaceous parts from each other, and escapes with considerable intumescence

(h) Some native cinnabars, according to Bruckman, (*Epistol Itiner.*) are so hard, that they are polished, turned in a lathe, and wrought like marble

(i) CINNAMON From 16 oz of the best cinnamon scarcely more than two scruples and a half of essential oil can be obtained This oil may be raised by distillation with water, but scarcely with spirit of wine The whole taste and flavor of cinnamon may be extracted by digestion with spirit of wine. *Neuman.*

(k) CIVET is an odoriferous unctuous animal juice, soluble in oils, but not in spirit of wine, nor in water, even by means of sugar *Neuman*

(l) Dr. Lewis found from experiments, that pure clay softened with water to a due consistence to be worked upon a potter's wheel, contracted by drying $\frac{1}{12}$th part of every dimension.

7 If

7 If pure clay, previously well dried, be exposed to a very violent fire, such for example, as the fire of a glass-house, it does not melt, and resists much more than sand does the action of fluxes and vitrifying matters By fire its parts are only very strongly agglutinated, and the mass of clay thus calcined is called *baked clay* During this baking it contracts in every dimension, and becomes as hard as flint, so that it is capable of striking fire with steel.

8 When clay has been thus baked by fire, it becomes no longer penetrable by water If it be ground and levigated, it mixes with water as very fine sand does, that is, it does not form, as the crude clay does, a tenacious, ductile paste, fit to be turned on a potter's wheel

9 Clay is entirely soluble in acids, and particularly in the vitriolic, with which acid it forms a vitriolic salt with an earthy basis, which is true alum *See* ALUM

10 Lastly, clay, which, when unmixed, perfectly resists the most violent fire without shewing any tendency to fusion, being mixed with equal parts of any calcareous or gypseous earth, and with two parts and a half, or three parts of any sand or vitrifiable stone, now becomes fusible, and disposes the other two earths to fusion

All the properties which we have enumerated are essential to argillaceous earth, when perfectly pure, that is, when free from any mixture of heterogeneous matter Clay so perfectly pure has never yet been found in the earth.

Mr. Macquer, in his Memoir upon clays given to the Academy in the year 1762, from which Memoir the greatest part of the present article is taken, observes, that clay being an earth miscible with water, is liable to mixture with many other matters, and that from this cause we never find pure clay, which ought eminently and exclusively to possess the argillaceous properties, and which ought to be always the same, without any peculiar differences, and lastly, that the only certain method of procuring this earth is to extract it from native clays, or from other bodies which contain it, by means of vitriolic acid, with which it forms alum, and then to decompose this alum by phlogiston or alkalis, which disengage the vitriolic acid, therefore, properly speaking, earth of alum well prepared can be considered as the only pure clay Further, this earth has so strong affinity with phlogiston, that we cannot expect to obtain it perfectly free from this principle The general properties of clay, described above, are then solely applicable to this kind of earth. *See the word* ALUM

Native clays possess more or less of these properties in proportion as they are less or more altered by mixture of heterogeneous matters

As clays are very useful in chemistry, in arts, and in many purposes of ordinary life, we shall mention some important parts of knowledge concerning them, as, the methods of discovering their purity, the places where they may be found, and the means of purifying them

The purity of clays is known by the general properties above related. The more any native clay possesses of these properties, the purer it is

The substances which hurt the purity of native clays are sand, phlogiston, bituminous matters, vitriolic acid, metallic earths, pyritous matters, calcareous earths, and mica.

Inflammable matters alter the color of clay, which when pure ought to be white. Its color is affected also by colored metallic earths, particularly by those of copper and iron, and by all pyritous matters.

Clay, which is colored only by an inflammable matter which is not metallic, loses its color by fire with access of air, and becomes white. Of this kind are most grey and brown clays, of an uniform color, and not veined.

Clays colored by pyritous matters, or by earths of iron or copper, are not rendered white by fire, till they are perfectly deprived of these metallic earths. A certain quantity of these heterogeneous substances in clay render it fusible. Such clays are known by their colors, which are yellow, red, green, or veined, and marbled with several of these colors. They are the most unfit of all clays for the making of utensils intended to sustain intense heat, such as chemical vessels, and the bricks, crucibles, or pots used in glass-houses.

We may observe, that even the purest native clays are never entirely free from a mixture of some parts of metallic, particularly ferruginous earth. Mr Macquer, who has examined above eight hundred clays, says, in the above quoted Memoir, that in all that number he did not find one, even amongst the whitest, that was entirely pure and free from metallic matter: but when a very small quantity only of ferruginous earth is in clays, when it is not uniformly mixed with them through all their mass, which is known by a beautiful and pure white color, but is dispersed in small yellow spots, as it frequently is, then such clays ought to be considered as being of a very good quality. The only practical method of separating these ferruginous parts, is to break the clay into small lumps, and to cut out the yellow spots. This ought to be done before the clay is mixed with water, because by washing the ferruginous parts are not separable, but are more intimately mixed with the purer part of the clay.

Pyritous matters, mica, and coarse sand mixed with clays render them brittle, and diminish their ductility. Clays are easily cleansed from the greatest part of these heterogeneous substances by washing, that is, by mixing the clay well with much pure water, which is left to rest till only the finest and lightest parts of the clay remain suspended in the water, the grosser parts having subsided to the bottom: the water then is to be decanted off from the gross sediment, and passed through a fine silken searce: the sediment which is deposited from this decanted and sifted water is the finest and purest part of the clay, and ought to be carefully and cleanly collected and dried. This purification of clay by washing is very necessary when good pottery or porcelain is to be made. *See* POTTERY *and* PORCELAIN.

The pyritous particles found in clays render them very fusible. A bit of pyrites left in clay which is exposed to a baking fire, always forms a cavity in the clay lined with a black leaden color.

The washing with water is an effectual method of separating from clay even the smallest particles of pyrites, because these particles have essentially a specific gravity much greater than that of clay. But sand and mica are not so easily separated from clay. Mr Macquer has shewn in his Memoir, that the most careful washing is insufficient for an entire separation of sandy particles contained in clays, because every native clay contains a considerable quantity of sandy particles as fine and as light as the clay itself.

MICA

Mica alſo cannot be ſeparated from clay for the ſame reaſon but theſe fine particles of ſand and mica, which cannot be ſeparated by waſhing, do not injure works made of the clay, but are rather uſeful by preventing cracks in drying and baking *See* POTTERY

The particles of calcareous earths which injure the purity of many native clays, are eaſily diſcovered by the effervеſcence which they make with nitrous acid This kind of earth cannot be ſeparated from clays by waſhing, from the fineneſs and lightneſs of its parts Clay containing a certain quantity of calcareous earth is by this mixture rendered fuſible, from the ſandy particles inſeparable from the clay hence all calcareous clays are improper for making utenſils intended to ſuſtain intenſe heat.

Laſtly, vitriolic acid, which appears to have been combined and diſtributed in a ſingular manner by nature in all clays, may be ſeparated from them by digeſting them in an alkaline liquor, and afterwards by edulcorating this clay with a ſufficient quantity of water but this purification of clays is not neceſſary for moſt purpoſes to which theſe earths may be applied, becauſe this acid is not injurious Vitriolic acid mixed with clays renders them capable of decompoſing nitre and common ſalt, and of diſengaging the acids of thoſe ſalts

Theſe extraneous matters being found naturally mixed with clays either ſingle, or ſeveral together, and in all proportions, occaſion a great variety of native clays No earth has ſo many different kinds, and undoubtedly from this great variety proceeds the multiplicity of names which are annexed to the ſeveral kinds of clay

The earths called *boles*, *bolar earths*, and *ſealed earths*, are true clays Theſe names have been chiefly applied to thoſe clays which ſtick ſtrongly to the tongue, and alſo to certain clays filled with a large quantity of ferruginous earth, by which they are uniformly colored red or yellow Other names are applied to clays from their particular uſes Such are *fuller's earth*, *tile-earth*, *brick-earth*, *potter's-clay*, *pipe-clay*, *porcelain-clay*

The earths called *marles*, as they are capable of dilution in water, have a certain degree of binding quality, effervеſce with nitrous acid, are fuſible with an intenſe heat, and appear to be nothing elſe than clays more or leſs ſandy, and mixed with much calcareous earth

Laſtly, epithets are given to many clays denoting their color, as *white clays*, *grey clays*, *blue clays*, &c

But theſe names communicate little knowledge on the true nature of the ſeveral native clays A more particular examination by chemical proofs is requiſite to inveſtigate the heterogeneous matters with which different native clays are mixed, the mixture of which alters the purity of ſimple and primary argillaceous earth, to which they owe all they poſſeſs of argillaceous properties, then names might be given which ſhould indicate their color and the heterogeneous matters with which they are mixed, or at leaſt thoſe which prevail moſt Thus amongſt theſe names we ſhould have *white*, *ſandy*, *micaceous*, or *calcareous clays*, *grey* or *blue pyritous clays*, *red* or *yellow ferruginous clays*, *black bituminous clays*, &c

As our intention in this work is not to enter into the details of natural hiſtory, we ſhall ſay no more upon this ſubject What we have ſaid concerning the properties of pure clay, and the different ſubſtances which alter its purity, and more or leſs diſguiſe the argillaceous properties of native clays, is ſufficient to give a notion of the light which chemistry can throw on natural history in this and many other instances

In Mr Gellert's table the substances capable of acting upon clays are set down in the following order Vitriolic acid, partly (see an explanation of this word *partly* at the article ALUM), liver of sulphur, fixed alkali, borax, calx of lead, calx of antimony, gypseous earth, calcareous earth

CLXX CLOVES (m)

CLXXI CLYSSUS By the word *clyssus* are meant the vapors which rise during the detonation of nitre with any inflammable body These vapors may be collected and condensed into a liquor by a proper apparatus of vessels

The vapors resulting from the detonation of nitre with charcoal are called *clyssus of nitre* To prepare this clyssus, an earthen retort must be employed capable of sustaining a great heat applied suddenly without injury

This retort, which ought to be tubulated, is to be placed in a furnace, and to it a very large balloon with a small hole is to be adjusted When the bottom of the retort has become red-hot, a small quantity, that is, a dram and a half, or two drams, of a mixture of purified nitre and charcoal powder, is to be thrown into the retort through the tubulated part, which must be immediately afterwards closed, the nitre then detonates, and the vapors are condensed in the receiver

Other parcels of the detonating mixture are to be thrown in successively with the same management, till a sufficient quantity of liquor is collected in the receiver If, instead of charcoal-powder, sulphur be employed to detonate with nitre in close vessels, the liquor obtained is called *clyssus of sulphur*, and if antimony be employed to detonate with nitre, the liquor is called *clyssus of antimony*

The old chemists who have practised these operations believed, that the liquors thus obtained had particular virtues for alchemical purposes For this reason, they made this preparation with great apparatus and trouble But now, when chemical operations are better understood, these liquors are believed to have no virtues The clyssus of nitre is made in laboratories, not for any use to which it can be applied, but to establish a theory concerning the nature of nitrous acid, and to prove that this acid is entirely destroyed and decomposed by detonation

For, when the operation is finished, nothing is found in the retort but the alkali which was the basis of the nitre, and the liquor contained in the receiver has no acid taste, does not redden the tincture of turnsol, makes no effervescence with alkaline matters, and is truly nothing but water, which is sometimes slightly

(m) CLOVES The pungency of cloves resides in their resin, or rather in a combination of resin with essential oil, for the spirituous extract is very pungent, but if the oil and the resin contained in this extract be separated from each other by distillation, the oil will be very mild, and any pungency which it does retain proceeds from some small portion of adhering resin, and the remaining resin will be insipid No plant, or part of any plant, contains so large a proportion of essential oil as cloves do From sixteen ounces Neuman obtained by distillation two ounces and two drams, and Hoffman obtained from the same quantity an ounce and a half This oil is specifically heavier than water *Neuman.*

alkaline,

alkaline, because the force of detonation is capable of raising some small part of the alkali of the nitre

The clyssus of sulphur is acid, because the vitriolic acid of the sulphur is not decomposed, as the nitrous is, by combustion, but is disengaged and set at liberty by the burning of the phlogiston of the sulphur Besides, one part of this vitriolic acid when disengaged acts upon the nitre, forms with its basis a vitriolated tartar called *Glaser's sal polychrestum*, and disengages the nitrous acid This portion of nitrous acid thus disengaged by the acid of sulphur, and which is no longer retained and fixed by an alkali, is not capable of inflaming with phlogiston wherefore it is not decomposed, and, together with the vitriolic acid which is not fixed by the alkali of the nitre, makes part of the clyssus

The clyssus of sulphur appears then to be composed, 1 Of a part of the nitrous acid destroyed by inflammation with the phlogiston of the sulphur 2 Of another portion of nitrous acid which is not decomposed, but is disengaged by the acid of sulphur 3 Of all the acid of sulphur which does not unite with the alkaline basis of the nitre

The clyssus of sulphur must differ considerably according to the proportions of nitre and of sulphur employed If a little nitre be added to much sulphur, the clyssus will be almost all pure acid of sulphur

An English chemist *, some time ago, found a method of obtaining very advantageously the vitriolic acid of sulphur, by burning sulphur in close vessels with a small quantity of nitre This method of decomposing sulphur for the extraction of its acid is said to be executed in great, and to be the cause of the great reduction of the price of that acid within these few years past This is an instance of practical utility from a clyssus, for the vitriolic acid obtained by detonation of nitre in close vessels is a true clyssus of sulphur

The clyssus of antimony is similar to that of sulphur, for the nitre in this operation chiefly detonates with the sulphur of the antimony · however, the phlogiston of the metalline part of the antimony contributes also to the detonation Besides, some flowers of antimony are mixed with this clyssus

Several necessary precautions ought to be taken to make this operation of a clyssus succeed, and to avoid accidents, for the rapidity and violence with which nitre detonates in certain circumstances may occasion a strong explosion and rupture of the vessels To prevent these accidents, the inflammable matters ought not to be very well mixed with the nitre, because the detonation is proportionably stronger and quicker as the mixture has been made more exactly Also, a small quantity only of the mixture ought to be detonated at once, and another quantity should not be added till the detonation of the former be finished *See* NITRE, DETONATION *of* NITRE, and GUN-POWDER

CLXXII C O A G U L A T I O N. This term is employed by chemists to denote certain operations in which fluid bodies become solid, for instance, the crystallization of salts *See* CRYSTALLIZATION

CLXXIII. C O A G U L U M. This Latin word is used to signify curdled concretions formed by the mixture of two liquors, such as the precipitate of silver in the formation of *luna cornea*, the *offa Helmontii*, the *miraculum chemicum*, and many others *See these words*

* Dr. Ward *See* SPIRIT *of* SULPHUR

CLXXIV. COAL. By the word *coal* is meant any ſubſtance containing oil which has been expoſed to fire in cloſe veſſels, ſo that all its volatile principles are expelled, and that it can ſuſtain a red heat without further decompoſition. Coal is a body ſolid, black, very dry, and conſiderably hard.

The ſpecific character of perfect coal is its capacity of burning with acceſs of air, while it becomes red-hot and ſparkles, ſometimes with a ſenſible flame which gives little light, no ſmoke or ſoot capable of blackening white bodies.

Coal is capable of communicating its inflammable principle either to the vitriolic acid, with which it forms ſulphur; or to the nitrous acid contained in nitre, with which it inflames; or to metallic earths, which it reduces into metals. But the phlogiſton cannot paſs from coal to form theſe new combinations without the aſſiſtance of red-heat.

Coal ſeems to be an unalterable compound in every inſtance but theſe mentioned, of burning in open air, and of communicating its phlogiſton to other bodies: for it may be expoſed in cloſe veſſels to the moſt violent and continued fire without ſuffering the leaſt alteration. No diſpoſition to fuſe, nor any diminution of weight can be perceived. It is a ſubſtance exceedingly fixed, and perhaps the moſt refractory which is known.

No change is produced upon coal by air or by water, nor by the moſt powerful menſtruums of chemiſtry, excepting perhaps by particular proceſſes. A trial might be made whether the concentrated mineral acids, or cauſtic alkalis, would not, when aſſiſted by heat, make ſome alteration upon coal in a long time. The younger Mr Rouelle propoſed as a problem, in the Journal de Medicine for October, 1762, to *diſſolve vegetable coal in the palm of the hand*. Why he propoſed it as a problem we do not know, ſince he adds, that Mr Wolf has reſolved it, and that this ſolution may be made by liver of ſulphur. He has not explained whether he means the ſolution of all the ſubſtance of the coal, or of its phlogiſton only.

Coal is evidently a reſult of the decompoſition of the compound bodies from which it is obtained. It conſiſts of the greateſt part of the earthy principle of theſe compound bodies, with which a part of the ſaline principles, and ſome of the phlogiſton of the decompoſed oil are fixed and combined very intimately.

Coal can never be formed but by the phlogiſton of a body which has been in an oily ſtate: hence it cannot be formed by ſulphur, phoſphorus, metals, nor by any other ſubſtance the phlogiſton of which is not in an oily ſtate.

Alſo every oily matter treated with fire in cloſe veſſels furniſhes true coal; ſo that whenever a charry reſiduum is left, we may be certain that the ſubſtance employed in the operation contained oil. *See* OIL.

Laſtly, the inflammable principle of coal, although it proceeds from an oil, is certainly not an oil, but is pure phlogiſton; ſince coal added to vitriolic acid can form ſulphur, to phoſphoric acid can form phoſphorus, to metallic earths can form metals, and can detonate with nitre; and ſince oil can produce none of theſe effects, till it has been decompoſed and reduced to the ſtate of coal. *See* SULPHUR, PHOSPHORUS, METALS, NITRE, *and* OIL.

Beſides, the phenomena accompanying the burning of coal are different from thoſe which happen when oily ſubſtances are burnt. The flame of charcoal is not ſo bright as that of oil, and produces no ſmoke or ſoot.

All

All the phlogiston of coal is not burnt in open air, particularly when the combustion is slow One part of it exhales without decomposition, and forms a vapor, or an invisible and insensible gas This vapor, or this phlogiston, disengaged from coal, is very pernicious It so affects the brain and nerves as to occasion instant death For this reason, to remain in a close place where charcoal or other coal is burnt, is dangerous Persons struck by vapor of charcoal are stunned, faint, suffer a violent head-ach, and fall down senseless and motionless If they are yet alive, the best method of recovering them is to expose them as quickly as is *possible to open air, and to make them swallow vinegar*, and breathe its steam Acids, and particularly vinegar, seem to have a property of fixing and restraining in some sort the action of phlogiston, and of the vapors of volatile inflammable matters, which produce similar effects on animals For this reason, vinegar diminishes the accidents of intoxication occasioned by spirituous liquors and by opium The vapor which exhales from liver of sulphur, particularly when a large quantity of it is decomposed by an acid, and the vapors which exhale from matters undergoing the spirituous or putrid fermentation, produce the same accidents as the vapors of coal, and are remedied by the same means

Amongst coals, some differences are observable, which proceed from the difference of the bodies from which they are made, particularly, some coals are more combustible than others This combustibility of coals seems to depend on the greater or less quantity of saline principle contained in coal, that is to say, that the more it contains of saline principle, the more easily it decomposes and burns For example, coals made of plants and wood, containing much saline matter capable of fixing it, the ashes of which contain much alkaline salt, burn vigorously and produce much heat, whereas the coals of animal matters, the saline principles of which are volatile, and cannot be fixed but in small quantity, and the ashes of which contain little or no alkaline salt, are scarcely at all combustible For they not only do not kindle so easily as charcoal does, nor ever burn alone, but they cannot be reduced to ashes without very great trouble, even when the most effectual methods are used to facilitate the combustion

I have kept the coal of bullock's blood very red-hot in a shallow crucible, surrounded with burning charcoal, six hours and more, and stirred it constantly that it might all be exposed to the air, but I could not reduce it to white or even grey ashes It remained still very black, and full of phlogiston

The coals of pure oils, or of concrete oily substances, and soot, which is a kind of coal raised during the inflammation of oils, are as difficultly burnt as animal coals These coals contain very little saline matter, and their ashes furnish no alkali

These coals, which are so difficultly burnt, are also less capable of inflaming with nitre than others more combustible, and some of them even in a great measure resist the action of nitre

The refractory quality of coals is a singular property This property is in so great a degree, that they are found to be the fittest substances for supporting bodies exposed to the focus of large burning glasses Nevertheless all coal is composed of an earth which is not perfectly refractory, of a saline matter which is fusible and assists the fusion of other substances, and of phlogiston which is

certainly

certainly the principle of the fusibility of metals, as their earths become so much more difficult to fuse as they are more dephlogisticated (n)

CLXXV COAL (FOSSIL) (o)

CLXXVI COATING (p)

CLXXVII COBALT This name is given by authors to several different minerals We shall here only talk of that kind of cobalt which contains the metallic matter whose calx furnishes a blue glass when vitrified, because the name *cobalt* ought to be confined to this mineral alone, to avoid the uncertainty and confusion too frequent in names of natural history and of chemistry

Cobalt is a very heavy mineral, of no determinate figure, of a grey color, more or less brilliant, of a fine, compact, close grain, the surface of which,

(n) To *make charcoal*, or vegetable coal, pieces of wood are so disposed as to form a pile, generally conical, which pile is covered with turf to prevent the too free draught of air, by which the wood would be reduced to ashes and not to coal The pile is then to be kindled, and the fire is to be continued till all the watery and the more volatile parts of the wood are dissipated, that is, till no more smoke arises, at which time the wood is thoroughly red-hot The external air is then to be totally excluded, by covering the pile with earth, and thus the fire is extinguished

(o) COAL (FOSSIL), or PIT-COAL, is a black or brown, laminated, bituminous substance, not very easily inflammable, but which once inflamed, burns longer and more intensely than any other substance Of this substance three kinds are distinguished by authors The residuum of the first after combustion is black, the residuum of the second is spongy, and like pounce stone, and the residuum of the third is whitish ashes Some fossil coal, by long exposure to air, falls into a greyish powder, from which alum may be extracted Fossil coal by distillation yields, 1 a phlegm or water, 2 a very acid liquor, 3 a thin oil like naphtha, 4 a thicker oil, resembling petroleum, which falls to the bottom of the former, and which rises with a violent fire, 5 an acid concrete salt, 6 an uninflammable earth remains in the retort These constituent parts of fossil coal are very similar to those of amber and other bitumens See BITUMEN For the exciting of intense heats, as of furnaces for smelting iron-ore, and for operations where the acid and oily vapors would be detrimental, as the drying of malt, fossil coals are previously charred, or reduced to *coaks*, that is, they are made to undergo an operation similar to that by which charcoal is made By this operation coals are deprived of their phlegm, their acid liquor, and of greatest part of their fluid oil Coaks therefore consist of the two most fixed constituent parts, the heavy oil and the earth, together with the acid concrete salt, which though volatile is detained by the oil and earth

(p) COATING, or LORICATION, is an application of clay, or mixture of clay with sand or other substance, to the external or internal surfaces of chemical vessels, to guard them against the effects of sudden heat, or of the corrosive quality of the matter to be contained Thus glass retorts intended to be exposed to what is called a naked fire, that is, to a fire without interposition of a sand bath or other substance, ought to be externally coated, by which means they will not be so liable to be cracked by the sudden application of heat and cold Retorts may be coated in the following manner Take of clay and sand equal parts, make them into a thin paste, with fresh blood prevented from coagulating by agitation till it be cold, and diluted with water, add to this paste *some hair and powdered glass*, with a brush dipt in this mass besmear the retort, and when this first layer is dry, let the same operation be repeated twice or oftener, till the coat applied be about one-third part of an inch thick For the compositions for coating crucibles, furnaces, and other instruments made of plate-iron, *see* CRUCIBLE

when

when it has been exposed to the air, is covered with a powder, or efflorescence of the color of a peach-blossom.

This mineral is not found in many places. Hitherto it seems to have been found only in Saxony and in the Pyrenean mountains (q). It contains several substances mixed and confounded together, and in this respect some cobalts differ from others. All of them contain sulphur, much arsenic, and the semi-metal the calx of which may be made into blue glass, and which Mr Brandt of the Swedish Academy calls *Regulus of Cobalt* when it is reduced to its metalline state. Besides these substances, some cobalts contain bismuth, silver, or both of these.

Of all these matters, the peculiar regulus of cobalt renders this mineral valuable from the fine blue which is manufactured from it, and which is the only blue that can be used in vitrification.

Nevertheless other substances are collected from cobalt in the operations practised on it, but only secondarily, because these substances may be obtained without additional labor or expence. For example, as it is necessary in the preparation of the blue to expel the arsenic, this mineral must be exposed to long roastings, instead of dissipating the arsenic which rises in vapors during the torrefaction, it is collected in long crooked chimneys, adapted to the furnaces in which the cobalt is roasted, and thus is obtained almost all the arsenic which is sold in commerce. *See* ARSENIC.

Likewise after the roasting, when the calx of cobalt is fused with vitrifiable matters to make the blue glass called *Smalt*, the bismuth and silver may be separated and collected.

(q) Cobalt has been found in Cornwall, Scotland, and probably in other parts of Europe. That it is in the eastern parts of Asia, appears from the blue coloring on old oriental porcelain. Probably also the mines discovered in these countries are nearly exhausted, as considerable quantities of zaffre and smalt are exported from Europe to China. Besides the grey or ash-colored cobalt described in the text, which is the most frequent, other cobalts are found of various colors and textures, mixed with various substances. Wallerius enumerates six species of cobalts. 1. The *ash-colored ore*, which is regulus of cobalt mineralised by arsenic, consisting of shining leaden-colored grains. Some ores of this kind are compact, resembling steel, and others are of a loose texture and friable. 2. The *specular ore* is black, shining like a mirror and laminated. This species is very rare, and is supposed by Wallerius to be a foliated spar, or selenites mixed with ore of cobalt. 3. The *vitreous*, or *slag-like ore*, is of a bluish, shining color, compact, or spongy. 4. *Crystallized ore of cobalt* is a grey, deep-colored ore of cobalt, consisting of clusters of cubical, pyramidal, prismatic crystals. 5. *Flowers of cobalt*, red, yellow, or violet. These flowers seem to be formed from some of the above described compact ores decomposed by exposure to moist air. This decomposition is similar to that which happens to ferruginous and cupreous pyrites. 6. The *earthy ore of cobalt* is of a greenish white or of a yellow color, and of a soft and friable texture. This species seems to be an ochre of cobalt, and is formed perhaps from the flowers of cobalt further decomposed, in the same manner as a martial ochre is formed from the saline efflorescence of decomposing pyrites, when this efflorescence is further decomposed by exposure to moist air, by which the vitriolic acid contained in it is expelled, and the efflorescence is changed from a saline state to that of an ochre or calx. Besides these proper ores of cobalt, it is also found in a blue clay along with native silver, in ores of bismuth, and in the mineral called kupfernickel. See NICKEL.

The

The silver, although a valuable metal, is generally in so small a quantity, that it would not be worth the trouble of obtaining on purpose from this mineral The cobalt is therefore always operated upon for the sake of the blue

If well-calcined cobalt be treated with phlogiston and fluxes, like other metallic calxes, it will be reduced to a semi-metal, called by Mr Brandt, who first discovered it, the *Regulus of Cobalt*

This regulus, and also the calx of cobalt, amongst other singular properties, has that of making a very curious sympathetic ink, by being dissolved in aqua regia. *See, for what further relates to cobalt, the articles* SMALT, ZAFFRE, AZUR, REGULUS *of* COBALT, *and* INK (SYMPATHETIC)

CLXXVIII. COCHINEAL. *(r)*

CLXXIX COERULEUM MONTANUM *(s)*

CLXXX COHESION By cohesion is meant the adhesion which the integrant or the constituent parts of bodies have to each other

CLXXXI. COHOBATION Cohobation is an operation by which the same liquor is frequently distilled from the same body, either with an intention to dissolve this body, or to produce some change upon it This is one of those operations which the ancient chemists practised with great patience and zeal, and which are now neglected

To make this operation easier, and to prevent the trouble of frequently changing or moving the vessels employed, a particular kind of alembic is contrived, very convenient and well adapted, called a *Pelican* *See* PELICAN

CLXXXII COLCOTHAR Colcothar is the substance which remains from the calcination and distillation of martial vitriol with a violent fire

Vitriolic acid does not adhere so strongly to the iron of the martial vitriol as to be capable of resisting the action of a strong fire, therefore when this vitriol is heated intensely and during a long time, it loses more and more of its acid, which is dissipated if the calcination be performed in open vessels, and which may be distilled with proper apparatus. When the vitriol loses its

(r) COCHINEAL From an ounce of cochineal Neuman obtained by distillation two scruples of phlegm, four scruples of urinous spirit, fifteen drops of oily spirit, twenty-two grains of volatile alkali, five scruples and two grains of empyreumatic oil, and two drams and two scruples of a residuum containing five grains of fixt lixivial salt The same author found that of four drams of cochineal, three drams were soluble in water, and nearly as much in spirit of wine

Cochineal infused or boiled with water produces a crimson tincture inclining to purple Fixed alkali renders the crimson deeper, but lessens its lustre Volatile alkali heightens the color without diminution of lustre The best method of applying volatile alkali for this purpose in dying was found by Mr Hellot to be, by dipping the cloth dyed with cochineal in a solution of sal-ammoniac, and then throwing into the solution some pot-ash, by which the volatile alkali of the sal-ammoniac is disengaged By a small quantity of vitriolic acid the crimson decoction of cochineal is rendered purple, by more of that acid it is rendered flesh-colored, and by still more colorless This color is first changed to a yellow, and afterwards destroyed by nitrous acid. Solution of tin in aqua regia heightens the color of this decoction to a scarlet French dyers give a scarlet tinge to this decoction by turmeric; but this tinge does not penetrate the cloth, and is not durable *See* DYING

(s) COERULEUM MONTANUM, *mountain-blue*, called by some authors *chrysocolla*, is a blue ore of copper. *See* ORES *of* COPPER.

acid,

acid, it acquires a red color, and becomes an earthy matter The calx of iron, whether it has been deprived of phlogiston by fire or by acids, is always of this red color but the iron contained in vitriol suffers this alteration during the calcination When the calcination is finished, what remains of the vitriol has still some taste, and even the property of becoming moist when exposed to air These qualities are caused by some remaining acid which adheres obstinately to the earth of the iron, and which the fire could not expel As this acid is very much concentrated, and is not combined with the calx of iron in the colcothar, as it was with the iron itself in the vitriol, because the phlogiston of the iron is lost by calcination, we need not wonder that this calcined vitriol should powerfully imbibe moisture from the air, although vitriolic does not

This remaining acid may be taken from the colcothar by washing with water The colcothar then has no taste, does not attract moisture from the air, and is called *Sweet Earth of Vitriol*

Unwashed colcothar is used in medicine, but only externally It may be properly applied to all putrid, sanious and fungous ulcers, because it is antiseptic, strongly tonic, astringent, and even corrosive, from its remaining uncombined vitriolic acid *See* VITRIOL (MARTIAL) *and* CALCINATION

CLXXXIII COLOPHONY Colophony, or rosin, is the resinous residuum after the distillation of the light oil from turpentine It has also the properties of other resins, and the same principles may be obtained from it by analysis *See* BALSAMS (NATIVE), TURPENTINE, *and* RESIN

CLXXXIV COLOCYNTH (t)

CLXXXV COLORS (u)

CLXXXVI COMBINATION By the word *combination*, we ought to understand the union of two bodies of different natures, from which a new compound body results For example, when an acid is united with an alkali, we say that a combination betwixt these two saline substances takes place, because from this union a neutral salt results which is composed of an acid and an alkali *See* COMPOSITION

CLXXXVII COMBUSTION Combustion is nothing else than the disengagement of the inflammable principle contained in several kinds of bodies, which are therefore called *combustible*

The principle of inflammability is united in greater or less quantity with bodies, and in several different manners, hence the diversity occasioned in the phenomena of combustion

If the phlogiston of a body be in large quantity, and in an oily state, this body is very combustible, and burns with a bright flame, accompanied with smoke and soot Wood, dry vegetables, resins, oils, fat, are combustible bodies of this kind

If the phlogiston of a body be not in an oily state, but in large quantity, or not very intimately combined, this body may also be very combustible, and may

(t) COLOCYNTH, or COLOQUINTIDA, is a bitter fruit, from an ounce of which Neuman extracted by spirit three ounces and a half, and by water seven ounces and a half

(u) *Colors* *See* BLACK, BLUE, &c *and* DYING.

even burn with flame But this flame is flighter and generally less luminous than the flame of oily bodies, besides, it is accompanied with no smoke or soot Spirit of wine, sulphur, phosphorus, charcoal, some metallic matters, and particularly zinc, are combustible bodies of this kind The flames of phosphorus and of zinc are nevertheless very luminous

Lastly, bodies containing phlogiston which is not in an oily state, and which is in small quantity, or strongly combined with other uncombustible principles, burn difficultly without any sensible flame, such are certain animal coals, soot, ashes of vegetables, containing very little phlogiston, and imperfect metals

The grand principle concerning combustion in general is, that no combustible matter can burn without access of air, and that the more immediate its contact with air is, the more rapid and compleat is its combustion *See* AIR

For this reason, even the most inflammable bodies, as spirit of wine and ethereal oils, do not burn but at their surface, because that only is exposed to air For the same reason, inflammable bodies, when reduced to vapor, burn rapidly and instantaneously, because they are all exposed to air at once Lastly, for the same reason, some bodies, though full of phlogiston, such as fat, oils, &c cannot burn without a heat sufficient to reduce them into vapor

The practical methods of promoting, accelerating, and of compleating the combustion of the inflammable principle of bodies may also be naturally deduced from what we have said on this subject These methods consist in applying as much of these bodies as possible to the air Thus by directing a current of air upon the burning bodies, their combustion is accelerated and augmented in proportion as this current is stronger, as the effects of bellows and air-furnaces evidently prove

Most oily bodies, as wood, burn with much flame, which lasts while any sensible quantity of oil remains after which the flame ceases They are not however yet deprived of all their inflammable principle, a part of which remains in the state of coal Then the remaining part of the body may continue to burn, if it contains much phlogiston, but without a luminous flame, and in the manner of charcoal

In proportion as the phlogiston is consumed by this second combustion, what remains of it becomes more and more difficultly combustible, not only because the least fixed and adherent part of it is first burnt, but also because the proportion of incombustible matter, to which this phlogiston is united, becomes greater and greater. Hence when this combustion has arrived at a certain point, that is, when a small portion of phlogiston only remains strongly combined, and also covered and defended by a large quantity of incombustible matter, this remaining phlogiston will not burn alone, and is nearly in the same state as that of most metallic matters. If, therefore, this combustion is to be compleated, which then is called *calcination*, fire must be applied from some other fuel, with which the body to be calcined or dephlogisticated is to be penetrated, and kept red-hot, and as much air is at the same time to be applied to the body, till no longer any marks appear of its inflammable principle Ashes of vegetables, soot, coals of oils and of animal matters, and several metallic substances, contain some phlogiston in this last state

When the phlogiston of these substances is to be entirely burnt or dissipated, all the means capable of favoring combustion ought to be made to concur

The

The substances ought to be first divided into very small parts, because then they present more surface to the air than when in one mass. They are then to be exposed to the action of fire in a convenient vessel, so that the air may have free access, as for example, in a wide-mouthed test, and under a muffle open on the side at which air is introduced into the furnace. To accelerate further this operation, a current of air may be directed upon the surface of these bodies, and they may be frequently stirred, that all their parts may be successively presented to it. The strongest fire which the matter can sustain without fusion ought to be applied, because a melted body forms always one mass, and presents less surface than when it is divided in small detached parts. Thus fusible bodies, as ashes, alkaline salts and metals, ought to be calcined with a moderate heat, and proportioned to their fusibility.

The last portions of the phlogiston of certain bodies are so difficultly combustible, that notwithstanding all these means united, they never can be entirely burnt.

Some of them even, as the perfect metals, are considered as bodies entirely incombustible, because they can sustain the most violent fire during entire months, without suffering any sensible alteration. Nevertheless, Junker affirms, that gold and silver may be calcined, if they are treated during six months, by reverberation, in the manner of Isaacus Hollandus.

Although the certainty of this experiment has not been sufficiently confirmed by repeated trials, the method of calcining these metals proposed by this chemist agrees so well with the great principles of combustion, that its success seems very probable. *See* CALCINATION.

CLXXXVIII. COMPOSITION *of* BODIES. Chemical composition is the union and combination of several substances of different natures, from which a compound body results. From this union of bodies of different nature a body is formed of a mixed nature, which Becker and Stahl have called a *mixture*, and which may be called a *combination* or *chemical composition*, to avoid the equivocal sense of the word *mixture*, by which may be understood only a mere interposition of parts, and which therefore would give a very false idea of chemical composition, in which a mutual adhesion takes place between the combined substances.

When the substances considered by chemists as *simple*, or *primary principles*, are combined together, they form the first compounds, to which Becker and Stahl give, by way of excellence, the name *Mixts*. The same chemists call the bodies formed from the union of these mixts, *compounds*. When they treat of more complicated combinations, they talk of *decompounds* and *surdecompounds*.

This distribution of bodies, more or less compounded, is just and conformable to experience. But the names given by Becker and Stahl are not sufficiently clear and accurate.

A more simple and clear method of distinguishing these several classes of bodies seems to be by numbers indicating their degree of composition. Thus we might say, compounds of the first, of the second, of the third degree, &c. as Mr Macquer proposes in his course of chemistry.

CLXXXIX. CONCENTRATION. The concentration of a body consists in approximating its proper and integrant parts, by taking away some

some substance interposed betwixt these parts, and which is extraneous or superabundant to the body to be concentrated Thus, for instance, a solution of any saline substance in water may be concentrated by expelling part of the water of this solution. But custom has applied the word concentration to the dephlegmation of acids, and particularly of vitriolic acid by distillation, and of vinegar by congelation We proceed to both these concentrations

CXC CONCENTRATION *of* VITRIOLIC ACID

Vitriolic acid, procured either from vitriol or from sulphur, is never sufficiently pure for chemical operations It always contains some extraneous substances from which it must be purified

The heterogeneous matters which chiefly affect the purity of vitriolic acid, are superabundant water by which it is weakened, and inflammable matter by which it is rendered black and sulphureous These two substances are separable by one and the same distillation, which is called the *concentration*, or the *rectification of vitriolic acid* This acid ought to be distilled, whether it be both watery and sulphureous, or have only one of these faults

To explain what passes in this operation, and the management which must be observed, we will first consider what happens in the concentration of vitriolic acid, which is only diluted with superabundant water, and not phlogisticated We will then proceed to the changes produced upon this acid by distillation, when it is sufficiently free from water, and is only phlogisticated

When vitriolic acid, diluted with superabundant water, is to be concentrated, if it contains a considerable quantity of water, it may be disengaged from the greatest part of this superfluous water in stone or glass bottles, without the apparatus of distillation The greater the quantity of water which is united with the vitriolic acid, the less strongly does a part of it adhere As this water is much more volatile than vitriolic acid, it evaporates by almost the same degree of heat which is requisite to the evaporation of pure water While the water exhales, the parts of the vitriolic acid remaining in the vessel are approximated, and the acid becomes more and more concentrated and strong Thus the operation proceeds very well to a certain point, and even better than by distillation But when the acid has arrived at a certain degree of concentration, it cannot be compleated in open vessels, because the smaller which the quantity is of water united to the acid, the more strongly it adheres, so that it cannot be separated without a heat sufficient to raise the acid also, which therefore in open vessels would be lost But also another and more remarkable inconvenience occurs, which is, that when vitriolic acid begins to be much dephlegmated and very strong, it becomes so greedy of moisture that it attracts that of the surrounding air, as Mr Beaumé has well observed, and perpetually combines with it; so that every instant it resumes as much water from the air as it loses by evaporation The concentration of this acid must therefore be compleated in close vessels by distillation

For this distillation, a retort of good glass, capable of resisting acids, must be filled half full with the vitriolic acid to be concentrated, and set in a sand bath covered entirely with sand After a receiver has been adapted to it, heat must be applied, and very gradually augmented till drops are distilled

If the vitriolic acid contains little water, the distillation does not begin but with a considerable degree of heat, and the drops which fall into the receiver

are

are very acid These drops fall very slowly, and the distillation must not be too much hastened As the concentration advances, the drops follow each other at longer intervals, although the acid contained in the retort acquires more and more heat Towards the end of the operation, and when the acid is much concentrated, care must be taken not to encrease the heat so much as to make the acid boil, which cannot be effected with less than a red heat By this heat all the acid may be raised at once, in drops and burning vapors, which pass precipitately, and generally burst the retort

When this accident happens, whether it proceeds from hastening the distillation too much, or from cold air striking the retort, the concentrated and burning acid is almost entirely reduced to white, thick, suffocating vapors which instantly fill the laboratory The operators ought to remove themselves from such hurtful vapors

The duration of this operation, and the quantity of phlegmatic acid to be distilled, so that the vitriolic acid shall be left highly concentrated, are absolutely indeterminate, as they depend on the degree of strength which this acid had before its concentration The vitriolic acid, which was formerly kept by druggists, required that one half of it should be drawn off by distillation to make the remaining part twice as heavy as water At present, it is much stronger, although cheaper Some may be got very concentrated, and which only requires to be dephlogisticated in the following manner

The vitriolic acid manufactured in the great, and sold in commerce, is always mixed with more or less inflammable matter, by which it is rendered black and opake It may be entirely disengaged from this extraneous matter by a distillation similar to that above described

The first portions of such an acid which passes in distillation are a very penetrating, volatile, sulphureous acid If the phlogisticated vitriolic acid which is rectified be also phlegmatic, the distillation may be so managed that the liquor shall slightly boil This liquor continues black till it is concentrated to a certain degree, when by help of a strong heat which it then acquires, the concentrated acid acts upon the inflammable matter, dissipates it, or completely burns it. The liquor in the retort becomes gradually clearer, and at length perfectly white and transparent If this acid has also the requisite degree of concentration, the operation is finished when it thus becomes perfectly white and transparent The retort must be left in the sand-bath till it is cold, and then the acid is to be poured into a clean, dry, crystal-glass bottle, considering that the smallest piece of inflammable matter is capable of phlogisticating and blackening rectified vitriolic acid, and that any moisture, besides weakening the acid, might occasion such heat as to break the bottle When the acid is poured into the bottle, the neck of this bottle ought to be wiped dry, and closed by a glass stopper, accurately fitted and well wiped The mouth of the bottle ought also to be guarded from dust by being covered with leather

The phlegmatic or sulphureous liquor, which passed over into the receiver, is called *Spirit of Vitriol* It is clear and white, and may be used in many operations where concentrated vitriolic acid is not requisite, or it may be concentrated and rectified

CXCI CONCENTRATION *of* VINEGAR *by* CONGELATION Vinegar produced by the acetous fermentation is a vegetable acid

acid much used in chemistry As this acid is mixed with much extractive matter and superabundant water, chemists have endeavored to render it more pure and strong

It may easily be disengaged by a single distillation from almost all its extractive matter, see VINEGAR (DISTILLED), but it cannot so easily be deprived of its superabundant water If vinegar be distilled with intention to concentrate it, as vitriolic acid is, the most watery and least acid part would always rise first; but the operation would succeed very imperfectly, because this acid is almost as volatile as water To procure the concentration of vinegar, other expedients must be used Chemists have discovered several which succeed well For instance, by combining this acid with fixed matters, such as fixed alkalis and metals, and afterwards subjecting to distillation the salts resulting from such combinations, a very concentrated acid of vinegar is obtained, called, *Radical Vinegar* *See upon this subject* TERRA FOLIATA TARTARI, SALT *of* LEAD, CRYSTALS *of* VERDIGREASE, and VINEGAR (RADICAL) We proceed here to describe another method of concentrating vinegar, by which indeed it cannot be so much dephlegmated as by the preceding methods, but it is much more simple, and has some peculiar advantages The method is effected by congelation, or freezing

Stahl seems to be the first who employed this method Since which time Mr Geoffroy has made many experiments on this subject, a relation of which is to be found in the Memoirs of the Academy for the year 1739

As acids resist congelation much more than water, if vinegar be exposed to a cold sufficient to sink the mercury of Mr Reaumur's thermometer eight or ten degrees below the figure 0, a considerable quantity of ice will be formed This ice, being separated from the rest of the unfrozen liquor, consists of scarcely any thing but pure water, and the unfrozen liquor is a much stronger vinegar By exposing again this vinegar to another and stronger frost, more ice is formed in it, less hard than the first ice, and somewhat resembling snow, because it contains a certain quantity of unfrozen acid, and may therefore be set aside for the extraction of this acid The acid remaining after the second congelation is greatly stronger This concentration of vinegar may be much encreased by repeating the congelation with greater cold Mr Geoffroy relates in the quoted memoir, that vinegar which has been already concentrated by frosts of preceding years, and eight pints of which had been reduced to two pints and a half by the frost of January 29, 1739, was at length so much concentrated, that two drams of this vinegar the saturation of which before these concentrations would have required six grains of salt of tartar, did now require forty-four grains for that purpose.

Stahl assures us, that wine may be well concentrated by the same method He says, that he exposed to frost different kinds of wine, and that he had procured by this means two thirds, or three quarters of pure phlegm

Wines thus concentrated had a thick consistence, were very strong, and were preserved without change many years, in places, where the free access of air alternately hot and cold, according to the seasons, would have soured or spoiled any other wine in a few weeks The general opinion that wines are spoiled and entirely weakened by frost proceeds undoubtedly from the ice not being taken

taken off, but left to mix again with the wine when it thaws. Perhaps also some delicate wines are considerably altered by frost.

Wallerius says, that in the northern countries cold is successfully used to concentrate sea-water, and to approximate the particles of salt, by separating the ice as soon as it is formed, and which is little else but pure water.

We might be induced to believe that the mineral acids might be concentrated by congelation, as indeed they might be, if they were mixed with a very great quantity of water: but their adhesion to water is so strong, that they cannot be much concentrated by this method.

CXCII. CONDENSATION. By the condensation of a body we ought to understand the approximation of its integrant parts, so that it occupies a smaller space, and that its specific gravity is augmented, without the loss of any heterogeneous matter. For instance, air, forced by compression to confine itself within a narrower space, is to be considered as condensed.

CXCIII. CONE. (x)

CXCIV. CONTRAYERVA. (y)

CXCV. COPAL. (z)

CXCVI. COPPER. Copper, called also by chemists *Venus*, is an imperfect metal of a red shining color. It is harder, more elastic and sonorous, but a little less ductile than silver. It is nevertheless considerably ductile, and may be drawn into wire as fine as hair, or beaten into leaves almost as thin as those of silver.

The tenacity of the parts of this metal is very considerable, since a copper wire, the diameter of which is a tenth part of an inch, is capable of supporting a weight of 299$\frac{1}{4}$ pounds without breaking.

(x) Cone (Melting). This is a hollow cone formed of copper or of brass, with a handle, and with a flat bottom adjoining to the apex of the cone, upon which it is intended to rest. Its use is to receive a mass of one or more metals melted together and poured into it. This mass when cold may be easily shook out of the cone, from the figure of the vessel. Also if a melted mass, consisting of two or more metals, or other substances not combined together, be poured into this vessel, its figure facilitates the separation of these substances according to their respective densities. The cone ought to be well heated before the melted mass is poured into it, that no moisture may be contained, by which a dangerous explosion might be occasioned. It ought also to be greased internally with tallow, to prevent the adhesion of the fluid matter.

(y) Contrayerva. The leaves of this plant are said to afford a poison employed by Indians for poisoning arrows, to which poison the root of the said plant is said to be an antidote. From an ounce of the root Neuman extracted, with water, three drams and half a scruple, and from the same quantity, with spirit of wine, five scruples and two grains.

(z) Copal, improperly called *gum copal*, is a hard, shining, transparent, citron colored, odoriferous, concrete juice of an American tree, but which has neither the solubility in water common to gums, nor the solubility in spirit of wine common to resins, at least in any considerable degree. By these properties it resembles amber. By digestion in linseed oil, with a heat very little less than sufficient to boil or decompose the oil, it may be dissolved. This solution, diluted with spirit of turpentine, forms a beautiful transparent varnish, which, when properly applied, and slowly dried, is very hard and very durable. This varnish is applied to snuff-boxes, tea-boards, and other utensils. It preserves and gives lustre to paintings, and greatly restores the decayed colors of old pictures by filling up the cracks, and rendering the surfaces capable of reflecting light more uniformly.

Copper weighed by the hydrostatical balance loses in water about an eighth or a ninth part of its weight (a). It has a very singular and disagreeable smell and taste. It cannot be fused without a violent degree of heat sufficient to make it white.

Copper, being an imperfect metal, may be burnt, destroyed, and calcined by the united action of fire and air; for which reason its quantity is always diminished by melting it without covering its surface.

When it is exposed to a great fire with free access of air, it smokes, loses part of its weight, and communicates to flame beautiful green and blue colors.

It resists more than any other imperfect metal the action of fire before it suffers any considerable alteration. When a clean and polished copper plate is gently and gradually heated, its surface is covered with all the colors of the rainbow. This appearance proceeds from the developement, and the different states of the phlogiston of the metal (b).

When this metal is exposed to red heat with contact of air, its surface becomes quickly tarnished, and its metallic lustre is changed into a dark and earthy appearance, and if this heat be continued during a certain time, the surface of the metal is burnt and destroyed, so that when it cools, it is found to have no longer any adhesion with the uncalcined copper, but to be separated in scales from the difference of the contraction, occasioned by cooling, upon the uncalcined copper, and upon its burnt surface.

When this surface is separated, the copper beneath it seems clean and shining, but it will soon suffer the same change as the former, if it be again heated, and thus a piece of copper may be entirely reduced to scales no longer possessed of brilliancy, ductility, or other metallic properties, and which are called *burnt copper*.

This calcined copper is less fusible than copper in its metallic state: when exposed to a great fire, but a very small quantity of copper is obtained from it, the rest of it is changed into a dark and opake vitrified scoria, except the scales have been mixed with some matter capable of restoring to them phlogiston, in which latter case a quantity of malleable copper is obtained nearly equal to that of the scales employed. *See* REDUCTION *of* METALS.

These copper scales, which are at first but imperfectly calcined, may be entirely deprived of phlogiston and of their metallic properties by a second calcination under a muffle continued sufficiently long.

(a) The specific gravity of European copper is to that of water as 8843, and of Japanese copper as 9000 to 1000.

(b) All metals are subject to receive these colors or irises by heat, and from the color of any part of a piece of metal we may discover what degree of heat has been applied to that part, as the same degree of heat always gives the same color to the same metal. Hence artists, by observing the colors acquired by steel exposed to fire, are enabled to apply to pieces of that metal the precise degree of heat which they have found by experience to produce the required hardness, in the operation of tempering steel. Thus they know, that the heat which gives a blue color to steel is sufficient to give the requisite hardness for springs. The irises, or different colors given to different parts of one piece of metal, are occasioned by the heat being unequally applied. These colors are produced by a more or less perfect calcination of the surface of the metal exposed to heat.

Copper

Copper is alſo affected by the combined action of air and water hence its ſurface is apt to tarniſh, and even to be covered with a green ruſt, called *verdegriſe*

This ruſt is copper partly decompoſed, and deprived of part of its inflammable principle, for it cannot be melted into copper without much loſs, excepting its phlogiſton be reſtored by ſome reductive flux These are alterations to which all the imperfect metals are ſubject *See* METALS (IMPERFECT)

This metal is eaſily ſoluble by all acids, and its ſolutions are green or blue (c)

Vitriolic acid, although the ſtrongeſt of all, diſſolves copper more difficultly than any other it muſt be concentrated and aſſiſted by conſiderable heat and time to diſſolve this metal From this ſolution reſults a neutral ſalt, which forms beautiful blue cryſtals, called *blue vitriol*, or *vitriol of copper* *See these words*

Nitrous acid diſſolves copper very quickly with violence and effervеſcence, and during the ſolution it takes from the metal part of its phlogiſton The nitre formed by this ſolution is a very deliqueſcent ſalt The ſalts formed by marine acid or by aqua regia with copper are alſo very deliqueſcent

Vegetable acids, and particularly thoſe of wine and of vinegar, may be eaſily united with copper. The former acid forms with it the verdegriſe uſed in painting (*See* VERDEGRISE), and the ſecond, when ſaturated, forms the ſalt called *cryſtals of verdegriſe*, or *cryſtal of Venus* *See* CRYSTALS *of* VERDEGRISE

All acids united with copper may be ſeparated from it without any intermediate ſubſtance, and merely by fire

Calcareous earths, fixed and volatile alkalis, ſeparate copper from any acid, and precipitate it in form of a beautiful green powder The color of theſe precipitates of copper is cauſed by a portion of the ſalts which remain united with them As the metal thus diſſolved and precipitated has loſt part of its phlogiſton, particularly when it has been diſſolved by vitriolic and nitrous acids, theſe precipitates of copper cannot be melted into malleable copper without addition of phlogiſton but if they be melted with glaſſes, or vitreſcible matters, and the fire be properly managed, they communicate their colors to theſe ſubſtances hence they may be applied to imitate precious ſtones of a green color, or nearly green, as the emerald, and beryl or aqua marina, and for ſeveral ſhades of painting upon pottery and porcelain

Some metallic matters, which have a ſtronger affinity than copper has to acids, are therefore capable of precipitating this metal from its ſeveral ſolutions. Iron particularly has this property, for which reaſon, if it be added to a ſaturated ſolution of copper in an acid, it will be attacked and diſſolved by this acid, and it will precipitate the copper, and thus the ſolution of copper is changed into a ſolution of iron While this happens, a remarkable phenomenon appears the copper thus precipitated is in its metallic ſtate and brilliancy This effect, which ſeems to be general whenever a metallic matter is ſeparated from an acid by means of another metallic matter, can only happen becauſe the

(c) Solutions of copper in vitriolic acid, vegetable acid, oil, or water, are green, that in marine acid is at firſt brown or yellow, and becomes afterwards green, and that in aqua fortis is of a bluiſh-green color volatile or fixed alkalis make the ſolutions of copper in acids blue a ſolution of copper in volatile alkali, expoſed to air, is blue.

precipitating metal separates entirely and exactly all the acid from the precipitated metal, which earths and alkalis seem incapable of doing, and because the precipitating metal supplies enough of phlogiston to the acid, to prevent the acid from retaining the phlogiston of the precipitated metal, which earths and alkalis are also incapable of doing

However that be, this precipitation of copper in its metallic state, by the intervention of iron, is capable of imposing upon, and actually has imposed upon persons ignorant of chemistry, who, perceiving that a piece of iron, dipt into a liquor in which they suspected no copper, became covered over with copper, imagined that this liquor had the property of changing iron into copper

This property which iron has of separating copper from acids has been applied to use In England, the water in a copper mine is impregnated with a great quantity of blue vitriol, and from which much copper is extracted by means of iron immersed in it In Germany some copper ores are so pyritous, that they cannot be advantageously treated by ordinary fusions, but are reduced into vitriol, and by means of the iron which is put into the lixivium of this vitriol, called *cement water*, a considerable quantity of copper is obtained, which would otherwise be lost *See* ORES, PYRITES, *and* VITRIOLS

Copper produces, with respect to mercury and silver dissolved in acids, the same effects which itself suffers from iron, that is, it separates these metals so exactly from the acids with which they are united, that they appear with their metallic lustre

This property of copper is employed to obtain silver dissolved by spirit of nitre in the operation of parting This silver is generally very pure

If a very clean plate of copper be immersed in a solution of mercury, particularly if this solution have an excess of acid, it will be very soon covered over with mercury, which adheres to it, and which, when wiped and washed, makes a very white and brilliant silvering This also is one of the experiments which exhibit an appearance of transmutation capable of astonishing those who are ignorant of chemistry. Every day credulous persons are deceived by tricks no better than this

No metal is more soluble than copper It is acted upon by almost all saline and metallic substances, and probably for this reason ancient chemists have called it *Venus*, considering it as prostituted to all substances

Fixed and volatile alkalis easily dissolve copper, either directly, or still better if it has been previously dissolved in acids *See* ALKALIS (FIXED *and* VOLATILE).

Most neutral salts corrode its surface, and reduce it into verdegrise The same effect is produced by all oils and fat matters, from the latent acid which they contain

Sulphur has considerable action upon copper, and even has a greater affinity with it than with any other metal excepting iron hence it may be separated from almost all metals by means of sulphur, which also renders it much more fusible Copper is formed into a mineral or pyritous state by union with sulphur, and if this compound be exposed to fire, so that the sulphur shall be burnt, its acid will act upon the copper, and reduce it to blue vitriol

Copper

Copper may be easily united with all metals and femimetals, and with them forms allays, of which *see* the detail at the articles ALLAY, BRONZE, TOMBAC, *and* SIMILOR.

As this metal is combustible, it may be separated from the perfect metals by calcination, which is accelerated by means of lead, as in refining, or by nitre, which generally much accelerates the calcination of all combustible bodies, so that by repeated projections of nitre upon melted gold and silver allayed with copper, the nitre burns the phlogiston of the copper, and reduces this metal into a scoria which floats upon its surface but the nitre must be added gradually, and but a little at a time, particularly if much copper be in the allay, because the detonation which it occasions is sufficient to dissipate some of the perfect metals *See* NITRE

The affinities of copper, according to Mr Geoffroy, are mercury and lapis calaminaris, or rather zinc, and according to Mr Gellert, gold and silver *(d)*

CXCVII COPPER (WHITE). White copper is an allay of copper, zinc, and arsenic, in certain proportions, and is white as silver The precise proportions cannot be easily determined, and the allay cannot without difficulty be made, because of the volatility of the two semimetals Nevertheless, a very beautiful and silver-like white copper is made by some artists, who carefully conceal their method of preparation

As this allay is not much used, from its very noxious quality, chemists have not considered it, otherwise any of them who knew the management of metals might probably discover it

The medicinal virtues of copper are treated of under the article BRASS.

CXCVIII CORAL *(e)*

CXCIX CORK *(f)*

CC CORK (FOSSIL) *(g)*

CCI CREAM This name is applicable to all substances which separate from a liquor, and collect upon its surface, but it is particularly given to the following substances

(d) Wallerius says, that if a mixture of calx of copper and sal ammoniac be exposed during a certain time to air, from that mass, by distillation with soap, mercury may be obtained, whence he infers, that either mercury is a component principle of copper, or that at least some part of the copper is convertible into it

(e) CORAL *and* CORALLINE are shells of marine animals of the polypus kind, and possess the same chemical properties as the fresh shells of oysters and other shell-fish, that is, they are calcareous earths impregnated with some animal principles *See* EARTHS (CALCAREOUS) From sixteen ounces of coral, Neuman obtained by distillation six scruples of a volatile, alkaline, oily spirit, two or three grains of empyreumatic oil, and a residuum containing five scruples and a half of fixed salt, probably sea-salt The quantities of these component parts were found to vary according to the freshness of the coral analised

(f) CORK is the bark of a tree of the oak kind, which grows in the southern parts of Europe From an ounce of cork Neuman extracted, by boiling in water, two scruples, and from the same quantity he obtained, by digestion in spirit of wine, two scruples and two grains.

(g) CORK (FOSSIL), *Suber montanum.* This name is given to a stone which is a species of amianthus, consisting of flexible fibres loosely interwoven, and somewhat resembling vegetable cork This is the lightest of all stones By fire it is fusible, and forms a black glass It possesses the general properties of amianthus, *See* AMIANTHUS

CCII. CREAM *of* LIME. The cream of lime is that most attenuated part of quicklime, and most approaching to a saline state, which is dissolved by water with which quicklime is slaked, or even in which slaked lime is boiled. This matter separates from lime-water by crystallization during the evaporation of the water; and as water only evaporates at its surface, this earthy crystallization is also formed there. It forms a semi-transparent pellicle, which becomes thicker and thicker till it separates into pieces, and falls to the bottom by its weight in form of scales. The cream of lime has the same properties as slaked lime has. See QUICKLIME. (*b*)

CCIII. CREAM *of* MILK. This is the most oily part of milk, which being naturally only mixed, and not dissolved in milk, and being specifically lighter than the other parts, separates from them by rest, and collects on the surface of the milk, from which it is generally skimmed to compleat the disengagement of the oily from the caseous and serous parts, that is, to make it into *butter*. See BUTTER *and* MILK.

Cream of milk, which is generally called simply *cream*, is not only an agreeable aliment when recent, but is also useful in medicine as a lenient, when applied to tetters and erisipelas accompanied with pain, and proceeding from an acrid humor.

CCIV. CREAM *of* TARTAR. Cream of tartar is, properly speaking, that part of the concrete acid of tartar which crystallizes first, and like a pellicle on the surface of water in which tartar has been boiled, with intention to purify it, and to separate from it its most saline part. Thus this substance called *cream*, from its manner of formation, does not essentially differ from the crystals of tartar which are formed in the liquor; and these crystals are accordingly, as well as the saline pellicle, generally called cream of tartar, these two matters being confounded together by one name, from which no inconvenience results. See TARTAR.

CCV. CRIMSON. (*i*)

CCVI. CROCUS. This Latin word, signifying *saffron*, has been applied as a name to earths of certain metals, which in color somewhat resemble saffron: such particularly are the earths of iron and of copper, each of which is therefore called *crocus*, the first being the *crocus of mars* or *of iron*, and the second *the crocus of copper*: but the word *saffron* is more commonly employed, and particularly applied to the earth of iron. See SAFFRON.

CCVII. CRUCIBLE. (*k*)

(*b*) Cream of lime is very different from slaked quicklime. The latter substance is calcareous earth deprived of fixable air, and combined with water: it is caustic, soluble in water, and possesses all the properties of quicklime, from which it differs only in containing a quantity of water. Cream of lime is calcareous earth, which having been deprived of fixable air by calcination, and dissolved by water, is, by exposure to air, again combined with fixable air; by which it is rendered mild, crystallizable, unsoluble in water, and restored to its original state before calcination. See AIR (FIXABLE).

(*i*) CRIMSON. A crimson color may be given to silks and woolen cloths by cochineal. See COCHINEAL. A less durable crimson may be given by Brazil wood. For the color called by dyers demi-crimson, the root of madder is mixed with cochineal. See RED *and* DYING.

(*k*) See POTTERY.

CCVIII CRYSTAL Cryſtal, called alſo *rock-cryſtal*, or *natural cryſtal*, is a hard, tranſparent ſtone, of the figure of a priſm with ſix faces, which is terminated at each of its extremities by hexagonal pyramids.

The moſt beautiful rock-cryſtal is that which is perfectly clear, white, and tranſparent It is frequently cut, and luſtres, vaſes, and toys are made of it, as of other beautiful ſtones Rock-cryſtals, like the precious ſtones, are of all colors, and they receive their color, as the precious ſtones do, from metallic and phlogiſtic ſubſtances Some of them are brown, and almoſt black, theſe may be rendered white and tranſparent, by making them red-hot, which muſt be done very gently and gradually, to prevent their cracking, which they are very apt to do as well as other vitrifiable ſtones *See* EARTH (VITRIFIABLE (*l*)

(*l*) *Cryſtal*, *rock cryſtal*, or *quartz-cryſtal*, is a tranſparent ſtone of the claſs of earths called by ſome ſiliceous, and by others vitrifiable Its form is that of an hexagonal priſm, one or both ends of which are terminated by hexagonal pyramids Some of them conſiſt of theſe two pyramids joined together at their baſes, without any priſm interpoſed Cryſtal is frequently found adhering to quartz, and, according to Cronſtedt, it is nothing but quartz, which he affirms always aſſumes this hexagonal form, when its accretion or cryſtallization has not been interrupted Cryſtals are either colorleſs, or colored Colored cryſtals are called by ſome authors *fluors* Thoſe which are red are called *falſe rubies*, the violet-colored, *falſe amethyſts*, or, according to Cronſtedt, the *true amethyſts*, the yellowiſh-red, *falſe hyacinths*, the blue, *falſe ſaphirs*, yellow, *falſe topazes*, the greeniſh-yellow, *falſe chryſolites*, the green, *falſe emeralds*, the ſea-green, *falſe beryls* Some cryſtals are duſky, brown, or blackiſh, but ſtill tranſparent Cryſtals poſſeſs the general properties of the earths called vitrifiable *See* EARTHS (VITRIFIABLE) Colorleſs cryſtals reſiſt the moſt violent and long continued fire *See* Mr D'ARCET's *Memoir upon Vitrification*, Academy of Sciences, 1766 Moſt of the colored cryſtals are fuſible by violent fire They probably receive this fuſibility, as well as their color, from metallic ſubſtances Colorleſs cryſtals may be tinged with various colors, ſo as to imitate precious ſtones For this purpoſe, Neri, in his *Art of making Glaſs*, directs that pieces of clear cryſtal ſhould be laid upon a mixture of four parts of orpiment, four parts of crude antimony, and one part of ſal ammoniac, placed in a crucible, to which another crucible inverted is well luted the crucibles are to be placed in a furnace, and ſurrounded with charcoal after a red heat has been gradually applied, and the fire extinguiſhed, the upper pieces of cryſtal will have acquired a fine golden color, reſembling opals, and variegated with beautiful ſpots the lower pieces of cryſtal will have acquired a fine color, reſembling that of the ſkins of vipers He gives another proceſs, in which he directs the cementing mixture to be compoſed of two parts of yellow orpiment, two parts of white arſenic, one part of crude antimony, and one part of ſal ammoniac He directs alſo, that no bellows or ſtrong current of air ſhould be applied to the fire, by which he ſays, that the cryſtals are apt to be cracked, probably by making the heat too intenſe, and that the crucibles ſhould not be opened till they have been gradually cooled Cryſtals thus treated reſemble rubies, opals, agates, turquois, marbles, chryſolites Mr Pott ſays, that he found the color of ſome cryſtals much improved by repeating the operation Baptiſta Porta directs, that cryſtals ſhould be colored by keeping them immerſed during four or five hours in a melted mixture of ſulphur, crude antimony, orpiment, arſenic, and tutty In theſe operations, the cryſtals ſeem to imbibe ſome of the vapors of the metallic ſubſtances The chief difficulties ſeem to be to prevent the cracks to which the cryſtals are very ſubject by this treatment, and to procure a ſufficient penetration Probably both theſe purpoſes might be effected by a very ſtrict attention to the gradual application, and to the maintenance of a due degree of heat

CCIX CRYSTAL (FACTITIOUS). The word cryſtal has been applied to glaſſes produced by art, which from their tranſparency and whiteneſs imitate rock-cryſtal In fact, ſome are made as beautiful as the fineſt rock-cryſtals, but not nearly ſo hard The heat of ordinary vitrification ſeem incapable of producing glaſs as hard as rock cryſtal, nor do our crucibles ſeem capable of ſuſtaining the requiſite heat, if it could be raiſed *See the method of making cryſtals at the words* GLASS *and* VITRIFICATION

CCX CRYSTAL (MINERAL) Mineral cryſtal, called alſo *Salt of Prunella*, is melted nitre detonated with a little ſulphur, and caſt into form of tablets

Nitre is one of the neutral ſalts which contains the leaſt water in its cryſtallization, or which loſes the leaſt water by a true fuſion, and is alſo one of the moſt fuſible ſalts

To make mineral cryſtal, very pure nitre muſt be put into a clean crucible, and quickly fuſed, taking care that no aſhes or coal fall in When the nitre is fuſed, it is to be detonated with ſulphur, in the proportion of a dram of the latter to a pound of the former It is then to be poured into a copper, or rather a ſilver baſon, in which it is to be agitated while yet fluid, that it may fix in form of cakes or tablets

No other effect is produced upon the nitre by the ſmall quantity of ſulphur with which it is detonated, than to introduce into it a proportionable quantity of vitriolated tartar, called *Sal Polychreſt of Glaſſer* In all other reſpects, chemical and medicinal, mineral cryſtal is nitre, and may be given like this, from four grains to ten or twelve, in a quart of proper drink It is cooling, ſedative, aperitive and diuretic This preparation then ſeems uſeleſs, ſince the ſame intentions may be better accompliſhed by well purified nitre *See* NITRE

CCXI CRYSTALLIZATION This word is ſometimes employed to ſignify ſubſtances which are cryſtallized, or whoſe parts are ſo arranged that they form regular figures In this ſenſe, we ſay *ſtony cryſtallizations*, *pyritous cryſtallization*, &c

CCXII CRYSTALLIZATION *of* SALTS *and of other Subſtances* If the word cryſtallization were to be confined to its moſt proper ſenſe, as it ſeems to have been formerly, it could only be applied to operations by which certain ſubſtances are diſpoſed to paſs from a fluid to a ſolid ſtate by the union of their parts, which ſo arrange themſelves that they form tranſparent and regularly figured maſſes, like native cryſtal, from which reſemblance the word cryſtallization has evidently been taken

But modern chemiſts and naturaliſts have much extended this expreſſion, and it now ſignifies a regular arrangement of the parts of any body which is capable of it, whether the maſſes ſo arranged be tranſparent or not Thus opake ſtones, pyrites, and minerals, when regularly formed, are ſaid to be cryſtallized, as well as tranſparent ſtones and ſalts

The opacity and tranſparency of ſubſtances are juſtly diſregarded in conſidering whether they be cryſtallized or not, for theſe qualities are perfectly indifferent to the regular arrangement of the integrant parts of ſubſtances, which is the eſſential object of cryſtallization

This being eſtabliſhed, cryſtallization ought to be defined an operation by which the integrant parts of a body, ſeparated from each other by the interpo-

ſition

ſition of a fluid, are diſpoſed to unite again and to form ſolid, regular, and uniform maſſes

To underſtand as much as we can of the mechaniſm of cryſtallization, we muſt remark,

1 That the integrant parts of all bodies have a tendency to each other, by which they approach, unite, and adhere together, when not prevented by an obſtacle

2 That in ſimple, or little-compounded bodies, this tendency of integrant parts is more obvious and ſenſible than in other more compounded hence the former are much more diſpoſed to cryſtallize

3 That although we do not know the figure of the primitive integrant molecules of any body, we cannot doubt but that the primitive integrant molecules of every different body have a conſtantly uniform and peculiar figure

4 That theſe integrant parts cannot have an equal tendency to unite indiſcriminately by any of their ſides, but by ſome preferably to others, excepting all the ſides of an integrant part of a body be equal and ſimilar, and probably the ſides, by which they tend to unite, are thoſe by which they can touch moſt extenſively and immediately The moſt general phenomena of cryſtallization may be conceived in the following manner

Let a body be ſuppoſed to have its integrant parts ſeparated from each other by ſome fluid If a part of this fluid be taken away, theſe integrant parts will approach together, and as the quantity of intervening fluid diminiſhes, they will at laſt touch and unite They may alſo unite, when they come ſo near to each other that their mutual tendency ſhall be capable to overcome the diſtance betwixt them If, beſides, they have time and liberty to unite with each other by the ſides moſt diſpoſed to this union, they will form maſſes of a figure conſtantly uniform and ſimilar For the ſame reaſon, when the interpoſed fluid is haſtily taken away, ſo that the integrant parts ſhall be approximated, and be brought into contact before they have taken the poſition of their natural tendency, then they will join confuſedly by ſuch ſides as chance preſents to them, they will in ſuch circumſtances form ſolid maſſes, whoſe figures will not be determinate, but irregular and various

In every cryſtallization all that we have deſcribed may be obſerved

If cryſtallization be taken in the general ſenſe we have given to it, ice is a true cryſtallization Water, for inſtance, is to be conſidered as a body whoſe integrant parts are ſeparated from each other by the interpoſition of the matter of fire Melted metals are alſo to be conſidered in the ſame manner The fluidity of theſe bodies is to be attributed to this matter of fire, with which theſe bodies are penetrated When therefore theſe liquefied bodies cool, which can only be by taking away this igneous matter which penetrates them, if the approximation of the integrant parts, which is a neceſſary conſequence of this cooling, be made ſo ſlowly that they ſhall have time and liberty to unite by the ſides moſt diſpoſed to this union, they will always form maſſes of a conſtant and ſimilar figure.

Thus when water freezes ſlowly, and is not agitated by any motion which can diſturb the order in which the integrant parts tend to unite, it forms regular cryſtals of ice, and always of the ſame form.

These

Theſe cryſtals which may be called cryſtals of water, are long, needle-like maſſes, flattened on one ſide, joined together in ſuch a manner that the ſmaller are inſerted into the ſides of the greater, and thus theſe compound cryſtals have the appearance of feathers, or of leaves of trees

The moſt remarkable circumſtance attending this cryſtallization is, that the angle formed by the inſertion of the ſmaller needles into the ſides of the larger ones is always of the ſame width, that is, ſixty degrees However, it is ſometimes double, that is, 120 degrees, but it is conſtantly one of theſe two angles, and it is to be remembered that theſe angles are complements to each other, that is, they are together equal to two right angles We are obliged to Mr Mairan for theſe fine obſervations, which he has given at full length in an excellent diſſertation on ice

Metals, ſulphur, and ſeveral other bodies not much compounded, which fix and become ſolid after fuſion, aſſume always a regular arrangement whenever they are ſlowly enough cooled for that purpoſe The ſtar of the regulus of antimony has been long obſerved with wonder Alchemiſts, who ſaw wonders in all their operations, conſidered this ſtar as ſomething myſterious and ſignificant, but the wonder ceaſed when the cauſe of it was inveſtigated by ſo good a philoſopher as Mr Reaumur, and diſcovered to be the tendency which the integrant parts of the regulus of antimony have to arrange themſelves in an uniform manner, for this arrangement always happens, when the regulus of antimony has been well fuſed, and ſlowly cooled Mr Macquer and Mr. Beaume having fuſed ſilver with great heat, and afterwards very ſlowly cooled it, obſerved that this metal alſo arranged itſelf in a regular manner Mr Beaumé obſerved the ſame effect upon applying to all the other metals and ſemi-metals the ſame treatment Every metallic ſubſtance was found to have its peculiar form, which Mr Beaumé propoſes to determine

What we have ſaid concerning bodies, which being fuſed by fire, are cryſtallized when they become ſolid by cold, may alſo be applied to all thoſe whoſe integrant parts ſwim ſeparately from each other in a fluid ſuch as water. Thus all kinds of earths, and of metallic and mineral matters, which are found in that ſtate, may be cryſtallized by taking away ſome of the watery fluid which ſeparates their integrant parts A ſlow evaporation of the water which contains theſe ſubſtances allows their parts to approximate and to unite together by the moſt ſuitable ſides, and to form maſſes of a determinate and conſtant figure

In this manner are formed the cryſtallizations of precious ſtones, of rock cryſtal, of ſpars, of certain ſtalactites, and of all ſtony bodies found ſo frequently well cryſtallized The regular forms of moſt pyrites, of many ores and metallic minerals, and even of ſome pure metals, ſuch as gold, ſilver, copper, which are found regularly arranged and ramified, ought to be attributed to the ſame mechaniſm, that is, to the ſlow ſeparation of their integrant parts from the water in which they are ſuſpended

But of all the ſubſtances thus ſuſceptible of cryſtallizing by their ſeparation from water, ſalts are moſt diſpoſed to it, and afford the beſt examples of cryſtallization, becauſe all ſaline ſubſtances being eſſentially ſoluble in water, are liquefied by this fluid in a much greater quantity than the bodies we have mentioned, which, properly ſpeaking, are only miſcible with water

This

This property which salts have of being soluble by water must depend on a certain affinity or adhesion of their integrant parts to those of water, and from this adhesion we can deduce the phenomena peculiar to the crystallization of salts, and the differences observable betwixt the crystallization of these, and that of other substances to which water has not the same affinity We shall relate what is most necessary to be known concerning the crystallization of salts, an object of great importance in chemistry

The crystallization of a salt dissolved in water may be procured, as evidently appears from what we have said, by taking away the dissolving water and as most salts are less volatile than water, and may even be considered comparatively as fixed substances, this substraction may be commodiously made by the evaporation of a sufficient quantity of water The parts of the salt, being sufficiently approximated by this evaporation, will unite together and form crystals, as we have already explained concerning other substances But as the saline parts adhere to those of the water, this circumstance occasions an essential difference in the crystallization, which is, that the salt when crystallizing, does not separate itself from all the water with which it was united in solution, but retains some part of it with some force, and this portion of water adhering to, and even combined with the parts of salt, makes with it one whole or entire body; whence saline crystals are compounded of crystallized salt, and of water which makes part of these crystals This water is called by chemists the *water of crystallization*

As this water of crystallization is superabundant to the essence of the crystallized salt, it may be taken from it by evaporation with a certain degree of heat, without any change produced upon the essential properties of the salt, so that it may be again dissolved and crystallized as at first But we must observe, that the water of crystallization cannot be taken from any salt without destroying the form, or at least the consistence and transparency of the crystals, and when the salt is to be re-dissolved and re-crystallized, it retains in this second crystallization the same quantity of water precisely as it had in the first

Hence we ought to conclude that this water of crystallization is not essential to a salt, as a salt, but that it is essential to a salt as being crystallized, since to it the saline crystals owe their form, transparency, and even the cohesion of their parts.

The quantity of water of crystallization varies much in different salts. Some of these, as alum, Glauber's salt, and martial vitriol, contain about half their weight of water, and others, as nitre and sea salt, contain but a small quantity Selenites contains an almost insensible quantity of water This difference seems to depend on the state of the acid in these salts, and in general the more firmly an acid is combined with its basis, the less water it retains in crystallization.

A very important remark to be made upon this water of crystallization, is, that when the crystallization is properly managed, this water is perfectly pure, and contains no substance foreign to the crystallized salt To Mr Beaumé we owe this discovery. By many experiments he was convinced that no neutral salt, with a basis of fixed alkali, retains in its crystals either superabundant acid or alkali, or any other matter foreign to the neutral salt, although even this falt had been cryftallized in a liquor that was acid, alkaline, or impregnated with any other fubftance foreign to the falt, and that if fometimes thefe heterogeneous fubftances are found included in faline cryftals, they have no adhefion to them, fince they may be feparated merely by draining upon brown paper, without any change produced upon the cryftals of the falt, whereas the water of cryftallization cannot be taken away without a deftruction of the cryftals The caufe of this phenomenon will eafily appear when we recollect that falts retain the water of their cryftallization by the adhefion of thefe falts to water, and that if a falt be diffolved in water impregnated with acid, alkali, or other fubftance foreign or fuperabundant to the falt diffolved, this falt does not adhere either to the fuperabundant acid, or alkali, nor to the other extraneous fubftances, but to the water alone

Evaporation of water, in which a falt is diffolved, is not the only method by which the falt can be cryftallized Another method which may be ufed with fuccefs, at leaft for the cryftallization of moft falts, is by application of cold to the water fufpending the falt The reafon of this is as follows

All falts are foluble in water, but not with equal facility, fome of them requiring much water, and others very little moft of them are more eafily diffolved, and in greater quantity, by hot than by cold water, and others with nearly equal facility, and in equal quantity by both hot and cold water This being eftablifhed, when boiling water, that is, water heated as much as poffible, fufpends in folution all that it can diffolve of thofe falts which are more foluble by hot than by cold water, if this water be cooled, the portion of falt which was diffolved merely by the heat of the water, will be collected and cryftallized as faft as the water cools We may alfo obferve, that when this cooling of the water is very quick, the cryftals it occafions are fmall, irregular, and ill-fhaped, and that the more flowly the cooling is produced, the larger and better formed the cryftals are

What has been hitherto faid concerning the regular forms taken by certain liquefied matters during their fixing or becoming folid, is entirely applicable to this kind of cryftallization of falts This cryftallization is not effected by a fubftraction of water but of fire, by which fubftraction a condenfation of the faline liquor is produced, and confequently a fufficient approximation of the parts of the diffolved falt to difpofe them to unite, and to form cryftals, and as in this cafe, the fluidity or the folidity of the falt is folely occafioned by the prefence or abfence of the matter of fire, thefe falts diffolved by heat, and cryftallized by cold, may be compared to melted metals, the parts of which are regularly arranged by a flow cooling But with regard to falts we muft obferve, that as their cryftallization is performed in a fluid to which they have an adhefion, they retain the fame quantity of water of cryftallization, whether the operation was performed by cold or by evaporation

Hence we may perceive, that evaporation and cooling are the two principal methods of cryftallizing falts Sometimes it is proper to employ one only of thefe methods, and at other times both together, according to the particular nature of the falt to be treated If it be one of thofe falts which are better cryftallized by cooling than by evaporation, fuch as nitre, for inftance, then the former method ought to be ufed, for nitre cannot be well cryftallized by

evapo-

evaporation alone, becaufe the water which keeps it diffolved would be reduced almoft to nothing before the cryftallization would begin, and the liquor would be fo concentrated that the parts of the falt would not arrange themfelves properly

When, therefore, nitre is to be cryftallized, the water is to be evaporated fo far only that when it cools cryftals fhall be formed This degree of evaporation is known by taking a few drops of the hot liquor, and cooling them quickly, if the evaporation has been fufficient, fmall cryftals may be perceived inftantly formed As the evaporation here mentioned does not occafion the cryftallization of the nitre, but is only preparatory to it, this evaporation may be either quick or flow without inconvenience The liquor may be made to boil as faft as poffible, and the cryftals of nitre will be no lefs perfect, provided that this liquor when fufficiently evaporated be flowly cooled when it is perfectly cooled, no more cryftals will be formed in it It ought then to be poured off, and again evaporated, when by a fecond cooling it will furnifh more cryftals, and this treatment is to be continued to the end

But if well formed cryftals are to be obtained of one of thofe falts which are nearly as foluble in cold as in boiling water, and which confequently cannot be cryftallized by cold, evaporation is the only method to be ufed Common falt is a proper inftance of this kind

Water impregnated with common falt muft be evaporated to obtain cryftals, and when the liquor contains much more water than is neceffary to the folution of the falt, the evaporation may be carried on as faft as poffible till the cryftallization is ready to begin This point is known by a thin, faline pellicle, which floats on the furface of the liquor, and feems as if duft had fallen upon it This pellicle is compofed of the firft portions of falt beginning to cryftallize It is always formed at the furface, becaufe this falt cryftallizes by evaporation only, and evaporation is only at the furface

Mr Rouelle, in his Memoir concerning the Cryftallization of Sea-falt, fays, that he has obferved, that when the evaporation has been very flow, and with a heat not much exceeding that of fummer, the cryftals of common falt are formed at the bottom and not at the furface of the liquor. As this appears quite contrary to the manner in which this falt cryftallizes in all other circumftances, have we not reafon to believe, that in this infenfible evaporation the cryftals of fea-falt are formed firft at the furface, as in all other evaporations, but that they cannot be perceived from the extreme fmallnefs of their fize at firft, and becaufe the heat is too weak to dry their upper furface, and to make them adhere to the air, thefe fmall cryftals fall to the bottom without being perceived, and there become larger by the union of other fmall cryftals, formed and precipitated in the fame manner?

If the evaporation when brought to the point of cryftallization was to be ftopt, and the liquor to be cooled after it has been filtrated, and put into a bottle to prevent further evaporation from the remaining heat, fcarcely any cryftals would be formed in it, but the falt would remain diffolved in the water If, on the contrary, the evaporation fhould be haftily continued, falt would indeed be formed in great quantity; but as its parts would not have time to arrange themſelves properly, the cryſtals would be ſmall and ill-formed * The evaporation therefore ought to be continued, but ſlowly: and by this method very beautiful cryſtals will be obtained, partly in cubes, partly in hollow pyramids formed by cubes †

The rules of cryſtallization moſt ſuited to the nature of each ſalt muſt be obſerved, not merely to obtain well-formed cryſtals, for if their figure was once determined, the regularity of their cryſtallization would be afterwards of no conſequence but the cryſtallization of ſalts relates to an affair of much more importance, which is their purity

We have already ſaid, that, when a ſalt is well cryſtallized, the water of its cryſtallization is very pure, and contains none of the heterogeneous matters which happened to be mixed with the ſolution of the ſalt before cryſtallization. This obſervation may be extended to other ſalts which may happen to be diſſolved in the ſame liquor If then ſeveral ſalts be diſſolved together, we may almoſt always ſeparate them exactly from each other, by cryſtallizing each of them according to their character, for amongſt the almoſt infinite number of ſalts now known, ſcarcely two ſhow preciſely ſimilar phenomena in cryſtallization We may, from the example of ſeparating nitre and common ſalt when diſſolved together in the ſame liquor by cryſtallization, ſhow how ſuch ſeparation may be done in general, even when ſeveral ſalts happen to be ſo confounded This is certainly one of the fineſt and moſt uſeful problems in chemiſtry

Let us then ſuppoſe that nitre and ſea-ſalt, diſſolved in the ſame liquor, are to be ſeparated from each other. The method of effecting this will appear evidently from conſidering what we have ſaid concerning cryſtallization, and this method will be found to conſiſt in employing alternately evaporation and cooling First of all then, the liquor muſt be evaporated If, during the evaporation, a pellicle appears on the ſurface, and no cryſtals of nitre appear in a ſmall quantity of the liquor when haſtily cooled, then we diſcover that common ſalt is in greater quantity than the nitre In this caſe the evaporation muſt be continued, and the common ſalt ſeparated as faſt as it is formed, till a ſmall quantity of the liquor, when haſtily cooled, ſhews ſmall needle-like cryſtals of nitre,

* Although cryſtals of ſea-ſalt are generally leſs regular when formed by a haſty than by a ſlow evaporation, this irregularity is, however, leſs ſenſible in this ſalt than in moſt others, and its cryſtals always tend to a cubic form, or at leaſt appear compoſed of cubes From this obſervation we have reaſon to believe that the primitive integrant molecules of this ſalt are cubes hence we may conceive that as all the ſides of this ſalt are equal and ſimilar, from their union regular ſolids ought to reſult, more or leſs approaching to the cubic figure, by whatever ſide they may have been united *Note of the Author*

† Although in a moderate evaporation a very large quantity of cryſtals of common ſalt is formed in quadrangular, hollow, and inverted pyramids, the cubic figure is nevertheleſs the primitive and eſſential form of this ſalt, for theſe pyramids are all compoſed evidently of cubes Beſides, they are only formed accidentally, by the union of ſeveral quadrangular priſms compoſed of cubes, which are ſucceſſively applied to the ſides of a firſt cube, which being formed at the ſurface of the liquor, remains ſuſpended there, by the adheſion of its upper dried ſurface to the air As this cube is beſides a little ſunk into the liquor by its weight, ſo that the liquor riſes along its ſides, it becomes by that means a very proper foundation for the formation of this pyramid This mechaniſm is explained at length in Junker's book, and in a Memoir of Mr Rouelle concerning the cryſtallization of ſea-ſalt, printed in 1745, *Note of the Author*.

nitre, then the liquor is to be left to cool, that the nitre may have an opportunity of cryſtallizing by cooling, after which the evaporation is to be reſumed that more common ſalt may be ſeparated, and to diſſipate ſo much water that cryſtals of nitre ſhall again be formed by cooling. Thus theſe ſalts may be alternately cryſtallized, one by cooling and the other by cryſtallization, till they are entirely ſeparated

If, in the beginning of the operation, the liquor had, upon trial in ſmall quantity, given cryſtals of nitre by cooling, before any pellicle had appeared upon its ſurface, the common ſalt would then have been known to be in much leſs quantity than the nitre In this caſe, the nitre would have been cryſtallized firſt, but always by cooling The quantity of nitre, which exceeds that of common ſalt, having been thus ſeparated, the common ſalt would then begin to cryſtallize in its turn by evaporation

Several eſſential remarks are to be made upon this ſeparation of ſeveral ſalts from each other by cryſtallization

Firſt, although the two ſalts, the method of ſeparating which we have given as an example, are the moſt capable of ſuch a ſeparation, becauſe ſea-ſalt is one of the ſalts which are leaſt of all to be cryſtallized by cooling, and on the contrary, nitre is one of thoſe which are beſt cryſtallized by this method, nevertheleſs, after a firſt cryſtallization of theſe two ſalts, ſuch as we have deſcribed, they are not entirely and perfectly ſeparated from each other the ſea-ſalt contains ſome nitre, and the nitre contains ſome portion of ſea-ſalt, becauſe in cryſtallization one ſalt always takes with it a ſmall portion of another but when two ſalts are ſo different from each other in this reſpect as theſe two, a perfect ſeparation may be eaſily made by diſſolving each of them ſeparately in more water, and by proceeding to their cryſtallization by the ſame method As a new ſeparation is made by each cryſtallization, they may be obtained at laſt perfectly pure by repeating ſufficiently this management

The ſecond remark to be made on the ſeparation of ſalts by cryſtallization is, that this ſeparation is ſo much more difficult and long, in proportion as the ſalts to be ſeparated are more ſimilar to each other in their manners of cryſtallization For inſtance, if two ſalts, which are only capable of cryſtallizing by evaporation, as ſea-ſalt and vitriolated tartar, or by cooling, as nitre and Glauber's ſalt, they cannot be ever obtained quite pure and ſeparated from each other by any management nevertheleſs, even in this caſe they may be in great meaſure ſeparated, firſt, becauſe the preciſe degree of evaporation, or of cold, which is neceſſary for the cryſtallizing of one ſalt, is generally ſomewhat different from that which is requiſite for the cryſtallization of another ſalt, ſecondly, becauſe although they ſhould reſemble each other much in this reſpect, ſome differences, which muſt be obſervable in the ſize and form of their cryſtals when well formed, will furniſh means of making at leaſt an imperfect ſeparation, which may be made more perfect by repeating this management

But the ſeparation of ſome ſalts is attended with ſingular and even inſuperable difficulties Such are the ſalts which have ſome action upon each other, and the parts of which have ſome adheſive power together. This action of neutral ſalts upon each other has been very little obſerved it is, nevertheleſs, very ſenſible in ſome of them, ſuch are ſal ammoniac and corroſive ſublimate, which not only act as intermediate ſubſtances to each other, by which they can be

diſſolved

dissolved in greater quantities in water and in spirit of wine than they can singly, but which being dissolved together in the same menstruum, cannot be again crystallized separately by any method; as Mr Macquer has shewn in his Memoir concerning Mr Garay's Tincture of Mercury, printed in the Collection of the Academy for the year 1755

Some salts have so great affinity with water, and are so soluble by this menstruum, that they can scarcely be crystallized The solution of these salts requires to be evaporated almost to dryness, or to a thick consistence, and then by cooling they generally form needle-like crystals applied longitudinally or transversely to each other. When they are exposed to the air, they attract humidity, and resolve into a liquid state Mr Rouelle was the first who described, in his Memoir concerning Salts in the year 1744, the crystallization of deliquescent salts, such as marine salt and nitre with bases of calcareous earth, of copper, and of iron, terra foliata tartari, and the salts formed by the union of the acids of vinegar and of tartar with iron and with copper

All these so difficultly crystallizable salts may be easily separated from salts which may be readily crystallized, with which they happen to be mixed, because the former salts in the evaporations and coolings are always the last to crystallize

Two of these salts, namely nitre and marine salt, with bases of calcareous earth, are found mixed with nitre and marine salt with bases of fixed alkali, both of them in the lixiviums of the manufacturers of nitre, and the latter in almost all the waters in which common salt is found to be naturally dissolved hence, when the proper operations are made to obtain nitre and sea-salt, after all the evaporations and crystallizations, a very heavy saline liquor remains from which no crystals can be procured, called the *mother water* These mother-waters of nitre and of common salt are, then, nothing but these salts with earthy bases almost pure, and if a crystallization of them were required, the method described by Mr Rouelle in the quoted Memoir ought to be practised. But this is not a matter worthy the attention of the manufacturers, to whom the perfect purification of nitre and of sea-salt, from an adhering portion of the salts with earthy basis, is of much more importance, as we shall see when we shall treat of these salts

Chemists have given much attention to this subject, the crystallization of salts; and particularly Mr Rouelle has made many interesting researches concerning it, which may be seen in his Memoir of 1744. But nevertheless, much remains yet to be done The true form of all crystallizable salts, and the best methods of crystallizing them, are not yet determined, which will not appear surprizing to those who understand this subject, and who know that one and the same salt, although constantly tending to the same form, is nevertheless capable of disguising itself in many ways, and of taking many different forms, according to the circumstances during crystallization. The quickness or slowness of evaporation, the quantity of water evaporated, the more or less hasty cooling, and the different degrees of cold applied, the state of the air and of the liquor with respect to rest or motion, even the form and matter of the vessel in which a salt is crystallized, are so many causes, which, acting successively or together in many different ways, are capable of producing numberless varieties in the crystallization.

Of

Of all the causes which we have mentioned, capable of varying crystallizations, the nature of the vessel employed seems to deserve least our attention, yet this may produce some change from the greater or less adhesion which the salt may have to the several matters of which these vessels are made For instance, we can only attribute to the adhesion of salts to the sides of the vessels employed the property which most of them have to branch out in various manners, and to creep along the sides of these vessels, particularly when the crystallization is very slowly performed, so considerably that they frequently go even on the outside of the vessels Mr Beaumé has prevented this phenomenon by hindering the adhesion of the salts to the sides of the vessels, by rubbing these sides with some oil

From what has been said concerning the action of neutral salts upon each other we may conceive that when such salts happen to be mixed together, they must produce considerable differences in crystallizing

Many other important observations might be made on the crystallization of certain salts, but they will be better placed under the articles of the several salts which they concern We are obliged also to leave to the understanding and reflection of our readers to draw from what we have said many corollaries, the detail of which would be too long We shall only mention a manner of crystallizing salts which is different from the methods by evaporation and by cooling, but which consists also in taking away from the salt a portion of water which keeps it dissolved This method of crystallization is well effected by adding to a solution of a salt a sufficient quantity of a substance which has no action upon that salt, but which has greater affinity than it with the water which keeps it dissolved Spirit of wine, for instance, has these properties with regard to many salts Thus by adding a sufficient quantity of rectified spirit of wine to a strong solution of Glauber's salt, of vitriolated tartar, or of sea-salt, this spirit of wine seizing the water necessary for the solution of the salts, obliges them to crystallize immediately but as this crystallization is very hastily made, and almost instantaneously, the crystals are always very small and ill-formed In this respect they resemble the crystals of salts produced from a liquor which contained too little water to keep them dissolved This happens, for instance, when a strong solution of alkaline salt is combined with concentrated vitriolic acid, to form vitriolated tartar, for this salt, which requires much water to keep it dissolved, does not find enough in the liquor, and appears immediately in form of very small crystals like sand The same thing may be said of vitriols of silver and of mercury, of luna cornea, and of other metallic salts of this kind produced by adding vitriolic or marine acids to the white metals dissolved in nitrous acid These salts appear immediately as precipitates, whenever they do not find water enough in the liquors to dissolve them, and Mr Rouelle justly observes, in his Memoir that they are not precipitates, but true salts, which not finding water sufficient for their solution, are obliged to be immediately crystallized, but in crystals so small, from the rapidity of their crystallization, that they cannot be known to be crystals but with the help of a microscope

Notwithstanding what has been said concerning the irregularity of the crystals procured by adding a substance, which seizes the water of the solution of salts, yet if this addition was managed and gradually made, perhaps it might produce very beautiful and very regular crystals. Mr. Beaume has actually observed, that when salts were crystallized in acid or alkaline liquors according to their nature, their crystals were infinitely larger and more regular than they would have been without this circumstance *Vegetable salt*, for instance, and *salt of Saignette*, require to be crystallized in an alkaline liquor, and *sedative salt* requires an acid liquor, when it is obtained from borax by the intervention of an acid, if we desire to have fine crystals of these salts. The cause of this must be, that acids or alkalis, having in general more affinity with water than neutral salts have, diminish the adhesion of these neutral salts with the water of the solution, for a too great adhesion of a salt to water may evidently be a great impediment to its crystallization *See the words* SALT, SALTS (NEUTRAL), *and the several sorts of neutral salts under their respective names*

CCXIII. CRYSTALS All neutral salts with metallic bases susceptible of crystallization are commonly called by chemists *Crystals*, when they are actually crystallized, and the name of the metal contained in the salt is added to distinguish it Thus we say, *crystals of gold*, *of silver*, *of copper*, *of lead*, &c But as these names do not indicate the acid contained in each salt, they ought to be disused Here we shall only mention two of these salts called crystals, because they are almost always distinguished by that name These are the *crystals of silver*, and *crystals of verdegrise* or *of copper*

CCXIV CRYSTALS *of* SILVER, or LUNAR CRYSTALS Crystals of silver are neutral salts with metallic bases composed of nitrous acid saturated with silver When very pure silver is dissolved by very pure nitrous acid, if the acid be strong, crystals will be perceived merely by the cooling of the solution. These crystals are white, flattened like thin scales, and not very hard When the nitrous acid used to dissolve the silver is weak, no crystals are formed, because the water in the acid is sufficient to keep the newly formed salt dissolved, but lunar crystals may easily be obtained from this dilute solution by evaporating the superabundant water, and letting the liquor cool

Very beautiful and white lunar crystals may also be obtained, although the silver employed be allayed with copper or iron because the salts formed by these two metals with nitrous acid are deliquescent, and are not so easily crystallizable as the salt with basis of silver In this case the solution ought to be evaporated, if it be necessary, and the crystals of silver will be crystallized by cooling, while the copper or iron will remain dissolved When the colored liquor is poured off, crystals willl be found sufficiently white and almost pure, but to purify them perfectly, they ought to be drained, dissolved again in very pure water, and again crystallized then after they are well drained from the liquor, they will be found perfect and beautiful This even is a method of separating silver from the allay of copper, or of iron, and of obtaining from standard silver, or silver allayed with copper, as fine and colorless a solution as if tested silver had been employed

Lunar crystals then are a true *lunar nitre*, or *nitre with basis of silver*, and they accordingly have the property of deflagrating upon burning coals, almost as well as nitre, with basis of fixed alkali When this experiment is made, silver is found after the detonation incrusted upon the surface of the coal in its metallic state.

Notwithstanding this property which lunar nitre has of detonating with coals, a property which shews a strong adhesion of nitrous acid with silver, yet this adhesion is not sufficiently strong to resist a certain degree of heat, so that by calcination or distillation these two substances may be disjoined

Lunar crystals may be melted with a very gentle, and less than a red heat They easily lose the water of their crystallization, and then congeal into a black mass, which is generally cast into moulds, and is called *Lapis infernalis*, or *lunar caustic* *See* CAUSTIC (LUNAR)

This salt is very caustic, as the effects of the lunar caustic shew in surgery, although it has lost a part of its acid in the fusion which it receives This corrosive quality of lunar crystals seems to render it unfit for internal use as a medicine, yet some physicians prescribe it as a powerful evacuant of water Boyle, though not a physician, but assisted by some persons of the faculty, proposes a method of rendering these crystals of silver milder, and boasts much of them as a remedy His method consists in adding to a solution of them in water another solution of an equal quantity of nitre, and evaporating the whole to dryness and whiteness, with a very gentle fire, by which a portion of the spirit of nitre is intended to be taken away without fusing the saline mass, after which, this saline powder is to be made into pills, by forming it into a paste with some bread and water

Little skill in chemistry is requisite to shew, that nitre thus mixed with lunar crystals, being incapable of acting upon it, cannot render it milder, but must leave it unchanged

Secondly, by the manner of drying this mixture of lunar crystals and nitre, less of the causticity of these crystals is destroyed than by forming them into lunar caustic, in which operation they sustain a heat sufficient to fuse and to blacken them, and consequently lose more of their acid After these considerations, we cannot believe that this remedy of Mr Boyle is so mild and innocent as it has been represented This is certain, that, notwithstanding the praises given it by this philosopher, its use has not yet been established in medicine

Lunar crystals are called by Lemeri *vitriol of silver*, but as they contain no vitriolic acid, this name does not suit them, and ought only to be given to the salt formed by the union of vitriolic acid with silver *See* SILVER

CCXV CRYSTALS *of* COPPER, or *of* VENUS By these names is meant a salt formed by the union of the acid of vinegar with copper

This combination may be made by dissolving directly copper in good distilled vinegar, but it is made much more commodiously, and more expeditiously, when the copper employed has been previously formed into verdegrise, because the copper in the verdegrise is already divided and penetrated by a certain quantity of acid of wine verdegrise therefore is always used for the preparation of crystals of copper

This operation is very simple It consists in dissolving verdegrise in good distilled vinegar till this acid be saturated For this purpose a matrass is to be used, and to be set in a sand-bath with a gentle heat When the vinegar dissolves the verdegrise, it takes a fine greenish-blue color Some chemists call it also Tincture of Venus When it ceases to act on the verdegrise, it is to be decanted, evaporated, and crystallized The beautiful greenish-blue crystals formed are crystals of copper When this salt is exposed to a dry air, it loses easily the water of its crystallization, and its surface is reduced to a lighter-colored sea-green powder.

The acid of vinegar does not ſtrongly adhere to the copper in this combination It may be entirely ſeparated from it by diſtillation, and as it had loſt moſt of its ſuperabundant water when it united with the copper, it may by this method be obtained in its greateſt concentration It is called *radical vinegar*, and improperly *ſpirit of Venus* See *theſe words.*

The principal intention of chemiſts in making cryſtals of Venus is to obtain radical vinegar But this preparation is alſo uſed by painters, for which reaſon large quantities of it are manufactured, and it is generally ſold under the name of *diſtilled verdegriſe*, probably becauſe diſtilled vinegar is employed in its compoſition *See* Copper *and* Vinegar

CCXVI C U C U R B I T A cucurbit is a chemical veſſel employed in diſtillation, when covered with its capital or head Its name comes from its lengthened ſhape, by which it reſembles a gourd ſome cucurbits, however, are ſhallow and wide-mouthed Cucurbits are made of copper, tin, glaſs, and ſtone-ware, according to the nature of the ſubſtances to be diſtilled A cucurbit provided with its capital conſtitutes the veſſel for diſtillation called *Alembic* See *this word, and* Plates

CCXVII C U P E L A cupel is a wide-mouthed earthen veſſel, like a flat cup, from which reſemblance it has been named

The uſe of cupels is to contain gold and ſilver mixed with lead in the operations of refining and of eſſay, and to abſorb the litharge and other ſcorified matters formed in theſe operations

For this reaſon cupels ought to be made of dry, porous earths, capable of reſiſting the action of ſtrong fire, and of fluxes

The aſhes of wood and of bones are the moſt proper earths for cupels Theſe aſhes ought to be perfectly burnt and calcined, that is, till they become white, ſo that they contain no more inflammable principle, which might revivify the ſcorified metals, and occaſion an ebullition during the operation They ought alſo to be well lixiviated, and deprived of all ſaline matter to avoid their fuſion

To form cupels, aſhes thus prepared ought to be mixed with water into a paſte, to which a proper form is given by means of a mould Sometimes they are made into a paſte with ſome beer, a ſmall quantity of clay is added, that they may be moulded more conveniently *Roaſting teſts* made of clay are alſo called by ſome artiſts *cupels*, becauſe they have the ſame form as the refining and eſſay cupels *See* Essay, *and* Plates

CCXVIII C U P E L L A T I O N Cupellation is an operation by which gold and ſilver are refined or eſſayed by ſcorification with lead upon the cupel *See* Refining *and* Essay

D.

CCXIX DAMPS These are noxious and even fatal exhalations or vapors, which infest subterranean places, and particularly mines, if the air be not frequently renewed

The instances of fatal accidents caused by these vapors are too frequent. Most of them kill animals so suddenly that no assistance can be given

Although all these vapors produce similar effects, and occasion sudden and mortal faintings and syncopes, yet some differences may be observed in the properties and modes of acting of these vapors in different places From which we may presume, that they are not all exactly of the same nature.

Some of them are visible, and appear in form of a fog such is that which is found in a quarry near to the mineral waters of Pyrmont, and of which Dr Seip has given a description in the Philosophical Transactions This vapor has a sulphureous smell, destroys insects, birds, and in general all animals which approach it, with symptoms similar to those which animals suffer when placed under an exhausted receiver of an air-pump

Others, though perfectly invisible, produce the same effects Such are, says the learned translator of Lehman, those which issue from a cave in Hungary, situated near Ribard, at the foot of Crapack mountains These vapors are so fatal that they kill birds, while in their flight they approach too near to the mouth of the cave

Amongst the noxious mineral exhalations we may also place those which are found in the mines of Sal-gem in Poland These frequently appear in form of light flocks, threads, and webs, like those of spiders They are remarkable for their property of suddenly catching fire at the lamps of the miners with a terrible noise and explosion They instantly kill those whom they touch. This explosion is a true subterranean thunder. Similar vapors are found in some mines of fossil-coal

As arsenic is the greatest poison of all mineral substances, as it is volatile, and abounds in almost all mines, many authors have supposed that damps contained something arsenical But this opinion is so far from being proved, that strong reasons induce us to believe that they are of a different nature We are certain, and I know it from my own experience, that a person may be a considerable time exposed to a large quantity of vapors of arsenic without suffering any of the symptoms occasioned by damps, and even without being much incommoded.

 Secondly.

Secondly, the effects produced by arſenic taken internally, even in a large quantity, although terrible, and always fatal, are not nearly ſo ſudden as thoſe occaſioned by damps, which inſtantaneouſly kill. Thirdly, no obſervation or experience have aſcertained the arſenical nature of any damps, and it is even demonſtrable, that many of theſe noxious mineral vapors are nothing elſe than volatile ſulphureous acid.

Laſtly, all thoſe which are not evidently volatile ſulphureous acid appear to be pure, or almoſt pure phlogiſton diſengaged from bodies without burning. They occaſion exactly the ſame accidents as exhalations of liver of ſulphur, of burning coals, and of matters undergoing the putrid or ſpirituous fermentations. The great inflammability of theſe vapors, when they are confined, and condenſed to a certain degree, ſuch as thoſe of coal-mines, is a demonſtrative proof of this opinion.

By art we may perfectly imitate theſe vapors. We know that when acids diſſolve imperfect metals, they take from them a conſiderable part of their inflammable principle. This principle is almoſt totally diſſipated in vapors during theſe ſolutions; and if the operation be made in a cloſe veſſel, when this is uncorked, and a lighted candle brought near its mouth, the vapor contained inſtantly catches fire, and occaſions an exploſion ſo much more violent as the quantity of vapor was greater. This phenomenon may be chiefly obſerved in the ſolution of iron in vitriolic acid diluted with a certain quantity of water. If after this exploſion the bottle be left open, ſuppoſing the ſolution of the metal to be continuing, and the flame of a candle applied to the mouth of the containing veſſel, the phlogiſton, which is continually diſengaging and forming vapors, but freely and without condenſation, will continue to burn in ſuch a manner, that a light-bluiſh flame will be ſeen at the mouth of the veſſel, ſuch as the flame of phlogiſton always is when this is not in an oily ſtate.

Although theſe experiments are generally made by means of a ſolution of filings of iron in vitriolic acid, I doubt not that, by employing proper management, ſimilar vapors might be produced from other imperfect metals, eſpecially thoſe which moſt eaſily part with their phlogiſton when diſſolved by acids, as tin, zinc, and regulus of antimony; and I doubt not that if theſe metallic vapors were collected in a ſufficient quantity in a cloſe place, where the air was not renewed, that they would produce the ſame fatal accidents as theſe called damps.

All theſe conſiderations induce us to believe, that moſt of theſe noxious ſubterranean vapors are nothing but phlogiſton diſengaged from certain ſubſtances, and circulating within the earth. It proceeds from bitumens and from ſulphur, which undergo different alterations and decompoſitions.

Almoſt all chemiſts and metallurgiſts agree in believing, that mineral exhalations contribute to the production of metals. This opinion is ſo much more probable, that, as phlogiſton is one of the principles of metals, (if it be true that theſe mineral exhalations are nothing elſe than phlogiſton) and as this principle is then in ſtate of vapor, and conſequently much divided, perhaps reduced to its ſmalleſt integrant particles, it is then in its moſt favorable ſtate for combination: it is therefore probable, that when theſe exhalations meet earths diſpoſed to receive them, they combine more or leſs intimately with theſe earths, according

cording to their nature. Perhaps this is the chief operation of the grand mystery of metallisation. *See* METALS and PHLOGISTON. (*m*)

CCXX. DECANTATION. By this word is meant the separating of a clear liquor from a sediment, by pouring it gently.

CCXXI. DECOCTION. This word is applied to signify either the action of boiling a substance in water, or the water itself in which the substance has been boiled.

Decoction is only applicable to matters containing some principles soluble in water; such, particularly, are vegetable and animal matters; and this operation is rather used for the purposes of medicine than of chemistry.

It is nevertheless very necessary to know well the nature and principles of substances subjected to decoction, that it may be properly managed, and that the principles with which the water becomes impregnated may be known.

These principles must evidently be such as are not sufficiently volatile to rise with the heat of boiling water, if the decoction shall be long continued.

Hence it follows, that plants, or other matters containing volatile principles, cannot be proper subjects of decoction, when these principles are required. In this case the matters may be infused with water in close vessels without heat, or with a heat less than that of boiling water.

(*m*) The damps or vapors mentioned in this article are of two kinds, *inflammable* and *uninflammable*. The inflammable kind is probably, as the author believes, similar to the vapors produced by the solutions of iron, zinc, tin, and perhaps of other metallic substances in vitriolic and marine acids. *See* AIR (FIXABLE). This vapor is chiefly found in coal mines, and sometimes in lead mines, as in those of Mendip hills. Like the inflammable vapor of metallic solutions, it is lighter than atmospherical air, and consequently floats chiefly near the roofs of mines: miners, therefore, when it is accidentally inflamed, or when they purposely set fire to it, to destroy it, lie flat on the ground, and thus escape burning. This inflammable vapor may perhaps be produced by the decomposition of pyritous matters, with which most mines, especially coal mines, abound. In this decomposition of pyrites exposed to air and moisture, the vitriolic acid of the sulphur attacks and dissolves the iron, while the inflammable principle of the sulphur is disengaged, and forms this vapor.

The *uninflammable vapors* of mines and subterranean places are much more noxious than the former. They seem to be similar to the uninflammable vapors produced by the combustion of inflammable bodies, as of charcoal, and by fermenting and effervescing substances. *See* AIR (FIXABLE). Like these, they are noxious to animals, extinguish flame, and are heavier than atmospherical air, for they are chiefly placed at the bottom of the pits in which they are found: accordingly, in the cavern near Pyrmont, mentioned in the text, a man may stand upright without any other inconvenience than an uncommon heat of his lower extremities, but he cannot without danger keep his head bent down. The symptoms attending persons exposed to such vapors shew sufficiently that they are not noxious merely by interception of common air, but by some quality which almost instantly affects and destroys the powers of animal life. Some persons digging in a cellar in Paris were found dead, stiff as statues, with open eyes, and standing in the posture of digging. At Chartres, in France, a person going down into a cellar into which a baker had been used to throw hot embers from his oven, was instantly killed, and when his body was opened, his lungs were found spotted with black marks, his intestines swoln, red and inflamed, and the muscles of his legs, thighs, and arms, seemed to be separated from each other and from the adjacent parts. *See Bomare's Dict. d'Histoire Naturelle, at the word* EXHALAISON.

But on the contrary, when it is not intended to preserve the volatile parts, or when the matters contain none that are volatile, then decoction may be employed. It even becomes necessary when the matters to be treated are solid, and of a compact and close texture, because then the water could not extract its principles without a boiling heat.

Most soft animal matters, as flesh, tendons, skins, may be boiled conveniently in water, because they contain no principle volatile with a boiling heat. Water extracts from them nothing but a gelatinous substance, and some oily parts which float on the surface of the water.

Decoction is the only method by which all the gelatinous substance of the solid parts of animals, as bones and horns, can be extracted.

All vegetable matters which are inodorous, and particularly those which are hard, as roots, barks, are generally boiled when an extraction of their principles by water is required.

However, many of these substances ought not to be boiled, those particularly, the principles of which, when extracted by water, suffer some change by a continued heat. Peruvian bark, for instance, which is inodorous, and contains nothing volatile, seems capable of being treated without any inconvenience by boiling, nevertheless, Mr Beaumé observes, in his Elements of Pharmacy, that the infusion of this bark made without heat really contains more of its principles than the decoction. The cause of this is, that water extracts from bark not only the substances of which it is naturally a menstruum, such as the gummy and extractive matters, but also a considerable quantity of resinous substance, which keeps well dissolved in the water by means of the former matters, till it is exposed to heat, and then it immediately separates and precipitates.

Many other vegetable matters exhibit the same phenomenon, therefore a general rule may be established, that decoction ought not to be employed but when absolutely necessary, that is, when the same principles or the same quantities of these principles cannot be obtained by an infusion, and that without heat, if it can be so done, considering that the proximate principles of vegetables are generally so delicate, and so susceptible of change and decomposition, that frequently the most gentle heat changes much their nature and properties. *See* EXTRACTS.

CCXXII. DECOMPOSITION *of* BODIES. The chemical decomposition of bodies consists in the disunion and separation of their principles and constituent parts.

This decomposition ought necessarily to be distinguished from a mere mechanical division, as the following reflections will shew.

All bodies in general, or portions of any matter, may be considered as composed of parts separable from each other.

We cannot, for instance, conceive an atom of matter so small, but that this atom may be considered as divisible into parts still smaller, and this undoubtedly has given the idea of the infinite divisibility of matter, a subject which we do not mean to examine here, because it does not belong to chemistry, besides that, it is like all those in which the consideration of infinity is concerned, that is, an absurdity seems to be joined with evidence.

As chemistry is a science solely founded on experience, we shall confine ourselves to what experience teaches concerning the divisibility of bodies.

But

But we are certain that bodies may be very ſoon reduced to ſo ſmall parts that we cannot further divide them, from the deficiency of our ſenſes and of our inſtruments

One thing is very remarkable in this diviſion, called mechanical, becauſe it is performed by cutting or bruiſing inſtruments , this is, that however ſmall the parts be into which it reduces bodies, theſe parts are always entirely of the ſame nature as the body from which theſe parts were taken Theſe ſmall parts of bodies are called their integrant parts Thus, for example, the ſmalleſt atoms into which iron, ſalt, reſin, or other ſubſtance, can be mechanically divided, have all the ſame properties, excepting quantity, which the maſs had before the diviſion

Hence we ought to conclude, that this mechanical diviſion cannot ſeparate bodies but into homogeneous parts, or parts of the ſame nature and if we had no other method of dividing bodies, the compounds would always remain ſuch as nature offers to us, without cauſing any other change than a diminution of quantity

The ſame thing would happen, if all natural bodies were equally ſimple, or equally compounded But all chemical experiments ſhew, that in this reſpect there is a very great diverſity

Some bodies are ſo ſimple that no change can be produced upon them by any effort of art Theſe are called by chemiſts elements, or primitive principles But theſe ſimpler bodies, the parts of which are evidently more ſmall and fine than thoſe of bodies leſs ſimple, become in the hands of chemiſts inſtruments capable of dividing theſe latter much further than can be done by mechanical inſtruments. Theſe ſimple bodies are capable of dividing molecules, which would be ſtill imperceptible by our ſenſe , although they were much larger than they are when they have undergone this inviſible diviſion

To illuſtrate this by an example Let us ſuppoſe a metallic maſs compoſed of mercury and gold, in ſuch proportion that no mercury can be forced out from the maſs by expreſſion, which is a mechanical method I ſay then, that the mechanical diviſion which could be made of this compound, would only ſeparate it into ſmaller and ſmaller molecules, each of which would be of the ſame nature as the original maſs, that is to ſay, compoſed of an equal proportion of mercury and gold

If indeed we had inſtruments and ſenſes ſufficiently fine, we might at length come to molecules, each of which would be compoſed of one atom of mercury and gold, which by one diviſion more would be ſeparated into two atoms, one of each of the two metals diſtinctly Thus we might obtain the mercury and the gold ſeparately, and conſequently effect a decompoſition of the compound ſubſtance ſubjected to this mechanical diviſion but the impoſſibility of ſuch a diviſion is ſufficiently demonſtrated

Yet what mechanical inſtruments cannot do, fire, which is one of thoſe ſimple bodies we have mentioned, is capable of performing. The primary parts of this element, much finer than thoſe of gold or of mercury, become in the hands of chemiſts inſtruments inconceivably fine, which effect a ſeparation of mercury from gold, conſequently reduce to its elements or principles the compound

pound which has been subjected to their action, and thus analyse or chemically decompose it See ANALYSIS

CCXXIII DECREPITATION By decrepitation is meant the quick separation of the parts of a body, occasioned by a strong heat, and accompanied with noise and crackling This effect is most frequently produced by water contained betwixt the parts of a decrepitating body, when these parts have a certain degree of adhesion together This water being quickly reduced into vapors by the heat suddenly applied to it, rarefies and bursts with noise the parts which compress it

The bodies most subject to decrepitation are certain salts, such as *common salt*, *vitriolated tartar*, *nitre of lead*, the decrepitation of all which proceeds from the water of their crystallization, *clays* which are not perfectly dry, and *flints*

CCXXIV. DELFWARE This is a kind of pottery of baked earth, covered with an enamel or white glazing, which gives it the appearance and neatness of porcelain

Some kinds of this enamelled pottery differ much from others, either in their sustaining sudden heat without breaking, or in the beauty and regularity of their forms, of their enamel, and of the painting with which they are ornamented

In general, the fine and beautiful enamelled potteries, which approach the nearest to porcelain in external appearance, are at the same time those which least resist a brisk fire Again, those which sustain a sudden heat are coarse, and resemble common pottery

The basis of this pottery is clay, which is to be mixed when too fat with such a quantity of sand, that the earth shall preserve enough of its ductility to be worked, moulded, and turned easily, and yet that its fatness shall be sufficiently taken from it, that it shall not crack or shrink too much in drying or in baking

Vessels formed of this earth must be dried very gently to avoid cracking. They are then to be placed in a furnace to receive a slight baking, and which is only meant to give them a certain consistence or hardness And, lastly, they are to be covered with an enamel or glazing, which is done by pouring upon the vessels thus prepared, the enamel which has been ground very fine and diluted with water

As vessels on which the enamel is applied are but slightly baked, they readily imbibe the water in which the enamel is suspended, and a layer of this enamel adheres to their surface. These vessels may then be painted with colors composed of metallic calxes mixed and ground with a fusible glass When they are become perfectly dry, they are to be placed in the furnace included in cases of baked earth, called *seggars*, and exposed to a heat capable of fusing uniformly the enamel which covers them

This heat given to fuse, the enamel being much stronger than that which was applied at first to give some consistence to the ware, is also the heat necessary to compleat the baking of it The furnace and the colors used for painting this ware are the same as those employed for porcelain See PORCELAIN

The glazing, which is nothing but white enamel, ought to be so opake as not to shew the ware under it Many receipts for making such enamels may be found in Neri's Treatise on the Art of Making Glass, with Kunkel's Notes, and in the Encyclopedia, both which books may be consulted on this subject We shall

ſhall only obſerve in general, that all theſe enamels for delf ware are compoſed of ſand or flints, vitrifying ſalts, calx of lead, and calx of tin, and that the ſand muſt be perfectly vitrified ſo as to form a glaſs conſiderably fuſible. Somewhat leſs than an equal part of alkaline ſalt, or twice its weight of calx of lead, is requiſite to effect ſuch vitrification of ſand. The calx of tin is not intended to be vitrified, but to give a white opake color to the maſs, and one part of it is to be added to three or four parts of all the other ingredients taken together.

From theſe general principles, various enamels may be made to ſuit the different kinds of earths to which they are to be applied.

To make this enamel, lead and tin are calcined together with a ſtrong fire, and the ſand is alſo to be made into a fritt with the ſalt or aſhes. The whole is then to be well mixed and ground together. This matter is then to be placed under the furnace, where it is melted and vitrified during the baking of the ware. Then it is to be ground in a mill, and applied as we have directed. *See* CLAY, POTTERY, PORCELAIN, *and* VITRIFICATION.

CCXXV. DELIQUESCENCE. We underſtand by deliqueſcence the property which certain bodies have to attract moiſture from the air, and of becoming thereby liquid.

This property is never found but in ſaline ſubſtances, or in matters containing them. It is cauſed by the great affinity which ſaline ſubſtances have with water. Hence, the more ſimple theſe ſubſtances are, the more alſo they are deliqueſcent. Acids, for inſtance, and certain alkalis, which are the moſt ſimple of ſaline ſubſtances, are alſo the moſt deliqueſcent. Mineral acids are ſo deliqueſcent that they ſtrongly imbibe moiſture from the air, although they are already mixed with a ſufficient quantity of water to be fluid. For this purpoſe it is ſufficient that they only be concentrated to a certain degree.

Many neutral ſalts are deliqueſcent, chiefly thoſe whoſe baſes are not ſaline ſubſtances. Their acids are but imperfectly ſaturated, and although they do not give the ſame marks of acidity as when quite diſengaged, they may be conſidered as ſtill poſſeſſing enough of their activity to exerciſe it on the moiſture of the circumambient air. This proves that the acids of neutral deliqueſcent ſalts are in an intermediate ſtate betwixt that of an acid quite diſengaged, and that of one perfectly ſaturated and combined.

All the phenomena which ſalts preſent relatively to their deliqueſcence, are ſo many proofs of what we have affirmed on this ſubject.

Salts formed by vitriolic acid with fixed or volatile alkalis, earths, or metallic ſubſtances, are not deliqueſcent, although this acid be the ſtrongeſt of all, and which, when diſengaged, moſt powerfully attracts moiſture from the air. But its greater ſtrength is the real cauſe of its forming ſo complete and intimate combinations with theſe ſeveral ſubſtances as to form neutral ſalts which are not deliqueſcent.

The nitrous and marine acids form with abſorbent earths and certain metallic ſubſtances, particularly with iron and copper, deliqueſcent ſalts, from the weakneſs of the union which they contract with theſe matters. Theſe acids form with ſilver, mercury, lead, and biſmuth, ſalts which are not deliqueſcent, becauſe they combine more intimately and completely with theſe latter metals.

Singular phenomena are presented by vegetable acids relatively to the deliquescence of the neutral salts formed by them The acid of vinegar united with fixed vegetable alkali forms a very deliquescent salt, called *terra foliata tartari* The same acid forms with copper a salt that is not deliquescent, as we see in the instance of *crystals of copper* These effects are directly contrary to those produced by the nitrous and marine acids united with the same substances, for these acids form with fixed vegetable alkali salts which are not deliquescent, and with copper salts which are very deliquescent

The acid of tartar, which when disengaged is in a concrete state, and far from being deliquescent, since it is scarcely soluble in water, forms with iron (another substance still less soluble) a very deliquescent soluble tartar, known by the name of *tartarised tincture of iron*

Many researches and experiments remain yet to be made to explain entirely the causes of these singular effects But probably the deliquescence or opposite quality of salts will be found to depend on the state of their acids, as we have already said

The fixed vegetable alkali is deliquescent, the mineral is not The cause of this undoubtedly is, that the saline principle of this latter is combined more intimately, or with a greater quantity of matter not saline, than that of the former, as the other properties of these two alkalis indicate *See* ALKALI

Fixed vegetable alkali treated with quicklime becomes more deliquescent Volatile alkalis, which are naturally not deliquescent, become by treatment with quicklime deliquescent We cannot explain these phenomena without supposing that quicklime takes from alkalis in general a portion of oily or other matter, which binds and saturates their saline principle, when in their natural state

The dry extracts of almost all vegetable matters easily moisten in the air. But they certainly possess this property so much more evidently, as a greater quantity of earthy or resinous matter, which is always deposited during the evaporation, has been previously separated from their infusions and decoctions

Before we finish this article we ought to observe, that some bodies which are not deliquescent attract moisture from the air, and even become liquid, that is, if they be saline or soluble in water This happens when bodies are much colder than the air to which they are exposed The reason of it is, that the moisture contained in the air being always in the state of insensible vapors, is condensed by the cold of the bodies it touches, and is collected in drops This effect is very different from a true deliquescence, but it deserves to be taken notice of, to prevent mistakes in experiments

Lastly, we must remark, that some bodies, after having been a long time exposed to the air, may remain apparently dry, although they really be in the disposition of deliquescent bodies, that is, attract much moisture from the ambient air Such, for instance, is quicklime, which imbibes from the air its equal weight of moisture, and retains, notwithstanding, its dry and powdery appearance This proceeds from the great quantity of earthy parts with which those parts of the quicklime are mixed, which may be considered as deliquescent, although, in fact, they do not resolve into a liquor

CCXXVI DELIQUIUM This term is frequently employed by chemists to characterize a body which is resolved into a liquor by exposure to

air

air In this sense they say the deliquium of a salt, as of salt of tartar, for instance This word is also frequently used instead of deliquescence Thus we say, that a salt falls into a deliquium, to signify that it is deliquescent

CCXXVII DEMI-METAL The same as SEMI-METAL, *which see*

CCXXVIII DEPHLEGMATION Dephlegmation is an operation by which the superabundant water of a body is taken from it, and it is principally effected by evaporation or distillation Dephlegmation is also called concentration, particularly when acids are the subject *See* CONCENTRATION

CCXXIX DETONATION By the word *detonation* chemists understand an explosion with noise made by the sudden inflammation of some combustible body Such are the explosions of *gun-powder*, *fulminating gold*, and *fulminating powder* As nitre is the cause of most explosions, the word *detonation* has been appropriated to the inflammation of the acid of this salt with bodies containing phlogiston, and it is frequently given to those inflammations of nitrous acid which are not accompanied with explosion Thus nitre is said to detonate with sulphur, with coals, with metals, although in the ordinary method of making these operations, that is, in open crucibles, and with small quantities of detonating substances, the nitre does not truly explode

CCXXX DETONATION *of* NITRE The detonation of nitre is one of the most important phenomena of chemistry It consists in the instantaneous inflammation and decomposition of the acid of nitre, when it immediately touches combustible bodies, the phlogiston of which is ignited, or when the acid is ignited

By two methods then may nitre, or rather its acid, be inflamed. The first method is by applying it to a red-hot combustible body, and the second is by making the acid itself red-hot, and applying a combustible body to it in that state

A very necessary remark is, that nitre cannot detonate without the concurrence of these circumstances now mentioned Nitre may be made red hot, or of any degree of heat, without shewing any sign of inflammation, provided it does not touch any inflammable matter

On the other side, nitre may be heated, and a combustible body applied to it without any inflammation For this purpose, the nitre need only be not sufficiently hot to kindle the inflammable bodies applied to it Messrs Macquer and Beaumé show, in their Course of Chemistry, an experiment which clearly proves this truth Some nitre is put into a crucible, and there completely fused by a heat just sufficient for that purpose when a black coal is thrown into this fused nitre, no inflammation arises, because the nitre may be melted with a degree of heat which is not sufficient to kindle combustible bodies, and this degree of heat is necessary for the success of the experiment.

But when nitre is red-hot, and a coal is applied to it, kindled, or not kindled, then it is inflamed with violence, and makes the coal burn rapidly The same event happens when nitre is thrown upon burning coals This inflammation lasts while these two substances touch, and any acid remains in the nitre During this detonation a considerable smoke rises, but this smoke contains no acid, as the experiment of the clyssus of nitre made in close vessels sufficiently proves *See* CLYSSUS *of* NITRE

When all the nitrous acid is thus burnt, and no longer any inflammation is excited, although more coals are added, if we examine what remains in the crucible, we shall find that it is the fixed alkali which was the basis of the nitre This alkali is called *fixed* or *alkalised nitre* See *these words, and* ALKALI (FIXED VEGETABLE)

The detonation may be rendered more easy and sudden by making the nitre touch the inflammable matter in a greater number of parts, so that when these two substances are divided into very minute parts, which are well mixed and interposed betwixt each other, the detonation is almost instantaneous, and is as strong as it can be made When the substances are thus prepared, they may be at once inflamed by a small spark of ignited matter, because the ignition is very quickly and almost instantaneously communicated by small intervals From the accurate mixture of the two detonating substances proceeds the great force and violence of *gun-powder* *See* POWDER (GUN)

Hence we may learn to avoid the violence of detonations in chemical operations, by mixing very imperfectly the nitre with the combustible substances

Let us now consider what passes in the detonation of nitre Mr Macquer, in his Elements of Chemistry, conjectures that the detonation of nitre, which is, properly speaking, the inflammation of the nitrous acid, cannot take place, unless a combination be previously formed betwixt this acid and the phlogiston of the combustible substance used for the detonation, that this combination is entirely similar to that of vitriolic acid with phlogiston when sulphur is formed, and that, in the present instance, *a nitrous sulphur* is produced, but that this sulphur is infinitely more combustible than the vitriolic sulphur, for a reason we shall soon see, and even so combustible, that it cannot exist an instant without being entirely burnt, hence it is inflamed with extreme rapidity and violence as soon as it is formed

The most essential circumstances attending the detonation of nitre concur in rendering this opinion probable, that is, to establish the preliminary existence of this nitrous sulphur

First, vitriolic sulphur cannot be formed by vitriolic acid engaged with a fixed alkali, unless this acid be deprived of all the water superabundant to its saline essence, and in a dry state, when it is applied to phlogiston

In the second place, to effect this combination, a degree of heat equal to that of ignition must be applied

Thirdly, as in sulphur not a particle of oil exists, but the vitriolic acid is united to pure phlogiston, as the illustrious Stahl has fully demonstrated, if, therefore, an inflammable matter, which is in an oily state, be used for the formation of sulphur, it must be first decomposed, and reduced to the state of coal, before the sulphur can be produced *See* SULPHUR But these are precisely the same conditions which are necessary for the detonation of nitre, for since the acid of nitre cannot detonate unless it be ignited, it must be evidently deprived of all the water superabundant to its saline essence.

In the second place, experience shews that nitre cannot detonate with any matter which is in an oily state, for if nitre be ignited in a crucible, and oil, resin, fat, or other inflammable matter of this kind be added to it, no detonation will happen while the inflammable matter remains in its oily state, or till it be burnt, decomposed, and reduced to a coal, then the detonation commences, and is always proportionable to the quantity of coal produced by the inflammable matter.

Some ſubſtances, the phlogiſton of which is certainly in an oily ſtate, ſuch as tartar, ſaw-duſt of wood, and others of this kind, do indeed detonate with nitre almoſt as readily as powder of charcoal: but we may eaſily perceive that the cauſe of this is, that the oil of theſe ſubſtances, being divided by the interpoſition of a large quantity of incombuſtible matters, may be exceedingly ſoon reduced to the ſtate of coal by the heat of ignition.

Several facts intimately connected with the detonation of nitre may be naturally deduced from this theory, and conſequently become additional proofs of it.

Let nitrous acid, as much dephlegmated as poſſible, be poured upon black coals, as dry and hot as they can be made, under a red-heat, no detonation or inflammation will enſue. This is not ſurpriſing, ſince all the neceſſary conditions for the production of nitrous ſulphur are wanting here, and ſince in ſimilar circumſtances ſulphur could not be formed by vitriolic acid.

If an ardent coal be plunged into the ſtrongeſt nitrous acid, a detonation begins at the ſurface of the coal, which very ſoon ceaſes, the coal is extinguiſhed, becomes black, and is not affected by the acid. The ſhort detonation upon the ſurface of the coal may be conſidered as accidental, and not belonging to the experiment, otherwiſe the detonation would continue while the acid laſted. This detonation can only be cauſed by a ſmall quantity of nitre, formed inſtantaneouſly by the acid uniting with ſome ſmall portion of alkaline ſalt contained in the aſhes of the coal, which happen to lie on its ſurface: therefore, when this ſmall quantity of nitre is conſumed, the coal is extinguiſhed, and the detonation ceaſes, and all this ought to happen becauſe the moſt dephlegmated nitrous acid contains always a conſiderable quantity of water ſuperabundant to its ſaline eſſence, and as it is not in the preſent experiment retained or fixed by any baſis, it diſſipates in vapors before it can be totally dephlegmated by the heat of the ardent coal: hence in this experiment no nitrous ſulphur can be formed, neither can vitriolic acid form vitriolic ſulphur in ſimilar circumſtances, but only volatile ſulphureous acid.

From theſe facts we may conclude, that nitrous acid, while free, that is, not engaged in any baſis, cannot ever contract with phlogiſton ſuch an union, as that a ſulphureous compound, or nitrous ſulphur, ſhall be formed, not only becauſe of the ſuperabundant water it always contains, but alſo becauſe, from its want of fixity, it cannot be deprived of this ſuperabundant water in the very act of combination: we may therefore affirm as a general and eſtabliſhed principle, that diſengaged nitrous acid is not capable of detonation. If then this pure acid inflames oils mixed with it, this inflammation proceeds from a very different cauſe than the true detonation of nitre, as Mr Macquer has ſhewn in his Elements of Chemiſtry, nitre and diſengaged nitrous acid being very different from each other, particularly with regard to detonation. *See* INFLAMMATION *of* OILS.

What we have ſaid on this ſubject clearly ſhews why combinations of nitrous acid with certain baſes form nitres ſuſceptible of a ſtrong detonation, while others of the ſame acid with different baſes detonate weakly or not at all, theſe differences depending on the greater or leſs adheſion of the nitrous acid with its baſis. All these

nitrous

nitrous salts in which the acid is so firmly fixed and retained by its basis, that it may be entirely dephlegmated and ignited, are susceptible of a strong detonation, such are *ordinary nitre, cubic nitre, nitrous ammoniacal salt, nitres of silver, of mercury, of lead, and of bismuth*, of all which ordinary nitre detonates most violently, and is the only one of which good gun-powder can be made; because the fixed vegetable alkali, which is the basis of nitre, has a stronger adhesion to nitrous acid than any other of the substances soluble by this acid

On the contrary, all combinations in which nitrous acid is only weakly united, do not detonate, or very weakly Such are *nitres with bases of calcareous earths, of copper, of iron, of tin, of regulus of antimony*, these being all nitrous salts in which the acid adheres weakly, as their deliquescent quality, and the facility with which fire detaches this acid from them, sufficiently shew

We shall now examine what happens in the very act of the detonation of nitre, or rather in the deflagration of nitrous sulphur We have seen that this sulphur is formed in the same circumstances as vitriolic sulphur but if these two compounds resemble each other in the manner of their production, they differ entirely in the phenomena of their combustion

Vitriolic sulphur burns very weakly, produces a flame which is very little luminous, requires for the continuance of its burning a constant supply of new air, and its acid undergoes no change by this combustion Nitrous sulphur, on the contrary, appears incapable of existing an instant without burning Its vivid, dazzling flame, accompanied with noise, resembles the flame of a fire strongly actuated by a blast of air, it needs not the contact of external air, it burns with the same violence and rapidity in close vessels, no obstacle is capable of containing it, and if it be confined, it bursts with a terrible noise the sides of the confining vessels, lastly, after its combustion no trace is found of its acid

What can be the cause of so considerable differences? and how are so singular phenomena produced? We cannot do better than adopt entirely the theory of Stahl This great chemist has explained all these effects in a manner the most satisfactory, and the most conformable to the principles of rational chemistry

Stahl considers nitrous acid as composed of a watery principle, and of an earthy principle, as well as all other acids but he also admits a third element to enter into this acid, by which it is characterised, and by which it differs from vitriolic acid This third principle of nitrous acid is phlogiston, but this principle is so proportioned and combined with the other two, that nitrous acid is not inflammable while alone, even when it is ignited but if a new quantity of inflammable principle unites with nitrous acid, (which happens in the production of nitrous sulphur) then the proportion of this principle being encreased, it accordingly assumes all the properties, and particularly the inflammability, which is essential to it Hence nitrous acid cannot be combined with a body containing phlogiston, so disposed as to be capable of forming with it an intimate union, that is, a nitrous sulphur, without producing an inflammation If, then, phlogiston united intimately with vitriolic acid forms vitriolic sulphur, which is much less inflammable, this happens because phlogiston is not one of the principles of vitriolic acid, and does not enter into its combination, as it enters into that of nitrous acid

From this cause also, namely the existence of phlogiston in nitrous acid, as a principle, Stahl deduces the destruction or total decomposition of this acid, when

when it is inflamed, and this he does upon good grounds, for then not only the phlogiſton which is combined ſuperabundantly with nitrous acid is inflamed, but alſo this ſuperabundant phlogiſton, finding itſelf mixed and confuſed with the phlogiſton which is a principle of nitrous acid, takes this along with it in its inflammation, and the whole is entirely conſumed

This being eſtabliſhed, we ought not to wonder that no nitrous acid is found after the detonation, for every compound body, from which one of its principles is taken, is thereby neceſſarily decompoſed If the inflammable principle of this acid could be conſumed without deſtroying the connexion of the other principles, we ſhould not indeed find after detonation any nitrous acid, becauſe the phlogiſton, its diſtinguiſhing principle, would have been taken from it, but as, according to Stahl, the union of the two principles, the watery and the earthy, is ſufficient to conſtitute an acid, we ſhould ſtill find an acid ſubſtance of a different nature from nitrous acid, nearly in the ſame manner that we find pure vitriolic acid after the portion of phlogiſton which had conſtituted it volatile ſulphureous acid has been taken from it but things paſs quite otherwiſe in the inflammation of nitrous acid, not a veſtige remains of this, or of any other acid, nothing is found again but earth and water This ſhews the connexion of the principles of nitrous acid to be ſuch, that one of its conſtituent parts cannot be taken from it without an entire disjunction of the others, ſo that after its inflammation, it does not exiſt neither as nitrous, nor as any other acid

We may eaſily perceive how much theſe facts, and the conſequences reſulting from them, give probability to the opinion of Stahl, who thinks that every acid, in general, reſults from an union of a watery with an earthy principle, and that the particular and ſpecific properties of the ſeveral acids are cauſed by ſome other principle, which enters into their combination with theſe two eſſential conſtituent parts

The exploſion accompanying the detonation of nitre, and which is ſo much more violent as the matters have been more perfectly mixed, and more cloſely compacted, proceeds from a great and ſudden dilatation of ſome very expanſible body Moſt natural philoſophers have attributed it to air contained in nitre, and in matters with which the nitre detonates, becauſe air included and rarefied is capable of producing, and does produce, very violent exploſions nevertheleſs, we muſt obſerve, that none of the exploſions of air are equal in violence to thoſe of gun-powder, of fulminating powder, and of fulminating gold, which are certainly effects of the inflammation of nitrous acid

Theſe conſiderations alſo incline us to adopt the opinion of Stahl on this phenomenon This chemiſt thinks, that theſe exploſions ought not to be attributed to the air, but to the water of the nitre, or rather of its acid, which is capable of producing much more violent exploſions than thoſe of air, when a ſtrong heat, ſuch as that of red-heat, is ſuddenly applied to it, as happens in the detonation of nitre See WATER

The ſame chemiſt goes farther He advances, not without much probability, that water, the aggregation of which is entirely broken, acquires the properties of air Upon this ſuppoſition we may well explain why nitre is capable of burning with combuſtible ſubſtances, without the acceſs of air, and in cloſe veſſels The reaſon of this is, that it contains in its own ſubſtance a matter which diſengages itſelf from it while it burns, and which, if it is not air, has is

[illegible]

well, or better, the property of maintaining combuſtion. The flame iſſuing from nitre when made to detonate ſo ſlowly that it can be obſerved, ſeems to prove what we have advanced on the ſubject; for it has, as we have ſaid, all the appearance of the flame of a body excited ſtrongly by a blaſt iſſuing from its own centre. (*n*)

Nitre detonates with ſulphur, and with thoſe metallic ſubſtances the phlogiſton of which is ſo diſpoſed that it can eaſily burn; ſuch are iron, tin, zinc, and others of this nature. This detonation has nothing peculiar: it muſt happen not only from the combuſtibility of the phlogiſton of theſe ſubſtances, but alſo becauſe this phlogiſton is not in the ſtate of oil. What we have ſaid concerning the detonation of nitre by coals, is applicable to thoſe which are now treated. However, attention muſt be given to the other principles of theſe ſubſtances, and to the greater or leſs quantity, and degrees of combuſtibility of their phlogiſton.

CCXXXI. D E W. Formerly this name was given to the phlegm that roſe firſt in the diſtillation of ſeveral ſubſtances. Thus the *dew of vitriol*, *the dew of honey*, were watery liquors which roſe firſt when theſe ſubſtances were diſtilled.

CCXXXII. D I A M O N D. Diamonds are ſtones of the vitrifiable kind, which are found naturally cryſtallized, nearly as rock-cryſtal is, in form of ſix-ſided priſms, each extremity of which is terminated by a pyramid alſo of ſix ſides. Some diamonds, however, are differently cryſtallized.

Diamonds are the moſt beautiful and the deareſt of all precious ſtones. They are of different colors, particularly yellow; but the greateſt part of them are white, and amongſt theſe, the whiteſt and moſt tranſparent are of higheſt value. No ſtone is harder than the diamond; it is alſo very refractory, and even apyrous; it has all the properties of vitrifiable ſtones, with this difference, that it requires more fire, and a larger quantity of flux to produce its vitrification than any other of the ſubſtances of the ſame kind. *See* STONES (VITRIFIABLE). (*o*)

(*n*) The exploſion of nitre deflagrated with inflammable ſubſtances is cauſed by an elaſtic fluid, which is produced from the nitre and theſe ſubſtances by deflagration. This fluid is not the water of the nitre rarefied and converted into air; for the water of the nitre is only rarefied by the heat of the deflagration, and is afterwards by cold condenſed, forming the water called clyſſus of nitre. *See* CLYSSUS *of* NITRE. But the elaſtic fluid produced by deflagration is permanent, and not condenſible into a liquid. Mr Robins found, by accurate experiments, that the fluid produced by firing gun-powder, when confined within a ſpace equal to that of the gun-powder which was fired, and reduced to the heat of the atmoſphere, was capable of ſuſtaining a preſſure equal to 244 times the preſſure of the atmoſphere; and that the elaſtic force of the fluid was increaſed probably about four times by the heat produced by the firing of the powder; and conſequently that it is thereby rendered capable, at the inſtant of exploſion, of ſuſtaining a preſſure nearly equal to a thouſand times the preſſure of the atmoſphere. *See* Robin's *Principles of Gunnery*.

(*o*) Diamonds are the moſt hard, heavy, tranſparent, and brilliant of all ſtones. They are either hexagonal priſms terminated by eight-ſided points or pyramids; or they are flat, or cubical, or rounded. Whether this difference of form be original, or adventitious, has not been determined. The firſt kind are the beſt and hardeſt, and may therefore have preſerved their original form againſt accidents better than the others, eſpecially than thoſe which are rounded, which are ſaid to be the leaſt hard, and conſequently moſt liable to have their forms altered by attrition.

CCXXXIII DIAPHORETIC ANTIMONY This is a white calx of antimony, made by calcining antimony with thrice its quantity of nitre *See* ANTIMONY.

CCXXXIV DIGESTION Digeſtion is an operation which conſiſts in expoſing bodies to a gentle heat, in proper veſſels, and during a certain time.

This operation is very uſeful to favor the action of certain ſubſtances upon each other as, for example, of well calcined, fixed alkali upon rectified ſpirit of wine When theſe two ſubſtances are digeſted together in a matraſs, with a gentle ſand bath heat, the ſpirit of wine acquires a yellowiſh color and an alkaline quality It is then called *alkaline tincture*, or *tincture of ſalt of tartar* See TINCTURE *of* SALT *of* TARTAR The ſpirit would not ſo well acquire theſe qualities by a ſtronger and ſhorter heat

attrition Diamonds are ſaid to conſiſt of laminæ or plates, and probably they have ſome uniform texture, becauſe lapidaries find that they may be poliſhed much more eaſily in one than in any other direction This ſtone becomes luminous in the dark by expoſure during a certain time to the rays of the ſun, by heating it in a crucible, by plunging it in boiling water, or by rubbing it with a piece of glaſs By friction it acquires an electrical property, by which it attracts the ſubſtance uſed for foils, called black maſtic, and other light matters The author of the Dictionary ſays, that diamonds are refractory in the fire, and even apyrous Nevertheleſs, experiments have been made, which prove that diamonds are capable of being diſſipated not only by the collected heat of the ſun, but alſo by the heat of a furnace A diamond, by expoſure to a concave ſpeculum, the diameter of which was forty inches, was reduced to an eighth part of its weight See *Phil Tranſ* No 386 In the *Giornale de Letterati d Italia, Tom* VIII *Art* 9 we may read a relation of experiments made on precious ſtones, by order of the Grand Duke of Tuſcany, with a burning lens, the diameter of which was two thirds of a Florentine ell, near the focus of which was placed another ſmaller lens By theſe experiments we find that diamonds were more altered by ſolar heat than moſt of the other precious ſtones, although not the leaſt appearance of a commencing fuſion was obſervable A diamond weighing thirty grains, thus expoſed during thirty ſeconds, loſt its color, luſtre, and tranſparency, and became of an opake white In five minutes, bubbles appeared on its ſurface, ſoon afterwards it burſt into pieces, which were diſſipated, and the ſmall fragment which remained was capable of being cruſhed into fine powder by the preſſure of the blade of a knife Neither the addition of glaſs, flints, ſulphur, metals, or ſalt of tartar prevented this diſſipation of diamonds, or occaſioned any degree of fuſion By this heat, rubies were ſoftened, and loſt ſome of their color, but preſerved their form and weight By addition of a third lens, a further degree of fuſion was given to rubies Even then rubies could not be made to unite with glaſs By having been expoſed to this heat, the ſurface of the rubies which had ſuffered fuſion, loſt much of their original hardneſs, and were nearly as ſoft as cryſtal But their internal parts, which had not been fuſed, retained their hardneſs Emeralds by this heat were rendered white, or of various colors, and ſoon afterwards were fuſed They were found to have loſt part of their weight, and to be rendered leſs hard and brittle

Experiments were alſo made by order of the Emperor Francis I on precious ſtones, from which we find, that diamonds were entirely diſſipated by having been expoſed in crucibles to a violent fire of a furnace during twenty-four hours, while rubies by the ſame heat were not altered in weight, color, or poliſh By expoſing diamonds during two hours only at a time, the alterations produced on them by fire were obſerved Firſt, they loſt their poliſh, then they were ſplit into thin plates, and, laſtly, totally diſſipated By the ſame fire, emeralds were fuſed See *Magaſin de Hambourg, tom* XVIII

Digestion is also used to soften and open certain bodies designed to undergo further operations, or to excite in them a certain degree of fermentation,

CCXXXV DISTILLATION Distillation is an operation by which the fluid and volatile principles of bodies may be separated and collected with a convenient degree of heat

If compounds containing volatile and fixed principles be exposed to fire, the former being rarefied by heat will endeavor to separate themselves from the latter, and if the effort which they make for this purpose be superior to the cohesion which they have with the fixed principles, a separation will happen, and they will be dissipated in state of vapor

The different fixity and volatility, which the several principles of almost every compound body have, furnishes a very extensive method of separating and obtaining their principles This chemists effect by distillation

Distillation requires an apparatus of vessels suited to the nature of the substances to be treated, and of the principles to be obtained

If the substance to be distilled be very compound, very susceptible of alteration by heat, and containing very volatile principles, such as most odoriferous plants, spirituous liquors, and others of this nature, a vessel must be used called an *alembic*, which must also be provided with a water-bath. *See* ALEMBIC

As in the distillation made with an alembic the vapors rise vertically, and are condensed in the upper part of the vessel called its *capital* or *head*, this method of distillation has been called *per ascensum* By this method may be distilled all matters volatile enough to rise with a degree of heat not exceeding that of boiling water such are the *spiritus rector of plants*, *ardent spirits*, and all *essential oils*

When compound bodies are to be distilled, the most volatile parts of which require a heat superior to that of boiling water, *retorts* must be employed, because these vessels may be conveniently placed either in a sand-bath or in a naked fire, and may be so disposed in a reverberatory furnace, that the matter which it contains shall be equally heated on all sides

The shape of a retort is such, that principles reduced to the state of vapor cannot issue but laterally through the neck of the vessel, which is accordingly placed on one of its sides This distillation has thence been called *per latus*. *See* RETORT

This second method of distilling is very useful, and may be applied to obtain essential oils, heavy acids, especially mineral acids, and sometimes even very volatile substances; as for example, the volatile alkali from sal ammoniac, or from animal matters which have not undergone putrefaction

A third kind of distillation is called *per descensum*, because it consists in applying the heat above the bodies whence the volatile parts are to be extricated, and by this method these volatile parts are obliged to descend into a vessel prepared for their reception But this method of distillation has many faults, is absolutely unnecessary, and is entirely neglected

We may easily conceive what passes in distillation Volatile substances are rendered by a suitable heat specifically lighter, are reduced to the state of vapor, and would be dissipated, if they were not retained, and obliged to pass into colder

colder places, where they are condensed and become liquors, if such be their nature, or else they collect in small solid particles called *flowers*, and in this case the operation changes its name, and is called *sublimation* See SUBLIMATION

As distillation is always performed in close vessels, the matters which rise are excluded from the access of air, which accelerates the ascent of volatile bodies *See* AIR

Hence distillations and sublimations, which are, properly speaking, only evaporations in close vessels, are more disadvantageous than evaporations in open air This is an inconvenience in all cases where distillation may be carried on very fast without any accident Such, for instance, is the distillation of water alone This inconvenience may be in a great measure remedied by introducing into the cucurbit a current of air by means of a ventilator, according to a method proposed by an English chemist to accelerate the distillation of sea-water, with a design to obtain by that means fresh water from it

But in distillations of almost all other substances, this slowness occasioned by want of air is rather useful than disadvantageous, because the more slowly a volatile substance is separated from a fixed substance, the more perfect is the separation For this reason, when a distillation is required to be performed according to the rules of the art, it must be so conducted that no more heat shall be applied to raise the volatile body than is necessary This management is particularly necessary when there is not a great difference betwixt the volatility of the principles of the body distilled We have an evident example of this in all concrete oily matters When we intend to separate the acid and the oil of which these matters consist, as these two principles have nearly the same volatility, they rise together, and are not disunited, so that the compound body passes in distillation without suffering any decomposition *See* BUTTER Notwithstanding the most careful management of most distillations, the volatile principles are seldom obtained perfectly free from the other principles of the compound, and therefore, to be purified, must be submitted to new distillations, called *rectifications*

We may then establish, as general and essential rules of distillation, that no greater heat ought to be applied than is just necessary to raise the substances to be distilled, and that the slowness of the operation is no less advantageous than the hurrying of it too much is prejudicial

These rules ought also to be observed for some other very strong reasons Such is the prevention of the breaking of vessels, which frequently happens in those of glass or of earthen ware when they are too suddenly or too strongly heated, and most certainly happens when the vapors rise more quickly than they can be condensed

These accidents are chiefly occasioned by vapors which are very elastic and not easily condensible Some vapors, as these of the smoking nitrous and marine acids, have these qualities so strongly, that much of them is lost, by the necessity of giving frequently a vent to them, by unstopping a small hole made in the balloon employed as a receiver in such distillations, and which might be conveniently made in all receivers*.

* *See* PLATES, where the vessels used in distillations are represented.

CCXXXVI. DITTANY *of* CRETE. (*p*)

CCXXXVII. DIVISION. *By diviſion* we ought to underſtand that ſeparation which is occaſioned in the parts of a body by help of mechanical inſtruments.

The mechanical diviſion of bodies does indeed ſeparate them into ſmaller, homogeneous, ſimilar parts, but this ſeparation cannot extend to the primary integrant molecules of any body, and conſequently is incapable of breaking what is properly called their aggregation: alſo, no union is formed betwixt the divided and dividing bodies, in which reſpect diviſion eſſentially differs from *ſolution*.

Diviſion is not properly a chemical operation. It is only employed preparatorily to facilitate other operations, and particularly ſolution. For this purpoſe it is very uſeful, as it encreaſes the quantity of ſurface, and conſequently the points of contact of any body.

Different methods are uſed to divide bodies according to their nature. Thoſe which are tenacious and elaſtic, as horns and gums, require to be cut, raſped, or filed. Metals, becauſe of their ductility, require the ſame treatment: but as they alſo are fuſible, they may be quickly and conveniently reduced into grains ſmall enough for moſt operations, by pouring them, when melted, into water.

All brittle bodies may be reduced conveniently into fine parts by being bruiſed in a mortar with a peſtle.

Very hard bodies, ſuch as glaſs, cryſtals, ſtones, particularly thoſe of the vitrifiable kind, before they are pounded, ought to be plunged when red hot into water, by which they are ſplit and cracked, and rendered more eaſily pulverable.

Bodies of this kind may alſo be bruiſed or ground by means of a hard and flat ſtone, upon which the matter is to be put, and bruiſed by another hard ſtone, ſo ſmall as to be held and moved upon the larger ſtone with the hand. The larger ſtone is called a *porphyry*, from its being generally of that kind of ſtone; and the operation is called *porphyriſation*. Inſtead of porphyriſation, a mill may be uſed, compoſed of a hard grit millſtone, moving round upon another ſtone of the ſame kind, which muſt be fixed. In the upper ſtone is a groove, or channel, through which the matter to be ground paſſes. By this method a ſubſtance may be more quickly reduced to a fine powder than by porphyriſation. But theſe mills can be only employed for conſiderable quantities of matter, as for manufactories of pottery and porcelain.

Theſe methods of mechanically dividing bodies are attended with ſome practical inconveniences, the moſt conſiderable of which is, that ſome parts of the dividing inſtruments are always ſtruck off, and mixed with the matter to be divided.

(*p*) DITTANY *of* CRETE. Sixteen ounces of the leaves of this plant yield about half a dram of a ſtrong, aromatic, eſſential oil, which coagulates by cold, reſembling camphor. From an ounce of this plant Neuman obtained with water two drams and a ſcruple of extract, and from the ſame quantity, with ſpirit of wine, he obtained a dram and a half of reſinous extract. He obſerves, that the green color of the leaves reſides in the reſin, and is extractible by ſpirit, eſpecially after water has previouſly extracted the gummy part, ſome of which being alſo ſoluble by ſpirit along with the reſin, alters the color of the ſpirituous tincture.

vided This may greatly affect the operations For instance, instruments of iron and copper furnish coloring metallic parts, and the latter metal is hurtful to health Porphyry is colored by a reddish-brown matter, which injures the color of crystal-glasses, enamels, and porcelain, made with matters ground upon this stone These matters, therefore, must be cleansed after their porphyrisation, or else no instruments ought to be employed capable of injuring the intended operations Thus, for the preparation of all medicines to be taken internally, no copper instruments, as mortars, pestles, ought to be used, those made of iron are preferable, and, instead of porphyries, mortars, grinding stones, and mill-stones, made of hard and white stones, ought to be employed for substances which are to enter into the composition of enamels, crystal-glass, and porcelain, the whiteness of which is a most necessary quality

CCXXXVIII DOCIMASTIC ART This name is given to the art of essaying, by operations in small, the nature and quantity of metallic or other matters, which may be obtained from mineral or other compound bodies The most important operations of the docimastic art are found under the words, REFINING, ORES, ESSAYS *of* ORES

CCXXXIX DOME The upper piece of furnaces, and particularly of portable furnaces, is called the *dome* It has the form of a hollow semisphere or small dome Its use is to form a space in the upper part of the furnace, the air of which is continually expelled by the fire, hence the current of air is considerably encreased which is obliged to enter by the ash-hole, to pass through the fire, to supply the place of the air driven from the dome The form of this piece renders it proper to reflect or reverberate a part of the flame upon the matters which are in the furnace, which has occasioned this kind of furnace to be called a *reverberatory furnace* See FURNACE

CCXL DORONICUM (q)

CCXLI DRAGON's BLOOD (r)

CCXLII DUCTILITY Ductility is a property possessed by certain solid bodies, which consists in their yielding to percussion, pressure, and in receiving different forms, without breaking

This property is nothing else than a continual adhesion of the integrant parts of those bodies which have this property, although these parts change place respectively to each other A body, therefore, cannot be ductile, excepting its integrant parts be so disposed, that, while some of its contiguous parts are forced to separate, others apply themselves, so that the whole shall be still one continued substance

(q) DORONICUM From two ounces of the dry root were obtained by water fourteen drams of extract, and from the same quantity, with spirit four drams and a half This root is supposed by some to be poisonous, especially when fresh *Neuman*

(r) DRAGON's BLOOD is a red colored, inodorous, and insipid resin, insoluble in water, soluble in spirit of wine and in oils, to both which liquors it communicates a red color By fire it is fusible, inflammable, and it emits an acid vapor like that of benzoin A solution of dragon's blood in spirit of wine is used for staining marble, to which it gives a red tinge, which penetrates more or less deeply according to the heat of the marble during application But as it spreads at the same time that it sinks deep, for fine designs, the marble should be cold Mr Du Fay says, that by adding pitch to this solution, the color may be rendered deeper

The

The figure of the integrant parts of ductile bodies contributes also probably to their ductility but as we have not any certain knowledge of the form of the integrant parts of any body, we cannot explain ductility more precisely and particularly

Some bodies are ductile both when they are hot and when they are cold, and in all circumstances Such are metals, and particularly gold and silver Other bodies are ductile only when they have a certain degree of heat, such as wax, and substances of the same kind, and glass *(s)* The degrees of heat requisite to render these bodies ductile vary according to their different natures In general, the heat must be such as to be in a middle state betwixt solidity and perfect fusion or fluidity As wax, for instance, is fusible with a very small heat, it may be rendered ductile by a still smaller heat, and glass, which requires a most violent heat to be perfectly fused, cannot acquire its greatest ductility without being made red-hot and almost ready to fuse Lastly, some bodies are rendered ductile by the interposition of the parts of a fluid Such are certain earths, and particularly clays When these earths have absorbed a sufficient quantity of water to bring them into a middle state betwixt liquidity and solidity, that is, to the consistence of a considerably firm paste, they have then acquired their greatest ductility Water has precisely the same effect upon them in this respect as fire has upon the other bodies mentioned

CCXLIII DULCIFICATION When caustic and corrosive bodies are rendered milder by being combined with another substance, they are said to be *dulcified.* This term is most commonly applied to the effect produced upon mineral acids by their union with spirit of wine *See* SPIRITS *of* NITRE, *of* SALT, *and of* VITRIOL (DULCIFIED)

CCXLIV DYING The art of dying consists in extracting from various substances coloring particles, and applying them to stuffs or other matters intended to be dyed, so that they shall adhere as firmly and durably as possible *(t)*

(s) Lastly, other bodies, as some kinds of iron, namely, those called by workmen *red-short*, brass, and some other metallic allays, are ductile only when cold, and are brittle when hot Concerning the ductility of metals, *see* METALS.

(t) DYING Notwithstanding the labors of Messrs Hellot, Astruc, Du Fay, Jussieu, and of some other authors, by which many processes for dying are ascertained, and notwithstanding the attempts of Mr Hellot to explain these processes, yet the theory of dying is far from being known or established. We do not sufficiently understand the nature of the colorific particles of dying substances, nor the action of the salts and other matters used in most of the processes for durable dyes, nor the causes of the differences of the several stuffs made of wool, silk, cotton, or thread, with regard to their aptitude to receive certain dyes. Many experiments are required to elucidate these subjects

Before we mention Mr Hellot's Theory of Dying, we must observe, that dyers enumerate five colors which they call primary, from the mixtures of which the other colors are produced These are blue, red, yellow, nut-color, and black *Good dyes* are those which can resist the action of water, air, and of certain saline and saponaceous liquors which are used as proofs of the durability of colors *False dyes* are those which cannot resist these proofs We may easily conceive the action of false dyes, that a colored decoction should color any stuff dipped into it by the adhesion of part of it to the stuff, and that when the stuff has become dry by the evaporation of the water of the decoction, it may again be deprived by washing with water of the coloring substance, which being soluble,

Although the principles of all the mechanical arts have a singlar dependance on chemistry, as we have endeavoured to shew in many parts of this work, few of them are so intimately related to this science as the art of dying, all the operations of which are so many chemical operations These operations must be described at full length to shew all their relations to chemistry, but these de-

soluble, as it was originally, in water, may easily be washed out of the dyed stuff but the action of those dyes which, although once dissolved or suspended in water, cannot again, after they are applied to stuffs, be washed out, is not so easily understood We shall here treat only of this latter sort, or good and durable dyes Dyes of different colors require different treatment Stuffs to be dyed of a *red* or *yellow* color must be boiled in water with alum and tartar before they are dipped into the dying decoctions the red coloring materials are *kermes*, *cochineal*, *gum-lac*, and *madder*, the yellow materials are *luteola*, or *dyers weed*, and other *yellow flowers* The stuffs for *blue* dyes require no previous preparation These blue dyes are made of *indigo*, or the blue fecula obtained from *woad* (*see* INDIGO and WOAD), dissolved in a lixivium of fixed alkali, or in urine, with or without the addition of some green vitriol The stuffs intended to receive a *root color* require no previous preparation but to be soaked in warm water These dyes are chiefly decoctions of *wallnut shells*, *wallnut-roots*, *alder-bark*, *sumach*, and *saunders* To these no saline or other matter is added. The *black* dyes, which are *inks*, or decoctions of *galls*, mixed with *green vitriol*, require no previous preparation of the stuff

Mr Hellot's Theory of Dying is, that the coloring particles are fixed into the pores of stuffs chiefly by means of a vitriolated tartar, which he believes to exist in each process, to be produced by the acid of alum and alkaline basis of tartar in the process for red and yellow dyes, to exist originally in the pot-ash employed in the blue dye, and in the nuts and roots employed in the root-colored dye He supposes that the pores of the stuff are cleansed and enlarged by the preparatory salts, and by the boiling water, so as to receive the coloring particles, which particles are afterwards detained by the contraction of the pores occasioned by cold, and further, that these pores are lined with a saline crust of vitriolated tartar, or of tartar, which salts being difficultly soluble in water, retain firmly the coloring particles But this theory cannot be admitted, when we consider that vitriolated tartar does not exist in any of the materials used in some of the processes for dying, as in the root-color materials, from which no vitriolated tartar can be obtained, unless accidentally, till they have been by burning reduced to ashes, and even then the quantity is exceedingly small, that although common pot-ash generally contains some vitriolated tartar, yet Mr Hellot has not shewn that pure fixed alkali is incapable of producing the same effect, and lastly, that vitriolated tartar and tartar, although they require much water to be dissolved, are yet soluble by water, and therefore if the coloring particles were fixed chiefly by means of these salts, they might be washed out by a large quantity of water, which we find to be contrary to experience

We shall find it more difficult to substitute a true theory, than to refute that of Mr Hellot Many experiments ought to be previously made Nevertheless we shall observe, that the colorific particles used in dying seem to be unsoluble in water, in spirit of wine, and even in alkaline lixiviums, that their diffusion through these liquids is caused merely by their adhesion to certain gummy and resinous particles, and that they may be disengaged from those gummy and resinous matters, by applying a piece of stuff, to which they have a greater adhesive power, which seems to be the case of the root-colored and blue dyes, or by applying another substance to which they have a greater power of adhesion, such as the earth of alum, in those dyes where that salt is used together with some substance, as fixed or volatile alkali, capable of decomposing alum, or as the ferrugineous earth of the green vitriol in black dyes, to which the colorific particles of the galls adhere, which earths are capable of applying themselves, and of adhering to the stuffs The separation of the coloring particles from the gummy and resinous matters is probably facilitated by the addition of acid

t l s wou l lead us too far from our object We must confine ourselves to shew the most general principles of dying These have been already explained in a preliminary discourse to the *Art of Dying Silk*, which is one of the dissertations upon the arts published by the Royal Academy of Sciences We shall here only give an extract of what is said there, to oblige those readers who have not their collection

Most vegetable and many animal substances contain coloring principles which may be extracted and applied to other bodies but these coloring principles are not always nearly of the same nature, and in the same state and their differences require that different methods should be employed for the extraction and application of them

Some of these coloring particles reside partly in a saponaceous extractive substance, and partly in an earthy and resinous matter When substances, the coloring particles of which are in this state, are boiled in water, they impregnate the water with their color, because a part of the resinous earthy portion is mixed and diffused in the water by means of the saponaceous extractive prin

and neutral salts, which may coagulate in some measure the vegetable matters, and leave the coloring particles disengaged, so that they may apply themselves to the stuff, or to the above-mentioned earths These salts are also useful by heightening certain colors, all acid salts and alum having the property of heightening the red colors of vegetables The metallic salt used in the *scarlet* dye (which consists of a decoction of *cochineal*, to which a solution of tin in aqua regia, and some tartar are added) has also the effect of changing the crimson color of cochineal to a vivid scarlet, and probably has also the other effects of alum, of affording an earth, namely that of tin, to which the coloring particles may adhere, and of coagulating the vegetable matters, so that they shall leave the coloring particles detached and suspended in the water The chief difference then betwixt the false and true dyes is, that the coloring particles in the former dyes are applied to stuffs, together with some gummy or resinous matter to which they adhere, and are therefore liable to be washed out along with these matters by any liquid capable of dissolving gums or resins, while the coloring particles of the true dyes are applied to stuffs, either alone, or adhering to some fine earth, as the earth of alum or of tin, and as both the coloring and the earthy particles are unsoluble in any liquids, to which they are most apt to be exposed, as water, soap-suds, &c they are capable of resisting the action of these liquids, and are therefore durable. Some dyes are also called *false*, because their colors are depraved by exposure to the sun and to the air These effects cannot, I fear, be explained without a further knowledge of colors, and of the action of light and air upon colors, than has hitherto been communicated We here treat not of the causes or changes of colors, but of the application and adhesion of coloring particles To confirm our conjectures on this subject, we may observe, that when the coloring particles of vegetables and animals are diffused in an alkaline lixivium, by means of gummy, resinous, or oily matters to which they adhere, they may be separated from these adhesive matters by adding alum, the acid of which unites with the alkali of the lixivium, while the coloring particles apply themselves to the basis or earth of the alum, now disengaged, with which they form what are called by painters *lakes*, the coloring matter of which is not now soluble in water or in spirit of wine although these liquids are capable of extracting that coloring matter from the vegetable and animal substances which contain it, by the intervention, as we suppose, of some gummy or resinous matters

For further particulars concerning dying, *see* Black, Blue, Crimson, &c and Cochineal, Indigo, Flowers, Fruit, Leaves, &c The *details* of the particular processes in this art are described fully by *Mr Hellot*, in his Treatises on the *Art of Dying*

ciple If a ſtuff be plunged in a decoction of ſuch ſubſtances, the coloring particles are thereby made to touch and apply themſelves to it, and even to adhere firmly, becauſe the reſinous earthy coloring principle, when once united to the ſtuff, and ſeparated from the extractive principle, is no longer ſoluble either by water, ſoap, ſalts, or other active matters Several ſubſtances are known, the coloring principles of which are in this ſtate Of theſe the chief are the *green ſhells of wallnuts*, the *root* of the *wallnut-tree*, *ſumach*, *ſaunders*, *bark of elder*, and the ſhell-fiſh called *murex*, ſuppoſed to be the purple dye of the ancients Excepting this latter ſubſtance, which gives a fine red, all the reſt give a dun color, called a *root color*, but which is valuable notwithſtanding its little luſtre, becauſe it is very uſeful as a ground upon which other brighter colors may be applied From the nature of theſe coloring ingredients we may perceive that no preparation is neceſſary for the colors, or for the matters to be dyed. They furniſh the ſimpleſt and moſt practicable kind of dying, for all the operation conſiſts in boiling the dying materials in water, and in dipping the ſtuff to be dyed in this decoction

The coloring principle of another kind of ſubſtance is contained in a matter altogether reſinous, which is ſo diſpoſed that it cannot be rendered miſcible with water by means of the ſaponaceous extractive principle of the ſame ſubſtance The principal ingredients of this kind are *indigo*, which furniſhes the blue dye, and the flowers of *cartamus*, or *baſtard Saffron*, from which a very beautiful red is procured Pure water cannot extract the colors from theſe matters The blue reſinous part of indigo is alſo of the nature of thoſe which ſpirit of wine cannot diſſolve but as fixed alkaline ſalts are capable of acting upon all reſinous matters, they are uſed ſucceſsfully to extract the coloring parts of theſe ingredients, and to render them fit for dying

The coloring principles of almoſt all the other vegetable and animal matters which furniſh colors for dying, and which are very numerous, are of a purely extractive ſaponaceous nature, and may conſequently be eaſily extracted by water alone, but as they are ſoluble in water, they might eaſily be waſhed away from the ſtuffs to which they have been applied, if theſe ſtuffs had not previouſly been impregnated with ſome matter capable of producing ſome change or decompoſition on the coloring part

A method has been found of fixing colors upon ſtuffs by different ſalts, with which the ſtuffs are impregnated before they are dyed The extractive coloring particles are ſo changed by theſe ſalts, that they loſe their property of being ſoluble in water, and are even rendered capable of reſiſting the action of ſoap, and other ſubſtances which are apt to deſtroy moſt colors, and are therefore uſed to prove the durability of theſe

Of all the ſalts which may be employed for this purpoſe, allum is found to be the fitteſt it is therefore generally employed for all extractive tinctures, which are very numerous, the principal of which are *luteola*, or *dyer's-weed*, and all the herbs which give a yellow color, *madder*, *vegetable kermes*, *cochenil*, *Braſil-wood*, *log-wood*, and other woods and roots uſed in dying Allum is not the only ſalt which has this effect All neutral ſalts with metallic baſes are alſo capable of fixing the extractive colors but ſome of theſe are very dear, and others change and ſpoil the colors, ſo that allum is ſolely employed for this purpoſe

All theſe dyes cannot be equally well fixed by alum, or by the other ſalts above-mentioned Some of them are only ſo much fixed by alum as to reſiſt the action of water, but not of the other ſubſtances uſed to prove the fixity of colors, nor even of the air, during a long time This latter kind of dyes are called *falſe* or *ſmall tints*, to diſtinguiſh them from the more fixed dyes, called *great* or *good tints*

Theſe differences muſt proceed from the particular nature of each of the coloring materials but very accurate analyſes of theſe materials, and a great number of new reſearches muſt be made, before this obſcure ſubject can be explained It will even appear ſtill more obſcure, when we conſider that the different nature of the ſubſtances to which the dye is applied, ſurprizingly affects the beauty and fixity of colors For inſtance, the red color of madder, which is ſufficiently beautiful and fixed upon wool and cotton, gives but a falſe tint upon thread, alſo cochenil, which gives a vivid and bright flame-colored red to wool, and even to moſt animal matters, does not adhere to ſilk, cotton, or thread In the particular details of the proceſſes for dying the different kinds of matters many other ſingular differences may be found, which require particular attentions to be explained. The moſt general inference from theſe particular details is, that wool and all animal matters are the moſt eaſily dyed, next to them, ſilk and other ſubſtances, which ſeem to be intermediate betwixt the animal and the vegetable nature; and laſt of all, thread, and vegetable matters.

The few facts and general principles we have advanced on the art of dying are ſufficient to ſhew its connexion with chemiſtry, and how much it may be improved by this ſcience.

E

CCXLV EARTHS Earth is one of the four simple substances called elements, or primitive principles, because they are indeed the most simple of all those which enter into the combination of compound bodies We cannot doubt, in particular, that the greatest part of the compounds which we can analyse contain earth as one of their principles, for after art has exhausted all its efforts to decompose them, a fixed and solid matter always remains, upon which no change can be produced, and this is what is generally called earth It has the solidity, weight, fixity, and other principal properties of the mass of solid matter which forms the globe we inhabit, called also *the earth*

These general considerations are sufficient to convince us, that in nature a substance exists whose properties are different from those of fire, air, water, and which is, like these other substances, one of the elements of compound bodies But a vague assertion like this does not satisfy chemists Besides the ascertaining of the existence of the different substances submitted to their examination, they require to know the properties of these substances in their greatest degree of purity and simplicity but they have found much difficulty and uncertainty in investigating the essential properties of the purest and simplest terrestrial element

Earth is not found so pure as the other elements, fire, air, and water, which, though not entirely free from mixture, are however so pure, that we may certainly and easily discover their fundamental properties These properties of each of these pure elements are so well ascertained, and so evident, that nobody has yet attempted to distinguish different kinds of fire, air, or water, notwithstanding the differences which may arise from the heterogeneous substances with which they are almost always mixed

But we cannot say the same of earth, for a considerable number of substances are called earths, because they possess the principal properties of the terrestrial element but these substances, when examined more particularly, are always found to differ from each other so much in other respects, and to be so difficultly purifiable from heterogeneous matter, that we have not ascertained whether only one simple and elementary earth, or several ones essentially different, although equally simple, exist

The most general and most probable opinion is that as only one kind of fire, of air, and of water, so only one kind of simple elementary earth, exists Alchemists chiefly have endeavoured to discover this primary earth, not with an intention to ascertain its properties, but because they imagine that as gold is the purest of metals, the earth of which it is partly composed must be also the most pure; they have, therefore, searched every where for this earth, which they call *pure earth* and *virgin earth*. They have endeavoured to obtain it from dew, rain, the [illegible] of vegetables, animals, [illegible] and metals; but it was impossible to find it in compound bodies; for we shall see that when once this element makes part of a compound body, it cannot be disengaged from the substances with which it has united.

Some of the best philosophical chemists have rather chosen to admit different kinds of elementary earths, than to investigate the nature of the most simple and elementary earth. Becher admits three principles, which he calls *earths*, namely, *the vitrifiable*, *the inflammable*, and *the mercurial earth*, which are known by the name of *the three earths of Becher*.

Mr Pott, examining the principal natural earths, divides them into four kinds, *the vitrifiable*, *the calcareous*, *the argillaceous*, and *the gypseous earths*. This able chemist shews the essential properties of these four kinds of earths, without affirming that they are all equally simple, and without even determining which of them he considers as most simple.

As earth is an element which enters into the composition of almost all bodies, and which seems chiefly to affect their properties, it deserves an accurate investigation to discover which is the most simple and elementary of all the substances to which the name *earth* has been applied. This subject seems capable of decision by considering, first, what are the essential properties by which earthy substances differ from other elements, and then by determining that earth to be the most pure and simple, which possesses these properties most eminently and decisively; for we cannot doubt, that the properties distinguishing earthy matters from the other elements are the essential and specific characters of the earthy element; and also, that the more eminently any substance possesses these characteristic properties of the earthy element, the nearer it approaches to this element considered in its state of purity and simplicity.

This being established, if we compare with the other elements all the substances which may reasonably be considered as earths, we shall soon be convinced, that these possess much greater *weight*, *hardness*, *fixity*, and *infusibility*, than any other element; for these qualities are insensible, or do not exist, in the element of fire; they are in an exceedingly small degree in the air, and are more sensible and considerable in water; but are infinitely less than in any thing which can be considered as earth. Hence we ought to conclude, that the qualities above mentioned are the distinguishing and characteristic essential properties of the earthy element. But these qualities are not so eminently united in any of those substances which are considered as earthy, as in that which is called by chemists, *vitrifiable earth*. We say then, that this earth is the heaviest, hardest, most fixed, and most infusible; and even the most *apyrous* of all earths, when it is very pure; and also that it is the most homogeneous, the most simple, and elementary earth, as we shall prove by a more particular examination of its properties, and by a comparison of these with the properties of the other earthy substances.

We

We call that *vitrifiable earth*, the integrant parts of which [illegible] in masses of matter or stones, absolutely white and colourless, [illegible] more [illegible] and hard than any other natural substances, and which suffers no alteration, or even fusion, by the strongest fire which we can [illegible].

Amongst the hard stones called vitrifiable, we [illegible] which [illegible] the qualities we have [illegible], because in [illegible] the vitrifiable earth is pure. Most of these stones, as [illegible] flint, free stone, agates, quartz, rock crystal and [illegible], are deficient in some of the qualities required to [illegible] the purest vitrifiable earth. Some of them are opake, or only semi-transparent; others are coloured; some are fusible by a great heat, [illegible] harder than any other kind of stones, [illegible] that they are mixed with heterogeneous substances [illegible], or even earthy, of a different kind.

The purest of all the vitrifiable stones is the diamond, which is perfectly white, free from all colour or stain, and transparent. This stone is also known to be the hardest of all, is absolutely apyrous, that is, incapable of receiving any alteration by the most violent heat. We, therefore, consider the matter of this stone as the purest, simplest, and most elementary earth that is known. The properties, then, of this stone, and of the other vitrifiable stones which resemble it, may give us notions of the properties of primary, elementary, unchanged earth. In this our opinion is conformable to that of the illustrious Stahl, who indeed admits the three earths of Becker, but, at the same time, corrects the theory of this chemist, by declaring that he only considers the first earth of Becker, or vitrifiable earth, as the proper terrestrial or earthy element. *Specimen Beckerianum*, p. 44. No. 25.

But before we particularly enumerate the properties of this earth, we ought to make some observations on those hard, earths, and other matters called by chemists *vitrifiable*.

Our first observation shall be concerning the name *vitrifiable earth*, because it may produce false notions of the nature of these stones.

We say then, that the epithet, *vitrifiable*, is given, first, because some stones of this kind are, by means of their heterogeneous matters, capable of fusion and conversion into glass, without addition, and merely by the action of a very violent heat; and secondly, because other stones of this kind which are less fusible than these now mentioned, but which are yet more so than stones of other kinds, require for their perfect fusion and vitrification a less quantity of flux, and a less degree of heat.

In the second place, as all the earths and stones called vitrifiable have, notwithstanding their impurities, more hardness and transparency than others, and are fitter to communicate these good qualities to glass, they are employed preferably to any other earths in the composition of glass, or artificial crystal. These are the only reasons why this kind of earth has been called vitrifiable. But we ought not from thence to conclude, that the earthy substance which [illegible] entirely composes them is more fusible and more vitrifiable than other earth. On the contrary, I again say, that vitrifiable earth, when very pure, is of all earths the least fusible, and the least vitrifiable. [illegible] is [illegible] experiment made relatively to this subject. Some diamond powder was mixed with a

fusible [illegible]

sufficient quantity of fixed alkali to vitrify any other earthy matter, and the mixture exposed to a heat sufficient for the most difficult vitrifications. After the operation, no glass was found in the crucible, but part of the alkali had been dissipated by the violence of the heat, and the diamond powder did not shew any signs of a beginning fusion. Thus we may consider it as an established truth, that the earths and stones called vitrifiable are not essentially and really so, that the fusibility of some of these, by which property they are rendered the fittest earths for vitrification, proceeds from heterogeneous matter with which they are mixed, and that, in general, the whitest, clearest, most transparent and hardest of these stones are also the most refractory and unfusible *See* VITRIFICATION

Our second observation shall relate to the weight of vitrifiable earths We have already said, that the purest and simplest of all earths ought to be also the heaviest, and accordingly we find that pure vitrifiable earth is specifically heavier than calcareous, argillaceous, gypseous, or other earths We are, nevertheless, no less certain, that metals, metallic earths, and several kinds of spars, both calcareous and selenitic, are much heavier than the most compact vitrifiable stones but we must consider that these earthy matters are very compound bodies in comparison of the purer earths An objection may be made, that if elementary earth be essentially the heaviest of all matters, then any body compounded of this earth and other matters ought to be lighter than pure earth This objection would be unanswerable, if the specific gravity of a body was always equal to the specific gravities of the integrant and constituent parts which compose it but as these parts may be so arranged that void spaces may be left betwixt them, sometimes larger, and sometimes less, therefore a body composed of parts essentially lighter, may yet have a greater specific gravity than another body whose parts are essentially heavier, and this happens in all metals and metallic matters *See* METALS and METALLISATION Thus the gravity of metals and of metallic earths and stones ought not to prevent our considering the pure and elementary earthy principle as the heaviest of all natural substances

After these explanations, we may consider the properties of elementary earth in the purest vitrifiable stones, and may compare them with the properties of the other elements Since of these elements water is the most capable of our examination, we shall compare it with the purest vitrifiable earth, observing always, that we consider these elements in their state of aggregation, for we have no method by which their primary integrant parts can be known and considered separately.

If then, on one side, we consider a mass of water, absolutely pure, exposed to a cold sufficient to form it into hard, compact, solid ice, and if, on the other side, we compare to this a mass of vitrifiable earth, as a diamond, or even a very fine and clear rock-crystal, we shall easily perceive that these two matters resemble perfectly each other in their appearance, we shall find that both of them are colorless, inodorous, and tasteless, and that their transparency is alike therefore, if we could no further examine their properties, we must consider them as being of the same matter but when the other properties of these substances are examined, as weight, hardness, fusibility, and fixity, then we shall perceive differences, which indeed are only in the degrees of these properties

possessed

possessed by each of the two substances but the difference of these degrees is very great Thus the specific gravity of rock-crystal is almost four times that of ice their hardness also is so different, that the earthy substance resists the point of the hardest steel, without being scratched, and when struck by steel, elicits ignited sparks, while ice may be easily cut by instruments of steel, and does not elicit sparks when struck their difference of fusibility is still more sensible, the ice becoming fluid by a gentle warmth, which does not sensibly affect rock-crystal in any respect I say, *sensibly*, because with the least diminution of cold it is certainly somewhat affected, so far as to be expanded, and consequently to be less hard and heavy But these two latter affections, particularly, are so inconsiderable in a vitrifiable stone with the heat necessary to thaw ice, that probably it cannot be estimated Lastly, if we continue to examine these two substances by a heat gradually augmented, we shall see the water totally dissipated in vapors, before even either of these substances has become red-hot, and the vitrifiable stone support a heat almost infinitely encreased, till it is white and dazzling, without becoming fluid, or without any part of it exhaling in vapors, for it may be afterwards found to have lost no weight by having been exposed to this heat

So far we can extend our examination, for I do not believe that a pure vitrifiable earth, as a diamond, can be fused even in the focus of the best burning speculums but supposing that a sufficient heat might be produced to procure this fusion, or that this stone were exposed to infinitely greater heat, such as we conceive to be in the body of the sun, it would then melt, and would even be reduced to vapors, if the heat were sufficiently violent, and when this heat should cease, it would, when it cooled, fix again, and become such a substance as it was before The same would happen to vitrifiable earth in these circumstances, which does happen to water rendered fluid, and reduced to vapor by a certain heat, and which is again frozen into solid ice when that heat is removed The differences, therefore, betwixt these two substances are only, as we have already said, in the degrees, but also these differences are very considerable

From these considerations an inference seems deducible, that the elements or the simplest substances which we know are essentially only one and the same matter, and only differ from each other in the quantity and in the form of their primary integrant molecules, which, from this difference of form and quantity, have a greater or less tendency to unite together, and we might be inclined to believe that a certain kind of analogy or gradation exists betwixt them thus, for example, that earth should be to water, what water is to air, and what air is to fire, or rather to some unknown intermediate substance betwixt air and fire, for the difference betwixt these two latter elements appears too great to be compared with the differences amongst the three former But these are speculations entirely systematic, for we are very far from being capable of estimating the essential properties of elements sufficiently exactly, to be able to determine any thing precisely and positively in this respect

However that may be, we cannot doubt but that earth chiefly differs from the other elements by the powerful tendency which its parts have to each other, and by the force of their cohesion For its hardness, fusibility, fixity, and even its gravity, are evidently the necessary consequences of this principal and essential property And by this property does the earthy element act in the system of nature. By this it is the cause of the consistence of all solid bodies

It unites, fixes, and incorporates in ſome meaſure the other elements.

Laſtly, as without fire the whole world would be one maſs of ſolid and immoveable matter, ſo without earth it would be a confuſed heap of fogs, vapours, a chaos of incoherent atoms, deſtitute of that harmony and equilibrium which ſuſtain it.

We have already had occaſion to ſhew in ſeveral parts of this work, that the general tendency of the parts of matter to each other is the grand ſpring of the univerſe, that by this power, all combinations, ſolutions, and, in a word, all the movements and operations of nature are performed: and as we have ſhewn that the earthy element poſſeſſes this tendency in the greateſt degree, we ought to conſider earth as being in this ſenſe the moſt active and powerful of all elements. This notion is contrary to the opinions of chemiſts and philoſophers, who from not having ſufficiently examined this ſubject, and being deceived by the ſeeming inactivity of earth conſidered in its ſtate of aggregation, have affirmed it to be an element purely paſſive, and only capable of impulſe from other elements. Indeed when the parts of earth are united together, they appear to be, and really are, incapable of acting upon other bodies, becauſe they then exhauſt all their action mutually upon each other. But the force with which they adhere together, and which renders them incapable of forming other unions, the extreme hardneſs and inſolubility of a maſs of pure earth, ought to demonſtrate to a true philoſopher, that if we ſuppoſe the parts of earth ſo ſeparated from each other, that they cannot unite, and exhauſt their action upon each other, they muſt then poſſeſs all their force of tendency, which muſt be very great, they muſt be in a ſtate of violent effort, and conſequently muſt tend with extreme force to unite with any parts of matter which may be within their reach, and to which they can apply themſelves. We do not indeed know any pure earth which is in this ſtate of broken aggregation: but we know compounds in which the primitive integrant parts of the earthy element are only combined with the parts of water, which are incapable of ſatisfying all their tendency to union. Theſe are the moſt ſimple ſaline ſubſtances, ſuch as acids and alkalis; and we may judge by the force and vehemence of the action of theſe ſolvents, how violent the action of the parts of earth would be, which ſhould be capable of exerting all the attractive force which belongs to them.

Although the entire maſs of our globe be probably formed by an immenſe heap of elementary, vitrifiable, and even actually vitrified earth, as the illuſtrious Buffon believes, we do not find upon its ſurface but a very ſmall quantity of this earth, unaltered, and in its primary ſtate. Perhaps even none of it exiſts in that ſtate: for, as we have obſerved, the common vitrifiable ſtones, which are chiefly formed of it, are very far from the degree of purity of primary elementary earth; and even perfect diamonds, which ſeem of all theſe ſtones to approach the neareſt to this purity, ſeem to have been elaborated by the waters, if we can judge from their regularly cryſtallized form.

We ſhall not be ſurprized at the ſcarcity of pure earthy element, if we conſider that the ſurface of the earth, which alone we are acquainted with, has been from the beginning of the world expoſed to the conſtant action of the other elements, and that by uninterrupted operations, nature, aſſiſted by

fire,

fire, air, and water, has gradually disunited the integrant parts of elementary earth, and by combining them in manners and proportions infinitely various with parts of the other elements, has formed the numberless compound bodies, which occupy a certain thickness near the circumference of the globe, probably very small in comparison of the diameter of the earth, but very large with regard to us, whose greatest efforts only extend to a few hundred feet below its surface

All the portions of elementary earth, which, having been thus disunited, have afterwards been combined with parts of matter of other kinds, have received very sensible changes, the effects of which always remain, and prevent them from appearing afterwards, notwithstanding future decompositions, in their original purity and simplicity They then assume different forms according to the nature of the compounds into the combination of which they have entered Thus, for example, the earth which makes parts of crustaceous animals, or rather of their shells and scales, takes the character of that earth which is called *calcareous*, and which is capable of conversion into quicklime by the action of fire The earth which has entered into the composition of plants, and even of the bodies of animals, after having been deprived as much as is possible of the principles of these compounds to which it was united, forms all the *argillaceous earths* Some of these are found which partake both of the calcareous and of the argillaceous properties, and are called *marles* Marles have not yet been sufficiently well examined by chemists They are either a mixture of clay and calcareous earth, or they have been so elaborated by nature as to be transformed into a particular earth, partly calcareous, and partly argillaceous, such as the earth of animal bones seems to be

As the earth which forms sands and the common impure vitrifiable stones retains more than the rest the essential properties of elementary earth, notwithstanding the heterogeneous, phlogistic, and other parts with which it is mixed, we cannot easily know whether it has once made a part of some very compound bodies, from the principles of which it has been more perfectly separated than the argillaceous and calcareous earths, or whether it be the primitive earth, which, without having made part of any intimate combination, has only been divided and conveyed by waters, and the parts of which have afterwards reunited, having only contracted a slight union with some phlogistic, metallic, and other matters, with which it is found mixed This latter supposition appears to me to be the most probable But very extensive researches in natural history and in chemistry are requisite to determine this question

From what we have said concerning the principal kinds of earths which form the surface of the globe, we may conclude, that excepting the purest vitrifiable earth, all the others are mixed with heterogeneous matter By these remaining heterogeneous matters are the different kinds of earth specified and characterized and as they all preserve and retain their peculiar character, we ought to conclude from thence that these extraneous matters are very intimately united To purify and simplify these mixed earths, so that they shall be assimilated to the purest vitrifiable earth, would be a fine problem But, probably this problem is beyond the power of our art For as in general the perfect separation of two substances, united together, is exceedingly difficult, this difficulty must greatly increase, when one of the two substances to be separated has a very strong attractive power, as earth has This is the true reason why we find so small a portion of pure earth amongst the bodies within our reach, and that on the contrary, the globe is covered with so great a quantity of earthy substances differing from each other so much, that we might be inclined to believe them to be bodies essentially different *See the articles*, EARTH (CALCAREOUS), EARTH (VITRIFIABLE) (*u*)

CCXLVI EARTH (ANIMAL) (*x*)

(*u*) In this article the author has advanced some ingenious speculations, but in my opinion several of his propositions are affirmed without proof, and some of his inferences are not conclusive The subject does not appear to me capable of being treated so decisively Most philosophers, ancient and modern, have enumerated, according to their theories, the *elements* of which they believed all substances to be constituted Nevertheless, they have not yet proved the existence of any one element The impossibility even of such a proof appears from considering, that the only reason which can induce us to believe that any substance is an element is, that we are incapable of decomposing that substance, and that our incapacity to decompose does not necessarily imply an impossibility of decomposition The improbability of the conjecture that fire, air, water, earth, are the only elements, might easily be shewn If we mean by element whatever substance we are incapable of decomposing, (and this is the only precise meaning which can be formed of it) then many other substances are entitled to be enumerated amongst elements According to this meaning the number of elements will decrease, when means of decomposing some of those which cannot now be decomposed are discovered The author believes that only one kind of elementary earth exists, and he further believes that this earth is that which he and some other authors call *vitrifiable* But besides that the class of earths called vitrifiable contains many substances, the properties of which are exceedingly different, no proof can be given that those substances which are believed to be the purest of this class of earths, as diamonds, are more simple and elementary than calcined calcareous earths, argillaceous earths, earth of magnesia, metallic or many other earths, all which, when purified by ordinary methods, are as incapable of decomposition as diamonds are, and consequently as well entitled to be considered as elementary

Earths are divided by Mr Pott into vitrifiable, argillaceous, calcareous, and gypseous The author of the Dictionary follows this division Other authors have invented other divisions, and enlarge the number of classes, by which their dispositions are more comprehensive and distinct

But although these arbitrary arrangements of natural substances may assist learners, yet as they are all very imperfect, our knowledge will be also very imperfect, unless we consider separately each species In the notes to this Dictionary, therefore, the chemical properties of each species, as well as of the genera and classes of earths, (in which are comprehended, not only substances, commonly called earths, but also stones, slates, spars, and talks) shall be mentioned as the names of these species occur in the alphabetical order

(*x*) EARTH (ANIMAL) is the earth of shells of animals, or that which is obtained by calcination or putrefaction of animal substances 1 The *earths of the shells of Sea Fishes* have the general properties of calcareous earths See EARTHS (CALCAREOUS) It differs from the mineral calcareous earths in being difficultly soluble by vitriolic acid, and in being less disposed to vitrify along with salts and metallic glasses The *shells of eggs* are also calcareous, but are somewhat fusible by fire 2 The *earths of calcined bones and horns* are soluble by nitrous, marine, and vegetable acids, and with difficulty by vitriolic acid, but are not calcareous They are said to be unfusible, even when mixed with salt, metallic glasses, and other fusible mixtures They are therefore used in the composition of enamels and opake white glasses

CCXLVII. EARTH (ARGILLACEOUS). *See* CLAY.

CCXLVIII. EARTH (CALCAREOUS). Chemiſts have given this name in general to all earths and ſtones, which being burnt acquire the properties of quicklime.

Nature preſents to us a conſiderable quantity of calcareous earths and ſtones, which have peculiar differences depending on their greater or leſs purity, but which reſemble each other by eſſential properties common to all, and particularly by their capacity to receive calcination.

The principal kinds of theſe earths or ſtones are, chalks, all the calcinable ſhell-ſtones employed for building, all marbles, calcinable ſtalactites, the alabaſters and ſpars which are convertible into quicklime by fire.

Amongſt theſe ſtones a great number are evidently impure and mixed, particularly thoſe which are colored. But amongſt the whiteſt, we cannot eaſily aſcertain which of them contains the pureſt earth, becauſe they have not been chemically compared with this view. We ought certainly to conſider thoſe as the pureſt which poſſeſs in the higheſt degree the eſſential properties of calcareous earth.

All calcareous ſtones are leſs hard than vitrifiable ſtones; none of them ſtrike fire with ſteel, and they all may be eaſily cut with ſteel inſtruments; ſome of them may be found, whoſe parts having been divided, conveyed by waters, and afterwards depoſited ſucceſſively upon each other, form concretions, or rather cryſtallizations, very neat and even tranſparent. Their tranſparency however is always leſs than that of the pureſt vitrifiable ſtones.

The ſpecific gravity of the different kinds of calcareous ſtones has not been compared with the ſpecific gravity of the vitrifiable. We only know that ſome calcareous ſpars are much heavier than the precious ſtones, and are therefore called *heavy ſpars*. But as we are very certain that the weight of theſe bodies is cauſed by extraneous and not calcareous matter, this does not prevent our eſtabliſhing a general rule that calcareous earth is leſs heavy than vitrifiable; for, excepting the inſtance now mentioned, they all are ſo.

If any calcareous earth or ſtone be divided by trituration and moiſtened with water, it abſorbs a certain quantity of it, particularly if it be very dry; and it forms a kind of paſte, the parts of which have a certain adheſion together. But this paſte is not ſo ductile as that formed by clay and water. It alſo dries and diſunites much more quickly.

glaſſes. Nevertheleſs, Wallerius affirms, that the earth of calcined bones, by intenſe heat, was changed, without addition, to a green glaſs. *See Mem. Sued.* 1760. The ſame author ſays, that the earth of the whites and yolks of eggs was eaſily fuſible, and that in general the fuſibility of animal earths is in proportion to the ſoftneſs of the parts from which they were obtained. 3. The *earth of blood, fleſh, and ſkins* of animals, is ſoluble by all acids, and is fuſible by fire; that of blood and of other animal fluids being moſt fuſible. This earth, like that of burnt bones and horns, is not calcareous; but both theſe kinds of earth are ſaid to be rendered calcareous by being diſſolved in acids, precipitated by fixed alkali from thoſe acids, and afterwards calcined. They probably contain ſome oleaginous ſubſtance, from which they cannot be entirely diveſted by fire without a previous ſolution in acids.

All acids are evidently capable of acting upon calcareous earth, they attack and diſſolve it with more or leſs effervescence. This action of acids upon calcareous earths and ſtones furniſhes us with an eaſy method of diſtinguiſhing them from other earth and ſtony matters, which they reſemble externally.

Calcareous earth ſaturates all acids, and forms with them different *neutral ſalts with baſis of calcareous earth*, according to the kind of acid.

With vitriolic acid, it forms a cryſtallizable ſalt, not very ſoluble in water, called *Selenites*.

With nitrous and marine acids, it forms acrid, bitter, and very deliqueſcent ſalts. They are called *nitre*, and *marine ſalts with calcareous baſes*.

With the acid of vinegar, calcareous earth forms a ſalt not deliqueſcent, and ſuſceptible of a ſilky and ramous cryſtallization like a kind of vegetation. This is *acetous ſalt with calcareous baſis*.

Laſtly, with acid of tartar, this earth forms a neutral cryſtallizable ſalt, a *ſoluble tartar with calcareous baſis*. This ſalt is much more ſoluble in water than pure acid of tartar.

Calcareous earth has alſo the property of decompoſing all ammoniacal ſalts, from which it diſengages the volatile alkali, and unites with their acids, when aſſiſted by a certain heat.

Calcareous earths and ſtones, being expoſed to the action of fire, loſe part of their weight, and much of their conſiſtence, which proceeds from the fire carrying off a conſiderable quantity of water which enters into their combination, and as the laſt portions of water are powerfully retained by earth, a very ſtrong heat is requiſite to diſſipate them, and in this principally conſiſts the change produced upon calcareous ſtones when reduced into quicklime. See QUICKLIME.

The moſt violent fire we can make is incapable of melting and vitrifying calcareous earths and ſtones, when they are very pure (y), but a very remarkable thing is, that theſe ſubſtances, ſo refractory when alone, become true fluxes, and facilitate the fuſion and vitrification of ſeveral other ſubſtances, as ſands and clays. This phenomenon, the cauſe of which is hidden, and not eaſily to be diſcovered, ſeems to depend on a particular diſpoſition of the inflammable principle from which none of theſe matters is entirely exempt, and perhaps on ſome remaining portion of watery principle, ſo ſtrongly retained by calcareous earth, that fire cannot entirely extricate it. See VITRIFICATION.

The other characteriſtic properties of calcareous earth are the ſame as the properties of this earth when converted into quicklime, which we ſhall relate and explain under the article QUICKLIME. We ſhall only here obſerve, that if we add to theſe the properties of calcareous earth before calcination, we ſhall evidently ſee that all theſe properties, and the phenomena ariſing from them, depend on the intimate union of a certain quantity of watery principle with the earthy principle in calcareous earth, an union which produces an incipient ſaline combination, according to Stahl's theory, and a ſtrong diſpoſition in cal-

(y) Mr D'Arcet found that chalk, limeſtone, and one calcareous ſpar, reſiſted a violent, long continued heat, but that other ſpars, ſtalactites, and other calcareous ſubſtances, ſhowed a beginning fuſion. See *Mem. l'Acad. des Sc. ſur l'Action d'un feu violent, egal, & continue*, 1766.

careous

careous earth to pass into a more compleat saline state by a more perfect combination with water. We may hence easily perceive, that as calcareous stones in their natural state do not differ from vitrifiable stones but in being less hard, less heavy, and less fixed, which are precisely the essential qualities by which pure water differs from pure earth; that as, besides the action of fire deprives calcareous stones of much water, calcareous earth chiefly differs from vitrifiable earth by its union with water; and lastly, that as we cannot doubt but that all calcareous earth has been once one of the principles of organized animal bodies, we cannot also doubt, but that the water, the portion of phlogiston *(z)*, perhaps also some remaining small part of saline matter, which are found in these earths, and which distinguish their different kinds, are the remains of the principles with which the elementary earth was found combined in these compounds, and which continue firmly united with them. *(a)*

CCXLIX. EARTH (GYPSEOUS). This name is applied by some chemists to gypsum, and to the earth contained in selenites. As the

(z) Most, perhaps all calcareous earths contain such a portion of phlogiston, as to enable them, by means of heat, to reduce metallic calces, especially those of lead and bismuth, which are easily reducible, and even in some measure those of copper and iron. By means also of this phlogiston they acquire a phosphoric quality when united with nitrous acid. *See* PHOSPHORUS *of* BALDWIN. A curious experiment is mentioned by Mr Pott, which shewed this phosphoric quality of calcareous earth united with nitrous acid. He saturated that acid with quicklime, and distilled it. He repeated this operation frequently, always using the same acid and the same quicklime. He perceived that the vapors which passed in these distillations through a hole in the receiver appeared luminous sparks, which afterwards kindled, and flowed out like a stream of fire. He also perceived another remarkable circumstance in this operation, namely, that the effervescence which happened on the mixing these two substances, became each time greater than it had been in the preceding experiment. Whence did the quicklime acquire the fixable air which caused these effervescences? Was it from the acid? *See* POTT's *Dissertation on Quicklime.*

(a) Calcareous earths may be combined with acids, with which they form neutralized earthy salts. *See* SALTS. They also readily unite with fixable air, in which state of combination they are always found native. When uncombined with fixable air, or in the state of quicklime, they may be combined with water, forming lime-water. *See* WATER (LIME), AIR (FIXABLE), CREAM *of* LIME, *and* QUICKLIME. In this uncombined state they also may be united in some degree with sulphur, forming a kind of hepar of sulphur, and imperfectly with oleaginous substances forming kinds of soaps.

Calcareous earth, although infusible by fire *(see the above note* [y]*)*, may be rendered fusible and vitrescible by addition of fixed alkaline salt, of borax, of sedative salt, of salt of urine, of metallic calxes, of gypseous and argillaceous earths, of fusible spars, and according to Mr Pott, of sparry quartz, of glass gall, and of fixed ammoniac. Mr Gellert, in his Table of Solutions, places calcareous earth amongst the substances incapable of uniting with gypseous earths. Nevertheless the experiments of Mr. Brandt and of Mr D'Arcet evince the fusibility of calcareous earths mixed with gypsum. This however may be observed, that I have found from experiments, that such mixtures are fusible only when exposed suddenly to a violent fire, and that by a gradually raised fire they are calcinable into quicklime. The cause of which seems to be, that the vitriolic acid of the gypsum is necessary to the fusion, and that this acid, by a long continued heat not sufficiently intense to occasion a fusion of these two earths, may be dissipated, leaving its calcareous basis behind, which together with the calcareous earth forms an unfusible mass or quicklime.

earth of gypſum, when ſeparated from the vitriolic acid, does not appear to be different from pure calcareous earth, we refer to the articles GYPSUM, SELENITES, *and* EARTH (CALCAREOUS)

CCL EARTH (MERCURIAL) Mercurial earth is a ſubſtance, which, according to Beccher and other chemiſts, enters into the compoſition of many bodies, particularly the metallic, together with *vitrifiable earth*, and phlogiſton, which that chemiſt calls the *inflammable earth* But the exiſtence of this mercurial earth has not yet been ſatisfactorily demonſtrated Metals and marine acid, of which alſo Beccher ſuppoſes the mercurial earth to be a conſtituent part, do indeed preſent ſome phenomena which may induce us to ſuſpect that theſe ſubſtances contain a principle different from all thoſe which we know But theſe phenomena are not ſufficient to eſtabliſh with certainty the exiſtence of this principle *See what is ſaid on this ſubject under the articles* ACID (MARINE), MERCURIFICATION, METALS, *and* METALLISATION

CCLI EARTH (VEGETABLE) *(b)*

CCLII EARTH (VITRIFIABLE) The earth ſo called by chemiſts is the pureſt, ſimpleſt, and moſt elementary of all known earths As we have mentioned all the eſſential properties of this earth under the general article EARTH, we refer for theſe properties to that article We ſhall only obſerve here, that the ſtones formed principally by the union of the parts of this earth, and therefore called vitrifiable ſtones, are eaſily diſtinguiſhed from all the others by their hardneſs, which is ſo great, that they cannot be cut by ſteel tools, and that they can elicit ſparks from ſteel They have alſo the property of giving ſparks of light when one of them is ſtruck againſt another, but it is then an internal fire, and ignited ſparks are not emitted, as when they are ſtruck by ſteel This property of giving light by percuſſion alſo belongs to glaſs, porcelaine, and other vitrified matters. It ſeems to be a phenomenon depending on electricity

(b) EARTH (VEGETABLE) From numerous experiments made by Wallerius we find that earths or aſhes of vegetables have not all the ſame chemical properties, but may be reduced into three kinds or claſſes The firſt claſs is the earth obtained by burning ſoft, ſpongy, and farinaceous plants It is partly ſoluble by vitriolic acids It is more fuſible by fire in proportion as the plant from which it has been obtained was more nouriſhing Thus the aſhes of rye, barley, oats, muſtard, and eſpecially thoſe of wheat and rice, were eaſily fuſible, forming green tranſparent glaſſes This fuſion is not occaſioned by any mixture of alkaline ſalt, for no ſuch ſalt could be obtained from the aſhes of the above-mentioned grains by lixiviation The ſecond claſs of vegetable earths is produced by burning the harder and leſs ſucculent plants This earth is more ſoluble than the former in nitrous and marine acids, but is leſs ſoluble in vitriolic acid This earth, after lixiviation, ſtill abſorbs moiſture from the air It is alſo fuſible by fire, but not ſo eaſily as the former earth, and is leſs fuſible in proportion to the hardneſs of the plant The third claſs of vegetable earth is that which is obtained by burning wood This earth is calcareous, and is more difficultly fuſible in proportion as the wood from which it was obtained was harder Accordingly, it has been obſerved by manufacturers of glaſs, that aſhes of the hardeſt woods make the moſt unfuſible glaſs Garden mould, which conſiſts chiefly of the earth of decayed vegetables, was alſo found to be fuſible by fire *See the Swediſh Memoirs for the year* 1760 By putrefaction of vegetable ſubſtances, a calcareous earth is ſaid to be obtainable

Vitrifiable earth, when pulverised into very fine parts, and moistened with water, absorbs but a very small quantity of this liquid, and forms a paste which has considerable adhesion, but no ductility. When it is made thin by water, it pours like an oily or viscid matter: when it is of a thick consistence, it does not preserve the form given to it, but it sinks and collapses: it also dries very quickly and easily. If, on the contrary, this finely ground vitrifiable matter be left at rest under water, its parts will unite and adhere together so strongly, that a mass shall be formed almost as hard as a stone. Hence when vitrifiable stones are ground with water, the matter must be continually agitated and stirred, and the mill must be turned without interruption; for if they are left but a little at rest, they harden, and adhere so strongly to the bottom of the mill, that the mill-stone cannot without difficulty be again set in motion. This inconvenience may be much diminished by mixing the vitrifiable earth to be ground, with different earths, calcareous or argillaceous.

No vitrifiable stone or earth is soluble in any acid, unless its nature has been changed by having been intimately united with some other substance; as, for instance, by fusion with a sufficient quantity of fixed alkali: but it cannot then be considered as pure vitrifiable earth, as it has not then the properties of that earth.

As some stones externally resemble vitrifiable stones, and which also resist the action of acids, although they are not vitrifiable, the proof by acids is not sufficient to ascertain the nature of these stones. To this proof must also be added that of hardness, which is the most decisive. Many impure and mixed vitrifiable earths and stones differ from each other by their colors, and other accidental particulars depending on the heterogeneous matters with which they are united.

Nature presents to us many mixed earths and stones, or such as are composed of many kinds of different earths, as the vitrifiable, calcareous, talky, argillaceous, gypseous or selenitic, and even the pyritous or metallic. But we cannot enter into these details, which are the object of mineralogy. We shall observe, that when an accurate examination of these compound bodies is required, the nature and proportions of the component parts may be discovered by submitting them successively to the decisive proofs which we have mentioned under the articles of the principal kinds of earths and stones, by which their nature may be discovered and ascertained. *See in particular for the vitrifiable earths and stones, the general article* EARTH, *and the word* VITRIFICATION.

CCLIII. EARTH-WORMS (c).

(c) EARTH-WORMS. Earth-worms, when moistened with wine, or with vinous spirits, to prevent their putrefaction, and set in a cellar in a wide-mouthed vessel, are in a few days almost wholly resolved into a slimy liquor. Stahl supposes that they are impregnated with a nitrous salt which they receive from the putrid matters amongst which they live. When this liquamen of worms is mixed with a little fixed alkali, and, after the evaporation, is set to shoot, the crystals are nothing else than nitre. Six drams of extract were obtained by ardent spirit from four ounces of worms; and from the same quantity of these, one ounce, six drams, and a scruple of extract, by means of water. Thirty-two ounces of dried earth-worms yielded, by distillation, thirteen ounces and a half of volatile urinous spirit, one ounce of concrete volatile salt, four ounces and a half of empyreumatic oil, and eight ounces of a residuum, from which were obtained by calcination and lixiviation, an ounce and a half of fixed alkali. *Neumann.*

CCLIV.

CCLIV. E A U D E L U C E Eau de luce is a kind of volatile, liquid ſoap, of a ſtrong, penetrating ſmell

This liquor is compoſed of the liquid volatile alkali made from ſal ammoniac with quicklime, and of the rectified oil of amber, ſo mixed together as to produce a white milky liquor

Eau de luce cannot be prepared without certain management, for if the volatile ſpirit of ſal ammoniac and rectified oil of amber be ſimply mixed and ſhook together, a milky liquor will be produced, ſuch as is required, but this color diſappears ſoon when the liquor is allowed to reſt, either becauſe the volatile alkali compleatly diſſolves the oil of amber when in ſmall quantity, or becauſe this oil diſengages itſelf from the volatile alkali, and floats a-part when in conſiderable quantity In both caſes the liquor becomes clear and tranſparent, but the milky color is required in eau de luce By the following receipt excellent eau de luce may be made

Take four ounces of rectified ſpirit of wine, and in it diſſolve ten or twelve grains of white ſoap, filtrate this ſolution, then diſſolve in it a dram of rectified oil of amber, and filtrate again, mix as much of this ſolution with the ſtrongeſt volatile ſpirit of ſal ammoniac, in a cryſtal-glaſs bottle, as when ſufficiently ſhook, ſhall produce a beautiful milky liquor If upon its ſurface be formed a cream, ſome more of the oily ſpirit of wine ought to be added

This receipt is given by the author of the French edition of the London Diſpenſatory The receipt given in that work is very good, but is much improved by the obſervations, experiments, and remarks made by that author.

CCLV E D U L C O R A T I O N. Edulcoration is, properly ſpeaking, the rendering ſubſtances more mild Chemical edulcoration conſiſts almoſt always in taking acids and other ſaline matters from ſubſtances to which they adhere, and this is effected by waſhing in much water The waſhing of diaphoretic antimony, and of the powder of algaroth, till the water comes off from theſe ſubſtances quite pure, may be given as inſtances of edulcoration

In Pharmacy, juleps, potions, and other medicines, are ſaid to be *edulcorated*, by adding ſugar or ſyrup

CCLVI E F F E R V E S C E N C E Effervèſcence is an inteſtine motion excited betwixt the parts of two bodies of different natures, when they reciprocally diſſolve each other Effervèſcences are commonly accompanied with bubbles, vapors, ſmall jets of the liquid, and noiſe or hiſſing All theſe phenomena are occaſioned by the air which diſengages itſelf in almoſt all ſolutions Frequently alſo effervèſcences are accompanied with a conſiderable heat, ſometimes exceeding that of boiling water This heat is occaſioned by the colliſion of the parts during their union The degree of heat produced in effervèſcences is proportionable to the activity with which bodies are diſſolved, to the quickneſs with which the ſolution is made, and to the quantity of ſubſtances reacting upon each other

The moſt ſenſible effervèſcences are obſerved in the combination of concentrated mineral acids with calcareous earths, alkaline ſalts, metallic ſubſtances, and oily matters

Generally the ſubſtances which contain a ſenſible quantity of inflammable principle are thoſe which in ſimilar circumſtances produce the moſt heat in

effervèſcing

effervescing with acids Of all acids, the nitrous produces the greatest heat, when it dissolves these bodies

Thus, for instance, the heat arising from a solution of calcareous earth in nitrous acid is not nearly so great as that which arises from a solution of a metallic substance in the same acid, although these solutions are performed equally fast, and the heat which is produced by the combination of nitrous acid with oils is so great, that a flame is quickly produced

Formerly the word *fermentation* was commonly applied to effervescences, but now that word is confined to the motion which is naturally excited in animal and vegetable matters, and from which new combinations amongst their principles take place This distinction is very proper, for a simple effervescence is very different from a true fermentation *See* FERMENTATION

CCLVII EFFLORESCENCE By this expression chemists denote what happens to certain bodies, upon the surface of which a kind of meal or powder is formed

Efflorescence is occasioned either by decomposition or by drying. That which happens to Cobalt, and most martial pyrites, is of the former kind, and the efflorescence observed on crystals of marine alkali, of Glauber's salt, of alum, of green and blue vitriols, and of several other salts, is of the latter kind

CCLVIII EGGS The eggs of hens, of birds in general, and of several other animals, are composed of several distinct substances, 1 Of a shell or external coat, which in the eggs of birds has a certain hardness and consistence, although it is brittle. The matter of this shell is a fine, absorbent earth, soluble in acids, hence if these eggs be steeped in vinegar, or any other acid, they are rendered quite soft, because the acid dissolves and takes away all the earth of their shells. (*d*)

The parts of this earth are bound together by a small quantity of gelatinous matter This matter becomes very sensible by an empyreumatic animal smell, and by the black color which shells acquire when exposed to fire

The shell of an egg is lined internally with a very white, fine, and strong membrane It resembles a very fine skin, and is entirely of animal nature

These external coverings contain the substance of the egg, which is of two kinds, namely, a lymphatic, white, transparent, gelatinous, viscous, and gluey substance, called *the white of the egg*, and another substance also gelatinous, but almost opake, yellow, less gluey and viscous than the white This latter, which is called *the yolk*, is of a spherical form, and is surrounded by the white To the yolk is annexed a small portion of white gelatinous matter, thicker and tougher than the rest of the white in which the embryo is contained.

We do not intend here to examine anatomically the uses of these several parts of the egg, we will consider them only relatively to their chemical properties and principles As eggs contain the embryo of the animal, and the nourishment proper for it in its first increase, they are proper to give as an example of the analysis of animal seed

(*d*) The shells of eggs are not only absorbent, that is, soluble by acids, but also calcareous, or convertible into quicklime The earth of the shells, and also the earth obtained by calcination of the other parts of the eggs, are fusible and vitrescible by fire. *See* EARTH (ANIMAL)

The white of an egg cannot be diſſolved by acids or by ſpirit of wine This latter ſolvent, far from dividing it, on the contrary coagulates it, by taking from it a great part of its water which renders it liquid

The white of an egg is ſoluble and miſcible with water, but difficultly, becauſe of its viſcidity Spirit of wine poured into water which keeps it diſſolved ſeparates it, and precipitates it in form of a curd In this reſpect, the white of an egg reſembles gummy, mucilaginous, and gelatinous matters It is, in fact, a matter entirely of the nature of animal jellies, but of that kind which are coagulable by heat The white of an egg, expoſed to a leſs heat than that of boiling water, is coagulated, hardened, and its tranſparency is almoſt entirely changed to a milky white color This ſubſtance contains no other principles which are volatile with the heat of boiling water, than water, for if whites of eggs be diſtilled in a water-bath, nothing but water is obtained While they loſe this water, they become more and more hard and horny, they reſume their tranſparency, and acquire a yellow-reddiſh color, ſo that when they are dried as much as poſſible, they perfectly reſemble horn

If they are to be further analyſed, they muſt be put into a retort, and expoſed to a naked fire then fetid empyreumatic oil with much volatile alkali is obtained, and in the retort, when the diſtillation is finiſhed, a coal is left like that of other animal matters. From this analyſis we ſee that the white of an egg is a perfectly animaliſed ſubſtance *See* JELLY (ANIMAL)

The yolk of an egg is chiefly compoſed of a gelatinous matter like the white, for it alſo coagulates and hardens by heat, but it alſo contains a conſiderable quantity of mild fat oil, which is in ſome meaſure ſuperabundant, and not combined, and, in ſhort, in the ſame ſtate as thoſe oils which may be obtained from vegetable emulſive ſeeds by expreſſion Thus the raw yolk of an egg when mixed with water is not entirely diſſolved, as the white is, but forms with it, on account of this oily part, a white milky liquor or emulſion This animal emulſion is vulgarly called *hen's milk*

This ſuperabundant oil of the yolk of an egg may be ſeparated from it, like that of moſt vegetable grains, by expreſſion But to make this operation ſucceſsful, the yolk of an egg ought to be deprived as much as is poſſible of its water For this purpoſe, the eggs are to be previouſly hardened, and the yolks are to be ſeparated, dried, and even roaſted in a proper veſſel, till they become ſomewhat ſoftened by the ſweating out of the oil, they are then to be put into a preſs, and a fat, unctuous, yellowiſh, and ſufficiently mild oil is procured, which readily fixes itſelf in the cold This oil has the ſmell of roaſted or fried eggs, from the drying and roaſting given to the yolks before the expreſſion Probably this oil might be obtained by a ſlower and more careful drying without roaſting, and conſequently without any change or ſmell

From this quantity of ſuperabundant oil in yolks of eggs, we may perceive a remarkable reſemblance betwixt the eggs of animals and vegetable ſeeds This oil is found in all ſeminal matters probably for the ſame reaſon *See* OILS (SWEET EXPRESSED)

As all eggs in general are compoſed of a very nouriſhing ſubſtance, and that thoſe of many animals have a very agreeable taſte, they have been much uſed as aliment They are alſo employed in medicine and in the arts The white of an egg is an ingredient in collyriums and cataplaſms for diſeaſes of the eyes; and

both

both the white and yolk in emollient and resolvent cataplasms The oil of eggs is softening, relaxing, and lubricating It is employed either singly, or formed into a pomatum with fat matters, in burns, chaps, contractions, and other similar diseases

The white of an egg, from its solubility in water, and from its coagulating by fire or in spirituous liquors, is very successfully employed in pharmacy, for many uses of the kitchen, and for clarifying the juices of plants, whey, sugar, syrups, &c *See* FILTRATION

The white of an egg alone forms a varnish very white and very shining, which is applied to several kinds of work, and particularly to pictures Lastly, the yolk of an egg, from its oily and viscid parts, is a proper intermediate substance for the mixture by trituration of oils with watery liquors, so as to form emulsions Several good remarks are found upon this subject in Mr. Beaumé's Treatise on Pharmacy (*e*)

CCLIX ELECAMPANE (*f*)

CCLX ELEMENTS Those bodies are called by chemists *elements*, which are so simple, that they cannot by any known method be decomposed, or even altered, and which also enter as principles, or constituent parts, into the combination of other bodies, which are therefore called compound bodies

The bodies in which this simplicity has been observed are fire, air, water, and the purest earth, for by the most complete and accurate analyses which have been made, nothing has been ever ultimately produced but some one, or more, of these four substances, according to the nature of the decomposed bodies

These substances, although reputed simple, may possibly not be so, and may even result from the union of several other more simple substances but as experience teaches us nothing on this subject, we may without inconvenience, and we ought to consider, in chemistry, fire, air, water, and earth, as simple bodies, because they really act as such in all chemical operations

The elements are also called by chemists *primary principles*. *See* PRINCIPLES, FIRE, AIR, WATER, and EARTH

CCLXI ELIQUATION (*g*)

CCLXII ELUTRIATION (*h*)

(*e*) Mr Reaumur found that eggs might be preserved during months or years, by being covered with mutton suet, or any other fat substance, which, by filling up the pores of the shell, excluded the air, which is necessary to putrefaction

(*f*) ELECAMPANE From thirty-two ounces of the roots of elecampane were obtained, by distillation, three scruples and a half of concrete oil, similar in many, but not in all its properties to camphor This concrete oil is soluble in spirit of wine. Geoffroy remarks, that it resides in the exterior part of the root, near to the bark From an ounce of the dry root six drams and a half of extract may be obtained by water, and from the same quantity two drams and a half by spirit. *Neuman*

(*g*) ELIQUATION This is an operation by which a more fusible substance is separated from one less fusible, by means of a heat sufficiently intense to melt the former, but not the latter Thus an allay of copper and lead may be separated by applying a heat which shall melt the lead, but not the copper

(*h*) ELUTRIATION is an operation performed by washing solid substances with water, stirring them well together, and hastily pouring off the water, while the lighter part remains suspended in the agitated water, that it may be thereby separated from the heavier part. By this operation metallic ores are cleansed from earth, stones, and other lighter unmetallic particles adhering to them.

CCLXIII EMERALD (i)

CCLXIV EMERY (k)

CCLXV EMPYREUMA Empyreuma is a ſmell proceeding from burnt animal and vegetable matters, when they are expoſed to a quick fire, particularly in cloſe veſſels

Empyreuma is the peculiar ſmell of burnt oils No other but oily ſubſtances can produce it As all vegetable and animal matters contain oil, and as no other ſubſtance contains it, hence the empyreumatic ſmell muſt be peculiar to burnt animal and vegetable matters, and hence alſo we may diſcover oil wherever it may be by this ſmell, which is ſo diſtinguiſhable, that it is very ſenſible even when the quantity of oil is too ſmall to be diſcovered by any other method If then we perceive an empyreumatic ſmell when we burn a ſubſtance in cloſe veſſels, we may conclude that this ſubſtance contains oil If, on the contrary, no empyreuma be perceived, we may be aſſured that the ſubſtance does not contain oil

CCLXVI EMULSION An emulſion is a watery liquor, in which ſome oily matter is diſperſed and diffuſed (but not diſſolved), by the intervention of a mucilaginous or gelatinous ſubſtance

The ſtate of the oil in emulſions is the cauſe why they are opake, and of a milky-white color, for this milky appearance is given to all tranſparent bodies by others that have not a very diſtinct color, when they are mutually interpoſed and divided to a certain degree

Nevertheleſs, water and oil ſlightly adhere together in emulſions, by the intervention of the mucilaginous matter, for oil agitated with water gives but a momentary appearance of an emulſion, and only during the agitation When it is left to reſt, the oil preſently riſes to the ſurface.

All vegetable and animal ſubſtances containing an uncombined oil, and mucilage or jelly, being triturated with water, yield emulſions

Moſt ſeeds and grains, all gum-reſins, gummy and reſinous juices, and yolks of eggs, are capable of forming emulſions with water Laſtly, the milky juices of plants, milk, and the chyle of animals, ought to be conſidered as natural emulſions

(i) EMERALD, *Smaragdus*, is a precious ſtone, contained by ſeveral unequal ſides and obtuſe angles, forming irregular priſms. Its color is green with a moderately ſtrong heat it becomes blue, but recovers its original green color when cold By expoſure to collected ſolar heat, emeralds were rendered white and of various colors, and ſoon afterwards were fuſed, by which they loſt part of their weight and hardneſs *See* DIAMONDS. Emeralds have the property of ſhining in the dark after having been heated They are the fourth in hardneſs from diamonds, nevertheleſs they are ſuſceptible of impreſſion from a file Emeralds may be imitated by adding forty-eight grains of pulveriſed calcined verdegriſe, and eight grains of martial crocus, to four ounces of minium and two ounces of pure rock-cryſtal, previouſly calcined and levigated, and by keeping that mixture fuſed during twenty-four hours

(k) EMERY *Smiris* Emery is a very refractory mineral containing a ſmall portion of iron It is exceedingly hard, and is therefore uſed for the poliſhing of metals, glaſs, and hard ſtones Some pieces of emery contain ſmall ſpecks of gold, and of copper. The mineral called by alchemiſts *ſmiris Hiſpanica*, and employed to adulterate gold, is with probability believed to be the metal now called platina

CCLXVII. E N A M E L. Enamel is in general a vitrified matter, betwixt the parts of which is diſperſed ſome unvitrified matter: hence enamel ought to have all the properties of glaſs excepting tranſparency. Enamels then are opake glaſſes, and their opacity and colors proceed from the unvitrified matter which they contain. The unvitrified matters which give opacity and various colors to enamels, are almoſt always metallic calxes. Receipts for making ſeveral kinds of enamel may be found in ſeveral books, particularly in Neri's Treatiſe on the Art of Making Glaſs, with Notes by Merret and Kunkel.

Enamels ought to be very fuſible. They are employed to color or to paint ſeveral kinds of work which are made by great heat. The white enamel is uſed to cover the earthen ware called *Delf*, to which it gives the appearance of porcelain. With the other colored enamels this Delf ware, porcelain, and alſo the white enamel, are painted. *See* DELF-WARE. *(l)*

CCLXVIII. E N S M A R T I S, and E N S V E N E R I S. Theſe Latin names are given to the flowers of iron and of copper made with ſal ammoniac, or rather to theſe two metals ſublimed by this ſalt. *See* FLOWERS.

(l) Enamels are glaſſes containing ſome opake ſubſtance, that is either unvitrifiable or incapable of being vitrified with the degree of heat requiſite for the fuſion of ordinary glaſs. Of the latter ſort are almoſt all the enamels uſed, they being moſtly compoſed of glaſs mixed with metallic calxes, all which, not excepting the calx of tin, by more intenſe heat might be reduced to tranſparent glaſſes. The white vitreous compoſition which is the baſis of all enamels is prepared, according to Neri, by melting together a hundred parts of frit of calcined flints, one part of pure ſalt of tartar, and a hundred parts of a calx of lead and tin. This calx is prepared by calcining together equal parts of tin and lead, and reducing the ſubſtance ſo calcined to a very fine powder, by bruiſing it, paſſing it through a ſieve, boiling it in water, decanting the water in which the finer parts are ſuſpended, evaporating the water, and drying the powder, and by repeating the calcination and ſubſequent operations upon the groſſer particles, till they become as fine as the former. This compoſition when ſlightly fuſed is to be reduced to a powder, and formed into all the various colored enamels, by adding to it coloring ſubſtances. Thus by adding to ſix pounds of this compoſition, forty-eight grains of magneſia, a *fine white enamel* may be prepared; an *azure blue enamel*, by adding to the ſame quantity three ounces of zaffre, and ſixty grains of calcined copper; a *turquois blue enamel*, by adding three ounces of calcined copper, ninety-ſix grains of zaffre, and forty-eight grains of magneſia; a *green enamel*, by adding three ounces of calcined copper and ſixty grains of ſcales of iron; a *ſhining black enamel*, by adding three ounces of zaffre and as much magneſia, or by adding ſix ounces of red tartar and three ounces of the ſame magneſia; a *purple enamel*, by adding three ounces of magneſia; a *yellow enamel*, by adding three ounces of tartar and ſeventy-two grains of magneſia; *a ſea-green or beryl-colored enamel*, by adding three ounces of calcined braſs and ſixty grains of zaffre; and a *violet-colored enamel*, by adding two ounces of magneſia and forty-eight grains of calcined copper. Theſe are the receipts given by Neri, approved by Kunkel, and now ſucceſsfully uſed. The intenſity and continuance of the heat muſt be attended to, as the colors both of enamels and of the tranſparent glaſſes imitating colored precious ſtones, eſpecially of thoſe which contain magneſia, depend much on theſe circumſtances. White enamels may be compoſed of other ſubſtances beſides calx of tin. Merret propoſes to ſubſtitute regulus of antimony. Calcined bones, and perhaps other white earths, may be uſed for the ſame purpoſe. Mr D'Arcet found that gypſum mixed with white clay, or with clay and hard ſpar, formed very beautiful enamels. Perhaps ſome of theſe enamels would form preferable glazings to that made with calx of tin, for covering thoſe kinds of earthen ware which require, in the baking, greater heat than is ſuitable to the common enamel.

CCLXIX. ESSAY. Eſſays are chemical operations made in ſmall, to determine the quantity of metal or other matter which is contained in minerals, or to diſcover the value or purity of any maſs of gold or ſilver

We ſhall treat ſucceſſively of each kind of eſſay

CCLXX ESSAY *of* ORES. Before eſſays of ores can be well made, a preliminary knowledge of the nature of the ſeveral metallic minerals ought to be attained Each metal has its proper and improper ores, which have peculiar characters and appearances hence perſons, accuſtomed to ſee them, know pretty nearly, by the appearance, weight, and other obvious qualities, what metal is contained in a mineral A good eſſayer ought to be very intelligent in this matter, that he may at once know what the proper operations are which are requiſite to the eſſay of any given mineral. Some remarks may be found on this ſubject under the article ORES.

As metals are very unequally diſtributed in their ores, we ſhould be apt to make falſe and deceitful eſſays, if we did not uſe all poſſible precautions that the proportionable quantity of metal produced by any eſſay ſhall be nearly the medium contained in the whole ore This is effected by taking pieces of the mineral from the ſeveral veins of the mine, if there be ſeveral, or from different places of the ſame vein All theſe minerals are to be ſhook together with their matrixes The whole is to be well mixed together, and a convenient quantity of this mixture is to be taken for the eſſay This is called the *lotting* of the ore

As eſſays, particularly the firſt, are generally made in ſmall, eſſayers have very ſmall weights correſponding to the weights uſed in the great, that is, to the *quintal or hundred pounds weight, to pounds, ounces, drams, &c* The eſſay quintal and its ſubdiviſions vary according to the difference of weights in different countries, and this occaſions ſome confuſion, when theſe weights are to be adjuſted to each other Tables of theſe weights are found in treatiſes of eſſaying, and particularly in that written by Schlutter, and tranſlated and rendered more complete by Hellot, which contains all the details neceſſary for the ſubject

The cuſtom is to take, for the eſſay quintal, a real weight of a gros, or dram, which in France is equal to 72 grains, but as the whole dram repreſents 100 pounds, each grain repreſents a pound and a fraction of a pound, and hence ſome difficulty and confuſion ariſe in making the ſubdiviſions A better method is that of Mr Hellot, which is to make the fictitious or eſſay quintal equal to a hundred real grains, and then each grain repreſents a real pound This eſſay quintal is ſufficiently exact for ores of lead, tin, copper, iron, antimony, biſmuth, and mercury But for ores of ſilver and gold another repreſentation is convenient, for theſe metals, as Mr Hellot ſays, are generally in ſo ſmall quantity, that the button or ſmall piece of metal obtained in the eſſay could not be accurately weighed, if a hundred real grains were made to repreſent a quintal, and the difficulty of ſeparating the gold from ſo ſmall a quantity would be ſtill greater Theſe motives have induced Mr Hellot to uſe for theſe ores a fictitious quintal ſixteen times bigger, that is, equal to 1600 real grains, which repreſent 1600 ounces, that is, 100 lb or quintal The ounce being repreſented by a grain, its ſeveral ſubdiviſions muſt be repreſented by fractions of a grain

Thus

Thus 12 grains of the fictitious quintal correſpond with $\frac{5}{48}$ of a real grain *(m)*, and this latter quantity may be accurately weighed in eſſay ballances, which when well made, are ſenſible to a much leſs weight.

When a quintal of an ore to be eſſayed has been weighed, and lotted, as we deſcribed above, it is to be roaſted in a teſt under a muffle. It is to be waſhed, if neceſſary, and, in ſhort, the ſame operations are to be made in ſmall which are uſually done in great. Additions alſo are to be made, and in proper proportions, according to the peculiar nature of the ore. The fluxes generally mixed with the ore in eſſays are three, four, or five parts of black flux, one, two, or three parts of calcined borax, and one half of that quantity of decrepitated common ſalt. The more refractory the ore is, the more neceſſary is the addition of theſe fluxes: then the whole mixture is to be fuſed either in a forge, or in a melting or eſſay furnace.

To make eſſays well, all poſſible attention and accuracy are to be employed. This object cannot be too much attended to, for the leaſt inaccuracy in weighing, or loſs of the ſmalleſt quantity of matter, might cauſe errors, ſo much greater, as the diſproportion betwixt the weights employed and thoſe repreſented is greater. The moſt minute accuracy therefore is neceſſary in theſe operations. For inſtance, the eſſay ballances ought to be ſmall, and exceedingly juſt. The ore ought not to be weighed till it has been reduced to groſs powder fit for roaſting, becauſe ſome of it is always loſt in this pulverization. When the ore is roaſted, it ought to be covered with an inverted teſt, becauſe moſt ores are apt to crackle and diſperſe, when firſt heated. To make the fuſion good and compleat, the preciſe degree of fire which is requiſite ought to be employed, and when it is finiſhed, the crucible ought to be ſtruck two or three times with ſome inſtrument to facilitate the diſengagement of the parts of the regulus from the ſcoria, and to occaſion their deſcent and union into one button of metal. The crucible ought not to be broken, nor its contents examined till it is perfectly cold.

Upon breaking the crucible, we may know that the fuſion has been good, if the ſcoria be neat, compact, and equal, if it has not overflowed or penetrated the crucible, if it contain no metallic grains, and if its ſurface be ſmooth, and hollowed in the middle. The regulus or button ought to be well collected, without holes, or bubbles, and to have a neat convex ſurface, it is then to be ſeparated from the ſcoria, well ſcraped and cleaned, and, laſtly, is to be weighed. If the operation has been well made, its weight ſhows the quantity of metal which every real quintal of ore will yield in the great. If the perfect ſucceſs of this eſſay be in any reſpect doubtful, it ought to be repeated, but the beſt method at all times is to make ſeveral eſſays of the ſame ore. Some ſmall differences are always found, however well the eſſays may have been made. By taking the medium of the reſults of the ſeveral operations, we may approach, as nearly as poſſible, the true product of the ore.

Laſtly, as mines are not worked, nor founderies eſtabliſhed (which cannot be done without conſiderable expence) till the ore has been eſſayed, ten or twelve

(m) The pounds, of which a hundred are here ſuppoſed to make a quintal, are called Paris pounds, one of which contains 9216 troy grains. See WEIGHTS.

real

real pounds of the ore ought to be previously essayed, and essayers ought to be furnished with necessary furnaces and instruments for these larger essays

We now proceed to give some examples of essays of ores To essay a lead ore, for instance, which is not very refractory, let one or more quintals of this ore be grosly powdered, and roasted in a test till no more sulphureous vapors be exhaled, and then reduced to a finer powder, it is then to be accurately mixed with twice its weight of black flux, a fourth part of its weight of clean filings of iron and of borax These proportions are given by Mr Cramer The mixture is to be put into a good crucible, or rather into a test, it is then to be covered with a thickness of two or three fingers of decrepitated sea-salt, the crucible is to be closed, and placed in a melting furnace, which is to be filled with unlighted charcoal, so that the top of the crucible shall be covered with it Lighted coals are then to be thrown upon the unkindled charcoal, and the whole is left to kindle slowly, till the crucible be red-hot, soon after which a hissing noise proceeds from the crucible, which is occasioned by the reduction of the lead the same degree of fire is to be maintained while this noise continues, and is afterwards to be suddenly encreased, so as to make a perfect fusion, in which state it is to be continued during a quarter of an hour, after which it is to be extinguished, and the operation is then finished

The filings of iron are added to the mixture, to absorb the sulphur, a certain quantity of which generally remains united with the lead ore, notwithstanding the roasting We need not fear lest this metal should unite with the lead and alter its purity, because although the sulphur should not hinder it, these two metals cannot be united The refractory quality of the iron does not impede the fusion, for the union it forms with the sulphur renders it so fusible, that it becomes itself a kind of flux

This addition of iron in the essay of lead ores would be useless, if the ores were sufficiently roasted, so that no sulphur should remain

Lead ores generally contain some silver, and sometimes a considerable quantity of it, wherefore, after the ore has been essayed, and the regulus of lead collected and weighed, it ought to be tested, to discover the quantity of silver it contains, and as sometimes these lead ores contain also gold, the button of silver remaining upon the cupel ought to be essayed by parting, to ascertain the quantity of gold, if there be any

The details for the essays of all other ores and minerals are too numerous to be inserted in this work. They are themselves the subject of several books, which may be consulted The best of these books are Cramer's Art of Essaying, (*Ars Docimastica*), and Schlutter's Work translated into French by Mr Hellot We shall find many things relating to this matter under the articles, ORES, SMELTING *of* ORES (*n*)

(*n*) The essaying of ores is a matter of such importance to chemistry, to arts, and to the wealth of nations, that we shall endeavor to supply what the author of the Dictionary has omitted on this subject, by adding to the several articles of the ores of metals the methods of essaying these ores *See* ORES We shall here only observe in general, that the methods generally practised for essaying ores of imperfect metals, and semimetals especially, are insufficient to procure the whole quantity of metal contained in ores, or even so much as is obtained in the smelting of large quantities of ores, and that therefore the result of essays is not to be considered as the precise quantity contained in an ore, but generally

CCLXXI ESSAY *of the* VALUE *of* SILVER, to examine its purity, or the quantity of alloy mixed with it The common method of examining the purity of silver, is by mixing it with a quantity of lead proportionable to the quantity of imperfect metals with which it is supposed to be alloyed, by testing this mixture, and afterwards by weighing the remaining button of silver The loss of weight which the silver suffers by cupellation shews the quantity of imperfect metals which it contained

We may hence perceive, that the essay of silver is nothing else than the refining of it by cupellation The only difference betwixt these two operations is, that when silver is tested merely for the purpose of refining it, its value is generally known, and it is therefore mixed with the due proportion of lead, and tested without any necessity of attending to the loss of weight it sustains during the operation, whereas in the essay all possible methods ought to be employed to ascertain precisely this loss of weight The first of these operations, or the mere refining of silver, is made in the great, in the smelting of silver ores, and in mints for making money *See* REFINING The second operation is never made but in small, because the expences of small operations are less than of great, and the requisite accuracy is more easily attended to The last operation is our present subject, and is to be performed in the following manner

We suppose, first, that the mass or ingot of silver, of which an essay is to be made, consists of twelve parts perfectly equal, and these twelve parts are called penny-weights Thus if the ingot of silver be an ounce weight, each of these twelve parts will be $\frac{1}{12}$ of an ounce, or if it be a mark, each of these will be $\frac{1}{12}$ of a mark, &c Hence if the mass of silver be free from all allay, it is called silver of twelve penny-weights, if it contains $\frac{1}{12}$ of its weight of allay, it is called silver of eleven penny-weights, if $\frac{2}{12}$ of its weight be allay, it is called silver of ten penny-weights, and these ten penny-weights or parts of pure silver are called *fine penny-weights*

We ought to observe here concerning these penny-weights, that essayers give also the name *penny-weight* to a weight equal to twenty-four real grains, which latter real penny-weight must not be confounded with the former, which is only ideal and proportional, and such a confusion is the more likely to take place, as this

generally only as an inaccurate approximation to that quantity Mr Gellert ascribes one cause of the want of success of these operations to the alkaline salts employed as fluxes to the ores, by which most metallic calxes are partially soluble, but more especially so, when any of the sulphur of the ore remains, which, by uniting with these salts, forms a hepar of sulphur, which is the most powerful of all solvents He proposes therefore to omit the black flux, and other alkaline salts, and to add nothing to the ore but powder of charcoal, and some fusible glass This method, he says, he learned from Mr Cramer, and has himself used with much success in the essays of iron and copper but finding that other imperfect metallic substances could not sustain the heat necessary to effect the fusion and vitrification of the unmetallic parts of the ore without being partly dissipated, he found it necessary to add in the essays of these latter metallic matters some borax, by which the fusion might be completed with less heat As we consider this as a considerable improvement in the art of essaying ores, we shall, to the articles of the several ores, add not only the processes commonly prescribed, but also these of Mr. Gellert, according to the method here mentioned I have sometimes essayed ores very successfully by this method, from which I could obtain little, if any metal, by means of the black flux *See* ORES

ideal penny-weight is alſo, like the former, divided into twenty-four ideal grains, which are called *fine grains*

An ingot of fine ſilver, or ſilver of twelve penny-weights, contains then 288 fine grains, if this ingot contains $\frac{1}{288}$ part of allay, it is ſaid to be ſilver of eleven penny-weight and twenty-three grains, if it contains $\frac{2}{288}$ of allay, it is called ſilver of eleven penny-weight and twenty-two grains, if it contains $\frac{14}{288}$, it is called ſilver of eleven penny-weight and ten grains, and ſo on Laſtly, the fine grain has alſo its fractions, as $\frac{1}{2}$, $\frac{1}{4}$ of a grain, &c

As eſſays to diſcover the value of ſilver are always made in ſmall, eſſayers only take a ſmall portion of an ingot for the trial, and the cuſtom in France is to take thirty ſix real grains for this purpoſe, which is conſequently the largeſt weight they employ, and repreſents twelve fine penny-weights This weight is ſubdivided into a ſufficient number of other ſmaller weights, which alſo repreſent fractions of fine penny-weights and grains Thus eighteen real grains, which is half of the quantity employed, repreſent ſix fine penny-weights, three real grains repreſent one fine penny-weight, or twenty four fine grains, a real grain and a half repreſent twelve fine grains, and $\frac{1}{32}$ part of a real grain repreſents $\frac{1}{4}$ part of a fine grain, which is only $\frac{1}{1152}$ part of a maſs of twelve penny weights

We may eaſily perceive that weights ſo ſmall, and eſſay balances, ought to be exceedingly accurate These balances are very ſmall, ſuſpended and incloſed in a box the ſides of which are panes of glaſs, that they may be preſerved from duſt, and that their motion may not be affected by agitated air, ſo as to diſorder their action

When an eſſay of a maſs or ingot of ſilver is to be made, the cuſtom is to make a double eſſay For this purpoſe, two fictitious ſemi-marks, each of which may be equal to thirty-ſix real grains, are to be cut from the ingot Theſe two portions of ſilver ought to be weighed very exactly, and they ought alſo to have been taken from oppoſite ſides of the ingot

Perſons accuſtomed to theſe operations know pretty nearly the value of ſilver merely by the look of the ingot, and ſtill better by rubbing it on a touchſtone By the judgment they form of the purity of the ingot, they regulate the quantity of lead which is to be added to it, as this quantity muſt be always proportionable to the quantity of imperfect metal mixed with the ſilver

Nevertheleſs, this proportion of lead to the alloy has not been preciſely determined Authors who treat of this ſubject differ much They who direct the largeſt quantity of lead ſay, that thereby the alloy is more certainly deſtroyed, and others who direct a ſmall quantity of lead pretend, that no more of that metal ought to be uſed than is abſolutely neceſſary, becauſe it carries off with it always ſome portion of ſilver Every eſſayer uſes his own particular method of proceeding, to which he is attached

To ascertain theſe doubtful points, three chemiſts of the Academy of Sciences at Paris, Meſſrs Hellot, Tillet, and Macquer, were appointed by the French Government They were directed to aſcertain every thing concerning the eſſay of gold and of ſilver by authenticated experiments, made under the inſpection of a miniſter whoſe ſuperior knowledge is equal to his deſire of public good, and in preſence of the officers of the mint

It appeared that the beſt proportions were, to add from two to three parts of lead to one part of ſilver of eleven penny-weights, and twenty three grains value,

value, that is, which contains $\frac{1}{48}$ of alloy, from four to ſix parts of lead to one part of ſilver of eleven penny weight, twelve grains value, or which contains $\frac{1}{24}$ of alloy, which is nearly the value of ſilver employed for plate from ſix to eight parts to one part of ſilver of eleven penny weight, which contains $\frac{1}{12}$ of alloy, ſuch as that of ſilver coin, and ſo on in proportion (o)

Two cupels of equal ſize and weight are to be choſen The cuſtom is to uſe cupels of ſuch a ſize that their weigh ſhall be equal to that of one half of the lead employed in the eſſay, becauſe ſuch cupels have been found capable of imbibing all the litharge formed during the operation Theſe cupels are to be placed together under a muffle in an eſſay-furnace The fire is to be kindled, and the cupels to be made red-hot, and to be kept ſo during half an hour at leaſt before any metal be put into them This precaution is neceſſary to dry and calcine them perfectly, becauſe if they contained any moiſture or inflammable matter, an ebullition and effervescence would be occaſioned in the eſſay When the cupels are heated ſo as to become almoſt white, the lead is to be put into them the fire is to be encreaſed which is done by opening the door of the aſh-hole ſo as to admit air, till the lead becomes red, ſmoking, and is agitated by a motion of its parts called its *circulation*, and till its ſurface becomes ſmooth and clear

Then the ſilver previouſly beat into ſmall plates, for its eaſier fuſion, is to be put into the cupels, the fire is to be continued, and even encreaſed, by putting hot coals at the mouth of the muffle, till the ſilver ſhall have *entered the lead*, that is, till it have melted and mixed with the lead When the melted matter circulates well, the heat is to be diminiſhed by taking away, partly or entirely, the coals put at the mouth of the muffle, and by cloſing more or leſs the doors of the furnace

The heat ought to be regulated ſo, that the eſſays in the cupels ſhall have ſurfaces ſenſibly convex, and ſhall appear ardent, while the cupels are leſs red, that the ſmoke ſhall riſe almoſt to the roof of the muffle, that undulations ſhall be made in all directions upon the ſurfaces of the eſſays, which are called *circulations*, that their middles ſhall be ſmooth and ſurrounded with a ſmall circle of litharge, which is continually imbibed by the cupels

The eſſays are to be kept in this ſtate till the operation is finiſhed, that is, till the lead and alloy have ſoaked into the cupel, and the ſurfaces of the buttons of ſilver being no longer covered with a pellicle of litharge, become

(o) The imperfect metals are deſtructible by ſcorification with lead, but when they are allayed with ſilver or gold, a larger quantity of lead is required to produce the ſcorification of any given quantity of imperfect metals, than when they are not allayed and defended from the action of the lead and fire by mixture with the perfect metals And further, the quantity of lead requiſite for this purpoſe muſt be encreaſed, when the quantity of ſilver or gold, with which the given quantity of imperfect metal is allayed, is encreaſed Thus, for inſtance, an ounce of pure copper may be conſumed by ſixteen ounces of lead But if an ounce of copper be allayed with eight ounces of ſilver, about ſix times the above quantity of lead, or ninety-ſix ounces, will be required to deſtroy the ounce of copper, and if the ounce of copper be mixed with thirty-ſix times its weight of ſilver, its ſcorification will require 128 ounces of lead The quantity of lead muſt be ſtill further encreaſed for another reaſon, namely, that almoſt all lead, as Cramer ſays, contains ſome portion of copper

suddenly bright and shining, and are then said to *lighten* If the operation has been well conducted, the two essays ought to become bright nearly at the same time When the silver has been by this operation well refined, we may see, immediately after it has brightened, the surface of the silver covered with rainbow colors, which quickly undulate and cross each other, and then the buttons become fixed or solid

The management of the fire is an important article in essays For if the heat be too great, the lead is scorified and imbibed by the cupel so quickly, that it has not sufficient time to scorify and carry along with it all the alloy , and if the heat be too little, the litharge is gathered upon the surface, and does not penetrate the cupel The essayers say then that the essay is *chooked* or *drowned* In this case the essay does not advance, because the litharge covering the surface of the metal defends it from the contact of air, which is absolutely necessary for the calcination of metals. *See* CALCINATION *and* COMBUSTION

We have above related the marks of a successful essay The heat may be known to be too great, from the convexity of the surface of the melted metal , from a too strong circulation , from the too vivid appearance of the cupel, so that the colors given to it by the litharge cannot be distinguished , and lastly, by the smoke rising up to the roof of the muffle, or not being at all visible, from its being so ardent and red-hot as not to be distinguishable In this case the heat must be diminished by shutting the door of the ash-hole Some essayers, for this purpose, put round the cupels small, oblong, cold pieces of baked clay, which they call *instruments*

If on the contrary, the melted metal have a surface not very spherical, relatively to its extent, if the cupel appear dark colored, and the smoke of the essay do only creep upon the surface, if the circulation be too weak, and the scoria which appears like bright drops have but a dull motion, and are not soaked into the cupel, we may be assured that the heat is too weak , much more may we be assured of it when the metal *fixes*, as the essayers call it In this case, the fire ought to be encreased by opening the door of the ash hole, and by placing large burning coals at the mouth of the muffle, or even by laying them across upon the cupels

As soon as the lead is put into the cupels, the fire is to be encreased, because they are then cooled by the cold metal, and the lead ought to be quickly melted, to prevent its calx from collecting upon its surface in too great quantity before it be formed into litharge, which it would do, and be difficultly fused, if the heat were too weak

When the silver is added to the lead, the heat must be still encreased, not only because the silver cools the mass, but because it is less fusible than lead. And as all these effects ought to be produced as quickly as possible, more heat is at length given than ought to be continued , and therefore, when the silver has entered the lead, the heat is to be diminished till it becomes of a due intensity for the operation

During the operation the heat ought gradually to be augmented to the end of it, both because the metallic mixture becomes less fusible as the quantity of lead diminishes, and also because the lead is more difficultly scorifiable, as it

is

is united with a larger proportion of silver. Hence the essays must be rendered very hot before they brighten.

When the operation is finished, the cupels are left in the same heat during some seconds, to give time to the last portions of litharge to be entirely absorbed; because if any of it remained under the buttons of silver, it would stick to them. The fire is then allowed to extinguish, and the cupels to cool gradually, till the buttons have entirely fixed, particularly if they be pretty large; because if they cool too quickly, their surfaces fix and contract before the internal mass, which is thereby so strongly compressed as to burst through the external solid coat and form vegetations, or even to be entirely detached from the rest of the mass and dissipated. This is called *the vegetation of the button*. It ought to be carefully prevented, because small bits of silver are sometimes thrown out of the cupel.

Lastly, when the buttons are thoroughly fixed, they are to be disengaged from the cupels by a small iron utensil while they are yet hot, otherwise they could not be disengaged clean and free from part of the cupels which strongly adhere to them when the heat is much diminished.

Nothing then remains to compleat the essay but to weigh the buttons. The diminution of weight which they have sustained by cupellation will show the purity or value of the ingot of silver.

We ought to observe, that as almost all lead naturally contains silver, and that after cupellation this silver is mixed with the silver of the ingot in the button of the essay, before we employ any lead in this operation, we ought to know how much silver it contains, that we may subtract this quantity from the weight of the button, when we compute the fineness of the silver of the ingot essayed. For this purpose essayers generally cupel a certain quantity of their lead separately, and weigh accurately the button of silver it yields; or, at the same time when they essay silver, they put into a third cupel, in the muffle, a quantity of lead equal to that employed in both their essays; and when the operation is finished, and the buttons are to be weighed, they throw the small button produced from the lead alone into the scale which contains the weights; and as this exactly counterpoises the small portion of silver which the essay buttons have received from the lead employed in the cupellation, the weights will show precisely the quantity of silver contained in the ingot, and thus the trouble of calculating is prevented. The small button of silver procured from the cupellation of lead alone is called the *witness*. But to prevent this trouble, essayers generally employ lead which contains no silver, such as that from Willach in Carinthia, which is therefore procured by essayers.

In the second place we shall observe, that a certain quantity of silver always passes into the cupel, as refiners in the great have long observed, and which happens also in essaying small quantities. The quantity of silver thus absorbed, varies according to the quantity of the lead employed, and the matter and form of the cupels; all which objects will undoubtedly be determined [illegible] above mentioned chemists.

The cupellation which we have now described is exactly the same [illegible] by which the produce of a silver ore, or of an ore of another metal c[illegible] silver, is determined. But as these ores contain frequently gold, and [illegible] in considerable quantity, when these essays are made, the buttons of silver obtained by the essays ought to be subjected to the operation called *parting* *See* SILVER, REFINING, FURNACE (ESSAY), MUFFLE, *and* CUPEL

CCLXXII ESSAY *of the* VALUE *of* GOLD The fictitious weights used to determine the purity of gold, and to essay this metal, are different from those of silver *See the preceding article* A mass of gold perfectly pure, or which contains no alloy, is ideally divided into 24 parts, called *carats* , this pure gold is therefore called gold of 24 carats If the mass or ingot contain $\frac{1}{24}$ part of its weight of alloy, the gold is then of 23 carats , and if it contains $\frac{2}{24}$ or $\frac{1}{12}$ of alloy, it is gold of 22 carats, &c Hence we see that the carat of gold is only a relative and proportional weight, so that the real weight of the carat varies according to the total weight of the mass or gold to be examined If this mass of gold weighs a mark, the real weight of the carat will be $\frac{1}{24}$ of eight ounces, which is equal to a mark If the mass weigh an ounce, the carat will be $\frac{1}{24}$ part of an ounce, or 24 grains If it is only a penny-weight or 24 grains, the real weight of a carat will be one grain , and so on

For greater accuracy, the carat of gold is divided into 32 parts, which are relative and proportional weights, as the carat itself is Thus $\frac{1}{32}$ of a carat of gold is $\frac{1}{32}$ of $\frac{1}{24}$, or the $\frac{1}{768}$ of any mass of gold , and the gold which contains an alloy equal to the $\frac{1}{768}$ part of the whole mass is called gold of 23 carats and $\frac{31}{32}$, gold which contains $\frac{2}{768}$ of alloy is gold of 23 carats and $\frac{30}{32}$, and so on

The real weight now generally used in the operation for determining the purity of gold, is six grains This weight then represents 24 carats The half of this weight, or three real grains, represents 12 carats According to this progression, we shall find that $\frac{1}{4}$ of a real grain represents one carat, and the $\frac{1}{128}$ parts of 1 grain represents the $\frac{1}{32}$ of a carat, or the $\frac{1}{768}$ part of a mass of gold to be essayed

As these weights are exceedingly small, some essayers employ a weight of 12 grains, which must be very convenient

When a mass or ingot of gold is to be essayed, six grains are to be cut off, and exactly weighed also 18 grains of fine silver are to be weighed These two metals are to be cupelled together with about ten times as much lead as the weight of the gold This cupellation is conducted precisely like that of the essay to determine the purity of silver, excepting that the heat must be raised a little more towards the end of the operation when the essay is going to brighten, Then the gold is freed from all alloy but silver If the quantity of copper or other alloy destructible by cupellation be required to be known, the remaining button is accurately weighed The diminution of weight from the sum of the weights of the gold and of the silver determines the quantity of this alloy

The button containing gold and silver is then to be flattened upon a polished piece of steel, and care must be taken to anneal it from time to time, to prevent its splitting and cracking By this method it is reduced to a thin plate, which is to be rolled up, in order to be parted by aqua fortis. *See the word* PARTING The diminution found after the parting from the original weight of of the gold eſſayed, ſhews the whole quantity of alloy contained in that gold

The eſſay for determining the purity of gold is then made by two operations the firſt, which is cupellation, deprives it of all its imperfect metals, and the ſecond, which is parting, ſeparates all the ſilver from it By antimony alſo gold may be purified, which is a kind of dry parting By this ſingle operation, all the imperfect metals, and ſilver with which gold is allayed, are ſeparated *See* PURIFICATION *of* GOLD *by* ANTIMONY *See alſo* GOLD, SILVER, REFINING, ESSAY *to* DETERMINE *the* PURITY *of* SILVER

CCLXXIII ESSENCES Eſſential oils are ſometimes called *eſſences* Thus we ſay, eſſence of cinnamon, of turpentine, &c to denote the eſſential oils of theſe ſubſtances *See* OILS (ESSENTIAL)

CCLXXIV ETHER Ether is a white, tranſparent liquor, of a peculiar and penetrating ſmell Ether is very volatile it may be entirely diſtilled without leaving any reſiduum, or ſuffering any decompoſition or alteration It is more volatile and inflammable than rectified ſpirit of wine Its flame reſembles the flame of ſpirit of wine, but it is ſenſibly much greater, whiter, and more luminous It is alſo accompanied with a ſlight ſmoke or ſoot, which ſpirit of wine is not

Ether does not mix with water, as ſpirit of wine does, in all proportions, but ten parts of water are required to diſſolve one part of ether This liquor has alſo a power of acting upon all oily and fat ſubſtances

From theſe eſſential properties ether appears to be a ſubſtance exactly intermediate betwixt ardent ſpirits and oils, as has been proved in the elements of chemiſtry *See* SPIRIT (ARDENT), *and* OIL

Ether has been but lately known by chemiſts From certain paſſages indeed of ſome old chemical books, we may infer that ether was not entirely unknown to their authors, but they have not mentioned it diſtinctly, nor have they ſufficiently deſcribed its properties, or the manner of making it wherefore no attention was given to it, till the curioſity of chemiſts was excited by a publication in the Philoſophical Tranſactions for the year 1730, by a German who calls himſelf Frobenius, (which however is ſuppoſed to be a feigned name) in which he relates the experiments he had made on that liquor, to which he firſt gave the name *ether* Since that time, many chemiſts have made experiments on this matter At firſt they made ether difficultly and in ſmall quantities, and at length abundantly and eaſily, particularly ſince Mr Hellot communicated to ſeveral artiſts a proceſs which he received from a foreign chemiſt This proceſs has been printed in the Encyclopedia, with conſent of Mr Hellot

Since that time, Mr Beaumé has operated more than any other chemiſt on ether He has publiſhed the details of his experiments and reflections, not only upon ether, but upon all the other ſubſtances produced from a combination of ſpirit of wine with vitriolic acid This forms the completeſt treatiſe on this ſubject which has hitherto been publiſhed

Vitriolic acid is not the only acid from the mixture of which with ſpirit of wine ether may be produced The nitrous, marine, and acetous acids have alſo been found capable of forming, with ſpirit of wine, liquors poſſeſſed

oi

of all the eſſential properties of ether, but differing from ether, properly ſo called, or vitriolic ether, by properties peculiar to each. We ſhall ſpeak ſucceſſively of theſe different ethers, beginning with the vitriolic, called ſimply *ether*, becauſe it is the chief one and the firſt diſcovered. The following proceſs for making this ether, which is the beſt hitherto publiſhed, is extracted from Mr Beaumé's diſſertation.

Put two pounds of perfectly rectified ſpirit of wine into a glaſs retort, and pour upon it at once two pounds of well concentrated vitriolic acid.

This acid being much heavier than the ſpirit of wine, ſinks directly to the bottom, and does not mix with the ſpirit of wine. Shake the retort gently, and repeatedly, that the two liquors may mix. The mixture will boil, and become very hot. Vapors will iſſue from it with a loud hiſſing noiſe, and a ſweet penetrating ſmell. The mixture will then aſſume a yellow-reddiſh color. Place the retort in a ſand-bath, warmed by degrees to the ſame heat with itſelf. Lute to it a receiver, in the ſide of which is a ſmall hole, and diſtill the mixture by a heat ſufficiently intenſe to make it quickly boil and to keep it boiling. At firſt a very ſweet ſpirit of wine will paſs into the receiver, after which the ether will come, which may be diſtinguiſhed by ſtriæ formed on the upper part and neck of the retort. Continue the diſtillation with the ſame degree of fire, and from time to time unſtop the ſmall hole of the receiver, till you perceive, upon applying your noſe near this ſmall hole, a ſuffocating ſmell of volatile ſulphureous acid. Then the receiver ought to be unluted, and the contained liquor, which will be nearly eighteen ounces, muſt be quickly poured into a glaſs bottle, which ought to be well ſtopped. This liquor is a mixture of a very dephlegmated part of the ſpirit of wine, of a ſweet penetrating ſmell, which paſſes at firſt, of ether, which was formed during the diſtillation, of a little oil, and ſometimes alſo of a ſmall quantity of ſulphureous acid, both which ſubſtances paſs frequently with the laſt portions of the ether, particularly if the diſtillation has been too long continued. To ſeparate the ether from theſe other ſubſtances, put the whole mixture into a glaſs retort, with a little deliquiated fixed alkali, to abſorb and retain the ſulphureous acid, and diſtill very ſlowly in a ſand-bath, with a very gentle lamp heat, till you have made one half of the liquor paſs over. The liquor that riſes in this diſtillation, called alſo *rectification*, is ether. (*p*)

Before the Count de Lauraguais had diſcovered that ether was miſcible with water in a certain proportion, the cuſtom was to put the ether after this diſtillation into a phial with diſtilled water, and to ſhake together theſe two liquors. The ether roſe quickly to the ſurface, and floated on the water, from which it might be ſeparated by a funnel, as oil may from water, and obtained unmixed. But this is evidently bad management: for in the firſt

(*p*) Mr [illegible] ſays, that by diſtilling together ſix pounds of concentrated vitriolic acid with an equal quantity of highly rectified ſpirit of wine, about 15 ounces of aromatic ſpirit of wine will be firſt diſtilled, and then ſome ether. By continuing a heat ſufficient to make the liquor boil, white vapors of a volatile, ſulphureous ſmell, together with ſome ether, will riſe, and thus in 15 or 16 hours, about three pounds and a half of liquor will have paſſed into the receiver. If another receiver be adapted to the retort, by continuing the diſtillation, from ten to ſixteen ounces of volatile ſulphureous ſpirit will

place, the water thus mixed dissolves about one tenth part of its weight of ether before it is saturated, all which is lost; and in the second place, for the same reason that water dissolves some ether, the ether also dissolves a certain quantity of water, by which it is weakened, and its properties altered, as Mr Beaumé has observed.

The production of ether is one of the most beautiful and instructive phenomena of chemistry. Spirit of wine, which is at once inflammable, and miscible with water in all proportions, differs from any oil by containing a more considerable quantity of water, which enters its composition as a principle or constituent part. This being established, if we deprive spirit of wine of part of that aqueous principle by which it differs from oils, it ought to assume the characters of oil, and to approach so much more to an oily nature, as it has been deprived of a greater quantity of the watery principle which constitutes it spirit of wine, and by which it differs from oil. But this is precisely what happens to it in the production of ether, and in the analysis of the remaining mixture after the formation of ether.

Concentrated vitriolic acid having a power of attracting water strongly, does, when mixed with spirit of wine, accordingly at first unite with the water which the spirit of wine may contain superabundantly: and its action would not extend farther, and it would not separate the watery principle from the spirit of wine, if a heat were not applied sufficient for distillation; for ether cannot be obtained from this mixture but by distillation. But when by the distilling heat the power of the vitriolic acid to attract water is encreased, that acid then becomes capable of separating the watery principle of the spirit of wine and of uniting with it.

As this is done gradually, so the spirit of wine which rises in distillation ought to be more and more changed by the action of the vitriolic acid.

will pass over, and from two to four gros * of oil. By distilling the liquor in the first receiver, together with a small quantity of oil of tartar, by a very gentle heat of a lamp furnace, about two pounds and four ounces of pure ether may be obtained; and afterwards when a new receiver is adapted, and a stronger heat applied, from eight to ten ounces of aromatic liquor, which makes a good anodyne mineral liquor of Hoffman, will be distilled. The ether which is first distilled is the purest, and that which passes afterwards has a smell of the oil of wine, improperly called sweet oil of vitriol, and of the volatile sulphureous acid. To obtain the largest possible quantity of ether, and free from the other liquors which are distilled in this operation, are the chief objects of attention: and, considering how much more volatile ether is than any of the liquors which affect its purity, we have reason to believe, that a larger quantity, and a purer ether than is procured by the ordinary process, might be obtained by using an apparatus for the distillation and rectification, so contrived, that vents of different heights from the retort or matrass shall be given to the vapors of the different degrees of volatility, to each of which vents a receiver shall be adapted; so that none but the purest ether can be found in the receiver communicating with the highest vent, and the ether which happens to be mixed with the other liquors in the receivers communicating with the inferior vents may be again rectified with less heat, till the whole quantity of pure ether be thus collected.

* A gros is equal to 72 grains.

This accordingly happens, and very distinctly The first liquor which rises in this distillation is a portion of spirit of wine, very volatile, penetrating, and dephlegmated, but which has not been deprived of its watery principle, and therefore retains the essential properties of spirit of wine.

The liquor which rises next is spirit of wine, deprived of part of its watery principle by vitriolic acid It consequently is spirit of wine essentially altered, and approximated to the nature of oil, in proportion to the quantity of watery principle which it has lost This is ether, which differs from spirit of wine in being no longer miscible with water in all proportions, and in emitting a whiter and more brilliant flame, accompanied with some fuliginous smoke

These properties by which ether differs from spirit of wine characterize so well its oily nature, that most chemists consider this liquor as a very volatile oil It seems, however, to be rather an intermediate substance betwixt oil and spirit of wine. The solubility of ether by water makes us chiefly consider it in this light, for what oil, properly so called, can be dissolved by water as ether can?

If the distillation of the mixture be continued after the ether has risen, the vitriolic acid, still continuing its action upon the spirit of wine already altered, takes at length from it all the watery principle by which it differs from a true oil, and hence ought to leave it in the state of oil. Accordingly, after the ether has passed over in distillation, an oil rises which wants none of the essential properties of true oil, as it is not miscible with water, burns with a fuliginous smoke, leaves a resinous coal, &c This oil, thus created in some measure during the operation, is known by the name improperly given to it, of *Sweet Oil of Vitriol*

From all this we might infer, that if ether ready prepared were mixed and distilled with concentrated vitriolic acid, it ought to be changed and transformed into sweet oil of vitriol Accordingly Mr Beaumé observed, that this did happen in an experiment he made, an account of which is given in his Dissertation on Ether

When the sweet oil of vitriol is distilling, the vitriolic acid acts also upon the phlogiston of the remaining part of the spirit of wine, and unites with one part of the inflammable principle Hence we may see at the same time much sulphureous, volatile, suffocating acid pass in distillation But as the vitriolic acid which forms it then becomes charged with all the water which it has taken from the spirit of wine, this first sulphureous acid, although very quick and penetrating, is very aqueous, and has not much acidity

By continuing this distillation, with a graduated fire, to perfect dryness, more of this sulphureous acid is raised, which becomes more and more acid, sometimes also a *little concrete sulphur is sublimed to the neck of the retort* towards the end of the distillation, and a fixed coal remains, as we ought to suppose, for the same substances are obtained by distilling to dryness a mixture of any oil with concentrated vitriolic acid *See* OIL

From all that has been said concerning the nature and properties of ether we may conclude, that this substance is nothing else than spirit of wine deprived by vitriolic acid of a part of its aqueous principle, and thereby approximated to the nature of oil. Some chemists believe that vitriolic acid is a constituent part

part of ether. This opinion, although it is not demonstrated, is not however destitute of probability, and deserves to be examined by experiments. For, on one side, a more copious and distinct acid is contained in all oils than in spirit of wine; and on the other side, the particular properties by which ethers formed by the nitrous, marine, and acetous acids differ from vitriolic ether, seem to be owing to adhering portions of the acids with which these ethers are prepared. This question requires a particular examination.

Ether is not employed in the arts, although it appears capable of being usefully employed in many cases, and particularly in the solution of certain concrete oily matters for the preparation of varnishes; but its high price prevents its introduction into the arts.

As ether is the most volatile and evaporable of all known liquors, and as in general liquors produce a degree of cold proportionable to the quickness of their evaporation, as Mr Beaume discovered, and several others have observed; therefore a very great degree of artificial cold may be produced by means of ether. Mr Beaumé has sunk the mercury of Reaumur's thermometer to 40 degrees below the freezing point, by applying linens soaked in ether to the ball containing the mercury; and he makes this fine experiment every year in his course of chemistry conjointly with Mr Macquer. (q)

Ether, like all thin and volatile oily matters, has the property of taking gold from aqua regia; but as it is more subtle than any other of these matters, it produces this effect better. For this purpose, ether ought to be poured upon a solution of gold in aqua regia, and the two liquors mixed together by shaking the containing phial. When this mixture is left to rest, the ether soon disengages itself from the aqua regia, and floats on the surface of the acid liquor, which being deprived of its gold is rendered white, while the ether has now acquired a yellow color from the gold it contains. This is an expeditious method of making a tincture of gold, or potable gold. We ought to observe that the gold which thus passes into the ether still retains a certain quantity of aqua regia.

Ether is employed in medicine. As a very thin and volatile inflammable matter, it acts powerfully on the nervous system, like all the matters of this kind. Frederic Hoffman was one of the first who employed it as a sedative and antispasmodic. The famous mineral anodyne liquor of this physician is nothing else than spirit of wine, in which are dissolved some ether and sweet oil of vitriol. It owes all its medicinal virtues to the ether.

Since ether has become more common and better known, many physicians prescribe it singly, in the dose of seven or eight drops upon a bit of sugar, which is to be eat or to be dissolved in some proper liquor and drank. It is given in flatulent colics, obstinate hiccups, convulsive, hysterical affections, and other disorders of this kind. It certainly produces frequently excellent effects; but, like all other antispasmodic remedies, it sometimes produces none.

(q) Mr Amontons, in a Memoir of the Academy of Paris, (1699) and more particularly, M Richman, in a Memoir of the Academy of Petersburg, (1747) have observed that cold was produced by evaporating fluids. Dr Cullen discovered, that the cold thus produced by evaporating fluids was considerably greater in vacuo than in air. *See Essays Phys. & Liter.* Edinburgh, vol. 2, 1756.

Several persons have affirmed, that ether applied externally to the back of the neck, or to the temples, dissipated instantaneously, and as it were by enchantment, head-achs and meagrims I have tried it in all doses upon myself for these disorders, but without success, but we cannot from thence infer that it may not have better effects upon other persons (r)

CCLXXV ETHER (ACETOUS) Since the discovery of the ether described in the preceding article, chemists have endeavoured to obtain such a liquor from spirit of wine by means of other acids, and accordingly they produced it first by means of the nitrous acid, then by the acetous, and lastly, by the marine. We shall speak successively of these several ethers.

The discovery of the production of ether by the acetous acid was made by the Count de Lauraguais This ether is made by mixing together equal parts of rectified spirit of wine, and concentrated acid of vinegar obtained by distilling crystals of copper, called the Spirit of Venus, or radical vinegar This mixture is to be distilled in the manner directed for vitriolic ether, and a considerable quantity of a liquor is obtained, which is possessed of the essential qualities of ether, as described in the former article, but which has also some of the acidity and peculiar smell of radical vinegar

When this ether is mixed with liquid fixed alkali, and again distilled, or rectified by a lamp heat, an acetous ether is obtained free from superabundant acid, and much liker to true ether It retains, however, the smell, not of the acid, but of the inflammable part of vinegar

We observe, that by this process a greater quantity of ether is obtained than by distillation with vitriolic acid, which shews that the acid of vinegar is essentially fitter to produce ether than the vitriolic acid This difference must undoubtedly be attributed to the great quantity of ardent spirit, which is one of the principles of the acid of vinegar, and which perhaps already approaches the state of ether *See* VINEGAR (RADICAL)

As this discovery has been but lately made, the properties of the acetous ether, and the phenomena which its residuum may afford, have not yet been sufficiently examined

CCLXXVI ETHER (MARINE) The discovery of the true process for making ether by means of the marine acid, is the latest which has been made on this subject The Marquis de Courtanvaux has communicated his process to the Academy of Sciences

The difficulty with which marine acid unites in general with inflammable substances has retarded the discovery of marine ether, for no ether can be obtained by treating the most concentrated marine acid with spirit of wine in the ordinary method, by which the other ethers are procured Able artists, and particularly Mr Rouelle and Mr Beaumé, had attempted unsuccessfully to procure ether by distilling smoking marine acid with spirit of wine Mr Beaumé, indeed, in his Dissertation concerning Ether, had given a process, by which he affirms that he had obtained a small quantity of marine ether This

(r) Ether dissolves all essential and expressed oils, animal empyreumatic oil, resins, and almost entirely ambergrise It dissolves difficultly petroleum and oil of amber. It precipitates regulus of antimony from aqua regia, and silver from nitrous acid It takes spots of grease from silks without affecting their colors

process

process consists in making the fumes of the marine acid and of the spirit of wine meet together in the same receiver But the quantity of ether obtained by this method was very small The process also is troublesome, and even imperfect, as Mr Beaumé himself declares He would not have published it in that imperfect state, but because the possibility of the fact had been denied What he says may be seen in his Dissertation on Ether.

Others, and particularly German chemists, had attempted to employ for this purpose a marine acid which was united with a metallic substance, such as the butter of antimony, and had observed the singular phenomena which happened in these mixtures The Marquis de Courtanvaux has perfectly succeeded by employing the smoking spirit of Libavius, which is a highly concentrated marine acid, obtained from corrosive sublimate by tin, and impregnated with a considerable quantity of this metal

This smoking liquor, mixed with an equal part of spirit of wine, and distilled together, easily produces a considerable quantity of a liquor possessed of all the essential properties of ether, and which may be considered as a true marine ether The tin contained in the spirit of Libavius is separated and precipitated in form of a white powder. This ether, like the others, must be rectified to be obtained in its greatest purity Some reflections concerning its nature will be found at the end of the following article

CCLXXVII. ETHER (NITROUS) This ether is obtained by mixing nitrous acid with spirit of wine, but with peculiar circumstances

In the writings of ancient chemists traces of the nitrous as well as of the other ethers may be found, but these traces are neither clear nor precise The first person who published a satisfactory account of this liquor, and who shewed the true method of obtaining it, was Mr Navier, a Physician, at Chalons-sur-Marne, and Correspondent of the Academy of Sciences His process, which he communicated to the Academy in 1742, is very simple, as it consists only in mixing together spirit of wine and spirit of nitre in a bottle, which is to be exactly closed, and left at rest, till the ether is formed and collected like an oil upon the surface of the liquor. This ether is made, as we see, without distillation

Since Mr Navier has published his discovery, other chemists have endeavored to improve the process A very good process is published in the Encyclopedia, which is attributed to Mr Rouelle Mr Beaumé also has published one in his Dissertation on Ether, which is very accurate, and is the result of many trials and researches Mr Beaumé's process is as follows

Put six ounces of rectified spirit of wine into a bottle made of strong and thick glass, large enough to contain a pound of water Place this bottle in a bucket of fresh water, which will be still better for the purpose if it has been rendered colder by throwing into it two or three pounds of ice, in small bits. Pour upon the spirit of wine, at four or five times, four ounces of smoking spirit of nitre, so concentrated, that a phial, capable of containing an ounce only of water, shall be capable of containing an ounce and a half of this spirit of nitre observing, during the whole time of pouring the spirit of nitre, that the spirit of wine be kept in a state of perpetual rotation. As soon as the two liquors are mixed, stop the bottle quickly with a good cork, which must be driven firmly into the neck of the bottle, and covered and fastened with a piece of leather doubled, and bound with packthread I leave it at rest in the cold water, which ought to be sometimes renewed

Two or three hours afterwards, the liquor loses some of its transparency by the interposition of many small drops of ether, which are disengaged throughout the liquor. This ether gradually collects and floats upon the surface Within twenty-four hours the mixture will have become clear, and the ether formed, which will be about two ounces, may be separated But as more ether will still be produced, the method is to leave it seven or eight days before any of it be separated After this time no more ether is formed Pierce then the cork with a pointed instrument, and a considerable quantity of air will escape with a hissing noise, which had disengaged itself during the production of the ether, and which is compressed in the bottle When the air has escaped, uncork the bottle, and pour quickly its contents into a glass funnel that the ether may be separated

The ether will amount to about four ounces, and the residuum will weigh five ounces and a half, so that half an ounce shall have been lost during the process This ether ought to be put into a well closed crystal-glass bottle

Nitrous ether in this state has a smell like that of the vitriolic ether, but somewhat stronger and less agreeable It has a light citron color, and as soon as the bottle which contains it is uncorked, it bubbles and effervesces When the stopper is put in loosely into the neck of the bottle, it may be observed to rise and fall alternately, which appearance is occasioned by vapors escaping from the ether The cause of these phenomena is a considerable quantity of air which remains interposed betwixt the parts of ether, for when all this air has been once disengaged from the ether, these phenomena do not happen.

Nitrous ether is not, in this state, pure, as it retains some of the acid employed from which it may be purified by mixing it with some fixed alkali, and rectifying it with a lamp-heat In this rectification, it suffers a loss of nearly one half its quantity

The properties of this rectified nitrous ether are, that it burns with a more luminous flame than the flame of vitriolic ether, that this flame is accompanied with a more sensible quantity of soot, that after the ether is burnt, a residuum of coal is perceptible, and, lastly, that if it be evaporated on the surface of water in open air, it leaves upon the water some oil, as the vitriolic ether does, but in a little larger quantity In other respects, but in these which shew that the nitrous ether is of a more oily nature than the vitriolic, these two ethers are perfectly similar

The activity and violence with which nitrous acid acts upon the spirit of wine is the most remarkable circumstance of this operation The action of nitrous acid is so much stronger than that of vitriolic acid upon spirit of wine, that equal parts of concentrated nitrous acid and spirit of wine cannot be mixed and contained for notwithstanding all the precautions that can be taken to moderate the action of these two liquors upon each other, they mix with so much violence when that proportion is used, that the mixture is instantly heated almost to inflammation, is reduced to vapors, and bursts the vessels with a terrible explosion

In Mr Beaumé's Dissertation upon Ether, an account of the trials which he made upon this subject, and of the resulting phenomena, may be seen.

In

In the second place, when spirit of wine and nitrous acid are mixed in proper proportions, ether may be obtained without distillation, which is peculiar to this acid The effects peculiar to the nitrous acid, in the preparation of ether, are caused by the action which this acid has, not only on the watery principle, but also on the inflammable principle of the spirit of wine We have therefore reason to believe that nitrous acid converts spirit of wine into ether, not only by depriving it of its watery principle, but also by acting upon its inflammable principle with which it combines, or to which perhaps it joins its own inflammable principle This is so true, that nitrous ether may be made with a nitrous acid which does not smoke, and which is, in some measure, saturated with water For this purpose, a larger proportion of spirit of wine ought to be added. But if nitrous acid converted spirit of wine into ether, merely by depriving it of its watery principle, a diluted acid ought not to have the same effect as a smoking and concentrated acid, particularly as it cannot concentrate itself during the operation, since this is performed without distillation Besides, as nitrous acid has a greater affinity than any other with the inflammable principle, and contains a greater quantity of it, we ought not to be surprized that nitrous ether is produced without distillation, and more easily than any other.

Marine acid, on the contrary, having the least disposition of all the acids to unite with the inflammable principle, and seeming to contain less of it than any other acid, does therefore produce ether with most difficulty, or, properly speaking, does not produce any ether, when pure, but only when it has been combined with metallic substances, as tin and antimony, part of the phlogiston of which it may have acquired *See* ETHER (MARINE) It probably becomes more proper to combine with the inflammable principle of the spirit of wine, or to communicate that which it has received, after it has already begun to unite itself with the inflammable principle of metallic matters

From these considerations we are inclined to believe, that in the production of ether, the acids act at the same time upon the watery and inflammable principles of the spirit of wine, by depriving this spirit of the former, and by combining partly with the latter, or by encreasing its proportion of acid, and thereby approximating it to an oily nature.

All acids, and particularly mineral acids, suffer singular alterations, and even transmutations, when they are distilled to dryness with a sufficient quantity of spirit of wine Mr. Pott, in his Dissertation on the Vinous Acid of Nitre, says, that this acid by being combined with spirit of wine loses the disagreeable smell peculiar to it, and acquires a penetrating and agreeable smell, that it does not rise in form of red vapors, but that it rises with a less degree of heat than when pure, and that it acts less powerfully on fixed alkalis and absorbent earths He adds, that by distilling this mixture, oil and a residuous coal may be obtained, and that if nitrous acid previously combined with spirit of wine be saturated with a fixed alkali, a salt is formed which does not detonate like nitre, but burns like an oily salt, without waste or diminution

Pott reasonably thinks, that this experiment may suggest hints concerning the transmutation of acids, and he believes that the nitrous acid in that experiment

loses

loses its detonating and other eſſential qualities, becauſe the phlogiſton which enters its compoſition as a principle is joined and confounded with the inflammable matter of the ſpirit of wine The marine acid ſeems to ſuffer leſs alteration in combining with ſpirit of wine, for Mr Pott ſays alſo, in his Diſſertation on the Vinous Acid of Salt, that having ſaturated with an alkali ſome marine acid previouſly treated with ſpirit of wine, he obtained a regenerated common ſalt, which poſſeſſed all the eſſential properties of common ſalt Nevertheleſs, Mr Pott, having diſtilled to dryneſs the thick matter which remains after the moſt fluid and volatile part had been diſtilled from a mixture of marine acid and ſpirit of wine, obtained a reſiduous black fixed coal which proves that one part of the acid of ſalt contracts in this experiment a very intimate union with the principles of ſpirit of wine, for the marine acid and ſpirit of wine diſtilled ſingly do certainly not leave any reſiduum

CCLXXVIII ETHIOPS (MARTIAL) Martial ethiops is iron divided into exceedingly fine parts by the action of water

This preparation was introduced into medicine by the younger Lemeri, who called it *ethiops* from its black color To make ethiops, filings of iron are taken, very clean and free from ruſt, and are put into a glaſs veſſel, on theſe pure water is to be poured, to the height of three or four fingers thickneſs above the filings, the filings are to be frequently ſtirred with a ſpatula, till they become ſo fine a powder, that when agitated they remain long ſuſpended in the water the water thus rendered turbid by the ſuſpended powder of iron, is to be decanted, and the ſediment which is depoſited is to be dried and ground on a porphyry This is the martial ethiops

Iron is a metal which is ſoluble in many menſtruums Its ſurface is ſenſibly affected by the combined action of air and water, and is in ſome meaſure corroded It is thereby deprived of part of its inflammable principle, and partly reduced to an earth or calx, called *ruſt* but to produce this effect, theſe two elements muſt concur, for iron is not ruſted nor altered by expoſure to dry air, or to water alone, without contact of air *(s)*

Nevertheleſs, the operation of ethiops martial ſhows that water alone, without the concurrence of air, is capable of a certain action upon iron, ſince this metal is by this action, continued ſome time, reduced to parts exceedingly ſmall. Whether this effect is cauſed by ſome heterogeneous particles in the water or in the iron, has not yet been determined The iron thus reduced into martial ethiops is certainly very different from ruſt It is black, attractable by magnets, and ſoluble in all acids, which proves that it is not deprived of its inflammable principle Ruſt, on the contrary, has none of theſe qualities

Theſe properties of martial ethiops have induced ſome perſons to propoſe it as a remedy much ſuperior to other preparations of iron This manner of preparing iron for medicinal purpoſes is certainly good and unexceptionable, but

(*s*) Iron is not ſo readily ruſted when kept immerſed in water, as when it is firſt moiſtened and then expoſed to air, but it is nevertheleſs ſubject to ruſt if it be kept a few days under water, as thoſe workmen know who have occaſion frequently to keep pieces of iron under water, to ſoften and render the metal more ductile, and alſo to preſerve the ſurface from ruſt during a ſhort time When they have occaſion to preſerve iron from ruſt a longer time, they immerſe it in lime-water.

Mr.

Mr Lemeri certainly ought not to have declaimed against all other preparations of iron indiscriminately, nor to have advised their total disuse in medicine He pronounced this general proscription without sufficiently understanding the matter He would probably have been more indulgent, if he had known that several martial saffrons, such as those called aperitive, and which are nothing but rust, are capable of easily resuming, and by the humid way all the phlogiston which is necessary to restore to them all the properties of martial ethiops, and that this change is actually produced upon them when they are taken internally, by the fat matters which they meet in the stomach, in the intestines, and in the aliments and digestive juices This is proved by the blackness of the excrements of those who have taken these martial saffrons

Mr Lemeri had certainly not examined the nature of the precipitates obtained from solutions of iron in acids, and particularly in the vitriolic and marine acids, by a phlogisticated alkali, for he must have observed that such precipitates receive from the alkali a sufficient quantity of phlogiston, to give it a dark and blackish color, and to render it soluble in any acid consequently these precipitates, which are at least as fine as the martial ethiops, are also equal to it in solubility, and preferable from the greater facility of their preparation

When well phlogisticated precipitates are required, they ought to be dried in close vessels, and by distillation This is an operation which is also necessary for martial ethiops, although the author does not direct it, for the iron, being moist and much divided, rusts with the greatest facility from the contact of air

Martial ethiops, and the martial precipitates and saffrons above-mentioned, are successfully employed in medicine as excellent tonic and fortifying remedies *See upon this subject* IRON

CCLXXIX ETHIOPS MINERAL Ethiops mineral is a combination of mercury with a sufficiently large quantity of sulphur The color of this compound is black, and hence it has been named ethiops

Ethiops mineral may be made either by fusion, or by trituration without fusion

To make ethiops mineral by fusion To sulphur melted in an unvarnished earthen vessel, an equal quantity of very pure mercury is to be added, the vessel is at the same time to be taken from the fire, and the mixture is to be stirred with a spatula till it be cold and fixed, the mixture is then become a black and friable mass, which is to be pounded and sifted This is ethiops

To make this preparation without fire, two parts of mercury are triturated in a glass or marble mortar with three parts of flowers of sulphur, till the mercury no longer appears

Mercury and sulphur have a strong disposition to unite together For this purpose, their integrant parts must be made to touch, and then they contract an adhesion, but not so strong as that which they acquire by sublimation in the process for making cinnabar

The black color of ethiops is always taken by mercury, when it is much divided and mixed with inflammable matters In this respect it resembles silver, lead, and other metals, which acquire a black color from the superficial union which they contract with sulphur or other phlogistic matters

Although the union of mercury with sulphur in ethiops is not so strong as in cinnabar, we must not believe that in ethiops these two substances are not united,

 but

but only mixed and interposed, for they really adhere and are combined together. The proof of this is, that they cannot be separated from each other without intermediate substances. These substances are the same as those which are capable of procuring a similar separation by decomposing cinnabar See CINNABAR

The difference betwixt ethiops prepared by fusion and ethiops prepared by trituration is, that the former contains a less quantity of sulphur than the latter.

Mr Lemeri has observed, in his Course of Chemistry, that when ethiops is made with fire, one half of the substances employed is lost, but the proportion in which each of the substances is dissipated is not known we are, however, certain that more sulphur is lost than mercury, notwithstanding which, each kind of ethiops contains more sulphur than is necessary for the saturation of the mercury, as evidently appears from the operation of making artificial cinnabar

The chief use of ethiops mineral is in medicine It may be given from six grains to half a dram, incorporated with other suitable remedies It is employed as a resolvent in the asthma, scrophula, obstructions and diseases proceeding from a stoppage or thickness of humors Some physicians prescribe it in venereal diseases others affirm, that ethiops has no medicinal virtue however, it certainly occasions salivation sometimes, although seldom *See* MERCURY

CCLXXX EVAPORATION Evaporation is a chemical operation, by which, with a certain degree of heat and access of air, volatile substances are separated from others less volatile

The effect of evaporation is essentially the same as that of distillation, with this difference, that distillation is almost always employed to separate and collect a volatile substance, whereas evaporation is always employed to separate and collect the fixed or less volatile substance only, the more volatile part being necessarily lost in the operation

Evaporation is always made in open air, and with open vessels, for air contributes much to the volatilisation of bodies, and evaporation is only performed from their surfaces hence the general rules for evaporation are, to place the body from which volatile parts are to be evaporated in a flat, shallow, wide vessel, so that it shall present to the air a large surface, towards which even a current of air ought to be directed

In all evaporations the degree of heat ought to be proportioned to the volatility of the substance to be evaporated, and still more to the degree of fixity of the substance intended to be left, and of its adhesion to the volatile parts Thus, the less fixed the remaining substance is, and the more strongly it adheres to the volatile substance, the less the heat ought to be For instance, if we would obtain the portion of oil which is found in rectified spirit of wine and ether, these liquors ought to be evaporated, as Mr Beaume did, upon the surface of water in open air, and without any other heat than that of the atmosphere, for, however little the evaporation of these liquors is urged by a heat somewhat too strong, the volatility of this small portion of oil differs so little from that of spirit of wine and of ether, that it would entirely exhale with these liquors without any separation, as it does when they are rectified Thus Mr Duhamel having discovered, by his experiments, that the volatile alkali of sal ammoniac

carries

carries off with it a considerable portion of the fixed earthy intermediate substances employed to disengage it, could not afterwards separate this earthy part from the concrete volatile alkali, but by allowing this latter to dissipate itself by the heat alone of the air, and by an evaporation which continued several months, because this earthy part, although very fixed, is so well combined, and adheres so strongly to volatile alkali, that it is always carried along with the salt in evaporation, whenever the heat exceeds that of the atmosphere *See Mr Duhamel's Memoirs concerning Sal Ammoniac amongst the Memoirs of the Academy*

On the contrary, in some cases evaporation may be urged by a strong heat, and even by a current of air directed upon the surface of the body This is practised when the part to be evaporated is not very volatile, and requires considerable heat to raise it, and when the remaining substance is very fixed, and does not adhere much to the volatile part Such, for example, is the evaporation of regulus of antimony in the *purification of gold by antimony* See *that operation*

The vessels employed in evaporation are basons, tests, crucibles, and these vessels are made of glass, metal, or of earth, according to the nature of the bodies on which the operation is to be performed

CCLXXXI EUPHORBIUM (*t*)

CCLXXXII EXCREMENTS (LIQUID) *of* ANIMALS

See Urine

CCLXXXIII. EXCREMENTS (SOLID) *of* ANIMALS

Alchemists who have sought every where for their great work, as they called it, have particularly operated much on the excrements of men and other animals, but philosophical chemistry has acquired no knowledge from all these alchemical labors, from the obscurity with which their authors have described them The philosophic chemists have not much examined animal excrements Of these, Homberg is the only one who has particularly analysed and examined human ordure, and this was done to satisfy an alchemical project of one of his friends, who pretended that from this matter a white oil could be obtained, without smell, and capable of fixing mercury into silver The oil was found by Homberg, but mercury was not fixed by it

The labors of this able chemist were not however useless, like those of the alchemists, because he has clearly related the experiments he made on this matter, in the Memoirs of the Academy of Sciences These experiments are curious, and teach several essential things concerning the nature of excrements The result of these experiments is as follows.

Fresh human fœces, being distilled to dryness in a water bath, furnish a clear, watery, insipid liquor, of a disagreeable smell, but which contains no volatile alkali, which is a proof that this matter, although nearly in a putrefactive state, is not however putrefied; for all substances really putrid furnish with this degree of heat a manifest volatile alkali *See* Putrefaction.

(*t*) Euphorbium is a very acrid, gummy, resinous juice From an ounce of euphorbium five drams were extracted by spirit, and from another ounce five drams also were extracted by water. Both these extracts, but chiefly the spirituous, were acrid and corrosive *Neuman.*

The dry residuum of the foregoing experiment, being distilled in a retort with a graduated fire furnishes volatile alkaline spirit and salt, a fetid oil, and leaves a residuous coal These are the same substances which are obtained from all animal matters *See* SUBSTANCES (ANIMAL)

Human fœces, diluted and lixiviated in water, furnish by filtration and evaporation of the water an oily salt of nitrous nature, which deflagrates like nitre upon ardent coals, and which inflames in close vessels, when heated to a certain degree

This same matter yielded to Homberg, who treated it by a compleat fermentation or putrefaction, excited by a digestion during forty days in a gentle water bath heat, and who afterwards distilled it, an oil without color, and without bad smell, and such as he endeavored to find, but which did not, as we said before, fix mercury into silver

CCLXXXIV EXPRESSION Expression is a mechanical operation, by which the juices of many plants are obtained, and sweet oils, which are not volatile, may be extracted from many substances in which they reside superabundantly and uncombined Such are all emulsive seeds, and some fruits, as oranges, citrons, lemons, olives, &c An oil may also be obtained from yolks of eggs by expression

This operation is performed by putting the substance to be expressed, previously bruised, in a machine called a press

The plants from which the juices are to be extracted, having been bruised in a mortar, ought to be wrapped up in a strong and closely woven linen cloth, and then put into the press The plants which are not very succulent, or too mucilaginous to give their juices by expression, ought to be mixed with some water when they are bruised in a mortar

Grains or seeds must also be bruised before they are expressed to obtain their oil, so as to form them into a greasy paste, the oil of which exudes spontaneously They are then to be wrapped in a strong linen cloth, and expressed To obtain as much oil as is possible, this paste ought to be expressed betwixt two hot iron plates But this method renders oils rancid, and therefore ought not to be used in the preparation of oils for medicinal purposes

To obtain oil from yolks of eggs by expression, they ought previously to be hardened by baking, or even a slight torrefaction *See* JUICES (EXPRESSED), *and* OILS (SWEET)

CCLXXXV EXTRACT This word, taken in the most general sense of which it is capable, is applicable to substances separated from any compound body by a proper menstruum But it is generally confined to denote substances separated from vegetables by water

To make an extract from any vegetable substance, it must be infused or boiled in a sufficient quantity of water, to extract from it all the substances soluble in this menstruum If the vegetable matter of which the extract is to be made is itself succulent and watery, it need not then be infused or boiled The juice which contains all the matter of the extract may be expressed, for in this case, the water in the plant has the same effect as the water employed in infusion or decoction

Then

Then the infusion, decoction, or expressed juice of the plant must be evaporated till they acquire more or less firm consistence For some extracts are made as soft as paste, and are called *soft extracts* , others are evaporated till they become dry, and are called *dry* or *solid extracts*

The liquor from which the extract is to be made by evaporation is always more or less charged with feculent matters, earthy or resinous, which render it turbid, because these matters are not soluble in water These matters are generally separated before the liquor is evaporated to the consistence of an extract, which may be done by clarification with the white of an egg, or otherwise By this separation of feculent matter, soft extracts are rendered less liable to ferment and to become mouldy But as the intention of making an extract is to preserve all that can be preserved of the principles of plants, the liquor of the extract ought not to be clarified, but it ought to be evaporated till it becomes dry, and thereby rendered not subject to change

As extracts ought to resemble, as nearly as is possible, the vegetables from which they are obtained, they ought to be evaporated with a gentle heat, and in a water-bath , because the delicate and compounded principles of vegetables are liable to be changed by a strong heat But to avoid the inconveniencies attending a tedious evaporation, by which a fermentation of the matter might be induced, this evaporation may be accelerated by encreasing the surface of the liquor, which therefore ought to be distributed in many flat and wide-mouthed vessels *See* EVAPORATION In this manner the Count de la Garaye prepared what he called *essential salts*, which are nothing but solid extracts, the best and most perfect which can be obtained

From what has been said concerning extracts, we may conclude, that they are collections of the proximate principles of vegetables, and chiefly of those which are soluble in water, and which are not so volatile as to be capable of dissipation by the heat of boiling water They contain, therefore, when well made, all the gummy, mucilaginous, saponaceous, (that is, the oil rendered soluble in water by some saline substance) bitter, or saccharine matters , and lastly, all the essential salts, acid or others, or any other saline matters, which are contained in vegetables In well made extracts are also found portions of the oily, resinous, and earthy principles of vegetables, which, although insoluble in water, have been extracted along with the other principles into the juice, infusion, or decoction , excepting, for particular reasons, these principles are required to be excluded If extracts are required which shall possess as much as they can of the properties and virtues of plants, we ought not only to extract by water but also by spirit of wine, and to mix together the substances thus extracted by these two menstruums *See* ANALYSIS *by* MENSTRUUMS

The taste of almost all extracts is bitter or saline, and somewhat like that which sugar or other vegetable substances acquire by slight burning But this latter quality is faulty It proceeds from a too strong heat having been employed to evaporate the extracts, by which some of the substances contained in the extract are considerably changed or even destroyed

Several

Several dry extracts, or essential salts of the Count de la Garaye, attract moisture from the air, and even become liquid. This property is occasioned by a separation of the saline from the resinous and earthy parts of the vegetable, and which are therefore uncombined, and consequently apt to attract moisture

These extracts ought to be preserved in well closed bottles

CCLXXXVI EXTRACT (MARTIAL) This name is given to a pharmaceutical preparation, which is not, properly speaking, an extract, since it is only a combination of iron with tartar, called *Tincture of Mars*, reduced to the consistence of an extract *See* TINCTURE *of* MARS

F.

CCLXXXVII FALSE GALENA This is a mineral which resembles at first view the lead ore called galena, but from which no metal is extracted (u)

CCLXXXVIII FALSE PRECIPITATE This name is given to a matter which has the appearance of a precipitate, but which has not been separated from a menstruum Such is mercury reduced into a red powder without addition, and merely by heat, improperly called *precipitate per se*, or mercury precipitated by itself such also is *red precipitate*, which is mercury dissolved in spirit of nitre, and afterwards deprived of most of the acid by fire, without any intermediate substance Silver, lead, mercury, separated from nitrous acid by marine or vitriolic acids or salts, are also generally considered as precipitates, and are really so, as they are actually separated from one substance by the intervention of another but as this separation is made by the union of the precipitated metal with the precipitating acid, such precipitate ought to be distinguished from those which are nothing but the precipitated matter uncombined and single *See* PRECIPITATES *and* PRECIPITATION.

CCLXXXIX FAT Fat is an oily concrete substance, deposited in different parts of animal bodies.

To obtain fat very pure, it must be cut into pieces, and cleaned from the interposed membranes and vessels, it must then be cleansed from its gelatinous matter by washing with water, till the water comes from it colorless and insipid; it is afterwards to be melted with a moderate heat, in a proper vessel, with a

(u) FALSE GALENA, *Pseudo Galena*, called also *Black-jack*, or *Blend*, is an ore of zinc, containing, besides that semimetal, generally some iron, together with the mineralizing substances sulphur and arsenic It is frequently intermixed with the lead ore called galena, and sometimes with the cupreous pyrites In England the former kind is found in the lead mines of Derbyshire, and the latter in the copper mines of Cornwall This mineral, formerly neglected as useless, has lately been employed, after a careful calcination, instead of calamine, for the manufacture of brass, and might also be employed as calamine is, for the extraction of zinc. For these purposes, that kind of blend is fittest which contains most zinc, and least of iron and arsenic Such is the blend of Derbyshire, which is a very rich ore of zinc This kind is more laminated in its texture, and of a greyish color when scratched, whereas the blend found in Cornwall has a more tessellated texture, consisting of oblong parallellipipedons, is of a reddish color when scratched, and contains a larger quantity of iron and arsenic

little water, and it is to be kept thus melted till the water be entirely evaporated, which is known by the discontinuance of the boiling, which is caused by the water only, and which lasts till not a drop of it remains it is afterwards to be put into an earthen pot, where it fixes, then it is exceedingly white, sufficiently pure for the purposes of pharmacy or chemical examination

Fat thus purified has very little taste, and a weak, but peculiar smell

Mineral acids exhibit the same phenomena with fat, as they do with the fixed sweet oils of vegetables, which contain nothing gummy or resinous, and which do not dry Such is the oil of ben, oil of olives, and all those which chemists call *fat oils*

Alkalis dissolve fat, as they do these oils, and form a similar soap Fat contains no principle so volatile as to be raised with the heat of boiling water It does not inflame but when heated in open air so as to rise in vapors Lastly, by age it contracts an acrid and rancid quality.

When fat is distilled with a heat superior to that of boiling water, which must therefore be done in a retort, and in a naked fire, first an acid phlegm arises, and a small portion of oil which remains fluid As the distillation continues, the acid becomes stronger, and the oil thicker, and at last it congeals in the receiver No other principle arises during this distillation. and lastly, when the retort is red, nothing remains but a very small quantity of that kind of coal which cannot be burnt without very great difficulty *See* COAL

If the congealed oil which is found in the receiver be again distilled, more acid is obtained, and an oil which does not congeal, and thus by repeating the distillations the oil is more and more attenuated While it is thus deprived of its acid, it acquires a more and more penetrating smell, and thus by distillation alone it may be rendered as volatile as essential oils, and capable of rising with the heat of boiling water!

From all these properties of fat we may perceive it is a sweet concrete oil, not volatile, and perfectly analogous to butter and wax, and that its consistence, as well as the consistence of these analogous substances, is caused by an acid intimately united with it, which cannot be separated but gradually and by repeated distillations Fat, and all other analogous oily matters, cannot be heated sufficiently to be raised into vapors, without suffering a considerable alteration, and even decomposition The vapors which rise from it, when heated in open air, are the same as those which rise when distilled in close vessels They consist of acid and attenuated oil This acid is remarkably penetrating, acrid, and volatile, it irritates and inflames the eyes, the throat, and lungs, it makes the eyes shed tears, and excites a cough as much as volatile sulphureous acid does, although its nature be very different

When fat is in its natural state, and has not yet suffered any alteration, its acid is so well combined with its oily part, that none of its properties can be perceived Thus fat, in good condition, is very mild, and used successfully in medicine, particularly externally, for its lenient quality but, notwithstanding its great mildness, before it has been heated sufficiently to decompose it, and while it is yet fresh, it becomes exceedingly acrid, irritating, and caustic, when its acid is partly disengaged by fire or by time

When fat is become very rancid, not only its medicinal effects, but also many of its essential properties, are totally changed, particularly its property of resisting the action of spirit of wine for this menstruum, which does not affect pure and unchanged fat, dissolves some portion of fat which has been strongly heated, or which has become rancid This effect can certainly proceed from no other cause, than that the acid of the fat disengages itself in both these cases Mr Macquer has shewn this in his Memoir concerning the Cause of the different Solubility of Oils in Spirit of Wine We shall speak more fully on this matter at the article OIL Mr De Machy, an intelligent apothecary of Paris, and an able chemist and observer, has made a remark upon this subject which corresponds with this opinion, which is, that all the rancidity of fat may be taken from it by treating it with spirit of wine Now, this evidently happens, because the spirit of wine dissolves all the portion of fat which is disengaged from its acid, that is, all the rancid part, while it does not touch that which is not changed This practice may be advantageously employed for the preservation or recovery of some fats used in medicine, but which are rare, and not to be procured in their recent state

The decomposition of fat, from which may be obtained acid, oil, a very small quantity of residuous coal, and not a particle of volatile alkali, proves evidently, that this substance, although elaborated in animal bodies, of which it makes a part, has not the marks of an animalised matter, it therefore seems to make a separate class, and to be produced from the oily parts of the aliments which could not enter into the composition of the nutritive juices it is consequently an oil superabundant to nutrition, which nature deposites and reserves for particular purposes One of the chief uses of fat probably is to receive into its composition, to blunt and correct a great part of the acids of the aliments, and which are more than are requisite to the composition of the nutritive juice, or which nature could not otherwise expel This is certain, that the greater the quantity of aliments is taken by healthy animals above what is necessary for their nourishment and reproduction, the fatter they become Hence animals which are castrated, which are not much exercised, or which are come to an age when the loss and production of the seminal fluid is less, and which, at the same time, consume much succulent aliment, generally become fatter, and sometimes exceedingly so

Although fat be very different from truly animalised substances, and appears not easily convertible into nutritive juices, it being generally difficult of digestion, and apt to become rancid, as butter does in the stomachs of many persons, yet in certain cases it serves to the nourishment and reparation of the body Animals certainly become lean, and live upon their fat, when they have too little food, and when they have diseases which prevent digestion and production of the nutritive juice, and in these cases the fatter animals hold out longer than the leaner The fat appears to be then absorbed by the vessels designed for this use, and to be transformed into nutritive juice

The fats of different animals differ little They have all the same essential properties, and only vary sensibly in consistence Frugivorous animals, and particularly sheep, have very firm fat, most reptiles, and particularly fish, which are almost all carnivorous, have a soft and sometimes a liquid fat *See* BUTTER, WAX, *and* OIL

CCXC. FEATHERS (x)

CCXCI FENNEL (y)

CCXCII FENUGREEK (z)

CCXCIII FERMENT A ferment is a substance actually fermenting, or strongly disposed to ferment, and which is employed to determine and excite another body to fermentation, such are yeast, leaven, and other such substances *See* FERMENTATION

CCXCIV FERMENTATION Fermentation is an intestine motion, excited spontaneously, with the assistance of proper heat and fluidity, betwixt the integrant and constituent parts of certain very compound bodies, from which result new combinations of the principles of these bodies

All vegetable and animal matters, into the composition of which enter a certain quantity of fluid oil and earth, rendered perfectly soluble in water by the intervention of a saline matter, being diffused in a sufficient quantity of water to become liquid, or at least soft, and being exposed to heat from a few degrees above the freezing point to twenty-five and more, and when the communication with air is not entirely stopt, suffer spontaneously the fermentative motion, which entirely changes the nature and proportion of their principles

But this fermentation, and the new compounds produced by it, differ considerably both in properties and proportions, according to the nature of the fermented substance, and the circumstances of the fermentation

We may distinguish three particular kinds of fermentation, or three degrees of the same fermentation, which refer to the three principal products which result from it

The first is called *vinous* or *spirituous fermentation*, because it changes into wine the liquors which undergo it, and because from this wine may be obtained an inflammable spirit, miscible with water, called *spirit of wine*

The second kind of fermentation is called *acid* or *acetous*, because the product of it is an acid, or *vinegar*

The third fermentation is called the *putrid* or *putrefactive* It might also be called the *alkaline* fermentation, because much alkali is disengaged by it

All matters susceptible of the spirituous fermentation may afterwards undergo the acid, and, lastly, the putrid fermentation, but some substances are not susceptible of the spirituous fermentation, but proceed first to the acid, and afterwards to the alkaline or putrid fermentation, and lastly, some substances are susceptible of the putrid fermentation only Further, a substance which

(x) FEATHERS From sixteen ounces of feathers Neuman obtained six ounces, two drams of spirit, two ounces and two drams of salt, one ounce two drams of oil, and a residuum, from which, after calcination, twenty six grains of saline matter were elixated

(y) FENNEL The leaves and seeds of common fennel contain an essential oil The oil obtained from the leaves on the upper part of the plant is much finer, lighter, and more subtle than the oil obtained from the lower leaves The former oil swims on water, and the latter oil sinks *Neuman*

(z) FENUGREEK The seeds of this plant contain an expressible oil blended with resin and mucilage, but no essential oil From sixteen ounces, eleven drams were extracted by water, and from the same quantity, four drams and a half were extracted by spirit of wine *Neuman*

having undergone the ſpirituous fermentation, has proceeded to the acid fermentation, cannot be again made to undergo the ſpirituous, but paſſes neceſſarily to the putrid. Alſo thoſe ſubſtances which have undergone the acid fermentation directly, that is, without previouſly paſſing through the ſpirituous, are only then ſuſceptible of the putrid, and not of the ſpirituous fermentation; and the ſubſtances which paſs directly to the putrefactive fermentation cannot be made to undergo, at leaſt ſenſibly, the acid, and ſtill leſs the ſpirituous fermentation. Laſtly, any matter ſuſceptible of the ſpirituous fermentation cannot be made to putrify without previouſly paſſing through the ſpirituous and acid fermentations.

Theſe conſiderations have induced moſt chemiſts, and particularly the great Stahl, to conſider theſe fermentations leſs as three operations diſtinct and independant of each other, than as three principal and diſtinguiſhed degrees of one and the ſame fermentative motion, by which nature endeavors to reſolve, and to reduce into a ſimilar condition, all the moſt compounded bodies, into the combination of which enters the oily principle; that is, all animal and vegetable ſubſtances.

We may add, that while vegetable and animal ſubſtances ſuſceptible of fermentation make part of the living vegetable or animal, they undergo fermentation only in a ſlow and inſenſible manner, becauſe they are preſerved from it by the vital motion, and becauſe this ſlowneſs is neceſſary for the vegetable and animal economy: but when the life of organiſed bodies ceaſes, then, as nothing in their juices or proximate principles prevents their diſpoſition to change their nature and to be decompoſed, all theſe ſubſtances ſenſibly acquire the fermentative motion, and paſs with more or leſs rapidity and regularity through the periods of change which they have ſtill to undergo, according to the concurrence of circumſtances which generally favor fermentation.

According to this idea, fermentation, taking it altogether, would be nothing elſe than putrefaction, to which all animals and vegetables naturally and continually tend, during their life, ſlowly and inſenſibly; but after their death, quickly and ſenſibly.

At the beginning of this article we obſerved what the neceſſary conditions were for fermentation of any body, and hence the means by which it may be prevented or ſuſpended are eaſily deduced. Theſe means are, intenſe cold, want of air and of water, and laſtly, a diſproportion of the principles of the bdoy expoſed to fermentation.

The moſt fermentable liquors, as the juices of grapes and other ripe fruits, do not ferment when expoſed to too great cold. The blood and fleſh of animals are preſerved from corruption by froſt. They may be alſo preſerved under the exhauſted receiver of an air-pump, or by drying perfectly. They may particularly be preſerved by this latter method any time, without ſuffering the leaſt alteration.

We are to remark upon this ſubject of preventing fermentations in fermentable ſubſtances, that when only the neceſſary degree of heat is employed to deprive them of their ſuperabundant moiſture, and their compoſition conſequently is not changed, we may, by mixing them again with the proper quantity of water, reſtore to them the ſame tendency to ferment which they had before they were dried. This obſervation is particularly applicable to matters ſuſceptible of the firſt and laſt degrees of fermentation; and we ought to conclude

 from

from thence, that although the products of the spirituous and alkaline fermentation are more volatile than water, yet the fermentable substances contain no principle which is not less volatile than water

The last method of preventing or retarding fermentation in fermentable substances is, as we said, to change the proportion of their proximate principles, which is conveniently done by mixing them with some substance which can unite itself to these principles, and which is not itself fermentable Such are spirit of wine, acids, and even all saline substances For this reason wine is preserved in the same state by penetrating it with sulphureous acid, and also animal matters are preserved from corruption by mixing them with spirit of wine, common salt, or any other salts

Those vegetable and animal substances only are properly fermentable which contain oil The action of minerals, or of their principles on each other, nor even the action of decompounded vegetable and animal substances, can be considered as true fermentations, except we so far extend the meaning of the word fermentation as to include the spontaneous and intestine motion of decompounding pyrites, by which new salts are formed, the changes produced upon the imperfect metals by air and by water, the rancidity of oils, and other changes, which appear to differ essentially from the fermentation of animal and vegetable matters

The effervescences which happen betwixt bodies not much compounded, when they mutually dissolve each other, such as the effervescences perceived when acids unite with earths, alkalis, or metals, are much more different from true fermentation, and have never been confounded together but by persons entirely ignorant of chemistry

We may judge from what we have said concerning fermentation in general, how important this matter is for the attainment of a knowledge of animal and vegetable substances, but we cannot form an adequate notion of it, without considering attentively the particular phenomena which appear in the several kinds or degrees of fermentation Wherefore, upon this the articles KINGDOM (VEGETABLE), KINGDOM (ANIMAL), WINE, SPIRIT *of* WINE, TARTAR, VINEGAR, *and* PUTREFACTION, may be consulted

CCXCV FILTRATION and FILTERS Filtration is an operation by which the heterogeneous parts mixed with a liquor are separated, or by which certain matters are freed from an useless liquid Filtration is generally performed by means of filters A heap of small parts of any substance, as sand, may also be employed for filtration in some cases

The rules of filtration are very simple The chief of these are, that the filter shall contain nothing which the liquor that passes through is capable of dissolving, that it shall not be liable to be attacked or corroded by the liquor, and that its pores shall be smaller than the particles of the matter to be separated from the liquor

A liquor cannot be filtrated unless its fluidity and thinness be proportioned to the pores of the filter Liquors which are viscid and thick, as syrups and mucilages, and those which are very thick, as very strong solutions of some salts, do not pass, or with great difficulty, through filters, whose pores appear otherwise sufficiently large in proportion to the fineness of their parts This proceeds from the adhesion which these parts have to each other

The

The filtration of these liquors is generally much forwarded by heat. Strong solutions, for instance, of salts, large proportions of which are soluble in water, as nitre, Glauber's salt, and others, require to be filtrated when boiling hot

When the parts of a matter diffused in this liquor adhere to this liquor, they cannot be separated by filtration. This adhesion must be previously destroyed. For instance, the expressed juices of plants are impregnated with a resinous, earthy, fine matter, adhering to these juices, and destroying their transparency The whey of milk also is turbid from the many fine caseous parts adhering to it These liquors cannot be clarified by filtration without a previous preparation, for they cannot pass through the pores of a filter close enough to retain the heterogeneous particles which disturb their transparency, and through a filter open enough to give them passage, they would pass in their turbid state

Such liquors are rendered capable of filtration by coagulating and collecting the heterogeneous parts This is effected by boiling, and still better by whites of eggs mixed and boiled together with these turbid liquors Whites of eggs, when they coagulate, collect and agglutinate the heterogeneous parts, which then appear in larger molecules, and float freely in the liquor without adhering to it This liquor is then in a state of filtration, it passes clear, and the matter which rendered it turbid remains upon the filter The fine caseous parts which disturbed the transparency of whey are so well mixed in it, that, besides whites of eggs, some cream of tartar must be added, to procure the required coagulation.

The matters generally used as filters are woollen stuffs, linen cloths more or less fine, and brown paper The form of filters varies according to the quality and quantity of the matters to be filtrated Some of them are hollow inverted cones These are more used in pharmacy and cookery than in chemistry With these syrups are filtered The filter most frequently used in chemistry is paper, in the making of which no paste or size has been employed

When a small quantity only of matter is to be filtrated, the paper must be folded so as to take the form of a funnel, and to be placed in a glass funnel, with straw interposed betwixt the filter and the sides of the funnel, to prevent the filter from applying itself immediately and in all its extent to the funnel, when it is filled and wet

When much matter is to be filtrated, a cloth is to be fixed to the four corners of a wooden frame, so that it shall not be stretched tight to the cloth is fitted paper, upon which the liquor is to be poured

The first portions of liquors which pass in filtration are almost always more or less turbid, wherefore they ought to be poured again upon the filter, and even more than once till it passes perfectly clear This happens because the pores of the filter, at first too open, are afterwards contracted by the swelling occasioned by the liquor, or they are partly stopped up by the sediment which is deposited upon them

CCXCVI FIRE Chemists consider fire, as also the other elements, in two very different views first, as it enters into the composition of many bodies, of which it is a principle or constituent part, and secondly, as being pure, free, not entering into any compound, but acting sensibly and strongly upon all natural bodies, and producing effects as a powerful agent in all chemical operations

operations In this latter point of view we ſhall conſider fire in this article. It will be conſidered as a principle under the article PHLOGISTON

Pure, free, uncombined fire ſeems to be a collection of particles, the matter of which is ſimple, homogeneous, and entirely unalterable All the properties of this element ſhew that its particles are infinitely ſmall, have no ſenſible adheſion to each other, and that they have a very rapid, continual motion in all directions, which is eſſential to them

From this definition, fire appears to be a body eſſentially fluid, and many facts concur to prove that it is the only body eſſentially fluid, conſequently the cauſe of the fluidity of other bodies, and that as it alone counterballances the general tendency of all the other parts of matter towards each other, they are prevented by it from uniting into one immenſe, homogeneous, and perfectly hard maſs

Whence can ſo aſtoniſhing a difference proceed between the properties of the primitive integrant molecules of fire, and thoſe of the integrant parts of all other matter? Is fire then not material, or not compoſed of matter, as its properties have induced ſome philoſophers to think? Is it matter of a peculiar kind? Or does, as a great geometrician thinks, the attraction of the parts of matter become negative, and changed into repulſion, when theſe parts become infinitely ſmall, and can come infinitely near to each other, which ſeems very probably to be the caſe with the particles of fire?

We have not facts enough to decide concerning theſe different opinions We ſhall, therefore, confine ourſelves to inveſtigate the eſſential properties of fire, chiefly thoſe which influence moſt in chemical operations and chemical phenomena

Fire can with great facility penetrate, or ſeparate itſelf from, any body however denſe, that is, any body whatever may be heated by expoſure to fire, or cooled to its former temperature, by removing it from this expoſure

From this effect we may infer the infinite ſmallneſs of the integrant parts of fire, and we may perceive the cauſe of its equal diſtribution through all bodies, when it is not determined by ſome particular cauſe to penetrate one body in greater quantity than another

In fact, all ſubſtances whatever, which are placed in any given degree of heat, and obliged to remain there, acquire preciſely the ſame degree of heat This fact has been aſcertained by inſtruments fit for meaſuring the degrees of heat

The effects which the fire produces, or rather heated bodies, upon our ſenſes, are ſenſations of heat and light, but theſe ſenſations are not excited but when the fire is in a certain quantity, for every known body contains a certain portion of uncombined fire, and yet not any body which is not lighted or ſtrongly heated, excites in us any ſenſation of heat or light Beſides, in certain circumſtances, a body may appear luminous, although it has no more ſenſible heat than the ſurrounding bodies This is proved by the effects of ſeveral phoſphoric bodies, ſuch as the ſcales of fiſh, rotten wood, glow-worms, all which ſhine in the dark, although no more heated than the ſurrounding bodies Alſo certain ſubſtances may be ſo penetrated with free and active fire, as to excite ſenſations of heat, and even to burn, although they do not appear luminous even in the dark Amongſt theſe ſubſtances are ſtones, metals, and even

water,

water, all which may be so heated as to excite pain to persons touching them, although they are not luminous.

Hence we ought to conclude, that the sensations of heat and light are in many cases insufficient to prove the presence of any given quantity of fire in bodies.

We ought also to remark, that although all bodies penetrated with much fire are necessarily hot and luminous, heat, and not light, is the only certain sign of the presence of fire. The reason of this is, that bodies may be very luminous, without any change being induced into any of their essential qualities in these two contrary states, whereas the difference of more or less heat produces in all bodies alterations of their properties very sensible and proportionable to the difference of heat.

These considerations seem to have induced some philosophers to imagine, that light is a being which is indeed rendered sensible by fire, but distinct and different from it. According to this opinion, heat is only a property of fire, whereas light is a distinct and independant substance. This opinion appears to be even demonstrated, when we consider that light may be decomposed by refraction, as Newton's experiments shew, and that it is not, as pure fire is, capable of pervading all bodies, is proved by the opacity of many bodies, and by the reflexion of light.

However that may be, as heat occasions more or less sensible changes in the qualities of all bodies, and that its whole action by which it influences any body consists in the single quality, or, to speak more accurately, the essential fluidity of fire, of which heat is only an effect, we ought here only to consider the general effects produced by fire upon all bodies by heating them more or less.

These effects, although diversified, depend nevertheless on one principle and primary change produced upon all bodies, by which they are rarefied or made to occupy a larger space. In fact, every solid and fluid body, when penetrated by a greater or less quantity of disengaged fire, is more or less encreased or diminished in size than it was before.

This principle has suggested to philosophers several different instruments by which this dilatation of heated bodies, or rather the heat which is the cause of it, may be measured, and quantities of fire, too small to be estimated by our senses, may be appreciated. The chief of these instruments is the THERMOMETER, *which see*.

As bodies are dilated by fire, their specific gravity must consequently be diminished, and the adhesion of their integrant parts must also be diminished. *See* AGGREGATION, INTEGRANT PARTS, *and* GRAVITY.

These two great effects, produced by fire upon all bodies, are the most important and most necessary to be considered, relatively to chemistry. We may indeed say, that they are the only effects, for excepting combustion, which is a peculiar property of inflammable bodies, every chemical operation is performed either by a diminution of specific gravity, or by a greater or less disjunction of the integrant parts of bodies, as we shall see.

Some substances are capable of a greater dilatation or diminution of their specific gravity, than others, by fire. Thus certain matters are so much rarefied by even a moderate heat, that they seem to lose all their specific gravity, or become at least specifically lighter than all the surrounding bodies hence these substances, when heated to a certain degree, are raised as bodies would be without gravity. All substances which have this property are called in general *volatile substances* See VOLATILITY Other bodies are so little dilatable by fire, relatively to their density, that the greatest heat that can be given to them produces an almost insensible diminution of specific gravity These are called, from their being almost unalterable in this respect by fire, *fixed bodies* See FIXITY.

Hence, if we expose to fire a compound body containing some fixed and some volatile principles, the former becoming specifically lighter ought to rise in vapors, and to separate themselves from the latter, which are unalterable in this respect But as almost all compounds contain principles differing so much in volatility and fixity, that some of them may be raised and sublimed, while others shall remain fixed with some given degree of heat, we may therefore, by heat alone, make many analyses and decompositions. If, for example, we expose a compound of regulus of antimony, which is a volatile semi-metal, and of gold, which is a fixed metal, to a heat so strong that the volatility of the regulus of antimony shall take place, then this semi-metal, being raised by its acquired levity, will be sublimed in vapors, and will be separated from the gold, which will remain fixed and pure. See DISTILLATION, SUBLIMATION, EVAPORATION

The observation we have just made concerning the changes in the specific gravity of bodies, which the dilatation occasioned by heat produces, ought also to be applied to the diminution of the adhesion of their integrant parts, which is an effect of the same cause, for if a body be dilated by heat, the contiguity, and consequently the adhesion, of its integrant parts must be diminished but in this respect the several natural substances differ very much, for the integrant parts of some bodies, when dilated by heat, are so separated and disjoined, that they seem no longer to cohere If these bodies be naturally solid, they become fluid when they are penetrated with a sufficient quantity of disengaged fire, and are called *fusible bodies* Those bodies, the integrant parts of which cannot be entirely disjoined by fire, are called infusible or refractory but as the aggregation of a body is broken when it is fused, and as this destruction of aggregation is a necessary condition for the combination of bodies with each other, fire therefore, by rendering solid bodies liquid, has influence as a principal agent in all combinations See COMBINATIONS, SOLUTIONS, FUSIBILITY, and REFRACTORY

As all chemical operations may be reduced to decompositions and combinations, fire is therefore in chemistry, as in nature, an universal agent Thus we know that, although decompositions and analyses may be made by menstruums without any more than the natural heat, yet as these menstruums can only act when rendered sufficiently fluid by heat, fire therefore acts in these analyses as necessarily as in those which are occasioned by the immediate application of heat

We ought to observe concerning this subject of the volatility, fixity, fusibility and infusibility of bodies, first, that all these qualities are properly only relative Not any body is entirely fixed and unfusible, and those which we consider as such would be reduced into vapors, as volatile bodies are, if they were exposed to a heat infinitely stronger than any we can excite. Thus a body will appear fixed, or infusible, when compared with other very volatile and very fusible substances, while it shall be considered as volatile or fusible, when compared with others more fixed and less fusible.

In the second place, as volatility and fusibility are effects of one and the same cause, namely, of the dilatation occasioned by the presence of a certain quantity of uncombined fire in bodies, these two qualities are properly the same, in more or less eminent degrees, and in this sense, volatility ought only to be considered as the highest degree of fusibility Accordingly, substances which are habitually liquid, and which ought therefore to be considered as the most fusible, are all very volatile, and may be raised into vapors with very little heat, while, on the contrary, matters that are hard, and not very dilatable, those, in short, the aggregation of whose parts is the firmest and most difficultly to be broken, and which are therefore the least fusible, are also the most fixed

The aggregation of all bodies, when reduced into vapors or fused, is broken, but more so when reduced into vapors, than when merely fused Accordingly, the most effectual of all methods for combining substances which cannot be easily united, or which cannot be joined while the aggregation of one of them is sensibly preserved, is, if possible, to reduce them into vapors, and to make these vapors meet

All the effects which fire produces, as an agent in chemical operations, are reducible, as we see, to those we have mentioned The quantity of uncombined fire which flows perpetually from the sun, and diffuses itself through all its sphere, is sufficient to produce all the separations and combinations which we daily see effected by nature but as the heat caused by the sun is very limited, chemistry would be confined almost to the contemplation of natural operations, if we had not methods by which pure and uncombined fire may be made to enter bodies, or to quit them in greater or less quantities

The methods of encreasing the quantity or the activity of uncombined fire in bodies may be comprehended in the following three

First, by concave mirrors and by convex glasses, a number of the rays of the sun, proportionate to the size and good quality of the instruments, may be collected into one point, called the *focus* Bodies exposed to such a focus are penetrated with an infinitely greater quantity of uncombined and active fire than they have naturally They are then ignited, inflamed, dilated, fused, or volatilised, according to their particular natures The heat of such a focus is the greatest that art has produced It is even exceedingly too strong for most chemical operations, and ought to be applied to the most fixed and refractory bodies only As such a focus is also very small and inconvenient for the performance of any operation, and as large mirrors and lenses are very rare and dear, this fire is not much used for chemical operations. Nevertheless, several very important chemical experiments were performed by collected solar heat, as the decomposition of gold, published by Homberg, if it be true, the fusion of platina, by Messrs Macquer and Beaumé, and of several other bodies which could not be fused by other fires, without addition of other substances, by other chemists, at different times.

Secondly, experience has long ago taught us, and even the most ignorant nations know, that heat and all the effects of fire may be occasioned by friction and percuſſion of hard bodies The heat excited by this method may be very conſiderable, and even comparable to that of collected ſolar fire It is in general proportionable to the force, rapidity, intenſity of friction and of percuſſion, and to the hardneſs of the bodies rubbed or ſtruck This heat is alſo not much uſed in chemical operations it, however, frequently occurs in many chemical experiments, as in fermentations, effervescencies, and ſolutions It occurs whenever bodies unite together, and is proportionable to the rapidity and force with which they act upon each other It is produced by the friction and colliſion of their integrant parts, which ſhows, that the primary integrant parts are exceedingly hard, even in bodies generally ſoft or fluid, for theſe ſubſtances, when diſſolving, produce as much heat as thoſe which are moſt hard, and whoſe aggregation is moſt firm

The third cauſe which produces or excites heat is the combuſtion of compound bodies, in the combination of which fire enters as an element or principle, and which are therefore called inflammable or combuſtible bodies

The principal phenomenon preſented by theſe bodies is, that by mere contact with any other body, inflammable or not, but which is ignited, they are kindled, inflamed, give much heat and light, in a word, produce all the ſame effects as the collected ſolar heat, or the alliſions of hard bodies This continues till the whole ſubſtance of fire, which entered into their compoſition, and which was inactive, has reſumed all the activity of pure and uncombined fire, and is entirely diſſipated

This inflammation of combuſtible bodies is undoubtedly one of the greateſt and moſt aſtoniſhing phenomena of nature but it is alſo one of the moſt difficult to be conceived We cannot expect to underſtand it well, till we know better than we do at preſent the eſſence and true ſtate of fire when combined, and conſtituting a principle of the bodies containing it, called *phlogiſton* See PHLOGISTON

We muſt obſerve at preſent, that as the combuſtion of inflammable bodies produces all the effects of fire, pure, uncombined, and active, it is alſo the moſt convenient method, by which fire can be applied by chemiſts to ſeveral bodies

The moſt common inflammable ſubſtances, ſuch as wood, foſſil coal, charcoal, are moſt generally employed in chemiſtry, in the arts, and in the ordinary purpoſes of life, in all operations where fire is requiſite

As chemiſts have occaſion to employ all the ſeveral degrees of heat, from the weakeſt to the ſtrongeſt, they have diſcovered methods of applying any required degree through intermediate ſubſtances, and ſtill better by the diſpoſition and conſtruction of furnaces, in which the combuſtible matters, and thoſe to which the fire is intended to be applied, are contained *See upon this ſubject* BATHS, COMBUSTION, FURNACES. (a)

CCXCVII FISH (b)

(a) *See the Supplement* I *article* FIRE

(b) FISH Neuman obtained from ſixteen ounces of fiſh analyſed by diſtillation, thirteen ounces two drams and a half of volatile alkaline ſpirit, five drams of concrete ſalt, three drams of oil, and an ounce four drams and a half of reſiduum, from which, by calcination and elixation, twenty-five grains of ſaline matter were extracted The proportion of volatile ſalt thus obtained from fiſh is conſiderably greater than that from fleſh.

CCXCVIII. FIXITY. Fixity is a property, by which a body resists the action of fire, without being raised and dissipated in vapors. It is the opposite quality to volatility.

The degree of resistance which a body ought to give to fire, to entitle it to the character of being fixed, is not determined. Thus substances are considered to be fixed almost always relatively to others which are less fixed.

As we do not know the ultimate degrees of the activity of fire, we cannot say whether any bodies in nature be capable of resisting this extreme degree of fire without sublimation, or be absolutely fixed.

Those substances, however, are generally considered by chemists as absolutely fixed, which lose nothing of their quantity by exposure to the most intense heat which they can produce. The purest and simplest earthy principle is a substance of this kind, and is perhaps the only one which can be considered as naturally fixed, and is the principle of fixity of all the rest.

Chemists commonly call many substances fixed, which do not deserve that name, but comparatively with others, as we have already mentioned. In this sense, for instance, vitriolic acid is sometimes called a fixed acid, by which is only meant that it is less volatile than others. For the same reason, regulus of antimony, and other semi-metals, may be considered as fixed substances when compared with essential oils and ether, particularly in operations where they remain fixed, when exposed to a heat sufficient to evaporate essential oils or ether; whereas these semi-metals may be considered as volatile, when compared with metals properly so called.

The fixity of bodies seems certainly to proceed from their little dilatability by fire, and this defect of dilatability is occasioned by the attraction or adhesion of the integrant parts of these bodies. *See* FIRE *and* VOLATILITY.

CCXCIX. FLAME. Flame is a collection of vapors of combustible bodies actually burning, and which are themselves in the motion of combustion. (*c*)

(*c*) FLAME is generally said to be an ignited vapor, or red-hot smoke. Nevertheless, *Flame*, *Vapor*, and *Smoke*, are things distinct from each other, and ought not to be confounded together. We shall endeavor to describe and distinguish these: and first, of *Vapor*.

By the action of certain determinate degrees of heat, with or without access of air, all liquid and some concrete bodies are so dilated, as to occupy a much larger space than before this exposure to these determinate degrees of heat, acquire a considerable expansive power, or elasticity, and become transparent and invisible. They are then properly vapors. This state they retain while exposed to the same heat by which it was produced; but by application of cold, they are condensible into palpable substances, similar to those from which they were formed, if they happened to consist of homogeneal parts, as water and mercury do; or they are condensible into palpable substances which are the constituent parts of the bodies subjected to heat, if these bodies happened to consist of parts not homogeneal, as plants do of water and essential oil. If the vapor consists of inflammable parts, it may be kindled by contact with any ignited body; by which means, together with access of air or nitrous acid, it may be made to undergo those effects which are produced upon all bodies during their combustion, namely, the decomposition of its parts, the dissipation of its phlogiston, and emission of heat and light: but vapor thus ignited, rendered visible, and in the act of combustion, by access of air, or nitrous acid, is *flame*. This flame, or vapor decomposed by combustion, is not condensible, as we may easily conceive, into such palpable substances

As bodies cannot burn but by touching immediately the air, and as for this reason they only burn at their surface, flame, which is the only truly burning part of bodies which appear in actual combustion, is always at their surface. It is luminous and ardent throughout its whole thickness, because it is only a mass of adjacent, but disunited inflammable parts, which touching the air on every side, burn altogether and throughout their whole substance.

substances, as the undecomposed vapor is, but into some only of the constituent parts of these substances, the rest being destroyed by the combustion. Thus the vapor of spirit of wine is again condensible into spirit of wine, but from the flame of spirit of wine little can be obtained by condensation but the water, which was one of the constituent parts of that spirit, the other parts, especially the phlogiston, being destroyed by the combustion.

Not only the vapor of an inflammable body, but also the inflammable body itself, without being previously changed into vapor, may, by contact with an ignited body, or any other mode of application of heat, as friction, percussion, &c. together with access of air or nitrous acid, emit a flame, which consists, as in the former case, of particles of that body in the act of combustion. Thus by applying a hot iron to sulphur, we may see a flame immediately produced upon the surface of the sulphur. We may easily conceive that bodies thus kindled can only flame at their surfaces, because there only they are contiguous to air: but when nitre is intimately mixed with the inflammable substance, as in gun-powder, the whole substance, its interior as well as its exterior parts, are instantly inflamed, because the nitrous acid has, like air, the property of maintaining combustion. Hence also we may easily conceive why the external surface of a flame, by being contiguous with air, is much hotter than its internal parts, as may easily be shewn by applying any substance, alterable by heat, alternately to the exterior and interior parts of the flame of a candle; and when the flame has a considerable diameter, as of a foot or eighteen inches, and is maintained only by the air contiguous to it, as when the vapor issuing at the upper mouth of a furnace for smelting iron ore is kindled by contact of any ignited body, the flame will then be found to have a thickness only of an inch or two, while the vapor near the center surrounded by this flame, is not inflamed, as appears from paper or other easily combustible matter being held in it without being kindled.

Smoke consists of palpable particles elevated by means of the rarefying heat, or by the force of the ascending current of air, from bodies exposed to heat. These particles vary much in their properties according to the substances from which they were produced. Vapors also rising from heated bodies, when condensed by the coldness of air or other contiguous bodies, become palpable, and therefore have the appearance, and may be considered as smoke. The smoke arising from combustible bodies consists of parts, some of which are generally combustible, but so difficultly combustible, that a greater heat is required than they possess while they are smoke, to effect their combustion. The flame also of combustible bodies may be so cooled by the application of cold air, or other cold substances, as that the combustion of the particles composing it shall be checked, and these particles shall become smoke. Thus the flame of a candle is, by the coldness of the air, diminished more and more as it rises higher, till at last it is extinguished, before all its inflammable parts are consumed, and its point terminates in smoke.

The smoke of burning inflammable substances, when collected, is called *soot*. The smoke of uninflammable substances, or of inflammable substances not exposed to air, and consequently not burning, consists of the substances not altered or decomposed, but only divided, as the flowers of sulphur raised by heat in close vessels, and the flowers of sal ammoniac; or it consists of parts of these substances decomposed merely by heat, and not by combustion, as the flowers of sulphur and of arsenic, from the mineral containing these called pyrites, exposed to heat in close vessels, and the flowers of benzoin, sublimed by heat from the resin of that name.

No

No combustible body really burns without flame Those, indeed, whose inflammable principle is firmly united with a great quantity of incombustible matter, such as charcoal or ashes almost entirely burnt, and most metals, seem to be consumed without sensible flame, but this appearance does not impose upon an accurate observer The appearance of a body which really burns is very different from that of a body which is only made red-hot by being penetrated with a fire proceeding from some other substance, which does not itself burn Let a bar of iron be compared with a flint, when both are taken out of a fire so intense as to give to each of them a white heat, and the surface of the metal will seem covered over with a small flame, which is indeed very low, but bright and sparkling, while nothing similar will appear on the surface of the flint Besides, the flint will lose its vivid color much sooner than the iron If we observe lead while it is scorified in a cupel under a muffle, we shall see in a striking manner that the metal shall be much more ardent and luminous than the cupel, although these two bodies are exposed precisely to the same degree of heat, but this difference can certainly proceed only from the small flame which necessarily accompanies the combustion of the metal, while the cupel which contains no combustible principle, and which consequently cannot burn, does not exhibit any such appearance

All bodies, therefore, which do really burn, seem to burn with flame, but the flames proceeding from the different combustible bodies differ very much from each other, according to the nature of these bodies, and to the particular state of their phlogiston I do not know whether the flame of any combustible body be entirely pure Such a flame would be nothing else than phlogiston separated from all other substances, reduced into vapor, and actually ignited The flames of rectified spirit of wine and of perfect coal seem to be the purest of all, because they are accompanied with no smoke nor fuliginous matter Nevertheless, the flame of spirit of wine is accompanied with much water *See* SPIRIT *of* WINE All other flames are evidently mixed with heterogeneous substances, which discover themselves by different qualities

The least pure of all flames is that of oils and of all oily matters, because it proceeds from very compound bodies This flame is always mixed not only with all the volatile principles of the oil, or oily body, but also with a considerable quantity of the fixed principles which are raised by the deflagration Besides, although it is considerably luminous, all the phlogiston which it contains is not burnt a portion of it remains combined in the state of coal with earth. Hence the flame of all oils is accompanied with a fuliginous smoke, which blackens bodies that it touches As this property belongs to the flames of all oils and oily matters, and to none else, it is a mark by which we may discover whether the phlogiston of any body be in an oily state *See* OIL, FULIGINOSITY, SMOKE, *and* SOOT

The flame of metals is also accompanied with a sensible smoke, which is even very considerable and thick in certain metals But this flame does not, like that of oils, blacken substances which it touches, because metals are not in an oily state *See* METALS

Lastly, the flame of sulphur would be very pure, if it was not for the vitriolic acid, a large quantity of which is mixed with it. Perhaps the flame of this compound would be very pure, if the sulphur was previously mixt with fixed

fixed alkali to absorb the acid, in Stahl's manner, and if it was made to burn so weakly as not to be capable of kindling combustible bodies See SULPHUR

CCC FLINTS See EARHTS (VITRIFIABLE) (d)

CCCI FLOWERS By this name is generally understood bodies reduced into very fine parts, either spontaneously, or by some operation of art, but it is applied chiefly to volatile solid substances, reduced into very fine parts, or into a kind of meal by sublimation

Some flowers are nothing else than the bodies themselves, which are sublimed entire, without suffering any alteration or decomposition and other flowers are some of the constituent parts of the body subjected to sublimation, as we shall see in the following articles, when we define the principal matters distinguished by the name of flowers

CCCII FLOWERS *of* ANTIMONY Antimony, which is a mineral composed of the semi-metal called regulus of antimony and sulphur, is entirely volatile, and capable of being sublimed into flowers

To make flowers of antimony, an earthen pot or large crucible, in the upper and lateral part of which is an opening, is placed in a furnace, and three or four aludels are fitted to it The pot is to be made red-hot, and powdered antimony is to be thrown into it through the lateral opening, and the sublimation is then to be made These projections of antimony are to be repeated till the operator judges that the inner surface of the aludels is sufficiently covered with flowers, which are to be detached from thence with a feather

The vessels employed for this sublimation must not be exactly closed, for two reasons, first, that access of air favors and accelerates all sublimations, and particularly this Lemery observes justly, that the operation is accelerated greatly by directing a blast of wind upon the surface of the antimony In the second place, if the vessels were perfectly closed, they would be burst by the expansion of the vapors, or of the contained air

Although flowers of antimony be composed of regulus of antimony and of sulphur, as the antimony itself is, they nevertheless differ from it essentially in many respects They have not the same metallic brilliancy Their color is different shades of white, grey, and yellow They are powerfully emetic These

(*d*) FLINTS are semi-transparent or opake stones, generally of a roundish form, and covered with a white crust, of a smooth, uniform, shining texture, so hard as to strike fire with steel, calcinable by fire so as to become white, brittle, and, according to Henckel, heavier than before calcination, not soluble by acids, and vitrifiable only by the very violent heat of the largest speculums, such as that of Vilette, and not even by the focus of a lens of Tschirnhaus, according to an experiment of Neuman They are found generally in beds of chalk and of sand, but never forming entire strata of rock, as jasper does By long exposure to air and to the sun, they seem to decay, to lose their lustre, their firmness of texture, and to be changed to a white calcareous earth or chalk Hence they are almost always found covered with a white chalky crust They are also convertible into calcareous earth by fusion, or vitrification with so much fixed alkali, that they shall resolve into a liquid mass called the liquamen of flints, and by precipitation from the fixed alkali by means of acids See LIQUOR *of* FLINTS

Flints are of the class of earths called *vitrifiable*, because these earths are generally employed, together with fixed alkali, as materials in the making of glass See GLASS, *and* EARTHS (VITRIFIABLE)

differences prove that antimony sustains a considerable alteration by this sublimation This alteration consists in the diminishing the connexion betwixt the sulphur and the regulus of antimony

The difference of colors in flowers of antimony proceeds from the variable action of the fire and of the air upon this mineral during the operation Probably the emetic quality of flowers of different colors also differs But this difference has not been observed, as the flowers of antimony have not been much employed, because of their uncertainty

CCCIII RED FLOWERS *of* ANTIMONY Lemery gives a process for making the red flowers of antimony It consists in distilling eight ounces of antimony, mixed with fourteen ounces of sal ammoniac, or of flowers of sal-ammoniac Some volatile alkali is raised from the sal-ammoniac, and red flowers are sublimed

The portion of volatile alkali which rises in this operation is disengaged by the reguline part of antimony, and as one part of this volatile alkali acts at once upon the sulphur and upon the regulus of antimony, an antimoniated volatile liver of sulphur is formed These red flowers are a kind of kermes, and differ from the ordinary kermes in having a volatile instead of a fixed alkali They are emetic, purgative, diaphoretic, incisive, &c as kermes is, and may be given in the same dose as kermes is, but are seldom used However, a kermes made with volatile alkali may have peculiar virtues, and deserves the attention of physicians, but in this case it ought to be prepared in a more certain manner by employing uncombined volatile alkali

CCCIV FLOWERS (ARGENTINE) *of* REGULUS *of* ANTIMONY To make these flowers, regulus of antimony is put into an unvarnished earthen pot, which is to be placed in a furnace so that its bottom may be red-hot, while its upper part shall be much colder. The pot is to be covered with a lid, without luting it, and heat is to be applied during an hour or more When the pot is cold, its internal surface, and also the remaining part of the regulus, is found covered with white flowers, in form of beautiful, transparent, and shining needles These flowers are to be gathered with a feather After this, a second sublimation may be commenced, and managed as the former was, and thus the whole regulus may be changed into flowers, which requires much time

Lemery directs that a small lid or diaphragm shall be placed within the pot, at the height of three or four fingers thickness above the regulus But this appears to be unnecessary Mr Beaumé does not use this second lid He only inclines the pot so, that all the upper part of it shall be out of the furnace He makes the bottom of it very hot, and thus obtains a large quantity of flowers

These flowers appear to be nothing else than the earth of regulus of antimony deprived of almost all its phlogiston They are not emetic nor purgative They are not very volatile, and cannot easily be reduced into regulus They are soluble in aqua regia All these properties, together with their remaining degree of volatility, shew that they contain some inflammable principle They have also considerable marks of a saline substance They have not only the appearance of a crystallized salt, but are also entirely soluble in

water,

water, as Mr Beaume observes, although a large quantity of water, which must also be boiling, is required for that purpose Eight ounces of boiling water are capable of dissolving half a grain of these flowers From this property we may suspect that regulus of antimony contains a saline matter as one of its constituent parts, which is conformable to the opinion of some chemists concerning salts and metals

Nevertheless, if we consider that regulus of antimony cannot be deprived of all the sulphur with which it is united in its mineral state, we may suppose that part of the acid of sulphur may, by uniting with the earth of the regulus of antimony, give the saline qualities to the flowers of this metallic substance.

CCCV FLOWERS *of* ARSENIC The white flowers of arsenic are nothing but white arsenic itself, which being a volatile substance, unalterable by sublimation, may be raised altogether, without any change

Flowers of arsenic are made, as all other flowers are, by subliming arsenic. *See* SUBLIMATION

We ought to observe that they are not perfectly white, unless the arsenic from which they have been sublimed has been perfectly dephlogisticated and white If the arsenic which is sublimed be mixed with a little sulphur, the flowers will be more or less yellow, or red, according to the quantity of sulphur which is sublimed along with them If the arsenic be in a reguline state, or considerably phlogisticated, its flowers will be more or less greyish or brown Hence we see veins of these different colors among the arsenic which is found in commerce, and which is obtained by sublimation in great works from arsenical minerals

As arsenic is very fusible, when these flowers fix themselves to any substance considerably heated, they suffer a kind of fusion, are agglutinated together, and form the dense, compact, heavy, shining masses which are in the shops of druggists The nature and properties of flowers of arsenic do not differ from those of arsenic *See* ARSENIC

CCCVI FLOWERS *of* BENJAMIN, *or* BENZOIN To make flowers of benjamin, let a quantity of benjamin be put into a varnished earthen pan, which is to be covered with another inverted pan of stone ware The edges of these two pans ought to have been ground upon a stone, so that they fit well to each other They are to be luted together with paper dipped in paste The earthen pan containing the benjamin is to be put upon a gentle fire, and which is not capable of raising the oil of the benjamin With that heat the sublimation is to be performed, when the vessels are cooled, they are to be unluted, and great care is to be taken that they be not shook If the sublimation has been performed, the inner surface of the upper earthen pan will be found covered with fine sparkling flowers like a very pure salt, forming crystals like flattened needles. A considerable quantity also of these flowers is generally found, which are not raised, and which cover the surface of the remaining benjamin The flowers are to be swept off with a feather

The success of this operation depends on the degree of heat given, and the time employed. If the heat be too great, a part of the oil of benjamin will rise together with the flowers, which will thence receive a dirty yellow tinge In this case they must be again sublimed, and with a less heat If, on the contrary,

trary, a sufficient degree of heat is not given, or the operation has not been long enough continued, all the flowers which the benjamin is capable of furnishing will not be procured The same benjamin will, by repeating the operation, furnish more flowers

The process formerly used to make these flowers consists in putting the benjamin in an earthen pot, to the mouth of which is fitted a paper, or pasteboard conical head But the method described above, which is proposed by Mr Beaumé, seems to be preferable because the paper or pasteboard heads absorb many flowers, which are consequently lost, and also because the earthen vessel employed by Mr Beaumé has a greater surface than the pot used in the ancient method, and quantity of surface is always favorable to sublimation

The flowers of benjamin are a true concrete, volatile, and oily essential salt of benjamin They have the smell of benjamin, and are inflammable, from the essential oil which enters their composition They are soluble in water and in spirit of wine, which sufficiently proves their saline nature Accordingly, Mr Geoffroy observes, that this salt may be obtained by treating benjamin with water, and by crystallization

Benjamin is probably not the only resin from which an essential salt of this kind may be obtained perhaps, even all resins contain such essential salt, in greater or less quantity, and this is certainly one of those which contain a great quantity of it

Flowers of benjamin are considered in medicine as incisive, dividing, and favoring expectoration, and are therefore given in the viscous asthma They may be given from six grains to twelve *See* RESINS, *and* SUBLIMATION

CCCVII FLOWERS *of* SAL AMMONIAC The flowers of sal ammoniac are nothing else than sal ammoniac sublimed, for this semi-volatile salt suffers no decomposition by sublimation The process for making these flowers contains nothing singular, excepting that an equal part of decrepitated common salt is generally mixed with the sal ammoniac, in order to divide this latter salt, and to facilitate its sublimation By this sublimation, sal ammoniac may be purified from fuliginous and other matters, with which it is generally mixed. But it may be better and more conveniently purified by solution in water, by filtration, and by crystallization For this salt has the property of raising along with it in sublimation very fixed matters, as we see from the example of the flowers of sal ammoniac tinged with copper and with iron, called *ens martis*, and *ens veneris*, which are nothing else than sal ammoniac sublimed with iron and with copper *See* AMMONIAC (SAL)

CCCVIII FLOWERS *of* SULPHUR Flowers of sulphur are crude sulphur sublimed in an apparatus of aludels Sulphur cannot be decomposed without an intermediate substance in close vessels Therefore flowers of sulphur have no properties different from those of pure sulphur in masses *See* SULPHUR

CCCIX FLOWERS *of* ZINC Flowers of zinc are the metallic earth of zinc, deprived of almost all its phlogiston, and raised in light flocks from deflagrating zinc

To make these flowers, zinc is to be put into a large open crucible, set in a furnace which draws air well When a white heat is raised, the zinc kindles and burns with a white, vivid, dazzling flame, accompanied with a considerable quantity of white ſmoke This ſmoke is condenſed in white light flocks, which float all round the laboratory The greateſt part of theſe flocks, however, fix themſelves to the ſides of the crucible and to the zinc. They are called *flowers of zinc*, *nihil album*, or *pompholix*

Although theſe flowers are raiſed into ſmoke in this operation, like a very volatile ſubſtance, they are really very fixed, as metallic earths are, when well dephlogiſticated, and are ſo incapable of being again ſublimed, that they reſiſt the moſt violent fire, and are ſooner melted than ſublimed If they are then raiſed in ſmoke during deflagration, this effect is produced by the activity with which the zinc burns, and for the ſame reaſon, earths and coals extremely fixed are found in ſoot of wood and of moſt other combuſtible matters

The flowers of zinc are ſoluble in acids, nearly as zinc is *See* ZINC The cauſe of this may be, that they retain ſome phlogiſton But they are difficultly reducible into zinc, and were even believed to be incapable of reduction, till Mr Margraaf publiſhed a method of reviving them, by expoſing them to a ſtrong heat together with ſome inflammable ſubſtance in cloſe veſſels

In the crucible uſed for the preparation of flowers of zinc, a conſiderable quantity of theſe flowers is found fixed to its ſides, and to the ſurface of the zinc, if any remains unburnt Theſe latter flowers are much leſs white and light than the former They have been produced by the part of the zinc which burnt leſs vehemently than the reſt Their color is greyiſh, from a certain quantity of phlogiſton which they retain

Flowers of zinc alſo are obtained from furnaces in which minerals containing zinc are ſmelted, particularly that of Rammelſberg They adhere in great quantities to the upper part of the internal ſurface of the walls of the furnaces But as theſe flowers ſuſtain a great heat, they are half fuſed and agglutinated together, forming maſſes, which muſt be taken off frequently in order to clear the furnaces Flowers of zinc in this ſtate are called *cadmia fornacum*, or *pompholix* *See* CADMIA *and* ZINC

CCCX FLOWERS *of* VEGETABLES (*e*)

(*e*) FLOWERS In this article, which is extracted from Dr Lewis's notes on Neuman's Chemiſtry, the *colors* only of flowers ſhall be conſidered Very few of the colors of flowers of vegetables are durable, or can be made durable by any means known The only permanent color is *yellow* The *red*, the *blue*, the *purple*, the *crimſon*, and the *violet* are very periſhable Many flowers loſe theſe colors merely by being dried, eſpecially by being ſlowly dried in a ſhady and not warm place The colors of all of them periſh by keeping, even in the cloſeſt veſſels The more haſtily they are dried, and the more perfectly they are ſecured from air, the longer they retain their beauty The coloring matter of flowers extracted and applied on other bodies is ſtill more periſhable.

BLUE FLOWERS The color of many blue flowers is extracted by infuſion in water, but from others, water acquires only a purpliſh hue Of thoſe which have been tried, not one gives a blue color to ſpirit of wine ſome give no color, and ſome give a reddiſh color The expreſſed juice of theſe flowers is generally blue The blue juices and infuſions are rendered red by all acids, and the moſt florid red is given to them by *marine* acid. The flowers alſo, by maceration, impart a red color to acid liquors Alkalis fixed and volatile, and lime water, change theſe blue colors to green And thoſe infuſions or juices which have nothing of the color of the flower, ſuffer the ſame changes from the addition of acid and alkaline liquors Even when the flowers have been kept

CCCXI FLUIDITY Fluidity is the state of a body whose integrant parts are so disunited and incoherent, that no sensible resistance is opposed to their separation in any direction, but which are nevertheless sufficiently attracted by each other, to remain adjacent, and to form an aggregate body

Hence fluidity is a middle state betwixt hardness, in which the integrant parts of bodies adhere together firmly, and the entire want of aggregation, in which the integrant parts of bodies are so separated and removed from each other, that their mutual attraction is no longer sensible

kept till their colors are lost, their infusions acquire a red color from acids, and a green color from alkalis, but in a less degree than when the flowers were fresh The red color produced by acids is scarcely more durable than the original blue applied upon other bodies, and exposed to air, it gradually degenerates into a faint purple, and at last disappears, without leaving a stain behind The green produced by alkalis changes to a yellow, which does not fade so soon The green made by lime-water is more permanent and beautiful Green lakes, prepared from blue flowers by means of lime water, have been used by painters The flowers of *cyanus* have been much commended for affording elegant and blue pigments But Dr Lewis has not been able to extract from them any blue color They retain their color, when hastily dried, longer than other blue flowers, but do not communicate their original color to any menstruum

Red Flowers readily communicate their color to water, and those of a full red color give to a rectified spirit also a deep red tincture, brighter, though somewhat paler than the watery infusion But the lighter red flowers, and those which are purplish, impart little color to pure spirit The colors of infusions of these flowers are supposed to be heightened by acids, and to be rendered green by alkalis But this is not universal For amongst those examined by Dr Lewis, the rose colors and purplish red were changed by acids nearly as blue flowers are, but the full deep reds were not The deep infusion of red poppies was turned by alkalis not to a green, but to a dusky purple

Yellow Flowers communicate to water and to spirit of wine durable yellow colors, not alterable but in degree by acids or by alkalis, the former only rendering them paler, and the latter, as also alum, rendering them deeper Wool, or silk, impregnated with a solution of alum and of tartar, receives, on being boiled with the watery infusion or decoction, a durable yellow dye. A durable yellow lake is prepared by precipitating with alum an infusion of yellow flowers made in an alkaline ley In some of the *orange-colored flowers* the yellow matter seems to be of the same kind as that of the pure yellow flowers, but the red matter seems to be different from that of the pure red flowers The yellow matter is extracted from these flowers by water, and the remaining red matter is extracted by spirit of wine, or by a weak solution of fixed alkali in water Such are the saffron-colored flowers of *Carthamus* These flowers, after the yellow matter has been extracted by water, are said to give a red tincture to ley, from which a deep red fecula subsides, called *Safflower*, *Spanish red*, and *China-lake* This pigment gives a beautiful red color to spirit of wine, but none to water The yellow farina or fine dust, resting on the tips of the stamina of flowers, gives a fine bright yellow color to spirit of wine, and a duller yellow color to water The colors of both the watery and spirituous tinctures were heightened by alkalis rendered red by acids, and again restored to a yellow by adding an alkali This is the only known instance of the yellow color of a vegetable being rendered red by acids

White Flowers, or their expressed juices, impart a green color to alkaline leys, but have not been observed by Dr Lewis to give a red color to acids The white flowers of the common wild *convolvulus* give a deep yellow or orange color to water, which is affected by acids, by alkalis, and by alum, as the infusions of yellow flowers are The white flowers of *Xeranthemum* give a beautiful yellow color to water acidulated with spirit of nitre.

A body may be fluid in two manners; first, by the figure of its primitive integrant parts, so that each of these parts shall not touch any other but in one point, or in one infinitely small side, and consequently have but little or no adhesion. Such a body must necessarily and naturally be fluid. Fire seems to be the only body possessed of this essential fluidity.

The second manner by which a body may be rendered fluid is, to lessen the contact of the integrant parts, to disjoin them, or even to separate them from each other by the interposition of a fluid. All bodies, which can only be fluid in this manner, are evidently not essentially fluid. On the contrary, they are naturally more or less hard and solid, and can only have a mediate or secondary fluidity. Such all bodies in nature appear to be, excepting fire. Hence, without fire no fluid would exist, all bodies would cohere together, and form a single, solid mass, and hence fire is the principle of all fluidity. But when a body is rendered fluid by fire, it may then be capable of giving fluidity to other bodies. Water, for instance, the fluidity of which is certainly caused by fire, may by interposing itself betwixt the integrant parts of gums and salts, give to them a fluidity similar in some respects to its own.

We must not confound the fluidity received directly from fire with the fluidity received from bodies rendered fluid by fire. Some substances are incapable of receiving fluidity directly from fire, but only through the intervention of some other substance previously rendered fluid by fire. Such are gums, which are rather decomposed than rendered fluid by fire, but which are readily soluble in water. Other bodies may be either rendered fluid directly by fire, or secondarily through the intervention of another body previously rendered fluid by fire. Such, for instance, are salts. They become fluid when exposed alone to the action of fire, and are also capable of liquefaction by water.

The principal difference betwixt a body rendered fluid merely by the action of fire, and another body rendered fluid by the interposition of a fluid substance, is, that the integrant parts of the latter body adhere to those of the interposed substance, and that this adhesion or affinity is the cause of the fluidity of that body.

This secondary fluidity, therefore, given by interposition of a fluid substance, is nothing else than a solution. The fluidity given immediately by fire is called by chemists, *fusion*, we therefore say that a salt is dissolved in water, but not fused or melted. This latter expression is frequently used, though very improperly.

These evident and important differences betwixt the fluidity of fire, which is essentially fluid, the fluidity of bodies fused merely by the action of fire, and the fluidity of bodies rendered fluid by the interposition of others already fused, require that these different kinds of fluidity should be distinguished by names appropriated to each. At present no such precise expressions have been used to denote them. Bodies habitually fused might be called *fluid*, and those which have only a secondary fluidity might be called *liquid*. But what name shall be given to the primary and essential fluidity of fire?

This want of suitable expressions shews the little attention given by chemists and natural philosophers to fluidity, and to the properties of bodies by which they give and receive fluidity. From not having reflected on the properties of fire, and upon the effects which it produces upon other bodies,

we

we have considered those substances as having an independent fluidity, which we have generally seen in a fluid or fused state, such as air, ethereal spirits, mercury, spirit of wine, and even water and oils, although we frequently see these two last mentioned substances become solid by cold, or want of active fire. The fixation of mercury by a sufficient degree of cold, the possibility of which is suspected in the *Elements of the Theory of Chemistry*, and is ascertained by experiments of some members of the Academy at Petersburg, induces us to conjecture, that every body is naturally solid or hard, and that all fluid bodies receive their fluidity from fire, which is the only substance essentially fluid.

However that may be, this is evident, that as the aggregation of every body which is fluid or liquid must be broken, or much diminished, fluidity is the most favorable state for the formation of new unions, and that every substance which forms a new combination must necessarily have or acquire this state. Therefore a precise and extensive knowledge concerning fluidity, and the properties of bodies by which they give and receive fluidity, is exceedingly important in chemistry. *See* AGGREGATION, SOLUTION, FIRE, FUSION, *and* LIQUEFACTION.

CCCXII. FLUOR. This word, used as an adjective, is applied to signify the habitual fluidity of any substance, or that property by which a substance cannot be rendered solid, and is employed as an epithet to distinguish such substances from others of the same kind, but which are habitually solid, or which may be rendered solid. Acids, for instance, which are habitually fluid, as all the mineral and some vegetable acids, are called *fluor acids*, in order to distinguish them from the acid of tartar and acid essential salts, which are naturally concrete. Also volatile alkali treated with quicklime, or with metallic earths, so that it is always liquid and not crystallized, is called *fluor volatile alkali*, to distinguish it from the concrete and crystallizable volatile alkali.

By *fluor*, used substantively, is meant a certain kind of stone which is fusible, or which facilitates fusion. Such are the greatest part of *spars*, which are called fluors. Thus, for example, in talking of a white or colored spar, which is found in the matrix of an ore, we say that this matrix is mixed with a white, green, or yellow fluor. *See* SPAR. *(f)*

(f) FLUORS. Mineralogists differ very much in describing fluors, some giving that name to colored quartz crystals, called also false emeralds, false rubies, &c. (*See* CRYSTAL), and to crystallized, prismatical, cubical, or pyramidal colored stones, more or less transparent, and others making the word *fluor* synonimous with *fusible spar*, their descriptions of which also are very different. Nevertheless, as the stones called fusible spars are distinguishable from *spars* properly so called, a characteristic mark of which is to consist of particles of a rhomboidal or other determinate figure, whereas those called fusible or vitreous spars are seldom so formed, we think that these fusible spars may be comprehended under the name *fluors*, to which also all stones possessing the following properties may be properly referred, whether they be transparent or opake, colored or not colored, crystallized or possessing no determinate form.

1. They are not sufficiently hard to strike fire with steel. By this property the colored quartz crystals are excluded.

2. They are not soluble by acids.

3. They have not the distinguishing properties of gypseous or of argillaceous earths.

4. They are fusible by fire without addition. Pott, Cronstedt, and others say, that they are not fusible, but Mr Engeström, the Translator of Cronstedt's Mineralogy, affirms, that he has fused all the fluors which he has tried by means of a blow pipe, and Mr D'Arcet found, by his experiments, that

CCCXIII FLUX This word is sometimes used synonimously with *fusion* For instance, an ore, or other matter, is said to be in liquid flux, when it is completely fused

But the word flux is generally used to signify certain saline matters, which facilitate the fusion of ores, and other matters which are difficultly fusible, in essays and reductions of ores Fixed alkalis, nitre, borax, tartar, and common salt, are the saline matters of which fluxes are generally composed But the word *flux* is more particularly applied to mixtures of different proportions of only nitre and tartar, and these fluxes are called by particular names, according to the proportions of these ingredients, as we shall see in the following articles

CCCXIV FLUX (WHITE) White flux is made with equal parts of nitre and of tartar detonated together, by which they are alkalised The residuum of this detonation is an alkali composed of the alkalis of the nitre and of the tartar, both which are absolutely of the same nature As the proportion of nitre in this mixture is more than is sufficient to consume entirely all the inflammable matter of the tartar, the alkali remaining after the detonation is perfectly white, and is therefore called *white flux*, and as this alkali is made very quickly, it is also called *extemporaneous alkali* When a small quantity only of white flux is made, as a few ounces, for instance, some nitre always remains undecomposed, and a little of the inflammable principle of the tartar, which gives a red or even a black color to some part of the flux but this does not happen when a large quantity is made of white flux, because then the heat is much greater This small quantity of undecomposed nitre and tartar which remains in white flux is not hurtful in most of the metallic fusions in which this flux is employed but if the flux be required perfectly pure, it might easily be disengaged from those extraneous matters by a long and strong calcination, without fusion *See* CALCINATION

CCCXV FLUX (CRUDE) By crude flux is meant the mixture of nitre and tartar in any proportions, without detonation Thus the mixture of equal parts of the two salts used in the preparation of the white flux, or the mixture of one part of nitre and two parts of tartar for the preparation of the black flux, are each of them a crude flux before detonation. It has also been called *white flux*, from its color, but this might occasion it to be confounded with the white flux above described The name therefore of crude flux is more convenient

that they were fusible I have also, by a very considerable heat, fused some of those white opake fluors, which are said to be similar to the *petuntse*, one of the materials of which the Chinese compose their porcelain

5 With much more moderate heat they greatly facilitate the fusion of calcareous and argillaceous earths, and of the topaz, according to Mr Pott For which quality they have been much employed in the smelting of ores, as they promote the fusion of the adhering earths

6 When heated slowly and gradually, they emit a phosphorescent light, and by being made red-hot they lose this property.

Many of these fluors are very heavy, and indeed the heaviest of all unmetallic substances, if they be unmetallic Mr Pott says, that by fusing them with marble he has obtained sometimes, but not always, a small portion of lead

Crude

Crude flux is detonated and alkalised during the reductions and fusions in which it is employed, and is then changed into white or black flux, according to the proportions of which it is composed. This detonation produces good effects in these fusions and reductions, if the swelling and extravasation of the detonating matters be guarded against. Accordingly, crude flux may be employed successfully in many operations, as, for instance, in the ordinary operation for procuring the regulus of antimony.

CCCXVI. FLUX (BLACK *or* REDUCING). Black flux is produced from the mixture of two parts of tartar and one part of nitre detonated together. As the quantity of nitre which enters into the composition of this flux is not sufficient to consume all the inflammable matter of the tartar, the alkali which remains after the detonation contains much black matter, of the nature of coal, and is therefore called *black flux*.

This flux is designedly so prepared, that it shall contain a certain quantity of inflammable matter, for it is thereby capable not only of facilitating the fusion of metallic earths like the white flux, but also of reviving their metals by its phlogiston. From this property it is also called reducing flux; the black flux, therefore, or crude flux made with such proportions of the ingredients as to be convertible into black flux, ought always to be used when metallic matters are at once to be fused and reduced, or even when destructible metals are to be fused, as these require a continual supply of phlogiston to prevent their calcination. *See* NITRE, REDUCTION, *and* TARTAR.

CCCXVII. FORGE. An ordinary forge is nothing but a pair of bellows, the nozzle of which is directed upon a smooth area, on which coals are placed. The nozzle of a pair of bellows may be also directed to the bottom of any furnace, to excite the combustion of the coals placed there, by which a kind of forge is formed. In laboratories, there is generally a small furnace consisting of one cylindrical piece, open at top, which has at its lower side a hole for receiving the nozzle of a double bellows. This kind of forge-furnace is very convenient for fusions, as the operation is quickly performed, and with few coals. In its lower part, two inches below the hole for receiving the nozzle of the bellows, may be placed an iron plate of the same diameter, supported upon two horizontal bars, and pierced near its circumference with four holes diametrically opposite to each other. By this disposition, the wind of the bellows, pushed forcibly under this plate, enters at these four holes, and thus the heat of the fire is equally distributed, and the crucible in the furnace is equally surrounded by it. This contrivance is used in the forge-furnaces for melting copper, with this difference only, that these furnaces are square, which is a matter of no consequence.

As the wind of bellows strongly and rapidly excites the action of the fire, a forge is very convenient when a great heat is to be applied quickly; but it is not suitable when the heat is to be gradually encreased.

The forge, or blast of bellows, is used in several operations in small, as, to fuse salts, metals, ores, &c. It is also much used in works in the great, which require strong heat, without much management, and chiefly in the smelting of ores, and fusion of metallic matters.

CCCXVIII. FRITT. Fritt is a mixture of several substances intended to be fused together for the purpose of making glass. After these substances have been

been mixed together, they are generally exposed during a certain time to a more or less strong heat, which is, however, incapable of compleatly fusing them The intention of this operation is either to effect a slight union betwixt these matters, or to free them more perfectly from any inflammable or extraneous matter, by this calcination *See* VITRIFICATION

CCCXIX FRUITS (*g*)

CCCXX FULIGINOSITY By this word is meant soot, or the black matter which accompanies the flame of oils and of oily substances *See* SOOT

CCCXXI FULMINATION Fulmination is the sudden and violent explosion and inflammation of certain bodies, which are therefore called *fulminating* Such are the explosions of fulminating powder and of fulminating gold The explosion of these matters is called *fulmination*, from the noise accompanying it, by which it resembles thunder

CCCXXII FURNACE Furnaces are chemical instruments used for containing combustible matters, by the burning of which the heat requisite for operations is procured, and also for containing the substances themselves to which the heat ought to be applied.

As chemists require for different operations all the possible degrees of heat, from the weakest to the strongest, and as the form of furnaces contributes greatly,

(*g*) FRUITS are considered only as *coloring materials* in this article, the greatest part of which is extracted from a note of Dr Lewis to his Translation of Neuman. The red juices of fruits, as of *currants*, *mulberries*, *elder berries*, *morello and black cherries*, when inspissated and dried, may be again dissolved in water, to which they give nearly the same red color as they do when fresh Rectified spirit extracts the tinging particles, and acquires a brighter color than the watery solution, because much of the mucilage is left undissolved by the former The red solutions and the juices are sometimes made dull, and sometimes more florid, by acids, and are generally rendered purplish by alkalis The colors of these juices are generally perishable They are not destructible by the fermentation of the liquors, but they quickly decay when the juice is spread thinly on any substance, and dried in open air The bright lively reds are soonest changed The dark, dull red stain of the black cherry is considerably durable The bright red fruit of the *opuntia* or *prickly pear* is an exception to the above rule, as it gives, according to Labat, a beautiful red dye The ripe berries of *buckthorn* stain paper of a green color From these is prepared the substance called *sap-green*, which is a pigment sufficiently durable, soluble in water, but not miscible with oil The same berries dried whilst green, and macerated in alum-water, are said to yield a yellow pigment, and when they have grown over ripe, a purple pigment Woollen cloth, prepared with alum and tartar, receives, on being boiled with the berries, a perishable yellow dye. The *French berries*, or *graine d'Avignon*, one of the most perishable yellow dyes, is a berry of the species of buckthorn It is said, that the berry of the *heliotropium tricoccum* stains paper of a green color, and that this green is soon changed to a blue, that the common blue paper receives its color from this juice, and that the red rags called *turnsol*, employed for coloring wines and other liquors, are tinctured by the same juice turned red by acids Mr Nissole says, that the coloring juice is obtained, not from the berries, but from the tops of the plant. The Dutch are said to prepare these rags from other materials, of which archil is a principal one

The seeds of some plants, as of *peony*, are covered with a fine shining red membrane. The pellicles of the seeds of an American tree afford the red masses called *annotto*, *orlean*, and *roucou*. *See* ANNOTTO

greatly, as we ſhall ſee, to produce the different degrees of heat, they have contrived many furnaces of different forms and conſtructions, but all theſe furnaces may be reduced to a ſmall number of general diſpoſitions, which we ſhall now deſcribe

The *ſimple furnace* is a kind of hollow tower, cylindrical or priſmatical, wit two doors or principal openings, the one below, called the *door of the aſh-hole*, and the other immediately above this, called the *door of the fire-place* Betwixt theſe two doors a grate is placed horizontally acroſs the interior part of the furnace, dividing the whole cavity of the furnace into two parts the lower part is called the *aſh-hole*, becauſe it receives the aſhes which fall from the fire-place The door of the aſh-hole gives admittance to the air neceſſary for maintaining the fire within the furnace The upper cavity of the furnace is called the *fire-place*, becauſe it contains the combuſtible matters Through the door of the fire-place, freſh fuel is to be introduced, to ſupply the place of what is conſumed.

This ſimple furnace, ſimilar to that uſed in kitchens, is ſufficient for many chemical operations In the fire-place, amidſt the coals, crucibles may be placed for the fuſion of fuſible matters, ſuch as lead, tin, biſmuth, &c or for the calcination of matters which require but little heat for their calcination, ſuch as the alkali for making Pruſſian blue, bezoar mineral, &c.

On this furnace may alſo be placed baſons for evaporations, alembics for diſtilling in the water-bath, pots filled with ſand for digeſtions and diſtillations to be performed by means of a ſand-bath and a gentle heat, either with alembics or with retorts

As ſeveral of the operations made with this furnace are of long duration, and as the furnace requires a continual ſupply of fuel, chemiſts have contrived to adapt to it a magazine of coals in form of a hollow tower, cloſed in its upper part, and ſo diſpoſed, that while the coal of the fire-place is conſumed, that of the tower falls down and ſupplies its place The furnace thus diſpoſed is called an *athanor*, or the *furnace of ſluggards* *See* ATHANOR *See* PLATES

The *lamp-furnace* is a kind of athanor, in which the heat is produced and maintained by the flame of a lamp introduced within it This furnace has evidently no occaſion for an aſh-hole, a grate, or a fire-place It has only one opening below, through which the lamp is introduced, and a kind of ſmall chimney made in its upper and lateral part, for circulation of air, to keep up the flame of the lamp, and to give vent to the ſmoke. This furnace is very convenient for diſtillations which require little heat A water-bath or ſand-bath may be fitted to it It is particularly uſeful for digeſtions *See* PLATES

The *reverberatory furnace* is the ſimple furnace, the fire-place of which is covered with a piece of the ſame diameter and form as the furnace, which is generally cylindrical This piece is croſſed in its lower part by two bars of iron placed horizontally and parallel to each other, and at its upper edge it has a ſemi-circular cut This piece conſequently forms a third cavity, which is called the *Laboratory*, becauſe it is intended to receive the retorts containing the matter to be diſtilled The ſemi-circular cut is made to give paſſage to the neck of the retort, which, as we have ſaid under the article DISTILLATION, ought to be inclined at an angle of 45 degrees The uſe of the two bars at the bottom of the laboratory is to ſupport the veſſel placed there

Above the piece we have now described is a fourth piece placed, the form of which is that of a spherical cap, or of an inverted dome it is accordingly called the *dome* This dome has an equal diameter to the other piece, to which it is to be fitted, and in its lower edge it has a semi-circular cut, which corresponds with the similar cut of the lower piece, and these together form a circular opening the dome has in its top another opening or short tube, through which the air contained in the furnace passes, and is a kind of chimney

The use of the dome is to keep up the heat all around the retort which is placed in the furnace, and to apply a certain degree of heat to the upper part or vault of the retort, by reflecting or reverberating it hence it is called a *reverberatory* By this disposition the vapors which rise in the retort are determined more efficaciously to pass through its neck We may judge after this description, that reverberatory furnaces are only used for distillations with a retort, in which a certain degree of heat is necessary

Distillation may be performed in reverberatory furnaces, either in naked fire, by placing the retort immediately upon the bars, or in a sand-bath, by placing upon these same bars an iron vessel, in the upper edge of which is a semi-circular cut Into this iron vessel is put fine sand to the thickness of one or two fingers then the retort is to be placed in it, and, lastly, it is to be filled with sand up to the arch of the retort If the heat be required to be of a certain strength, the iron vessel must have a diameter so much less than the internal part of the furnace, that an empty space of about the thickness of a finger shall be left betwixt them, excepting on the side where the neck of the retort is, and there the hollow cuts of the furnace and iron vessel that correspond to each other ought to join exactly *See* PLATES

The *melting furnace*, or wind furnace, is intended to produce the greatest degree of heat that can be excited without bellows This furnace ought to be so constructed, that a current of air shall constantly pass through the fire-place, and the more strongly and rapidly this air passes, the more intense will be the heat in the furnace

The chief method for producing this effect is to leave in the upper part of the furnace a space close on every side, excepting above and below, because the air contained in this cavity being rarefied and expelled by the heat produced by the fuel burning in the furnace, a vacuum is here formed, which the external air necessarily tends to occupy from its gravity

This being established, the furnace ought evidently to be so disposed that the external air shall be obliged to enter at the ash-hole, and to pass through the fire-place, to fill the vacuum which is continually forming both in the internal part of the furnace and in its upper cavity

We ought to observe, that the column of air which corresponds with the upper part of the furnace, being a little shorter, and consequently lighter, than the column which corresponds with the lower part, the air appears naturally determined to enter at the bottom, and to go out at the the top of the furnace, so that if this furnace was a hollow cylinder, the lower and upper mouths of which were equal, and if the fire-place was in the middle, the air would probably pass through it from bottom to top, but this difference of the two columns being almost infinitely small, the velocity of the current of air would be as small but if, instead of this disposition, the furnace be contracted in its upper part, and if it be made to become a tube of less diameter, then the rarefied air is obliged conſiderably to accelerate its courſe in paſſing through a ſtraiter ſpace, and thereby overcomes more eaſily the preſſure of the ſuperior air: hence the air introduced through the lower part of the furnace, in order to fill the vacuum which is continually forming in its upper part, paſſes ſo much more rapidly through the fire-place as it finds leſs obſtacle above; and conſequently this diſpoſition of the furnace neceſſarily determines a ſtrong and rapid current of air to paſs through it, from the bottom to the top.

From what has been ſaid we may eaſily perceive, that the more the ſpace or air is rarefied in the upper part of the melting furnace, the ſtronger and more rapid is the external current of air which is obliged to enter the furnace to fill up this vacuum, and conſequently the more intenſely the coals muſt burn. Hence theſe furnaces produce ſo much more heat, as the tube which is at their upper part, called the *tube of aſpiration*, is longer. But we muſt obſerve, that although the activity of this furnace is owing in great meaſure to the contraction in its upper part or to its tube, nevertheleſs a too great contraction of the tube would be very inconvenient, becauſe the air rarefied, and obliged to go out at the upper part, can only acquire a certain determinate velocity: whence it follows, that if this tube, through which the rarefied air is to go out, were ſo ſtrait that this air could not paſs, unleſs it had a greater velocity than it is capable of acquiring, then the air, finding an obſtacle in its way, would be retarded in its progreſs, and conſequently too great ſtraitneſs in the tube impedes rather than facilitates the courſe of the air: accordingly, I have found by experience, that a melting furnace to which too ſtrait a tube, however long, has been adapted, produces little effect, compared with that cauſed by a tube of ſufficient diameter.

Hence the diameter of the tube muſt have a certain relation to the capacity of the furnace, and to the door of the aſh hole. I have found that the diameter of the tube ought to be to the diameter of the furnace as 2 to 3 nearly, particularly when the tube is long enough (*b*). The opening at the bottom of the furnace may be equal in width to the body of the furnace, or it may be contracted, if the air be required to ſtrike the fire with more force and rapidity. After all theſe principles, we now proceed to the conſtruction of a good melting furnace. The body of this furnace does not differ from that of a ſimple furnace, except that it is, or may be open, or almoſt

(*b*) The diameter of the tube ought to have a certain proportion, not to the door of the aſh-hole, but to the ſpace left by the intervals of the grate, and both theſe ought to bear a certain proportion to the diameter of the fire-place. The proportion mentioned by the Author, which the diameter of the tube ſhould hold to the diameter of the fire-place, as two to three, ſeems to allow too great a width to the tube. When the tube is too wide, more air paſſes through the furnace than is neceſſary for the maintenance of the fire and conſumption of the fuel, by which means the furnace is greatly cooled; and even, if the air ſhould be prevented from paſſing through in too large a quantity, by narrowing the door of the aſh-hole, the air will paſs down the wide tube, which will then contain two diſtinct columns of air, one aſcending, and the other deſcending. The following proportions ſeem to me to be preferable. If the area of the fire-place contain 144 ſquare inches, let the area of the tube, and the ſum of the ſeveral intervals of the grate be, each of them, 36 ſquare inches: but in certain ſtates of the fire, for inſtance, when it is thoroughly kindled, the upper vent may be advantageouſly ſtill further contracted by regiſters, by which much fuel may be ſaved, and the fire kept more equally intenſe.

entirely open, below, and supported upon feet, or a kind of tripod, which serves as an ash-hole. An elliptical form is generally given to it, with intention to concentrate the heat (i). The upper part of this furnace is terminated by a dome higher than that of the reverberatory furnace, called the *cap*. This cap has two openings, one of which is placed laterally and in the front; it ought to be large, and to be capable of being closely shut by a door: the other is at the top, and ought to be a tube of a convenient diameter, upon which other tubes of indeterminate length are adjusted.

This furnace has no laboratory, or rather its laboratory is the fire place itself, for the matters to which the heat is to be applied are placed in the fire-place, and surrounded by the burning coals.

The melting furnace may have a door to the fire-place, but this door ought to be kept shut during the operations. It only serves for the more convenient examination of the condition of the crucibles or other matters placed in the furnace, and not for the introduction of fresh fuel, for which purpose the door of the cap is intended. This latter door ought to be very large, that a considerable quantity of coal may be thrown in at once. The reason why this door is preferable to the door of the fire place for the introduction of the fuel is, that the current of air may not be disturbed in its direction; and therefore the lateral door ought to be kept open as little as possible.

When the internal diameter of such a furnace is 12 or 15 inches, when the diameter of the tube is 8 or 9 inches, and its height 18 or 20 feet, and when the furnace is well supplied with fuel, an extreme heat is produced: in less than an hour the fire will be white and dazzling, like the sun; its heat will be equal to the strongest degree of heat in a glass-house furnace. In less than two hours may be melted whatever is fusible in furnaces (k). The hottest part of this furnace is 4 or 6 inches above the grate.

Chemists generally believe that the power of a melting furnace is greatly encreased by a wide and high ash-hole, or by bringing the air which is to enter it through a long pipe from without the house in which the furnace stands: but these advantages are either imaginary, or only relative to the vacuum formed in the upper part of the furnace. If indeed a furnace be so placed that the opening of its ash-hole shall be fitted to the mouth of a great cavity, as to a cave, for instance, in the roof of which a hole is made, into which this furnace is to be fitted; and if this cave has no other opening than through the bottom of the furnace, then a very strong current of air will pass from the cave across the furnace, although the furnace had neither cap nor tube: but we must observe, that this current of air will always be stronger if the furnace is provided with a dome and tube; and secondly, if the air be determined to pass from the cave across the furnace, even without dome or tube, this must proceed only

(i) The inequality of the surface of the sides of the furnace would prevent any advantage from the elliptical form of furnaces, even if heat were supposed to diffuse itself, like light, only in right lines, and to be thereby capable of concentration by reflexion, a supposition, however, which cannot be admitted.

(k) Most fusible substances may be fused in a much less time: nevertheless we find from M. D'Arcet's Memoir concerning the effects of a violent and long-continued heat, that by prolonging the action of fire, he had been able to vitrify substances which had resisted the most violent fires continued only during a shorter time.

only from the heat of the furnace rarefying the ambient air, by which the more condensed air of the cave is determined to pass through the furnace to supply the place of this rarefied air In this case, the chamber in which the furnace is placed, serves instead of the dome and tube This happens in a glass house furnace These furnaces are built upon subterranean vaults, which serve as ash-holes The internal capacity of these furnaces is very great, and is occupied only partly by the combustible matters, and by the pots containing the glass hence the air of the ash-hole is continually introduced there to fill this empty space besides, the heat is always very great in the domes under which the furnaces are built, the contained air is therefore continually rarefied, so that they serve as the domes and tubes of furnaces to draw the air from the vaults

The pipe which is sometimes fitted to the ash-hole of melting furnaces does not contribute to the draught of the furnace, excepting the laboratory in which the furnace stands be small and confined for then the air of this laboratory, being soon heated and rarefied, becomes less proper for exciting fire than the colder external air which the pipe supplies *See* PLATES

The furnace called the *essay* or *cupelling furnace* is of a prismatic quadrangular figure, and is chiefly used to make essays of the value of silver, or of silver ores This furnace is composed of an ash-hole, a fire-place, and an upper part which terminates it above, like a quadrangular truncated pyramid The fire-place and ash hole are not, properly speaking, separated from each other, because this furnace has no grate *(l)*, hence the coals in this furnace fall to the bottom in the lower part of the furnace are three small doors, two in the sides, and one in the front above this latter door is a fourth door, placed like that of the fire place of a simple furnace, and at the bottom of this door are two iron bars, placed within the furnace horizontally and parallel to each other These bars are intended to support a muffle, the mouth of which corresponds exactly to the last mentioned door In this muffle the cupels and vessels capable of containing the matter to be heated are to be placed

The top of this furnace is truncated, and forms a pretty large aperture, through which the fuel is to be introduced Some of these furnaces have a small hole in the front of this upper part, through which an iron rod is introduced to push the coals down, and which also serves to shew the state of the fire In some of these furnaces the upper part is terminated by a short tube, which on some occasions is convenient, for although the internal capacity of this furnace, including its upper part, makes a sufficient draught for these operations, a greater heat may possibly be required, and this is effected by adapting a tube to this furnace *See* ESSAYS

Some operations, which must be made either in a muffle or in a reverberatory furnace, require the strongest melting heat The distillation of Kunckel's phosphorus, for instance, requires a heat much superior to that of ordinary distillations Essays also of porcelain and vitrification, which ought to be done very cleanly, and therefore under a muffle, require a very violent heat, which cannot be procured in an ordinary essay furnace In these cases a tube may be fitted to the distilling

(l) A grate would certainly render this furnace much more convenient, in the plate therefore which we have added of this furnace a grate is represented.

or to the effay-furnaces, like that of the melting furnace, and thus as ftrong a heat as is wanted may be procured *See* PHOSPHORUS, PORCELAIN, VITRIFICATION (*m*)

Chemifts have contrived many other furnaces, and fome very complicated, for particular purpofes, but they are moftly embarraffing, ill contrived, and even ufelefs for by the furnaces above defcribed an able operator may perform perfectly well every chemical operation

All thefe furnaces may be either portable, and compofed of baked earth hooped with iron rings, or covered with iron plates, if they are intended to be more durable, or they may be fixed and ftationary, and made of bricks and tiles This depends on the fize and difpofition of the laboratory

The matter of all chemical furnaces is always a clay which ought to be of a good quality Common clays do well enough for furnaces that are not intended to fuftain very violent heats, by which furnaces are apt to be cracked and deftroyed, even before the operation is finifhed, unlefs they are made of the moft pure and refractory clay *See the clays moft proper for this purpofe under the article* CLAY

In thefe furnaces no iron bars or fupports ought to be ufed, as that metal is very quickly melted, calcined, and deftroyed All the fupports within thefe kinds of furnaces ought to be of the fame clay of which the furnace confifts As the heat is much lefs in the tube than in the body of the furnace, this tube is frequently made of iron plates, excepting its lower part, which ought always to be made of clay Thefe tubes of iron plate have many advantages, as they are light and manageable, but they have a great inconvenience, which is, that their inner furfaces are fubject to calcine, hence when much flame paffes through them, fcales fly off from the iron with noife, which falling upon the crucibles and muffles, difpofe them to vitrify, becaufe iron is a powerful flux to clay The whole tube ought therefore to be made of clay

When the tube is long, it ought to be ftrengthened by iron rings and hooks, but thefe ought to be fo arranged that the tube may be lengthened and fhortened, according as the greater or lefs heat may difpofe it, otherwife it might crack.

The furnaces defcribed in this article are employed, and are neceffary, for the feveral operations of chemiftry Many of them are alfo ufed in the arts, in manufactures, and in works in the great fuch are the furnaces for glafs, pottery, porcelain, and for fmelting of ores What is peculiar to any of thefe furnaces may be found under the article of the art in which it is employed In other refpects their ftructure is conformable to the general principles eftablifhed in the prefent article (*n*)

CCCXXIII FUSIBILITY Fufibility is a quality which renders bodies fufceptible of becoming fluid, when expofed to a certain degree of heat

(*m*) See a plate and defcription of a very commodious furnace for experiments on vitrification, and on the making of porcelain, and for many other purpofes

(*n*) *See* PLATES, where feveral furnaces are reprefented, and the defcriptions annexed, in which the proper compofitions for lining the infides of furnaces made of plated iron, and the methods of applying them, are related.

Fufibility

Fusibility is the reverse of the refractory quality; so that the less the heat is which is requisite for the fusion of any substance, the more fusible it is.

Bodies differ much from each other as to their degrees of fusibility. Some of them, as air and mercury, are so fusible that the heat of the atmosphere is always sufficient to keep them fluid: others, as some oils and water, which are naturally solid with the degree of cold marked o in Reaumur's thermometer, are presently melted when they are exposed to a greater heat: other substances again, as lead, tin, bismuth, &c. are habitually solid in the greatest natural heats; but are fusible with a degree of heat less than is requisite to make them red: and, lastly, others are not fusible till they become red, and even white, by heat: such are silver, gold, copper, iron, glass, &c.

As the fusion of a body is caused by the interposition of fire betwixt its integrant parts, by which their adhesion is destroyed, we cannot conceive any other cause of the greater or less fusibility than a more or less intimate contact, and a more or less strong adhesion of the integrant parts of different bodies; which are dispositions depending on the figure of these parts. *See* HARDNESS *and* FLUIDITY.

CCCXXIV. FUSION. Fusion is the state of a body rendered fluid by fire. *See* FLUIDITY *and* FUSIBILITY.

G.

CCCXXV. GALANGAL. (o)
CCCXXVI. GALBANUM (p)
CCCXXVII. GALLEY. This name is given to reverberatory furnaces, in which several retorts may be placed at the sides of each other. As these furnaces are oblong, and have lateral openings, they have been supposed to resemble galleys, and have thence received their name.
CCCXXVIII. GALENA. (q)
CCCXXIX. GALLS. (r)

(o) GALANGAL. The Indian root called *greater galangal* resembles ginger in smell, taste, and chemical composition. The *smaller galangal* has a stronger and more agreeable smell than the former, and a more pungent and hot taste, like that of pepper. From 16 ounces of this root scarcely two scruples of oil were obtained, and this oil possesses little of the pungency of the root. Six ounces of extract were obtained by means of water from 16 ounces of the root, and an ounce and a half from the same quantity by means of spirit of wine. The watery extract was the more pungent of the two. *Neuman.*

(p) GALBANUM is a gum-resin, containing more of a resinous than gummy matter. Spirit of wine extracted from a pound of it nine ounces and a half, and water extracted from the same quantity only three ounces. The smell, flavor, and peculiar taste of galbanum resides in an essential oil, which may be raised in distillation either by means of water or of spirit of wine. From a pound of galbanum six drams of essential oil may be obtained. This oil, or a great part of it, is of a blue color, sometimes of a deep bright blue. By exposure to air this blue color is changed to a purple. *Neuman.*

(q) GALENA is the name of a lead ore, consisting of cubic particles, and composed of lead mineralised by sulphur, with which also a little silver is almost always united. *See* ORES *of* LEAD.

(r) GALLS are excrescencies found upon oak trees, and are amongst the strongest vegetable astringents. Extracts made from galls, either by water or by spirit, possess all the astringency of these vegetable substances. From sixteen drams of galls fourteen drams were extracted by water, and from the same quantity twelve drams and two scruples were extracted by spirit. Galls, like other vegetable astringents, or the infusions of these substances, being added to solutions of green vitriol, or to dilute and saturated solutions of iron in any acid, change the color of these solutions to a deep blue or black. The black liquor thus produced is the basis of inks, and of many black dyes. *See* BLACK *and* INK. When the green vitriol is dissolved, and when the galls are infused in distilled water, or in common spring waters, the color produced by mixing them is, according to Dr Lewis, blue; but if the smallest portion of alkaline salt be dissolved in the water, or if this water has any putrid tendency,

CCCXXX GAMBOGE (s)

CCCXXXI GANGUE Gangue is the matrix of ores See MATRIX

CCCXXXII. GARLIC (t)

CCCXXXIII GARNET (u)

CCCXXXIV. GAS. This name is given by chemists to the volatile in-

tendency, however small, the color produced will be purplish or reddish These colors, when rendered more intense, by adding more of the coloring substances to the water, appear of a black color The blackness produced by this mixture proceeds from a coloring matter which is only diffused through the liquor, and may be separated from thence by dilution with water, and by deposition The separation may be prevented, as is done in the preparation of ink, by adding some mucilaginous matter, as gum arabic This coloring matter is evidently a ferruginous precipitate, for altho' it is not magnetical, it may be rendered magnetical by a slight calcination To this precipitate some of the inflammable matter of the vegetable astringent adheres and gives color When by calcination this adhering matter is made to combine in some measure with the ferruginous precipitate, this precipitate, though not perfectly metallized, is however sufficiently metallized to be rendered magnetical In these properties this precipitate corresponds with the blue ferruginous precipitate, which forms Prussian blue, to which also some phlogistic matter adheres and gives color, but it differs from Prussian blue by this property, that it is soluble by acids, whereas the latter precipitate is not soluble Thus, the black coloring matter of inks may be dissolved by acids, and their color thereby destroyed. Alkalis also destroy the blackness of inks, by dissolving the astringent or inflammable adhering matter, and leaving the iron in an ochery state, similar to the precipitates of iron, formed by adding alkalis to solutions of that metal in acids The blackness destroyed by adding acids to ink is recovered by addition of alkalis, and conversely

I have not found that galls precipitate other metallic substances, but I have observed, that when added to metallic solutions, the precipitates afterwards formed from these by fixed alkalis, were deeply colored, and generally purple

(s) GAMBOGE is an acrid gum-resin, the gummy parts of which are so intimately blended with the resinous, that greatest part of it is soluble either by water or by spirit of wine It forms a beautiful yellow pigment, and is much used as such by painters Dr Lewis says, that it gives a beautiful and durable citron-yellow stain to marble, whether rubbed in substance on the hot stone, or applied, as Dragon's blood is, in form of a spirituous tincture When it is applied on cold marble, the stone is afterwards to be heated, to make the color penetrate

(t) GARLIC The roots of garlic contain a considerable quantity of mucilage some resin, and a very small portion of essential oil, in which the whole smell, taste, and peculiar qualities of garlic reside. From thirty-two ounces of garlic distilled with water, Neuman could obtain scarcely half a dram of this oil

(u) GARNET, *Granatus gemma*, is a stone ranked amongst those called gems, tho' less brilliant than any other gem, it is transparent, sometimes more and sometimes less, generally of a dark-red color, but sometimes yellowish or brown, the eighth stone in hardness from diamonds, and fusible by fire Cronstedt forms a distinct order of the garnets and the basaltes, which he calls *terræ granatæ* The distinguishing property of these garnet earths is, that they are more fusible in proportion as they contain less metallic matter, and are more transparent and glassy in their texture. In other respects they resemble the siliceous order of earths. *See* BASALTES. All garnets contain iron, most of them contain tin also, and some, according to Mr Swab, contain iron and lead Their forms are various, some having six sides, and others having a greater number To imitate garnets Neri directs, that twenty pounds of crystal frit, sixteen pounds of calx of lead, three ounces of manganese, half an ounce of zaffre, should be fused together during twelve hours, and that the vitrified mass, after it is separated from any lead which may have been revived by the fusion, must be again kept in fusion during ten hours

visible parts which escape from certain bodies, and which cannot be retained and collected, at least without great difficulty, and mixture of other substances

Thus, for example, the noxious vapors which rise from burning charcoal, and from matters undergoing the spirituous and putrid fermentations, the volatile part of spirituous mineral waters, the spiritus rector of some substances, such as musk, may be called the *gas* of these bodies

The gas of most substances, particularly those which affect the nerves, seems to be nothing but pure, or almost pure phlogiston, which is disengaged from bodies without ignition The mineral noxious vapors called *damps* may be also ranked amongst vapors called *gas*, at least those of them may which are invisible *See* DAMPS

CCCXXXV GELATINOUS, *and* GELLY (x)

CCCXXXVI GEMS (y)

CCCXXXVII GENTIAN (z)

CCCXXXVIII GILDING Gilding is the art of applying exceedingly thin layers of gold upon the surfaces of certain substances, to give them the external appearance of gold

The lustre and beauty of gold have occasioned several inquiries and discoveries concerning the different methods of applying it to different substances Hence the art of gilding is very extensive, and contains many particular operations, and various management

A color of gold is given by painting and by varnishes, without employing gold, but this is a false kind of gilding Thus a very fine golden color is given to brass and to silver, by applying upon these metals a gold-colored varnish, which being transparent, shews all the brilliancy of the metals beneath Many ornaments of brass are varnished in this manner, which is called *gold lacquering*, to distinguish them from those which are really gilt Silver-leaves thus varnished are put upon leather, which is then called gilt leather. (a)

(x) GELATINOUS *and* GELLY *See* JELLY.

(y) GEMS are certain stones consisting of the *siliceous*, or what is improperly called *vitrifiable* earth, much valued for their lustre, transparency, color, hardness, weight, and rarity These are, diamonds, rubies, saphirs, topazes, emeralds, chrysolites, amethysts, garnets, hyacinths or jacinths, berylls or aqua marinas The order in which they are enumerated shows their relative degrees of hardness See *each of these articles*, DIAMONDS, RUBIES, &c

(z) GENTIAN From sixteen drams of the root of gentian Neuman obtained six drams and a half of resinous extract by means of spirit of wine, which contained all the bitterness of the gentian, and from the same quantity he obtained nine drams of gummy extract, which was considerably bitter, but less so than the spirituous extract

(a) The basis of these lacquers is a solution of the resinous substance, called seed-lac, in spirit of wine The spirit of wine must be very much dephlegmated, and for this purpose authors direct dry pot-ash to be thrown into it, which attracts the water, and with it forms a liquid distinct from the spirit, which being collected at the bottom of the vessel, may be separated by decanting the spirit. By this method the spirit is much dephlegmated, but, at the same time, it dissolves a part of the alkaline salt, by which it acquires color, and also communicates a property to the lacquer of imbibing moisture from air These inconveniences are prevented by adding to the spirit of wine thus dephlegmated some calcined alum, the acid of which unites with the alkaline salt remaining in the spirit, and forms with it a vitriolated tartar, which not being soluble in spirit of wine, falls to the bottom, together with the earth of the decomposed alum, and the superfluous alum, if more be added than is necessary. To a pint of the spirit thus dephlegmated,

Amongst the false gildings may also be reckoned those which are made with thin leaves of copper or brass, called *Dutch leaf* In this manner are made all the kinds of what is called gilt paper

In the true gilding, gold is applied to the surface of bodies The gold intended for this purpose ought in general to be beat into thin leaves, or otherwise divided into very fine parts

As metals cannot adhere well merely by contact to any but to other metallic substances, when gold is to be applied to the surface of some unmetallic body, that surface must be previously covered with some gluey and tenacious substance, by which the gold shall be made to adhere These substances are in general called *sizes.* Some of these are made of vegetable and animal glues, and others of oily, gluey, and drying matters Upon them the leaves of gold are applied, and when the whole is dry, the work is to be finished and polished Wood chiefly is gilt in this manner, but it must be previously covered with ten or twelve layers of chalk, mixed with glue dissolved in water That forms a body or coat, which hurts the sculpture and mouldings upon the wood, but is necessary for furnishing the gold with a softer support, otherwise, if the gold was applied to the wood without the interposition of this size, it would be apt to be torn and rubbed off, when burnished, that is, polished with a hard instrument, called a *dog's tooth*, to give it lustre. *(b)*

dephlegmated, about 3 ounces of powdered shell lac are to be added, and in a day or two, by help of moderate heat, the spirit will have acquired a reddish color: It ought then to be poured off, strained, and cleared by settling then as much gamboge and annotto are to be added as are sufficient to give it the color required, which must be discovered by frequently trying the mixture upon silver leaf These two substances are readily soluble in the above described tincture of lac For the greater conveniency of mixing them in any proportion, the best method is to dissolve them separately in two quantities of the tincture of lac, and thus the color of the lacquer may be adjusted by mixing together the solution of gamboge, which is yellow, with that of annotto, which is reddish-yellow Generally two parts of the solution of gamboge are added to one part of the solution of annotto Saffron, dragon's blood, turmeric, and other red and yellow coloring materials, are sometimes used for the same purposes, but are not preferable to the two above-mentioned The varnish is then to be laid, with a brush, upon the leaves of silver or of tin, previously fixed upon the piece of work by the intervention of some size, and when the varnish is dry, other layers are to be spread till it be sufficiently thick A varnish containing less of the coloring materials than the above is applied upon works of brass, to heighten the color, and preserve it from tarnishing

(b) When wood, paper, and such substances are to be gilded, they must be previously covered with some glutinous substance, upon which, when almost dry, gold leaf is to be applied, and pressed down with a little cotton, or hare's foot When the matter is dry, the gold is to be burnished When the work is required to be capable of resisting rain or moisture, it ought to be previously covered with a composition of drying oil and yellow ochre ground together, otherwise a water-size may be used, which is prepared by boiling cuttings of parchment or white leather in water, and by mixing with this some chalk or whiting several layers of this size must be laid upon the wood, and over these a layer of the same size mixed with yellow ochre Lastly, another mixture, called *gold size*, is to be applied above these, upon which the gold leaves are to be fixed This gold size, the use of which is to make the gold leaf capable of being burnished, is composed of tobacco-pipe clay, ground with some ruddle or black lead, and tempered with a little tallow or oil of olives The edges of glasses may be gilt by applying, first, a

The method of applying gold upon metals is entirely different The surface of the metal to be gilt is first to be cleaned, and then leaves are to be applied to it, which, by means of rubbing with a polished blood-stone and a certain degree of heat, are made to adhere perfectly well (c)

Gold is applied to metals in several other manners. One of these is by previously forming the gold into a paste or amalgam with mercury *See* AMALGAM

With this amalgam the surface of the metal to be gilded is to be covered, then a sufficient heat is to be applied to evaporate the mercury, and the gold is lastly to be burnished with a blood stone (d)

a very thin coat of varnish, upon which the gold leaf is to be fixed, and when the varnish is hardened, may be burnished This varnish is prepared by boiling powdered amber with linseed oil in a brass vessel to which a valve is fitted, and by diluting the above solution with four or five times its quantity of oil of turpentine, and that it may dry sooner, it may be ground with some white lead

(c) In this manner silver leaf is fixed and burnished upon brass in the making of what is called *French plate*, and sometimes also gold leaf is burnished upon copper and upon iron

(d) This method of gilding by amalgamation is chiefly used for gilding copper, or an allay of copper, with a small portion of zinc, which more readily receives the amalgam, and is also preferable for its color, which more resembles that of gold than the color of copper Of the method of preparing the amalgam of gold, *see the word* AMALGAM The proportion of mercury to gold is generally as six or eight to one When the metal to be gilt is wrought or chased, it ought to be previously covered with quicksilver, before the amalgam is applied, that this may be easier spread but when the surface of the metal is plain, the amalgam may be applied directly to it The quicksilver or amalgam is made to adhere to the metal by means of a little aqua-fortis, which is rubbed on the metallic surface at the same time, by which this surface is cleansed from any rust or tarnish which might prevent the union or adhesion of the metals The use of the nitrous acid in this operation is not confined merely to cleanse the surface of the metal to be gilt from any rust or tarnish it may have acquired, but it also greatly facilitates the application of the amalgam to the surface of that metal, in the following manner It first dissolves part of the mercury of the amalgam, and when this solution is applied to the copper, this latter metal having a stronger disposition to unite with the nitrous acid than the mercury has, precipitates the mercury upon its surface, in the same manner as a polished piece of iron precipitates upon its surface copper, from a solution of blue vitriol When the metal to be gilt is thus covered over with a thin coat of mercury, it readily receives the amalgam In this solution and precipitation of mercury, the principal use of the nitrous acid in the process of gilding appears to me to consist The amalgam being equally spread over the surface of the metal to be gilt, by means of a brush, the mercury is then to be evaporated by a heat just sufficient for that purpose, for if it be too great, part of the gold may also be expelled, and part of it will run together, and leave some of the surface of the metal bare while the mercury is evaporating, the piece is to be, from time to time, taken from the fire, that it may be examined, that the amalgam may be spread more equally by means of a brush, that any defective parts of it may be again covered, and that the heat may not be suddenly applied to it when the mercury is evaporated, which is known by the surface being entirely become of a dull yellow color, the metal must then undergo other operations by which the fine golden color is given to it First, the gilded piece of metal is rubbed with a scratch-brush, (which is a brush composed of brass wire) till its surface is made smooth, then it is covered over with a composition called *gilding wax*, and is again exposed to the fire till the wax be burnt off This wax is composed of bees-wax mixed with some of the follow-

ing

Finally, some metals, particularly silver, may be gilt in the following manner

Let gold be dissolved in aqua regia In this solution pieces of linen are to be dipt, and burnt to black ashes These ashes being rubbed on the surface of the silver by means of a wet linen rag, apply the particles of gold which they contain, and which by this method adhere very well The remaining part of the ashes is to be washed off, and the surface of the silver, which in this state

ing substances, red ochre, verdegrise, copper-scales, alum, vitriols, borax By this operation the color of the gilding is heightened, but must be further improved by another operation This consists in covering over the gilt surface with a saline compound, in exposing it thus covered to heat till the saline matters acquire a certain color and appearance, known to artists, and lastly, in suddenly quenching it when thus brought to its proper degree of heat, in urine, water, or other liquid Different artists use different receipts for the preparation of the saline compound, but all, or most of these receipts contain nitre, sal ammoniac, or common salt, alum, or some vitriolic salt, to which they add verdegrise, borax, or other matters, all which must be powdered and mixed, or boiled, with urine Some artists think that they give an additional lustre to their gilt work, by dipping it after it has undergone the foregoing operations in a liquor prepared by boiling some yellow material, as sulphur, orpiment, or turmeric, in water or in urine, together with tartar, common salt, and other saline substances These operations cannot be well explained, unless experiments were made to discover by what of the numerous substances used at the same time, the effects are produced In the mean time, I will hazard some conjectures concerning this subject The effect produced by flaming off the gilding wax is the heightening of its color, and seems to me to be caused by a more thorough dissipation of some mercury remaining after the first evaporation of it, which is well effected by this equable application of heat The effect produced by the saline compound is that of giving the genuine color of gold, entirely similar to that of a piece of gold dipped in aqua regia, by which any tarnish upon its surface is dissolved, and its true color is made to appear Accordingly, in all the receipts which I have seen for the preparation of this saline compound, I have always found one ingredient to be nitre, another to be common salt or sal ammoniac, and a third to be alum or some vitriol Now, by exposing these to the fire, an aqua regia is actually produced, the vitriolic acid of the alum or of the vitriolic salt decomposing the other two salts containing the marine and nitrous acids, by which means these acids are so disengaged that they can, thus formed into an aqua regia, dissolve some of the surface of the gold, and thus give it its genuine color The action of the marine and nitrous acids upon the gold must evidently be continued but an exceeding short time, the artist therefore watches the appearance of the saline compound, which, from the urine or other substance containing some inflammable matter, becomes black, upon the application of a certain degree of heat, and then he quickly plunges it in water Lastly, the only advantage from the last operation is, that a part of the yellow matter, as the sulphur, or turmeric, remains in some of the hollows of the carved work, in which the gilding is apt to be more imperfect, and to which it gives a rich and solid appearance

Iron cannot be gilt by amalgamation, unless, as it is said, it be previously coated with copper by dipping in a solution of blue vitriol Iron may also receive a golden coat from a saturated solution of gold in aqua regia, mixed with spirit of wine, the iron having a greater affinity with the acid, from which it therefore precipitates the gold Whether any of these two methods be applicable to use, I do not know, but the method commonly employed of fixing gold upon iron is that above-mentioned, of burnishing gold-leaf upon this metal when heated so as to become blue, and the operation will be more perfect if the surface has been previously scratched or graved

Another

does not seem to be gilt, is to be burnished with a blood-stone, till it acquire a fine color of gold This method of gilding is very easy, and consumes a very small quantity of gold Most gilt ornaments upon fans, snuff-boxes, and other toys of much show and little value, are nothing but silver gilt in this manner

Gold may also be applied to glass, porcelain, and other vitrified matters As the surface of these matters is very smooth, and consequently is capable of a very perfect contact with gold leaves, these leaves adhere to them with some force, although they are not of metallic nature This gilding is so much more perfect, as the gold is more exactly applied to the surface of the glass. The pieces are then to be exposed to a certain degree of heat, and burnished slightly to give them lustre (e)

These are the principal methods of gilding *Silvering* is performed by processes very similar to these, and founded on the same principles (f)

CCCXXXIX GILLA VITRIOLI This name is given to white vitriol purified by crystallization, which was formerly given as an emetic, from half a scruple to a dram *See* VITRIOL

CCCXL GINGER. (g)

Another method is mentioned by authors of gilding upon metals, and also upon earthen ware, and upon glass, which is, to fuse gold with regulus of antimony, to pulverize the mass which is sufficiently brittle to admit that operation, to spread this powder *upon the piece to be gilt, and expose it* to such a fire that the regulus may be evaporated, while the gold remains fixed The inconveniencies of this method, according to Dr Lewis, are, that the powder does not adhere to the piece, and cannot be equably spread. that part of the gold is dissipated along with the regulus, that glass is fusible with the heat necessary for the evaporation of regulus of antimony, and that copper is liable to be corroded by the regulus, and to have its surface rendered uneven.

(e) A more substantial gilding is fixed upon glass, enamel, and porcelain, by applying to these substances powder of gold mixed with a solution of gum arabic, or with some essential oil, and a small quantity of borax, after which a sufficient heat is to be applied to soften the glass and the gold, which is then to be burnished With this mixture any figures may be drawn The powders for this purpose may be made, 1 By grinding gold leaf with honey, which is afterwards to be washed away with water, 2 By distilling to dryness a solution of gold in aqua regia, 3 By evaporating the mercury from an amalgam of gold, taking care to stir well the mass near the end of the process, 4 By precipitating gold from its solution in aqua regia by applying to it a solution of green vitriol in water, or some copper, and perhaps some other metallic substances

(f) *Silvering* by amalgamation is seldom practised, as it does not succeed nearly so well as the gilding by amalgamation The common method of silvering metals, as brass, or of making French plate, is that mentioned above of burnishing silver leaves, from twenty to sixty, upon the piece of metal previously heated

(g) GINGER From sixteen ounces of the root of common ginger, about a dram of oil possessing the smell and flavor, but not the pungency of the ginger, may be obtained by distillation The same quantity of root yielded with rectified spirit an ounce and two scruples of resinous extract, containing all the pungent matter of the root Water also extracted four ounces from sixteen ounces of the root The watery extract was considerably pungent, but it seems to receive its pungency from some part of the resin which is mixed with it, for the resin remaining in the root after the extraction by water, contains greatest part of the pungent matter *Neuman*

CCCXLI GLACIES MARIÆ. (*h*)

CCCXLII GLASS. Glass is a hard, solid, brittle, transparent substance. It resists, when it is of a good quality, the action of air, water, acids, and all other menstruums. Lastly, it is not fusible without a very strong heat.

The large quantity of vitrifiable earth which enters into the composition of glass, gives it all these qualities. But as this earth is so difficultly fusible, when it is pure, that it cannot be fused and vitrified by the greatest fires of our furnaces, other matters, and particularly salts, must be mixed with it, by which its fusion is facilitated, and so intimate an union is formed, that it makes with them but one body. These fluxes therefore enter into the composition of glass. We only give here the definition of glass, and refer to the article VITRIFICATION for what we have to say on this important subject.

CCCXLIII GLASS *of* ANTIMONY. The method of preparing glass of antimony, is by calcining crude antimony with a moderate heat till no more vapors of sulphur rise, and till it be reduced to a grey ash-colored earth or calx. This calx is then to be put into a crucible, placed in a good melting furnace, and a sufficiently strong heat is to be applied during an hour, or an hour and an half, or rather till it be converted into a transparent glass. The operation may be known to have been well made, by dipping an iron rod into the crucible. In that case, some vitrified matter will adhere to the end of the iron rod, and will be capable of being drawn out into fine wire, like ordinary glass. The crucible is then to be taken from the furnace, and the glass is to be cast upon a smooth plate of copper, which ought to have been previously heated to dry it perfectly. This glass, when cold, is of a transparent hyacinthine color, more or less yellow or reddish.

The earths of all metallic matters are disposed to fusion and vitrification, when they still retain a portion of their inflammable principle. If this portion be too large, they may be melted more easily, but the mass will be opake, and more or less approaching the metallic state. If, on the contrary, these earths are too much dephlogisticated, they are so much more refractory, as they have lost more of their phlogiston, and at last become entirely unfusible, at least in the fires of our furnaces, when so much dephlogisticated as to possess only the properties of pure earths. Therefore metallic glass ought to be considered as in a state intermediate betwixt that of metals and of earths. Accordingly the glass of antimony, like all the others, is so much more colored, fusible, heavy, and less transparent, as the antimony employed has been less calcined.

As glass of antimony is chiefly prepared for the purposes of medicine, and as its emetic quality, which is its chief virtue, depends on the quantity of inflammable principle which it retains, this glass, to be well conditioned, ought to be moderately fusible and transparent, of a hyacinthine color, not too clear, nor too deep, lastly, it ought to smoke, while it remains fused.

(*h*) GLACIES MARIÆ, or *lapis specularis*, is a transparent, laminated, selenitic or gypseous stone. For its properties *see* GYPSUM. Its appearance is very similar to that of talk, but differs from it in this circumstance: that the plates of which talk consists are flexible, while those of glacies mariæ are inflexible. Some of these laminated gypsums have a rhomboidal form, and are then called *selenites*, or *gypseous spar*: others have no determinate form.

When

When the glaſs is poured out, this ſmoke condenſes partly in white flowers, which fix upon the ſurface of the glaſs and upon the plate of copper

Hence the eſſential point for making beautiful and good glaſs of antimony is, to give the antimony the preciſe degree of calcination which is neceſſary, which is not very eaſy Accordingly the operation ſometimes fails, but the exceſs or defect of the calcination may be remedied If the calx be too fuſible, and if it flow into a fluid matter which is not tranſparent, nor is capable of being drawn out into wire, as glaſs is, we may conclude that the calx has not been ſufficiently calcined In this ſtate, the fire ought to be diminiſhed, the crucible uncovered, and, after the matter has been allowed to ſmoke during a certain time, the fire may be encreaſed, and a tranſparent glaſs will be obtained But if, on the contrary, the calx cannot be made to flow or vitrify well, this ſhows that the calx has been too much calcined This fault may be remedied by throwing into the crucible about a ſixteenth part of the weight of the calx, of crude antimony, and then fuſing the whole This ſmall quantity of crude antimony not only gives phlogiſton to the calx, which thereby becomes more fuſible, but alſo ſome mineral ſulphur, which produces the ſame effect, for glaſs of antimony ſeems always to retain a certain quantity of ſulphur

When the calx of antimony employed for the preparation of this glaſs is evidently of difficult fuſion, a very ſtrong heat ought to be applied quickly, for by being kept long moderately hot in the crucible before it is fuſed, it is more and more calcined, and at laſt rendered unfuſible Some calxes are ſuppoſed to have been too much calcined for this operation, becauſe they were not expoſed to ſtrong fire ſufficiently quickly.

Glaſs of antimony is more eaſily and perfectly ſoluble in acids, and particularly in oily acids, than the regulus, wherefore, when taken internally, it produces more conſiderable effects as an emetic For this reaſon alſo, it is combined with cream of tartar for the preparation of *ſtibiated* or *emetic tartar*

Formerly it was given medicinally without other preparation than levigation. But its uſe has been relinquiſhed by prudent phyſicians from the violence and uncertainty of its effects, which are produced by the ſame cauſes as thoſe explained under the article TARTAR (EMETIC) Nevertheleſs it is given ſucceſsfully by very able phyſicians in ſome diſeaſes, as in the colic of miners But notwithſtanding the experience which has eſtabliſhed the uſe of it in theſe caſes, probably emetic tartar might be adminiſtered with equal ſucceſs and greater certainty, and, if neceſſary, in more frequent and larger doſes than in ordinary caſes *See* TARTAR (EMETIC)

CCCXLIV GLASS *of* ANTIMONY CORRECTED *by* WAX A method has lately been practiſed in England to render the glaſs of antimony milder, and this preparation has been commended as an excellent remedy in dyſenteries, and lochial hemorrhages It is made by melting a dram of yellow wax in an iron ladle, and by adding to this an ounce of levigated glaſs of antimony, in a fire continued during half an hour, and juſt ſtrong enough to diſſipate almoſt entirely the wax without inflaming it When the matter is cooled, it appears of a brown color It is again to be levigated,

levigated, and is called the glass of antimony corrected by wax, or *vitrum ceratum antimonii*. The dose of it is from six grains to ten or twelve.

The emetic quality of glass of antimony is indeed diminished by this preparation, because the wax evidently furnishes a certain quantity of phlogiston, and approximates it more to the state of the regulus, or rather of the liver of antimony, both which are less emetic than the glass. But this waxed glass must evidently be subject to the inconveniencies of these other preparations of antimony, particularly to the inequality of their effects, and for the same reason. By introducing this new remedy, therefore, a kind of preparations essentially faulty, and relinquished for good reasons, has again been brought into use, without considering, that the diseases, for which it is recommended, proceed from different causes, and ought not to be treated with the same remedies; as Mr Baron has judiciously remarked in his edition of Lemery's Chemistry.

CCCXLV. GLASS *of* BORAX. Borax is, as we have said under that article, a neutral salt, which when exposed to fire, loses the water of its crystallization; and by a stronger heat is further fusible into a matter which may be drawn out, while hot, into wire, like ordinary glass, and which when cold, has the appearance of a very white, transparent glass. Borax thus perfectly fused has been called a glass, from its resemblance to vitrified matters. This glass of borax differs nevertheless from true glass by the saline properties which it retains; it being entirely soluble in water, and again crystallizable into its original form of borax. It is susceptible of the same decompositions as borax; in a word, it does not differ essentially from borax, but only in being more dry, or deprived of water.

To obtain very beautiful glass of borax, it ought to be guarded against ashes and coals, which is conveniently done by melting it in a muffle. As this matter is very fusible, and at the same time capable of facilitating much the fusion and vitrification of sand, and other earthy matters, it is advantageously used in the essays of ores, and as an ingredient in compositions for glasses and artificial crystals. But for this latter purpose a very small proportion only ought to be used, as it imparts to glass the same property it has itself, of losing its lustre by exposure to air. Glass of borax is preferred to borax for these purposes, because it is deprived of all superfluous moisture, and is not subject to swell, as the borax is. *See* BORAX.

CCCXLVI. GLASS *of* LEAD. Lead is a metal easily calcinable; but it has a singular property, that when it has lost so much of its phlogiston that it cannot be reduced into metal without addition, it then retains the remaining part of its phlogiston more strongly than any other metallic matter. Hence cerus or white lead, minium, litharge, and all the other preparations and calxes of lead, retain always great fusibility, and are much disposed to vitrification. All these matters, by a moderate fire only, are easily fused, and formed into a transparent glass of a deep yellow color. But this glass is so penetrating and so powerful a flux, that it passes through crucibles as soon as it melts; and when it has been kept long enough in the fire to be perfectly fused and vitrified, none of it is to be found in the crucible, which is then glazed over internally and externally.

This property of glass of lead proceeds from its powerful action upon all earthy matters, by which it disposes them to vitrify Hence the difficulty of obtaining a pure glass of lead A greater consistence must be given to it, and its activity must be repressed, by uniting it with sand, in the following manner, to render it fit for use

Take two parts of a calx of lead, minium for instance, and one part of sand or powdered flints Put this mixture into a good crucible made of refractory clay, baked into a very compact body Place this crucible in a melting furnace, after having closed it well with a luted lid This crucible is to be heated by degrees, and very slowly, not only to prevent the breaking of the crucible, to which this kind of crucible is very subject, when heated too quickly, but to hinder the matter from swelling too much, and flowing over the crucible in the beginning of the fusion. During an hour or an hour and a half, the fire must be thus managed in the beginning of the operation, and afterwards it may be encreased, to obtain a compleat fusion, and continued in that state during an hour or an hour and a half, after which the crucible is left to cool in the furnace, and when it is broken, a very transparent yellow colored glass is found in it Some chemists direct the addition of some nitre and common salt to the above mixture, as these salts promote the fusion, and the more equal distribution of the sand

This glass, which, as we have seen, is not a pure glass of lead, but in which the lead is the prevailing ingredient, has a considerable specific gravity, and its lower part is always the heaviest. As it is very fusible, and easily re melted with a moderate fire, and as it is besides a very powerful flux, it is advantageously employed in essays of ores to facilitate their scorification. *See* LEAD *and* VITRIFICATION

CCCXLVII GLASS-GALL This is a saline matter which rises as a scum in the pots or crucibles in which glass is made

This matter is chiefly composed of Glauber's salt, common salt, vitriolated tartar, or other neutral salts which cannot enter into vitrification, and which were originally contained in the ashes or alkalis employed in the composition for glass Glass-gall is used to facilitate the fusion of certain ores, and in essays, but this matter must vary much, according to the kinds of alkalis or ashes from which it is produced (*a*)

(*a*) *Glass-gall*, called also *Sandiver*, is said to contain the vitriolic acid, although no vitriolic salt was employed in the composition for the glass The vitriolated tartar which is in all pot-ash and wood-ashes employed in the manufacture of glass, might account for the existence of vitriolic acid in common glass-gall, but Pott affirms, that by melting together fixed alkali, flints, and common salt, a salt of Glauber may be produced, which he thinks very similar to glass-gall in many of its properties, but from which, however, it differs in this, that it deliquiates by exposure to air, whereas the salt of Glauber falls into a dry powder Tachenius supposes that the vitriolic acid of glass-gall proceeds from the flints Its crystals resemble, as Mr Pott says, partly vitriolated tartar, and partly the salts of mineral water. It differs from vitriolated tartar in being more fusible, more soluble in water, and in being even deliquescent. It is used as a flux in essays of ores, and in the fusion of filings of gold or silver, in the same manner as borax is It is even said to increase the malleability of metals. *See Pott's Dissertation on Glass-gall.*

CCCXLVIII. GOLD. Gold, called also by chemists the *Sun*, *Sol*, and the *king of metals*, is a perfect metal, of a yellow splendid color, and unalterable by all the operations of art This is the most perfect of all metals, its principles are the best combined, and it possesses most eminently the metallic characteristics

When gold is very pure, it has no taste nor smell, even when heated and rubbed It loses in water betwixt $\frac{1}{19}$ and $\frac{1}{20}$ part of its weight A cubic foot of gold weighs 1326 pounds It is the heaviest of all metals, and consequently of all known bodies

The hardness of gold is intermediate betwixt that of the hard and of the soft metals. Its ductility is surprizingly great, and exceeds that of all metals From calculations made by experimental philosophers concerning the extension of gold upon silver, a single ounce of gold, the bulk of which is very small on account of its great weight, is found to be capable of covering and gilding perfectly a silver wire 444 leagues in length

The gold beater's art, by which gold is formed into such thin leaves that they are made to float in the air by a light breath, is a further proof of its great ductility, and is also a proof of its extreme opacity for these gold leaves are still perfectly opake Light may indeed be perceived through them, but this is owing to cracks, which may be easily perceived upon examining the leaves, and which are occasioned by the repeated strokes of the hammer

When gold is struck during a certain time by a hammer, or when violently compressed, as it is by gold-wire-drawers, it becomes more hard, elastic, and stiff, and less ductile, so that it is apt to be crackt and torn The same thing also happens to the other metals by percussion and compression Ductility and tractability may be restored to metals in that state, by making them red-hot, which is called *annealing* them Gold seems to be more affected by percussion and by annealing than other metals

The tenacity of the parts of gold is also much greater than of any other metal. For 500 pounds can be supported by a wire of $\frac{1}{10}$ of an inch in diameter made of gold, but not of any other metal

Gold is unalterable by air and by water It never contracts any rust, and when its surface loses its lustre, this is occasioned by the adhesion of extraneous matters, and not by any destruction of the metal The action of fire does not occasion any alteration upon gold When exposed to fire it soon becomes red, and when it has acquired a vivid redness, like that of a burning coal, it soon melts. Its surface has then a light green color, like that of a beryl No vapor or smoke rises from gold during its fusion, and it suffers no loss of weight by that operation, however long continued, or with the most violent fire. Kunckel kept gold in a glass-house furnace during a month, and Boyle kept some still longer exposed to great heat, without the loss of a single grain or any alteration.

Gold resists also, while its aggregation is entire, the action of the strongest simple chemical menstruums, either in the dry or in the humid way It is not soluble either by the strongest mineral acids when they are pure, nor by sulphur, nor by alkalis Two compound bodies, nevertheless, are powerful solvents of gold. The first is a mixture of the nitrous and marine acids, called by chemists *aqua regia*, because it dissolves gold, the king of metals, and the second solvent of gold is a combination of sulphur with fixed alkali, called *liver of sulphur*.

The solution of gold in aqua regia is very easy. A very small quantity of nitrous acid, or even of inflammable matter, mixed with marine acid, gives this latter acid the property of attacking gold. Also a very small quantity of marine acid, or of any of the salts containing it, mixed with nitrous acid, renders this nitrous acid capable of dissolving a certain quantity of gold. But experience has shown, that an aqua regia composed of four parts of nitrous acid, and one of sal ammoniac, dissolves perfectly well a fourth or a third part of its weight of gold, according to the strength of the acid. *See* AQUA REGIA.

To make this solution, the gold is to be reduced into filings or thin plates, and put into a small matrass. Upon this gold the aqua regia is to be poured, and the matrass is to be placed in a sand-bath moderately heated. As soon as the aqua regia is sufficiently heated, it attacks the gold with all the usual phenomena which accompany solutions of metals in acids. But in this solution the effervescence is only moderate. While the aqua regia dissolves the gold, it acquires a beautiful yellow color, which becomes more and more intense, till it has a golden, or even an orange color. When the menstruum is entirely saturated with gold, the solution is very clear and transparent.

The power which the nitrous and marine acids acquire by their union, of dissolving gold, which neither of them have separately, is one of the most remarkable facts in chemistry, and favours much the opinion which admits the three earths or principles of Becker as the constituent parts of metals, because that fact is well explained by this doctrine. If marine acid contains the mercurial principle, as nitrous acid contains the inflammable principle, and if, on the other side, both these principles constitute metals, by their union with the earthy principle, we may easily conceive that all those metallic matters, in which the union of these principles is weak and imperfect, may be attacked indiscriminately by the nitrous and marine acids separately; because when any of these acids finds in the metallic matter the principle which is analogous to it, weakly combined, it may be capable of attacking that metallic matter, by means of this analogous principle. But if these principles be strongly united together, as many reasons concur to prove they are in gold, since it is the most perfect and indestructible of metals, then we may easily conceive that while these acids act on the gold separately, the mercurial principle may be defended from the action of the marine acid by the inflammable principle, and reciprocally the inflammable principle may be defended from the action of the nitrous acid by the mercurial principle, and that thus gold cannot be dissolved by either of these two acids separately.

But we may at the same time easily perceive, that if two acids united make a combined attack upon gold, that is, if the marine acid attacks the mercurial principle of the metal, while the nitrous acid attacks the inflammable principle, the action of this compound menstruum will be twice as strong as that of any of the two acids separately, and they may therefore perform the solution conjointly, which neither of them could do singly.

Gold

Gold receives no alteration in its composition from the acids of aqua regia. This solution is corrosive, as also all other metallic solutions are. It gives a violet color to the fingers, or to any animal matters, for the same reason that solutions of silver and mercury in nitrous acid tinge these matters black. If the solution be evaporated and cooled, yellow transparent crystals like fossil topazes will be formed. But if the evaporation be carried too far, the acids with which the gold is united may be driven from it by heat alone, and the gold will be left in the state of a yellow powder called *calx of gold*.

Gold may be precipitated from its solution by those intermediate substances which generally precipitate metals from acids; that is, by alkalis fixed and volatile, by calcareous earths, and by some other metals. But volatile alkali seems to precipitate gold more easily than fixed alkalis; at least gold is very slowly precipitated from an aqua regia made without sal ammoniac by fixed alkali, but is copiously and instantly precipitated by volatile alkali. Fixed alkali also precipitates it copiously and speedily from aqua regia made with sal ammoniac; but in this case the volatile alkali in the nitrous ammoniacal salt, contained in this aqua regia, is evidently disengaged by the fixed alkali, and contributes to the precipitation.

All these precipitates of gold, although yellow, have not a metallic brilliancy, because they retain part of the dissolving and precipitating salts. In other respects, they, and also the calx of gold above-mentioned, are nothing but gold unaltered; and when melted without addition, become entirely like the metal before it was dissolved.

Gold precipitated by a volatile alkali from its solution in aqua regia has an astonishing property, namely, its power of exploding with violence and terrible noise, when heated to a certain degree. It is accordingly called *fulminating gold*. *See* GOLD (FULMINATING). This property has not been observed in any other metal.

Although a mass of gold, that is, gold, the aggregation of which is entire, resists the action of simple solvents, as we have seen, we must not conclude that it is absolutely incapable of solution by any of these simple solvents. On the contrary, Mr Margraaff has discovered, that this metal, precipitated by an alkali from its solution in aqua regia, is then rendered soluble by any, even the vegetable, acids. Besides, gold dissolved in aqua regia is not precipitated, when the proportions of the two acids of this compound menstruum are changed, by adding to this solution any quantity of nitrous or of marine acids. Lastly, gold may be dissolved in alkalis by the process of the martial alkaline tincture of Stahl; that is, by pouring into a concentrated solution of fixed alkali in water, a small quantity of solution of gold in aqua regia in which the acids are not too much saturated, the gold will be quickly seized and dissolved by the alkali.

All these experiments prove, that the just proportion and intimate connection of the principles of the gold are not the only causes which render it insoluble, or difficultly soluble by menstrua which easily attack the other metals, but that its great density and strength of its aggregation contribute also much to this effect; since, when this aggregation is broken by a previous solution in aqua regia, it easily yields to the action of other solvents.

Most metals are capable of separating gold from aqua regia by precipitation the precipitate occasioned by adding tin is the most remarkable of these It has not the metalic splendor, as metals precipitated by other metals generally have, but it is of a beautiful purple color, when well made This precipitate, called *Cassius's precipitate of gold*, is used to give a crimson color to vitrified matters *See* PRECIPITATE *of* GOLD (CASSIUS'S)

Oily, thin, ethereal substances have great affinity with gold If a light, essential oil, and still better if ether, be poured upon a solution of gold in aqua regia, and the mixture be shook, the gold will be seen to pass into the oily matter, which will float upon the aqua regia now deprived of its metal This is one of the best methods of making potable gold *See* GOLD (POTABLE)

Neither sulphur nor fixed alkali can act separately upon gold But the liver of sulphur, which is composed of these two substances, is also a great solvent of this metal This solution can be well made only by the dry way To make it succeed, gold leaves are to be mixed with liver of sulphur, put into a crucible together, and very quickly fused The gold will be attacked by the liver of sulphur, and will very soon disappear If this liver of sulphur thus impregnated with gold be dissolved in water, the metal remains suspended, and may be even passed through a paper filter

This is also a method of making potable gold, the taste of which is very disagreeable, from the liver of sulphur Stahl has written a dissertation concerning this method of dissolving gold, by which, he thinks, Moses might have dissolved and rendered potable the golden calf mentioned in scripture (*k*) As the liver of sulphur is decomposed by time, and changes into vitriolated tartar by exposure to the air, the gold therefore must also separate from it

When a solution of gold in liver of sulphur is precipitated by an acid, the sulphur and gold are precipitated together, and in this case the precipitate is not white, as it is from a pure liver of sulphur, but acquires a yellow color from the gold The gold and sulphur thus precipitated together are not united, but are easily separable by fire, which consumes the sulphur, and leaves the metal pure

Gold may be allayed with all metals, but these allays are not much used, excepting with silver and copper, for coins and gold plate, with mercury, in the extraction of gold from the ore or matrix containing it, and for gilding, with lead and with regulus of antimony, for its purification by these substances

Gold allayed with any metallic substance is always less ductile than when pure, which observation is applicable in general to all allays *See* ALLAY.

The color of gold is considerably altered and rendered paler by silver, and is, on the contrary, much exalted and heightened by a mixture of copper. Cop-

(*k*) Moses was probably a good chemist, as he had been instructed in all the wisdom of the Egyptians, and possibly might have known the solubility of gold by liver of sulphur, but those persons who cannot be convinced that he was assisted by divine power, in this and all other instances of his administration, will scarcely believe that he could persuade the Israelites to swallow so fetid and perhaps so poisonous a potation, as a solution of gold by liver of sulphur, or that he knew no better method of employing this precious calf, than by applying it as an emetic to his countrymen.

per alſo diminiſhes very little the ductility of gold, and gives it more firmneſs and ſolidity Accordingly the allay of copper with gold is much uſed

Gold cannot be ſeparated from ſilver but by expoſing this allay to the action of menſtruums, which can only diſſolve one or the other of theſe two metals, that is, acids and ſulphur *See* PARTING

All other metals may be ſeparated from gold by ſcorification with lead, by nitre, and by antimony, or rather by the ſulphur of the antimony *See the details of all theſe operations, under the words* REFINING, CUPELLATION, PURIFICATION *of* GOLD, *and* SMELTING *of* ORES

All that we have ſaid concerning the properties of gold ought to make us conſider it as a metal, indeſtructible, fixed, and not to be decompounded But this does not prove that it is a ſimple body, and abſolutely unalterable On the contrary, we have reaſon to believe that its reſiſtance to all our operations is owing to our inability to raiſe a ſufficient heat, and that if it were expoſed to a fire infinitely ſtronger, ſuppoſe near the ſun, or even within the ſun, it would be burnt and decompoſed, as the imperfect metals are, in a moderate fire, and perhaps would be reduced into vapors

Some chemiſts pretend that they have been able to calcine gold Homberg ſays, in the Memoirs of the Academy of Sciences, that having expoſed gold to the focus of Tſchirnhauſen's great lens, he ſaw this metal ſmoke, and become a glaſs But according to the tradition preſerved in the Academy, this experiment is not ſufficiently authenticated, and is one of thoſe which require to be repeated with great care (*l*)

Kunckel ſays, that he changed gold into an irreducible calx, by long calcination, without fuſion, and by reverberation in the manner of Iſaacus Hollandus This experiment alſo is not very well aſcertained, becauſe no chemiſt has had patience enough to repeat it.

Laſtly, the true alchemiſts do not make any doubt of the poſſibility of decompoſing, or entirely deſtroying gold Their books are filled with proceſſes by which they affirm, that this metal may be radically diſſolved, its principles ſeparated, its ſulphur, as they call it, its tincture, and its ſoul, may all be extracted

In Junker's Chemiſtry we find, that Langelot, and Borrichius in his Treatiſe concerning the Wiſdom of Hermes and of the Egyptians, ſay, that if gold leaves be triturated upon a porphyry during fourteen days and nights, the gold will at laſt be changed into a black powder, which contains ſome thing viſcous, volatile, of a ſulphureous ſmell, and which being diſtilled with a graduated heat in a ſhallow retort, furniſhes ſome drops of a very red liquor

This experiment is evidently very long, laborious, and liable to error, as moſt of this kind are. For it is almoſt impoſſible, but that during ſo long a

(*l*) Homberg ſays, that part of the gold was vitrified, and ſuppoſes only that the reſt might alſo have been vitrified But he did not aſcertain the purity of the gold which he employed, and therefore the glaſs produced in this experiment might proceed from copper or other metal with which the gold might have been allayed, or from the aſhes of the charcoal which ſupported it, which we find was the opinion of ſome perſons who had been preſent at that experiment

trituration, a sensible quantity of heterogeneous matters should be mixed with the gold, if it were only those which are continually floating in the air (m)

Borrichius says also in the same work, that a plate of gold, being made red-hot and extinguished in water many times, gives an astringent taste to the water, which seems to shew a kind of solution of gold by water But was the gold, and also the water employed by Borrichius in this experiment, perfectly pure? We know with what difficulty gold can be obtained perfectly pure, and that no water but distilled water is fit to chemical experiments

Becker in his second Supplement to the *Physica Subterranea*, gives a process to render gold as soft as lead, and to encrease its fusibility This process consists in throwing melted gold a number of times into a liquor composed of spirit of sal ammoniac and rectified spirit of wine I do not believe that this experiment has been repeated by any chemist If it succeeds, the softness and fusibility which the gold acquires may probably be caused by a superabundance of inflammable principle communicated to it by these two liquors

The author of a treatise called *Alchymia Denudata* affirms, that if half an ounce of gold be melted with two ounces of copper, and the copper be afterwards separated from the gold with eight times as much aqua fortis not depurated, and if this work be repeated nine times, the gold will receive so lively a red color that it would scarcely be known to be gold, and so fixed as to sustain all the ordinary trials without hurt or loss This experiment deserves to be repeated We do not see why the author directs the use of undepurated aqua fortis, or of such as probably contains some marine acid Such an aqua fortis seems, on the contrary, very unfavorable to the experiment, for as it is a little of the nature of aqua regia, it may dissolve some of the gold

Roth advances in his Chemistry, that gold may be dissolved in spirit of nitre distilled in Glauber's manner, the vapors of which have been received and condensed by highly rectified spirit of wine In this experiment, nitrous ether must be formed, and we know that ether has a strong disposition to unite with gold therefore this solution ought to succeed better, as the ether is here assisted by the action of the nitrous acid But this solution of gold probably does not differ much from the ordinary tincture of gold made with nitrous ether *See* GOLD (POTABLE)

Kunckel, in his Chemical Laboratory, proposes as an excellent solvent of gold, but which acts exceeding slowly, the subtle vapor which arises during the re-action of deliquiated fixed alkali with vitriolic acid This vapor seems indeed to be very subtle and active, by the impressions it makes upon our organs of smelling, but these qualities are only apparent, and we cannot easily believe

(m) Junker also relates from Borrichius and Olaus, that by a long trituration of an amalgam of gold with distilled water, a black powder was formed, which was convertible into green glass, and that the water became impregnated with a saline matter, and that by this method the gold may be destroyed Dr Lewis observes, that the green glass probably proceeded from abraded parts of a glass mortar, that the saline matter had probably pre existed in the water or was extracted from the glass, and that the black powder was produced by the trituration of the mercury The same author says, that he has triturated an amalgam of gold during a week, without destroying any part of the gold.

lieve that this vapor is capable of dissolving gold, excepting the vitriolic acid be impure and sulphureous I collected a considerable quantity of this vapor by saturating fixed alkali with vitriolic acid in a tubulated glass alembic The vapor when condensed into a liquor seemed to be nothing but pure water Its poignant smell, therefore, seems to be nothing but the air which is disengaged in all these effervescencies, and which by interposing itself betwixt the parts of the water, gives this spirituous quality to the water, which Mr Venel has shewn to exist also in the mineral, aerial, and spirituous waters *See* WATERS (MINERAL)

Cassius, in his Treatise *de Auro*, mentions a process to obtain very red crystals of gold of a violet smell For this purpose he directs gold leaves to be dissolved by help of a long continued heat, in a liquor composed of a pound of the phlegm of ordinary aqua fortis, and of four ounces of common salt When the solution is made, the crystals above mentioned may be obtained by crystallization, in the ordinary method As this is merely a solution of gold in aqua regia, the peculiar color and smell of the crystals probably proceed from matters extraneous to this metal Besides, marine acid when weakly attached to a basis without smell, always emits an odor similar to that of violets

Glauber, in his Treatise *de Lapide Animali*, gives a process for dissolving gold, by which also it is remarkably altered. This process consists in dissolving two or three ounces of hartshorn in an aqua regia made by distilling together nitre and decrepitated common salt (by means undoubtedly of some substance capable of disengaging the acids) Then a dram of gold leaf is to be put into this liquor, which is to be afterwards distilled off from the gold in a glass cucurbit, during which distillation the gold is dissolved, and when the liquor is drawn off, at the bottom of the vessel, a mass will be found composed of all the ingredients employed This mass is then to be fused very quickly in a forge fire, and in an open crucible, by which it is changed into a black scoria, under which the gold is found rendered white and brittle like regulus of antimony If this experiment be true, we cannot easily conceive why the gold should acquire this whiteness and brittleness, except we impute it to the mercurial principle of the marine acid, which acid, being retained by the union it forms with the earth of the hartshorn, may be supposed capable of a partial decomposition by the gold and by the fire, and thus a portion of the mercurial principle, which many chemists believe to be one of the constituent parts of the marine acid, might apply itself to the gold, and unite with it superabundantly Such an experiment well confirmed, would certainly indicate the presence of the mercurial principle in the marine acid

As most chemists have made wonderful experiments on gold, their books are filled with many other processes of this nature, by which very curious and interesting phenomena result, and which therefore deserve to be repeated But as they are at the same time almost always obscure, confused, and full of tedious and embarrassing operations, they require a very careful examination Those processes which we have described as examples of this kind were chosen as the most practicable, and which give the most hopes of success

Mr Limburg, who has written a Dissertation, which obtained the prize from the academy at Rouen, concerning chemical affinities, gives a table of affinities, in which he establishes those of gold in the following manner; aqua regia, liver of sulphur, mercury, ether, silver, iron, and lead

The principal uses of gold are well known It is very proper to be formed into coin, and into various ornaments, from its lustre, beauty, and undestructible quality By means of the art of gilding, much external beauty, neatness, and richness is given to many utensils and toys A fine color also is obtained from gold for enamel and porcelain painting Many persons have been of opinion, and many still are, that a remedy superior to all others may be extracted from gold, capable of procuring long life The truth of this opinion is more than doubtful *See* GOLD (POTABLE) With gold, an explosive powder more terrible and destructive than gun-powder may be made This powder is called fulminating gold *See* GOLD (FULMINATING) (*n*)

CCCXLIX GOLD (FULMINATING) This preparation is gold precipitated from its solution in aqua regia It is called fulminating, because, when it is heated or rubbed so as to acquire a certain heat, it makes an explosion similar and perhaps superior to that of thunder

The method always used to prepare fulminating gold, consists in dissolving this metal in a sufficient quantity of aqua regia, which is generally made with spirit of nitre and sal ammoniac, from which the gold is to be afterwards precipitated by adding fixed alkali A copious precipitate of a yellow and somewhat reddish color is soon formed This precipitate washed and dryed is fulminating gold

The phenomenon of fulmination is certainly one of the most striking and wonderful which chemistry affords The cause of this fulmination is not easily to be discovered But the following facts may suggest hints to explain it

(*n*) For further particulars concerning gold, *see the articles* ESSAY *of the* VALUE *of* GOLD, PURIFICATION *of* GOLD *by* ANTIMONY, PARTING, ORES *of* GOLD, GILDING, *and* ALLAY Every thing almost that is known concerning gold, its natural history, its chemical properties, and its use in arts, are treated copiously and accurately by Dr Lewis, in his very useful work, intitled, *Philosophical Commerce of Arts*

We shall here make some additions to the metallurgic history of gold 1 The color of gold is rendered paler by fusion with borax, which substance, or other flux, is used to facilitate the fusion of filings of gold The paleness acquired by gold from borax may be prevented or corrected by fusion with nitre, or with sal ammoniac 2 The color of gold is heightened by an allay of copper, which also encreases its hardness, and when in small quantity, as in the proportion of one to twelve, does not much diminish its malleability Other metals render it paler *See* ALLAY See also the methods of heightening the color of gilding at the article GILDING 3 The malleability of gold is diminished by cooling it, when fused too hastily To prevent which, artists heat the mould into which the gold is to be cast 4 The malleability of gold is destroyed by fumes of lead and of most other metallic substances, and may be recovered by fusion with nitre Many authors say that the malleability of gold is injured by the fumes of charcoal, but Dr Lewis believes this to be a mistake 5 Gold may be melted with a low white heat, and when melted has a bright bluish green color Dr Lewis observes, that although its expansion is less than that of other metallic substances with small degrees of heat, it nevertheless expands more than most of the other metals when fused, and that this property, by which it shrinks more when it becomes solid than most other metals, renders it less capable of receiving sharp and perfect figures, when cast into moulds, than silver, copper, lead, and tin, which do not shrink so much, and far less so than iron or bismuth, which expand in their passage from a fluid to a solid state

First,

First, if gold be dissolved in an aqua regia composed of nitrous acid, and of marine acid or common salt, and to which no sal ammoniac is added, and if this gold be precipitated by fixed alkali, this precipitate does not fulminate On the contrary, it fulminates strongly, if it be precipitated from this same aqua regia by a volatile alkali These facts were well known to chemists One of the menstruums employed by them to dissolve gold, is the liquor which they call *menstruum sine strepitu*, this solvent is a compound of equal parts of alum, nitre, and common salt, with which the gold is first to be ground, water is then to be added, and the whole digested, that the salts may act upon the gold By this method the gold is found to be entirely dissolved In this operation the vitriolic acid of the alum disengages the acids of the nitre and of the common salt, and thus an aqua regia is formed, in which no sal ammoniac, and consequently no volatile alkali, enters Hoffman and Etmuller affirm, that if gold be precipitated by a fixed alkali from its solution in this menstruum sine strepitu, this precipitate of gold does not fulminate, but that it fulminates strongly when the precipitate is made by volatile alkali

Secondly, when gold is dissolved in an aqua regia in which sal ammoniac enters, its precipitate, whether by a fixed or by a volatile alkali, always fulminates

Thirdly, when fulminating gold is prepared, and all the precipitate carefully collected, we find that its weight sensibly exceeds that of the gold employed, that is, a fourth more of fulminating gold is obtained, than the gold which was dissolved

Fourthly, sulphur, or vitriolic acid, or fixed alkalis, being well mixed with fulminating powder, deprive it of its fulminating quality

The first and second of these experiments prove clearly, that in order to procure fulminating powder, a nitrous ammoniacal salt must be formed in the operation The augmentation of the weight of the gold shews also that this ammoniacal nitrous salt applies itself to the gold during the precipitation, and incorporates with it

Lastly, the methods, by which the fulminating property of this precipitate may be destroyed, are also capable of decomposing the nitrous ammoniacal salt The acid of sulphur, or vitriolic acid, separates its nitrous acid, and forms a vitriolic ammoniacal salt, by uniting with its volatile alkali, and the fixed alkali disengages its volatile alkali, and forms ordinary nitre with its nitrous acid

All these facts seem to prove, that the fulminating property of the gold is occasioned by the nitrous ammoniacal salt formed during the precipitation, and which very strongly and intimately unites with the metal Further, this nitrous ammoniacal salt is known to be susceptible of detonation when heated to a certain degree, and without addition of any combustible matter, which property is occasioned by the quantity of inflammable matter which its volatile alkali contains This detonation of nitrous ammoniacal salt is indeed very small, when compared with that of fulminating gold. But all explosive bodies are known to produce explosions so much the stronger as they are more confined and compressed But the parts of the ammoniacal salt may be so combined with the gold as to be strongly included within the particles of the metal.

If the exploſion of the fulminating gold only proceeds from the detonation of the nitrous ammoniacal ſalt which it contains, as we have reaſon to believe, it muſt certainly be the effect of the inflammation of the nitrous ſulphur, in which chiefly conſiſts the detonation of nitre. *See* DETONATION *of* NITRE.

M. Beaumé has a particular opinion on this ſubject. He thinks that the nitrous ſulphur which occaſions the fulmination of gold, is formed during the precipitation, by the union of phlogiſton with nitrous acid; that this nitrous ſulphur exiſts mixed with the gold, and ready formed before its fulmination; and conſequently that the nitrous ammoniacal ſalt does not contribute to the production of this effect.

The chief proof which he brings to ſupport this opinion, is, that if fixed alkali be poured upon fulminating gold, no ſmell of volatile alkali ariſes. Mr Beaumé further affirms, that fulminating gold may be boiled in any quantity of water, provided that water be pure, that is, diſtilled, without loſs of its fulminating quality; which experiment ſeems to ſhew, that the fulminating quality is not occaſioned by any ſaline ſubſtance ſoluble in water, as the nitrous ammoniacal ſalt, but rather by ſome ſubſtance inſoluble in water, as the nitrous ſulphur probably is, from its analogy to vitriolic ſulphur. This is certainly an ingenious thought, and we wiſh that Mr Beaumé would proſecute, prove, and explain it fully, as it deſerves. *See* SULPHUR (NITROUS).

But whatever be the cauſe of the fulmination of gold, we are certain that the exploſion occaſioned by it is one of the moſt violent which are known in chemiſtry. It is not neceſſary that fulminating gold ſhould be touched by an ignited matter, or that it ſhould be heated till it becomes red, to make it explode. The heat requiſite for this purpoſe is intermediate, betwixt that of boiling water and the heat which makes metals of an obſcure red color. Friction alone, and even a friction not very conſiderable, is ſufficient to make it fulminate, and this effect is produced either in open or in cloſe veſſels. Theſe circumſtances render fulminating gold very dangerous. Several chemiſts, from not ſufficiently knowing its effects, have been hurt or killed, while they were pounding and drying it. I was witneſs to the following accident. A young man, who worked in a laboratory, had put a dram of fulminating powder into a glaſs bottle, and had neglected to wipe the inner ſurface of the neck of the bottle, to which ſome of the powder adhered. When he endeavoured to cloſe this bottle, the turning the glaſs ſtopper round, to make it fit more cloſely, occaſioned ſuch a friction, that heat enough was produced to make part of the powder explode. By this exploſion the young man was thrown ſome ſteps behind, his face and hands were wounded by the fragments of the bottle, and his eyes were put out. Notwithſtanding the violence of this exploſion, the whole dram of fulminating gold did certainly not explode. Probably even very little of it was exploded, for much of it was afterwards found ſcattered about in the laboratory, in its unexploded ſtate.

A misfortune of this kind is ſo terrible, and at the ſame time ſo difficult to be prevented by thoſe who are not ſufficiently initiated in chemiſtry, that I thought a relation of this accident ought to be publiſhed.

The gold is not altered by this ſudden and violent inflammation. Of this we may be aſſured by detonating ſo ſmall a quantity of fulminating gold under a glaſs bell, that nothing is to be feared from the exploſion. The gold may

be

be afterwards obſerved to adhere, in its proper metallic ſtate, to the inner ſurface of this ball (o)

CCCL. GOLD (POTABLE). Alchemiſts have always believed that gold poſſeſſes admirable virtues for the cure of many diſeaſes, and for the prolongation of life. They have conſequently laboured much to procure remedies from this metal, and they have accordingly invented many preparations, any one of which, if we believe the inventor, is capable of curing all evils. But the conſtant obſervation of the moſt intelligent practitioners not having confirmed theſe pretended qualities, this metal is not employed by phyſicians. Many ignorant people have ſtill the prejudice of its great virtues, and empyrics, who know how to profit by the weakneſs of men, keep up and ſtrengthen this prejudice, by continually boaſting of their elixirs and tinctures of gold, and of their potable gold, which they always declare to be wonderful ſecrets.

The indeſtructible quality of gold ſufficiently ſhews, that no effect can be produced upon it in our body, for we are certain that it is voided unaltered, and it is only uſed in pharmacy to cover and conceal other remedies, or to give them an air of wealth and grandeur which pleaſes ſome people.

This inactivity of gold in its natural ſtate, ſeems to be acknowledged by the moſt ignorant; for all the quacks who boaſt of their golden remedies declare that they can radically diſſolve it. But this pretenſion is as uſeleſs to an intelligent phyſician as it is ill founded, ſince the example of many other metallic matters, the virtues of which are aſcertained, although they are not diſſolved radically, proves that ſuch a ſolution of gold, ſuppoſing even that this metal had virtues, would be very unneceſſary. Accordingly, when we examine the preparations given for potable gold, we find that a part of them contains no gold, and the gold which others do actually contain may be eaſily extracted, and reduced to its natural ſtate.

(o) The expanſion of fulminating powder ſeems to be more ſudden and quick, but leſs forcible than that of an equal quantity of gunpowder. The quickneſs of the expanſion of fulminating gold, is inferred from the loudneſs of its exploſion, which is much greater than that of gunpowder, and from its perforating or impreſſing a metalline plate, upon which it is laid unconfined, and is exploded, which effect is not produced by gunpowder, the cauſe of which ſeems to be, that the force of the exploſion of gunpowder is applied ſo ſlowly and gradually, that it may be communicated from the part of the plate which the powder touches to the other parts of the plate, and thus the force is reſiſted by the vis inertiæ of the whole plate, whereas in the exploſion of fulminating gold, the whole force is ſo ſuddenly applied to the contiguous part of the plate, that it is capable of perforating or impreſſing that part before it can be communicated to the reſt of the plate. Now, though the force applied during the inſtant of the exploſion of fulminating gold, be greater than the force of exploding gunpowder during that inſtant, yet the ſum of the forces of exploding gunpowder, in the ſeveral inſtants of its exploſion, is probably much greater than the whole force of fulminating gold, becauſe a quantity of aurum fulminans ſhut up in a ſtrong hollow iron ball, and heated in the fire, did not ſeem to explode, while gunpowder treated in the ſame manner burſt the ball. This experiment is related in *Dr Birch's Hiſtory of the Royal Society*, vol I.

Dr Black attributes the encreaſe of weight, and alſo the exploſive property of fulminating gold, to adhering fixable air. See his *Eſſay on Magneſia*, among the *Eſſays Phyſical and Literary*, publiſhed at Edinburgh, vol II.

To render gold potable, it must be previously dissolved This may be done in aqua regia, or even in any of the acids, with proper management, but by this method gold and the other metals are rendered corrosive This is so well known, that the preparers of potable gold affirm that their solutions are made without any acid But as all the very thin and volatile oily substances have a strong disposition to unite with gold, and do really unite with it when they find it much divided, by their means may be made several tinctures of gold, or kinds of potable gold. If these preparations do not acquire any virtue from the gold which they contain, they have at least that of the inflammable subtile matter, which is the vehicle of the gold *See* Oils (Essential) *and* Ether

Subtle essential oils, ethereal liquors such as the vitriolic and other ethers, being mixed and agitated with a solution of gold in aqua regia have a property of depriving this aqua regia of its gold, which it seizes, so as to carry it to the surface of the liquor, where it floats upon the aqua regia Many receipts for potable gold are upon these principles One of these is in the Dispensatory of the Faculty of Medicine in Paris It consists in mixing and agitating sixteen parts of essential oil of rosemary with one part of gold dissolved in aqua regia, in separating afterwards this aqua regia thus deprived of gold from the essential oil which contains it, and in dissolving this essential oil in five times its weight of rectified spirit of wine This preparation is the same as that described in the last edition of Lemery's Chemistry, under the name of *potable gold of Mademoiselle Grimaldi* As all essential oils have the same property of taking gold from the aqua regia, potable gold may be made with any of these, as well as with the oil of rosemary

As ether possesses eminently all the properties of the most attenuated and volatile oils, it produces the same effect, and better than essential oils, upon the solution of gold, so that potable gold may be made by any of the ethers in the same manner as by the essential oils Mr Pott having perceived a smell of ether in a potable gold, sold under the name of *Drops of General de la Motte*, imagined that this preparation was made with ether But as these drops are miscible with water in any proportion, a quality which does not belong to pure ether, this smell of ether probably proceeds from a small quantity of nitrous ether formed by the mixture of the nitrous acid of the solution of gold with spirit of wine, both which are certainly ingredients in this preparation

All these tinctures of gold are nothing but gold in its natural state, exceedingly divided, and suspended in an oily liquor They are not therefore, properly speaking, tinctures Neither can they be called potable gold in any other sense than that it swims in a fluid, and is divided into so fine parts, that it may be drank under the appearance of a liquor, as Mr Baron well remarks in his edition of Lemery

We ought to observe, that all these preparations we have mentioned contain a certain quantity of the acids of aqua regia, and that they are, notwithstanding, apt to deposite in time a considerable quantity of the gold they contain, unless the contained quantity be very small Gold is deposited, particularly from the mixture of ether, in its metallic state, and is even very brilliant

Lastly,

Laſtly, as gold may be diſſolved and reduced into a liquor, as well by liver of ſulphur as by aqua regia, a potable gold may alſo be made by that ſolvent. Nevertheleſs we have not ſeen any potable gold made in that manner, probably from the inſupportable ſmell and taſte of the liver of ſulphur.

CCCLI. GRAIN. A grain is the ſmalleſt weight uſed in the ordinary operations of chemiſtry. It is nearly equal to the weight of a grain of corn, from which it has received its name. A grain is the 24th part of a ſcruple, $\frac{1}{72}$ part of a gros, the $\frac{1}{576}$ part of an ounce, &c. (*p*)

CCCLII. GRAINS. The ſeeds of moſt vegetables are ſo called. Two principal kinds of ſeeds are diſtinguiſhed in chemiſtry, relatively to the predominant ſubſtances which are obtained from them. Some of them contain at the ſame time a conſiderable quantity of mucilage and oil, which may be ſeparately extracted from them, the former by infuſion in water, and the latter by expreſſion, or both together by trituration with water, in form of an emulſion. Theſe are therefore called emulſive grains or ſeeds. Of this kind are almonds, and the ſeeds of almoſt all fruits. The other grains are called farinaceous, becauſe they contain no ſuperabundant oil like the former, but are entirely compoſed of a dry ſubſtance eaſily reducible into a fine powder, called meal, from which water can extract a large quantity of mucilaginous, nutritive, ſaccharine matter, and which is very ſuſceptible of the ſpirituous fermentation. Of this kind are the grains of all gramineous and leguminous plants, the fruits of which are only coverings including grains.

CCCLIII. GRANITE. A granite is a ſtone formed by the coheſion of ſmall ſtones of different colors, and of different natures.

This diſpoſition conſtitutes it a ſtone compoſed of ſmall particles, called grains, and hence it is called granite.

Moſt granites are formed by particles of quartz, ſpars, ſand, and mica or talk, of different colors. As quartz and ſand generally predominate in granites, theſe ſtones ſtrike fire with ſteel, and are claſſed amongſt the hard ſtones. Nevertheleſs, granites differ much in this reſpect. Granites are found in large maſſes. Some of them are very beautiful, when cut and poliſhed. Many beautiful granites are found in Brittany. The moſt valuable granites are brought from Egypt. (*q*)

CCCLIV. GRANULATION. Granulation is an operation by which metallic ſubſtances are reduced into ſmall grains or roundiſh particles, the uſe of which is, to facilitate their combination with other ſubſtances.

This operation is very ſimple. It conſiſts in pouring a melted metal ſlowly into a veſſel filled with water, which is, in the mean time, to be agitated

(*p*) The weights mentioned in the text are French. A grain is $\frac{1}{24}$th part of an Engliſh troy pennyweight, or $\frac{1}{480}$th part of a troy ounce. *See the article* WEIGHTS.

(*q*) Granites are very various in their appearance, as they are in the colors and proportions of their component particles. Theſe particles conſiſt of common quartz, of that ſpecies of quartz called *feltſpar* or rhomboidal quartz, and of mica, with which alſo are often accidentally mixed particles of other ſtones, as of ſteatites, baſaltes, garnets, and metallic earths. The rocky ſummits of the higheſt mountains generally conſiſt of this compound ſtone, or of porphyry, which is alſo a compound ſtone, and different from granite only in containing, beſides quartz, feltſpar, and mica, a great deal of the opake colored ſiliceous ſtone called jaſper.

v . a broom. Lead is alſo granulated by pouring it when melted into a box, the internal ſurface of which is to be rubbed with powdered chalk, and by ſhaking ſtrongly the box, till the lead has become ſolid. What paſſes in theſe operations may be eaſily imagined. Metals are granulated becauſe their ductility renders them incapable of being pounded, and becauſe filing is long, tedious, and might render the metal impure by a mixture of the iron of the file. (*r*)

CCCLV. GRAVITY. Gravity is the property of bodies, by which they endeavour to approach each other. Thus, for example, we know that a body reſting upon the earth cannot be raiſed but by a force ſuperior to what is called its weight, and that this body thus raiſed, returns precipitately to the earth, when it is no longer ſupported. Men in general have always obſerved this phenomenon without attending to it. But philoſophers have always admired it, and have endeavoured to diſcover its cauſe, but without ſucceſs, which is not ſurpriſing, for we do not yet know all the circumſtances attending gravity. We are not yet certain, that all the particles of matter have this property. The gravity of the air was not diſcovered till the laſt age. We will not therefore attempt to reaſon upon this obſcure ſubject. But as the particular effects of gravity influence much all chemical phenomena, and as the particular gravity of the integrant parts of different ſubſtances is probably the primary cauſe of the action of theſe ſubſtances upon each other, we muſt enter into ſome detail upon this ſubject.

The gravity of a body may be conſidered in two manners. Firſt, every body, conſidered as heavy, cannot be compared but to greater or leſs quantities of the ſame kind of matter. In this caſe, we may obſerve that the greater the quantity of matter of any body is, the greater is the effect of its gravity. Hence the gravity of bodies is directly as their maſſes or quantities of matter. The gravity of bodies conſidered in this view is called their *abſolute gravity*, that

(*r*) The granulation of metals by agitation in a box, is thus explained by Cramer. The metals capable of this kind of granulation, as lead, tin, and braſs, are very brittle, when they are ſo hot as to be almoſt fuſed. The chalk with which the inſide of the box is rubbed, increaſes the reſiſtance to the motion of the agitated metal, and preſerves the box from being burnt. When the melted metal is ſhaken and daſhed againſt the ſides of the veſſel, it no ſooner becomes ſolid, and conſequently exceedingly brittle, than it is ſhivered into a fine duſt. Thoſe metals which are rendered more tenacious by being *heated almoſt to fuſion, as gold and ſilver*, muſt evidently be incapable of this kind of granulation.

The other method of granulation may be performed by pouring the metal upon a broom, interpoſed betwixt it and the water, by which means the fluid metal is divided into ſlender ſtreams which are further broken by the circular motion of the water. See a deſcription of an apparatus for granulating copper for the purpoſe of making braſs, in a note to the article BRASS. Melted metals may alſo be granulated by being poured from a certain height into a veſſel of water, or of other fluids capable of fixing by their coldneſs the drops as ſoon as they fall, and thereby preventing them from again running together into large maſſes. This granulation may be thus explained. The ſeveral parts of a fluid poured out of a veſſel, begin their falls at ſucceſſive inſtants of time. The velocity acquired by each of theſe parts from the accelerating power of gravity, is proportionable to the time from the beginning of its fall. *This acceleration of velocity produces a con*tinual increaſe of the interval or ſpace betwixt any two parts of a fluid, which have begun to fall at different times. Hence the ſeveral parts of a falling fluid tend to ſeparate from each other, or to form diſtinct maſſes or drops; and they accordingly do ſeparate, when this tendency is ſtronger than the force of cohesion by which they are held together.

is,

is, their weight, or the constant effect of the gravity of any certain quantity of matter Thus we judge, that the quantities of any two substances, however dissimilar, are equal, if they produce equal effects of gravity The weight, therefore, and the quantity, of a substance are the same thing Men have agreed to determine the weights and quantities of matter of all substances by certain effects of gravity, and have given different names to more or less considerable weights, as *grains*, *drams*, *ounces*, *pounds*, &c so that two quantities of different substances, which produce the same effect of gravity, that is, of a grain, or of a dram, of an ounce, &c are justly considered to be equal In this sense we say, that a pound of lead is not heavier than a pound of cotton This absolute gravity, weight, or quantity of matter of any body, is measured by means of an ordinary ballance, which is a lever suspended freely on its center of gravity, which ought to be exactly in the middle of its length Two quantities of matter, being suspended at the two extremities of the lever, are considered as equal, or of the same weight, when this lever maintains itself in an horizontal direction

This is the best and justest method to determine the quantity of matters employed It is much used in commerce, and in the ordinary purposes of life It is also the only one which ought to be employed in all the operations of chemistry, which require accuracy

In the second place, we may consider a body as heavy, relatively not only to its mass or quantity of matter, but also to the space it occupies, that is, to its bulk A great difference is found in this respect, among natural bodies This difference proceeds from the greater or less number or size of empty spaces, called pores, which are in every body Bodies which are not very porous, must evidently contain under the same bulk, a greater quantity of matter than those which are more porous, and consequently a body of a certain size, but not very porous, must have a greater absolute gravity than another body of the same size, but more porous As these differences depend on the particular species of each body, gravity estimated in this manner is called *specific gravity*. It may also be called *relative*, because we judge of it by comparing bodies with one another This gravity is the same thing as the density of bodies. The specific gravity or density therefore of bodies, consists in the relation betwixt their absolute gravity or weight and their bulk and the specific gravity of any body is so much greater as its absolute gravity is more considerable, and as its bulk is less, or, in the language of geometricians, it is in a direct ratio of the mass, and in an inverse ratio of the size Hence if two bodies be equal in size, they will be to each other as their real weights or masses and if they are equal in weight or mass, their specific gravities will be reciprocally as their sizes, that is, the specific gravity of the less bulky body will so exceed that of the more bulky body, as the bulk of this latter body exceeds that of the former

As the density of bodies is one of their internal and essential qualities, the knowledge of which contributes much to distinguish them, and to throw light upon their nature, philosophical chemists have always applied themselves to determine this matter By this method the purity of metals, and of several other substances, the degree of concentration of acids, of liquid alkalis, of spirits, and of other solvents, may be ascertained, and thus important discoveries may be made For inſtance, they have diſcovered that by allaying metals and ſemimetals, metallic maſſes are formed, the ſpecific gravity of which ſeldom correſponds with what it ought to be, if theſe metals were not condenſed or expanded by the allay These experiments, however, are but yet begun, and we may preſume that in proſecuting them, the ſame phenomena will be obſerved, and perhaps ſtill more varied in the ſolutions and combinations of all other ſolid and liquid bodies, and that we may find by this means explanations of many obſcure and intereſting facts

The ſpecific gravity of bodies may be conveniently determined by ſeveral methods As this gravity is only relative, and can be eſtimated by compariſon only, a ſubſtance ſimple and invariable, or which at leaſt might eaſily be made as pure as poſſible, was judiciouſly choſen, to the weight of which the weight of all other ſubſtances might be compared All theſe conditions are found in pure and diſtilled water Accordingly by weighing very accurately a determinate quantity, an ounce, for inſtance, of pure water in a phial, and marking preciſely the ſpace it occupies in the phial, the relation of the ſpecific gravity of any other fluid to the ſpecific gravity of this water may be eaſily determined For this purpoſe, let ſuch a quantity of this fluid be put into the phial, that it ſhall exactly occupy the ſame ſpace which the water did, and let it be accurately weighed As the bulk of the two ſubſtances thus compared are equal, and as their ſpecific gravities are to each other in this caſe as their abſolute weights, if the liquor compared with water weighs exactly an ounce, its ſpecific gravity will be equal to that of water, and if, on the contrary, it weighs more or leſs than an ounce, its ſpecific gravity will be ſo much more or leſs great than that of water, according as it ſhall weigh more or leſs than an ounce If, for example, this bulk of liquor equal to that of an ounce of water, weighs two ounces, its ſpecific gravity will be double that of water, if, on the contrary, this liquor weighs only half an ounce, its ſpecific gravity will be only half as much as that of water

This method is very juſt, convenient, and the beſt which can be employed to determine the ſpecific gravity of liquid ſubſtances, from the facility with which they may be all reduced to an equal bulk But ſome management and addreſs are requiſite to give preciſely the ſame bulk to two ſolid bodies To do this preciſely we may even affirm to be impoſſible, therefore another method muſt be uſed, to determine the ſpecific gravities of ſolid bodies We have obſerved, that the ſpecific gravities of bodies of equal bulk are to each other as their abſolute gravities or weights, and upon this principle the method we have explained is founded, but that when the maſſes or weights of two or more bodies are equal, their ſpecific gravities are to each other in the inverſe ratio of their bulks From this ſecond principle we may more eaſily determine the ſpecific gravities of ſolid bodies. The method uſed for this purpoſe conſiſts in reducing the bodies to be compared to the ſame real weight, and then in comparing their bulks to each other, or (which is the ſame thing) the effects of theſe bulks upon the ſame or equal quantities of water, as we ſhall ſee

When, therefore, the ſpecific gravity of two ſolid bodies is to be determined, an equal quantity, an ounce, for example, of each of them is to be weighed very accurately in the ordinary method, whatever be the difference of their bulks. Each of theſe bodies is afterwards to be weighed in pure water, by the

the *hydrostatical ballance*, and the difference between their real weights and their weights when they are immersed in water, that is, the loss of weight which each of them sustains by this immersion, is to be observed These losses of weight are then to be compared, and the body which has lost the least exceeds the other in specific gravity in the same proportion that the loss of weight of the latter exceeds that of the former

To understand well what happens in this experiment, we must remark, that if a solid body be immersed in water, and if it be left in the water unsupported, and without giving it any impulse, the bulk of this body will occupy the room of a quantity of water exactly equal in bulk to that of the immersed body, and if the specific gravity of this body be equal to that of the water, it will remain motionless in the same place where it was left, because its real weight being the same as that of an equal bulk of water, it remains suspended in the water, like an equal quantity of water, that is, counterpoised by the gravity of all the surrounding parts, and consequently at rest, and in an equilibrium But if the specific gravity of this body be different from that of water, then no equilibrium can exist If its weight be greater than that of the water, it must necessarily descend to the bottom of the vessel, and if it be less, it must rise to the surface of the water and the force with which that body will rise or descend, will be proportionable to the difference betwixt its gravity and that of water If, for example, when it occupies the place of an ounce of water, it really weighs two ounces, it will fall to the bottom of the vessel, but with a force only proportionate to the excess of its weight above the weight of water, for as it cannot fall without continually displacing the bulk of an ounce of water, therefore one ounce of its weight will be employed in ballancing or counterpoising an equal weight of water, and the body will descend by the effect of the weight of the remaining ounce, or with half its real weight Hence, if that body be suspended at one of the arms of a ballance, it may be counterpoised by an ounce weight, placed in the scale suspended by the other arm of the balance, in air, and consequently it will appear to be one half less heavy in water, than in air

This being established, as a body of a determinate weight loses so much less of this weight in water as its bulk is less, and as these two things are in the same relation, we may therefore substitute one for the other, and when we weigh in water two bodies of equal weight, we may judge of the relation of their bulks, and consequently may appreciate their specific gravities, by determining and comparing the diminution of weight which they sustain when weighed in water This is much more easy and exact than a mensuration of their bulks Thus, for example, if we weigh in water two bodies of equal weight, and if the one loses a tenth part of its weight in the water, and the other loses only a twentieth part, we may conclude from thence, that the bulk of this latter body is one half less than that of the former, and consequently its specific gravity is double, because the specific gravities of bodies of equal weights are in the inverse ratio of their bulks *See what ought to be observed in weighing bodies in water, under the article* BALANCE (HYDROSTATICAL)

From what has been said concerning the gravity of bodies, we may perceive, that in examining their nature and properties, the specific gravity only of bodies is attended to, and that the absolute gravity, or rather the weights used to determine it, are things arbitrary and conventional, which, however, determine well the absolute gravity, when they themselves are determinate and accurate But we must observe, that weights, like measures, have a great inconvenience in not being uniform They are fixed arbitrarily and differently in different countries, so that an ounce, or a pound, is not always the same in one country as it is in another, which necessarily introduces confusion and errors in commerce and in the arts As weights cannot be fixed but by an exact measure or bulk of the bodies intended to be used to fix these weights, the measures must evidently be first rendered uniform in all nations, which is not to be expected The thing, however, is very possible The length of a pendulum, which vibrates every second under the equator, is a fixed and invariable measure to which all others may be referred, and would be very proper to be universal, if nations would agree to it This project, the execution of which would certainly be very favorable to commerce, arts, sciences, and consequently mankind, was proposed by M de la Condamine, in a memoir which he read at the Academy of Sciences

To compleat this article, we must examine what effects are produced by the gravity of bodies in their combinations and decompositions, that is, in all chemical operations It is undoubtedly the most important and decisive object for the general theory of chemistry, but it is not within our province, as it cannot be well treated but by help of mathematics In this point these two sciences, which appear so remote from each other, meet A man sufficiently intelligent and able in both, might, by treating this matter accurately, throw much light upon it, and lay the foundation for a new physico-mathematical science, or rather, might render the application of algebra and geometry to natural philosophy much more general Several persons, and lately Mr Sage, in a Dissertation, which gained the prize of the Academy of Rouen, concerning the Cause of Chemical Affinities, have advanced some steps in this path, but great difficulties will probably occur Perhaps chemistry is not yet sufficiently advanced to be subjected to calculation, perhaps even it will never be so far advanced, and although men of genius have, since the restoration of the sciences, carried mathematics to a greater perfection than it was believed could have been attained, the problems which chemical phenomena offered to geometricians may be so complicated, as to be above the reach of human understanding

However that may be, in these latter ages a most happy application has been made of the theory of universal gravity to the system of the world, and to explain very satisfactorily the celestial phenomena If this universal gravitation of the heavenly bodies, so happily observed, and so well calculated, be an essential property of matter in general, as many reasons induce us to believe, its effects cannot be confined to very large bodies separated from each other by immense distances, but must necessarily act betwixt the small particles of matter at very small distances from each other, and consequently in chemical combinations and solutions Although we do not precisely know the bulks, the masses, the forms, nor the distances of the integrant and constituent parts of bodies, we see them act upon each other, unite or separate, adhere more or less strongly, or resist all union, and we must believe that these effects are produced by the same power, such, for example, as the reciprocal gravitation of these small particles to each other, which is variously modified, according to their

size,

ſize, their denſity, their figure, their extent, the intimacy of their contact, or the greater or leſs diſtance of their approach

By teleſcopes and other inſtruments, aſtronomers have indeed diſcovered the ſize, diſtance, and motions of heavenly bodies, and by applying calculation and geometry to theſe diſcoveries, they have perceived the gravitation of theſe great bodies, and have even determined the law of that gravitation But the microſcope has been found ineffectual to ſhew the primary and elementary parts of bodies, and when geometricians have endeavoured to apply the theory of univerſal gravitation to the phenomena of terreſtrial bodies, they found that this gravitation did not follow the rule of the inverſe ratio of the ſquare of the diſtance, when this diſtance was very ſmall. The law of gravitation in ſmall diſtances does not appear to have been yet well determined, whether this proceeds from a want of a ſufficient number of facts, or becauſe it has not been examined by the ableſt geometricians But although we cannot preciſely determine this point, would it not be deſirable to approximate it indirectly, and by making ſuppoſitions? This appears ſo much the more eaſy, as the velocities, the times, the ſpaces paſt, need not be obſerved and calculated, nor periodical revolutions to be determined for the motions of the elementary parts of bodies, although certainly very regular, and ſubjected to the ſame fixed laws, cannot be perceived minutely, and only by their effects They are made in indiviſible inſtants They are not conſtant, but perpetually variable, according to the circumſtances which determine them We cannot therefore conſider theſe objects but in general, or rather in a vague manner But, however, I aſk thoſe who are capable of deciding ſuch queſtions, if, ſuppoſing that the ſmalleſt atoms of matter are affected by the ſame power by which the heavenly bodies gravitate to each other, may we not conſider their tendency to the center of the earth as of no effect, when we attend to the almoſt infinite ſmallneſs of theſe elementary particles, and the infinitely ſmall diſtance at which they may approach each other? The effect of their gravity ought in this caſe to be, to make them tend to each other They are, as it were, ſmall worlds ſeparated from the reſt, or, being at liberty to yield to their reciprocal tendency, they re-act upon each other, without being diſturbed by the great counterpoiſe which keeps the whole univerſe in an equilibrium In the ſecond place, as the diſtance betwixt theſe molecules of bodies is infinitely ſmall, or none at all, may not contact be ſubſtituted for it? And in this caſe, would not the force with which theſe molecules tend to each other, or adhere together, be in a compound ratio of their denſities and contacts? Hence it ſhould follow, that bodies whoſe primary integrant molecules ſhould have the greateſt denſity, and whoſe figure ſhould allow them to have the moſt extenſive and immediate contact, would be the hardeſt of all bodies, or thoſe whoſe aggregation would be the firmeſt, ſuch, for example, as we conceive that of vitrifiable ſtones to be and that, on the contrary, bodies whoſe primary integrant molecules ſhould have the leaſt denſity, and ſuch a figure that they could not have but the ſmalleſt poſſible contact, would be the leaſt hard of all bodies, or rather would be fluid, ſuch pure fire appears to be, and the other ſubſtances eſſentially fluid, if any ſuch are

In the third place, if we ſuppoſe ſubſtances whoſe primary integrant molecules have a very great denſity, but can have only very ſmall contacts, whether that may depend on their figure, or the interpoſition of ſome other ſubſtance with the

the parts of which they can alſo have but ſmall contacts, then we may evidently perceive, that the force with which theſe molecules tend to unite together will not be ſatisfied, and conſequently will be in a continual niſus or effort, and, if we may be allowed to ſay it, in a ſtate of violence, ſo that when they ſhall have within their reach any other ſubſtance upon which they may exerciſe the tendency which they have to unite with that ſubſtance, that is, with which they ſhall have a greater contact, they will then actually unite with that ſubſtance with an activity and impetuoſity proportionate to their remaining tendency to unite, or their unſatisfied gravitation Such appear to be mineral acids, and in general all chemical ſolvents, the action of which cannot be conceived, unleſs we ſuppoſe that the force with which their integrant parts tend to unite with the particles of the bodies which they diſſolve, is much greater than the force with which theſe latter are kept united

Hence, if the parts of the diſſolved body be ſo denſe, or be capable of having ſuch contact with the parts of the ſolvent, that the activity of theſe latter parts ſhall be entirely ſatisfied by their mutual union, the ſolvent will then be in a ſtate of reſt, or in a kind of equilibrium, and will have no more diſſolving power This is called in chemiſtry the *ſtate* or *point of ſaturation* To make this ſaturation compleat, each of the integrant parts of the ſolvent muſt have met an integrant part of the diſſolved body, upon which it may exhauſt all its activity.

If, on the contrary, the parts of the diſſolved body be not ſufficiently denſe, and cannot have a ſufficient contact with the parts of the ſolvent to ſatisfy entirely all the tendency of theſe latter, from ſuch a combination, an imperfect ſaturation only of the ſolvent will reſult, and it will ſtill retain force enough to act upon other bodies. This may be obſerved in the neutral deliqueſcent ſalts, and other combinations of this nature *See* SALTS, *and* DELIQUESCENCE

Fourthly, we may perceive from what has been ſaid, that the force which makes the integrant and conſtituent parts of bodies tend to each other, although much ſuperior to their gravitation towards the center of the earth, is however limited, that it muſt be very variable in its effects, and even of no effect in certain circumſtances In the ſame manner as the adherence of the integrant parts of a body which yields to the action of a ſolvent, ought not to be conſidered as any thing in compariſon of the force which makes them tend to the parts of this ſolvent, ſo that after the ſolution they cannot any longer be united together, but only to the parts of this ſolvent, ſo in the ſame manner, I ſay, we may conceive that the force which unites the principles of a compound body to each other ought to become ineffectual, when, on one ſide, the tendency of the parts of theſe principles is entirely exhauſted by their union, and when, on the other ſide, to this compound is applied another body, with the parts of which thoſe of one of the principles of the compound may contract an union, infinitely ſuperior to that which they had with the parts of the other principles of the compound In this caſe, the principles of the compound muſt evidently be diſunited, one of theſe principles muſt form a new compound with the new ſubſtance applied to it, and the molecules of the other principles, being now diſengaged, muſt exerciſe their tendency upon each other, and form ſmall aggregates, which, when they have arrived at a certain maſs, muſt yield to the gravity

gravity by which they tend to the center of the earth. Thus we may conceive how *precipitations* are effected.

This will become clearer by an example, and for this purpose, let us choose a compound, such as that which results from the union of nitrous acid with silver. From experience we know that when copper is applied to this compound, the nitrous acid quits the silver to combine with the copper, with which it forms a new compound, and that silver thus separated from this acid, by the presence and contact of the copper, has no longer any adherence with the acid, unites again into larger molecules, the mass of which becomes so large, that they cannot yield to any other tendency than to the general gravitation which all bodies of a certain mass have towards the center of the earth, and accordingly we see the molecules of silver fall to the bottom of the vessel in which this operation is made. I say, first, that we cannot conceive what happens in this operation, unless we suppose that the force which unites the parts of the silver with those of the nitrous acid evanishes, or becomes ineffectual, in comparison of that force which tends to unite, and which does unite, these parts of the nitrous acid with the parts of the copper. In the second place, supposing always that all chemical combinations and decompositions are the effects of a mutual and particular gravitation of the integrant and constituent parts of bodies to each other, which is in a ratio of the density and contact of these same parts, I say, that if in the present case, the parts of the nitrous acid quit the silver to unite with the copper, the integrant parts of this latter metal must have infinitely more density, or must be capable of having a much more extensive and intimate contact with the parts of the nitrous acid than those of the silver. Whence the action of the parts of the nitrous acid, which is only very imperfectly satisfied by their union with the parts of the silver, is in some measure exhausted by the new union with the parts of the copper, so that only an infinitely small force of adhesion to the parts of the silver remains, and then we may easily conceive that the tendency of the parts of the silver to each other may be more than is sufficient to overcome this slight adhesion, and consequently the parts of silver may really separate from the nitrous acid, and may form sensible masses capable of yielding to the general gravitation to the center of the earth.

Hence also, if, at the same time that the parts of the nitrous acid are determined by the presence and contact of the parts of the copper, to separate from those of the silver, these parts of silver shall find within their reach some other substances, with the parts of which they have a still greater disposition to unite than with each other, they will unite with this substance, and form a new compound, which circumstance ought to facilitate the separation of silver from the nitrous acid, and which also, when the silver has a strong affinity with the matter presented to it, might effect the same decomposition, although even the copper had not a sufficiently strong affinity with the nitrous acid to separate it from the silver. This seems actually to happen in the case of two new decompositions and combinations, which can only be performed by *double affinities*.

All the other phenomena which happen in chemical combinations and decompositions may be easily deduced from the suppositions we have made, and are only the necessary consequences of these suppositions. For these phenomena, we refer to the articles AFFINITY, AGGREGATION, COMPOSITION, COMBINATION, DECOMPOSITION, SOLUTION, PRECIPITATION, *and* PRECIPITATES.

I am

I am sensible that this interesting matter is liable to great difficulties and objections, and is here but superficially treated. Perhaps time, experience, the encrease of chemical knowledge, lastly, the zeal of persons skilled in mathematics and chemistry, will hereafter throw much more light upon these subjects, of which now we have but confused notions. However, I cannot but consider them as the true key of the most hidden phenomena of chemistry, and consequently of all natural philosophy.

CCCLVI. GREAT WORK. The great work is the alchemical process by which gold is made, or pretended to be made.

CCCLVII. GRITT-STONE. (s)

CCCLVIII. GUMS. Gums are mucilaginous juices which separate spontaneously from several plants or trees, and which have acquired a solid consistence by the evaporation of the greatest part of their superabundant water. Formerly all concrete juices collected from trees, whatever their nature was, were called gums. Hence many of these juices, which are entirely or partly resinous, are still called gums, such are *gum copal*, *gum elemi*, *gum anime*, *gumma gutta*, and many others; but modern chemists and naturalists have with propriety considered only the concrete mucilages soluble in water as true and pure gums. We shall therefore treat of these gums only in this article.

Gums have a firm and solid consistence, a certain degree of elasticity, and great tenacity of their parts. These latter properties render them capable of resisting percussion without being broken, by which they are rendered very difficultly pulverisable in a mortar. They are more or less white and transparent; some of them, nevertheless, are of a yellow or brown color, but the matters by which they are colored are foreign to them. Very pure gums have no smell, scarcely any taste, or a very mild and slight taste. They are not soluble, either by oils, or by spirit of wine, but are perfectly soluble in water, and when the quantity of water used for this solution is but moderate, they form with it a thick, viscid, transparent fluid, and they again become mucilages, such as they were originally.

Although gums are obtained from many trees and plants of very different kinds, all gums, nevertheless, are very similar, and do not properly differ from each other but by the quantity of mucilage which they are capable of forming with water. Three principal kinds of gums are distinguished. These are *gum tragacanth*, *gum arabic*, and *ordinary gums*.

Gum tragacanth issues from a thorny shrub called *tragacanth*, which grows in Syria and other oriental countries. It consists of small twisted bits, the surfaces of which, when broken, are shining. It contains more mucilage, and is therefore dearer than any other gum.

Gum arabic is obtained from a kind of acacia, and perhaps from several other trees which grow in Arabia and in Africa. It consists of round, rough pieces, some of which are beautiful, white, and transparent.

(s) GRITT STONE is a stone consisting of particles of sand agglutinated together. The differences of these stones proceed from the different sizes of the particles of sand composing them, the different properties of these sands, and their different degrees of compactness and of agglutination. Some of these stones are employed for building, others for grinding, others for whetting sharp steel instruments, and others for filtrating water.

Ordinary gums are those which are gathered from most fruit-trees, such as almond, apricot, plumb, and cherry trees, &c It is generally less white and less transparent than gum arabic, though sometimes it is as beautiful Druggists pick the best pieces of these gums, and sell them for gum arabic, from which no inconvenience proceeds, as they do not essentially differ from that gum

As gum and mucilage are only one and the same substance united with a greater or less quantity of superabundant water, these matters have absolutely the same properties, and in their analysis furnish the same principles For a further knowledge, therefore, of the nature of gums, we refer to the article Mucilage

CCCLIX GUM-RESINS Gum resins are juices, partly mucilaginous and partly oily, which flow from many kinds of tree, and which become concrete by the evaporation of their finest fluid parts

The oily and mucilaginous parts which form gum-resins are intimately mixed, but not absolutely combined with each other hence these concrete substances are not perfectly soluble, either by water, by oils, or by spirit of wine, singly When indeed any of these solvents, for example, water, is applied singly to most gum-resins, and when the action of such solvent is assisted by trituration, a kind of solution is effected The gummy part is entirely soluble in water, and forms a mucilage with it, while the resinous part, which was originally much divided and intimately mixed with the gummy part, remains suspended in the water, and consequently forms a kind of milk or emulsion but this oily part is then evidently divided only, but not dissolved *See* Emulsion Thus the gum-resin is reduced nearly to its original state, I say, nearly, because the oily substance loses by drying its most fluid and volatile part, which is not restored to it by treating it with water in the manner above-mentioned

We may also make a kind of solution of these gum-resins, by employing solvents, which are partly watery, and partly oily or spirituous, such as wine, vinegar, or aqua vitæ but these solutions are always milky, from the water which hinders the spirituous part from combining intimately with the resin To dissolve, therefore, completely a gum-resin, the resinous part must be separated from the gummy part, by applying alternately a spirituous menstruum, and a watery menstruum

From these properties of gum-resins, relating to their solubility, chemists have discovered their true nature, for from most of their other properties, and particularly from their external appearance, they might be confounded with pure resins, to which they have a strong resemblance Here we ought to remark, that the proportion of the gum and of the resin is not constantly the same in different gum-resins, in some of which the gummy part is very small in proportion to the resinous hence, upon a more particular examination of the concrete juices which issue from trees, many of them are classed among the gum-resins, which formerly had been considered as pure resins, and this subject is still very unc[illegible]n Nevertheless, as all gum-resins are mixtures of substances which are not [illegible]ually solub[illegible] by each other, and as from such a mixture the compound bod[illegible] which r[illegible] must be opake, we may discover, merely by the view, whe[illegible] any conc[illegible] a gum-re[illegible]n or not All those which are opake, or are [illegible] evidently t[illegible] may reasonably be suspected to be of a gummy-resinous, or extractive resinous nature Of this kind are *myrrh*, *bdellium*, *sagapenum*, *opoponax*, *assa-fætida*, and others which are evidently gum-resins. On the contrary, all those which are very transparent may be certainly considered either as pure gums or pure resins such are the gums *tragacanth* and *arabic*, and the pure resins *mastic*, *sandarac*, *gum-copal*, and other diaphanous substances, which may be discovered to be pure resins, and distinguished from pure gums, by their smell, inflammability, and other qualities peculiar to oily matters

This rule, which certainly may be useful in determining without trouble concerning the nature of concrete juices, ought not to prevent us from making other suitable trials, and particularly those by applying different menstruums, when we would certainly determine the nature of the matter to be examined These trials are particularly necessary for those concrete juices which are but little transparent, and are strongly colored Such are *gum-lac*, *gumme gutta*, *sanguis draconis*, *aloes*, *opium* for these latter concrete juices are still more compounded than pure gum-resins, and contain different coloring and extractive matters *See* OILS, MUCILAGE, EXTRACTS, EMULSIONS, GUMS, *and* RESINS

CCCLX GUN-POWDER *See* POWDER

CCCLXI GUYAC Guyac is a very hard, heavy, compact wood of a tree which grows in hot countries, particularly in the Antilles Islands, and in other parts of America It contains much resin, which may be extracted from it by spirit of wine, in the same manner as the resins of jalap, turpentine, &c may be extracted from the vegetables which contain them *See* ANALYSIS *by* MENSTRUUMS, *and* RESINS

Guyac wood, when distilled with a heat not exceeding that of boiling water, is not, properly speaking, decomposed, since nothing passes over but a pure, or almost pure, phlegm, which seems to be nothing else than the superabundant water it contains a naked fire, therefore, is necessary for the decomposition of this and all other woods When guyac is to be distilled, it is to be cut into thin shavings, and put into a stone-ware retort, to which is to be adapted a large glass receiver with a small hole pierced in its side, and the distillation is to be promoted by a graduated fire At first, a liquor almost purely watery is obtained, and then, upon encreasing the fire, an acid, reddish, empyreumatic liquor passes over, together with a little fluid reddish oil These results rise in white vapors, and, at the same time, a considerable quantity of air is disengaged, which would burst the receiver, if it was not allowed to escape through the small hole, which is sometimes opened for that purpose. The acid and oil continue to rise thus to the end of the distillation, the acid becoming stronger and stronger, and the oil becoming more and more empyreumatic, black, and thick, so that, at last, its consistence is equal to that of turpentine Lastly, when the retort is thoroughly red-hot, the distillation is finished In the retort, the shavings of guyac are found reduced to perfect coal, but still retain their original form The acid, called also the *spirit*, and the oil are found together in the receiver, and may be separated from each other by a funnel

This analysis of guyac is well known by chemists, because the empyreumatic oil produced was one of the first which was observed to be capable of inflammation by mixture with spirit of nitre, and because this analysis is generally given as an example of the distillation of vegetables with a naked fire

Thus,

Thus, for instance, all the odoriferous plants from which the spiritus rector, essential oil, and other volatile principles, have been extracted by a degree of heat not exceeding that of boiling water, being afterwards distilled with a naked fire without which they cannot be decomposed, yield principles analogous to those obtained from guyac wood

The analysis of guyac wood exhibits some phenomena deserving attention The great quantity of air disengaged during this operation is very remarkable. It proves that this element is truly combined in certain bodies, and particularly in this, that is to say, that its integrant parts are disunited from each other, and adhere to some of the united parts of the guyac This is proved by the long time during which the air disengages itself from the guyac, for this element being much more volatile than water, if it was not combined and retained by some fixed principle to which it is united, it would be soon disengaged, and with a heat much less than that which is sufficient to raise the superabundant and uncombined water of the guyac Besides, this air seems to be deprived of its elasticity while it remains in this compound, otherwise, it could not be condensed into so small a space, but by a violent compression But this privation of the elasticity of the air proves also that its aggregation is broken, in the same manner as the phlogiston, or combined fire, has neither light, heat, nor fluidity, which are properties essential to it, when it is in its state of aggregation

The acid obtained in distillation with a naked fire from guyac and other similar vegetables is still united, and even intimately, with a considerable portion of oil This appears from its color, and particularly from its empyreumatic smell, for this smell cannot be contracted by any thing but oil besides, the acid may be deprived of much of this empyreumatic oil, by further operations, and particularly by saturating it with alkalis, from which it may be afterwards separated by a second distillation In both these operations much of the oil is separated, and thus the acid is rectified

This portion of empyreumatic oil is found to be well combined with the acid after the first distillation, for it no longer disturbs its transparency, even when it is mixed with much water, because the acid serves as an intermediate substance to keep the oil and water suspended or dissolved

This rectification of empyreumatic vegetable acids has not been carried so far by chemists, as it might be

The oil obtained in this distillation is acrid and empyreumatic, it being one of those which are incapable of being distilled but by a heat much superior to that of boiling water, by which heat all oils are much altered, acquire a burnt and empyreumatic smell, and allow much of their acid to escape *See* OIL The oil of guyac is employed, as all those equally acrid, to facilitate the exfoliation of carious bones

Lastly, the coal found in the retort is a perfect coal, when the distillation has been continued till the retort has been red-hot, otherwise the residuum would contain some thick and half-burnt oil, but it is contrary to the nature of coal to contain any oil *See* COAL

CCCLXII GUHR (*t*)

(*t*) GUHR, *Creta fluida*, *Medulla fluida*, *Marga fluida* Those names are given to a liquid calcareous or chalky substance, white or ash colored, found generally in mines and subterranean

CCCLXIII GYPSUM Gypſum is a ſoft, friable, ſtony matter, which does not ſtrike fire with ſteel It is found in large quantities in many parts of the earth, forming large mountains, and very extenſive chains of mountains and hills, as in the neighbourhood of Paris

Gypſum is always cryſtallized, or regularly diſpoſed In its cryſtallization it affects ſeveral different forms The firſt form is that of large, tranſparent, ſhining, thin laminæ applied to each other, ſo exactly, that they conſtitute maſſes as tranſparent as cryſtal Theſe are called by naturaliſts, *lapis ſpecularis*, from their large ſhining ſurfaces, like thoſe of mirrors

In the ſecond place, a large quantity of gypſum is found cryſtallized in ſtriæ, like threads applied longitudinally to each other This is called *ſtriated gypſum* Laſtly, a very large quantity of gypſum is found in ſmall irregular cryſtals, agglutinated to each other, forming conſiderable maſſes of ſemi-tranſparent granulated ſtones, commonly called *gypſeous alabaſter*, when they are very white and pure, which gives them a more beautiful and perfect ſemi-tranſparency *See* ALABASTER (*u*)

All theſe gypſums, although very different in external appearance, are perfectly ſimilar as to their chemical and eſſential properties

When expoſed to a very moderate heat, they quickly loſe their tranſparency, and acquire an opake white color They alſo become very friable by expoſure to this heat, and the laminæ of the lapis ſpecularis ſeparate from each other

Gypſum in this ſtate, mixed and kneaded with water, forms a kind of mortar, which ſoon hardens into a ſolid body This property renders it very uſeful for buildings, in the conſtruction of which it is employed under the name of *plaſter* And, in fact, nothing can be more convenient than a ſtone which in its ſoft ſtate is capable of receiving any form, which it afterwards preſerves many years by its property of hardening.

The properties above-mentioned are peculiar to gypſeous matters, and diſtinguiſh them from *talcs*, *amianthus*, *asbeſtus*, with which they frequently have an external reſemblance

Gypſum by other properties reſembles calcareous earths Thus, when it is calcined and put into water, a pellicle like the cream of lime is formed upon the ſurface of the water This water makes the ſyrup of violets green, as lime-water does Laſtly, gypſum acts a little upon ſulphur, and makes it a kind of earthy hepar of ſulphur, as quicklime does but, nevertheleſs, gypſeous and calcareous ſtones ought not to be confounded together

Gypſum differs from calcareous earth in this, that it does not diſſolve and effervesce with acids Mr Pott obſerves, that vitriolic and nitrous acids being treated with gypſum, do not loſe their acidity; whereas theſe acids are eaſily

ſubterranean places, where it drops and forms ſtalactitical concretions There are alſo *metallic guhrs*, or liquid maſſes, ſometimes found in mines, containing metallic particles, and which, by dropping, form metallic ſtalactitical concretions

(*u*) Beſides the gypſums above-mentioned, a rhomboidal gypſeous ſtone is found, called alſo *ſelenites*, ſometimes laminated, and ſometimes not It is diſtinguiſhable from rhomboidal calcareous ſpars by the general properties of gypſeous earths, and by its truncated angles Other gypſums are found, conſiſting of differently formed cryſtals, as hexagonal parallelipipedons and pyramids.

neutralised by calcareous earth, with which they form neutral salts with earthy basis Mr. Beaumé remarks, that gypsum may indeed be dissolved in some measure by acids, but that the gypsum thus dissolved is afterwards separated by crystallization, and is in the same state as it was before that solution, without retaining any part of the acid. Besides, quicklime does not harden, as gypsum does, without addition of sand or cement

These differences are sufficient to distinguish gypseous from calcareous earths But this distinction is further established by experiments which have been lately made by chemists to determine the nature of gypsum

Mr Pott, in his Lithogeognosia, places gypsum amongst the four principal kinds of earths, to which he refers all the others, and consequently distinguishes it very accurately from the three other principal earths, and particularly from calcareous earth He relates in that work many experiments made upon gypsum, to shew its nature and properties Gypsum, according to him, cannot be fused without addition by the most violent fire of furnaces Some chemists had affirmed that it was fusible by the heat of solar rays collected by mirrors Mr Pott did not repeat that experiment

I have exposed lapis specularis to the focus of a good burning mirror, and I remarked, that while the focus of rays fell upon its flat surface, the stone was only calcined, and not fused, but that when the focus was applied to the side of the stone formed by the edges of the plates or laminæ placed upon each other, this gypsum was immediately fused with a considerable ebullition (*x*)

From Mr Pott's experiments we chiefly learn, that gypsum or gypseous alabaster, (for that was the kind which he made the subject of his experiments) may be fused and vitrified when mixed with argillaceous earths, to which it serves as a flux, as calcareous earth does but in this fusion with argillaceous earth, gypsum bubbles and swells much more than pure calcareous earth does

This fusion of clay procured by gypsum, as by calcareous earth, as well as the other properties common to gypsum and calcareous earth, are occasioned by the greatest part of the gypsum being really composed of calcareous earth, which earth has been proved to be united in this compound with vitriolic acid Mr Macquer, in his Memoir upon Quicklime and Plaster, printed amongst the Memoirs of the Academy for the year 1747, mentions the vitriolic acid as one of the constituent parts of gypsum

Mr Pott, in his Lithogeognosia, says, that several Authors rank amongst gypsums a composition resulting from the union of vitriolic acid with a calcareous earth, and that they call this compound *selenitic earth*, or *artificial gypsum* Although Mr Pott found some slight differences betwixt this compound and natural gypsum, yet the former had all the essential properties of the latter

Mr Macquer, treating of hard waters, in his Elements of Chemistry, says, that their hardness is occasioned by a gypseous selenites which is dissolved in

(*x*) From Mr D'Arcet's Memoir upon the Effects of violent and long-continued Heat, we find that all gypseous stones and earths are fusible by the fire of furnaces This, however, we may observe concerning the fusibility of gypsum, that if it be exposed long to a moderate fire not sufficient to fuse it, much of its vitriolic acid will be expelled, and part of it will be reduced to a calcareous earth, as unfusible as chalk, or the other earths of that kind, therefore, a violent heat suddenly applied is necessary to the fusion of gypsum

them Laſtly, Mr Margraaf ſays, that from gypſum diſtilled with powder of charcoal he obtained a volatile ſulphureous acid and true ſulphur, that having treated it with the alkali of tartar, by the dry and by the humid way, he obtained from it a vitriolated tartar, that the remaining earth was calcareous, that gypſum is entirely ſoluble in water, and that it may be artificially compoſed by ſaturating vitriolic acid with calcareous earth *Opuſc Chem* 13 *Diſſ*

We may then conſider, that gypſum has been demonſtrated to be nothing elſe than calcareous earth ſaturated with vitriolic acid It is a vitriolic ſalt with baſis of calcareous earth, that is, it is a true *ſelenites* *See* SELENITES

From this account we may explain all the properties of gypſum Its want of hardneſs, its tranſparency, its cryſtallization, its ſolubility in water, proceed from its ſaline character It cannot be combined with any acid, becauſe it is naturally ſaturated with the vitriolic acid It requires much water to diſſolve it, which proceeds from its ſelenitic quality, that is, from the great quantity of earth which it contains, and the intimacy with which this earth is united with the vitriolic acid Its calcination, by which the coheſion of its parts are deſtroyed, is nothing elſe than the ſubſtraction of the water of its cryſtallization *See* CRYSTALLIZATION

The properties of quicklime which gypſum acquires by calcination, ought alſo to be attributed either to the ſuperabundant calcareous earth which it may contain or rather to the ſubſtraction of a portion of the vitriolic acid, which is diſengaged during the calcination, chiefly by touching ſome inflammable matters, with which this acid unites and forms ſulphur Laſtly, the hardening of plaſter, when calcined and mixed with water, may proceed from a mixture of thoſe parts, which by calcination have become quicklime, with thoſe other parts which have not acquired that quality, and which ſerve to the former as a cement, as Mr Macquer conjectures in the above quoted memoir (*See* QUICKLIME) or elſe this hardening proceeds from the gypſum reſuming the water of its cryſtallization, and again cryſtallizing precipitately and confuſedly, as many chemiſts think, and particularly Mr Pott, who ſays, "As plaſter mixed with water "does not harden, but when it is left at reſt, (for if it be ſtirred too long, it "will not become hard) we ought to conclude, that in this caſe a cryſtalli-"zation very ſuddenly happens, which conſequently ſuppoſes a very divided "ſaline ſubſtance, uniformly diffuſed through the plaſter, as Stahl has obſerved "This alſo is the reaſon of the want of durability of plaſter in the air, becauſe "the air alters and attacks the ſaline ſubſtance which it contains"

Some chemiſts and naturaliſts have given to gypſum the name of *ſpar*, or rather diſtinguiſh a kind of ſpar by the appellation, *gypſeous*, becauſe this ſpar has the principal properties of gypſum. *See* SPAR

H.

CCCLXIV HARDNESS. Hardness is a quality of certain bodies which consists in an intimate union and strong adhesion of their integrant parts, which cannot therefore be easily disjoined.

We cannot precisely determine what disposition of parts occasions the greatest hardness but this probably depends on the perfection and extent of the contact of these parts, and this quality depends essentially upon their figure, which we do not know

The hardest bodies which we know are vitrifiable stones, and amongst these, the hardest are those which are the most pure and homogeneous, that is, diamonds

Not any one of all known bodies is perfectly hard Perfect hardness belongs undoubtedly to the primary, elementary, and constituent parts of matter, which of all beings we know the least of

CCCLXV HELLEBORE (y)

CCCLXVI HEMATITES (z)

(y) HELLEBORE Two ounces of the root of *white hellebore* yielded, with water, nine drams and a scruple of gummy extract, and the same quantity of root yielded with spirit of wine seven drams of resinous extract From six ounces of the root of *black hellebore*, six drams and a scruple were extracted by spirit, and from the same quantity of root six drams and two grains were extracted by water Borrichius relates, that the distilled water of the whole plant possesses emetic and purgative qualities

(z) HEMATITES, or *Bloodstone*, is a hard mineral substance, red, black, or purple, but the powder of which is always red, sometimes of an intermediate figure, and sometimes spherical, semi-spherical, pyramidal, or cellular, that is, like a honey-comb, consisting of pyramids generally small, the apices of which appear, in a transverse section, in the center It contains a large portion of iron Forty pounds of this metal have been extracted from a quintal of the stone But the iron is obtained with such difficulty, and is of so bad a quality, that this ore is not commonly smelted The great hardness of hematites renders it fit for burnishing and polishing metals

CCCLXVII HEPAR. (*a*)

CCCLXVIII HETEROGENEOUS, *and* HOMOGENEOUS. Heterogeneous signifies of different natures, and homogeneous signifies of the same nature.

CCCLXIX HOPS. (*b*)

CCCLXX HYDROMEL. Hydromel is honey diluted in nearly an equal weight of water. When this liquor has not fermented, it is called *simple hydromel*, and when it has undergone the spirituous fermentation, it is called the *vinous hydromel*, or *mead*.

Honey, like all saccharine substances, vegetable or animal, is susceptible of fermentation in general, and particularly of the spirituous fermentation. To induce this fermentation, nothing is necessary but to dilute it sufficiently in water, and to leave this liquor exposed to a convenient degree of heat. To make good vinous hydromel, or mead, the whitest, purest, and best-tasted honey must be chosen, and this must be put into a kettle with more than its weight of water; a part of this liquor must be evaporated by boiling, and the liquor scummed, till its consistence is such, that a fresh egg shall be supported upon its surface without sinking more than half its thickness into the liquor; then the liquor is to be strained, and poured through a funnel into a barrel: this barrel, which ought to be nearly full, must be exposed to a heat as equable as is possible, from 20 to 27 or 28 degrees of Mr Reaumur's thermometer, taking care that the bung-hole be slightly covered but not closed. The phenomena of the spirituous fermentation will appear in this liquor, and will subsist during two or three months, according to the degree of heat, after which they will diminish and cease. During this fermentation, the barrel must be filled up occasionally with more of the same kind of liquor of honey, some of which ought to be kept apart on purpose to replace the liquor which flows out of the barrel in froth. When the fermentation ceases, and the liquor has become very vinous, the barrel is then to be put in a cellar and well closed. A year afterwards the mead will be fit to be put into bottles.

The vinous hydromel or mead is an agreeable kind of wine, nevertheless it retains long a taste of honey, which is unpleasing to some persons; but this taste it is said to lose entirely by being kept a very long time.

The spirituous fermentation of honey, as also that of sugar, and of the must of vinous liquors, when it is very saccharine, is generally more difficultly effected, requires more heat, continues longer, than that of ordinary wines made from the juice of grapes; and these vinous liquors always preserve a saccharine taste, which shews that a part only of them is become spirituous. The cause of this probably is, that they contain less acid, or that they contain an acid less disengaged than the must of ordinary wine. *See* FERMENTATION *and* WINE.

(*a*) HEPAR. *See* LIVER.

(*b*) HOPS are usually added to malt liquors, and are said to render these liquors less apt to become sour, less viscid, and more wholesome by their aromatic bitterness. They contain a subtle odorous principle, which promotes the vinous fermentation. When infused, or but slightly boiled in wort, they encrease its spirituosity. *Neuman.*

CCCLXXI. HONEY Honey is a saccharine fermentable juice collected by bees from flowers For the nature and properties of honey see SUGAR

CCCLXXII HORN *of* ANIMALS The horn of animals is of the same nature as their gelatinous matter, and is only that matter charged with a less quantity of water, with a larger quantity of earth, and sufficiently condensed to have a firm and solid consistence By digesting horn with water in Papin's digester, it may be entirely converted into jelly

Horn is a perfectly animalised matter, and furnishes in distillation the same principles as all animal matters, that is, at first a pure phlegm, with a degree of heat not exceeding that of boiling water, then a volatile alkaline spirit, which becomes more and more penetrating and strong, a fetid, light, and thin oil, a concrete volatile salt, which forms ramifications upon the sides of the receiver, much air, fetid oil, which becomes more and more black and thick, and lastly, it leaves in the retort a considerable quantity of almost incombustible coal, from which, after its incineration, scarcely any fixed alkali can be obtained

Animal oil, and particularly that which is drawn first in the distillation of horn, is susceptible of acquiring great thinness and volatility by repeated distillations, and is then called *the oil of Dippel* See that article

The horns of stags, and of other animals of that kind, are the most proper to furnish the animal oil to be rectified in the manner of Dippel, because they yield the largest quantity These horns also differ from the horns of other animals in this, that they contain a larger quantity of the same kind of earth which is in bones, hence they seem to possess an intermediate nature betwixt horns and bones

CCCLXXIII HORN (HART'S) CALCINED *to* WHITENESS The phlogiston of the coal of hart's-horn, although very difficultly combustible, may nevertheless be burnt with more ease than the coal of other horns, and with nearly the same facility as bones may This coal, by being calcined with a long continued and strong fire, is changed into a very white earth called hart's horn calcined to whiteness This earth is employed in medicine as an absorbent It is given in dysenteries and labor-pains which are supposed to be caused by acrid and ill-digested matters. Hart's-horn calcined to whiteness and levigated is the basis of Sydenham's *white decoction*, which is commonly prescribed in these diseases.

CCCLXXIV HORN (HART'S) PREPARED PHILOSOPHICALLY. This name is given to hart's-horn deprived by water of almost all its gelatinous part, so that it becomes brittle, and when its outer part is taken off, it is thus rendered very white, and is applicable to the same uses as that which is calcined by fire

CCCLXXV HORN-BLEND. (*c*)

(*c*) HORN-BLEND is a black or green indurated bole or clay, consisting of scaly particles, which are distinguishable from those of mica, by being less shining, thicker, and rectangular It is generally found amongst iron ores, and sometimes intermixed with mica, forming a compact stone

CCCLXXVI. HORNSTEIN. (d)
CCCLXXVII HYACINTH (e)

(d) HORNSTEIN, *Petrosilex Wallerii* This name is given by German authors to the siliceous stone called in England chertz See CHERTZ

(e) HYACINTH, or JACINTH, is a precious stone, polygonal, more or less transparent, of a yellowish red color, the ninth in degree of hardness from diamonds, and fusible by fire

CCCLXXVIII

I.

CCCLXXVIII. JACINTH. *See* HYACINTH.
CCCLXXIX. JALAP (*f*)
CCCLXXX. JAPONIC EARTHS. (*g*)
CCCLXXXI. JASPER (*h*)
CCCLXXXII. ICHTHYOCOLLA *See* ISINGLASS
CCCLXXXIII. JELLY From many vegetables, mucous ſubſtances capable of forming kinds of jelly are obtained, but theſe are more frequently called *mucilages* and *gums*. The name *jelly* or *gelatinous matter* is particularly applicable to the mucous ſubſtance obtained from animals

The bodies of moſt animals ſeem to be chiefly compoſed of gelatinous matter For if we boil in water, fleſh, bones, membranes, tendons, nerves, horns, ſkin, in a word, any of the ſeveral ſolid or ſoft parts which compoſe animal bodies, and if we evaporate ſufficiently this water, the liquor by cooling will become a true jelly. If the evaporation be continued till the matter be dry, but with a heat incapable of decompoſing this jelly, it forms at firſt a glue, and afterwards a horny ſubſtance more or leſs tranſparent, hard and ſolid

(*f*) JALAP. From ſixteen ounces of root of jalap, ſpirit of wine extracted five ounces, and four ſcruples of reſinous matter, and from the reſiduum, water extracted two ounces and a half of gummy-matter This root is obſerved to have a conſiderable power in promoting the ſpirituous fermentation of ſweet vegetable juices, as of melaſſes *Neuman*

(*g*) JAPAN-EARTH This name is improperly given to a gum-reſin, obtained by inſpiſſating the juice or decoction of the fruit of a certain palm-tree, which grows in the Eaſt Indies It is almoſt entirely ſoluble, when pure, by water, or by ſpirit of wine Its taſte is at firſt bitteriſh and ſtyptic, and is afterwards agreeably ſweet *Neuman*. The Indians are ſaid to cut the fruit of this tree into ſmall pieces, which they wrap in the leaves of the maritime plant *betel*, together with ſome quicklime, and to chew theſe balls, the taſte and ſmell of which they find to be very agreeable

(*h*) JASPER is an opake ſiliceous ſtone, of various colors, white, green, red, yellow, black, or variegated with ſpots or with veins of different colors It differs from flints and chertz in being opake, in being more eaſily fuſible by fire, in having a granulated texture, and in frequently compoſing large maſſes, or rocks, whereas flints and chertz are generally in form of nodules or lumps From ſome jaſpers, iron may be obtained They are ſufficiently hard and compact to receive and retain a fine poliſh

When jaſpers are ſpotted with ſpecks of onyxes or agates, they are called *jaſponyxes*

The

The blood, lymph, and seminal fluid of animals are scarcely any thing but pure gelatinous matter. Milk contains a large quantity of it. *See* CHEESE. In a word, almost all animal liquors, excepting the excrementitious, such as urine and sweat, are nothing but kinds of watery jellies.

Hence we ought to conclude, that the gelatinous matter of animals is the true animal substance. It constitutes almost entirely the body of animals; it is that which nourishes, repairs, and reproduces them; it is in the animal kingdom, what mucilage is in the vegetable kingdom, from which it seems to be derived, and which it resembles in many of its properties. *See* GUMS *and* MUCILAGES.

This matter in its natural state has scarcely any smell, or any acid or alkaline quality. Its taste is sweet and faint. When diluted with water, and by the help of other circumstances necessary to fermentation, it easily ferments as soon as it is deprived of vital motion, and sometimes even during the life of the animal to which it belongs. It occasions several diseases, and considerably deranges the animal economy. At first it tends slightly to the acid fermentation, as may be observed in milk, in blood, in flesh, and broths; and then it passes very quickly to a compleat putrefaction, which reduces it to a very fetid liquid substance. *See* FERMENTATION *and* PUTREFACTION.

When it is very fresh, and exposed to a degree of heat not exceeding that of boiling water, nothing rises from it but its superabundant phlegm, or water. By losing this superabundant water it becomes more and more gluey, and at length acquires nearly the consistence of horn. In this state, when it has suffered no other alteration than this kind of drying, it may be again dissolved in water, and resume its former liquid gelatinous state.

Nevertheless, some gelatinous matters, such as the whites of eggs, and the white part of the blood which is not watery, are coagulated and hardened by heat; and these, when once well dried, cannot be again redissolved in water, or at least without great difficulty and particular management.

Acids and alkalis, the latter particularly, attack and dissolve jelly, with great ease. The results of these combinations have not yet been sufficiently examined.

Oily substances appear to have no action upon gelatinous matter. Neither can rectified spirit of wine dissolve it. This spirit does not act upon it when it is dry, and only takes from it part of its water when it is liquid, and thus coagulates it. It then appears a precipitate composed of little white flocks. To this property which spirit of wine has of coagulating jelly, is with much probability attributed, the thickening of the lymph, the stuffing and breaking of the lymphatic vessels, whence extravasation and dropsy follow; in a word, the principal diseases of those who drink too much of spirituous liquors.

When dry gelatinous matter is exposed to a degree of heat superior to that of boiling water, it swells, rises into bubbles, emits an acrid, empyreumatic, fetid fume, and is with difficulty, and not without a very violent heat, inflammable.

If it be distilled in a retort with a graduated heat, at first a little phlegm is obtained, then some liquid volatile alkali, a thin and penetrating oil, solid volatile alkali, and a very empyreumatic oil, which becomes more and more thick, follow in the order they are here mentioned. In the retort a considerable quantity of that kind of coal remains, which cannot be burnt without

great

great difficulty From the ashes of this coal an exceeding small quantity of fixed alkali, and a little common salt may generally be obtained These are exactly the same substances which may be obtained from all animal mattters As many things are common to jelly and to vegetable mucilage, *see the word* MUCILAGE

CCCLXXXIV JET (*i*)

CCCLXXXV INDIGO (*k*)

CCCLXXXVI INFLAMMATION *of* OILS *by* NITROUS ACID The vivid inflammation occasioned by mixing highly concentrated nitrous acid with most oils, is one of those surprizing phenomena, which excite the admiration even of people the most unintelligent, and least conversant in matters of chemistry and experimental philosophy No wonder, therefore, that it has particularly excited the attention of chemists Glauber, Borrichius, Tournefort, Homberg, Rouviere, Dippel, Hoffman, Geoffroy, and Mr Rouelle, have particularly applied themselves to this matter These chemists have successively found methods of inflaming different oils, and have published their processes in their writings

Borrichius, a Danish chemist, had affirmed in the Copenhagen Transactions for the Year 1671, that oil of turpentine may be inflamed by mixing it with nitrous acid But as in that time a highly concentrated nitrous acid was very rare, most of the chemists who attempted to repeat this experiment, did not succeed Tournefort, in the year 1700, inflamed by this method the oil of sassafras Homberg in the year 1701 says, in the Memoirs of the Academy, that he inflamed oil of turpentine by mixing it with nitrous acid, but he says that

(*i*) JET, *Gagates*, *Succinum nigrum*, is a black bitumen, resembling fine black ebony wood, hard, light, compact, and smooth It is very inflammable, and burns with a bituminous smell By distillation it yields, 1 an acid liquor, 2 a thin black oil, 3 a thick black oil By friction it becomes electrical, as amber does *See* BITUMEN

(*k*) INDIGO is a blue fecula, obtained from the American plant *anil* by means of fermentation, in the following manner The herb is put into a vat and covered with water In a few hours the liquor begins to ferment, becomes hot, throws up a froth, and acquires a blue or violet color The liquor is then emptied into another vat by means of a cock inserted near the bottom of the first vat In the second vat, the liquor is to be continually and strongly agitated by sticks and buckets annexed to sticks, by which means the blue coloring matter is made to unite together, or is disposed to separate from the liquor, and to subside When the blue matter has subsided, the water is let off by cocks, and the sediment, when drained and dried in the air, is indigo

Indigo may be almost entirely consumed by fire With water it may be formed into a paste, diffusible through more water, but at last the coloring matter subsides By means of fixed alkaline salt it becomes permanently diffusible in water Woollen stuffs previously steeped in warm water, being dipped in the above liquor, are dyed of a green color, which is almost instantly, by exposure to air, changed to a fine blue Volatile alkaline spirits extract yellowish or brownish red tinctures, and spirit of wine a reddish tincture, by digestion with indigo Indigo gives no color to lime-water, or to water acidulated with vitriolic, nitrous, or marine acids The concentrated vitriolic acid unites with indigo into a smooth paste, especially if the indigo be previously ground with powdered glass, or sand By this method, the indigo is rendered soluble in boiling water along with the acid, so as to pass through a filter This solution, when hot is of a bright green color, and, when cold, becomes brown The above experiments are mentioned by Dr Lewis in a note to his translation of Neuman's Works

that the oil must be thick. Rouviere, in the year 1706, inflamed the empyreumatic oil of guyac, and his experiment was much talked of, because it succeeded more easily than the others, because this inflammation is very vivid, and because it is attended by a surprizing circumstance, namely, that from amidst the flames arises a black, thin, spongy body, of a considerable height, which is, as we shall see, only the thickest part of the oil rarefied and burnt during the inflammation This inflammation of oil of guyac was solely attended to, and was shewn to students in courses of chemistry and experimental philosophy, till Hoffman, a German chemist, and Geoffroy, a French chemist, having made many experiments on this matter, discovered at the same time, that smoking nitrous acid mixed with concentrared vitriolic acid, succeeded infinitely better for the inflammation of oils, and particularly of the oil of turpentine, which had been almost relinquished Mr Rouelle then resumed this subject, and published in the year 1747, a Memoir filled with many experiments, which shewed, that by nitrous acid may be inflamed all essential oils, including oil of turpentine, and even those sweet expressed oils which are capable of quickly thickening and drying, such as oils of nuts, linseed, hemp, provided that the acid be sufficiently concentrated Lastly, the same chemist discovered that even the sweet oils least disposed to dry, that is, those called *fat oils*, may also be inflamed But to make their inflammation succeed, the method mentioned by Hoffman and Geoffroy was necessary, that is to say, some concentrated vitriolic acid must be previously mixed with the nitrous acid As these last mentioned oils are of all oils the least inflammable, we have reason to believe that every oil may be inflamed by a mixture of these two acids

Mr Rouelle further remarks, in the above quoted Memoir, that flame is more certainly produced in all these experiments, when the nitrous acid is poured on at intervals, and when it is applied to that part of the oil which the portions of acid first poured on had thickened, heated, and dried The inflammation of oils by acids is now become an experiment easily performed The following circumstances are remarked to be peculiar to the inflammation of the several kinds of oil

All essential oils, and even the sweet drying oils, may be inflamed by the nitrous acid alone, provided that the vessel in which the inflammation is to be made be of a convenient size and form, that the nitrous acid be sufficiently concentrated, and that a sufficient quantity of acid and oil be employed The vessel ought to be sufficiently wide-mouthed, and the nitrous acid, for greater certainty, ought to be so concentrated that a phial capable of containing exactly an ounce of pure water, shall be capable of containing one ounce four gros and two scruples of this acid Lastly, an ounce of this acid, and as much of the oil to be inflamed, ought to be employed although less quantities may succeed, but less certainly The oil is first put into the vessel in which the inflammation is intended to be Then the vessel containing the nitrous acid is to be tied to one end of a rod, that the operator may not be hurt by the part of the mixture which is generally thrown out of the vessel, and sometimes at a considerable distance One half or two-thirds of the acid is poured at once A considerable ebullition is excited by the reaction of these two liquors The oil becomes black, thick, and sometimes inflames If it does not inflame

within

within four or five seconds, more nitrous acid must be poured upon the part which appears thickest and dryest, and then the mixture never fails to be inflamed.

The oils of almonds, olives, rapes, and other fat oils, have not been hitherto inflamed by the nitrous acid alone. But their inflammation is effected, as Mr Rouelle practises, by mixing with them first equal quantities of the concentrated vitriolic and nitrous acids, which occasion less quick and violent ebullition than in the preceding instances; but when this ebullition is at its height, some pure nitrous acid must be poured on the thickest part of the mixture. Then the inflammation generally happens, but is less strong than when any other kind of oil is used.

Although these phenomena be surprizing, their theory is easy. All oils contain phlogiston as a constituent part. Nitrous acid also contains phlogiston. Hence we may understand the cause of the powerful action of these two substances upon each other. The heat resulting from their reaction is equal to that of ignition; and hence the oil and even the nitrous acid being capable of inflammation, must consequently be inflamed.

The reaction becomes more strong, and the inflammation more certain, when the nitrous acid is applied to the part of the oil which has already been thickened and dried, either by the nitrous acid alone, or by that acid mixed with vitriolic acid. But ought this portion of thickened and dephlegmated oil to be considered as a pure coal? And ought the action of the disengaged nitrous acid upon this thickened oil, to be compared to the action of nitre detonating with coal? We cannot be easily persuaded of this, when we consider that nitrous acid, however much concentrated, when not retained by some base, has no action upon any kind of coal, even when heated as much as possible. See DETONATION of NITRE.

The effect produced by the addition of the vitriolic acid, may be explained in the following manner. This acid does much promote these inflammations; since, on the one hand, it makes them succeed more certainly, and with less doses than can be done with the nitrous acid alone; and on the other hand, some oils have never hitherto been made capable of inflammation without it. But although this acid acts powerfully upon oils, it cannot singly inflame any of them. Mr Rouelle considering, that as the vitriolic acid is essentially stronger, and has a greater affinity to water than nitrous acid, believes that it renders the nitrous acid more capable of inflaming oils by dephlegmating it. Probably the vitriolic acid may from this cause facilitate the inflammation of oils; but has it not also as great an affinity with the water contained in the oils, as with that contained in the nitrous acid? and may not, consequently, its power of facilitating these inflammations proceed from the dephlegmation of the oils, as well as of the nitrous acid?

CCCLXXXVII. INFUSION. Infusion, taken in its most general sense, consists in placing compound bodies in a liquor intended to be impregnated with some of their principles, either without heat, or with a heat less than that of the boiling liquor.

From this definition we may see that infusion is one of the principal operations of the analysis by menstruums, in the same manner as decoction is, of which infusion may be considered as the first degree.

Infusion

Infusion may be made in watery, spirituous, oily, acid, or alkaline liquors, according to the nature of the matters to be infused, and of the principles intended to be extracted It is nevertheless practised upon vegetable matters only, and almost always for the preparation of remedies which are also called *infusions*

Aromatic plants and other odoriferous vegetable matters are generally infused when their odoriferous principle is to be preserved, in which their virtue consists, and which is at the same time so volatile as to be dissipated and lost by the heat of ebullition To preserve still better these volatile principles, the smallest heat requisite for the extraction ought to be employed, and these infusions ought to be made in matrasses or other vessels, which may be exactly closed

The principles extracted by infusion are different according to the menstruum employed

Pure water may be impregnated with the odoriferous principle, or spiritus rector, with saline, saponaceous, mucilaginous, extractive principles Spirit of wine dissolves the spiritus rector, the essential oils, those resinous matters the base of which is an oil of the nature of essential oils, and greatest part of the saponaceous extractive matter Those infusions made by spirit of wine are particularly called *tinctures*, especially in pharmacy Oils dissolve the spiritus rector, and any oily matter Acids and alkalis dissolve the earthy substances of vegetables, and almost all their other principles but they disguise them, alter them, and change considerably their virtues by the combination They are therefore not much used for these kinds of extractions *See* ANALYSIS, DECOCTION, EXTRACTS

CCCLXXXVIII INK Ink is a liquor, generally black, used for writing Nevertheless some inks are of other colors

The basis of black ink is an infusion of galls, and of martial vitriol, known to druggists by the name of green copperas, both which are mixed together, and to them is added some gum-arabic The following receipt makes good ink In four pints of common water or beer let a pound of bruised galls be infused twenty-four hours without boiling, to this add six ounces of gum arabic, and when the gum is dissolved, six ounces of green vitriol, which will soon give it the black color the liquor is then to be strained through a hair sieve

Galls and all vegetable astringents have the property of separating iron, when it is united, either with vitriolic acid, or with any other acid, and the precipitate thus formed is black The blackness of these precipitates is caused by a certain quantity of oily matter which they receive from the vegetable substances

In the operation of making ink, something passes analogous to the precipitation of iron into Prussian blue, by means of a phlogisticated alkali Some chemists having even remarked that ink diluted with much water has a color approaching to blue, have considered the martial precipitate of ink as a Prussian blue, the color of which is so intense as to seem black when diluted in a small quantity of water, because a very deep blue has actually the appearance of a black but this opinion does not correspond with the properties of ink or of Prussian blue Iron precipitated in these two methods is essentially different, and the difference proceeds from the different natures of the two inflammable

matters

matters with which the iron unites itself in these two cases The inflammable matter which unites with iron in the preparation of ink is in an oily state, and that in the preparation of Prussian blue is not in that state *See* BLUE (PRUSSIAN) Accordingly the precipitate of iron in ink is easily soluble by all acids, but the precipitate of Prussian blue is not If a sufficient quantity of spirit of nitre, or any other strong acid, be mixed with ink, its color will disappear, and the blackest ink will thus be rendered clear and transparent as water Its blackness and opacity may be again restored to it by adding to the ink thus discolored a sufficient quantity of alkali to saturate all the acid which had dissolved the martial precipitate, by which means this precipitate resumes its former appearance Thus the black color of ink may be made to disappear and appear again as often as we please, by mixing with it alternately some acid and some alkali but this change of color cannot be produced upon the Prussian blue By adding any quantity of an acid to the water in which Prussian blue is suspended, its color, so far from being altered, becomes only the more beautiful by that addition

The color of Prussian blue may be indeed made to appear and disappear at pleasure by one method but this method is precisely the reverse of that used to produce those effects upon ink By mixing much alkali with Prussian blue, its color is destroyed, and by saturating this alkali with an acid, the color is restored This constitutes a very sensible difference betwixt these two martial precipitates

Inks of all colors may be made by using a strong decoction of the ingredients used for dying, mixed with a little alum and gum-arabic For example, a strong decoction of brasil wood with as much alum as it can dissolve, and a little gum-arabic to give it body and some consistence, forms a beautiful red ink (*l*)

(*l*) As the duration of records and other valuable writings depends much on the goodness of the ink employed, Dr Lewis has thought this subject worthy of his attention The chief imperfection of common inks is, that they decay in time, and at last the writing becomes invisible From experiments made by that author, he infers that the decay of inks is chiefly owing to a deficiency of galls, that the galls are the most perishable ingredient, the quantity of these, which gives the greatest blackness at first, (which is about equal parts with the vitriol) being insufficient to maintain the color, that for a durable ink, the quantity of galls cannot be much less than three times that of the vitriol, that it cannot be much greater without lessening the blackness of the ink, that by diminishing the quantity of water, the ink was rendered blacker and more durable, that distilled water, rain water and hard spring water, had the same effects, that white wine produced a deeper black color than water, that the color produced by vinegar was deeper than that by wine, that proof spirit extracted only a reddish-brown tinge, that the last mentioned tincture sink into, and spread upon, the paper, and hence the impropriety of adding spirit of wine to ink, as is frequently directed, to prevent mouldiness or freezing, that other astringents, as oak bark, bistort, sloe-bark, &c were not so effectual as galls, nor gave so good a black, the color produced by most of these, excepting oak-bark, being greenish, that the juice of sloes did not produce a black color with martial vitriol, but that, nevertheless, the writing made with it became black, and was found to be more durable than common ink, that inks made with saturated solutions of iron in nitrous, marine, acetous, acids, in tartar, or in lemon juice, were much inferior to the ink made with martial vitriol, that the color of ink was depraved by adding quicklime, which was done with an intention of destroying any superabundant acid which might be supposed to be the cause of the loss of the color of ink, that the best method of preventing the effects of this superabundant acid is probably by adding pieces of iron to engage it,

and

CCCLXXXIX INKS (SYMPATHETIC) Chemistry furnishes many methods of making the inks called sympathetic These inks are colorless liquors, with which an invisible writing is made, but which becomes very sensible when we please, by certain treatment appropriated to the particular kind of sympathetic ink employed

As ordinary ink is made black by a mixture of two liquors which are not, or but very little colored, it may become a sympathetic ink by several methods

If green vitriol be dissolved in water, and a little acid be added, to prevent the yellowish martial precipitate, which is always formed when there is not superabundant acid, with this solution invisible characters may be written, which may be rendered very black, by being moistened with a strong infusion of galls

If the blackness of ordinary ink be destroyed by a sufficient quantity of nitrous acid, the writing made by it will remain invisible, till it be moistened by liquid fixed alkali

Characters traced with the acid solution of green vitriol above-mentioned will become of a fine blue color, if they be moistened with the phlogisticated alkaline liquor used in the preparation of Prussian blue, and characters traced with this last mentioned liquor, which are absolutely invisible, may be rendered of a fine blue color by being moistened with a solution of green vitriol. The theory of these inks may be seen under the articles INK, *and* BLUE (PRUSSIAN)

Pure vitriolic acid, weakened by so much water that it shall not make too strong an impression upon paper, becomes a sympathetic ink, the characters written with which are invisible, but may be rendered sensible by heating the paper on which they are traced This effect is occasioned by the heat concentrating the acid, and rendering it capable of burning and blackening the paper But

and that this conjecture was confirmed by an instance the author had heard, of the great durability of the color of an ink in which pieces of iron had been long immersed, and lastly, that a decoction of logwood used instead of water, sensibly improved both the beauty and deepness of the black, without disposing it to fade The same author observes, that the addition of gum-arabic is not only useful, by keeping the coloring matter suspended in the fluid, but also by preventing the ink from spreading, by which means a greater quantity of it is collected on each stroke of the pen Sugar, which is sometimes added to inks, was found to be much less effectual than gums, and to have the inconvenience of preventing the drying of the ink The color of ink is found to be greatly injured, by keeping the ink in vessels made of copper, or of lead, and probably of any other metal, excepting iron, which the vitriolic acid can dissolve The foregoing experiments point out for the best proportions of the ingredients for ink, one part of green vitriol, one part of powdered logwood, and three parts of powdered galls The best menstruum appears to be vinegar or white wine, tho', for common use, water is sufficient If the ink be required to be of a full color, a quart, or, at most, three pints, of liquor may be allowed to three ounces of galls, and to one ounce of each of the other two ingredients Half an ounce of gum may be added to each pint of the liquor The ingredients may be all put together at once in a convenient vessel, and well shaken four or five times each day In ten or twelve days the ink will be fit for use, though it will improve by remaining longer on the ingredients or it may be made more expeditiously, by adding the gum and vitriol to a decoction of galls and logwood in the menstruum To the ink, after it has been separated from the feculencies, some coarse powder of galls, from which the fine dust has been sifted, together with one or two pieces of iron, may be added, by which its durability will be secured

this

this ink is not convenient for use, because the vitriolic acid, although weakened by water, always injures the paper, and at length destroys it

Amongst the most famous sympathetic inks is that made with the solution of bismuth in nitrous acid The invisible characters written with this ink may be rendered sensibly black without being moistened or heated, but by being exposed to the contact of phlogiston reduced into vapors, because this phlogiston revives the earth of bismuth, which is partly calcined by the nitrous acid, and even applies itself, superabundantly, to that metallic earth, which it blackens so much more, as it is in greater quantity

The phlogistic vapors exhaling from liver of sulphur are the fittest for producing this effect upon the solution of bismuth The authors who first described this sympathetic ink required that a solution of the scoria of regulus of antimony, or of a mixture of quicklime and orpiment, should be employed but as the former of these substances is an antimoniated liver of sulphur, and as the latter is an earthy liver of sulphur, mixed with arsenic, we may perceive that they produce their effects only as being livers of sulphur The ordinary liver of sulphur is found to succeed equally well

When therefore characters written with the sympathetic ink of bismuth are required to appear, exposure to the vapors of liver of sulphur is sufficient for that purpose, and these vapors are said to be capable of producing their effect across a quire of paper, or even a stone-wall This does not appear impossible, but it must require a long time We are certain, that the white precipitate of bismuth, nitrous crystals of bismuth, or of lead, although well covered with paper, become blackened on their surfaces by remaining in laboratories where phlogistic vapors float, particularly the vapors of liver of sulphur

We may easily perceive that the writing made by this ink of bismuth may be more readily made to appear by being moistened with a solution of liver of sulphur (*m*)

The most modern sympathetic ink, and, at the same time, one of the most curious, is that made with a solution of the regulus or calx of cobalt in aqua regia The process of this ink has been published in the Memoirs of the Academy of Sciences by Mr Hellot

This process was very troublesome, because he directed that cobalt itself should be employed, which must be first roasted, then dissolved in nitrous acid, and, lastly, to the solution some sea salt must be added, and also because good cobalt is very scarce. But this ink may be easily made. For this purpose, let the

(*n*) Instead of the solution of bismuth in nitrous acid, a solution of sugar of lead in water may be employed for the same purpose, and the writing made with this liquor is rendered black by vapors of liver of sulphur, or still more effectually by the solution of liver of sulphur in water But as these chemical liquors may require more management than can be conveniently applied, or perhaps comprehended by some lovers, and other persons engaged in mysterious correspondencies, Ovid, that admirable instructor, has recommended a more familiar and domestic method of communicating tender sentiments without danger of discovery from fathers or husbands This method consists in writing with milk, which, by being held near a fire, is rendered visible The juice of lemons has also been used with great success, for the same purposes, and in the same manner The color given to these two last mentioned liquors proceeds from a beginning decomposition of their oily and mucilaginous particles by means of heat Not only these liquors, but all the sympathetic inks, mentioned by authors, may be rendered more or less visible, by application of heat

 zaffre

zaffre be taken which is commonly sold by druggists, from which, by digestion in aqua regia, may be extracted all that this acid is capable of dissolving: this soluble part of zaffre is the calx of cobalt, which is used for giving a blue colo to glass This solution is then to be diluted with a little common water, to prevent it from making too strong an impression upon paper Characters written with this diluted solution are invisible when cold, and become of a fine greenish blue when heated, and have this singular property, that after they have been rendered visible by heat, they again disappear when exposed to cold, and may thus be made to appear and disappear alternately, by alternate applications of heat and cold but care must be taken to heat the paper no more than is just sufficient to make the writing appear, for when it is heated too much, the writing will not again disappear by exposure to cold

This ink may be applied to the drawing of landscapes, in which the earth and trees destitute of verdure, being drawn with common ink, give a prospect of winter, and which may be made to assume the appearance of spring, by exposure to a gentle heat, which covers the trees with leaves, and the earth with grass, by rendering visible those parts of the landscapes which are drawn with this sympathetic ink. This idea has been executed upon fire screens by an industrious artist (*n*)

By reflecting a little upon the properties of chemical agents, and on the phenomena of many operations, we may perceive that many new sympathetic inks with peculiar properties may be discovered

CCCXC INSTRUMENTS (CHEMICAL) The instruments employed in chemical operations are very numerous, and are described under their several articles They are also enumerated in a general manner under the article LABORATORY

CCCXCI INTERMEDIUM, *or* INTERMEDIATE SUBSTANCE Those substances are called *intermediate* by means of which other substances incapable of uniting together alone, may be united For example, saline, acid, or alkaline substances, by means of which oils are reduced to a saponaceous state, and are thereby rendered miscible with water, are the intermediate substances of this union of oil with water, because, without these saline substances, oil and water cannot be united, or even well mixed

Those matters are also called intermediate, which are employed to disunite others, which cannot be otherwise disunited In this sense vitriolic acid is an intermediate substance, by which nitrous or marine acids may be separated from any alkaline salt, with which they happen to be united

CCCXCII IPECACOANHA. (*o*)

CCCXCIII IRON Iron, called also *Mars*, is a metal of a white, livid, greyish color It is the hardest of all metals, the most elastic, and, ex-

(*n*) We may observe, that a solution of regulus of cobalt, or of zaffre, in spirit of nitre acquires a reddish color by application of heat Hence, some variety of color might be given to the landscapes proposed in the text Thus while the green solution of this semi-metal in aqua regia represented the leaves, the red solution might represent the fruits and flowers

(*o*) IPECACOANHA From sixteen ounces of good ipecacoanha, three ounces of resinous matter were extracted by means of spirit of wine, and from the same quantity, by means of water, five ounces of gummy matter were extracted *Neuman*.

cepting

cepting platina, the most difficult to be fused. This metal has, next to gold, the greatest tenacity of parts; an iron wire, the diameter of which is a tenth part of an inch, being capable of sustaining 450 pounds, without being broken.

Next to tin, iron is the lightest of the metals. It loses when immersed in water betwixt a seventh and an eighth part of its weight. A cubic foot of forged iron weighs 580 pounds.

Very pure iron is sufficiently ductile to be drawn into wire as fine as horse-hair. But these properties of iron are subject to vary much in their degrees, according to the different kinds of iron. This difference proceeds from a quantity, sometimes greater and at other times less, of an earth contained in iron, which is unmetallic, or at least which is not metallised, from the great difficulty of fusing perfectly its ore. See ORES of IRON and SMELTING of ORES.

Iron is the only known substance which is attracted by magnets, and capable of becoming itself a magnet, so as to attract other iron. By this property it may be discovered in mixtures where by other methods it could scarcely be perceived, and may be even separated, when it is only interposed betwixt other bodies, and not adherent to them. It preserves this property, although it be allayed with some other metals. Henkel says, in his Pyritologia, that iron allayed with two parts of copper is still magnetical. (p)

Iron is a very destructible metal. Its surface is quickly converted by the combined action of air and water into a rust or yellow calx, deprived of all its phlogiston. This calx is only an earth deprived of metallic properties, and which cannot recover these properties, without being again combined with its inflammable principle. The destruction of iron exposed to a moist air by rust, is universally known. The rust of iron, and the other calxes of this metal, are called *saffron of Mars, crocus martis*. See SAFFRON of MARS.

Water alone, without the help of air, seems to be capable of acting upon iron in some measure, without depriving it indeed of its inflammable principle; but it divides and considerably attenuates it; which seems to shew that this metal contains some saline parts. See ETHIOPS MARTIAL.

Iron is not fusible by the heat of ordinary furnaces, but it is easily burnt and calcined, by which it is changed into an earthy matter more or less reddish or blackish, called *astringent saffron of Mars*. See that word. This saffron of Mars is nothing but the proper earth of iron deprived of the greatest part of its phlogiston by calcination.

Iron heated as much as is possible, that is, till it becomes of a shining white colour, and just beginning to fuse, has the appearance of a combustible body, penetrated by a vivid and bright flame; and indeed the inflammable principle of this metal heated to that point, really burns in a sensible manner. A number of vivid and shining sparks shoot out from it, and burn with a kind of decrepitation. I have exposed iron to the focus of a large burning glass, where it quickly fused and boiled, and emitted an ardent fume, the

(p) A greatly smaller proportion of iron in an allay of copper with this metal, retains its magnetical quality. Gellert affirms, that the magnetical quality of iron is destroyed by allaying it with regulus of antimony. He observes, that the surface of his allay was covered with spots like rust, which circumstance induces a suspicion that his iron might have been injured by sulphur, some of which is frequently retained by regulus of antimony.

lower

lower part of which was a true flame At length it was changed into a blackish vitrified scoria The sparks struck from iron by flints are nothing but bits of iron heated by violent collision, and when collected upon paper, and viewed by means of a microscope, appear to be like scoria of iron or slag (*q*)

All the acids dissolve iron, and in their solutions exhibit particular phenomena

If filings of iron be put into a matrass, and a sufficient quantity of vitriolic acid added to dissolve it, the solution will be made with heat and effervescence The vitriolic acid, when it dissolves the iron in this manner, takes from it much of its inflammable principle for the vapors which exhale from this solution have not only a strong smell of volatile sulphureous acid, but they are so impregnated with phlogiston, that they are very inflammable An experiment may be made to render this truth sensible by sight Let the mouth of the matrass be stopt by a finger during thirty or forty seconds, and a lighted candle be brought very near the mouth when it is to be unstopped, a flame will then immediately appear within the matrass, and at the same time a strong explosion will happen This explosion would break the matrass, if the quantity of filings of iron was considerable, for instance eight or nine ounces, and if the neck of the matrass was straight. This inflammation and this explosion may be frequently repeated, when the solution is made with some activity, and if the matrass be left unstopt after the explosion, and the vapor be kindled, it continues to burn at the mouth of this vessel with a blue tranquil flame, while the solution continues *See* AIR (FIXABLE INFLAMMABLE), *and* DAMPS

From the solution of iron by vitriolic acid, a vitriolic salt with metallic basis is formed, which by evaporation and cooling is coagulated into green rhomboidal crystals This salt is called *martial vitriol*, *green vitriol*, or *green copperas*. See its properties at the article VITRIOL (MARTIAL)

Nitrous acid dissolves iron most actively and violently This acid cannot scarcely be saturated with iron, because when it has dissolved a large quantity of iron, and seems to be so saturated, that some of the metal is deposited under

(*q*) Iron is a combustible substance, as appears from the great waste or loss of quantity observable in iron exposed to a red, but especially to a white heat This combustion is maintained and excited, like that of all other combustible substances, by contact of air Dr Hook says, that having heated a bar of iron to that degree called white heat, he placed it upon an anvil, and blowed air upon it by means of bellows, by which it burnt brighter and hotter The sparks produced by the collision of steel with flint, appear to be globular particles of iron which have been fused, and imperfectly scorified or vitrified They are kindled by the heat produced by the collision, but their vivid light, and their fusion or vitrification, are the effects of a combustion continued in these particles during their passage through the air, and these effects are so great in so short a time, because the quantity of surface of these minute particles of iron, and consequently the quantity of air applied to excite the combustion, is so great in proportion to the quantity of matter This opinion, that the ignition, light, and fusion of the sparks are occasioned by the heat, excited by the combustion of their own inflammable matter, and not merely by the heat communicated by the collision, is confirmed by an experiment made and related by Mr Hawksbee, from which we find that these sparks struck by collision are not visible, that is, they are not ignited, and do not deflagrate, in an exhausted receiver; the air being necessary to maintain and excite their deflagration and combustion

form

form of martial saffron, if more iron be then added, it will be dissolved, while some of that which was before dissolved will be precipitated

The cause of this phenomenon is, that the nitrous acid takes from the iron much of its phlogiston during the solution, and also that iron has so much less adhesion to nitrous acid, as it is more deprived of phlogiston. This being established, we may perceive, that when iron containing its due quantity of phlogiston is added to nitrous acid saturated with a half dephlogisticated iron, this acid, greedy of the inflammable principle, quits the latter metal, and dissolves the former

The vapors of nitrous acid which dissolves iron are always very red, of a nauseous smell, more disagreeable, and apparently more volatile, than those of the uncombined acid. This observation may be applied to all solutions with nitrous acid of those metallic substances, which are capable of losing their inflammable principle. These qualities of nitrous acid proceed from the superabundant quantity of phlogiston, which it imbibes in every solution. Experiments might be made to try whether the vapors which exhale from this solution, and from solutions of several other metallic substances abounding in phlogiston, are inflammable, like those which exhale from a solution of iron in vitriolic acid. But these experiments ought to be made cautiously, lest explosions should happen

Marine acid also dissolves iron with ease, and even with activity, but it does not take from the metal its inflammable principle so efficaciously as nitrous acid does, and even as vitriolic acid, although it does produce some change upon it in this respect. A great chemist affirms, that marine acid treated with iron acquires the properties of nitrous acid (g)

Aqua regia dissolves iron with much impetuosity, and presents phenomena partaking of those of the solutions of this metal in the nitrous, and in the marine acids separately

Iron forms with the nitrous and marine acids, separately or conjointly, salts with metallic bases, of a deliquescent nature

When solutions of iron with any of the mineral acids are made with much superabundant acid, their color is more or less green, and they remain clear without making any deposition but when the acid is saturated with metal, the color of the solution is more or less yellow or reddish, and a certain quantity of yellow ferruginous earth called *ochre* or *saffron of Mars* is deposited. These differences proceed from this cause, that iron requires so much more acid to keep it dissolved, as it is more deprived of its phlogiston

Lastly, when solutions of iron, not too acid, and particularly when diluted with water, are heated, they become turbid, and immediately deposite a quantity of ochre, which they would not have deposited but in a long time, if they had not been heated

Ochres, or saffrons of Mars, which are deposited from solutions of iron, are not so soluble as iron they require a much greater quantity of acid, or cannot be again dissolved, particularly by nitrous acid, but by peculiar management

Vegetable acids also dissolve iron. The acid of tartar forms with this metal a sort of vegetable metallic salt, or of soluble tartar, which is deliques-

(g) This great chemist is Stahl. The experiment has not been confirmed by other chemists

cent,

cent, and is called TINCTURE (TARTARISED) *of* MARS, which *see* Martial or vulnerary balls are made by mixing acid of tartar with filings of iron, which being dissolved in water furnish a true soluble martial tartar, or tartarised tincture of Mars *See* BALLS (MARTIAL)

Iron, like other metals, dissolved in any acid, may be precipitated by absorbent earths and alkaline salts But this metal, like all others, presents, when precipitated by fixed alkalis, different phenomena, according to the particular state of the alkali

If the alkali employed to precipitate iron is as much dephlogisticated as it can be, the ferruginous precipitate is of the color of rust If this alkali contains any superabundant phlogiston, a part of this phlogiston will be transferred to the iron during its precipitation, and will give it an olive color, more or less deep This precipitate may be easily and instantaneously re-dissolved by pouring upon it a quantity of acid sufficient to saturate the alkali, and to dissolve the precipitate This precipitate, when dried with proper precaution, (*see* ETHIOPS MINERAL) forms an excellent saffron of Mars for the use of medicine. Lastly, if an alkali much impregnated, or still better, if saturated with phlogiston, be added, the precipitate will be of a blue color, and will form what is called *Prussian blue* *See* BLUE (PRUSSIAN)

Alkalis act upon iron as upon all other metals, and are even capable of dissolving it perfectly, when they can seize it sufficiently divided, as Stahl has discovered For this purpose a solution of iron by nitrous acid is to be poured into good liquid alkali Immediately afterwards a red precipitate appears, which, upon agitating the alkaline liquor, instantly dissolves, and communicates to the liquor its color By this method a considerable quantity of iron may be dissolved by an alkali When this solution contains much iron, it is called *martial alkaline tincture of Stahl* This operation cannot succeed but in certain circumstances These circumstances will be mentioned under the article TINCTURE (MARTIAL ALKALINE) *of* STAHL

When this tincture is well impregnated with iron, a part of the metal is deposited in form of a very fine yellow brick colored saffron of Mars, and at the same time the tincture loses much of its color All the iron may be quickly separated from it under the same form, by saturating this alkali with any acid This ferruginous precipitate is called *Stahl's saffron of Mars* It is rendered sufficiently soluble in acids by the phlogiston transferred to it from the alkali *See* SAFFRON *of* MARS

Iron precipitates metals dissolved in acids, and these precipitates have their metallic form and brilliancy, as all metallic precipitates, which have been separated from the acids of their solutions by other metals, have But iron may be separated from acids by zinc, and by some other substances *See* PRECIPITATION *and* PRECIPITATE All vegetable astringent substances, as galls, pomegranate rind, &c form inks, or black precipitates, with any solutions of iron *See* INK

Iron has a greater affinity than any other metal with sulphur hence it may be employed to separate most metals from sulphur, by fusion, and sulphur thus united with iron, considerably augments its fusibility *See* ESSAYS *of* ORES, *and* REGULUS (MARTIAL) *of* ANTIMONY

If

If a bar of iron be heated till it becomes white, and a roll of sulphur be applied to one of its extremities thus heated, the sulphur, uniting with the iron, makes it fuse so as to run down in red hot drops This experiment ought to be made over an earthen pan filled with water, to receive the melted iron and sulphur, while they flow down copiously, that they may be extinguished as fast as they fall down, and that their dissipation may be prevented In the earthen pan, after this operation, are found some parts of pure sulphur, which had melted without being combined with iron, and which are softened (*see* SULPHUR), and other pieces composed of iron combined with sulphur, and which had been fused together. These latter pieces are brittle They are iron artificially mineralised, or brought into a pyritous state by sulphur *See* PYRITES

Sulphur and iron act so strongly upon each other, that they can mutually dissolve each other even in the humid way. If five or six pounds of filings of iron be mixed with as much powdered sulphur, and the mixture be moistened with a sufficient quantity of water to form a paste, this mixture will in a certain time swell, become hot, melt, emit vapors, and even take fire This is an experiment of Mr Lemery the elder The residuum of this operation furnishes martial vitriol, which has been produced by a transposition of acid from the sulphur to the iron Here the same things happen as in the decomposition, effervescence, and inflammation of ferruginous pyrites This union of the acid of vitriol with iron, and the formation of martial vitriol, may be much accelerated by heating and burning the sulphur, immediately after the mixture *See* PYRITES, SMELTING *of* ORES, *and* VITRIOL

As the phlogiston of iron is copious, and not much engaged, the filings of this metal when heated are capable of detonating with nitre, vividly and briskly Hence they are said to be used by the Chinese in their fire-works

After this detonation, iron is reduced to a reddish calx, called *Zwelfer's Saffron of Mars*. *See* SAFFRON *of* MARS.

In whatever manner iron be treated and calcined, the calxes, the ochres, the rusts, and the precipitates of this metal, are always colored, and the colors of ferruginous earth, in these different states, are from the yellow pale of rust to a red brown or blackish brown Hence we are induced to believe that martial earth is never entirely deprived of phlogiston. This is also probably the cause that all these preparations of iron are easily susceptible of resuming phlogiston, and even in the humid way, for generally metallic calxes resume phlogiston so much more easily, as they have been less perfectly deprived of it

These colors retained by calxes of iron render them fit to be used in painting, not only with oil, but also to tinge glass. Hence they are successfully employed for coloring glasses or artificial precious stones, and for painting different shades of red upon pottery, enamel, and porcelain

Iron may be allayed with all metals excepting lead and mercury, with which it has not yet been rendered capable of uniting *See* ALLAY and TINNING

Lastly, one of the most interesting properties of iron is, that it is capable of being combined either by fusion or by cementation with a more abundant quantity of phlogiston, of being converted thereby into a more perfect iron called *steel*, which is capable of acquiring by sudden cooling or tempering a very great hardness, which renders it very useful for numberless necessary purposes See STEEL

The affinities of iron are, according to Mr Geoffroy's table, in the following order Regulus of antimony, silver, copper, and lead These three last are placed so as to mark an equal degree of affinity with iron But we must observe, that lead ought not to have been placed there, because it has no affinity with iron but as iron united with silver may be instantly separated from the silver by addition of lead, which unites with the silver, and obliges the iron to float upon the surface of this new mixture, Mr Geoffroy seems to have meant to have shewn this effect in this column of his table of affinities, which however is not very accurate for this experiment only shews, that silver quits iron to unite with lead. Mr Gellert's table of solutions gives for the affinities of iron, gold, silver, and copper. Lead and mercury might be placed at the bottom of the column, where substances are mentioned which cannot be united with that which is placed at the head of the column (s)

The uses of iron are so well known, and so numerous, that they need not be enumerated We shall only observe, that no metal is so useful It is, as it were, the soul of the arts, and is necessary for the existence of them all

This metal furnishes also very efficacious remedies, the virtues of which are well established by practice This is almost the only metal which is not virulent It may be taken internally in substance, provided it be well divided in form of calx or saffron, or even when united with some acid, and in a saline form, without any danger It never produces any bad effect, when applied in suitable quantity and circumstances

The great medicinal virtue of iron is caused by its tonic and strengthening qualities It produces a slight and gentle irritation of the fibres, the effect of which is, to constringe the sensible organic parts upon which it acts, and to encrease their force and elasticity

Iron particularly acts upon the fibres, and the vessels of the stomach and intestines hence it produces excellent effects in all diseases which proceed from laxity and inactivity of the digestive organs, such are crudities, bad digestions accompanied with diarrhea, flatulencies, flatulent colics, &c and in diseases which proceed from the former, as megrims, many hysterical, hypochondriacal, and melancholic affections, intermittent fevers, tertians and quartans, &c

Iron has also been always considered and administered by the best practitioners as a resolving and aperitive remedy. Stahl, however, and several other good physicians and modern chemists, acknowledge no other but the tonic and strengthening qualities of iron If their opinion be well founded, the cases in which iron has produced a resolving and aperitive effect, are such where the obstructions, and the defect of secretions and excretions, have proceeded from weakness and re-

(s) Iron like other metals is said to consist of earth, phlogiston, and a metallic or mercurial principle. Teichmeyer relates an experiment by which the existence of the mercurial principle is pretended to be proved He says, that by distilling iron filings, which had been exposed during a year to the air, then triturated, and afterwards exposed another year to the air, he had obtained a hard matter which stuck to the neck of the vessel, and along with it some mercury.

Concerning the *smelting of iron ores*, and the other parts of the *Metallurgical History of Iron*, *see* SMELTING *of* ORES *of* IRON, *and* STEEL.

laxation

laxation of the fibres and of the veſſels, rather than from a craſſitude of humors, as in the chloroſis, in ſome kinds of jaundice, and in other diſeaſes of the ſame ſort.

The excrements of perſons uſing martial remedies are blackiſh, or even black, which proceeds from a mixture of this metal diſſolved with the aliments. This proves, that if iron penetrates farther than the primæ viæ, it muſt be in very ſmall quantity, ſince the greateſt part of it is ejected with the excrements.

As the principal effect of iron is to change the tone, the tenſion, and the ſpring of the ſolid parts of the body, this effect cannot be continued without a continuance of the martial remedy for ſome conſiderable time, otherwiſe only a tranſient relief would be given, and the diſeaſe would ſoon recur.

CCCXCIV. ISINGLASS (*t*).

CCCXCV. JUICES *of* PLANTS. The juices of ſeveral plants are expreſſed to obtain their eſſential ſalts, and for ſeveral medicinal purpoſes, with intention either to be uſed without further preparation, or to be made into ſyrups and extracts.

The general method of extracting theſe juices is, by pounding the plant in a marble mortar, and then by putting it into a preſs. Thus is obtained a muddy and green liquor, which generally requires to be clarified, as we ſhall ſoon obſerve.

The juices of all plants are not extracted with equal eaſe. Some plants even when freſh contain ſo little juice, that water muſt be added while they are pounded, otherwiſe ſcarcely any juice would be obtained by expreſſion. Other plants which contain a conſiderable quantity of juice, furniſh by expreſſion but a ſmall quantity of it, becauſe they contain alſo much mucilage, which renders the juice ſo viſcid that it cannot flow. Water muſt alſo be added to theſe plants to obtain their juice.

The juices thus obtained from vegetables by a mechanical method are not, properly ſpeaking, one of their principles, but rather a collection of all the proximate principles of plants which are ſoluble in water, ſuch as the ſaponaceous extractive matter, the mucilage, the odoriferous principle, all the ſaline and ſaccharine ſubſtances; all which are diſſolved in the water of the vegetation of the plants. Beſides all theſe matters, the juice contains ſome part of the reſinous ſubſtance, and the green coloring matter, which in almoſt all vegetables is of a reſinous nature (*u*). Theſe two latter ſubſtances, not being ſoluble in water, are only interpoſed between the parts of the other principles which are diſſolved in the juice, and conſequently diſturb its tranſparency. They nevertheleſs adhere together in a certain degree, and ſo ſtrongly in moſt juices, that they cannot be ſeparated by filtration alone.

(*t*) ISINGLASS is a glue prepared by boiling the ſkin, tail, fins, ſtomach, inteſtines, and bladder of a certain large fiſh frequent in the Ruſſian ſeas and large rivers. It is totally ſoluble in water, but not at all in rectified ſpirit of wine. From eight ounces of iſinglaſs were obtained, by diſtillation, four ounces and two drams of urinous ſpirit, half an ounce of concrete volatile ſalt, an ounce and a half of empyreumatic oil, half a ſcruple of fixed ſalt, and nine drams of earth. Iſinglaſs is employed as a glue for many purpoſes, and for fining wines. *Neuman.*

(*u*) The coloring ſubſtance of vegetables does not ſeem to be a reſinous or gummy matter, but only to adhere accidentally to the reſinous or gummy matters of plants, for when it has been ſeparated from theſe ſo as to form with earth of allum the precipitates called *lakes*, it is not ſoluble either by water or by ſpirit of wine. *See* DYEING.

When

When therefore these juices are to be clarified, some previous preparations must be used by which the filtration may be facilitated Juices which are acid, and not very mucilaginous, are spontaneously clarified by rest and gentle heat The juices of most antiscorbutic plants abounding in saline volatile principles, may be disposed to filtration merely by immersion in boiling water, and as they may be contained in closed bottles while they are thus heated in a water-bath, their saline volatile part, in which their medicinal qualities chiefly consist, may thus be preserved Fermentation is also an effectual method of clarifying juices which are susceptible of it, for all liquors which have fermented, clarify spontaneously after fermentation But this method is not used to clarify juices, because many of them are susceptible of only an imperfect fermentation, and because the qualities of most of them are injured by that process

The method of clarification most generally used, and indispensably necessary for those juices which contain much mucilage, is by boiling with the white of an egg. This matter, which has the property of coagulating in boiling water, and of uniting with mucilage, does accordingly, when added to the juice of plants, unite with and coagulate their mucilage, and separates it from the juice in form of scum, together with the greatest part of the resinous and earthy matters which disturb its transparency And as any of these resinous matters which may remain in the liquor, after this boiling with the whites of eggs, are no longer retained by the mucilage, they may easily be separated by filtration *See* FILTRATION.

The juices, especially before they are clarified, contain almost all the same principles as the plant itself, because in the operation by which they are extracted no decomposition happens, but every thing remains, as to its nature, in the same state as in the plant The principles contained in the juice are only separated from the grosser, oily, earthy, and resinous parts, which compose the solid matter that remains under the press These juices, when well prepared, have therefore exactly the same medicinal qualities as the plants from which they are obtained They must evidently differ from each other as to the nature and proportions of the principles with which they are impregnated, as much as the plants from which they are extracted differ from each other in those respects

CCCXCVI. IVORY-BLACK (x)

CCCXCVII JUPITER By this name the old chemists distinguished tin *See* TIN.

(x) *See the article* BLACK

K.

CCCXCVIII KALI (y)

CCCXCIX KAOLIN (z)

CCCC KARAT This name is applied to the proportional parts which are supposed to be in any mass of gold, the value or purity of which is to be ascertained When therefore gold is considered with regard to its degree of purity, the whole mass of it, whatever be its real weight, is supposed to be divided into 24 parts, and these parts are called karats Hence, when gold is entirely pure, and without alloy, it is called gold of 24 karats If it contains $\frac{1}{24}$ part of alloy, it is called gold of 23 karats, because in such a mass $\frac{23}{24}$ are gold, and $\frac{1}{24}$ is alloy If the mass of gold be $\frac{2}{24}$ or $\frac{1}{12}$ of alloy, it is called gold of 22 karats, and so on For greater precision, the karat is supposed to be subdivided into 32 parts, which have no other name than the thirty-second parts of a karat (a) *See* ESSAY *of the* VALUE *of* GOLD *and of* SILVER.

(y) KALI is a maritime plant, from the ashes of which a considerable quantity of mineral fixed alkali is obtained by lixiviation *See* ALKALI (FIXED MINERAL). Henkel informs us, that by boiling the plant in water, and by evaporating the decoction, he obtained a considerable quantity of sea-salt

(z) KAOLIN is the name of an earth which is used as one of the two ingredients of the oriental porcelain Some of this earth was brought from China, and examined by Mr Reaumur He found that it was perfectly unfusible by fire He believed that it was a talky earth, but the author of this Dictionary justly observes, that it is more probably an argillaceous earth, from its forming a tenacious paste with the other ingredient called *petuntse*, which has no tenacity Mr Bomare says, that by analysing some Chinese kaolin, he found it was a compound earth consisting of clay, to which it owed its tenacity, of calcareous earth, which gave it a mealy appearance, of sparkling particles of mica, and of small gravel or particles of quartz crystals. He says, that he has found a similar earth upon a stratum of granite, and conjectures that it may be a decomposed granite *See* PORCELAIN

(a) The karat, or carat, in England is divided into four parts only, called grains, and in Germany into twelve parts Standard gold in England is gold of twenty-two carats, that is, which contains $\frac{1}{12}$ part of alloy, which is generally an equal mixture of copper and silver, as the whole proportion of the copper would make the gold too high-colored, and the whole proportion of the silver would make it too pale

The

The word karat, when applied to diamonds, signifies a real weight of four grains.

CCCCI KERMES (b)

CCCCII KERMES MINERAL Kermes mineral, so called from its color, which resembles that of vegetable kermes, is one of the most important antimonial preparations, both with regard to its chemical phenomena and to its medicinal uses

The use of kermes mineral was not established in medicine before the beginning of this century Some chemists, indeed, amongst others Glauber and Lemeri, had before that time mentioned in their works several preparations of antimony which approach more or less to kermes, but these preparations being little known, were confounded with many others which are entirely neglected, although much praised by their authors

The fame of kermes was occasioned by Friar Simon, apothecary to the Chartreux Friars This friar received this preparation from a surgeon called La Ligerie, who had procured it from a German apothecary who had been a scholar of the famous Glauber Friar Simon, from the commendations given to this new remedy by La Ligerie, administered it to a Chartreux Friar, who was dangerously ill of a violent peripneumony, by which the Friar was suddenly, and as it had been miraculously, cured From that time the Friar apothecary published the virtue of his remedy Several other remarkable cures were performed by means of kermes The public believed in its medicinal qualities, and called it *Powder of Chartreux*, because it was prepared only in the apothecary's shop belonging to these monks The reputation of kermes extended itself more and more, till at length the Duke of Orleans, then Regent of France, procured the publication of the process by La Ligerie

This is the history of kermes, as it is related by Mr Baron, in his edition of Lemeri's Chemistry Although the process for making this preparation be very accurately described in this and other books, we shall treat of it in detail, because it is a matter of much importance

The process for kermes, published by La Ligerie, consists in boiling, during two hours, pulverised crude antimony in the fourth part of its weight of the liquor of nitre fixed by coals, and twice its weight of pure water at the end of this time the liquor is to be decanted and filtrated, while boiling, through brown paper It continues clear while it is boiling hot, but when it cools, it becomes turbid, acquires a red brick color, and again becomes clear by the deposition of a red sediment, which is the kermes The boiling may be thrice repeated, and each time the same quantity of water is to be added to the antimony, and a fourth part less of the liquor of fixed nitre The several sediments from these three boilings are to be added together, washed with clean water, till the water acquires no taste, and the kermes is then to be dried La Ligerie directs, that aqua vitæ shall be once or twice poured upon it and burnt, and the kermes dried again

(b) Kermes are excrescencies formed by insects on the branches and leaves of the scarlet oak They communicate a red color to water or to spirit of wine Woollen cloth, previously dipped in a solution of alum and of tartar in water, receives from a decoction of kermes a more durable, but less vivid, scarlet dye than that usually procured from cochineal, together with a solution of tin.

We

We now proceed to explain the nature of kermes, and the phenomena of its preparation

Crude antimony is compofed of regulus of antimony and common fulphur, united naturally with each other, as in almoft all metallic minerals The fixed alkali with which the crude antimony is boiled, although it is diluted with much water, acts upon the fulphur of the antimony, and forms, with it liver of fulphur, and as this compound is a folvent of all metallic matters, it diffolves a certain quantity of the regulus of antimony In this operation then a combination is formed of fixed alkali, of fulphur, and of regulus of antimony Of thefe three fubftances the fixed alkali only is foluble in water, and is the intermediate fubftance by which the fulphur and regulus are fufpended in the water But we are to obferve, that the alkali becomes impregnated by this operation, and by boiling, with a larger quantity of regulus, and efpecially of fulphur, than can be fufpended in cold water, hence the decoction of kermes, which is clear, limpid, and colorlefs while boiling hot, becomes turbid, and depofites a fediment while it cools This compound, therefore, like certain falts, may be kept diffolved in larger quantity by hot than by cold water, and much of it is therefore depofited by cooling

Further, while the kermes is precipitating, the whole antimoniated liver of fulphur, which is diffolved by the boiling liquor, may be divided into two parts, one of which, that is the kermes, being overcharged with the regulus, and particularly with the fulphur, contains but a little alkali, which it draws along with it during its depofition The other part, as it contains much more alkali, remains diffolved even in the cold liquor, by means of this larger quantity of alkali All thefe propofitions are to be explained and demonftrated by the following obfervations

Firft, when the decoction of kermes is cold, and has formed all its fediment, if, without adding any thing to it, it be heated till it boil, it again entirely re-diffolves the kermes, the fediment difappears, the liquor becomes clear, and by cold is again rendered turbid, and depofites fediment as before Thus the kermes may be made to precipitate and to re-diffolve as often as we pleafe

Secondly, by digefting kermes in aqua regia, which diffolves its alkali and regulus, the fulphur is feparated pure The acids of aqua regia form a nitre and a febrifugal falt of Sylvius with the alkali of the kermes, and if a certain quantity of kermes be melted with black flux, after having deftroyed its fulphur by roafting, a true regulus of antimony may be obtained from it

Thefe experiments, which were made by Mr Geoffroy, and the detail of which is found in Memoirs given to the Academy in the years 1734 and 1735, upon the Analyfis of Kermes, fhew evidently the prefence of fulphur, of fixed alkali, and of regulus of antimony, in this compound From Mr. Geoffroy's experiments we find, that 72 grains of kermes contain about 16 or 17 grains of regulus, 13 or 14 grains of alkaline falt, and 40 or 41 grains of common fulphur

Thirdly, by repeating the boiling of the liquor upon the antimony, more and more kermes will be formed each time by cooling, as at firft, and this experiment may be repeated a great many times. Mr Geoffroy fays, that he repeated it 78 times, without any other addition than that of pure water, to fupply that which was loft by evaporation, and that each time a confiderable quantity of kermes

kermes was formed by cooling. This experiment proves, that the alkali transforms the antimony into kermes by overcharging itself with regulus and sulphur, and at each precipitation the kermes does not retain and take with it but a very small quantity of alkali.

Fourthly, if any acid be poured upon the liquor in which the kermes has been formed, and from which it has been entirely separated by cooling, Mr Beaumé has observed, that this liquor is again rendered turbid, and that a second sediment is formed of a yellow reddish color, which is nothing else than golden sulphur of antimony; that is, regulus of antimony and sulphur mixed together, but in very different proportions, and with different strengths of union, from those in which they are found in the crude antimony. *See* SULPHUR (GOLDEN) *of* ANTIMONY.

After this precipitation, in the liquor a neutral salt is left, which is formed by the contained alkali and the precipitating acid. From this experiment we find, that in the liquor from which the kermes has been deposited, a considerable quantity of antimoniated liver of sulphur remains, which differs from kermes by containing a much larger proportion of alkali; so that it can keep dissolved the regulus and sulphur with which it is united, even when the liquor is cold.

From what has been said concerning the manner in which kermes is formed, and the phenomena presented by this operation, we ought to understand well what it consists of. It is evidently nothing else than an antimoniated liver of sulphur, in which the sulphur predominates, and which contains too little alkali to be soluble in water. On this last article we may observe, that kermes after its spontaneous separation, and before it has been washed, contains much more alkali than after it has been washed; whence, if the kermes has been washed with very hot water, a part of it will be re-dissolved; but as the water always takes away the part which is most alkaline, the kermes which remains at last contains so little alkali that it is no longer soluble even in boiling water; and then it has all the qualities peculiar to it.

In the processes for several antimonial preparations, a kermes, or compounds like it, are formed. This always happens when crude antimony is treated by fusion with a quantity of alkaline salt, so that an antimoniated liver of sulphur results from it, overcharged with regulus and sulphur; that is, containing more of these two substances than it can keep dissolved in cold water. If any of these combinations be boiled in water, a matter analogous to kermes is always deposited by cooling. This happens, for instance, to the scoria of the regulus of antimony, and in an operation described by Mr Geoffroy to abridge the process for making kermes by fusion.

To make kermes by fusion, Mr Geoffroy fuses two parts of antimony with one part of alkaline salt; he powders this matter while yet hot, and keeps it during two hours in boiling water; he then filtrates it, and receives the liquor into more boiling water, from which, when it cools, about six gros of kermes is deposited, when an ounce of antimony has been used. This method of making kermes is much more expeditious, but less perfect; for, as the author confesses, the kermes produced is not so fine and soft as that made in the ordinary method.

Mr

Mr Lemeri the elder mentions also, in his Treatise concerning Antimony, an operation from which his son pretends that kermes may be obtained. This operation consists in digesting and afterwards boiling powdered crude antimony in a very pure liquor of fixed nitre. This liquor, if it be in sufficient quantity, is capable of dissolving quickly and entirely powdered crude antimony, and we cannot doubt but that by cooling a considerable quantity of a substance very analogous to kermes will be produced. Nevertheless, none of these short methods of making kermes is directed by dispensatories, or by the best books for describing the preparations of chemical remedies, and we must allow, that this is done prudently, for besides that all these kinds of kermes may be suspected to be less fine, or more charged with reguline parts than that which is prepared by the ordinary process, when the constant observation of medical practitioners has ascertained the effects of a compound remedy, such a remedy ought to be considered as it were consecrated by a respectable kind of empiricism, against which the finest theory and most specious reasonings ought not to avail. The least reformation or innovation ought then to be considered as a blameable rashness, particularly when a remedy of such importance is concerned.

Kermes is used in medicine only, and from it singularly excellent effects may be produced, when administered by able physicians. In kermes are united the citing and evacuant virtues of the emetic preparations of antimony, with the tonic, dividing, aperitive, and resolving properties of the liver of sulphur, that is to say, that it is capable of answering two principal indications in the treatment of many acute and chronic diseases. Properly managed, it may become an emetic, purgative, a diuretic, a sudorific, or an expectorant, as is required, and it is always attenuating and resolving. When seven or eight grains are taken at once, it chiefly acts upon the primæ viæ, generally as an emetic and as a purgative. A dose of three or four grains is seldom emetic, and more frequently purgative.

When taken in these quantities as an evacuant, a little of it passes also into the viæ secundæ & tertiæ. When it is administered in smaller doses, it passes almost entirely into the lacteal, blood, and lymphatic vessels. In these it occasions such spasms and oscillations as it does in the primæ viæ, so that it encreases all secretions and excretions, but particularly those of urine, sweat, and expectoration, according to the dose, to the nature of the disease, and to the disposition of the patient. It produces singularly good effects in those diseases of the breast which proceed from fullness and obstruction.

Kermes may be administered in linctus's, in oily or in cordial potions, in any vehicle, or incorporated in a bolus, with other suitable remedies. One precaution, hitherto little observed, is very necessary, that is, not to join it with acid matters, if it is intended to act as kermes. Anti-acid and absorbent substances ought to be joined with it, if the patient has an acid in the primæ viæ, or an acescent disposition, for as these acids saturate the alkali by which the kermes is rendered an antimoniated liver of sulphur, and by which alone it differs from golden sulphur of antimony, they accordingly render the kermes entirely similar to the golden sulphur of antimony, the properties of which are very different from those of kermes. *See* SULPHUR (GOLDEN) *of* ANTIMONY.
In some cases, we certainly ought to prefer the unwashed kermes to that which

has been washed, and therefore apothecaries ought to keep both the kinds, as Mr Baron proposes in his edition of Lemeri's Chemistry

CCCII KINGDOMS Most naturalists and chemists divide all natural bodies into three great classes, which they call kingdoms These are the *mineral*, the *vegetable*, and the *animal kingdoms*

This great and first division is founded on this consideration, that any plant or vegetable which is produced, which grows, which is organised, which contains a seed, and which produces its like, seems to be a being very distinct and different from a stone or a metal, in which we at most observe only a regular arrangement of parts, but not a true organisation, and which contains no seed by which it is capable of reproduction, and another foundation of this division is, that an animal differs no less from a simple plant, by sensation, by the use of its senses, and by the power of voluntary motion which it possesses, while these qualities do not belong to any thing which is merely vegetable

But notwithstanding these marks so distinctive, some philosophers pretend, that this division into classes of natural bodies is only ideal They affirm, that by observing nature attentively, we may perceive that all her productions are connected together by an uninterrupted chain, and that by surveying the several beings, we must be convinced that any one being differs very little from some other two, betwixt which it seems to be placed, so that we may descend from the most perfect animal to the rudest mineral by insensible degrees, and without finding any interval from which a division might be made

This idea is certainly great, sublime, and not improbable, for if we compare a *polypus* with the *sensitive plant*, or a *lichen* with a beautiful ore of ramified native silver, we shall be inclined to consider this opinion as conformable to the plan of nature

The opinions of naturalists are therefore divided upon this subject, and each opinion seems to be founded on observations, analogies, and reasonings more or less conclusive But as the discussion of this matter is foreign to our subject, we shall not enter into a more particular detail, but we shall consider natural bodies only in a chemical view, that is to say, relatively to the several principles which we obtain in the analysis of those bodies We proceed therefore to shew what experiments have taught us on this subject In the decomposition of all beings truly living, organised, and containing within themselves a seed by which they may be reproduced, such as vegetables and animals, we always obtain an inflammable, fat, or oily substance, and on the contrary, we do not find the smallest trace of this principle in any substance purely mineral, not even in sulphur, which is the most inflammable of all these substances On the other side, if we carefully examine and compare with each other the analogous principles obtained from the three kingdoms, such as the saline substances obtained in the analysis of animals, vegetables, and minerals, we shall easily perceive that all the saline matter which comes from the vegetable or animal kingdoms is altered by oil, while all the saline matter which comes from the mineral kingdom is entirely free from oil

We ought to observe here, that because any matter is found in one or more individuals of any kingdom, we must not therefore conclude, that it belongs to the kingdom of such individuals, for we may be convinced from a slight observation of nature, that by a thousand combinations, and particular circumstances,

substances

ſubſtances of quite different claſſes or kingdoms are daily found mixed and confounded together Thus, for example, within the earth, and even at great depths, that is, in the region appropriated to minerals, ſometimes ſubſtances are found evidently oily, ſuch as all *bitumens* but we at the ſame time can prove, and all the obſervations of natural hiſtory prove, that theſe oily ſubſtances are only accidentally within the earth, and that they proceed from the vegetable or animal bodies which have been buried in the earth by ſome of thoſe great revolutions which have happened from time to time upon the ſurface of our globe Alſo in decompoſing ſeveral vegetables and animals, ſalts are obtained, ſuch as common ſalt, Glauber's ſalt, and others, which contain nothing oily, and which are conſequently matters evidently mineral But, on the other ſide, we are certain that theſe mineral ſalts are extraneous to the animals and vegetables in which they are found, that they are only introduced into theſe living bodies, becauſe they happen to be mixed with the matters which have been applied to them as aliments, and that they ought not to be numbered amongſt their principles The proof of this is, that not only the quantity of theſe mineral ſalts is not uniform in animals and vegetables, but alſo, that not a particle of ſuch ſalts is contained in ſome plants and animals equally ſtrong and healthy, and of the ſame ſpecies as thoſe in which theſe ſalts have generally been obſerved

In the ſecond place, we obſerve, that oils do only exiſt in the proximate principles of vegetables and animals, that is, in thoſe of their principles which enter immediately into their compoſition, when theſe principles have not been altered by further decompoſitions, and conſequently when they ſtill preſerve their animal or vegetable character, for, by a natural putrefaction continued during a long time, or by chemical operations, not only the materials of which animal and vegetable bodies are formed, may be deprived entirely of oil, but alſo this oil may itſelf be entirely deſtroyed or decompoſed Theſe ſubſtances in that ſtate contain nothing by which they can be diſtinguiſhed from minerals The earths, for example, of vegetables and animals, when they are deprived, by a ſufficient calcination, of all inflammable matter, become entirely ſimilar to the calcareous and argillaceous earths found within the globe, and which may be conſidered as mineral ſubſtances, although probably they have been formerly a part of animal and vegetable bodies Further, if vegetable acids were deprived of all their oily parts, which is perhaps very poſſible, then they would entirely reſemble the mineral acids, probably the vitriolic and marine, and would loſe all the characteriſtic properties of vegetable acids

Hence we conclude, that when we conſider natural bodies in a chemical view, we ought to divide them into two great claſſes The firſt claſs is of ſubſtances inanimate, unorganiſed, and the principles of which have a degree of ſimplicity which is eſſential to them theſe are minerals The other claſs contains all thoſe bodies which not only have been diſtinctly organized, but which alſo contain an oily matter, which is no where found in ſubſtances which have not made part of animate bodies, and which, by combining with all the other principles of theſe animate bodies, diſtinguiſhes theſe principles from thoſe of minerals by a leſs degree of ſimplicity This ſecond claſs contains vegetables and animals We ought alſo to remark, that the oil contained in vegetable and animal ſubſtances renders them ſuſceptible of fermentation, properly ſo called,

 which

which cannot by any means take place in any mineral *See* ACIDS, BITUMENS, FERMENTATION, OILS, PUTREFACTION, *and* EARTHS

We shall now proceed to examine, if, by comparing the principles obtained in the decomposition of vegetables with those obtained in the decomposition of animals, we can find some essential character by which these two kingdoms may be chemically distinguished, in the same manner as we have seen that both of them may be distinguished from minerals From experiments we indeed learn, that the principles of vegetables differ evidently enough from those of animals, that in general the saline principles of the former are acid, and are transformable in great measure into fixed alkali by incineration, while the principles of the latter are volatile alkalis, or easily changeable into these, that vegetables are much farther removed from putrefaction than animals, lastly, that oils truly animal have a character different from vegetable oils, and are in general more attenuated, or at least more disposed to be attenuated and volatilised But we must, at the same time, confess, that these differences are not clear and decisive, like those betwixt these two kingdoms and the mineral kingdom, for we do not find any essential principle, either in animals or in vegetables, which is not also to be found in the other In some plants, chiefly the cruciform, as much volatile alkali, as little fixed alkali, and as much disposition to putrify, are found as in animal matters, and thence we conclude, that if these two great classes of natural bodies differ chemically from each other, this difference proceeds only from the quantities or proportions of their several principles and properties, and not from any thing distinct and peculiar, nor is it similar to the manner in which both vegetable and animal substances differ from minerals, namely, by containing an oil, and possessing a fermentable quality Besides, the degrees of the chemical differences betwixt these three great classes of natural bodies are found to be the same, in whatever manner we consider them or compare them together

CCCIV KUPFER-NICKEL (c)

(c) KUPFER-NICKEL is a reddish yellow mineral containing the semi-metal called nickel, together with iron and cobalt, mineralised by arsenic and by sulphur. It is sometimes of a vitreous texture, sometimes fine-grained, and sometimes consisting of scaly particles. *See* NICKEL.

L.

CCCCV LABORATORY (CHEMICAL) As chemistry is a science founded entirely on experiments, we cannot hope to understand it well, or to possess a certain degree of it, without making such experiments as shall verify most of the known fundamental operations, and also such as reasoning, analogy, and the spirit of inquiry, never fail to suggest to those whose taste and suitable talents lead them to this essential part of experimental philosophy Besides, when a person himself observes, and operates, he must perceive, even in the most common operations, a great variety of small facts, which must necessarily be known, but which are not mentioned either in books or in memoirs, because they are too numerous, and would appear too minute. Lastly, how many qualities are in the several chemical agents, of which no just notion can be given by writing, and which are perfectly well known as soon as they have been once made to strike our senses ?

Whoever therefore would become a chemist, must indispensably have a laboratory furnished with the most necessary instruments for the practice of this science, and we therefore think proper to mention what these are Our intention is not to speak in this article of laboratories designed for operations in the great, nor of those which are appropriated to some particular part of chemistry, as, for example, to essays, enamels, &c but of the kind of laboratory which is proper for a philosophical chemist, to make occasionally, in small, any chemical operation whatever Such a laboratory necessarily occasions certain expences, but not so much as is generally believed, when the operator knows how to manage his utensils, and to employ only the proper quantity of the several substances upon which he operates, and lastly, when he chuses the least expensive methods of attaining his purposes

Many people think, that a laboratory level with the ground is most convenient, for the sake of water, pounding, washing, &c It certainly has these advantages, but it is also subject to a very great inconvenience from moisture,

Constant

Conſtant moiſture, tho' not very conſiderable and ſenſible in many reſpects, is a very great inconvenience in a chemical laboratory. In ſuch a place, moſt ſaline matters become moiſt in time, the inſcriptions fall off, or are effaced, the bellows rot, the metals ruſt, the furnaces moulder, and every thing almoſt ſpoils. A laboratory therefore is more advantageouſly placed above than below the ground, that it may be as dry as is poſſible. The air muſt have free acceſs to it, and it muſt even be ſo conſtructed, that, by means of two or more oppoſite openings, a current of air may be admitted to carry off any noxious vapors or duſt.

In the laboratory a chimney ought to be conſtructed, ſo high that a perſon may eaſily ſtand under it, and as extenſive as is poſſible, that is, from one wall to another. The tube of this chimney ought to be as high as is poſſible, and ſufficiently contracted to make a good draught. As charcoal only is burnt under this chimney, no ſoot is collected in it, and therefore it need not be ſo wide as to allow a chimney-ſweeper to paſs up into it.

Under this chimney may be conſtructed ſome brick-furnaces, particularly a melting furnace, a furnace for diſtilling with an alembic, and one or two ovens like thoſe in kitchens. The reſt of the ſpace ought to be filled up with ſtands of different heights, from a foot to a foot and a half, on which portable furnaces of all kinds are to be placed. Theſe furnaces are the moſt convenient, from the facility of diſpoſing them at pleaſure, and they are the only furnaces which are neceſſary in a ſmall laboratory. A double bellows of moderate ſize muſt alſo be placed as commodiouſly under the chimney, or as near as the place will allow. Theſe bellows are ſometimes mounted in a portable frame, which is ſufficiently convenient when the bellows is not more than eighteen or twenty inches. Theſe bellows ought to have a pipe directed towards the hearth where the forge is to be placed.

The neceſſary furnaces are, the ſimple furnace, for diſtilling with a copper alembic, a lamp furnace, two reverberatory furnaces, of different ſizes, for diſtilling with retorts, an air or melting furnace, an eſſay furnace, and a forge-furnace. *See the enumeration and deſcription of theſe furnaces under the words* FORGE *and* FURNACE. *See alſo* PLATES.

Under the chimney, at a convenient height, muſt be a row of hooks driven into the back and ſide walls, upon which are to be hung ſmall ſhovels, iron pans, tongs, ſtraight, crooked, and circular pincers, pokers, iron rods, and other utenſils for diſpoſing the fuel and managing the crucibles.

To the walls of the laboratory ought to be faſtened ſhelves of different breadths and heights, or theſe ſhelves may be ſuſpended by hooks. The ſhelves are to contain glaſs veſſels, and the products of operations, and ought to be in as great a number as is poſſible. In a laboratory where many experiments are made, one cannot have too many ſhelves.

The moſt convenient place for a ſtone or leaden fountain to contain water is a corner of the laboratory, and under it a ciſtern ought to be placed with a pipe by which the water poured into it may diſcharge itſelf. As the veſſels are always cleaned under this fountain, cloths and bottle bruſhes ought to be hung upon hooks faſtened in the walls near it.

In the middle of the laboratory a large table is to be placed, on which mixtures are to be made, preparations for operations, ſolutions, precipitations,

ſmall

ſmall filtrations, in a word, whatever does not require fire, excepting that of a lamp

In convenient parts of the laboratory, are to be placed blocks of wood upon mats, one of which is to ſupport a middle-ſized iron mortar, another to ſupport a middle ſized marble, or rather hard-ſtone mortar, a third to ſupport an anvil Near the mortars are to be hung ſearces of different ſizes and fineneſs, and near the anvil are hung a hammer, files, raſps, ſmall pincers, ſciſſars, ſheers, and other ſmall utenſils, neceſſary to give metals a form proper for the ſeveral operations

Two moveable treſtles ought to be in a laboratory, which may ſerve to ſupport a large filter mounted upon a frame, when it is required This apparatus is removed occaſionally to the moſt convenient place *See* FILTRATION *and* FILTER

Charcoal is an important article in a laboratory, and it therefore muſt be placed within reach but as the black duſt which flies about it whenever it is ſtirred is apt to ſoil every thing in the laboratory, it had better be in ſome place near the laboratory, together with ſome furze, which is very convenient for kindling fires quickly. This place ſerves, at the ſame time, for containing bulky things which are not often wanted, ſuch as furnaces, bricks, tiles, clay, fire-clay, quicklime, ſand, and many other things neceſſary for chemical operations

Laſtly, a middle-ſized table, with ſolid feet, ought to be enumerated amongſt the large moveables of a laboratory, the uſe of which is to ſupport a porphyry, or levigating ſtone, or rather a very hard and denſe grit ſtone, together with a grinder made of the ſame kind of ſtone

The other ſmall moveables or utenſils of a laboratory are, ſmall hand-mortars of marble, iron, and glaſs, and their peſtles, earthen, ſtone, metal, and glaſs veſſels, *an enumeration of which ſee under the article* VESSELS, *and a deſcription under their reſpective names*

Some white writing-paper, and ſome paper not glued for filtrations, a large number of clean ſtraws, eight or ten inches long, for ſtirring mixtures in glaſſes, and for ſupporting paper filters placed in glaſs funnels

Glaſs tubes for ſtirring and mixing corroſive liquors, ſpatulas of wood, ivory, metal, and of glaſs

Thin paſteboards and horns, very convenient for collecting matters bruiſed with water upon the levigating ſtone or in mortars, corks of all ſizes, bladders and linen ſtrips for luting veſſels *See* LUTES.

A good portable pair of bellows, a good ſteel, for ſtriking fire, a glue pot, with its little bruſh, laſtly, a great many boxes of various ſizes, for containing moſt of the above-mentioned things, and which are to be placed upon the ſhelves

Beſides theſe things, ſome ſubſtances are ſo neceſſary in moſt chemical operations, that they may be conſidered as inſtruments neceſſary for the practice of this ſcience Theſe ſubſtances are

All metals and ſemi-metals, which ought to be very pure

Vitriolic acid, ſome of which ought to be concentrated and rectified, and alſo ſome of that ſort commonly ſold by druggiſts.

Aqua

Aqua fortis, such as is commonly sold, and is cheap, also spirit of nitre moderately strong, but very pure the same acid very pure, concentrated, and smoking

Common spirit of salt Some of the same acid very pure, very strong, and smoking All these acids ought to be kept in crystal glass bottles, and closed with glass stoppers

Some distilled vinegar, which may be kept in an ordinary bottle, some radical vinegar, which ought to be kept in a bottle with a glass stopper, some cream of tartar, in an earthen or glass vessel, or in a box

Common fixed vegetable alkali, very dry, such as pot-ash, which must be kept in a well closed bottle The same alkali in a liquid state

Very pure salt of tartar, some dry, and some liquid

Mineral alkali, liquid, that is, a solution of soda The same alkali dry and very pure, that is, well formed crystals of soda

The two fixed alkalis liquid, and rendered caustic by quicklime Alkalis, particularly those which are caustic, ought to be kept in bottles with glass stoppers Some phlogisticated fixed alkali, or even saturated so as to be fit for making Prussian blue

Some dry liver of sulphur kept in a well closed bottle The same liquid Some common sulphur

Very pure alkali of sal ammoniac, disengaged by a fixed alkali, some solid, and some liquid, kept in a bottle with a glass stopper

Fluor spirit of sal ammoniac disengaged by quicklime, as strong as is possible Some of this spirit may be kept of less strength

Lime water, and quicklime, in well closed bottles

The purest and highest rectified spirit of wine

Good vitriolic ether

Rectified essential oil of turpentine, oil of olives, soap

Galls, syrup of violets, tincture of turnsol, or turnsol in rags, fine blue paper, river or distilled rain-water

Besides these substances, most of which are solvents, certain neutral salts ought to be had which are frequently used in chemical operations, or are difficultly prepared These are

Vitriolated tartar, alum, and calcined alum, green vitriol, blue vitriol, nitre, decrepitated common salt, some of the same salt very pure dissolved in distilled water, purified sal ammoniac, calcined borax, sedative salt

A pure solution of silver in spirit of nitre, a solution of mercury in the same acid, butter of antimony All these to be kept in bottles with glass stoppers Corrosive sublimate

Cerus, litharge, minium, sand washed and ground, white marble, washed chalk, glass of lead, glass of borax *See the nature and properties of all these matters under their respective names*

A person, provided with the above-mentioned instruments and substances, may at once perform any chemical experiment He may indeed occasionally want several neutral salts which have not been named, but all these salts with bases of earths, metals, fixed or volatile alkalis, may be easily and instantly prepared, as most of them do not require distillation or sublimation They may nevertheless,

nevertheless, if they are not too numerous, be all previously prepared and kept ready for any occasions.

We ought not to finish this article without making some observations important to those who propose to give themselves up to the study of chemistry. They ought to be well persuaded that method, order, and cleanliness, are essentially necessary in a chemical laboratory. Every vessel and utensil ought to be well cleansed as often as it is used, and put again into its place. Inscriptions ought to be fastened upon all the substances. These cares, which seem to be trifling, are however very fatiguing and tedious; but they also are very important, though frequently little observed. When a person is keenly engaged, experiments succeed each other quickly; some seem nearly to decide the matter, and others suggest new ideas: he cannot but proceed to them immediately, and he is led from one to another: he thinks he shall easily know again the products of the first experiments, and therefore he does not take time to put them in order: he prosecutes with eagerness the experiments which he has last thought of; and, in the mean time, the vessels employed, the glasses and bottles filled, so accumulate, that he cannot any longer distinguish them; or, at least, he is uncertain concerning many of his former products. This evil is encreased if a new series of operations succeed, and occupy all the laboratory, or if he is obliged to quit it for some time: every thing then goes into confusion. Thence it frequently happens that he loses the fruits of much labor, and that he must throw away almost all the products of his experiments.

The only method of avoiding these inconveniences is to employ the cares and attentions above-mentioned. It is indeed disagreeable to stop continually in the middle of the most interesting researches, and to employ a very precious and considerable time in cleaning vessels, arranging them, fastening inscriptions on them, &c. These employments are capable of cooling or retarding the progress of genius, and are tedious and disgustful; but they are nevertheless necessary. Those persons whose fortune enables them to have an assistant operator, on whose exactness and intelligence they can depend, avoid many of these disagreeable circumstances; but they ought nevertheless to attend to the execution of these things. We cannot depend too much on ourselves in these matters, however minute, on account of their consequences. This becomes even indispensable when the experiments are to be kept secret, at least for a time; which is often necessary in chemistry.

When new researches and inquiries are made, the mixtures, results, and products of all the operations ought to be kept a long time, distinctly labelled and registered; for these things, when kept some time, frequently present phenomena that were not at all suspected. Many fine discoveries in chemistry have been made in this manner, and many have certainly been lost by throwing away too hastily or neglecting the products.

Lastly, we cannot too much recommend to chemical operators to be exceedingly upon their guard against imposing and deceitful experiments, which frequently present themselves in practice. A circumstance seemingly unimportant, or not easily perceptible, is frequently sufficient to give the appearance of a great discovery, by means of certain effects, which, nevertheless, are found to proceed from some other cause. Chemical experiments depend on so many necessary things, that all of them can seldom be attended to, particularly when the subject is new: hence we frequently find that very different results proceed from the same experiment, made at different times. We therefore must not decide after the first success, but the experiment must be repeated several times, and even varied, till no doubt can remain.

Further, as chemistry offers many views for the improvement of many important arts, as it presents prospects of many useful and profitable discoveries, those who apply their labors in this way ought to be exceedingly circumspect not to be led into an useless expence of money and time. Those researches which have some analogy with the philosopher's stone, from the hopes of wealth which they suggest, are also attended with similar danger. In a certain set of experiments some one is generally of an imposing appearance, although in reality it be nothing more. Chemistry is full of these half-successes, which serve only to deceive the unwary, to multiply the number of trials, and to lead to great expence before the fruitlessness of the search be discovered. By these reflexions we do not intend to divert from all such researches those whose taste and talents render them fit for them, on the contrary, we acknowledge that the improvement of the arts, and the discovery of new objects of manufacture and commerce, are undoubtedly the finest and most interesting part of chemistry, and which make that science truly valuable, for without these ends what would chemistry be but a science purely theoretical, capable of employing only some abstract and speculative minds, but useless to society? We acknowledge also, that the successes in this kind of chemical inquiry are not rare, and that their authors have sometimes acquired fortunes, so much the more honorable as being the fruits of their talents and industry. But we repeat, that in these researches, the more dazzling and near any success appears, the more circumspection and even distrust is necessary.

CCCCVI. LAC LUNÆ. (d)

CCCCVII. LAC. (e)

CCCCVIII. LAPIS INFERNALIS. *See* CAUSTIC.

(d) LAC LUNÆ, *Agaricus Mineralis*, is a very light, spongy, friable, and white calcareous earth. *See* EARTH (CALCAREOUS).

(e) LAC, *Lacca*, or *Gum-lac*, is a kind of wax, of which a species of winged ants form cells upon trees, like honeycombs. In these cells remain some of the dead insects, which give a red color to the whole substance of the lac. That called *stick lac* is the wax adhering to some of the small branches of the tree, and which is unprepared. This lac, when separated from the adhering sticks, and grossly powdered, and deprived of its color by digestion with menstruums, for the sake of dyes, and other purposes, is called *seed-lac*, and lastly, when the stick-lac is freed from impurities, by melting it over a gentle fire, and formed into cakes, it is called *shell-lac*. Lac is unsoluble in water, and difficultly soluble in spirit of wine, which for that purpose must be well dephlegmated. According to Neuman, sixteen ounces of seed-lac, distilled in an open fire, yielded nine ounces and six drams of a butter or thick oil, one ounce six drams of a watery liquor neither acid nor alkaline, and a residuum weighing two ounces and a half. It is used in the preparation of spirit varnishes, for the making of sealing-wax, and as a coloring material for dying scarlet. The color given by lac is less beautiful, but more durable, than that given by cochineal. To render the coloring matter of the lac diffusible in water, so as to be applied to the stuffs to be dyed, Mr Hellot directs the following process. Let some powdered gum-lac be digested during two hours in a decoction of comfrey root, by which a fine crimson color is given to the water, and the gum is rendered pale or straw-

CCCCIX. LAPIS LAZULI (*f*)

CCCCX LEAD Lead, called also *Saturn*, is an imperfect metal, white, but darker than tin, the softest, least ductile, least elastic, and least sonorous of all the metals

It also has the least tenacity, a leaden wire of $\frac{1}{10}$ of an inch in diameter being capable of supporting only 29$\frac{1}{4}$ pounds

This metal has a considerable specific gravity Next to gold, platina, and mercury, it is the heaviest metal It loses, when immersed in water, betwixt $\frac{1}{11}$ and $\frac{1}{12}$ part of its weight A cubic foot of lead weighs 828 pounds

straw colored To this tincture, poured off clear, let a solution of alum be added, and when the coloring matter has subsided, let it be separated from the clear liquor, and dried. It will weigh about $\frac{1}{5}$ of the quantity of lac employed This dried fecula is to be dissolved or diffused in warm water, and some solution of tin is to be added to it, by which it acquires a vivid scarlet color This liquor is to be added to a solution of tartar in boiling water, and thus the dye is prepared

(*f*) LAPIS LAZULI is a blue stone, generally intermixed with white veins and gold colored spots. Wallerius considers this stone as a species of jasper, and Cronstedt, more justly, as a species of that order of earths which have been lately called zeolites *See* ZEOLITES Mr Margraaf, and also Mr Cronstedt, have made experiments on this stone, carefully cleansed from all white, pyritous, or heterogeneous matters From these experiments we learn, 1 That this stone is soluble in acids without effervescence, and when it has been previously calcined, it forms gelatinous masses with acids 2 That by calcination it is not deprived of its blue color, till at least that operation has been long continued 3 By a violent fire it is fusible, and forms a frothy glass, sometimes whitish, and sometimes of a dusky, yellow-color, but always clouded with blue spots 4 Fused with nitre, and thrown red-hot into water, it tinged the water with a blue color, which disappeared in some hours By this operation the stone lost its blue color 5 Some of this stone, powdered and mixed with glass frit, produced a transparent citron-colored glass With borax, it produced a glass of a chrysolite-color 6 It gave no signs of its containing copper, notwithstanding it has been considered as an ore of copper by most authors 7 It shewed marks of iron, by forming a blue precipitate, like Prussian blue, when a phlogisticated alkali was added to a solution of this stone in acids 8 Margraaf says, that by adding vitriolic acid to solutions of this stone in nitrous and marine acids, a white precipitate was formed, which he supposes was calcareous earth Nevertheless, Mr Cronstedt affirms, that this stone does not effervesce with acids Perhaps the calcareous earth was not essential, but only accidental 9 Cronstedt says, that a precipitate is formed by adding a fixed alkali to a solution of this stone in vitriolic acid, which, being scorified with borax, yields a regulus of silver He says, that by scorification with lead, two ounces of silver have been obtained from a hundred pounds of the stone Mr Margraaf does not mention that he found any silver, or that he searched for any Perhaps it is only accidental

The fine blue substance called *ultramarine* is prepared from lapis lazuli in the following manner, according to Wallerius The stone, first finely levigated and mixed with linseed oil, is to be added to a paste, made by mixing together equal parts of yellow wax, colophony, pitch, that is, half a pound of each, with half an ounce of linseed oil, two ounces of turpentine, and two ounces of mastic To three or four parts of this paste one part of the levigated stone, mixed with linseed-oil, is to be added, and after the mixture has been digested together during three or four weeks, it is to be thrown into hot-water, and stirred till the blue color separates and diffuses in the water, which is then to be poured off The blue matter is allowed to settle, and, when dry, is the ultramarine required.

Like all imperfect metals, it has its peculiar smell and taste When it is cut by a very sharp instrument, its surface appears smooth, compact, and shining, but it quickly tarnishes in the air, and its surface becomes covered by a slight greyish rust It resists nevertheless much longer than iron or copper the combined action of air and water, before it is decomposed and destroyed It is very fusible, and melts nearly with the same degree of heat as tin, that is, before it is red

As soon as it melts, even with the least heat that is requisite, it calcines, and upon its surface greyish ashes are formed, in the same manner as tin is calcined

The color, softness, fusibility and calcinability of lead being similar to these qualities in tin, persons acquainted with only the common and superficial qualities of metals suppose that a great analogy subsists between lead and tin, nevertheless, we shall show that the properties of these two metals are essentially different

The grey calx, or ashes of lead, similar externally to those of tin, become of a very different appearance, if the calcination with a fire so moderate that it cannot melt them be continued, and particularly if they be exposed to flame Instead of becoming more and more white, they acquire at first a yellow color, and are then called *massicot*, or *yellow lead* The color becomes more and more intense, and at last entirely red It is then called *minium*, or *red lead*, *which see* If instead of calcining this calx with a gentle fire, it be fused, it then easily melts into a yellow vitrified substance, composed of small scales like those of talk Lead in this state is called *litharge*, *see* that word This happens in the operation of *cupellation* Lastly, if calx of lead be heated more than is necessary to keep it in fusion, it then soon changes into a true glass, which becomes so active and fluid, that it passes like water through the most compact crucibles Lead thus calcined and melted is called *glass of lead*, because in fact it has the transparency, brittleness, and all the essential properties of glass It is very useful in many arts, as may be seen under the article GLASS *of* LEAD

Of all the metallic calxes, that of lead is the most fusible, and most easily convertible into glass, in which respect it differs essentially from the calx of tin which is very refractory

This difference proceeds from the total privation which tin sustains of all its phlogiston, and from its capacity of a radical or perfect calcination Whereas lead, although it loses, as easily as tin does, as much of its phlogiston as is necessary to destroy its metallic appearance, and to calcine or vitrify it, yet it retains enough of its phlogiston to preserve a great fusibility, and even a considerable density For all the calxes and glasses of lead are very heavy

All these calxes and glasses of lead are easily revivable They can scarcely be melted but some part of the lead is revived, although no inflammable matter has been added This also is a proof that they retain much phlogiston For, in general, all metallic calxes are so much more easily reducible as they retain more of their inflammable principle

Lead is soluble by all acids, and presents with them phenomena similar to those of silver with the same acids Lead combined to saturation with nitrous acid forms, as silver does, a crystallizable nitrous salt with metallic base,

called

called *nitre of lead* This salt is capable of decrepitating and even of detonating without addition of inflammable matter, as several chemists pretend This detonation must therefore proceed from the phlogiston retained by the lead, which is sufficiently combustible for that purpose Kunkel, who seems not to have known this property of nitre of lead, relates, in his Treatise on the Art of making Glass, that when he attempted to distil this salt, his retort was suddenly burst with great noise and danger

Several chemists, among others Becker in his Second Supplement to the *Physica Subterranea*, and Kunkel in his *Laboratorium Chemicum*, give processes by which mercury may be obtained from lead Mr Grosse, who mentions these processes in the Memoirs of the Academy, gives one himself, which is more simple and more easily tried, since it consists only in saturating perfectly some good nitrous acid with lead By means of this saturation a grey powder is precipitated, according to this chemist, in which mercury is found But this process probably does not succeed with every kind of lead, for Messrs Macquer and Beaumé say, in their Course of Chemistry, that they have repeated with all possible attention this experiment of Mr Grosse, without having obtained mercury

Pure vitriolic acid, and that contained in neutral vitriolic salts, when mixed with a solution of lead in nitrous acid, unites with the lead, separates it from the nitrous acid, and forms with it a metallic salt, or vitriol of lead, which crystallizes, and appears therefore in form of a white precipitate, when the liquors do not contain a sufficient quantity of water to dissolve it This salt is the same as that made by dissolving directly lead in vitriolic acid

Marine acid, and all the neutral salts containing it, precipitate also lead from its solution in nitrous acid, and unite with it, forming a metallic salt called *plumbum corneum*, from the many resemblances that it has with the combination of silver with marine acid, called *luna cornea* Plumbum corneum differs from luna cornea in being much more soluble in water, which shews an abundancy of marine acid, or that it is less intimately combined in the lead than in the luna cornea Plumbum corneum may be made by several other methods, and particularly by disengaging the volatile alkali from sal ammoniac by lead, for, like all other metals, it has the property of decomposing this salt By this method, Mr Margraaf makes the plumbum corneum which he employs in the preparation of phosphorus

Several chemists affirm that the solution of lead in nitrous acid may be decomposed by water singly, and that a magistery of lead may be thus formed, in the same manner as that of bismuth But Mr Beaume, who has examined the affair with greater accuracy, found that this precipitation does not happen when very pure, that is, distilled water is used, and that consequently this precipitation is to be attributed to the salts, and particularly to the selenites, contained in almost all ordinary waters

Vegetable acids also dissolve lead with ease, but only the combinations of this metal with vinegar are known, because these are used in medicine and in the arts The first of these preparations is called *ceruss*, or *white-lead* It is a kind of rust of lead, or an admirable white color, made by the acid of vinegar, to the vapor of which the lead is exposed The chief use of this preparation is for painting in oil, and is the only white hitherto discovered for that purpose,

although

although its has two very great faults. The first is, that it gives painful colics to persons employed in its preparation, and the second is, that it is liable to become yellow or black, and, in a word, to lose much of its beauty in time; which proceeds from the disposition which this calx of lead, like all the other preparations of this metal, has to recover its phlogiston, and consequently its color. The discovery therefore of another white, possessed of the beauty and other advantages of white-lead, without its inconveniencies, would be of important service to painting, and even to mankind *See* CERUSS.

Cerufs contains too little of the acid of vinegar to be in the state of a neutral salt, but as it is lead much opened and divided, it may be easily completely combined to saturation with this acid For this purpose cerufs must be digested with a sufficient quantity of distilled vinegar, to dissolve it perfectly The liquor after this solution is called *vinegar of lead* If it be filtrated, evaporated, and crystallized, fine crystals are formed, capable of a perfect solution in water, of a saline, metallic, and saccharine taste, from which this salt is called *sugar* or *salt of lead* Salt of lead may be decomposed merely by the action of fire. By distillation a very concentrated acid of vinegar may be obtained from it, a kind of radical vinegar, similar to that obtained from crystals of copper *See* SALT *of* LEAD

Oils and fat matters, which in general are capable of acting upon metallic substances, have a distinguished action upon lead, and particularly upon its calxes In consequence of this action, cerufs, minium, and litharge, may be entirely and copiously dissolved in most oils by coction with moderate heat. Oils in which lead has been dissolved are thereby rendered thick and drying. Linseed oil thus thickened by lead is much used in painting The painters call it *drying oil* So large a quantity of calx of lead may be dissolved in oils, that a body is thence formed, which when cold is solid, tenacious, and of the consistence of plasters The consistence of many of the plasters used in surgery is caused by calxes of lead dissolved in oils. These masses of lead combined with oil, or plasters, resemble soap in smell, rancid taste, milkiness given to water, and lastly, in being decomposed by acids which unite with the lead, and separate the oil from it These observations were made by Mr. Geoffroy

Lead is easily united to sulphur, and is easily burnt and calcined by exposing it at once to the action of sulphur, fire, and air With sulphur alone it forms a compound resembling the ore of lead, or lead naturally mineralized by sulphur

This metal easily unites with all metals excepting iron, with which it cannot by any means be allayed Such is the antipathy of these two metals, that if silver allayed with some iron be melted with lead, the lead presently seizes the silver, and the iron floats upon the surface of the melted metals Nevertheless the calxes of lead and iron are very well united together by fusion, and the former facilitates the vitrification of the latter as much as it does that of the calxes of other metals Hence lead may be employed to purify the perfect metals from iron, as well as from other imperfect metals Of all the allays of lead, that with tin is most used, being employed for soldering by plumbers, and for tinning If an allay of lead and tin be exposed to an open fire, sufficiently strong to make the metal red-hot and to smoke, these two metals will burn and calcine together much

much more quickly and perfectly than either of them would do singly. The calx resulting from this operation is the basis of white enamels, and glazings for earthen ware. It is called *putty*.

The affinities of lead, according to Mr Geoffroy's table, are silver and copper: according to Mr Gellert's table, they are silver, gold, tin, copper. Iron is marked in this table as being incapable of uniting with lead.

Lead and its several preparations are of great use. It is used and formed into sheets and pipes, for containing and conducting water in buildings and gardens. Lead is not much used in medicine, only externally, from the colics and palsies which it occasions when taken internally. But its external applications are very useful, from its sedative, drying, and repelling qualities. The vinegar and the sugar of lead, also all the ointments and plasters which contain cerufs, minium, or litharge, eminently possess these qualities. We have seen that lead is much employed in painting with oil, both as a color and as a dryer. It is also used in the preparation of enamels and of porcelain as a flux, and makes the basis of the glazing of almost all pottery wares from the most ordinary kind to the finest. Lastly, by means of lead, the most perfect metals are refined and essayed. We may therefore say, that this metal is so generally used, and so necessary in the important arts we have mentioned, that they absolutely could not exist without it.

CCCCXI. LEATHER (FOSSIL). (*g*)

CCCCXII. LEAVES. (*h*)

(*g*) LEATHER (FOSSIL). *Aluta montana*. This is a foliated amianthus, consisting of soft fibres interwoven together. Frequently it contains sparry crystals enclosed in it. For the properties of this stone, *see* AMIANTHUS.

(*h*) LEAVES. The following remarks concerning the coloring substance of leaves are taken from Dr Lewis. The green color of the leaves of plants may be extracted by rectified spirit of wine and by oils. The spirituous tinctures are generally of a fine deep green, even when the leaves themselves are dull colored, or yellowish, or hoary. The color however seldom remains long in these liquors, and it remains a much shorter time when the coloring matter is separated in a solid form, and exposed to air. The *acanthus* gives a more durable green color to spirit than any other herb. Alkalis heighten the colors of the tinctures and of the juices, and acids weaken, destroy, or change them to a brownish color. Limewater improves the color, and also the durability of the color. By means of lime, not inelegant green lakes may be obtained from the leaves of *acanthus*, *lilly of the valley*, and of several other plants. Few herbs communicate any part of their green color to water, perhaps none give a green considerably deep. Nevertheless a green dye is said to be given to woolen by the leaves of some plants, as of the wild *chervil*, or *cow-weed*, the common *rag-wort*, and *devil's-bit*. The leaves of many kinds of herbs and trees give a yellow dye to wool, previously boiled in a solution of alum and tartar. *Weld* particularly affords a fine yellow dye. Mr Hellot observes, that all leaves, barks, and roots, which have an astringent taste, as the leaves of the *almond*, *peach*, and *pear* trees, ash-bark, roots of *wild patience*, &c. yield durable yellows. From the leaves of two plants, *blue* coloring substances are produced, namely, *indigo* and *woad*, which *see*. Mr Hellot suspects that a similar blue fecula might be produced from many other vegetables. He supposes the green color of vegetables to proceed from a mixture of blue and yellow particles, and that the former are frequently more permanent than the latter, so as to be capable of resisting the fermentation of the juice of the plants, while the yellow are destroyed by that fermentation. Dr Lewis has tryed, without success, to obtain blue dyes from other plants, by putrefying them in water.

CCCCXIII. LEY (CAUSTIC), *or the* LEY *of* SOAP-BOILERS. This name is given to lixiviums of fixed alkali rendered caustic by quicklime. To make these leys, two parts of soda or of potash are mixed with one part of quicklime; or equal parts of alkaline salt ready prepared and quicklime are added together. This mixture is to be put into a large vessel, and 12 or 15 times as much pure water is to be poured upon it, and the quicklime is to be thus slaked: after which the whole is to be boiled during some minutes, and the ley while yet hot is to be filtered through a brown paper filter supported upon linen, and the ley is to be concentrated by evaporation upon the fire, to such a degree as is judged necessary, according to the use for which it is designed.

Quicklime has the property of encreasing considerably the causticity of all fixed alkalis; and this is probably done, not only by taking from them their superabundant inflammable matter, but a part also of that which enters into their composition as a principle. Hence a considerable alteration is produced upon these alkalis by quicklime, similar to that produced upon volatile alkali; and we may consequently decompose entirely all alkalis by quicklime. But these experiments have not been hitherto prosecuted. The properties of fixed alkali rendered caustic have not been sufficiently examined. We know only that by this treatment the dissolving power of alkalis, and particularly upon oily matters, is much encreased; and they are therefore thus prepared, when they are to be combined with oils for the formation of soaps. (*i*)

The caustic ley, evaporated to dryness, furnishes an alkaline salt exceedingly acrid, which being melted in a crucible becomes what is called *common caustic*, because when it is applied to the skin, it makes an eschar, pierces it, and leaves an ulcer, the suppuration of which, when continued, is called an *issue*.

Caustic alkali has not only much greater dissolving power, but it is also much more deliquescent, and attracts much more powerfully the moisture of the air, than ordinary alkali. These properties must proceed from the developement of the saline principle by the quicklime. *See* ALKALI.

CCCCXIV. LILLY *of* PARACELSUS. *See* TINCTURE *of* METALS.

CCCCXV. LINNEN (FOSSIL). (*k*)

CCCCXVI. LIQUOR SILICUM. LIQUOR *of* FLINTS. The preparation of this liquor consists in uniting by fusion powdered flints or sand with a sufficient quantity of fixed alkali, so that a compound results from it in which the properties of the alkali prevail, and particularly a total solubility in water. For this purpose one part of ground flints or sand is to be well mixed with three or four parts of fixed alkali. The mixture is to be put into a crucible which ought to be very large, in proportion to the quantity of matter. The crucible is then to be placed in a forge or good melting furnace, and gradually heated.

When this mixture has acquired a certain heat, a considerable boiling and swelling are observable, occasioned by the action of these two matters upon

(*i*) The effect produced upon alkalis by quicklime is the absorption of their fixable air. *See* AIR (FIXABLE) *and* ALKALI.

(*k*) LINNEN (FOSSIL) is a kind of [illegible] which consists of flexible, parallel, soft fibres, and which has been celebrated for the use it has been applied to, of being woven, and forming an *incombustible cloth*. Paper has also been made of it, and wicks for lamps. *See* AMIANTHUS.

each

each other To prevent the matter in this state from flowing over the crucible, this ought to be large, and the fire gradually raised A part only of the mixture may be put into the crucible at once, and when its effervescence is over, the rest may be added at different times, taking care that each portion to be added be previously heated to prevent explosion from any moisture which it might contain, when mixed with red-hot melted matter

When the effervescence of all the mixture is over, it is to be kept in a good fusion during a quarter of an hour, and is then to be poured upon a greased stone or plate of iron The matter when cold is brittle, and seems vitrified It is even transparent like glass, when the quantity of alkali is only double or nearly double the quantity of flints It quickly and strongly attracts moisture from the air, and is entirely soluble in water, except a very small portion of earthy matter But a similar earth is also always separated from pure fixed alkali during its solution in water

The filtrated solution is at first clear, and limpid, but it afterwards becomes turbid, and forms an earthy sediment, like that formed by solutions of fixed alkali, only the former seems more copious This liquor has all the properties of liquid fixed alkali

All these properties of alkaline salts, and particularly its total solubility in water, are caused by the quantity of fixed alkali which enters into this kind of vitrified matter As compound bodies partake always of the properties of their component principles, and as the properties of the principle which predominates in the composition of any body do also predominate in that body, we may perceive why the properties of the fixed alkali in the present combination should be *more sensible than those of the earthy matter or flints* The alkali communicates to the earthy matter some of its strong disposition to unite with water The flints are really kept dissolved in water, and by this experiment they are consequently reduced into a liquor, and hence it has been called the *liquor of flints* If any acid be added to the liquor of flints so as to saturate the alkali, the flint which was kept dissolved in water by means of this alkali will be now precipitated in state of a fine earth Mr Pott mentions a very singular phenomenon which happens in this experiment, which is, that this earthy precipitate is entirely soluble by acids, so that if more acid be added than is sufficient to saturate the alkali, the precipitate will entirely disappear

As vitrifiable earths in their natural state, and even when divided as much as is possible by mechanical methods, are insoluble in acids, and as they become soluble by acids, when they have been combined by fusion with a sufficient quantity of fixed alkali, they must consequently undergo a singular alteration in this operation This property which they acquire of dissolving in acids, proceeds either from the great fineness to which their parts are reduced, or from a small portion of fixed alkali, or from some of its principles which remain united with them, and from which they cannot be entirely separated by the precipitating acid

The fixed alkali which enters into this combination receives also some alteration from the vitrifiable earth, one part of it is decomposed, and its earth is precipitated with the vitrifiable earth, and the remaining part is rendered much more caustic than it was before

In vitrifications something happens similar to what is observed in the compound designed to make the liquor of flints The glasses which contain too

 much

much alkaline salt in their composition, or which have not sustained a long or strong enough fire to unite the earth intimately with the fixed alkali, are partly soluble in acids, have sometimes even an alkaline taste, tarnish, and moisten in the air. *See* VITRIFICATION.

CCCCXVI. LIQUOR, *or* SPIRIT (SMOKING) *of* LIBAVIUS. This preparation is a marine acid very concentrated, smoking, and impregnated with much tin. It is obtained by distillation from a mixture of corrosive sublimate with tin.

To make the smoking liquor of Libavius, an amalgam must be made of four parts of tin and five parts of mercury: this amalgam is to be well mixed with an equal weight of corrosive sublimate, by triturating the whole together in a glass mortar. This mixture is to be put into a glass retort, which is to be placed in a reverberatory furnace. To the retort is to be luted with fat lute a receiver with a small hole in it, in the same manner as is done for the distillation of concentrated mineral acids. The distillation is then to be begun with a graduated and well managed fire. A very smoking liquor passes into the receiver, and towards the end of the distillation a very thick and even concrete matter. When the operation is finished, the liquor in the receiver is to be poured quickly into a crystal glass bottle with a glass stopper. When this bottle is opened, a white, copious, thick, and poignant fume issues, which remains long in the air without disappearing.

The very concentrated marine acid contained in the corrosive sublimate quits the mercury in this experiment to unite with the tin; and as this acid has the property of raising with it in distillation most metallic matters, a considerable quantity of the tin passes over in this distillation. Nevertheless this acid is far from being saturated with tin; it is still very acid, and capable of dissolving much tin in the ordinary way. From this imperfect saturation, together with its great concentration, proceeds partly its property of smoking so considerably. Nevertheless some other cause probably concurs to give it this property. For although this liquor smokes infinitely more than the most concentrated spirit of salt, distilled in Glauber's manner, its vapors are notwithstanding much less elastic. Another very essential difference betwixt this liquor and concentrated spirit of salt is, that by mixing the former, but not the latter, with spirit of wine, marine ether may be obtained. *See* ETHER (MARINE).

Lastly, if we attempt to dissolve, by the ordinary method, as much tin in concentrated spirit of salt as is contained in the smoking liquor of Libavius, this acid, so far from being thereby rendered more smoking, ceases entirely to smoke. A real difference therefore subsists betwixt the marine acid impregnated with tin by the decomposition of corrosive sublimate, and by distillation, and the marine acid treated with tin in any other manner. But we cannot easily determine whence this difference proceeds. Does this acid deposit in the mercury or in the tin some of its principles? If that be the case, with what principle is tin impregnated in this experiment? Is it with phlogiston? or with mercurial earth? These questions cannot be decided without further researches.

The smoking liquor has all the other properties of the most concentrated marine acid, when imperfectly saturated with tin. If it be diluted with much water, most of its tin will be separated from it in the form of white light flocks; when

when it is mixed with a solution of gold in aqua regia, it forms the purple precipitate of Cassius, as all other solutions of tin, and even pure tin not dissolved, do *See* PRECIPITATE (PURPLE) *of* CASSIUS It may be precipitated by absorbent earths, and by alkaline salts. In several dyes, particularly in those which are red, it produces the same effects as tin dissolved by marine acid *See* DYEING

The necessary management for making the smoking spirit of Libavius is not very troublesome or difficult This operation is much easier than the distillation of very smoking spirit of salt by means of vitriolic acid, from the greater elasticity and expansive force of the vapors of the latter

For the distillation of the smoking spirit of Libavius, the tin is previously amalgamated with mercury, because in this state it is much more easily miscible with corrosive sublimate If the distillation be continued, and the heat encreased, after the butter of tin, or the concrete part of the combination of tin with marine acid, has risen, the mercury revived from the corrosive sublimate may be obtained *See* ACID (MARINE), TIN, MERCURY, *and* CORROSIVE SUBLIMATE

CCCCXVII LIQUOR (MINERAL ANODYNE) *of* HOFFMAN This composition, which is used in medicine only, is a mixture of very rectified spirit of wine, of ether, and of a little of the sweet oil of vitriol This liquor is made by mixing an ounce of the spirit of wine which rises first in the distillation of ether, with as much of the liquor, and afterwards by dissolving in this mixture, which rises next, and which contains the ether, twelve drops of the oil which rises after the ether has passed This is what is called the mineral anodyne liquor of Hoffman It has precisely the same virtues as the ether, which physicians now begin to substitute for it As ether and oil of spirit of wine is now made from the nitrous, marine, and acetous acids, liquors may be made from these, in imitation of that of Hoffman from the vitriolic acid *See* ETHERS

CCCCXVIII LITHARGE Litharge is lead deprived of great part of its phlogiston by fire, and is in a state of imperfect vitrification

When silver is refined by cupellation with lead, this latter metal, which is scorified, and causes the scorification of the imperfect metals allayed with the silver, is transformed into a matter composed of small semi-transparent shining plates, resembling mica, which is litharge Litharge is more or less white or red, according to the metals with which the silver was allayed. The white is called *litharge of silver*, and the red is called *litharge of gold*

Litharge may be easily revived into lead, accordingly much of that which is produced by refining in great is reduced, by being melted upon burning coals The part of it which is least altered by mixture with other metals is thus reduced, and by this method good and saleable lead is obtained The rest of the litharge of these refineries is sold and used for various purposes Potters use much of it for glazing their ware It is employed for the preparation of some plasters, and other external remedies, and also in painting, to render linseed oil drying Lastly, it is added in the composition of some glasses, for it is very fusible, and assists the fusion of other substances It has in general the same properties as the other calxes of lead All the litharge which is commonly sold comes from refineries The quantity formed there is more than is sufficient for the demand, and therefore it is not prepared purposely. *See* REFINING *and* LEAD.

CCCCXIX. LIVER *of* ANTIMONY. Liver of antimony results from the detonation of antimony with an equal weight of nitre. These two matters reduced into powder are to be mixed together, and put into a large crucible. The matter is then to be kindled, and the detonation to be made. When it has detonated, it is to be kept in fusion and then cooled. When the crucible is broken, at the bottom two distinct matters are found, which may be separated from each other by the stroke of a hammer. The upper matter is a saline scoria, nearly of the same nature as the scoria of the regulus of antimony. This is a true antimoniated liver of sulphur, mixed with a certain quantity of vitriolated tartar. The lower matter is heavier. It is opake, compact, red, and brittle. This is the liver of antimony. Its colour and appearance have been supposed similar to those of the livers of animals, and thence it has received its name.

Liver of antimony is principally composed of the metallic part of antimony, half deprived of its sulphur, and dephlogisticated by nitre.

Some chemists consider the liver of antimony as an antimoniated liver of sulphur. Others affirm, that it is only the metallic earth of antimony, melted, by means of a remaining part of sulphur and phlogiston, into a substance the nature of which is intermediate betwixt those of antimony and of glass of antimony. It may possibly be sometimes in one state, and sometimes in the other, according as the matter has been more or less long in the fire, and more or less well fused. The true nature of this substance may easily be ascertained by a proper examination. But this preparation, which was considered as important when antimonial remedies were first introduced, deserves at present little notice. For it is not of any use in what is properly called Chemistry; and it is no longer employed in Medicine, since kermes mineral and emetic tartar have been introduced, which are remedies superior to all other antimonials from the certainty of their effects, when they are well prepared, and by which all the effects obtainable by any preparation of antimony may be obtained, by giving them separately or conjunctly in different proportions, according to the indications to be answered. *See* ANTIMONY, KERMES MINERAL, *and* TARTAR (EMETIC).

CCCCXX. LIVER *of* ARSENIC. Liver of arsenic is a combination of white arsenic with liquid fixed vegetable alkali, or by the humid way. Arsenic has in general a strong disposition to unite with alkalis. Mr Macquer, in his Memoirs upon Arsenic, mentions a singular kind of neutral salt, which results from the union of arsenic with the alkaline basis of nitre, when nitre is decomposed, and its acid is disengaged in close vessels, by means of arsenic. To this salt he has given the name of *neutral arsenical salt*. See that article. The liver of arsenic mentioned also by that chemist, although composed, like the neutral arsenical salt, of arsenic and fixed alkali, is nevertheless very different from that salt.

The operation for making liver of arsenic is easy and simple. To strong and concentrated liquid fixed alkali, previously heated, fine powder of white arsenic must be added. This arsenic easily disappears and dissolves, and as much of it is to be added till the alkali is saturated, or has lost its alkaline properties, although

although it is still capable of dissolving more arsenic superabundantly While the alkali dissolves the arsenic in this operation, it acquires a brownish color, and a singular and disagreeable smell, which however is not the smell of pure arsenic heated and volatilized Lastly, this mixture becomes more and more thick, and at length of a gluey consistence This matter is not crystallizable as the neutral arsenical salt is It is easily decomposed by the action of fire, which separates the arsenic. This does not happen to the arsenical salt Lastly, any pure acid is capable of separating arsenic from the liver of arsenic, in the same manner as they separate sulphur from liver of sulphur whereas the neutral arsenical salt cannot be decomposed but by means of the united affinities of acids and metallic substances Thus we see that arsenic may be combined with fixed alkali in two very different manners

The author has given to this combination the name of *liver of arsenic*, to distinguish it from the neutral arsenical salt, and in imitation of the name of the *liver of sulphur*, given to the combination of the fixed alkali with sulphur *See* ARSENIC *and* NEUTRAL ARSENICAL SALT

CCCCXXI LIVER *of* SULPHUR The liver of sulphur is the combination of sulphur with alkaline matters Ordinary liver of sulphur, or the combination of sulphur with fixed alkali, may be made either in the dry or humid way

To make liver of sulphur by the dry way, or by fusion, equal parts of fixed alkali and sulphur are mixed together This mixture is to be put into a crucible, and it is to be quickly fused to avoid the dissipation and combustion of the sulphur A strong heat, however, is not necessary, because the sulphur easily melts and facilitates the fusion of the alkali When this mixture is perfectly fused, it is to be poured upon a greased stone, and then the liver of sulphur congeals and acquires a brown color If it be required to be kept dry, it must be quickly broken in pieces, and put while it is yet hot into a bottle which is to be well corked, because it readily imbibes moisture from the air

To make liver of sulphur in the humid way, concentrated liquid fixed alkali and fine powder of sulphur are to be boiled together, till the alkali has dissolved all that it can the liquor is then to be filtrated and evaporated. This second method of making liver of sulphur is not much used, because it is longer and less advantageous than the former

Liver of sulphur is an important combination in chemistry, because it is in general a very powerful solvent This compound partakes, according to the general rule, of the properties of the two substances which enter into its combination The sulphur, by its union with the alkali, appears less volatile, less combustible than when alone, and may be entirely dissolved in water by the intervention of this alkali, and also this alkali, saturated with sulphur, shews less of its alkaline properties

As sulphur is composed of vitriolic acid and phlogiston, we may doubt to which of these its union with the fixed alkali is to be attributed But if we attend to the properties of liver of sulphur, we shall perceive that the sulphur is in all its substance combined with the alkali, and adheres to it by both its principles In fact, if we dissolve liver of sulphur in water, and pour into this solution any acid, the liver of sulphur will be instantly decomposed by this acid, which will unite with the alkali, and separate from it the sulphur in form of a white

white powder but this powder, when dried and examined, appears to be sulphur, such as it was before

Although vitriolic acid which is contained in sulphur be in general the strongest acid, the sulphur is nevertheless separated from the alkali by any acid, even by the weakest, as vinegar This phenomenon is another proof of what we have advanced concerning the manner in which sulphur is combined with alkali, for if the union of the inflammable principle of the sulphur did not considerably oppose the adhesion which the acid of this sulphur is capable of contracting with fixed alkali, the weaker acids certainly could not separate it *These effects may be explained by this general principle that the less simple any bodies are, the less strongly they are capable of adhering to other bodies*

The liver of sulphur exhibits also another phenomenon worthy of attention, and which depends also, as we shall see, on the same principle It is, that the connexion betwixt the phlogiston and the acid is much less in sulphur united to an alkali than in pure sulphur This is proved by the smell of the liver of sulphur, which is very strong and very fetid, even when it is not heated, while sulphur, not heated, has scarcely any smell

This smell of the liver of sulphur, which resembles much the smell of eggs beginning to putrify, becomes much stronger when it is decomposed by an acid It is certainly occasioned by an evaporation of part of the phlogiston of the sulphur, for it produces exactly all the effects of the inflammable principle when reduced into vapor, or when it disengages itself from bodies without burning It particularly affects the brain and nervous system, and causes stupefaction, intoxication, syncopes, and when in large quantity is even capable of instantly killing men and animals These are the same effects which are produced by the vapors of charcoal, and of substances undergoing the spirituous or putrid fermentations Mr Cartheuser, talking of the manner of decomposing sulphur with an alkali, to obtain from it the acid without sensible combustion, according to Stahl's process, expressly remarks, that the vapor which exhales during this operation affects the head, and causes stupefaction I know a chemist who, when he was decomposing at once a large quantity of liver of sulphur by an acid, was struck by the vapor so as to fall down and faint

Further, the emanations of liver of sulphur, which are nothing else than pure phlogiston reduced into vapor, and which must be distinguished from the vapor of burning sulphur, which are phlogisticated vitriolic acid, these emanations, I say, of liver of sulphur are easily applied to any body capable of receiving the inflammable principle, and combine more or less intimately with these bodies, according to their nature and actual state If silver, for example, be exposed to the vapor of liver of sulphur, or if it be immersed in a heated solution of liver of sulphur, the surface of this metal becomes tarnished and blackened by the phlogistic emanations, with which it readily is impregnated superabundantly Also, if solutions of silver, mercury, lead, or bismuth, be precipitated by liver of sulphur, all these precipitates, instead of being white, as they would have been if a pure alkali had been used, are rendered brown, black, or leaden colored, by the phlogiston which attaches itself to them hence *solutions of these metals become sympathetic inks*, which may be rendered visible by liver of sulphur, or by its vapor, and hence liver of sulphur may be successfully employed to discover lead contained in adulterated wine,

wine, and reciprocally, these metals, their solutions or calxes, may be properly applied to discover sulphur in mineral waters or other liquors See Ink (Sympathetic), Waters (Mineral), and Wine

We must observe, that in this application of the phlogiston of liver of sulphur to most metallic calxes, this phlogiston, although transmitted either in vapor, or by the humid way without fusion, combines nevertheless so intimately with these metallic earths as to revive them, and to restore to them all their metallic properties This truth, though long ago known to chemists, was alluded to by Mr Rouelle the younger, who, in the Medical Gazette, proposes this reduction in form of a problem, as a very great novelty The chemist who replied, judiciously used litharge to make this reduction visible, because this preparation of lead being in molecules or scales, which present surfaces very smooth and sufficiently large, is very proper to shew the metallic color and brilliancy which the litharge instantly assumes, when it is immersed even in a cold solution of liver of sulphur See Reduction

All these properties of liver of sulphur shew very clearly, that the adhesion of the phlogiston to the acid in sulphur is greatly diminished by the union of sulphur with alkali, and as the phlogiston is infinitely more volatile than the acid, it may therefore be more easily separated from the liver of sulphur The smell and emanations of liver of sulphur shew, that its inflammable principle is continually dissipating We may therefore consider sulphur, formed into liver of sulphur, as gradually decomposing, particularly when it is dissolved in water Accordingly, if we preserve liquid liver of sulphur in an open vessel, the quantity of sulphur diminishes more and more, and the liver of sulphur gradually changes into vitriolated tartar

We may form an explanation of this diminution of the connexion of the principles of sulphur in the liver of sulphur, if we suppose that all bodies have only a certain determinate degree of force by which they adhere to each other, which is very probable, and is even shewn by all the phenomena of chemistry, and if we suppose, in the second place, that in sulphur the phlogiston and acid have exhausted upon each other all their force or tendency or of combination Upon these suppositions, these two principles are either incapable of combining with a third body, as with the alkali, or if they combine with it, this new union must lessen the force of the former union, and this accordingly appears to be the reason why the simplest bodies are those which contract the strongest union See Affinity, Aggregation Combination, and Solution

Liver of sulphur is a great solvent of metallic matters, all which, excepting zinc, it attacks, particularly in fusion It seems to dissolve gold more effectually than other metals See Gold This compound dissolves also vegetable coals, even by the humid way, according to the observation of Mr Rouelle the younger This solution is of a green color, and when liver of sulphur has dissolved charcoal by fusion, it becomes of a much deeper red color than when pure, as may be observed in the making of artificial sulphur in Stahl's manner

Particular kinds of liver of sulphur may be formed by the combination of volatile alkali, of quicklime, or of absorbent earths, all which attack sulphur more or less The properties of these livers of sulphur may be referred to those of the

the ordinary one, but they have not been examined so much as they ought to be See SULPHUR

CCCCXXII LIXIVIAL Those salts are called lixivial which have been extracted by lixiviation, and these chiefly are fixed alkalis, which are therefore called *lixivial salts* See ALKALI

CCCCXXIII LUNA CORNEA This name is given to the combination of marine acid with silver Marine acid has in general a great affinity with metals, and particularly with those called *white*, or *lunar*, or *mercurial metals* Of these silver is the chief Marine acid can scarcely dissolve these metals in the ordinary methods They must be generally much divided, or the acid must be much concentrated, reduced into vapors, and assisted with a considerable degree of heat, to accomplish the solution This is particularly true as to silver and mercury But when these metals are previously dissolved in nitrous acid, then the marine acid, which has a stronger affinity with them than the nitrous has, seizes them quickly, separates them from the nitrous acid, and forms with them a new combination

To make this combination with silver, it is first dissolved in nitrous acid To this solution marine acid, or more commonly common salt dissolved in water, is to be added The mixture soon becomes turbid, and in it a copious precipitate is formed, which has always the appearance of curd The solution of salt is thus added till no more precipitate is formed The precipitate, when separated from the supernatant liquor, is called *luna cornea*

Marine acid has so great an affinity with silver, that it overcharges itself in some measure with the metal in this precipitation Luna cornea is much less soluble in water than the combinations of other metals with this acid This little solubility of luna cornea is the cause of its appearing in the form of a precipitate

The adhesion of the marine acid with silver is very strong in luna cornea If this matter be exposed alone to fire, the acid carries off with it a portion of the silver, although this metal be very fixed The remaining matter melts, and takes the form of a horn-like substance, as all chemists say, and hence it has been called luna cornea Some differences must occur in combining marine acid with silver, according to the manner in which it is done, and particularly according to the proportion of the two substances

Luna cornea is not employed either in medicine or in the arts *(l)*, and is even little used in chemistry, excepting for particular operations and researches This precipitation is very convenient for example, in the examination of mineral waters, or of any other liquor, to discover if they contain marine acid in whatever base it be engaged, excepting metallic bases, for if these waters contain the smallest quantity of marine acid, a luna cornea will be precipitated by

(l) Luna cornea mixed with sea-salt and tartar rubbed on brass, gives a silver-like appearance, and is the substance employed for the silvering of the dial-plates for clocks A more substantial silvering may be given by the above mixture, if the piece of brass to be silvered be previously heated considerably, and cleaned with a scratch-brush, and if the operation be repeated till the silver seems to be sufficiently thick The brass, having a stronger disposition to unite with the marine acid than the silver has, separates it from this latter metal, which is then precipitated upon the surface of the brass plate

them

them from a ſolution of ſilver in nitrous acid, and this luna cornea is eaſily known by its curd-like appearance *See* WATERS (MINERAL)

We may eaſily perceive that when the marine acid, which forms the luna cornea, is engaged in a baſis, it muſt quit its baſis to combine with the ſilver, and then the nitrous acid, which was united with the ſilver, is now diſengaged, and joins itſelf to the ſubſtance with which the marine acid was firſt united, ſo that two decompoſitions take place, from which two combinations reſult Thus, when luna cornea is made with a ſolution of common ſalt, the liquor after the operation contains ſome cubic nitre, and if marine ſalt with an earthy baſis was uſed, it would be transformed, in this operation, into a nitre with an earthy baſis

The beſt method of ſeparating ſilver from marine acid, or, as the chemiſts ſay, of reducing luna cornea, is to mix it very accurately, and to melt it in a crucible, with a very large quantity of ſome fixed alkali but the heat muſt be very gradually applied till the ebullition and ſwelling, which are cauſed by the action of the fixed alkali and marine acid, have ceaſed, then the heat is to be encreaſed, and the matter is to be thoroughly fuſed, after which, the ſilver is found revived at the bottom of the crucible This ſilver is juſtly eſteemed to be the pureſt of all, when the ſeveral operations have been well made But the luna cornea cannot eaſily be reduced without loſs, becauſe it is apt to evaporate partly, and even to paſs through crucibles *See* ACID (MARINE), *and* SILVER *

CCCCXXIV LUTE In many chemical operations, the veſſels muſt be covered with ſomething to preſerve them from the violence of the fire, from being broken or melted, and alſo to cloſe exactly their joinings to each other, to retain the ſubſtances which they contain, when they are volatile and reduced to vapor For this purpoſe, ſeveral matters are employed, called in general *lutes*

The lutes with which glaſs and earthen-ware retorts are covered ought to be compoſed of nearly equal parts of coarſe ſand and refractory clay Theſe matters are to be well mixed with water and a little hair, ſo as to form a liquid paſte, with which veſſels are to be covered, layer upon layer, till it is of the required thickneſs

The ſand mixed with the clay is neceſſary in this lute, to prevent the cracks which are occaſioned by the contracting of clay during its drying, which it always does when it is pure. The hair ſerves alſo to bind the parts of the lute,

* Mr. Margraaf has made experiments to diſcover the beſt method of reducing luna cornea, which he found to be the following Diſſolve half an ounce of fine ſilver in aqua fortis, precipitate it by ſea-ſalt, and edulcorate the precipitate, which will then weigh five drams and ſixteen grains For the reduction of this precipitate, mix it with an ounce and a half of dry volatile ſal ammoniac, triturate them well together with a little water during a quarter of an hour, then add three ounces of mercury obtained from cinnabar by means of quicklime, and continue to triturate during ſome hours with a little more water Thus an amalgam will be formed, which being waſhed from a white powder and dried, will weigh three ounces and half a dram By diſtillation of this amalgam, a reſiduum of ſilver, four grains leſs than the original half-ounce, will be obtained. By ſubliming the white powder, which weighs five drams, three grains of ſilver will be obtained but if the amalgam and white powder be together diſtilled, the operation will fail, and the luna cornea be recompoſed. *See* BERLIN MEMOIRS, 1749

and to keep it applied to the vessel for, notwithstanding the sand which is introduced into it, some cracks are always formed, which occasion pieces of it to tumble off

The lutes with which the joinings of vessels are closed, are of different kinds, according to the nature of the operations to be made, and of the substances to be distilled in these vessels

When vapors of watery liquors, and such as are not corrosive, are to be contained, it is sufficient to surround the joining of the receiver to the nose of the alembic, or of the retort, with slips of paper or of linen, covered with flour-paste In such cases also slips of wet bladder are very conveniently used

When more penetrating and dissolving vapors are to be contained, a lute is to be employed of quicklime slaked in the air, and beat into a liquid paste with whites of eggs This paste is to be spread upon linen slips, which is to be applied exactly to the joining of the vessels This lute is very convenient, easily dries, becomes solid, and sufficiently firm

Lastly, when saline, acid, and corrosive vapors are to be contained, we must then have recourse to the lute called *fat lute* This lute is made by forming into a paste some dried clay, finely powdered, sifted through a silken searce, and moistened with water, and then by beating this paste well in a mortar with boiled linseed oil, that is, oil which has been rendered drying by litharge dissolved in it, and fit for the use of painters This lute easily takes and retains the form given to it It is generally rolled into cylinders of a convenient size These are to be applied, by flattening them, to the joinings of the vessels, which ought to be perfectly dry, because the least moisture would prevent the lute from adhering. When the joinings are well closed with this fat lute, the whole is to be covered with slips of linen spread with lute of lime and whites of eggs These slips are to be fastened with pack-thread The second lute is necessary to keep on the fat lute, because this latter remains soft, and does not become solid enough to stick on alone

CCCCXXV

M.

CCCCXXV MACERATION Maceration is the steeping of bodies in a cold liquor, to soften, penetrate, and open them, or even to dissolve some principle of them This operation is essentially the same as digestion, and only differs in this, that it requires no more than the heat of the atmosphere Maceration is preferable to digestion, whenever heat is useless or hurtful to the operation For instance, when hard and woody aromatic vegetable matters are to be steeped, with intention to soften and open them, to extract afterwards more easily from them their essential oil, they ought to be macerated without heat, and not digested, considering that the smallest heat is capable of dissipating a great part of the spiritus rector, which ought always to be preserved as much as is possible, since it ameliorates the essential oil, and encreases its quantity

CCCCXXVI MADDER (*m*)

CCCCXXVII MAGISTERY This name is given to almost all precipitates Thus magistery and precipitate are frequently synonimous but lately chemists have chiefly used the term precipitate, and applied that of magistery to some particular precipitates only, which are used in medicine and in the arts Such are the magisteries of bismuth, coral, crabs-eyes, sulphur, &c *See* PRECIPITATION *and* PRECIPITATE

CCCCXXVIII MAGISTERY *of* BISMUTH The magistery of bismuth is the calx of that semi-metal, separated from the nitrous acid by water alone, and well washed

To make this preparation, very pure bismuth must be dissolved in nitrous acid, which must also be very pure To this solution when a very large quantity of clear water is added, the whole is rendered turbid and milky, and a

(*m*) MADDER The root of madder impregnates water with a dull red color, and spirit of wine with a deep bright red This root, when eat by animals along with their food, tinges their urine, and their most solid bones, of a deep red Wool, previously boiled in a solution of alum and tartar, receives from a hot decoction of madder and tartar a very durable, but not a very beautiful red color

very beautiful and ſhining white ſediment is afterwards formed. The ſupernatant liquor is then to be decanted, the ſediment is to be put upon a paper filter, and more pure water is to be added, till it comes off quite inſipid. The ſediment, which is the magiſtery of biſmuth, ought to be carefully dried, and kept in a well cloſed bottle

Biſmuth is one of thoſe metallic ſubſtances which are partly ſeparated from acids by dilution with much water, and which cannot be kept diſſolved but by acids concentrated to a certain point, or when the acid is more than is ſufficient to ſaturate the metal By the dilution of the acid, then, this operation is performed The precipitate is very white, both becauſe a ſmall portion of acid remains united with it, which the water cannot take from it, and becauſe the nitrous acid has taken from the biſmuth moſt of its phlogiſton

As biſmuth reſembles lead in many of its properties, ſome chemiſts obſerving that by mixing a ſolution of common ſalt with a ſolution of biſmuth in the nitrous acid, a white precipitate is formed, which alſo happens to ſolutions of ſilver and of lead, believed that in this precipitation the marine acid united with the biſmuth, and formed a *biſmuthum corneum* But Mr Pott, although he had been himſelf of this opinion, has ſhewn that the precipitation is cauſed merely by the water in which the common ſalt is diſſolved, ſince, when the ſolutions of biſmuth and of common ſalt contain the ſmalleſt poſſible quantity of water, no precipitation reſults from their mixture Biſmuth, therefore, differs eſſentially from lead in this reſpect

The chief uſe of the magiſtery of biſmuth is to enter into the compoſition of white paint uſed by ladies It is preferred to all other whites from its ſuperior beauty, its luſtre, and an almoſt inſenſible tint of carnation, which renders it more ſimilar to the fineſt and whiteſt ſkin

This advantage, which is very great, is counterbalanced by great faults. The ſkin is ſaid to be conſiderably ſpoiled by a continued uſe of it, it is alſo very apt to acquire a blackiſh color. Metallic ſubſtances and their calxes are known to be very apt to be impregnated with phlogiſton, when it touches them while it is in vapor, or in any other ſtate favorable to combination By this means, whether they recover a part of the phlogiſton of which they have been deprived, or whether they receive it ſuperabundantly, they always acquire dark and blackiſh tints But of all metallic calxes, that of biſmuth is one of the moſt ſuſceptible of this effect its fine white becomes brown, and even leaden-colored, by a very ſlight expoſition to the phlogiſtic vapors, ſuch as the exhalations from houſes of office, from garlic, eggs, and particularly from liver of ſulphur For this reaſon the white of biſmuth muſt be kept in well cloſed bottles, otherwiſe it would be injured by circulating vapors which pervade paper coverings From this property of biſmuth, it is rendered capable of affording a kind of ſympathetic ink. *See* INK (SYMPATHETIC)

Some artiſts prepare magiſtery of biſmuth by precipitating it from its ſolution in the nitrous acid, by a fixed alkali But this method does not produce ſo good a white as the precipitation by water alone. The cauſe of this alſo is, that the calx of biſmuth very eaſily recovers its phlogiſton. Alkalis, however pure, always contain ſome ſuperabundant inflammable matter, and apply it to the metallic calxes which are precipitated, and particularly to the calx of

biſmuth,

bismuth, which becomes more brown in proportion to the greater quantity which it takes of this inflammable matter See BISMUTH

CCCCXXIX. MAGISTERY *of* CORAL, CRABS-EYES, &c Coral, crabs-eyes, pearl, shells, chalk, and other substances of that kind, are all absorbent and calcareous earths, easily soluble in nitrous acid, with which they form a nitre with an earthy basis. If the solutions of these matters be treated like the mother-water of nitre, that is, if they are precipitated by a fixed alkali, and afterwards well washed, all these earths will be obtained in a very divided state The name of magistery is then given to them, together with the name of the substance which has been dissolved and precipitated All these magisteries are nothing else but absorbent earths, which differ little from each other, or from magnesia For the method of preparing these magisteries *see* MAGNESIA.

CCCCXXX. MAGNESIA ALBA Magnesia is a white earth precipitated from the mother-waters of nitre and of common salt by a fixed alkali It ought afterwards to be well edulcorated, to deprive it of all the saline particles it might retain.

To make magnesia, the mother-water of nitre, or of common salt, is placed in a large vessel, and diluted with a considerable quantity of common water; then a liquid fixed alkali is gradually poured upon it, and the mixture is to be agitated, which presently becomes turbid, and of a white milky color In this manner alkali is to be added at different times, till no more precipitate is perceived, the liquor is to be further diluted with common water, if that be necessary for facilitating the earthy sediment when this sediment is all formed, the liquor is to be decanted from it it is then to be poured upon a filter of brown paper, supported by a cloth pure water is poured upon it, till it is no longer capable of giving any taste to the water the earth is then to be formed into troches or cakes, and left to dry This is *magnesia*

The mother-waters of nitre and of common salt are almost entirely composed, the former of nitre and sea-salt with earthy bases, and the latter of sea-salt with an earthy basis. *See* WATERS (MOTHER), NITRE, NITRE *with* EARTHY BASIS, WATER *of the* SEA *and* SALT FOUNTAINS, SALT (COMMON), SALT (SEA) *with* EARTHY BASIS These salts are composed of nitrous and marine acids saturated with a calcareous earth, and are very deliquescent They therefore do not crystallize, and great quantities of them remain dissolved in the last portions of liquor from which no more crystals can be obtained. Fixed alkalis being capable of decomposing all salts with earthy bases, and of separating their earth, do actually separate it in the present operation Magnesia is then nothing else than a very much divided calcareous earth It is employed in medicine as an absorbent earth, and is a very good one, from the fineness of its parts.

The mother-waters from which magnesia is to be precipitated, must necessarily be diluted in a very large quantity of water, because the absorbent earth dissolved by the nitrous and marine acids, is there in so large a quantity, that when an alkali is added to it without dilution, no precipitation seems at first to take place The molecules of earth, not being capable of moving freely and of joining each other, do not form sensible molecules, and remain almost in the same state in which they were when they adhered to acids. But the separation

ration is nevertheless made, and so copiously, that the water of the mixture is found to be in too small a quantity, and that the whole becomes solid. This almost solid coagulation, which happens when two very fluid liquors are mixed, astonishes persons who do not understand the reason of it. It has accordingly been called the chemical miracle, *miraculum chemicum*. To prevent this coagulation, and to allow the earth to depolite itself, a sufficient quantity of water must be added.

After the precipitation is made, neutral salts with bases of fixed alkali remain in the liquor, which differ according to the kinds of acids which formed the salts with earthy bases, and according to the nature of the alkali employed for this decomposition. Thus, if the mineral fixed alkali had been employed, the neutral salt formed in the mother water of sea-salt will be common salt, and the neutral salt formed by that alkali in the mother-water of nitre will be cubic nitre. If a fixed vegetable alkali has been employed, from the mother-water of common salt, the febrifugal salt of Sylvius may be obtained, and from the mother-water of nitre, not only that febrifugal salt, but also ordinary nitre may be obtained.

Hence, if magnesia be made in a very large quantity, the water, after the precipitate has been procured, ought not to be thrown away, as from it much good nitre and common salt may be obtained, according to the kind of mother-water employed. To obtain nitre, fixed vegetable alkali ought to be used, and to obtain common salt, the mineral alkali: the liquor is then to be evaporated, and crystals of these salts will be formed.

If the magnesia is not washed, it contains much of these salts. In that case, it would not be a simple absorbent, but would partake of the virtues of these salts. It would even be purgative in a certain dose: but as the quantity of salts which remains is always uncertain, when we intend that the magnesia shall contain any, it ought to be prepared in the ordinary method, and afterwards such doses of these salts as we shall judge proper may be added to it.

Some artists prepare magnesia without precipitation by an alkali. Their method is by evaporating the mother-water, and calcining the residuum in a crucible, to dissipate the acids: but this method is improper, because the magnesia by calcination acquires the property of quicklime.

If, instead of pouring fixed alkali into the mother-water, vitriolic acid be mixed with it, and if the mother-water has not been diluted with common water, a large quantity of a very white precipitate will be formed in it. Some authors have improperly called this precipitate magnesia, but it is of a very different nature from the earth properly so called. *(n)*

(n) This substance, distinguished by the name *magnesia alba*, from the dark-colored mineral called also *magnesia*, or *manganese*, has been accurately examined by Dr Black. The experiments of that excellent chemist on this subject are related in the second vol. of the *Essays Philosophical and Literary*, published at Edinburgh. From these we learn the following results. 1. Magnesia is soluble with effervescence in vitriolic, nitrous, marine, and acetous acids. With vitriolic acid it formed crystals similar in all respects to those of the salt called *Epsom-salt*. With nitrous acid it formed crystals, which deliquiated in a moist air. With marine acid it did not form crystals, but the saline matter being evaporated to dryness, soon deliquiated by exposure to air. With distilled vinegar it formed no crystals by evaporation, but a saline mass, which, when warm,

The sediment formed by adding vitriolic acid, far from being a pure calcareous earth, consists of that earth which this acid takes from the nitrous and marine acids, and forms with it a selenites This selenites appears as a precipitate, because, as it is very little soluble in water, it cannot be all suspended or dissolved in the liquor but if a large quantity of water, especially hot water, be added, this pretended magnesia either does not appear, or afterwards disappears by being again dissolved This precipitate is not applied to any use See SELENITES

CCCCXXXI MAGNESIA (o)

warm, was viscid, resembling glue in color and consistence, and when cold, was brittle 2 By calcination, it lost ⅞ of its weight When calcined, it did not effervesce with acids, whence the substance lost by calcination was chiefly fixable air This air, and almost all its weight lost by calcination, was restored to it by solution in vitriolic acid, and precipitation from thence by a mild fixed alkali, the air of which it absorbed 3 By the last mentioned properties (2) it seemed analogous to calcareous earths, but differed from these earths, in the nature of the salts formed by it with acids (1), and also in other properties, but especially in this, that even when calcined, it was not soluble in water The Author of the Dictionary, therefore, improperly calls it a calcareous earth, this name being applicable to such earths only as are convertible into quicklime 4 It was precipitated from acids by volatile alkali 5 When uncalcined, it precipitated calcareous earth from acids When calcined, or otherwise deprived of air, it did not precipitate these earths hence its attraction to acids is not greater than that of these earths, but the cause of the former precipitation was this, that the sum of the forces which tended to join the calcareous earth with the fixable air of the magnesia, and the magnesia with the acid, was greater than the sum of the forces which tended to join the calcareous earth with the acid, and the magnesia with the fixable air 6 When uncalcined, or united with air, it precipitated lime from lime-water, which shews, that the calcareous earth had a stronger power to combine with fixable air than magnesia had, since the former earth took this air from the latter earth, by which means the former was rendered mild and unsoluble in water, and therefore was precipitated. This property suggested to Dr Alston a method of procuring sweet water at sea, by adding magnesia to water, the putrefaction of which had been prevented by the previous addition of quicklime 7 By distillation of three ounces of magnesia, five drams of water, containing some small portion of volatile alkali, were obtained

(o) MAGNESIA, or MANGANESE, is commonly considered as an ore of iron, but the experiments of Mr Pott and Mr Cronstedt shew, that this stone contains little or no iron, and therefore the latter author has made a distinct order of this earth, which he calls *terra magnesiæ* Its colors are dark-grey, black, red, or white Its texture is striated, or with concentric fibres, or indeterminate It has the following properties 1 It does not effervesce with acids, they, however, dissolve some part of it, especially when it is calcined spirit of vitriol acquires from it a rose color aqua regia also acquires color, especially from the black kind From these solutions fixed alkalis precipitate a white earth 2 A small quantity of this earth, mixed with glass frit, gives red or purplish colors to the glass By continuing the fusion, these colors disappear, and also other tinges which the glass may have accidentally received, hence it is used to produce colorless glass Larger quantities of it are added when a deep purple glass is required It is also used to give a glazing to pottery 3 Fused with nitre or with fixed alkali, it gives to warm water various colors, green, purple, red, or blue, which change by agitating the water 4 Cronstedt affirms, that it deflagrates with nitre Pott says, it does not 5 Cronstedt says, that he has sometimes extracted a small portion of tin from magnesia 6 The same author affirms, that the colors given by magnesia to glass are easily destroyed by calces of arsenic or of tin. Whence does its property

CCCCXXXII M A G N E T. *(p)*

CCCCXXXIII. M A L T. The grain is ſo called which has been made to germinate, and afterwards dried, ſo as to become fit for the ſpirituous fermentation, or for making beer. *See* BEER.

CCCCXXXIV. M A N N A. *See* SUGAR.

CCCCXXXV. M A R B L E. *(q)*

CCCCXXXVI. M A R C A S I T E. This name has long been given indifferently to all ſorts of minerals, to ores, pyrites, and to ſemi-metals. Lately it ſeems to be confined to pyrites, and Mr Wallerius propoſes to apply it only to ſuch pyrites as are regularly formed. This ſeems to be better than to leave it a vague and indeterminate ſignification, from the ambiguity and obſcurity which might thereby be introduced. *See* PYRITES.

CCCCXXXVII. M A R L E. *(r)*

CCCCXXXVIII. M A R S is the name of a planet which chemiſts have given to iron, and which is ſtill much uſed in medicine and chemiſtry. *See* IRON.

CCCCXXXIX. M A S T I C. *(s)*

CCCCXL. M A T R A S S. A matraſs is a bottle with a neck more or leſs long, uſed in chemiſtry for making digeſtions and macerations. Matraſſes are alſo uſed as receivers. Their form is different, ſome of them being ſpherical, which is the ordinary ſhape, others flattened at the bottom, called *matraſſes with a flat bottom*, and others having the figure of an egg, which laſt kind are called *philoſophical eggs*. Theſe matraſſes are choſen according to the operations intended. The moſt convenient of all, when we do not mean to operate on a large quantity of matter, are bottles of thin glaſs, known by the name of *medical phials*; becauſe theſe phials are very cheap, are made of good glaſs, and may be quickly heated, ſo that the liquor contained ſhall boil without danger of being broken. This advantage they owe to their thinneſs. Such phials are very uſeful in a laboratory, and therefore a number of them ought always to be kept there. *See* VESSELS.

of tinging glaſs proceed? Does it contain any of the known volatile metallic ſubſtances, or a new ſemi-metal?

(p) MAGNET. Magnets are iron-ores, from which a conſiderable portion of iron may be extracted. Neuman ſays, that they are almoſt totally ſoluble in ſpirit of nitre, and partially in the vitriolic and marine acids.

(q) MARBLES. All thoſe calcareous ſtones are ſo called, which are hard, which have a compact texture, are capable of receiving a fine poliſh, and which are conſidered as beautiful. For their properties, *ſee* EARTHS (CALCAREOUS).

(r) MARLE is an earth compoſed of different proportions of argillaceous and of calcareous earths. Its properties vary in degree according to the proportions of theſe earths. Marles effervesce with acids, which property they receive from the calcareous earth. They are fuſible by fire, as all mixtures of theſe two earths are. By a leſs heat, if the calcareous earth predominates, they are calcinable into a kind of quicklime, and if the clay predominates, they may be changed by fire into hard maſſes capable of ſtriking ignited ſparks from ſteel.

(s) MASTIC is a reſin almoſt totally ſoluble in ſpirit of wine, but not at all in water. It becomes ſoft and tough, like wax, by being chewed. It is uſed as an ingredient in varniſhes.

CCCCXLI

CCCCXLI MATRIX (*t*)

CCCCXLII MATT Ores not perfectly deprived of their sulphur, when fused, are called *matt* It is obtained in the first fusion for the extraction of metal from some ores. *See* SMELTING *of* ORES

CCCCXLIII. MENSTRUUM. Menstruum is a word synonimous with solvent *See* SOLUTION

CCCCXLIV MERCURY Mercury is the name of a planet, which is also given to the metallic substance called *quick-silver* But as mercury is the most general name, we shall here relate the principal properties of this metallic substance.

Mercury is a metallic substance of a shining white appearance, entirely similar to that of silver. It is habitually fluid, and consequently we cannot discover either its ductility or the tenacity of its integrant parts

Its specific gravity is very great next to gold and platina, it is the heaviest of all metallic substances, and even of all known natural bodies It loses about $\frac{1}{15}$ part of its weight in water, and a cubic foot of mercury weighs 947 pounds

Neither air, water, nor the united action of these two elements, appear to make any sensible impression upon mercury, nor is it more susceptible of rust than the perfect metals Its surface tarnishes, nevertheless, to a certain degree, and more quickly than gold and silver, when it is exposed to the air but this is because the dust which floats in the air quickly fixes upon its surface. The watery vapors also which float in the air seem also to be attracted by the mercury

Mercury may easily be cleansed from those extraneous matters which adhere only slightly to it, by making it pass through a new, clean, and close cloth, and afterwards by heating it. When mercury has been thus purified, and is free from all metallic allay, it is considerably fluid A phosphoric light is produced by shaking in the dark such mercury contained in a barometer. Its integrant parts, like those of melted metals, seem mutually to attract each other, and always acquire a convex or spherical form when they touch bodies with which they have no tendency to unite

Mr Lemeri the younger asserts, that mercury loses no weight by being kept in boiling water, and therefore that water dissolves none of it Nevertheless, many good physicians are of opinion, that water which has been boiled upon mercury has the property of killing worms and other insects, from which we may suspect, that some mercurial parts are dissolved by the water, although their quantity is too small to be rendered sensible by a balance These experiments deserve to be repeated with due attention

Mercury, when exposed to fire, presents many remarkable phenomena It seems to suffer no change from a heat that is not superior to that of boiling water With a greater heat it is entirely dissipated in vapors, like other volatile bodies It undergoes no alteration by having been thus reduced into vapor, for if the evaporation be made in close vessels, that is, if the mercury be

(*t*) MATRIX The matrix of ores is the earthy and stony substances in which these metallic matters are generally invelopea These are very various, generally spar, quartz, fluors, or horn-blend. *See note to the article* ORES

distilled, its vapors when condensed will form the same mercury as before the operation Mercury remains unchangeable by repeated distillations Boerhaave distilled 18 ounces of mercury 500 times, without perceiving any other change than that its fluidity and specific gravity were a little encreased, and that some grains of a fixed matter remained which small changes were probably produced by a purification of the mercury, rather than by any real alteration of it The vapors of mercury, like those of all other volatile bodies, if they cannot escape, or be condensed, cause violent explosions Mr Hellot, of the Academy of Sciences, says, that he was present at an experiment of this kind A person pretending to fix mercury had enclosed some of it in an iron box closely welded. When the mercury was heated, it burst the iron box, and dissipated in invisible vapors

By digestion in a strong heat, continued during several months, mercury undergoes a more sensible alteration, its surface being gradually changed into a reddish earthy powder, without any metallic lustre, which floats upon the surface of the fluid mercury, without incorporating with it Thus any quantity of mercury may be entirely converted into a red powder For this purpose only the proper time and vessels are required As mercury, thus changed, resembles a metallic precipitate, and as, for this purpose, no addition is necessary, this preparation is called *mercurius precipitatus per se*, or mercury precipitated by itself.

The strongest heat which mercury can sustain is necessary for the preparation of this precipitate *per se* For Boerhaave, who made long continued experiments upon this substance, with a patience unequalled even by the searchers for the art of making gold, kept mercury in digestion during 15 years, without observing any change, unless that upon its surface a little black powder had formed, which by trituration was easily reducible into fluid mercury *See* PRECIPITATE PER SE

Till lately it was believed that the fluidity of mercury was as essential to it in its natural state as its volatility so that those even who had labored to render it fixed and solid, expected to attain their purpose only by producing a great change upon its nature But at present we are assured that by a sufficient degree of cold it may be rendered solid and malleable like the other metals This truth, which had been conjectured by theoretical chemists, has been lately demonstrated by the Members of the Academy at Petersbourgh These philosophers availed themselves of the intense cold on Dec 25, 1759, which they further encreased by the artificial methods known, and particularly by the mixture of spirit of nitre with snow, till Mr de Lile's thermometer was sunk to the 213th degree They then perceived that the mercury in the thermometer no longer continued to mark the degrees of cold, and suspected that it had lost its fluidity Having broken their thermometer, they found that their mercury was actually consolidated. They repeated this experiment upon other thermometers, and found that it succeeded so completely, that after having broken one of these instruments, they extracted the mercury in a solid state, which resembled a small globe of silver, with a flexible silver wire attached to it They struck this mercurial globe several times with a hammer, and perceived that it was thereby flattened and extended like a ductile metal Mr Poissonnier, Physician of the Faculty of Paris, Physician to the King, and Member of the Academy at Petersbourgh,

Peterſbourgh, who then happened to be in Ruſſia, was preſent, and one of the operators at this important experiment, and was the perſon who firſt ſent a particular account of it to the Academy of Sciences at Paris (u) By this capital experiment it is then well eſtabliſhed and authenticated, that mercury is, like other metals, fluid or ſolid, according to the greater or leſs quantity of fire with which it is penetrated, that if we only ſee it in a fluid ſtate, it is becauſe it is ſo fuſible that ſo ſmall a degree of heat can keep it fluid, that even in the greateſt natural colds, a ſufficient quantity of heat always remains for that purpoſe

This exceeding fuſibility of mercury, and its great volatility, together with its great denſity and gravity, are properties which appear contrary and incompatible, to be found in the ſame body, and ſo eminently In fact, the denſity, gravity, and ſolidity of metals, leave no doubt but that the earthy element enters in a great quantity into their compoſition, and beſides, by the calcination of imperfect metals, this element is in ſome meaſure developed, and rendered ſo ſenſible by eſſential properties, that it undoubtedly makes part of metals. The extreme denſity and gravity of mercury ſeem to prove no leſs evidently that much of the earthy element enters into the compoſition of that ſubſtance But on the other ſide, ſolidity and fixity ſeem to be eſſential properties of the earthy principle How then ſhall we conceive, that a ſubſtance compoſed almoſt entirely of the moſt fixed and refractory principle, ſhould be exceedingly volatile, and perhaps the moſt fuſible of all bodies? This moſt undoubtedly proceeds from the preſence of ſome other principle which is eminently volatile and fuſible But what is this principle? Is it phlogiſton? or that principle which Becker has mentioned, but not aſcertained, and which he calls *mercurial earth?* Is it the union of the inflammable principle and of this mercurial earth? Theſe certainly are objects worthy the curioſity of thoſe who have taſte and talents for the ſublimeſt reſearches in chemiſtry

We proceed now to the other properties of mercury, which it diſcovers when combined with the principal chemical agents.

(u) The validity of this experiment, which ſeems to aſcertain the fixation of mercury by cold, has been queſtioned by counſellor Lehman According to this author, the mercury employed by profeſſor Braun in the recited experiment had been diſtilled in the common method through water, and the water only in that experiment was frozen, but not the mercury He alſo affirms, that having diſtilled mercury without water, and having carefully purified it from all watery particles, he could not congeal the mercury by artificial cold, altho he at the ſame time did congeal common mercury But I think that we muſt aſſent to the fixability of mercury by cold, as affirmed by the academicians of Peterſbourgh, unleſs we diſbelieve what they aſſert concerning the ductility of the mercury thus hardened, which could certainly not be given by the congelation of adhering water

Nevertheleſs, mercury is ſaid to attract powerfully moiſture from the air The exploſions occaſioned by expoſing mercury ſuddenly to heat in cloſe veſſels are ſaid by Mr Rouelle to be produced by water adhering to the mercury The water commonly obtained in diſtilling mercury which has been expoſed to moiſt air, has induced a belief of the convertibility of mercury into water Neuman ſays, that he has obſerved that the weight of mercury was greater in winter than in ſummer Probably this difference proceeded from the mercury having acquired more moiſture from the air in the former than in the latter ſeaſon *See* ENCYCLOP. tom. X. p. 373

Vitriolic acid in its original ſtate does not act, or but very weakly, upon mercury. Theſe two ſubſtances cannot be united together, unleſs the acid be very highly concentrated, and a very ſtrong heat applied These two conditions are united in diſtillation Vitriolic acid, poured upon mercury and diſtilled, becomes more and more concentrated, and as it acquires a great heat when it is concentrated, it then acts upon the mercury, diſſolves it, and reduces it to a ſaline, white maſs

In this operation we obſerve, that the portion of acid which paſſes in diſtillation is very much of the volatile ſulphureous nature, which might induce us to ſuſpect that the acid ſeizes part of the inflammable principle of the mercury Nevertheleſs, when we afterwards ſeparate the vitriolic acid from the mercury, we find that this metallic ſubſtance has received no alteration This volatile ſulphureous quality, therefore, ſeems more probably to be given to the vitriolic acid by ſome inflammable matter which the mercury had ſuperabundantly, as moſt other metallic matters generally have This deſerves a more particular examination

When the ſaline-mercurial combination which remains in the retort is mixed with pure water, it divides into two different matters, one of which is perfectly ſoluble in water, and the other precipitates in form of a white powder, if the water be cold, and of a yellow powder, if the water be hot, and in ſufficient quantity The portion which remains diſſolved in the water is a combination of mercury with as much vitriolic acid as is neceſſary to give it a ſaline quality It is a ſalt with a metallic baſis, cryſtallizable by evaporation of the water It ought to be called *vitriol of mercury* The precipitated portion is almoſt entirely pure mercury, which retains too little acid to give it a ſaline quality, or ſolubility in water It may be totally deprived of its acid, according to Mr Beaume, by a ſufficient lavation with hot water This precipitate becomes more and more yellow, when it is waſhed with hot water, it is a violent emetic, and is known by the name of *turbith mineral* *See that article*

If, inſtead of treating with water the combination of vitriolic acid and mercury which remains in the retort after diſtillation, it be cohobated ſeveral times with vitriolic acid, Lemery ſays, that the mercury becomes more and more impregnated with acid, and at laſt becomes a very corroſive liquor, which ſome chemiſts have improperly called *oil of mercury*

If the combination of vitriolic acid with mercury be expoſed to fire, the greateſt part of this acid will be expelled and this remarkable thing happens, that mercury treated thus with vitriolic acid ſuſtains a greater heat, and conſequently ſeems to be ſomewhat more fixed than when it is pure

Nitrous acid diſſolves mercury very readily and this ſolution preſents phenomena very ſimilar to thoſe of the ſolution of ſilver by the ſame acid This acid ought to be very pure, the ſolution may be made without heat, it is corroſive, and blackens the ſkin, in the ſame manner as the ſolution of ſilver does From this ſolution may be obtained by cryſtallization a nitrous mercurial ſalt, which may be called *mercurial nitre* If this ſalt be expoſed to the action of fire, much of the nitrous acid will be driven from it in the ordinary form of red vapors, and when the acid quits the mercury, the ſalt, which is at firſt very white, becomes yellow, then orange colored, and laſtly red Mercury treated with

with this acid becomes also more fixed Nevertheless, by a sufficient heat it may be sublimed

The red powder which remains after the evaporation of the nitrous acid has the appearance of mercury precipitated by itself It is called *red precipitate*, but improperly, for it is not a precipitate See PRECIPITATE When spirit of wine has been poured upon it and burnt off, it is called *arcanum corallinum* See PRECIPITATE (RED)

Marine acid when liquid does not act sensibly upon mercury in its ordinary state, even when assisted with a boiling heat But when this acid, very concentrated and reduced into vapors, meets mercury also in vapors, these two bodies easily unite together, and even intimately Hence results a marine salt with basis of mercury, the crystals of which have the form of flattened needles It is called *corrosive sublimate mercury*, or only *corrosive sublimate*, because it is always made by sublimation, and is at the same time a very violent corrosive

Corrosive sublimate may be made in several methods The most common is to take a solution of mercury evaporated to dryness, to mix it with a quantity of calcined martial vitriol and of decrepitated common salt equal to the quantity of mercury dissolved, and to proceed to sublimation by exposing the mixture to fire in a matrass set in a sand-bath On one side the acid of vitriol disengages the acid of common salt which rises in vapors On the other side, the mercury is reduced into vapors by the heat These two bodies combine together in that state, and form a salt, which being itself volatile, attaches itself in the upper and colder part of the matrass, where it forms a very white and shining crystallized incrustation, which is the corrosive sublimate The other methods of making this salt are founded on the same principles They will be found under the article CORROSIVE SUBLIMATE

This salt is of a singular nature, and differs much from all the other combinations of mercury with other acids Altho' it is extremely caustic, and is capable of receiving still a considerable quantity of mercury, as we shall afterwards observe when we speak of sweet mercury, (which qualities indicate an imperfect saturation of the acid) it nevertheless has none of the properties observable in those salts whose acids are imperfectly saturated It crystallizes well, and very easily, so far is it from being deliquescent, as all these salts are. it is difficultly soluble in water, and requires a large quantity of boiling water to dissolve it entirely It is consequently a salt which crystallizes by cold Its crystals are of the same form as those obtained by sublimation, and cross each other irregularly They resemble a heap of large sword blades or poniards thrown carelessly together

If corrosive sublimate be exposed to fire, it will again be sublimed in its original form, without being decomposed, or at least only insensibly The mercury then, so far from receiving any fixity from the marine acid, as it does from the vitriolic and nitrous acids, seems on the contrary to be rendered more volatile This phenomenon is analogous to those which are exhibited by other metallic substances with marine acid, the union of which renders all these substances more or less volatile This acid ought to produce this effect more strongly upon mercury, as it is itself considerably volatile

This property as well as the others which are peculiar to the combination of marine acid with mercury, are naturally deducible from the presence of mercurial earth existing abundantly in both these substances, if Becker's opinion upon this subject was sufficiently proved *See* SUBLIMATE (CORROSIVE)

The affinity of marine acid with mercury is so great, that it overcharges itself in some measure with a considerable quantity of that metallic matter. If corrosive sublimate be triturated in a glass mortar with fluid mercury, it will receive the mercury and acquire a blackish color By thus adding mercury till it no longer is extinguished (for this kind of combination is called *extinction*) which is known by the globules of mercury not disappearing, we shall find that corrosive sublimate is capable of absorbing or extinguishing about three quarters of its weight of fresh mercury And if this new mixture be subjected to sublimation, the combination of mercury with corrosive sublimate is compleated, and a new sublimate is formed, in which the quantity of mercury is much greater than in corrosive sublimate When this matter has been sublimed thrice, to render the combination more perfect and intimate, the sublimate is then called *mercurius sublimatus dulcis*, or more frequently *sweet mercury*, because the mercury which is then united to the marine acid forms a compound which is no longer caustic, and which is taken internally as a purgative *See* MERCURY (SWEET) It is also called *aquila alba*, the white eagle, and this Latin name is still in use

Corrosive sublimate is not only rendered less caustic by this addition of mercury, which changes it into sweet mercury, but also the properties of the marine acid, and even its saline qualities are, almost entirely abolished Sweet mercury has not then, properly speaking, but the external appearance of a saline matter It is almost entirely unsoluble in water, which is the most distinguishing mark of salts

If sweet mercury be six times sublimed, it loses more and more of its purgative quality, and at last all of it This change is produced either by a loss of part of the acid each time, or by the combination betwixt the acid and mercury being rendered more intimate In this state it is called *mercurial panacea*, or merely *panacea* The panacea taken internally in sufficient doses can then only produce salivation *See* MERCURY (SWEET) *and* PANACEA

The combinations of mercury with the vitriolic, nitrous, and marine acids, may be decomposed by all intermediate substances, which having in general a stronger affinity with acids than metallic substances, decompose all metallic solutions by acids These intermediate substances are absorbent earths, and alkaline salts, both fixed and volatile

Lime-water mixed with a solution of corrosive sublimate, precipitates the mercury in form of a red brick-colored powder This mixture is employed in surgery under the name of *phagedenic water* It is used for cleansing ulcers, particularly those which are venereal

Fixed alkalis precipitate mercury from its solutions in a reddish powder, volatile alkali precipitates corrosive sublimate in a white powder, and the solution of mercury in nitrous acid in a grey slate colored powder In general, the colors of the mercurial precipitates are various, and these colors depend, like those of all other metallic precipitates, on the degree of division of parts, and on the quantity of saline matter and of phlogiston retained by these precipitates *See* PRECIPITATE

Fixed

Fixed and volatile alkalis do not act, or but insensibly, on mercury, in its proper state, but they can dissolve it, as well as all other metallic matters, when they can be applied to these metallic matters very much divided, as, for example, previously dissolved by acids Thus when a solution of mercury, with more acid than is necessary to dissolve the mercury, is poured into a very concentrated alkaline liquor, the precipitate formed upon first mixing the liquors will be again dissolved, and will disappear The volatile alkali may by this management dissolve a very considerable quantity of mercury

Lastly, vegetable acids which scarcely have any action upon ordinary mercury, are also capable of dissolving it when it is sufficiently divided Thus if we pour a large quantity of distilled vinegar upon mercury precipitated by a fixed alkali from its solution in nitrous acid, this precipitate will be easily dissolved again by help of a little heat, and from this combination a mercurial salt of a singular nature will be formed

The acid of vinegar, and probably all other vegetable acids, seem to be capable of contracting a very intimate union with mercury, for the *acetous mercurial salt* which we have just mentioned is not only crystallizable, but is even difficultly soluble in water. Hence, the phlegm of the vinegar not being in sufficient quantity to keep the acetous mercurial salt dissolved without heat, when it is made by the process described, this salt crystallizes in great quantity, when the liquor cools Its crystals are small, shining, thin plates, floating in the liquor like pieces of silver leaf.

From all the solutions of mercury we have mentioned, we may see, that this metallic matter is capable of being combined with all acid or alkaline saline substances, but with more or less facility and intimacy Of all the acids, the nitrous dissolves mercury most easily, as it does in general all metallic substances but it has not the strongest affinity with mercury, on the contrary, it seems to be that which contracts with it the least intimate union, as we may see from the following experiments

If into a solution of mercury made by spirit of nitre, vitriolic acid be poured, or the solution of any neutral salt containing this acid, the liquors will be rendered turbid, and when they are hot, a yellow precipitate will be formed, exactly similar to that which is obtained by pouring water upon the combination of vitriolic acid with mercury, that is to say, turbith mineral This effect cannot happen but because the vitriolic acid is joined to the mercury, which it separates from the nitrous acid.

As this experiment is very manifest, as the turbith mineral is easily known, and as it may be formed from this solution of mercury in the nitrous acid, not only by the vitriolic acid when disengaged, but also by any salts which contain that acid, this solution of mercury, therefore, affords a convenient method of discovering the presence of that acid in many chemical experiments, and particularly in examining mineral waters. Accordingly, it is much used for that purpose, and is, with regard to the vitriolic acid, what the solution of silver in the nitrous acid is to the marine acid *See* WATERS (MINERAL)

Marine acid, common salt, and in general all salts which contain this acid, mixed in a similar manner with a solution of mercury in nitrous acid, occasion a precipitate by the action of the marine acid upon the mercury, which it separates from the nitrous acid, and with which it unites, forming a combination,

which

which appears as a white precipitate, and is accordingly known by the name of the *white precipitate.* We must observe upon this subject, that that precipitate which is only a combination of marine acid with mercury, appears in these experiments as a precipitate, only because it requires more water to keep it dissolved than is to be found in these liquors, otherwise this mercurial salt would remain dissolved, and would not become sensible In this respect it differs essentially from turbith mineral, which is insoluble in water

The reason why this mercurial salt is much less soluble in water than the nitrous mercurial salt, is, that the marine acid is more intimately joined than the nitrous acid with the mercury, and also because marine acid has so strong an affinity with mercury, that it overcharges itself with that metallic matter, whenever it meets with a sufficient quantity of it, as in the present experiment For if we add to the white precipitate, to corrosive sublimate, or to any other combination of marine acid with mercury, a much greater quantity of this acid disengaged, these saline mercurial matters will charge themselves with it superabundantly, and will become so much more soluble in water, as they shall have received a larger quantity of this acid, according to the general rule. *See* SALTS

Hence if white precipitate be made by pouring a considerable quantity of disengaged marine acid into a solution of mercury by spirit of nitre, the precipitate ought to be re dissolved and it accordingly is so, as Geoffroy, Junker, and Pott, have observed. As in this experiment, mercury is found dissolved in a liquor containing the nitrous and marine acids, some chemists have imagined that mercury was soluble in aqua regia Nevertheless nothing appears less certain than that conclusion For it is very possible that mercury may be kept dissolved by a superabundant quantity of marine acid, with which only it is really united, and that the nitrous acid should contribute nothing to this solution Besides, if the nitrous and marine acids could be both united to the same mercurial parts, why do the white precipitate and corrosive sublimate, both made by help of a large quantity of nitrous acid, contain only the marine acid? The smallest vestige of nitrous acid cannot be discovered in them

Mr Pott, in his Dissertation on Common Salt, mentions another fact, which seems to prove not only, that mercury is soluble in aqua regia, but also that nitrous acid may seize upon that metallic matter exclusively of the marine acid Mr Pott's experiment consists in pouring spirit of nitre upon corrosive sublimate, by which he observed that spirit of salt was disengaged in vapors

A modern author draws from this experiment a consequence against the greater affinity of the marine acid than of the nitrous with mercury, supposed by all chemists, and even against the doctrine concerning the tendencies of bodies to one another according to certain laws, called affinities But, I believe, we may affirm that this experiment is only capable of imposing upon us at first view, and not when we examine circumstances attentively

If indeed spirit of nitre be poured upon corrosive sublimate, and particularly if the mixture be heated, we may observe the usual phenomena of substances acting upon each other, that vapors are disengaged, not of pure marine acid, but of aqua regia, and if the quantity of nitrous acid be sufficiently large, that the corrosive sublimate will be entirely dissolved in it But we must observe upon this subject, that as the quantity of mercury is very considerable in corrosive

rosive

rosive sublimate, we cannot be surprized that nitrous acid, which has great dissolving power upon this metallic matter, and which probably finds it not sufficiently defended by marine acid, should exercise upon it part of its action, but on the other side, as nitrous acid fixes mercury a little, and as the mixture undergoes a certain degree of heat, it is scarcely possible but that a certain quantity of marine acid should disengage itself But we may easily perceive that this effect is produced by the concurrence of these two circumstances, rather than by a superior affinity of the nitrous acid to the marine, with mercury For when these two causes cease to act, that is, when the mixture becomes cool, and the action of the nitrous acid is over, the corrosive sublimate is seen to crystallize very quickly even in the nitrous acid, and in as large a quantity as before the experiment

This is not the only fact which furnishes specious objections against even the most manifest affinities But in good philosophy, when a single fact is found to contradict many others well established, it ought to be examined very attentively, and in all its circumstances, before the consequences it seems to contain ought to be inferred We shall now return to our examination of white precipitate

This combination of marine acid with mercury, being exposed to the action of fire in close vessels, is sublimed into a saline mass, which is considered by Lemery as a sweet mercury, by others as a corrosive sublimate, and, lastly, by some chemists as being in an intermediate state betwixt corrosive sublimate and sweet mercury The last opinion seems to be the most probable, for the sublimate formed by white precipitate is probably not often charged with a sufficient quantity of marine acid to form corrosive sublimate, at least if by that expression we understand mercury sublimed, and united with the greatest possible quantity of marine acid, and on the other side, this sublimate from white precipitate probably contains too little mercury to constitute sweet mercury But as the marine acid and mercury may be united in very different proportions, according to the state in which they are presented to each other, in this respect very considerable differences ought to be found in white precipitates, according to the methods of preparation If, for example, mercury be precipitated by a large quantity of disengaged marine acid, this mercurial precipitate will most probably contain a much larger quantity of acid, than a precipitate made by adding common salt to the solution of mercury If this be true, we need not be surprized that chemists should disagree in their opinions concerning the degree of corrosive quality to be attributed to this sublimate from white precipitate

We have seen above, that the combinations of mercury with acids may be decomposed, as all metallic solutions may, by earths and by alkalis both fixed and volatile They may be decomposed also, and particularly corrosive sublimate may, by several metallic substances, such as tin, regulus of antimony, and copper

Corrosive sublimate, being mixed with tin and subjected to distillation, may be decomposed The marine acid is applied to the tin, a part of which it carries with it in distillation, and with which it passes in form of an acid, smoking liquor This acid is called the LIQUOR (SMOKING), *or* SMOKING SPIRIT *of* LIBAVIUS, which *see*

Antimony or its regulus, being mixed and distilled with corrosive sublimate, also decompose it, the regulus taking the marine acid from the mercury, and passing with that acid in form of a thick liquor, which congeals by cold, and is known by the name of BUTTER *of* ANTIMONY *See that article*

If very clean plates of copper be steeped in a solution of corrosive sublimate, the acid of that salt will attack the copper, and the mercury will be deposited upon the surface of the copper, with its metallic lustre, which always happens when one metal is precipitated by another *See* PRECIPITATION *and* PRECIPITATE

As mercury revived is always fluid, and therefore capable of being allayed with any metallic matter which it can touch, it amalgamates in the present experiment with the surface of the copper, and forms there a beautiful, white, and shining silvering, capable of surprizing persons ignorant of these effects, and of making them believe that copper is thus changed into silver But to make this experiment succeed well, we must add some marine acid, or some sal ammoniac to the solution of corrosive sublimate This experiment succeeds equally well with the solution of mercury in spirit of nitre, but always better when the acid is larger in quantity than is sufficient to dissolve the mercury. The surface of the copper immersed in these liquors becomes instantly silvered, and then it must be immediately withdrawn, washed in clean water, and wiped by rubbing it with a dry cloth

When corrosive sublimate and the other combinations of mercury with acids are decomposed by proper intermediate substances, the mercury is always by that operation *revived*, that is, reduced to a fluid state, and is obtained in that state when the operation is made by distillation, by giving a heat sufficient to raise it But when the intermediate substance is a compound body, such as antimony, which contains a principle capable of uniting and subliming with mercury, then the mercury which is disengaged from the corrosive sublimate, instead of being revived, makes part of a new combination, and is sublimed in form of cinnabar, if antimony was used, from the union it contracts with the sulphur of the antimony *See* BUTTER *of* ANTIMONY, *and* CINNABAR

Sulphur acts strongly on mercury If these two substances be triturated together, the mercury will be easily divided, its molecules will be distributed betwixt those of the sulphur, and will adhere to it; the mixture will acquire a color more and more brown, or blackish, which is a certain sign of the division of the mercury, in a word, the mercury disappears entirely, because it is extinguished and incorporated with the sulphur When the sulphur has thus absorbed all the mercury which it can receive in this method, the mixture is called *ethiops mineral*, from its black color.

The same combination may be made by fusion, that is, by mixing the proper quantity of mercury with melted sulphur. These two substances unite together, as when triturated, and form a black compound, called *ethiops made by fire* By this method the union of the sulphur and of the mercury is made much more quickly, and somewhat more intimately *See* ETHIOPS MINERAL

When mercury and sulphur have been united together only by fusion or trituration, the union is not sufficiently strong, nor the proportions suitable for making the most perfect and most intimate combination, called *cinnabar*, for

for the preparation of which, sublimation is necessary By sublimation of the ethiops, the mercury and sulphur are raised together, and are more intimately combined But we must observe, that in this sublimation a part of the sulphur of the ethiops, which is superabundant to the combination of cinnabar, is separated, so that only one part of sulphur remains united in the cinnabar with six parts of mercury This superabundant sulphur is not entirely separated by one sublimation The sublimation must then be repeated several times, that the cinnabar may be entirely free from the superabundant sulphur The sublimate, which is at first black like ethiops, becomes more and more red, as the mercury and sulphur approximate more and more to their proper proportions, and lastly, it remains in form of a very weighty, deep-red, striated mass, when the cinnabar is perfect The red color of the cinnabar is so deep, because the matter is exceedingly dense, for when it is finely powdered, it acquires a fiery red color, and is then called *vermillion*, which is used in painting

This combination of mercury with sulphur is found native, and is called *native cinnabar*, to distinguish it from that made by art Native cinnabar is mercury mineralised, or the ore of mercury *See* ORES

The connexion of mercury and sulphur is so strong in cinnabar, that the principles of this compound are not disunited merely by the action of the fire, without burning the sulphur Thus cinnabar exposed to fire in close vessels does only sublime, without any decomposition or alteration To decompose, therefore, cinnabar, and to separate the mercury from it, some intermediate substance must be employed, which has greater affininity than mercury with sulphur These intermediate substances are calcareous earths, fixed alkalis, iron, copper, lead, silver, and regulus of antimony If, then, cinnabar be mixed with any of these substances, and be distilled, the mercury will disengage itself and pass into the receiver, where it will appear in its proper fluid form, and the sulphur will remain in the retort combined with the intermediate substance

The mercury obtained in these operations is said to be *revived from cinnabar* It is justly considered as the purest, and fittest for chemical and medicinal purposes, and even for the arts in some cases where very pure mercury is required

The mercury obtained by the decomposition of cinnabar is not only very pure, but the whole quantity which was in the cinnabar is thus obtained, when none of it is lost in the operation, which proves that mercury suffers no alteration from the sulphur *See* CINNABAR

Mercury, which, from what we have said at the beginning of this article, is to be considered as a melted metal, also acts as such with regard to all earthy and metallic matters Like other melted metals, it cannot contract any union with earthy substances, not even with metallic earths, but it may be very well allayed with almost all metallic matters in the following order Gold, silver, lead, tin, copper, zinc, regulus of antimony Iron is not numbered amongst the metals capable of uniting with mercury, because no method has yet been discovered by which they can be united together.

The allays of mercury with metals are called *amalgams*, and are employed for many important purposes. The amalgams of gold and silver are employed

Fff 2 for

for gilding and silvering, and for the extraction of these two metals from their ores, that of silver is employed for preparing the *arbor Dianæ*, that of tin for silvering looking-glasses, for mercurial balls, and for the preparation of the smoking spirit of Libavius. *See all these words, and the articles* ALLAY *and* AMALGAM.

All fat and oily matters, vegetable or animal, act upon mercury. If mercury be triturated with any grease, it suffers an alteration similar to that in the preparation of ethiops by trituration. The parts of the mercury are thereby very much divided, and made to unite with those of the grease. The mercury disappears, is perfectly extinguished, and acquires a black and leaden color. This combination of mercury and fat is called *mercurial ointment*, and is very useful in medicine, as we shall afterwards see.

The mercury in mercurial ointment must not be considered merely as distributed and intermixed with the parts of the fat: on the contrary, there is an adhesion and even intimate combination between the integrant parts of these two substances, for this fat very quickly becomes rancid, as all oily matters do when combined, and besides, when mercurial ointment has been made a considerable time, all the mercury cannot be separated from it even by fusion. This fact has been verified by Mr Beaume.

Mercury, exposed to the vapor of melted lead, or thrown into boiling linseed oil, loses its fluidity, and becomes so solid, that it may be formed into toys and small utensils. Although, properly speaking, this is only an apparent fixation of mercury, since all its fluidity is restored to it by a little heat, this experiment proves, nevertheless, that some principle in these substances, probably their phlogiston, is capable of acting sensibly upon mercury.

Persons engaged in the discovery of the art of making gold, or of meliorating metals, considering that mercury has the metallic lustre, and a gravity approaching to that of gold, have endeavored much to fix it, that is, to deprive it of its volatility and fluidity, intending always to give it the color of gold afterwards by a philosophical tincture. The false fixations of mercury above-mentioned seem to indicate, that if any method by which mercury could be fixed were discovered, which is not very probable, this method must consist in giving it some principle that it wants. Nevertheless, all the properties of mercury seem to shew, on the other side, that its fusibility and volatility depend on some metallic principle united with it superabundantly, and, consequently, that its fixation ought rather to be effected by depriving it of some principle, than by any addition. However, we are certain that it must be effected by the one or the other, or by both these causes united. *(x)*

(x) The *purification of mercury* from extraneous substances is important for the purposes of medicine and of the arts, and especially for some nice chemical operations. Mercury may be cleansed from dust, by straining it through shamoy leather, from grease, by washing it with an alkaline lixivium, from any alkaline matter, by vinegar, from lead, or bismuth, with which it is frequently adulterated, by distillation, from sulphur, by mixing it with quicklime or with filings of iron, and then distilling the mixture. The best method of purifying mercury is by reducing it into ethiops mineral, with which twice the quantity of quicklime or of filings of iron is to be mixed, and by distilling it from this mixture. Its purity may be known, by observing that it does not soil clean white paper, that it has no pellicle on its surface, that when triturated with

Mercury is one of the metals which best deserves to be well known, not only from its great importance to chemistry and to the arts, but also from the powerful remedies it furnishes against diseases incurable by other means, particularly those called venereal diseases The medicinal use of mercury has been known only since the introduction of those diseases into Europe The ancient physicians did not use it, but considered it as a poison This opinion seems to have been founded upon some accidents from mercury ill prepared, or given improperly, or perhaps from the tremblings and diseases to which artists who handle mercury much are subject However that may be, the Arabian physicians were the first who ventured to use mercury medicinally, and they employed it successfully against the itch, and other diseases of the skin

When the venereal disease first appeared in Europe, in the army of Charles VIII at the siege of Naples, a physician, called Beranger de Carp , considering that the new disease discovered itself by cutaneous pustules, similar to those of malignant itches, and encouraged by the example of the Arabians, attempted the cure by mercury, and succeeded Nearly about this time, chemists and alchemists directed much of their labors towards medicine, and discovered many chemical remedies, the best of which are preserved, and employed at this time with success The famous Paracelsus chiefly distinguished himself in this way,

with water, it does not soil the water, that when exposed to fire in an iron spoon or laddle, it does not crackle, and, lastly, that it is perfectly and entirely soluble in pure spirit of nitre, without any deposition

Mercury may be united with all metallic substances, excepting iron, arsenic, and the semi-metal called nickel *See a note under the article* IRON Dr Lewis observes, that in some cases mercury absorbs gold and silver from their solutions in acid and in alkaline liquors This it may do by precipitating these metals, from its greater affinity to those menstruums, and by uniting or amalgamating with the very minute particles thus precipitated

The mercury of an amalgam exposed to heat, raises along with it some of the amalgamated metal, even of gold, as happens in the gilding of metals by amalgamation Mere distillation, therefore, may not be sufficient to procure mercury perfectly pure from metals By the above-mentioned method of mixing it with sulphur so as to form an ethiops, and afterwards with quicklime, and by distilling the mercury from that mixture, it may be obtained well purified from metals, which will remain engaged in the sulphur, or rather liver of sulphur, formed by the sulphur and quicklime By no method can purer and brighter mercury be obtained than by distilling it from cinnabar, by intervention of filings of pure iron. In all distillations of mercury, the addition of filings of iron seems to render the mercury more fluid and bright, probably by giving phlogiston

The *volatility of mercury may be diminished* by several methods, some of which we shall mention 1 Mercury calcined by heat, called the precipitate *per se*, sustains during some time a red heat, and by exposure to the heat of a burning glass is vitrifiable 2 Dr Brandt relates a very curious experiment, from which mercury appears capable of being so detained and fixed by digestion with gold, that a considerable part of it cannot be separated from this metal by the most intense heat 3 Mercury may be rendered considerably less volatile by being combined with vitriolic acid, but especially with the vitriol of silver, or the salt formed by silver and vitriolic acid This salt may be united with a considerable portion of mercury, with which it forms a concrete substance fusible by fire, but capable of sustaining, according to Dr Lewis, the greatest heat that can be applied to glass vessels, without dissipation of the mercury 4 Neuman says, that if mercury sublimate be frequently sublimed with sal ammoniac, and each time the sublimed matter mixed with the residuum, the whole becomes at last so fixed in the fire, that it cannot be any more sublimed.

and

and treated venereal diſeaſes with aſtoniſhing ſucceſs, by internal remedies, in form of pills. Although he has not publiſhed his remedies, it is believed from their effect, that the baſis of them was *turbith mineral*. Since that time mercury has been uſed in a great variety of forms.

Crude and fluid mercury taken internally produces no effect in the body, becauſe the adheſion of its integrant parts to each other hinders their diviſion, and diſtribution, or ſolution, without which it cannot have any effect. In its crude ſtate, therefore, it does nothing but load the ſtomach and inteſtines. It falls downwards by its weight, and goes out of the body along with the fæces in the ſame ſtate in which it entered.

Several phyſicians have believed that mercury, ſwallowed in its crude ſtate, may be uſeful in the iliac paſſion, imagining, that by its weight it is capable of reducing the inteſtines to their proper ſituation. But the effects are not ſuitable to their expectations. We have even ſeen this diſeaſe rendered worſe by mercury, from the ſhooting pains it occaſioned in theſe parts, already pained and irritated by ſpaſms. The uſe of crude mercury is now aboliſhed in theſe diſeaſes.

But when mercury is much divided, ſo that its molecules cannot again unite and form fluid mercury, in whatever manner this diviſion may have been made, it then produces very ſtriking effects, and ſuch as may be expected from the moſt powerful remedies.

Mercury adminiſtered in this ſtate accelerates the pulſe, divides and carries off the thickened humors, augments in general all excretions and ſecretions, but ſome preferably to others, according to circumſtances. If it be in a ſaline ſtate, or capable of being eaſily put into one, and be thus introduced into the body by the ſtomach in ſufficient quantity, it acts as an evacuant, purgative, or emetic. Mercurial frictions and fumigations chiefly encreaſe the ſecretion of ſaliva, and this in proportion to the quantity and number of doſes. Mercury, in every form, if ſufficiently divided, cures diſeaſes, and every preparation has its peculiar advantages and diſadvantages, which render it more or leſs adapted to particular circumſtances. We ſhall here mention the effects of the ordinary preparations of mercury.

Mercury precipitated *per ſe*, being much divided, is capable of entering the blood-veſſels, and when given in doſes from two to ſix grains, properly repeated, produces ſalutary effects in venereal diſeaſes. Notwithſtanding that it contains no ſaline matter, it is frequently purgative and even emetic, and is then leſs diſpoſed to ſalivate. But we muſt obſerve, that this preparation is a mercury exceedingly divided, that every body in this ſtate, and mercury perhaps more than any other, is diſpoſed to be attacked by every ſolvent, that it meets in the primæ viæ ſeveral ſubſtances, even of the ſaline kind, which are capable of diſſolving it, and that then it muſt produce the effects of a ſaline mercurial combination, which effects are in general purgative or emetic. Theſe properties of the precipitate *per ſe* ſhew, that it may be ſucceſsfully employed in many caſes. Nevertheleſs, this preparation is not much uſed, perhaps becauſe it is very dear.

The combination of mercury with a ſufficient quantity of vitriolic acid, to render it ſoluble in water, is very corroſive, and therefore not given internally.

Turbith mineral taken internally produces nearly the ſame effects, and in the ſame doſes as the precipitate *per ſe*, and undoubtedly for the ſame reaſon, for

if

if it retains a little vitriolic acid, as most chemists have believed, this small quantity of acid seems to be sufficient to make it act as a saline mercurial combination and if, on the contrary, when it is perfectly washed, no acid remains, it will be entirely similar to the precipitate *per se*, and, like this precipitate, will be disposed to receive a saline state, and to act in the same manner Turbith mineral has been much commended, and is still used by some persons in venereal diseases

All the precipitates of mercury, when separated from any acid by an alkali, and afterwards edulcorated, ought to produce internally the same effects as the precipitate *per se*, and as turbith mineral, supposing it to be freed from all acid by lotions Thus the great number of such mercurial preparations nearly equivalent to each other, are but little used, which must be attributed to the want of attention to their nature and advantages

The solution of mercury in the nitrous acid, and mercurial nitre, are justly ranked amongst corrosives

Some persons, and Lemery amongst others, say, that they may be taken internally if they are diluted, an ounce of solution, for example, with 24 ounces of water or ptisan This is called *mercurial water*

Lemery says, that from half an ounce to an ounce of this mercurial water may be taken in a glass of ptisan, or broth, and that it vomits gently, and excites salivation Mr. Baron, in his notes on Lemery, justly exclaims against the use of that dangerous remedy Nevertheless physicians of great reputation have introduced, and even successfully, the use of corrosive sublimate for the cure of venereal diseases, although this preparation is no less corrosive than the solution of mercury in nitrous acid

A pomatum is made of two ounces of mercury dissolved in a sufficient quantity of nitrous acid, and mixed perfectly well in a mortar with two pounds of hog's-lard This pomatum admirably cures the itch The solution of mercury acts powerfully upon the hogs lard with which it combines, and to which it gives greater solidity, while at the same time it is itself rendered thereby much milder The pomatum is of a citron color, and is to be lightly rubbed upon the parts attacked by the itch, which by this treatment soon disappears This pomatum for the itch comes from the Hotel Dieu at Paris, where it is given to convalescents, by which they are quickly cured of the itch, which they all catch by remaining some time in the hospital The receipt of this pomatum is also found in the last edition of the Dispensatory at Paris

Red precipitate is not used internally, but is employed externally as a detergent and cicatrising escharotic, in the treatment of venereal ulcers

All the combinations of mercury with marine acid are used Of these the corrosive sublimate has been the least used, in France at least The terrible accidents and deaths occasioned by small doses of this preparation have confined its use to external application, as an escharotic, and even then it is generally rendered milder, or rather decomposed by mixture with quicklime. But some years ago Van Swieten, a disciple of Boerhaave, and principal physician to the Empress-Queen, introduced the internal use of corrosive sublimate for the venereal disease This great physician dissolved twelve grains of sublimate in two pounds of malt spirits, and gave this solution by spoonfuls, diluted copiously with emollient liquors

A great

A great number of trials made by Van Swieten and many others of the profession have proved, beyond any possibility of doubt, that corrosive sublimate, administered in this manner, is a powerful anti-venereal, capable of curing inveterate poxes, which have resisted the other ordinary preparations of mercury We know besides, that the internal use of corrosive sublimate has been long established amongst the Tartars and amongst the Russians, whose unrestrained manner of living with all sorts of women exposes them to a continual accumulation of venereal diseases

But notwithstanding these powerful motives to confide in this remedy, many excellent physicians are still deterred from the use of it They observe, that the use of corrosive sublimate seems only to agree with cold climates, and they believe that it always has disagreeable consequences in such as are hot or temperate They think that a number of compleat cures, without any seeming inconveniencies, do not justify the use of a substance which is so corrosive, that very bad consequences may be apprehended from it, when it has been once introduced into the body

Opinions therefore are still divided upon the internal use of corrosive sublimate Time and experience must decide concerning them But this is certain, that a remedy of this kind cannot be administered with too much caution, prudence, and discernment, that every one ought not to pretend to meddle with it, and that this, and most other very active substances, are kinds of poisons, and only become powerful remedies in the hands of able physicians

If it were once established, that corrosive sublimate given internally cures venereal diseases radically, and without troublesome consequences, we should think it certain, that the saline combinations of mercury with the other acids may be employed as safely for the same purposes, that is, the vitriolic and nitrous mercurial salts, for these salts are not more, perhaps less, caustic than corrosive sublimate and besides, the vitriolic and nitrous acids being more disposed to unite with oily matters than the marine acid, they are therefore more susceptible of being rendered milder within the body than the corrosive sublimate, which ought therefore to be considered as the most dangerous of all that are used in medicine

Sweet mercury, not being corrosive, may certainly be used internally, and has been so a long time But notwithstanding the great quantity of mercury with which the marine acid in this compound is charged, it still retains sensibly a saline quality, and is purgative, when taken from four grains to 15 or 18 It is used in the treatment of venereal diseases, particularly when it is intended to purge But it is not usual to attempt the cure of a true pox by this remedy only The *mercurial panacea*, which is only apparently saline, acts, when taken internally, simply as mercury deprived of its fluidity, but too little divided to acquire a saline quality in the alimentary canal accordingly it does not generally purge, but rather salivate, when given in a large enough quantity The dose of it is from ten grains to twenty-four or thirty It is to be repeated as occasion requires, and at proper intervals Several persons of the profession cure the pox by this remedy only

White precipitate, however it be made, is much more saline than sweet mercury Accordingly it excites vomiting, and must be given more cautiously and in less quantity, but it is little used. Nevertheless, if the propriety of using corrosive sublimate were established, this precipitate may also be advantageously

advantageously employed with proper management It would probably produce the same effects in a larger dose

No sensible effect is produced by the combinations of mercury with sulphur, whether *ethiops* or *cinnabar*, taken internally, and in large doses Some physicians therefore reject these mercurial preparations as useless and inactive This is certain, that mercury united with sulphur has no saline quality, and is very little acted upon by menstruums, because it is defended by the sulphur, nearly as the regulus of antimony is in antimony Cinnabar is used nevertheless in venereal diseases, and successfully on certain occasions, and then it is decomposed by burning The body of the patient is exposed to the vapors of mercury, which are disengaged by this burning These mercurial vapors insinuate themselves through the pores of the skin, excite salivation and cure the venereal disease This is called *the method by fumigation*

We know yet very little the effects which are produced by combinations of mercury with vegetable acids, if it be true that Keyser's pills have for their basis the acetous mercurial salt, as is very probable We may nevertheless suppose, that mercury administered in this form might produce good effects

Lastly, of all the preparations of mercury, the most generally employed is certainly that called *mercurial ointment* It is, as we mentioned above, mercury extinguished by trituration with fat The only method of using this ointment is by rubbing it on the body of the patient, and repeating this friction at proper intervals and in proper doses, till a sufficient quantity of mercury has been introduced to effect a cure This is called *the method of friction*

This method is more prevalent than the others It is recommended by the best physicians, and particularly by the learned Astruc The chief motives for this preference are, that mercury introduced by this method has no corrosive quality, and that as much of it as is necessary for the cure may be thus introduced without inconvenience

Mercury administered by friction or by fumigation produces no purgative or emetic effect, because it does not enter into the body by digestion, but is immediately introduced into the lymphatic and blood vessels There it circulates, and penetrates into their most remote recesses When sufficient doses of it are given, it produces almost always a salivation more or less strong, makes the symptoms disappear, and subdues at length the venereal poison

This is all that we know concerning the effects produced by mercury The nature of this poison, and the precise manner of the action of the mercury, are still unknown Many physicians believe, that, as mercury is capable of a division into very minute but weighty globules, these globules act mechanically by their number and by their weight upon the lymph, which they supposed to be thickened and coagulated by the venereal poison, and which by this action of the mercury was attenuated, divided, and restored to its ordinary state But this opinion, although one of the most specious that has appeared upon the subject, is nevertheless far from the truth, for if this opinion were just, mercury could only, while it was fluid and in its proper state, cure the venereal disease But experience has proved incontestably, that mercury in a saline state, such as it is in corrosive sublimate, and consequently deprived of all the properties of ordinary mercury, cures the pox effectually, and particularly in a dose infinitely less than when it is administered by friction or fumigation.

Hitherto it seems to have been believed, that mercury in the mercurial ointment is only divided, dispersed, and interposed betwixt the parts of the fat, without being truly dissolved and combined, and this undoubtedly has given cause to the above-mentioned opinion We are nevertheless certain, that much of the mercury contained in the ointment is really combined either with the acid, or with the whole substance of the fat This being established, may we not conclude, that mercury cannot cure the venereal disease but when it is really dissolved, and deprived of its properties of fluid mercury, that only the portion of mercury in the ointment, which is thus combined, affects the cure, and that the other portion of the mercury which remains in its natural state in the ointment (for much of the mercury is in this state) passes into the body without producing any effect, for which reason the mercurial salts cure in much less doses than the mercurial ointment, that, lastly, if the portion of mercury introduced into the body in its proper state by friction or fumigation contributes to the cure, the reason of it is, that the most divided part of this mercury unites within the body with some greasy or other substance with which it is capable of combining?

If this be true, ought we not to search for some new combination of mercury, which shall be at the same time very soluble and free from causticity? Such a remedy would certainly be very precious For although the mercury of the mercurial ointment is not caustic, and although the method by friction is undoubtedly the most advantageous and certain, it is not however free from inconveniencies It frequently exposes to dangerous salivations, accompanied with very troublesome accidents, and if to avoid them, the quantity of ointment be diminished, and the intervals of the several frictions lengthened, by which indeed these accidents are avoided, the cure then is not only of a tedious length, but is also sometimes imperfect, or less certain

But have we reason to flatter ourselves with the hopes of finding such a preparation of mercury? If we consider that mercury has been tried in a great variety of methods, and by very able chemists, and that, notwithstanding, no preparation has yet been found free from inconveniencies, we shall be apt to despair of success in this inquiry But on the other side, if we reflect on the nature and properties of mercury, if we consider that this singular substance, as we have seen in the present article, is perhaps one of those which may be combined in the greatest variety of manners, that it is acted upon by almost every solvent, we may still have hopes of finding a mercurial preparation, not only much superior to those hitherto known, but which perhaps shall be attended with no inconvenience

The use of mercury is not confined to the venereal disease We have already seen, that its antivenereal quality was discovered from its property of curing the itch, even the most malignant, and, in fact, it does cure much more readily and efficaciously than any other remedy, not only the several kinds of the itch, but also many other cutaneous diseases more or less similar to the itch, and which are very various

Another medicinal quality of mercury is, that of destroying the worms and insects of all kinds which are apt to infest the human body, either internally or externally In the cure of these two latter kinds of diseases, the same preparations of mercury, but smaller quantities, are employed as for the venereal disease

Lastly,

Laſtly, ſome obſervations made lately by able phyſicians ſeem to give hopes, that by mercury another ſcourge more terrible, but fortunately leſs frequent, than thoſe diſeaſes above-mentioned, namely, the madneſs occaſioned by the bite of a mad dog, may be cured But this effect of mercury is not ſufficiently eſtabliſhed, and requires to be confirmed by many new obſervations, which would require a conſiderable time, ſince happily the occaſions of trying them are not very frequent

Phyſicians, ſtruck with the ſurprizing ſucceſs of mercury in certain very obſtinate and otherwiſe incurable diſeaſes, were induced to try it in moſt of the other diſeaſes which were incurable by the ordinary remedies, and particularly in thoſe which were attributed, as well as the venereal diſeaſe, to a thickneſs or coagulation of lymph, ſuch as the ſcrophula, cancers, ſchirrhus, and others of this kind But mercury was not found to have any good effect in theſe diſeaſes, and ſome diſeaſes, ſuch as the ſcurvy, the ſymptoms of which are ſo like thoſe of the pox that they cannot eaſily be diſtinguiſhed, were not only not diminiſhed, but aggravated by mercury

We may ſtill however hope, that ſo powerful a remedy may be employed ſucceſsfully in other diſeaſes Perhaps for this purpoſe only ſome new method of preparing it is wanting But even at preſent, it is one of our moſt valuable remedies

CCCCXLV MERCURY (ANIMATED) This is mercury purified by alchemical proceſſes, for the preparation of the philoſopher's ſtone

CCCCXLVI MERCURY (SWEET) Sweet mercury, called alſo *aquila alba*, is corroſive ſublimate combined by further operations with all the mercury which it can receive, and afterwards ſublimed thrice

To make ſweet mercury, corroſive ſublimate is to be triturated carefully in a glaſs mortar with fluid mercury, which is to be added gradually as it diſappears This is to be continued till the corroſive ſublimate is ſaturated and will receive no more mercury, which is known by the globules not diſappearing by trituration Lemery ſays, that corroſive ſublimate can only receive about three quarters of its weight of freſh mercury, nevertheleſs a larger quantity, a half, may without inconvenience be added, becauſe thereby the corroſive ſublimate will be more perfectly edulcorated, and the ſuperabundant mercury will be eaſily diſengaged, as we ſhall ſoon ſee

The corroſive ſublimate receives from the mercury with which it is triturated a blackiſh-grey color, which color mercury always acquires when it is much divided, and ſtill retains its metallic ſtate This grey matter is to be put into one or more matraſſes with ſhort necks, or rather into the veſſels called medical phials, ſo that two-thirds of the containing veſſel ſhall be empty for the ſake of the ſublimation

Theſe matraſſes are to be placed in a ſand-bath, and ſunk in ſand to the height of the contained matter The fire is then to be gradually augmented till we ſee that the ſublimation begins It is then to be kept in this ſtate till it be all ſublimed, and attached to the top of the veſſel, excepting a ſmall portion of fixed matter which remains at the bottom When the matraſſes are cold, they are to be carefully broken The white compact ſublimate is to be ſeparated from ſome leſs white and denſe adhering to the neck of the veſſel, to be again powdered, and ſublimed a ſecond and a third time in the ſame manner, always taking care to ſeparate each time the compact white maſs from that part which

 has

has less of these qualities The sweet mercury is then in its most perfect state, a white, heavy, semitransparent mass, smooth as glass in its convex part, where it adhered to the vessel

In these operations no mortars must be employed, upon which the acid or the mercury of the corrosive sublimate can act therefore neither marble nor metal mortars are proper, but those made of glass

Although the crude mercury which is triturated with the corrosive sublimate is joined to it superabundantly, and contracts with it a certain degree of union, this union is not nearly so intimate as it may be, and as it is after the perfect dulcification of the corrosive sublimate, for if we take internally corrosive sublimate impregnated by trituration alone, with all the crude mercury which it can perfectly extinguish, it would produce nevertheless very violent corrosive effects By sublimation then the new mercury is completely combined with the acid of corrosive sublimate, which is thus rendered milder The external mark of this intimate combination is the change of color from an opake grey, which the matter had before sublimation, to a transparent white, which it afterwards acquires This opake grey color proceeds, as we said, from the mercury preserving its metallic state, which it does because it is not intimately enough combined with the acid, and the white, transparent, saline appearance is a certain sign of this intimate combination

One or two sublimations are not sufficient to change entirely the corrosive sublimate into sweet mercury, experience shews that three sublimations are necessary. The mercurial sublimate may then be taken internally without danger It is no longer corrosive, nor retains any more of its saline property than is sufficient to render it purgative in a dose from four or five to twenty-four or thirty grains and if sweet mercury be sublimed eight or nine times, or perhaps less, it loses its purgative quality, and is then called MERCURIAL PANACEA *See* PANACEA

The matter which adheres to the neck of the retort, particularly in the first sublimations, is an imperfect combination of crude mercury with corrosive sublimate, and must therefore be separated from the rest of the mass When the quantity of crude mercury triturated with corrosive sublimate is more than can be united with it into sweet mercury, the superabundant mercury remains in its metallic state, and gives a grey or blackish color to the sweet mercury This superabundant mercury may be disengaged by subliming in a retort, as Stahl proposes, and as Mr Baron remarks in his Notes on Lemery.

The fixed matter which remains at the bottom of the matrass is quite extraneous to the mercurial sublimate It is a portion of earthy substances proceeding from the salts employed in the preparation of corrosive sublimate, and which this sublimate had carried along with it in sublimation For, in general, volatile bodies are capable of carrying along with them a part of the fixed bodies with which they happen to be mixed, particularly when they are exposed to a stronger heat than is necessary for their sublimation For this purpose no union betwixt the fixed and the volatile bodies is necessary. This is done by a purely mechanical impulsion of the volatile parts against the parts of the fixed body Hence the heaviest volatile bodies must produce this effect more sensibly than those which are lighter. Accordingly, the sublimates of mercury, which are certainly the heaviest of all volatile bodies, produce this effect surprizingly. For in the operation for sweet mercury, sometimes fragments

of

of the matrasses in which the sublimation had been made, and which adhere to the matter which is again to be sublimed, are raised along with the mercurial sublimate. Mr Beaume has frequently found large fragments of glass in the middle of masses of the sublimates, which had been made in great works, where the same care and attention are not given as in the small operations of chemical laboratories.

Lemery remarks, that sweet mercury acquires a yellowish color when it is triturated. This color proceeds from the quantity of mercury being considerable with respect to the acid; for that is the ordinary color of mercury when it is much divided, and has not its metallic lustre, as we see from the example of the precipitate *per se*, of turbith mineral, and other preparations of mercury which are in this state. *See* MERCURY, *and* SUBLIMATE (CORROSIVE).

CCCCXLVII. MERCURY *of* PHILOSOPHERS. Alchemists have given the name of mercury to many other things besides the metallic substance generally so called. This latter they call ordinary mercury, and value it little. We cannot precisely say what they meant by their mercury, from the obscurity of their writings, and also from their different descriptions of the matter. No term is more frequently used by them than this. In every page of their writings we find the words mercury, mercurification, &c. Probably they had not all the same idea annexed to the term *philosophical mercury*. The most probable opinion upon this subject is, that this mercury is the metallic principle which Beccher has called *mercurial earth*. *See* EARTH (MERCURIAL), *and the following article*.

CCCCXLVIII. MERCURIFICATION. Mercurification is an alchemical operation, by which metals are said to be reduced into a fluid, heavy, opake, and shining liquor, like ordinary mercury; or by which the mercurial principle may be extracted from metals, and obtained in the form of quicksilver. But these mercurified metals, or their mercurial principle rendered sensible, are a kind of philosophical mercury, which, although they resemble ordinary mercury, are nevertheless said, by persons exercised in such studies, to differ from it considerably, by having a greater specific gravity, by more effectually penetrating and dissolving metals, by a stronger adhesion to these, and by a less volatility.

We may find in the books of many authors, who, though not alchemists, give more or less attention to these subjects, a great number of processes for mercurification, or for obtaining the mercury of metals, most of which are very long, laborious, confused, and consequently subject to fail. The detail of these processes would be too long. An account of the principal of these operations may be seen in *Junker's Conspectus Chemiæ*. We shall only mention some of the easiest mercurifications, extracted from the most modern authors, as *Wallerius* and *Teichmeyert*.

If cinnabar of antimony made with corrosive sublimate be distilled, we shall obtain, by reviving the mercury, a larger quantity of mercury than was originally in the corrosive sublimate.

If a corrosive sublimate be prepared with spirit of salt and fluid mercury, and if calx or filings of silver be several times sublimed together with this corrosive sublimate, a part of the silver will be changed into mercury.

Very fine filings of iron, exposed during a year to the air and afterwards well triturated in a mortar, and cleansed from dust and extraneous matter, then exposed

exposed during another year to the air, and, lastly, distilled in a retort, furnishes a hard matter which attaches itself to the neck of the retort, and with this matter a little mercury *Teichmeyer†*

If calx of copper be mixed with sal ammoniac, and this mixture exposed during a certain time to air, and distilled with soap, mercury will be obtained

If luna cornea or plumbum corneum be mixed with an equal weight of very concentrated spirit of salt, digested together during three or four weeks, then an equal quantity of black flux and Venice soap added to it, and the whole matter distilled in a glass retort, some mercury will pass into the receiver

These experiments are important and easily made, but have not been repeated by modern chemists; for which we see no other reason than the small hopes of their succeeding If they should succeed, they would ascertain the existence of a mercurial principle in metals, and would so much more confirm the theory of Beccher, as all the experiments above-mentioned are made with the marine acid, which that chemist supposes to contain the mercurial earth The conclusion deducible from these experiments would be, that, by introducing a superabundant quantity of mercurial earth into metals, a true mercury might be obtained from them *See* METALS

Many other processes for mercurification may be seen in authors who have treated of this matter, particularly in Junker's book above quoted, in which marine acid is not employed, but other saline matters, or sublimation through the burning fuel, with concourse of free air, in Geber's manner In this latter case, we must look for the mercurial substance in the metallic fumes and flowers, and if any such substance be obtained, it must evidently proceed from the decomposition of the metallic matter employed

Mr Grosse says, in the Memoirs of the Academy, that he obtained mercury from lead by an easier and simpler process than those above-mentioned This consists in saturating perfectly some good nitrous acid with lead, which may be done effectually by employing more lead than the acid can dissolve, and from this solution, according to Mr Grosse, a grey powder is precipitated, in which mercury is discovered This experiment being short, Messrs Macquer and Beaume repeated it with due attention in their Course of Chemistry, but they did not find the grey mercurial powder mentioned by Mr Grosse As the exactness and veracity of that able chemist are well known, we must believe that the lead which he employed contained some extraneous mercury, which might easily happen in a laboratory The same thing has possibly happened in other experiments of mercurification, and this proves how circumspect we ought to be in drawing conclusions

CCCCXLIX METALS *and* METALLISATION Under the general name *metal*, we comprehend here not only the metals properly so called, but also the semimetals, or all matters which have the essential metallic properties, which we shall here recount Thus the word *metal* and *metallic substance* will be synonimous in this article

Metallic substances form a class of bodies not very numerous, of very great importance in chemistry, medicine, arts, and the ordinary affairs of life These substances have very peculiar properties, by which they differ from all other bodies

The

The natural bodies from which metals differ the least are earthy and pyritous matters, on account of their solidity and density. Metals and stones are, nevertheless, very different, the heaviest stones which are unmetallic being much lighter than the lightest metals. A cubic foot of marble weighs 252 pounds, and an equal bulk of tin, the lightest of metals, weighs 516 pounds. The difference is much greater when the weight of such a stone is compared with that of gold, a cubic foot of which is 1326 pounds.

Opacity is another quality which metals possess eminently, the opacity of metals being much greater than the opacity of any unmetallic substance.

This great opacity of metals is a consequence of their density, and these two properties produce a third, peculiar also to metals, namely, a capacity of reflecting infinitely more light than any other body: hence metals whose surfaces are polished, form mirrors representing the images of bodies, more clearly than any other matter. Thus looking-glasses produce their reflexion merely by the silvering, which is a covering of metal upon their surfaces. To this reflective property metals owe their peculiar lustre, called the *metallic lustre*.

Although the several metallic substances differ considerably in hardness and fusibility, we may say in general, that they are less hard and less fusible than pure earths.

Metals cannot unite with any earthy substance, not even with their own earths, when these are deprived of their metallic state: hence when they are melted, they naturally run into globes, as much as the absolute gravity of their mass, and their pressure upon the containing vessels, will allow. Accordingly, the surface of a metal in fusion is always convex. A metal in that state always endeavors to acquire a spherical form, which it does more perfectly as the mass is less. This effect is very sensible in quicksilver, which is nothing but a metal habitually fluid or fused. A mass of several pounds of mercury, contained in a shallow, wide mouthed vessel, is so spread out, that its upper surface is almost flat, and the convexity is not very sensible but at its circumference: on the contrary, if we put very small masses of mercury into the same vessel, as, for instance, masses weighing a grain each, they become so round as to seem perfect globes. This effect is partly occasioned by the inaptitude of metals to unite with the vessels containing them when in fusion, by which quality the whole affinity which subsists betwixt the integrant parts of these metals is capable of acting, and partly also by this affinity, which disposes the integrant parts to come as near to each other as they can, and consequently to form a sphere.

This property is not peculiar to melted metals, but to all fluids, when contiguous to bodies solid or fluid, with which they have no tendency to unite. Thus, for instance, masses of water upon oily bodies, or oily masses upon bodies moistened with water, assume always a form so much nearer to the spherical as they are smaller. Even a large drop of oil poured upon a watery liquor, so that it shall be surrounded with this liquor, becomes a perfect sphere.

All metals are in general soluble by all acids, but often these solutions require particular treatment and circumstances, which are mentioned under the articles of the several metals. With acids, they form neutral salts with metallic bases. These salts have all more or less causticity, which proceeds from the little intimacy of union betwixt the acid and metal, and from the great weight of the latter substance. The affinity of metals is less than of absorbent earths

and

and alkaline ſalts to acids, and therefore any metal may be ſeparated from any acid by theſe earthy and ſaline alkalis

Alkaline ſalts are capable of acting upon all metallic ſubſtances, and of keeping them diſſolved by proper management

Metals may in general be united with ſulphur and liver of ſulphur With ſulphur they form compounds reſembling the peculiar ſubſtance of ores, which are generally nothing elſe than natural combinations of ſulphur and metal Metals have leſs affinity with ſulphur than with acids, hence ſulphur may be ſeparated from them by acids Some exceptions from theſe general rules, concerning the affinity of metals to ſulphur and liver of ſulphur, and concerning their ſeparation from ſulphur by acids, may be ſeen under the articles of the ſeveral metals. But theſe exceptions do probably take place, only becauſe we have not yet found the method of ſurmounting ſome obſtacles which occur in the ordinary methods of treating certain metals

All metals may in general be united with each other, with which they form different allays which have peculiar properties, but this rule alſo is not without ſome exceptions *See* ALLAY *and* AMALGAM

Metals have ſtrong affinity with the inflammable principle, and are capable of receiving it ſuperabundantly

Laſtly, oily ſubſtances ſeem to be capable of acting upon all metals Some metals are eaſily and copiouſly diſſolved by oils, and perhaps they might all be found to be entirely ſoluble in oils, if the methods known in chemiſtry were tried for the accompliſhment of theſe ſolutions

The properties above-mentioned agree in general to all metallic ſubſtances but, beſides the properties peculiar to each metal, ſome properties are common to a certain number of them, and hence they have been divided into ſeveral claſſes

Thoſe metallic matters which, when ſtruck by a hammer, or ſtrongly compreſſed, are extended, lengthened, and flattened, without being broken, (which property is called *ductility* or *malleability*) and which alſo remain fixed in the moſt violent and long continued fire, without diminution of weight, or other ſenſible alteration, are called *perfect metals* Theſe perfect metals are three, *gold*, *ſilver*, *platina*

The metallic matters which are ductile and fixed in the fire, to a certain degree, but which are deſtroyed by the continued action of fire, that is, changed into an earth deprived of all the characteriſtic properties of metals, are called *imperfect metals* Of this kind are four, *copper*, *iron*, *tin*, *lead*

The metallic ſubſtances which, as well as the imperfect metals, loſe their metallic properties by expoſure to fire, but which alſo have no ductility nor fixity, are diſtinguiſhed from the others by the name of *ſemi-metals* Of this claſs are five, *regulus of antimony*, *biſmuth*, *zinc*, *regulus of cobalt*, and *regulus of arſenic*

Laſtly, mercury, which has all the general properties of metals, makes a claſs ſeparate from the others, becauſe in purity and gravity it is ſimilar to the perfect metals, and in volatility to the ſemi-metals Its fuſibility alſo ſo far ſurpaſſes that of any other metallic matter, that it is ſufficient to diſtinguiſh it from all, and to give it a diſtinct claſs We have enumerated, therefore, in all, thirteen metallic ſubſtances, two of which only were unknown to the ancients

cients, namely, platina and regulus of cobalt We have reason to wonder that these two metallic bodies, and particularly platina, which is a perfect metal, should have remained unknown till lately

This may give us cause to hope, that if natural history and chemistry be carefully cultivated, as they have been since the renovation of the sciences, we may still make essential discoveries in this way Mr Cronstedt has given, in the Swedish Memoirs, a description of a metallic matter, which, as he says, appears to be a new semimetal distinct from the others In that case, this would be the fourteenth metallic matter known, and the third lately discovered but as, since the Memoir of Mr Cronstedt, this new semimetal has not been examined by chemists, it is yet but little known, and therefore further experiments seem requisite to decide whether it ought to be admitted as a new semimetal (y)

As chemists can only know compound bodies by being capable of separating the principles of such bodies, and even of re-uniting their principles so as to reproduce such compounds as they were originally, and as hitherto they have not been able to accomplish any such decomposition upon the perfect metals, hence, if all the other metallic substances were equally inalterable, we should be very far from having certain notions concerning metals in general but if we except gold, silver, and platina, all the other metallic matters are susceptible of decomposition and of recomposition, at least to a certain degree, and the experiments of this kind made by chemists, and chiefly by the modern chemists, have thrown much light on this important subject.

We may observe, that even if we had not been able to decompose any metallic substance, we might still, by reflecting on the essential properties of metals, discover sufficiently well the nature of their principles

The solidity, the consistence, and especially the gravity which they possess in a degree so superior to all other bodies, would not have allowed us to doubt that the earthy element, of which these are the characteristical properties, enters largely into their composition, and makes their basis

The facility with which they combine with almost all inflammable matters, and with all those which have great affinity with phlogiston, such as acids, joined to their incapacity of being allayed with meagre matters that are purely earthy or purely watery, which have no disposition to unite with phlogiston, would also have furnished very strong motives to believe, that the inflammable principle enters largely into the composition of metals

We must acknowledge, however, that these considerations would only have furnished concerning the existence of the inflammable principle in metals, but a simple probability, very far from the compleat proof we now have but the combustibility of all metals capable of decomposition by this method, and of a subsequent reduction with all their properties, by the rejunction of the inflammable principle, furnishes the clearest and the most satisfactory demonstration that we have in chemistry. We shall now mention what is known upon this subject, and the consequences necessarily resulting

(y) See NICKEL Mr. *Justi* pretends that he has discovered a new metallic substance contained in yellow mica This he says was of a blackish-grey color, but when mixed with gold heightened the lustre, without destroying the malleabity of that metal, though itself is brittle.

The deſtructible metals preſent exactly the ſame phenomena as all other bodies containing the inflammable principle do, in the ſtate of combuſtion When expoſed to fire, without acceſs of air, that is, in cloſe veſſels, they become red-hot, melt, or ſublime, according to their nature but they receive no alteration in their compoſition from fire applied in this manner, and they are afterwards found to be exactly in the ſame ſtate as before In this reſpect, they reſemble perfectly all bodies which contain no other inflammable matter than pure phlogiſton

But when imperfect metals are expoſed to fire, with acceſs of air, as, for inſtance, under a muffle in a furnace which is made very hot, then they burn more or leſs ſenſibly, as their inflammable principle is more or leſs abundant, or more or leſs combined Some of them, as iron and zinc, burn with a very lively and brilliant flame, but this flame is of the ſame nature as that of charcoal, of ſulphur, of all bodies, the combuſtible principle of which is pure phlogiſton, and is not in an oily ſtate, that is, furniſhes no ſoot capable of blackening

Alſo the imperfect metals detonate with nitre, when all the circumſtances which that detonation requires are united *See* DETONATION *of* NITRE Their phlogiſton is conſumed by this method much more quickly and compleatly than by ordinary calcination or combuſtion Their flame is alſo much more lively and brilliant, and ſome of them, as iron and zinc, are uſed in compoſitions for fireworks, from their very vivid and beautiful flame

Nitre is alkaliſed by theſe metallic detonations exactly in the ſame manner as in its detonation by coals

Laſtly, imperfect metals being treated with acids which have an affinity with phlogiſton, that is, with the vitriolic and nitrous acids, are deprived alſo by theſe acids of a more or leſs conſiderable part of their inflammable principle They give a ſulphureous quality to vitriolic acid, and are even capable of furniſhing ſulphur with that acid

Although the experiments now mentioned were the only proofs of the exiſtence of an inflammable principle in metallic ſubſtances, theſe would be ſufficient to eſtabliſh it inconteſtibly But we ſhall ſee, when we continue to examine the phenomena attending the decompoſition of metals, that thoſe are not the only proofs

If the inflammable matter which ſhews itſelf ſo evidently in the burning of metals, is really one of their conſtituent parts, their eſſential properties muſt be altered in proportion to the quantity of it taken from them, and this evidently happens upon trial, for the reſiduum of metallic matters, after calcination, departs from the metallic character, and approaches to the nature of mere earth The opacity, brilliancy, ductility, gravity, fuſibility, volatility, in a word, all the properties by which metallic ſubſtances differ from ſimple earths, diminiſh or entirely diſappear, by taking from them their inflammable principle; ſo that when their calcination has been carried as far as is poſſible, they reſemble mere earths, and have no longer any thing in common with metals Theſe earths can no longer be combined with acids or with metals, but are capable of uniting with pure earths They are then called *calxes* or *metallic earths*. *See* CALXES (METALLIC).

We

We muſt obſerve concerning the decompoſition of metals, 1 That when only a ſmall quantity of inflammable principle is taken from metals, a ſmall quantity only of calx is formed, and the remaining part continues in the metallic ſtate hence, as the portion of calcined metal can no longer remain united with the undeſtroyed metal, it ſeparates in form of ſcales from the ſurface of the metal, when the calcination has been performed without fuſion, as generally happens to iron and to copper, or theſe ſcales float upon the ſurface of the melted metal when the calcination is performed during fuſion, becauſe the calx is ſpecifically lighter than the metal, as happens to the very fuſible metals, as tin, lead, and moſt of the ſemimetals

2 The imperfect metals are not all equally eaſily and compleatly calcinable In general, as much of their phlogiſton may be eaſily taken from them, as is ſufficient to deprive them of their metallic properties, but the remaining portion of their phlogiſton cannot ſo eaſily be driven from them Some of them, as copper, reſiſt the firſt calcination more than the reſt, and others, as lead and biſmuth, may be very eaſily calcined, but only to a certain degree, and retain always obſtinately the laſt portions of their inflammable principle, laſtly, others, as tin and regulus of antimony, may not only be eaſily and quickly calcined, but alſo much more completely All the other metals partake more or leſs of theſe properties relating to their calcination In general, if we except the labors of alchemiſts, which are not much to be depended upon, we have not yet made all the proper efforts to arrive at a perfect calcination of the ſeveral metallic ſubſtances, which, however, is abſolutely neceſſary, before we can arrive at a complete knowledge of the nature of their earths, as we ſhall afterwards ſee

When metallic earths have loſt but little of their phlogiſton, and are expoſed to ſtrong fire, they melt and are reduced to compact maſſes, ſtill heavy and opake, although much leſs ſo than the metals, and always brittle and abſolutely unmalleable If the calcination has been more perfect, the metallic earths are ſtill fuſible by fire, but leſs eaſily, and convertible into brittle and tranſparent maſſes poſſeſſed of all the properties of glaſs, and are accordingly called *metallic glaſſes* Theſe glaſſes do not poſſeſs any of the properties of their metals, excepting that they are ſpecifically heavier than other glaſſes, that they are capable of being attacked by acids, and that the glaſſes of the ſemimetals are ſomewhat leſs fixed than unmetallic glaſſes Laſtly, when the calcination of metals has been carried to its greateſt height, their earths are abſolutely fixed, and unfuſible in the fire of our furnaces, and poſſeſs no longer the ſolubility in acids by which metals are characteriſed

Theſe are the principal changes which metals ſuffer by loſing their phlogiſton They are thus changed into ſubſtances which have no properties but thoſe of earth This is a certain proof that the inflammable principle is one of their conſtituent parts But we have alſo other proofs of this important truth The reduction of metallic calxes into metal, by the addition of phlogiſton alone, completes the proof, and the whole forms one of the cleareſt and moſt ſatisfactory demonſtrations in all the ſciences This reduction is effected in the following manner

If the earth of a metal be mixed with any inflammable matter, which either is, or can be changed into the ſtate of coal, together with ſome ſalt capable of facilitating fusion, but which, from its quantity or quality, is incapable of receiving the inflammable principle, and if the whole be put into a crucible, and the fusion promoted by a fire gradually raised, then an effervescence will happen, accompanied with a hissing noise, which continues a certain time, during which the fire is not to be encreased, afterwards, when the whole has been well fused, and the crucible taken from the fire and cooled, we shall find at the bottom, upon breaking it, the metal, the earth of which was employed for the operation, possessed of all the properties which it had before calcination and reduction *See* REDUCTION

We cannot doubt that this wonderful transformation of an earthy substance into a metal is solely caused by the phlogiston passing from the inflammable matter to the metallic earth, for, first, in whatever manner, and with whatever substance metallic earths be treated, they cannot be ever reduced into metals without a concurrence of some substance containing phlogiston 2dly, The nature of the substance which is to furnish phlogiston is quite indifferent, because this principle is the same in all bodies containing it 3 Lastly, if after the operation the substance furnishing the phlogiston be examined, we shall find that it has lost as much of that principle as the metallic earth has received

The facts related concerning the decomposition and the recomposition of metals prove incontestably, that they are all composed of earth and phlogiston But we do not yet certainly know whether these two be the only principles of metals We might affirm this, if we could produce metals by combining phlogiston with some matter which is certainly known to be simple earth But this hitherto has not been accomplished, for if we try to treat any earth, which has never been metallic, with inflammable matters, we shall perceive that these simple earths are not combinable with phlogiston, so as to form metals. We shall even perceive that the metallic earths resist this combination, and are incapable of reduction into metal, when they have been so much calcined as very nearly to approximate the nature of simple earths

These considerations, added to this, that we cannot easily conceive how, from only two certain principles, so many very different compounds as the several metallic substances are, should result, are capable of inducing a belief that *some other principle is added to these two already mentioned in the composition* of metals

Many great chemists, and particularly Becker and Stahl, seem to be convinced *of this opinion*, and chiefly *from the experiments concerning the mercurification* of metals, they believe that this third principle exists copiously in mercury, that it is of a mercurial nature, that it also exists in marine acid, to which *it gives its* specific character, that by extracting this mercurial principle from marine acid, or any other body containing it copiously, and by combining it with simple earths, these may acquire a metallic character, and be rendered capable of receiving phlogiston, and of being completely metallised

These chemists admit also, and with probability, a different proportion of metallic principles in the several metals, and believe, that particularly the principle which they call *mercurial earth* exists more copiously and sensibly in certain metals than in others The most mercurial metals, according to them, are mercury, silver, lead, and arsenic. Most chemists distinguish from the

the other metals, ſilver, mercury, and lead, which they call *white metals*, *lunar metals*, or *mercurial metals*

All theſe conſiderations being united, and others too many to be mentioned, give ſome probability to the exiſtence of the mercurial principle in metals We muſt however acknowledge, that the exiſtence of this principle is only merely probable, and, as Stahl obſerves, is not nearly ſo well demonſtrated as that of the inflammable principle we may even add, that we have ſtrong motives to doubt of this exiſtence

As marine acid, mercury, arſenic, and even the other ſubſtances in which the mercurial earth is ſuppoſed to abound, are very volatile, and that none of the properties attributed to it ſhew that it is fixed, it ſeems, if it does exiſt, to be neceſſarily volatile The chemiſts who admit it, conſider it as volatile, ſince one of the methods beſt atteſted for the mercurification of metals is by ſubliming them through charcoal in Geber's manner, and ſince it is chiefly in the ſoot formed by the metals, that chemiſts look for their mercurial principle

If then the mercurial earth be a volatile principle, when metals are decompoſed by combuſtion, or by detonation with nitre, a conſiderable part of this volatile mercurial principle muſt be diſſipated Hence we ought not to be able to remetalliſe the calxes of metals, without recombining not only their loſt phlogiſton, but alſo their loſt mercurial earth But from experience we know, that by addition of phlogiſton alone theſe calxes may be metalliſed, and that no mercurial principle is neceſſary We cannot anſwer to this difficulty, that all ſubſtances containing phlogiſton contain alſo a ſufficient quantity of mercurial earth for the reduction of metallic calxes, for if that were true, we ſhould be able to produce metals by treating unmetallic earths with inflammable matters, ſince in ſuch a combination all the principles of metals would be preſent But we have already obſerved, that this cannot be done.

When indeed metallic calxes are reduced, there is always ſome loſs of quantity, as the ſame weight of metal is never procured which exiſted previouſly to the calcination, and alſo the more complete the calcination has been, this loſs of weight will be ſo much the more conſiderable We may conſequently attribute this loſs to that of the mercurial principle, during the decompoſition of the metal, and which is not reſtored to it by reduction with phlogiſton alone.

But may we not as reaſonably believe, that if ordinary earths, or even metallic earths perfectly calcined, cannot be metalliſed, this proceeds only from the difficulty of commencing an union with ſubſtances ſo different as earth and phlogiſton? but when this union is once begun by nature, the earth is then much more diſpoſed to combine intimately with a ſufficient quantity of phlogiſton to conſtitute it a metal; that thus any earth, entirely free from phlogiſton intimately combined, is, relatively to us, an unmetallic earth, whether it be naturally found in that ſtate, as almoſt all ſubſtances are, which we call ſimply *earths*, or whether it be a metallic ſubſtance perfectly calcined Hence the mercurial earth would be nothing elſe than phlogiſton, or rather is not a diſtinct ſubſtance, ſince it conſiſts only in a beginning of union of phlogiſton with earth, or in a diſpoſition which an earth has of uniting intimately with the inflammable principle This is an idea of the celebrated Henkel, whom we we certainly cannot suspect of indifference or incredulity concerning the possibility of the artificial production of metals

If this opinion were well grounded and proved, the artificial production of metals would be, in fact, not only possible, but much less difficult than has hitherto been believed, for only two principles are, in this case, necessary to be combined to form a metal We should then have nothing to do with the mercurial principle, the most troublesome of all, the most untractable, the least distinctly known, and the existence of which is not even ascertained

But notwithstanding these considerations, we must not believe that the production of metals is not one of the most difficult problems in chemistry The reflexions we shall add upon this subject will be sufficient demonstration to every sensible person, that great knowledge is requisite in that science, to attempt with any hopes of success, the production even of the most imperfect semimetal, they will shew the folly of those who attempt to make gold and silver, without being possessed of any knowledge even of elementary chemistry, which they despise and call *vulgar chemistry*, of which they disdain to inform themselves, although elementary knowledge be in chemistry, as in every other science, the most essential, fundamental, and necessary for further attainments By a singular fatality, the most ignorant persons are the most presuming They who see what passes in the particular assemblies of the Academy of Sciences, know that this illustrious society is always beset with pretenders to geometry, who really believe they have discovered the quadrature of a circle, the perpetual motion, &c and who at the same time are so ignorant of the first elements of algebra and geometry, that they are incapable of perceiving the demonstrations of their errors Happily the persons who imagine that they have discovered the means of making gold, are not so communicative, and keep their secrets in hopes of enriching themselves, otherwise the Academy would be as much importuned by the adepts of the philosophers stone, as it is now by the squarers of a circle

To return to the artificial production of metals, we must observe, that even if we were certain, that it depends only on the intimate combination of the inflammable principle with a matter simply earthy, we should labor by chance, and without any reasonable expectation of success, if we were to attempt that combination, without having more knowledge than we now possess, concerning the true nature of the earthy principle which enters into the composition of metals, for we must acknowledge that chemistry has made but little progress in this matter

Metallic substances, although they resemble each other by the general properties mentioned in the beginning of this article, differ nevertheless from each other very evidently by the properties peculiar to each Do these differences proceed from the different proportion, and from the more or less intimate connexion of the inflammable principle with the earthy principle, supposing that this latter should be essentially the same in all metals? or ought they to be attributed to the difference of earths, which, in that case, would be distinct and peculiar to each metal? or, lastly, do metals differ from each other, both by the nature of their earths, and by the proportion and intimacy of connexion of their principles? All these things are entirely unknown, and we may easily perceive, that till they are known, we cannot discover what method to

pursue

pursue in our attempts to accomplish the combinations we are now treating of

The most essential point then is to arrive at a knowledge of the true nature of the earths which are in metals, and the only method of arriving at this knowledge is, to reduce them to their greatest simplicity by a perfect calcination But this cannot be accomplished but by long and difficult operations We have seen above, that all metals are not calcinable with equal ease, that the perfect metals have not been hitherto calcined truly, by any process, and that in general the last portions of phlogiston adhere very strongly to calcinable metals

Some metals, however, as tin and regulus of antimony, may be easily calcined so as to be rendered irreducible By carrying the calcination still further, by the methods known in chemistry, we might obtain their earths so pure, that all their essential properties may be discovered, by which they might easily be compared together This comparison would decide whether their nature be essentially different, or not

If they were found to be composed of earths essentially the same, we might next proceed to compare metallic with unmetallic earths If the former were found similar to some of the latter kind, we should be then assured that the earth of metals is not peculiar to them, and that ordinary unmetallic earths are susceptible of metallisation.

The greater the number of metals operated upon, the more general and certain the consequences resulting from these would be, so that, for instance, if the operation were extended to all calcinable metals, and if the result of each of these operations were, that the calxes, when perfectly dephlogisticated, do not differ from each other, and are similar to earths already known, we might conclude from analogy, and we should be almost certain, that the earths of the perfect metals are also of the same nature

They who know the extent and difficulties of chemical operations, will easily perceive that this would be one of the most considerable Nevertheless, after having determined this essential point, we should only have done half our work For a knowledge of the nature of the earth of metals, and where it is to be found, would not be sufficient, we must further endeavor to find a method of combining with this earth a sufficient quantity of phlogiston, and in a manner sufficiently intimate, that a metal might be formed by such a combination We here always suppose, that earth and phlogiston are the two only principles of metals I say, then, that the method of combining these two principles must be discovered, for we know that the ordinary processes, those, for example, which are employed for the reduction of metals, are insufficient in this case But this second difficulty is perhaps greater than the former

When we reflect on the fundamental rules of the union of bodies, we shall discover a road which may lead to this combination In fact, if it be true, as every thing seems to demonstrate, that all natural substances may be united together, and that the resistance made by some to this union proceeds from the too strong union of their integrant parts, then the difficulties which occur in attempting to combine intimately phlogiston with earth, which of all known substances has the strongest aggregation, can only proceed from the too great ad-

hesion

hesion of the integrant parts of earth to each other Hence the only method of disposing to this union, is to separate and insulate the primary integrant parts sufficiently, and to break the aggregation as much as is possible

The integrant parts of earth may indeed be well disjoined, when fused by a strong heat therefore, if it were possible to fuse perfectly a simple earth, previously mixed with some inflammable matter, and put into a vessel accurately closed (which circumstance is absolutely necessary to prevent the combustion of the inflammable principle) the phlogiston would probably unite intimately with this earth, and a metallic matter would result from it. But this method seems to be impracticable, because simple earths are too refractory to be fused without addition, by the strongest fire which can be made in furnaces.

We may indeed facilitate, as much as we please, the fusion of earths, by the addition of saline fluxes, but this method, which succeeds very well for the reduction of metallic earths, when they have not been too much dephlogisticated, and when therefore they preserve a disposition to be metallized, becomes insufficient to reduce these earths, when they have been too much calcined, and it must be much more insufficient with regard to simple earths, which have never been in a metallic state

The reason of this is, that to procure the union of one body with another, not only the aggregation of that body must be broken, but also when this disjunction of aggregation is occasioned or facilitated, as in the present case, by the interposition of the parts of some substance, this substance must not have a too great affinity with the body to be united to that whose aggregation is broken, as may easily be understood

But we are certain that all the saline matters, which may be employed to facilitate the fusion of earths, have themselves a very great affinity with the inflammable principle, and the greater this affinity is, the more it ought to weaken the tendency which the inflammable principle has to be combined with the parts of earth

Here then is a compensation For if, on one side, the salts, while they facilitate the fusion of the earth, place it in a more favorable state for combination with phlogiston, on the other side, the affinity of these salts with phlogiston diminishes in the same proportion the disposition which the phlogiston has of combining with the earth, and therefore we need not wonder that this combination should not take place

But the case is different, when the earth intended to be metallised by the addition of phlogiston, is previously united intimately with a certain quantity of that principle, as happens in metallic calxes not perfectly dephlogisticated For this phlogiston, strictly united with the earth, not only much diminishes the force of its aggregation, but it must also necessarily facilitate very greatly the accretion of a new quantity of phlogiston, from the strong disposition of bodies to unite with others of the same nature.

Hence we cannot hope to succeed in trials of this kind by fusion with an intense fire but these are not the only resources which chemistry offers to us We are very certain, that the metallic combinations formed daily by nature, are not effected by violent fusions Water kept in a fluid state by the little heat necessary for that purpose, is itself capable of keeping the integrant parts of bodies

bodies whose aggregation is broken, suspended and insulated from each other, and those of earth, as well as of other substances, as is evidently demonstrated by sediments, stalactites, crystallizations, stones of all sorts, which are formed every where by water Water also of all substances has the least affinity with phlogiston, and consequently has all the requisite conditions as a vehicle, to assist the combination of earth with phlogiston Lastly, we know from experience that metals may be decomposed, and that their calxes may be metallised as well by the humid as by the dry way *See* REDUCTION

Water, then, seems to be a very proper intermediate substance to form the first rudiments of metallisation, and is employed by nature for the production of metals minerals, and of all the compound bodies that we see According to the opinion of one of our greatest naturalists and philosophers, nature makes with water all that we make in our laboratories with fire, and many others which we cannot accomplish Water is her principal and almost only instrument By water, therefore, that is, by the humid way, the combinations now in question ought to be attempted

But, it may be said, nature employs an almost infinitely long time for most of her productions, and particularly for metallic combinations Can this time be shortened by chemical means? Does chemistry furnish a method of impregnating water with the primitive integrant molecules of earth, and with a sufficient quantity of inflammable principle? We have reason to presume it Nevertheless, to be able to affirm any thing upon this subject, a person ought to have made experiments with these views, which, I confess, I never have done

We shall not enter into a further detail upon this matter, that we may not prolong this discussion, perhaps too long already, and too conjectural for a work of this nature We thought some extent ought to be given to it, not only because the subject is itself interesting, but also because many persons, particularly those who are ignorant of the whole extent of chemistry, consider metallisation as the sole object of that science It has been almost the sole end of chemists, from time immemorial to the renovation of the sciences, that is, to late times

All the ancient chemists were solely engaged about metals Their views and inquiries were so directed to that point, that they entirely neglected whatever was not connected with it, so that the name of chemist gave the idea of a man who endeavored to make metals The insuperable obstacles they have met, have obliged them to multiply their experiments, and to work upon many bodies besides metals The properties of many substances have been thus discovered successively, and these multiplied discoveries, having been afterwards generalised, and arranged, have given birth to the philosophical chemistry now cultivated, to that chemistry which explains clearly, which proceeds with order and method, and which in this respect differs greatly from the ancient researches concerning the philosopher's stone

We do not now undertake with the same confidence and ardor as heretofore the solution of the most difficult problems The slow and circumspect progress of chemistry appears humble and timid, in comparison of the bold and rapid course of ancient alchemy but such is the consequence of experience and reflection.

When men have long wandered at random, when, after they have fatigued themselves with every trial that occurred, without rule or measure, they have failed in their attempts, their most reasonable conduct is to return as they came, to begin afresh, and not to engage in the pursuit till the proper road be well ascertained

We do not consider as certain guides the ideas which the nature of the subject, and the desire of contributing to the advancement of the art, and of inspiring a true taste for it, have induced us to suggest on metallisation in this article If, in pursuing these ideas, we should be able to produce the rudest beginning of a metal or semimetal, true chemists would certainly find much cause of astonishment and admiration Much farther are we from presuming that by this method the perfect metals, as gold and silver, can be produced We do not intend to excite too flattering hopes, but only to present a rational plan of such labors, and to shew the difficulties to those who chuse to undertake them

We ought to advertise here, that some famous chemical processes have been considered by many as metallisations, but which are really not so Such is Beccher's famous experiment of the *Minera arenaria perpetua*, by which that chemist proposed to the States General to extract gold from any kind of sand Such also is the process of Beccher and of Geoffroy, to obtain iron from all clays by treating them with linseed oil in close vessels In these, and many other such processes, we do only obtain metal that was already formed Every earth and sand, as the intelligent and judicious Cramer observes, contain some particles of gold Clays do not commonly contain iron ready formed, but all of them contain a ferruginous earth, naturally disposed to metallisation *See* CLAY. Accordingly we must conclude, that, by Mr. Geoffroy's experiment, iron is only reduced or revived, but is not produced

The great difficulties which occur in attempting to give a metallic quality to simple earths have induced a belief, that the nature of metals ready formed might be more easily changed, and the less perfect brought to a more perfect state To effect this, which is one of the principal objects of alchemy, and is called transmutation, numberless trials have been made As we have not any certain knowledge of what occasions the specific differences of metallic substances, we cannot decide whether transmutation be possible or not In fact, if each metallic substance have its peculiar earth, essentially different from the earths of the others, and consequently if the differences of metals proceed from the differences of their earths, then, as we cannot change the essential properties of any simple substance, transmutation of metals must be impossible. But if the earths and other principles of metals be essentially the same, if they be combined in different proportions only, and more or less strictly united, and if this be the only cause of the specific difference of metals, we then see no impossibility in their transmutation

Whatever be the cause of the differences of metals, their transmutation seems to be no less difficult than the production of a new metallic substance, and perhaps it is even more difficult. Alchemists, whom nothing astonishes or embarrasses, believe that transmutation is possible, and they even affirm that they have effected it They begin by supposing that all metals are composed of the same principles, and that the imperfect metals do not differ from gold and silver, but

but becauſe their principles are not ſo well combined, or becauſe they contain heterogeneous matters We have then only theſe two faults to remedy, which, as they ſay, may be done by a proper coction, and by ſeparating the pure from the impure As we have but very vague and ſuperficial notions concerning the cauſes of the differences of metals, we confeſs that we cannot make any reaſonable conjecture upon this matter, and we ſhall only adviſe thoſe who would proceed upon good principles, to determine previouſly, if metals have each a peculiar earth, or only one common to them all In the ſecond place, if it ſhould be demonſtrated that the earthy principle is the ſame in all metals, and if that be demonſtrated as clearly as the identity of the inflammable principle in metals is proved, they muſt then determine whether theſe two be the only principles in metals, whether the mercurial principle exiſts, and whether it be eſſential to all metals, or to ſome only, and what is the proportion of theſe two or three principles in the ſeveral metallic ſubſtances When we ſhall clearly underſtand theſe principal objects, we may then be able to determine concerning the poſſibility of tranſmutation, and if the poſſibility ſhould be affirmed, we ſhall then begin to diſcover the road which we ought to purſue

We have no reaſon to believe that any other principle enters into the compoſition of metals than thoſe above-mentioned, no veſtige is perceptible of either air or water Some chemiſts have nevertheleſs advanced that they contain a ſaline principle. If that were true, they would alſo contain a watery principle But all the experiments adduced to prove this opinion are either falſe, or only ſhew the preſence of ſome ſaline particles extraneous to the metals, or contained unknown to the chemiſts in the ſubſtances employed in the experiments For metals perfectly pure, ſubjected to all trials with ſubſtances which do not contain, and which cannot produce any thing ſaline, do not diſcover any ſaline property We muſt however except arſenic, and even its regulus, theſe being ſingular ſubſtances, in which the ſaline are as ſenſible as the metallic properties

Arſenic ſeems to be one of thoſe intermediate ſubſtances which nature has placed in almoſt all its productions betwixt two different kinds, and which partake of the properties of each kind Arſenic thus placed betwixt metallic and ſaline ſubſtances has properties common to both theſe kinds of ſubſtances, without being either entirely a metal or a ſalt *See* ARSENIC

As water ſeems to act to a certain degree upon iron, even without the concurrence of air, as the operation of martial ethiops ſhews, we might thence ſuſpect ſomething ſaline in that metal Nevertheleſs, I do not believe that what happens in that operation has been ſo well explained, that any certain conſequences can be deduced 1 The water employed ought to be perfectly pure, that is, diſtilled rain water 2 The iron employed ought alſo to be perfectly pure, and ſuch is very difficultly to be procured 3 The operation ought to be performed in a bottle accurately cloſed, that we may be aſſured that the air contributes nothing to the action upon the iron 4 After the water has remained a long time, ſuppoſe a year, upon the iron, the water ought to be carefully filtrated and examined, to aſcertain whether it really has diſſolved any part of the metal

In the mean time, we may conclude that metals do not ſeem to contain any ſaline principle And when we conſider well their general properties, they ſeem to be nothing elſe than earths combined more or leſs intimately with a large quantity of phlogiſton Although we can demonſtrate that their inflammable principle is not in an oily ſtate, and that it is pure phlogiſton, they have nevertheleſs an oily appearance, in this circumſtance, that they adhere no more than oils to earthy and aqueous ſubſtances, and that they always aſſume a globular figure when ſupported by theſe ſubſtances entirely free from phlogiſton

This reſemblance is ſo ſenſible, that chemiſts, before they knew the nature of phlogiſton, believed that metals contained an oily and fat matter, and even now many perſons, who talk of chemiſtry without underſtanding it, ſpeak of the *oil, or fat of metals*, expreſſions, which do not ſound well to genuine chemiſts The cauſe of this quality of metals is the quantity of phlogiſton which they contain Sulphur, phoſphorus, oils, and even fats, have this appearance merely from the inflammable principle which enters into their compoſition for this property is communicated by that principle to every compound which contains a certain quantity of it *See* PHLOGISTON

When the phlogiſton combines copiouſly and intimately with earthy matters ſo as to form metals, it probably ſo diſpoſes them that the primitive integrant parts of the new compound, that is, of the metal, approximate and touch each other much more than the integrant parts of ſimple earths can This is proved by the great denſity or ſpecific gravity, and other general properties, of metals

In fact, as we cannot conceive that a body ſhould be tranſparent, unleſs it have pores and interſtices through which rays of light can paſs, therefore the more denſe a body is, that is, the fewer ſuch interſtices it has, the leſs tranſparent it will be, ſo that the denſeſt bodies ought to be the moſt opake, as in metals The diſpoſition of the pores of bodies contributes alſo much to their greater or leſs tranſparency, and bodies, the pores of which are continued and ſtreight, are more tranſparent than thoſe whoſe pores are interrupted, tranſverſe, or oblique, ſo that a body may be much more tranſparent than another which is leſs denſe, as we ſee that glaſs is more tranſparent than charcoal But when other circumſtances are equal, the denſeſt bodies are the moſt opake. Therefore the opacity of bodies is proportionable to their denſity, and to the deviation of their pores from right and parallel lines

From the great opacity of metals, they probably poſſeſs both theſe qualities in an eminent degree We have ſeen, at the beginning of this article, that the luſtre of metals and their property of reflecting light much better than any other ſubſtance, are neceſſary conſequences of their opacity This is alſo ſelf-evident, becauſe the fewer rays any bodies can tranſmit, the more it muſt reflect

Laſtly, the ductility of metals proceeds alſo from their denſity, and from the diſpoſition of their pores, as we have explained under the word DUCTILITY Phlogiſton alſo appears to communicate ductility to moſt of the bodies containing it, as we ſee in ſulphur, and unctuous bodies, as reſins, wax, &c all which are more or leſs ductile, at leaſt when heated to a certain degree Laſtly, the ſoftneſs, fuſibility, and volatility of which all metals partake more or leſs, and which many of them poſſeſs in a ſuperior degree, being properties entirely contrary to thoſe of the earthy principle, probably proceed from the inflammable principle In general, if we reflect on the eſſential properties of the earthy and inflam-

mable

mable principles, we ſhall eaſily perceive that theſe properties, being combined and modified by each other, ought to produce the properties of metals In order therefore to underſtand all this article, the words EARTH and PHLOGISTON ought to be conſulted

The order in which metals compared with each other poſſeſs moſt eminently their principal properties, is the ſame as that in which they are here enumerated, beginning always with that metal in which the property is moſt conſiderable

1 *Specific gravity* or *denſity* Gold, platina, mercury, lead, ſilver, copper, iron, and tin

2 *Opacity* We cannot well compare metals with each other in this reſpect, becauſe it is ſo conſiderable in all that it ſeems complete If, however, they differ in this reſpect, the ſame order will ſerve for opacity as for denſity

3 *Metallic luſtre* or *brilliancy* The ſame obſervation which was made concerning the laſt-mentioned property is applicable to this alſo We muſt however obſerve, that as, by poliſh, bodies are rendered brighter, and that as whiteneſs contributes much to the reflexion of light, the whiteſt and hardeſt metals therefore reflect beſt Hence platina ought to be placed firſt, and then iron or rather ſteel, ſilver, gold, copper, tin, lead (z)

4 *Ductility* Gold, ſilver, copper, iron, tin, lead. The ductility of mercury and of platina are not yet determined

5 *Hardneſs* Iron, platina, copper, ſilver, gold, tin and lead.

6 *Tenacity* By tenacity we underſtand the force with which the integrant parts of metals reſiſt their ſeparation This force appears to be in a compound ratio of their ductility and hardneſs The comparative tenacity of metals is meaſured by the weight which wires of the ſame diameter, made of the ſeveral metals, can ſuſtain without breaking Gold is the moſt tenacious, then iron, copper, ſilver, tin, lead The tenacity of mercury is unknown That of platina is not yet determined, but is probably conſiderable

7 *Fuſibility* Mercury, tin, lead, ſilver, gold, copper, iron, and laſtly platina, which cannot be fuſed by the greateſt fire of our furnaces, but only by the ſolar focus, as Meſſrs Macquer and Beaume have determined

(z) Hardneſs of metals may contribute much to the duration of their poliſh, but certainly ſoft metals, if their texture be equally compact, are no leſs capable of receiving a poliſh than hard metals Some hard metallic allays have been found to be leſs liable to tarniſh than ſofter compounds, and have for this reaſon alſo been chiefly uſed for ſpeculums. The property of reflecting light ſeems chiefly to depend on the cloſeneſs of the particles, or on the denſity, on the ſmoothneſs of the ſurface, and on the color being moſt ſimilar to the color of the light to be reflected. The white metals, ſilver, mercury, tin, reflect light more abundantly than others Gold being the denſeſt metal, and perhaps becauſe the color of ſolar light has a ſlightly yellowiſh tinge, does alſo reflect light very copiouſly Hence ſpeculums made of [illegible]-gold have been found to be very effectual Iron or ſteel reflects much leſs light than any of the above-mentioned metals, although the author has conſidered it as capable of a greater reflective power Platina is generally in ſo ſmall grains, that its reflective power cannot eaſily be determined The preciſe degrees of that power which ought to be aſſigned to each of the above-mentioned metals, cannot without accurate experiments be aſcertained However, I think, their reflective powers will be found to be more nearly in the following order, than in that mentioned in the text Silver, quickſilver, tin, gold, copper, iron, lead

The

The table of affinities of Mr Geoffroy gives for metallic ſubſtances in general, marine acid, vitriolic acid, nitrous acid, vegetable acid Mr Gellert's table contains no column for metallic ſubſtances in general

The uſes of metals are numberleſs and great Their particular uſes ſhall be mentioned under the articles of the ſeveral metallic ſubſtances

CCCCL M I C A *(a)*

CCCCLI M I L F O I L *(b)*

CCCCLII M I L K, *and* W H E Y The milk of animals is a white liquor compoſed of three very different ſubſtances, namely, butter, cheeſe, and whey Theſe three matters are intimately mixed with each other in freſh milk Whey is the only fluid part of milk Butter and cheeſe, which are mixed with it, have each of them a certain ſolidity, and are not ſoluble by whey Theſe two matters, the former of which is entirely of an oily nature, and the ſecond is gelatinous or mucilaginous, are only interpoſed and ſuſpended in the ſerous part by being very much divided

Hence we ſee that milk is a true emulſion Butter compoſes its oily part, which by the interpoſition of its particles gives an opake white color, the cheeſe ſerves as a mucilage to keep the oily part ſuſpended, and, laſtly, whey, which is naturally tranſparent, is the aqueous ſubſtance, which is a vehicle for the other two Milk may then be juſtly called an animal emulſion From its properties we ſhall ſee that this name ſuits it in every reſpect

Milk, recently taken from a frugivorous animal in good health, and fed with proper aliments, gives not by chemical trials any marks of an acid or alkaline quality. It has a ſweet, agreeable, and ſomewhat saccharine taſte, it contains no parts that are volatile with the heat of boiling water, at leaſt in any ſenſible quantity, ſo as to be collected Its ſmell, which is peculiar to it, is very weak

This liquor is very ſuſceptible of alteration, the ſmalleſt quantity of acid is capable of coagulating it When an alkali is mixed with it, a kind of coagulation happens, which is very different from that which is occaſioned by an acid

(*a*) Mica, or *Talk*, is an earthy or ſtony ſubſtance conſiſting of thin, flexible, ſhining plates Theſe plates by expoſure to fire become brittle, crumple, and by violent heat are vitreſcible *See* Mr D'Arcet's Memoir on the effects of a long and violent fire Mica is either colorleſs and tranſparent, or it is colored, red, brown, green, or black, and ſemi-tranſparent The colored micas generally contain ſome metallic matters, chiefly iron, and as Mr Juſti ſays, a new metallic ſubſtance [*ſee the laſt note* (*y*)], and are much more fuſible than thoſe which are pure and colorleſs Micas have a ſoft touch reſembling that of unctuous ſubſtances They are not ſoluble by acids, they are incapable of eliciting ſparks when ſtruck by ſteel, as flints do, or of forming a tenacious paſte with water, as clay does, or of hardening, when mixed with water, as gypſum does Mica is therefore neither a calcareous, ſiliceous, argillaceous, nor gypſeous earth The colorleſs tranſparent mica, called *Muſcovite glaſs*, is uſed as panes for windows In Jemptland, a crumpled kind of mica is manufactured into kettles and other veſſels, and alſo for hearths. The powder of this ſtone is mixed with ſea-ſalt, and from the mixture marine acid is obtained by diſtillation

(*b*) Milfoil or Yarrow The flowers and tops of the common purpliſh-flowered milfoil afford a blue oil ſimilar to that of camomile Theſe flowers have an aromatic and not diſagreeable ſmell, and ſomewhat of a rough, bitter and pungent taſte The bitterneſs and aſtringency remain in the extracts made by water or by ſpirit From an ounce of milfoil-tops, water extracted three drams and a ſcruple, and ſpirit extracted from the ſame quantity two drams and a half *Neuman*

This difference proceeds from the action of the alkali upon all the parts of the milk, and especially upon the butyraceous part, to which it gives a saponaceous quality

Milk also very readily suffers several remarkable changes, without addition of other substance The oily or butyraceous parts of the milk, being specifically lighter than the rest, and adhering but weakly, separate in great quantity by rest alone, and are collected on the surface, precisely as the oily parts separate from emulsions They there form what is called *cream*, from which, when collected, butter is made Milk is also susceptible of a spontaneous fermentation, by which it becomes acid, and is coagulated

The coagulation of milk occasions a distinct separation of the caseous part from the serous, and as this latter continues to separate, the former acquires a greater solidity By coagulation then, these two parts of milk are obtained separately from each other But the manner, in which this coagulation is made, produces considerable differences in the qualities of both Wherefore milk is coagulated by different methods, according to the purposes for which the cheese and the whey are intended.

As the acid, which discovers itself in the milk when it curdles spontaneously, is more than is sufficient for its coagulation, and as it communicates its taste both to the cheese and to the whey, milk is not generally left to curdle spontaneously, either for the making of cheese for aliment, or of whey for medicine This sensible acidity is avoided, by mixing with the milk, before it has become too old, the smallest quantity of acid necessary for coagulation, and by accelerating this coagulation by a convenient heat

The common and also the best method is to dilute, in three or four spoonfuls of water, about 18 grains of runnet for every two pounds of milk, and to mix it with the milk, which is then to be placed upon hot embers The milk, by means of this runnet, curdles more or less quickly according to the degree of heat given to it When the curd is intended to be eaten before the whey is separated, the heat ought to be very gentle, and the coagulation slow If cheese be intended to be made of it, more expedition may be used, and as soon as the milk is curdled, it is to be cut, to allow the whey to separate from it by draining If this be done for the sake of the whey, more heat may be given, and the separation may be more expeditious It is then to be passed through a strainer

The butyraceous, caseous, and serous parts are separated by these operations only imperfectly Each of these three matters partakes of the other two The butter and the cheese are purified in the manners mentioned under their particular articles The whey must be cleared from the caseous particles it contains, and which had not been curdled sufficiently, by throwing in and mixing well with it a liquor made by boiling about 15 grains of cream of tartar in water, and also the white of an egg, after which the whey is to be filtered through brown paper

The runnet employed to curdle milk is nothing else than a milky matter found in the stomachs of calves This matter is usually salted that it may be kept It smells of old cheese, and coagulates milk, because it contains a sufficient but not sensible quantity of acid It is a kind of leaven capable of producing the acid fermentation of milk The same may be said of several other substances, such as the flowers of almost all thistles, of wall flower, hence

hence called curdle milk, &c All these matters which do not seem acid, and which do not communicate any sensible acidity to milk, curdle it very well, undoubtedly from the latent acid which they contain The operation for clarifying whey is necessary, because it could not otherwise be filtered from the caseous particles adhering to it, which must be curdled again, or more strongly by boiling with the cream of tartar and white of an egg See FILTRATION

Well clarified whey is very far from being a pure phlegm It is indeed the most watery part of the milk, but it is also impregnated with all the parts of the milk which are soluble in water It has accordingly a sensible taste, which becomes very evident, when the whey is evaporated to nearly one half of its quantity It is saccharine and somewhat saltish. In whey is contained dissolved a considerable quantity of extractive substance of the nature of saccharine juices, and it is accordingly susceptible of the spirituous fermentation The Tartars certainly make from it a spirituous drink, or kind of wine

Whey contains, besides this saccharine fermentable substance, several kinds of salts which may be obtained by crystallization If three fourths of clarified whey be evaporated, and if the remainder be then set in a cool place, a certain quantity of reddish crystals will be formed This is the essential salt of milk It is called the *sugar of milk*, from its taste, which is manifestly saccharine But this color and taste are extraneous to the salt, and proceed from the extractive matter of the liquor in which the salt was crystallized Accordingly, if the crystals are well drained, dissolved in pure water, and crystallized, they will be much whiter and less saccharine By repeating the operation a third or a fourth time, the crystals may be rendered perfectly white and almost tasteless

This salt is of a singular nature, but is little known, because it has not been well examined We know only that it is not deliquescent, and requires much water to dissolve it Mr Beaumé has promised in his Pharmacy, that he will publish some particulars relative to this subject, which cannot fail of being interesting

The liquor which furnished these first crystals contains also some more, which may be obtained by continuing the evaporation and crystallization If the evaporation be still continued after the formation of the second crystals, some common salt will be formed, and lastly the mother-water contains, as Mr Beaumé affirms in his Pharmacy, some fixed alkali, which consequently is obtained without burning As this alkali is not sensible either in milk or in whey before the above-mentioned operations, it probably exists in the milk, combined with some matter with which it is saturated, and which is separated from it by these operations. All this requires a further and more particular inquiry

Milk, and consequently whey, contains no principle more volatile than water, and therefore none of its other principles are lost by exposure to the heat of boiling water But if we distill in a naked fire the residuum of whey, evaporated in a sand-bath to dryness, as Mr Geoffroy has done, phlegm will be at first obtained, then a citron-colored acid spirit, and afterwards a thickish oil. lastly, a residuous coal will remain in the retort, which will become moist by exposure to air, from the saline substances with which it is mixed.

What we have said concerning whey, together with the explanations we have given under the articles, BUTTER *of* MILK, and CHEESE, are sufficient

to

to give just notions concerning the nature of milk The result is, that milk is a mixture, first, of butter, which is an uncombined oleaginous matter, of the nature of fat, and not volatile, sweet oils (*see* Oil), secondly, of cheese, which is a more earthy matter, containing oil combined nearly in a mucilaginous state, and, thirdly, of whey, which is a watery liquor containing several salts, together with a saponaceous substance, or oil combined in the same manner as the oils of saccharine juices

Milk is much employed in aliments and in medicine. It is softening, incrassating, cooling, restorative, and healing It is proper against a sharpness of humors, as tetters, erysipelas, or gout, when these diseases are not accompanied with fever, and against internal suppurations, phthisis, marasmus, and slow fevers Sick persons are frequently dieted with milk alone, and generally with good effect But we must observe, that although milk be a food already prepared by nature, and as it were half-digested, it does not agree with all constitutions. It is apt to occasion one of two very opposite disorders, fluxes and costiveness This is remedied by diluting it with water, or by proper correctives, or by chusing that kind of milk which suits best with the constitution, and the disease to be treated. The milk of goats, for instance, has been observed to suit better than cows milk, with those persons whose constitution disposes them to diarrheas.

Whey is not used as an aliment, because being deprived of the butyraceous and caseous parts of the milk which are alimentary, it is much less nourishing than milk. It affords, nevertheless, a little nourishment by means of the saccharine matter which it contains Like milk, it is softening and cooling, and may be employed as such in the same diseases, but it is much more diluting, aperitive and laxative. It is frequently used as a vehicle for other remedies

We are far from having concerning milk all the knowledge which is to be wished Many inquiries remain yet to be made on this subject For besides the salt of milk, which is almost only known by name, nobody has hitherto undertaken a chemical examination, and a comparison of the several kinds of milk drawn from different animals, which milks do nevertheless differ considerably from each other, as has been observed in the Elements of Practical Chemistry Considerable differences must also be observable in the milk of the same animal in different circumstances, and particularly with relation to the nature of the food which the animal has eat for we are certain, that milk partakes much of the nature of the aliment used by that animal which furnishes it *See* Cheese

The milk of nurses is well known to acquire the virtues of drugs taken by them, and thus remedies are frequently applied to children at the breast (*c*)

(*c*) Thus the color of saffron, the bitterness of wormwood, and the smell of garlic, are given to the milk of a woman who eats these plants, and also the purgative and inebriating effects of certain substances are communicated from the nurse to the child Hoffman found by experiments, that the milk of cows and of goats contained more of the butyraceous and caseous, and less of the serous and of the saccharine particles than human milk, and the milk of asses.

CCCCLIII MILK *of* LIME MILK *of* SULPHUR The name of milk is given to substances very different from milk properly so called, and which resemble milk only in color Such is water in which quicklime has been slaked, which acquires a whiteness from the small particles of the lime being suspended in it, and has hence been called the *milk of lime* *See* QUICKLIME Such also is the solution of liver of sulphur, when an acid is mixed with it, by which white particles of sulphur are made to float in the liquor *See* LIVER *of* SULPHUR

CCCCLIV MILK *of* VEGETABLES. For the same reason that milk of animals may be considered as a true animal emulsion, the emulsive liquors of vegetables may be called *vegetable milks* Accordingly emulsions made with almonds are commonly called *milk of almonds* But besides this vegetable milk, which is in some measure artificial, many plants and trees contain naturally a large quantity of emulsive or milky juices Such are lettuce, spurge, fig-tree, and the tree which furnishes the elastic American resin The milky juices obtained from all these vegetables derive their whiteness from an oily matter, mixed and undissolved in a watery or mucilaginous liquor Most resinous gums were originally such milky juices, which afterwards become solid by the evaporation of their most fluid and volatile parts

These natural milky juices have not been examined by any chemist. Such an examination would, however, procure much essential knowledge concerning vegetable economy We should probably find examples of all kinds of oils reduced into milky juices, and this knowledge cannot fail of throwing much light on the nature of resins and gum-resins. *See* GUM-RESINS *and* RESINS

CCCCLV MINES *See* ORES

CCCCLVI MINIUM Minium, or *red lead*, is a calx of lead, of a vivid yellowish red color This color is said to be given by a slow calcination and reverberation Nevertheless, the method of making minium is not well known, as it is not made in small quantities in laboratories All the minium which is in commerce is brought from Holland, where large quantities of it are manufactured

Minium is employed in painting, and may serve for all the same purposes as the other calxes of lead *See* LEAD. *(d)*

CCCCLVII MIRACLE (CHEMICAL). When a concentrated solution of fixed alkali is mixed with a strong solution of nitre or of sea-salt, with earthy bases, the earth is so copiously precipitated, that a solid mass is formed from the mixture of these two liquors As this experiment is something wonderful, it has been called by some chemists *miraculum chemicum*. *See* MAGNESIA

(d) Minium is generally prepared by exposing lead to a melting heat till it is converted into a greyish calx, which is afterwards ground, and again calcined in an oven or reverberatory furnace, during several days, with a moderate heat The action of the flame and of air is said to be necessary to produce the red color For which reason, the matter to be calcined is frequently stirred during the operation, that its surface may be changed, and thus the whole of it exposed to air and flame. Three parts of lead are said to produce nearly four parts of minium, but if the minium be revived, about $\frac{1}{2}\frac{2}{8}$th parts only of the lead originally employed, will be recovered A smaller quantity of the lead will be recovered by reduction of the minium, if the calcination has been performed more effectually.

CCCCLVIII MIXTION. Stahl and all his school use this expression to signify the union of the first principles in the most simple compounds Instead of it, we substitute the terms *combination* and *composition*, which *see*.

CCCCLIX MOLYBDENA (*e*)

CCCCLX MORTAR A mortar is a chemical instrument, very useful for the division of bodies, partly by percussion, and partly by grinding Mortars have the form of an inverted bell The matter intended to be pounded is to be put into them, and there it is to be struck and bruised by a long instrument called a *pestle* The motion given to the pestle ought to vary according to the nature of the substances to be pounded Those which are easily broken, or which are apt to fly out of the mortar, or which are hardened by the stroke of the pestle, require that this instrument should be moved circularly rather by grinding, or bruising, than by striking Those substances which are softened by the heat occasioned by rubbing and percussion, require to be pounded very slowly Lastly, those which are very hard, and which are not capable of being softened, are easily pounded by repeated strokes of the pestle They require no bruising but when they are brought to a certain degree of fineness But these things are better learnt by habit and practice than by any directions

As mortars are instruments which are constantly used in chemistry, they ought to be kept of all sizes and materials, as of marble, copper, glass, iron, grittstone, and agate The nature of the substance to be pounded determines the choice of the kind of mortar The hardness and dissolving power of that substance are particularly to be attended to As copper is a soft metal, soluble by almost all menstruums, and hurtful to health, good artists have sometime ago proscribed the use of this metal *See* DIVISION *of* BODIES

One of the principal inconveniences of pulverisation in a mortar proceeds from the fine powder which rises abundantly from some substances during the operation If these substances be precious, the loss will be considerable, and if they be

(*e*) MOLYBDENA, or *Black lead*, is a blackish friable substance, unsoluble by acids, capable of resisting the most intense heats in close vessels It has been generally considered as a talky substance, and as being apyrous but from some late experiments made by Mr Quist, this substance appears to be decomposed by a calcining heat in open vessels, and even to be almost entirely dissipated or consumed and, long before these experiments, Dr Lawson, in his Dissertation De Nihilo, had shewn that blue inflammable flowers were raised from black lead by a violent fire Mr Quist relates, that having exposed several specimens of this mineral to a strong heat on a scorifying dish under a muffle, they emitted sulphureous fumes and flowers, that from one specimen, one fifth part only of the original weight remained after calcination, and from another specimen, only a twentieth part remained, of a yellow or brown calx, which being treated with inflammable fluxes, yielded seven-tenths of its weight of a metallic regulus, which appeared to consist of iron and tin Mr Cronstedt has accordingly classed black lead amongst sulphureous substances, and calls it *sulphur saturated with iron and tin*

Black lead is easily dissolved or mixed with melted sulphur, and with this mixture some pencils are made much inferior to those which are made with slips of pure black-lead Crucibles and portable furnaces are made of black-lead mixed with clay Black lead is also used to lessen the friction of machines, which it does from the fineness, the want of tenacity, and a kind of unctuosity of its particles.

injurious to health, they may hurt the operator These inconveniences may be remedied, either by covering the mortar with a skin, in the middle of which is a hole, through which the pestle passes, or by moistening the matter with a little water, when this addition does not injure it, or, lastly, by covering the mouth and nose of the operator with a fine cloth, to exclude this powder Some substances, as corrosive sublimate, arsenic, calxes of lead, cantharides, euphorbium, &c are so noxious, that all these precautions ought to be used, particularly when a large quantity of them is pounded

Large mortars ought to be fixed upon a block of wood, so high, that the mortar shall be level with the middle of the operator When the pestle is large and heavy, it ought to be suspended by a cord or chain fixed to a moveable pole, placed horizontally above the mortar this pole considerably relieves the operator, because its elasticity assists the raising of the pestle

CCCCLXI MOTHER-WATER *See* WATER

CCCCLXII MUCILAGE Mucilage is a white, transparent substance, which has little or no taste or smell, the consistence of which is thick, ropey, tenacious, and viscid, when it is united to a certain quantity of superabundant water It is entirely and intimately soluble in water, and it does not appear to contain any disengaged acid or alkali

When mucilage is dissolved in a large quantity of water, it does not sensibly alter the fluidity of this liquor, but this water, by evaporation, grows more and more thick, and, lastly, acquires the viscous consistence of vegetable glue.

While the evaporation continues, the liquor becomes more and more thick, without losing any transparency, and this evaporation may be continued till the mucilage becomes quite solid it then does not differ from gums. If this evaporation or drying has been made with a heat not exceeding that of boiling water, this mucilage, thus rendered solid, and become a gum, may be entirely dissolved again in water, and may again form a liquid mucilage, as before.

Gums or solid mucilages, when well dried and very hard, being exposed to an open fire, are not liquefied as resinous matters are, they swell, and emit many fumes, which at first are watery, then oily, fuliginous, and acrid

This matter, at the same time, becomes black, and is then capable of being inflamed, but not before it is thoroughly dried, and almost reduced to the state of coal

If mucilage or gum be exposed to distillation in close vessels, nothing but water is obtained, with a heat not superior to that of boiling water, and the matter which remains in the retort seems to be nearly of the same degree of dryness as before the operation, which is a certain proof that distillation does only deprive the gum of its superabundant water If a greater degree of heat be then applied, more aqueous liquor will be obtained, which gradually becomes more and more acid and empyreumatic. By continuing the distillation with a fire gradually augmented, a little thick oil and volatile alkali pass, and, lastly, a considerable quantity of residuous coal remains in the retort, which burns difficultly in open air, together with some ashes, from which a very little fixed alkali may be obtained

Mucilages and gums are not soluble either by oils, or by spirit of wine, which latter menstruum has the property of taking from these substances the water in which

which they are dissolved, so that if spirit of wine be mixed with a liquid mucilage, or with water in which gum is dissolved, this spirit will take all the water of the solution, and will separate the gummy matter in form of an almost dry white precipitate We may easily perceive that this experiment cannot succeed but by adding a sufficient quantity of spirit of wine, that is, a quantity proportionable to the quantity of water united with the gummy matter

From what we have said concerning the general properties of the gummy vegetable principle, we may conclude, first, that excepting a portion of superabundant pure water, no substance is contained which is volatile with the heat of boiling water, consequently no volatile saline spirits, no essential oil, or spiritus rector, at least in any sensible quantity

Secondly, we may conclude, that this gummy matter is composed, first, of a certain quantity of oil of the nature of sweet oils, which are not volatile, nor soluble in spirit of wine, secondly, of water, thirdly, of vegetable acid, and, lastly, of an attenuated earth, that the oil which is a principle of gums is in small quantity, since they are not attackable by oily or spirituous solvents, and that they are difficultly combustible

Thirdly, that the portion of oil which is combined in gums is in them so intimately united with a sufficient quantity of acid, that it is rendered entirely soluble in water

Fourthly, that as all compounds, the principles of which are nearly in these proportions, and in this kind of union, are susceptible of fermentation, all gummy matters are fermentable, they are also nutritive This is confirmed by experience Some differences, however, exist in this respect betwixt the several mucous vegetable matters Some of them, particularly those called *gums*, are very transparent, insipid, little nutritive, and susceptible of only an imperfect fermentation, which passes soon to vapidity or mouldiness others, namely those which all the farinaceous substances furnish, are less transparent, less insipid, more viscid, more nutritive, and susceptible of a compleat spirituous fermentation, particularly when they are placed in circumstances favorable to fermentation. *See* BEER

Although the existence of mucilage in all vegetables and in all their parts is not equally sensible, we may nevertheless consider it as universally diffused through the vegetable kingdom Plants, or the parts of plants, from which no mucilage is obtainable by ordinary processes, do all impregnate water with an extractive matter, and this extractive matter includes always a certain quantity of mucilaginous substance, which remains mixed with the saline and saponaceous matters, and which might even be separated by certain processes, particularly by a proper application of spirit of wine.

The use of the mucilaginous matter appears to be in the vegetable kingdom exactly the same as that of the gelatinous matter in the animal kingdom These two substances, which, in many respects, resemble each other, are both of them singularly nutritive and reparative

Accordingly, nature has provided all the plants which have occasion for it with plenty of it, and has even produced a superabundant quantity of it for the encrease and support of each individual This superabundance of nutritive matter is reserved with economy in vegetables, as in animals, for the generation and reproduction of individuals of the same species

The

The feed and eggs of animals are then nothing elfe than a provifion of gelatinous matter, intended for the production and nutrition of their young. The fame obfervation is applicable to all the feeds and kernels of vegetables, which may be confidered as their eggs, all which contain fo much mucilage, that it may be eafily obtained abundantly from them by infufion or boiling in water

Some of thefe, fuch as the feeds called emulfive, furnifh eafily by infufion in water a confiderable quantity of the kind of mucilage which we mentioned above was tranfparent, not very nourifhing or vifcid, but they alfo contain a confiderable quantity of fweet oil, which may be obtained by expreffion alone The others, thofe called *farinaceous grains*, being bruifed and boiled in water, are almoft entirely reduced to a glue, which is nothing elfe than the kind of mucilage which we mentioned as being very nutritive Thefe grains do not, like the emulfive feeds, contain an expreffible oil, but a confiderable quantity of oil enters into the compofition of the mucilage Accordingly, thefe two kinds of feeds contain the fame materials, with this difference, that a large portion of fweet oil is difengaged in the emulfive feeds, and is combined in the farinaceous grains.

The kind of grains called *leguminous*, which are very numerous, contain a meal more mucilaginous than thofe properly called farinaceous, but they are likewife provided with a greater or lefs quantity of fapid or even faccharine fubftance, which alfo is a kind of mucilage, and of a truly nutritive nature *See* SUGAR

The roots of many plants are filled with much mucilage or faccharine matter. Some of them are farinaceous, efpecially thofe which produce the entire plant.

Mucilage is eafily obtained from the vegetable fubftances above-mentioned, by infufing or flightly boiling in water thofe which contain it moft abundantly, as linfeed, the feeds of pfyllium, of quinces, the roots of marfhmallows, &c. The water by this means foon becomes ropey and vifcous, like the whites of eggs. The water and heat neceffary for this extraction are incapable of caufing any alteration upon the mucilages, which are therefore obtained exactly in the fame ftate as in the vegetable itfelf

From many trees much mucilage iffues fpontaneoufly, which being dried by the air and fun, forms gums Thefe trees are chiefly the acacia, the almond, the peach, the apricot, the plumb, and even the pear and apple-trees May not this exfudation of nutritive fubftance, which might be confidered as the effect of a fuperabundant quantity of nutritive juice, rather proceed from a ftoppage or too great fulnefs of the veffels containing it? That this exfudation proceeds from a difeafe in the tree, is rendered probable by this remark, that all the trees from which much gum iffues, become languid and dry, and do at length perifh, with all the appearances of trees which die from want of nourifhment

Gummy and mucilaginous matters ferve for many different purpofes. Gums are employed in the arts, in dyeing, in painting with water-colors, and for giving luftre and firmnefs to ftuffs

Mucilages are the moft relaxing, emollient, and foftening remedies in medicine. But if we take the term *mucilaginous matter* in its moft extenfive meaning, and apply it, as we may with propriety, to all the farinaceous and faccharine vegetable fubftances, then the above mentioned advantages are nothing

in

in compariſon of their infinite utility to us, ſince that ſubſtance conſtitutes the chief and ſole matter of our nouriſhment, whether we obtain it directly from the grains and roots of vegetables which we eat, or that it has previouſly ſerved as food to the animals which we uſe as food.

CCCCLXIII MUFFLE *See* VESSELS (CHEMICAL).

CCCCLXIV MUSK (*f*)

CCCCLXV MUST By *muſt* is meant the ſaccharine juice of ſeveral fruits ſuſceptible of the ſpirituous fermentation, and particularly of grapes, before the commencement of this fermentation Accordingly muſt is, properly ſpeaking, what is commonly called *ſweet wine* *See* JUICES (SACCHARINE) *and* WINE

CCCCLXVI MYRRH. (*g*)

(*f*) MUSK is an animal juice, the moſt odoriferous of all known ſubſtances Its ſmell is very diffuſive, and adheres very tenaciouſly to ſubſtances perfumed with it From thirty grains, water extracted twelve grains, and from the ſame quantity, ſpirit of wine extracted ten grains. Spirit of nitre and oil of vitriol totally diſſolve it The former deſtroys the whole of its ſmell, and the latter the greateſt part of it. Spirit of ſalt, dilute ſpirit of vitriol, and vinegar, have no effect upon it Spirit of ſal ammoniac diſſolves a little of it Oil of tartar ſcarcely acquires any tinge from muſk, but extricates from it a volatile urinous ſmell Muſk is not ſoluble in oils expreſſed or diſtilled By diſtillation in a retort, musk yielded the animal principles, empyreumatic oil, volatile ſpirit and ſalt Musk is uſed medicinally, and as a perfume. In the diſtillation of odoriferous waters and ſpirit, a ſmall portion of musk included in a linen cloth, is generally hung in a ſtill-head, the vapors of both liquors extracting its ſcent Spirit diſtilled with musk immerſed in it acquires little of its ſmell But water by this method acquires both the ſmell and taſte A minute portion of musk greatly improves the fragrance of the diſtilled odoriferous waters, as thoſe of lavender and roſemary, and heightens the ſmell of other odoriferous ingredients, without communicating any of its own peculiar ſmell *Neuman*

(*g*) MYRRH is a gum reſin, from ſixteen ounces of which twelve ounces and a half were extracted by water, and from the ſame quantity five ounces were extracted by ſpirit of wine. The whole ſmell and taſte of the myrrh is received either by the water, or by the ſpirit, and the reſiduous ſubſtances are perfectly inſipid. By evaporating the aqueous infuſion, an extract is obtained, containing all the bitterneſs, but not the flavor of the myrrh, which ſeems to reſide in an eſſential oil; three drams of which may be obtained by diſtillation of a pound of myrrh. If ſome powdered myrrh be incloſed in the white of a hard boiled egg, and ſet in a moiſt cellar, the liquor into which the egg will be gradually reſolved, will extract nearly all the ſmell and taſte of the myrrh. This liquor, which is commonly called, *oil of myrrh per deliquium*, may be precipitated and coagulated by ſpirit of wine This coagulum is ſoluble by water.

N.

CCCCLXVII. NAPHTHA. This name is given to the petroleum which is the most white, volatile, and thin, whether this bituminous matter possess these qualities naturally, or has acquired them by rectification. See PETROLEUM and BITUMENS. (h)

CCCCLXVIII NATRUM or NATRON. This is a native alkaline salt of the nature of the mineral or marine alkali, which is found crystallized in Egypt, and in some other hot countries, in sands which surround lakes of salt water This crystallization is produced by the spontaneous evaporation of this water; and as that water contains other salts also, besides the mineral alkali, the natrum is not a pure mineral alkali, and is naturally found mixed with other saline matters, and particularly with common salt. This salt is said to be the nitre of the ancients. It is little known in this country. The soda, and salt obtained from it, being of the same nature as the natrum, supply all our purposes. See ALKALI (MINERAL).

CCCCLXIX NEPHRITIC STONE. (i)

CCCCLXX. NEPHRITIC WOOD. (k)

(h) Mr Rouelle thinks that naphtha is formed by a distillation of bitumens occasioned by subterranean fires

(i) NEPHRITIC STONE. This is a green, semi-transparent, foliated stone, unctuous to the touch, not compact, nor capable of being polished. By Wallerius it is ranked amongst gypsums, and by Pott, amongst calcareous earths Some other authors more justly consider it as a steatites, from its unctuosity, from its partial solubility in acids, and from its property of becoming hard by burning. Its green color is occasioned by copper, a small quantity of which metal Mr Pott extracted from this stone, by fusion with borax Neuman affirms, that by distilling the stone, he obtained a small portion of an empyreumatic oil, and of an ammoniacal salt.

(k) NEPHRITIC WOOD. This wood gives a blue color to spirit of wine, or to water. This color is changed to a yellow by acids, and afterwards restored to a blue by alkalis Dr Lewis observes, that it is the only woody matter which gives a blue tincture, and that this is the only vegetable blue which is thus destructible by acids

CCCCLXXI

www.ingramcontent.com/pod-product-compliance
Ingram Content Group UK Ltd.
Pitfield, Milton Keynes, MK11 3LW, UK
UKHW020227290926
15470UKWH00001B/410

9 781379 490265